World Population – Turning the Tide
Three decades of progress

Stanley P. Johnson

KLUWER LAW
INTERNATIONAL
THE HAGUE - LONDON - BOSTON

Published by Kluwer Law International
PO Box 85889   Tel. +31 70 308 1560
2508 CN Den Haag   Fax. +31 70 308 1515
The Netherlands

Distribution in the USA and Canada
675 Massachusetts Avenue   Tel. 617 354 0140
Cambridge, MA 02139   Fax. 617 354 8595
USA

ISBN 185966 046 0 (hardback)
ISBN 185966 047 9 (paperback)

© Stanley P. Johnson
First published 1994

Library of Congress and British Library Cataloguing-in-Publication Data is available.

Typeset in 10/11pt Janson by EXPO Holdings Malaysia
Printed and bound in Great Britain by Hartnolls Ltd, Bodmin, Cornwall

Contents

Foreword

by Dr Nafis Sadik, Secretary-General, International Conference on Population and Development, Executive Director, United Nations Population Fund

This book tells a remarkable story. Over the past three decades, many parts of the world have undergone remarkable demographic, social, economic and political change. Many countries have made substantial progress in expanding access to reproductive health care and lowering birth rates, as well as in lowering death rates and raising education and income levels, including the educational and economic status of women. The dramatic success of some countries provides a basis for optimism about what *all* countries can accomplish over the next twenty years. The world as a whole has changed in ways which create important new opportunities for addressing population and development issues. Among the most significant factors, as this book records, are the major shifts in attitude among the world's people and their leaders in regard to reproductive health, family planning and population growth.

A particularly encouraging trend has been the development of national population policies and family planning programmes in many Governments. A 'reproductive revolution' is under way in many parts of the world. The critical dimension of this reproductive revolution is a substantial decline in human fertility. Most importantly, it is now increasingly recognized that family planning is part of a broader concept of reproductive health and rights.

Significant changes in attitudes, leading to much greater demands for family planning information and services, have occurred at the grassroots level among individual women and men. Since the early sixties, contraceptive use in developing countries has increased five-fold, reflecting the growing strength of organized family planning programmes in a large majority of developing countries and relatively rapid reduction in family size norms. On average, family planning programmes account for about half the decline in average fertility rates for developing countries from between 6 to 7 children per family in the 1960s to about 3 to 4 children today.

Today, about 55 per cent of couples in developing regions use some method of family planning. In Europe, North America and much of East Asia, access to family planning is almost universal; contraceptive use is between 65 and 80 per cent and average family size is at or near replacement level fertility of two children per couple.

Stanley Johnson's book also emphasizes that, although much progress has been made, there is still a long way to go. In most countries, including many sub-Saharan African countries, many more women express a desire to space pregnancies or limit family size than are currently practising family planning. One indication of large unmet demand for more and better family planning services is the estimated 50 million abortions which occur every year, many of them unsafe.

The 1994 International Conference on Population and Development (ICPD) occurs at a defining moment in the history of international cooperation. With reductions in international and regional tensions, and with the growing recognition of global economic and environmental interdependence, the opportunity to mobilize human and financial resources for global problem-solving has never been greater.

The ICPD is the latest in a series of international conferences focusing on population. As this book recalls in some detail, twice before – at the 1974 World Population Conference in Bucharest and the 1984 International Conference on Population in Mexico City – the international community assembled to consider the broad issues of population growth and distribution and their implications for social and economic development. However, the 1994 International Conference on Population and Development has been given a broader mandate than its predecessors, reflecting the growing awareness that population change, poverty, inequality, patterns of consumption and threats to the environment are so closely connected that none of them can profitably be considered in isolation.

I am hopeful that the ICPD Programme of Action will commit the international community to making real progress over the 20-year period, 1995–2015: increased access to education, especially for girls; reduced infant, child and maternal mortality; and providing universal access to family planning and reproductive health services. Progress in each of these areas is mutually reinforcing and essential for meeting needs of individual women and men, and for attaining an early stabilization of world population and the achievement of sustainable development.

Nafis Sadik

Stanley Johnson is currently Special Adviser on the environment to Coopers and Lybrand, a major international management consultant and accountancy company. He previously served for several years as Adviser to the Director-General for the Environment in the European Commission, Brussels and was subsequently Director of Energy Policy. He was also elected Member of the European Parliament, and Vice-Chairman of the Parliament's Committee on Environment, Public Health and Consumer Protection.

Mr Johnson joined the staff of the World Bank in Washington, DC in 1966 and in 1968/69 served as the Project Director of the UNA–USA National Policy Panel on World Population under the chairmanship of John D. Rockefeller 3rd. From 1970 to 1973 he was international liaison officer for the International Planned Parenthood Federation (IPPF), and has also frequently acted as consultant to the United Nations Population Fund (UNFPA).

He is the author of numerous books in the field of population, development and environment including: *The Environmental Policy of the European Community* (with Guy Corcelle); *The Politics of the Environment; The Green Revolution; World Population and the United Nations; The Population Problem; and Antarctica – the Last Great Wilderness*. His last book, The Earth Summit, is a compilation of, and commentary on, documents relating to the United Nations Conference on Environment and Development (UNCED).

Mr Johnson is also the author of eight published novels. In 1984, he won the Greenpeace Prize for Outstanding Services to Conservation.

Acknowledgements

The author acknowledges with gratitude all the help and encouragement he has received during the preparation of this book from members of the staff of the United Nations Population Fund (UNFPA). Special thanks are due to Dr Nafis Sadik, Executive Director, UNFPA and the Secretary-General of the International Conference on Population and Development (ICPD), as well as to Jyoti Shankar Singh, Director of UNFPA's Technical and Evaluation Division and Executive Coordinator, ICPD; to Catherine S. Pierce, of UNFPA's Women, Population and Development Branch; and to Cecile Cuffley of the Interregional and NGO Programmes Branch who have commented on early drafts and offered useful suggestions.

A special debt is due to the United Nations and in particular to the staff of the UN's Population Division who sought out and assembled many of the early demographic reports which have been drawn on in the text. Material provided by the World Bank, the Population Information Program of Johns Hopkins University, and by Population Action International has also been extremely valuable.

The author also expresses his deep appreciation for the extensive help he received from the field staff of UNFPA and other United Nations bodies in the course of visits made to observe population and family planning programmes at work in Asia, Africa and Latin America.

Thanks are due too to the United Kingdom's Overseas Development Administration (ODA) for the practical support given. The insights provided by all these and others have without doubt enriched this book immeasurably. That said, unless they are clearly attributed to another source, the responsibility for the views and opinions expressed in this book rests firmly with the author.

Abbreviations

CELADE	Centro Latinoamericano de Demografía
CPR	Contraceptive Prevalence Rate
DFTR	Desired Total Fertility Rate
DHS	Demographic and Health Surveys
ECA	Economic Commission for Africa
ECAFE	Economic Commission for Asia and the Far East
ECE	Economic Commission for Europe
ECLAC	Economic Commission for Latin America and the Caribbean
ECOSOC	United Nations Economic and Social Council
ESCAP	Economic and Social Commission for Asia and the Pacific
ESCWA	Economic and Social Commission for West Asia
FAO	Food and Agriculture Organization of the United Nations
FPS	Family Planning and Health Surveys
IBRD	International Bank for Reconstruction and Development (or World Bank)
ICPD	International Conference on Population and Development
IPPF	International Planned Parenthood Federation
IUD	Intra-uterine contraceptive device
IUSSP	International Union for the Scientific Study of Population
NGO(s)	Non-governmental Organization(s)
OECD	Organization for Economic Co-operation and Development
TFR	Total Fertility Rate
UAR	United Arab Republic
UN	United Nations
UNA-USA	United Nations Association of the USA
UNCED	United Nations Conference on Environment and Development
UNDP	United Nations Development Programme
UNEP	United Nations Environment Programme
UNESCO	United Nations Educational, Scientific and Cultural Organization
UNFPA	United Nations Fund for Population Activities; United Nations Population Fund
UNICEF	United Nations Children's Fund
USAID	United States Agency for International Development
WCS	World Conservation Strategy
WHO	World Health Organization
WPPA	World Population Plan of Action

List of Tables

List of Figures

World Population –Turning the Tide: Three decades of progress Introduction and Summary

On May 1, 1969, Mr Robert S. McNamara, then the President of the World Bank, gave a speech at the University of Notre Dame, Indiana, on the subject of population. It was not the first time he had spoken on this topic. Indeed, Mr McNamara's first address to the World Bank's Board of Governors on September 30, 1968, had caused considerable controversy particularly among Latin American delegates since he pledged the Bank's assistance for a new area of lending, namely population projects and programmes. What made the Notre Dame speech remarkable was that it was delivered before a Catholic audience. And it was a model of eloquence and passion.

Mr McNamara opened his remarks by saying:

> I want to discuss with you this afternoon a problem that arose out of the recent past: that already plagues man in the present, and that will diminish, if not destroy, much of his future – should he fail to face up to it, and solve it. It is, by half a dozen criteria, the most delicate and difficult issue of our era, perhaps of any era in history. It is overlaid with emotion. It is controversial. It is subtle. Above all, it is immeasurably complex.
>
> It is the tangled problem of excessive population growth. It is not merely a problem, it is a paradox. It is at one and the same time an issue that is intimately private – and yet inescapably public. It is an issue characterized by reticence and circumspection – and yet in desperate need of realism and candour. It is an issue intolerant of government pressure – and yet endangered by government procrastination.
>
> It is an issue, finally, that is so hypersensitive – giving rise to such diverse opinion – that there is an understandable tendency simply to avoid argument, turn one's attention to less complicated matters and hope that the problem will somehow disappear.
>
> But the problem will not disappear. What may disappear is the opportunity to find a solution that is rational and humane. If we wait too long, that option will be overtaken by events. We cannot afford that. For if anything is certain about the population explosion, it is that if it is not dealt with reasonably, it will in fact explode: explode in suffering, explode in violence, explode in inhumanity.

A few months after Mr McNamara's Notre Dame speech, in October 1969, the Right Honourable Lester Pearson, a former Prime Minister of Canada, presented the report of the Independent Commission on International Cooperation for Economic Development, which he chaired, to the Board of Governors of theWorld Bank. Like its successors, the Brandt Commission, the Brundtland Commission and the South Commission, the Pearson report had a considerable impact at the time both on public opinion at large and among policy-makers concerned with aid, trade and development. Its recommendations for action were addressed to the developing countries, to the industrialized countries, and to international organizations.

As far as population was concerned, the Pearson report commented starkly:

> No other phenomenon casts a darker shadow over the prospects for international development than the staggering growth of population. It is evident that it is a major cause of the large discrepancy between the rates of economic improvement in rich and poor countries.

One more quotation – again from 1969, obviously a vintage year for quotations. Speaking in New York in his capacity as Secretary-General of the United Nations, U Thant said:

> I do not wish to seem overdramatic, but I can only conclude from the evidence that is available to me as Secretary-General, that the Members of the United Nations have perhaps ten years left in which to subordinate their ancient quarrels and launch a global partnership to curb the arms race, to improve the human environment, to *defuse the population explosion*, and to supply the required momentum to development efforts. If such a global partnership is not forged within the next decade, then I very much fear that the problems I have mentioned will have reached such staggering proportions that they will be beyond our capacity to control.

Looking back over a gap of twenty-five years, McNamara's moving and courageous speech, Pearson's sombre vision, U Thant's almost apocalyptic predictions encapsulate what seemed at the end of the 1960s to be the bitter realities of the time. McNamara, Pearson and U Thant did not speak just for themselves; they spoke for ever-growing number of men and women who believed that the population tide had sooner or later to be turned back if there was to be any hope for mankind. The issue, as McNamara so well put it, was whether the 'rational and humane solution' could be found.

The trumpet, as it turned out, gave forth no uncertain sound. The dark shadow has indeed begun to lift. In a world where news often means bad news, the purpose of this book is unusual. It seeks to tell a success story, possibly one of the most important success stories of all time. The heart of the story is the account which is given in the following chapters of national and international approaches to the population question over the last three decades and of the progress that has been made in reducing rapid rates of population growth and high levels of fertility. To use the metaphor which was current in the 1960s, this book is essentially about the efforts which have been made over the years to 'defuse the population bomb' and to provide to those who want it safe, reliable and preferably cheap means of contraception and family planning.

For the most part, the story is told chronologically. The book takes as it starting point the world demographic situation at the end of the 1960s and the beginning of the 1970s. It had taken mankind all of recorded time until the middle of the nineteenth century to achieve a population of one billion, less than a hundred years to add the second billion, and only thirty years to add the third. At the end of the 1960s, it was anticipated at then current rates of increase that there would be four billion people by 1975 and nearly seven billion people by the year 2000. What had begun as a plane taking off over an immensely long runway had turned in a frighteningly brief period of time into a rocket accelerating rapidly towards the stratosphere.

The immediate cause of the massive demographic expansion which the world was experiencing at the end of the sixties could be summarized in a single sentence. The fall in death rates in developing countries had not been matched by a fall in birth rates. The developing world had experienced one 'demographic revolution' – the transition from high mortality to low mortality. But it had yet to undergo the second demographic revolution, the transition from high fertility to low fertility. An increasing gap was opening up between the birth rates for countries in the developed regions of the world which ranged from 16 to 20 per 1000 and those of the developing regions which ranged from 36 to 49 per 1000.

The early chapters of the book describe the evolution of national population policies as governments came to understand the consequences of rapid population growth and high fertility both for their national development efforts as well as for the welfare of families and individuals. Several countries, particularly in Asia, actively promoted policies aimed at facilitating fertility reduction and lowering population growth rates. Indeed, by the end of 1969, the governments of about thirty less developed countries, comprising almost two-thirds of the combined populations of the less developed regions, had adopted national family planning programmes as integral parts of their development policies.

What successes had there been, by the end of the sixties, in turning the tide of human fertility? In what countries? Were those successes in any way replicable in other countries? Chapter 4, without seeking to be comprehensive, looks at a small number of countries – including Japan, Taiwan, Singapore and China – where significant reductions in fertility appeared to have been achieved. Chapter 5 looks at some other countries – India, Pakistan, Kenya etc – where substantial and long-standing efforts were being made to provide family planning services either through government programmes or through the private sector, for example through national family planning associations, but where the demographic impact of such programmes remained uncertain.

The growth in national concern over the implications of rapid population growth and the increasing number of official family planning programmes was reflected in the growth of international assistance in this field. Indeed, international assistance in the field of population, perhaps more than in most other fields, has played a vital role in reinforcing and underpinning national commitments. Chapter 6 presents the key players as they emerged on the international stage during the 1970s: the United Nations and its system of agencies, particularly the United Nations Population Fund (UNFPA); the World Bank (strictly a UN agency, but deserving a special mention); the International Planned Parenthood Federation (IPPF) whose local affiliates often played a pioneering role in pushing for action on family planning matters and in providing family planning services themselves either in the absence of, or as a supplement or alternative to, government services; and bodies such as the Population Council, the Ford Foundation, the Rockefeller Foundation who truly were pathfinders in the field. Total international assistance for population activities amounted to only about $2 million in 1960 and $18 million in 1965, but it increased rapidly to $125 million in 1970 and to nearly $350 million by 1977. Between the years 1970 and 1974, the average annual rate of growth in international population assistance was around 20 per cent.

As the patient reader works his or her way deeper into the book, it will be obvious that the present study draws heavily on documents and reports from those early days. At times, fairly extensive selections from the sources are included. It seemed more sensible to promote and protect authenticity than to attempt a paraphrase or a gloss which, though more economical as far as space is concerned, might fail to capture the flavour of the original. Chapter 7, for example, discusses the first (official intergovernmental) World Population Conference, held in Bucharest in 1974. It was at Bucharest that the World Population Plan of Action (WPPA) was adopted and an attempt made – not wholly successfully, as we shall see – to define, amongst other policy and programme objectives, the goals and targets for reducing high rates of population growth and high levels of fertility. The speeches made by national delegates at the Bucharest meeting (as at subsequent meetings) are of consuming interest because they reveal the way different countries actually felt at the time on the key issues: population growth, family planning, abortion etc. China came in out of the cold at Bucharest to denounce both the 'super-powers', arguing that 'of all things in the world, people are the most precious.'

The Bucharest conference witnessed the clash of competing ideologies and viewpoints. Put in its simplest terms, the contest was between those (like the United States) who saw population limitation as the precondition of, or vital concomitant to, economic growth and those of a different persuasion (e.g. the Marxist countries of Eastern Europe) who believed that economic growth would of and by itself 'solve' the problems of population. The position of the Vatican was an additional complication. Barely five years had passed since the publication of the Papal Encyclical *Humanae Vitae*. Astute lobbying by the representatives of the Holy See both before and during the Bucharest Conference ensured that most delegates were quite familiar with the Catholic church's position.

If Bucharest in the end managed to achieve a compromise, it was nonetheless a fairly fragile plant. There was no clear language about overall or global targets for population growth. Even the language which related to national target setting was fuzzy. Where the draft Plan indicated that 'countries which consider that their present or expected rates of population growth hamper their goals of promoting human welfare are invited, if they have not done so, to consider setting quantitative population growth targets,' the Plan as it emerged from the buffeting of the Conference merely invited countries to 'consider adopting population policies, within the framework of socio-economic development.'

Similarly, there was a proposal in the Draft Plan to 'make available, to all persons who so desire, if possible by the end of the Second United Nations Development Decade, but not later than 1985, the necessary information and education about family planning and the means to practise family planning effectively and in accordance with their cultural values.' The alternative text which the Conference adopted merely talked of the need to 'encourage appropriate education concerning responsible parenthood and make available to persons who so desire advice on the means of achieving it.'

In spite of the real disagreements on substance which existed, the Plan adopted at Bucharest was important in that it set the framework for national action and for international assistance in the field of population.

The decade which followed the Bucharest Conference saw rapidly falling birth rates in some parts of the world (what the UN has called a 'spectacular' decline). In 1950–1955, the birth rate for the world as a whole was 38.0 per 1,000 persons. The corresponding figures for the more developed and less developed regions were 22.7 and 45.4. By 1975–1980, the birth rate for the world had fallen to 28.9 and, for the more developed and less developed regions, to 15.8 and 33.5 per 1,000, respectively.

In all world regions except sub-Saharan Africa, there had been substantial declines in fertility. The picture was mixed in the case of Asia, the most populous and, demographically, the most heterogeneous continent. Fertility remained high in most countries of Western South Asia while declines in fertility had been recorded in many countries elsewhere in Asia. Not only had fertility declines been observed in city States, such as Singapore, and islands, such as Sri Lanka, but they had also been observed in parts of some of the largest countries of the region: India, Indonesia and the Philippines. China, which comprised approximately one third of the total population of all developing countries, had experienced a particularly rapid fertility decline. Its birth rate was much below the average for the developing countries of Asia. However, little or no change in fertility appeared to have taken place in Bangladesh, Pakistan or the Islamic Republic of Iran.

There was also diversity in Latin America, but the decline in fertility was not limited, as it was a few years previously, to the countries of Temperate South America and the Caribbean. There was evidence of decline in the largest countries in the region, including Brazil, Mexico, Colombia and Venezuela.

In all but a few of the developed countries, fertility was lower in 1980 than a decade earlier. In some countries, for example the (former) Federal Republic of Germany, crude birth rates had fallen almost to 10 per thousand. However, fertility in Eastern Europe remained higher than for the developed countries as a whole.

Evidence from the World Fertility Survey, a series of national inquiries using a comparable methodology in a large number of countries, indicated that, in most developing countries of Latin America, Asia and Oceania, preferences were for moderate-sized rather than large families. The Survey indicated that lack of access to modern contraception was a major problem. The evidence seemed to be that where effective governmental policies favoured their use, contraceptive methods could spread quite rapidly and accelerate the decline in fertility.

There remained, however, substantial differences in the approach to population questions which countries in different regions of the world adopted. The nations of East Asia remained in the vanguard but many Latin American and Caribbean countries developed over the decade an increasing consciousness of the social and economic consequences of their respective demographic situations, and – to a varying extent – showed a concern for associated problems such as adolescent pregnancy, though the question of abortion remained on the whole taboo. Many Latin American governments seemed to prefer not to look and not to know. Meanwhile in the Middle East and most of Africa the fairest assessment was that there was still a long way to go before the urgency of population issues began to impinge on the consciousness of policy-makers in any profound sense.

The culmination of the post-Bucharest decade came with the International Conference on Population, held in Mexico City in August, 1984. Once again, fairly full quotations are used to demonstrate the various national positions. Of particular interest was the position adopted by the United States whose representative threw a largish bombshell into the proceedings on the first day by arguing for 'market-based solutions' to population and by threatening to withdraw US funding for international population programmes run by the United Nations and the International Planned Parenthood Federation unless it could be demonstrated that these bodies were not, directly or indirectly, supporting coercive abortion in China.

Nonetheless, in spite of the fireworks, the Mexico City conference marked some solid progress. On the opening day, Mr Rafael Salas, the Conference's Secretary-General and the Executive-Director of UNFPA, said:

> Our goal is the stabilization of global population within the shortest period possible before the end of the next century.

This was possibly the most explicit commitment to a specific target so far made by a high official of the United Nations. Though the Mexico Conference did not itself adopt the goal of world population stabilization, there was nonetheless an underlying current of interest in such an idea and in the better provision of practical means to attain it. The final Declaration of the Mexico Conference observed that 'millions of people still lack access to safe and effective family planning methods' and called for major efforts to be made 'to ensure that all couples and individuals can exercise the basic human right to decide freely, responsibly and without coercion, the number and spacing of their children and to have the information, education and means to do so.' Demographic objectives are not, of course – as we shall see – the only purpose of family planning programmes. But the experience of the past decades seems to indicate that the provision of family planning services is a necessary, though not a sufficient, condition of successful attempts to limit human fertility.

Chapter 9 looks at some of the post-Bucharest landmarks, events or reports which helped – slowly but surely – to build a consensus. Brief summaries are provided of the key conclusions, including where appropriate direct quotation from the texts adopted. Some of the events, such as the Colombo Conference of Parliamentarians or the Rome meeting on Population and the Urban Future, were directly concerned with the population issue. Other reports, such as the Brandt Report or Global 2000 or the World Conservation Strategy, all of which came out in the early 1980s, treated population as part of a wider theme. It was the World Commission on Environment and Development chaired by Mrs Gro Harlem Brundtland, the Prime Minister of Norway, which, most famously, took a comprehensive view of the population–environment–development nexus. The Brundtland report *Our Common Future* is widely credited as having coined the concept, or at least the term, 'Sustainable Development'. The treatment of population issues given in the Brundtland report was a model of intelligent analysis and sensitive drafting. It set the stage for the last major highlight of the decade of the 1980s, at least as far as the great debate on population was concerned, namely the International Forum on Population in the Twenty-First Century, which was held in Amsterdam in November 1989.

The Amsterdam Declaration on Population and Sustainable Development is of outstanding importance for the development of this particular narrative. It made clear recommendations about national population goals ('a reduction in the average number of children born per woman commensurate with achieving, as a minimum, the medium variant population projections of the United Nations'). It indicated clear programme priorities ('an increase in contraceptive prevalence in developing countries so as to reach at least 56 per cent of woman of reproductive age by the year 2000'). It gave a realistic assessment of programme costs (a minimum annual cost of $US 9 billion, to be compared with the 1987 total of national and international expenditures for family planning and other major population activities in developing countries of around $4.5 billion).

However, the Amsterdam meeting, crucial though it was as far as the intellectual debate was concerned, did not carry the *political* weight which attaches to some other international meetings. Though the United Nations General Assembly would later 'take note with appreciation' of the Amsterdam Declaration, many looked to the Earth Summit, the United Nations Conference on Environment and Development (UNCED) which was to be held in Rio de Janeiro, Brazil, for a final political endorsement at the highest level of the Amsterdam verities.

In the event, UNCED's recognition of the centrality of population policies and programmes to the pursuit of sustainable development was less than vociferous. Though Agenda 21's Chapter 5 (on 'Demographic Dynamics and Sustainability') contains some workmanlike ideas amid the inevitable dense thickets of intergovernmental prose, UNCED cannot in the end be said to have taken the consensus on population as far as many hoped. Rio's delegates were, for whatever reason, unable or unwilling to be even as specific as Amsterdam's. Perhaps it was something to do with the climate. Because Rio was important in its own right, and because consideration of the Rio conclusions on population reveals how much still has to be settled at the next main event on the international calendar, the International Conference on Population and Development to be held in Cairo in September 1994, Chapter 10 looks in some detail at 'Population at the Earth Summit'.

The later chapters focus on the world population situation at the end of the 1980s and on the projections made around that time for future population growth under different scenarios. Under the United Nations so-called *medium* variant, total world population would grow from 5.3 billion in 1990 to 8.5 billion in the year 2025. The population of the more developed regions would increase by 12 per cent during that period and that of the less developed regions by 75 per cent. Europe's share of the world's population, which declined from 16 to 9 per cent between 1950 and 1990, would decline further, to 6 per cent by 2025. Africa's share, which increased from 9 to 12 per cent between 1950 and 1990, would rise to 19 per cent in 2025.

The medium variant assumes that the total fertility rate for the developing countries as a whole declines from 3.71 for the period 1990–1995, to 2.71 for the period 2010–2015 and 2.32 for 2020–2025.

Under the low variant, the world population would reach only 7.6 billion by the year 2025, and 7.8 billion by the year 2050. However, the low variant assumes more rapid falls in fertility. To achieve it, the total fertility rate for the developing regions as a whole would have to decline from 3.38 for the period 1990–1995, to 2.71 for the period 2010–2015 and 2.32 for the period 2020–2025. The long-range projection of the low variant, i.e. beyond the year 2025, would ultimately bring about an actual decline in total world population: to 6 billion in the year 2100 and 4.3 billion by the year 2150. So around one hundred and fifty years from now, world population could – hopefully in an orderly and rational manner and without the intervention of one or more of the Four Horsemen of the Apocalypse – have been clawed back to a level not seen since the beginning of the 1980s.

The stakes, whether we look at the near future, to the middle distance or to the far horizon, are thus almost unimaginably high. The difference between the high and the low projections is 327 million people by the year 2000, 1.8 billion by the year 2025, 4.6 billion by 2050 and 13 billion by the end of the next century. In other words we are talking about the difference between, on the one hand, a world which is demographically speaking out of control and, on the other hand, a world where the unprecedented proliferation of the human race (probably the single most distinctive feature of the history of the twentieth century) has at last been contained and even reversed.

Can the fertility levels implied in the 'low' projections actually be attained in practice? The last part of the book focuses on recent national and international efforts in the field of population and family planning. The book looks at key countries which have introduced population and family planning programmes and where significant declines in fertility either have already been achieved or seem likely to occur. Real progress appears to be linked not only to the availability of family planning supplies and services, but also – crucially – to other factors such as the quality of care, the level of female literacy, community participation etc.

By the beginning of the 1990s, important reductions in fertility had been achieved in many parts of the world. The region of East Asia, which included China, had already attained the replacement level fertility of 2.1 children per couple. In South-eastern Asia, Indonesia had achieved a fertility rate of just above 3 taking the country as a whole, but some major provinces had already attained or were on the verge of attaining replacement levels. In Latin America, fertility had declined by at least one child per woman since the 'seventies and stood at just above 3 at the beginning of the 1990s.

In Europe, fertility at 1.7 children per woman was below replacement level (with the highest fertility in Eastern Europe at 2.0 and the lowest in Southern Europe at 1.5, the world record low being held by that staunch Catholic country, Italy, with a rate of 1.3 children per woman, followed closely by another Catholic country, Spain, with a rate of 1.4). Like Europe, Northern America had already attained replacement level fertility at the beginning of the 1990s, as had Australia and New Zealand.

According to the World Bank, the *'central observable event in the reproductive revolution is a substantial irreversible decline in human fertility.'* That reproductive revolution is, however, by no means complete. Though substantial progress has been achieved in many areas of the world, there are other regions where reproductive revolution is either unfinished or has not properly started. The fertility rate per woman over the continent of Africa as a whole still stood at around 6 at the beginning of the 'nineties, the highest rate being found in Eastern Africa with 6.8 and the lowest in Southern Africa at 4.2. In Western Asia (or the Middle East) the fertility rate stood at 4.7 and in Southern Asia, an area which included Afghanistan, India, Iran and Pakistan, the rate stood at 4.3. The Johns Hopkins survey published in December 1992 and cited extensively in Chapter 13 indicates that between 20 per cent and 30 per cent of married women have an 'unmet need' for family planning.

Chapter 14 is entitled 'Effective Family Planning'. If family planning programmes met all of the existing potential demand, they would have a dramatic influence on contraceptive prevalence in the developing countries and hence on fertility levels. Surveys indicate that with an increase in contraceptive prevalence from the current level of 51 per cent to over 60 per cent, fertility would fall from an average of about 4 children per woman to about three, or halfway to replacement level. In most countries outside sub-Saharan Africa, a further rise in contraceptive prevalence – to levels of 70–80 per cent – could bring fertility close to replacement.

The challenge facing the world today is to consolidate existing gains while achieving new break-throughs in fertility reduction in those areas where progress has been so far limited. New insights may be required; new or different approaches may need to be pursued if these more demographically recalcitrant regions of the world are to be able to follow successfully the trail which others have blazed. From a global perspective, the second 'demographic revolution' – namely the transition from high fertility to low fertility – has still some way to go. Both national and international resources will be needed if further reductions in fertility are to be achieved.

Compared with other expenditures, the sums that appear to be needed are not enormous. It has been calculated that if the world was to reach an average family size of two children early in the twenty-first century, 70 to 80 per cent of all couples would need to use contraception by the year 2000. This would require a doubling of family planning users from about 350 million in 1990 to roughly 700 million by the end of the decade. Assuming that the cost of providing high quality family planning information and services is about $16 per couple per annum, annual expenditures on family planning would need to more than double from their current levels – to around $11 billion in constant 1990 dollars. Such a sum (which is less than one per cent of current Third World debt) could put the world firmly on the track towards population stability.

The last part of the book looks ahead to the preparations for the International Conference on Population and Development (ICPD). It examines the prospects for a new international consensus on population and a new World Population Plan of Action which builds on the achievements of Mexico, Bucharest and Rio de Janeiro to include, amongst other things, clear commitments on national and international population goals, programme objectives and resources. Such goals have indeed already been formally proposed to the ICPD's preparatory committee. In May 1993, Dr Nafis Sadik, the Conference's Secretary-General and Executive-Director of UNFPA, put forward for consideration a set of goals which included aiming at attaining the low variant population projection of 7.27 billion for the year 2015, reducing infant and maternal mortality in the developing countries to developed country levels and expanding contraceptive prevalence in the developing countries from the current 51 per cent to 71 per cent by the year 2015.

If a new international consensus on population is to emerge at Cairo, it must of course be based on the profound conviction that Cairo is a complement to, and not a substitute for, Rio; that coherent population programmes are the vital third side of the 'population–environment–development triangle' rather than a bargain-basement substitute for development; and that there are few areas of human endeavour where performance will not be significantly improved as a result of successful efforts to lower human fertility rates and rates of population growth.

Are such beliefs sufficiently widespread and sufficiently solid to generate the consensus which is needed if the Cairo conference is to achieve the success it deserves? Where, after the last thirty years, does the great population debate stand? What are the intellectual and other undercurrents which have determined the course of this particular river?

At any moment, one or more of several themes may appear to dominate the population discussion. Sometimes Malthusianism, having flown out by the window, seems to be creeping back through the door and books with titles like *The Population Bomb*, *Standing Room Only* or *Our Crowded Earth* reappear in the shop windows. At other times, the economic arguments predominate. It is not population growth *per se* which matters, we are told; it is the rate at which populations are growing in any particular country and the ability of the national economy to absorb the annual increase. This latter viewpoint certainly predominated in the 1960s and early 1970s when weighty volumes like the United States National Academy of Science's massive study, 'Rapid Population Growth: Consequences and Policy Implications', were to be found on the desks of officials in the World Bank, UNDP, USAID and the Ford Foundation. Or again, action in the field of population and family planning may be promoted or supported primarily for health or human rights motivations, with wider demographic considerations taking second place. As noted in Chapter 3, the right of couples to choose freely and responsibly the number and spacing of their children was enshrined as early as 1968 in the corpus of international law and was certainly one of the factors which led to increasing support at national and international level for maternal and child health programmes which included family planning or for stand-alone family planning programmes.

Over the years other themes began to emerge. The impact of population on the environment, and the contribution of population pressures to ecological degradation, began to be examined more closely and this in turn necessitated some rethinking. If there were after all 'limits to growth' in the long term, and real environmental problems in the shorter term (like desertification) associated with population pressures, perhaps the classic economic theories needed to be looked at again. Perhaps it was not just the rate of population growth; perhaps population *per se* was indeed a problem, particularly when seen in terms of its impact on non-renewable ecological resources.

In which case, of course, the matter could no longer be presented as an issue purely for the developing world since it was clear that the rich industrialised world – in particular, the United States, Western Europe and Japan – consumed far more resources on a per capita basis than did most of the inhabitants of Asia, Africa and Latin America. Thus even though the industrial world might have much lower rates of population growth, and in some cases might have already attained replacement levels of fertility or lower, the impact of the average American man (or even the average American dog for that matter) on limited world resources might far outweigh that of, say, 100 villagers in Bihar or Rajasthan. The text-books of the future may quite possibly treat the equation I = PAT, (where I stands for environmental impact, P for Population, A for affluence or per capita consumption, and T is a measure of the environmental damage done by technology in supplying each unit of consumption) with as much respect as they accord Einstein's historic formula $E = MC^2$!

This latter theme emerged quite strongly at the Earth Summit in June 1992. Principle 8 of the Rio Declaration on Environment and Development states that:

> To achieve sustainable development and a higher quality of life for all people, States should reduce and eliminate unsustainable patterns of production and consumption and promote appropriate demographic policies.

Chapter 4 of Agenda 21, the international action plan for achieving 'sustainable development', is devoted to 'Changing Consumption Patterns' and is followed by a chapter on 'Demographic Dynamics and Sustainability' which begins with the clear statement that 'The growth of world population and production combined with unsustainable production patterns places increasingly severe stress on the life-supporting capacities of our planet.'

In practice it is always easier to call for changes in consumption patterns than to achieve them. The Earth Summit gave no clear guidance on this front. Some see a linkage between reducing population growth in the developing world and reducing consumption in the industrialized world, reckoning that the one may be a *quid pro quo* for the other. Others see a danger in seeking to strike this kind of a global bargain. Reducing population growth, reducing consumption are objectives to be pursued in their own right without being part of some international package deal.

The process of urbanisation forced another rethink of the classic approaches to population. Urban problems were not purely economic problems, capable of being 'solved' through the application of economic measures. In the developing world, many urban problems are linked to the phenomenon of urbanisation, itself a function both of population growth and internal migration (the latter often a result of rural population pressures).

The new emphasis on women's rights and female emancipation has also led to an evolution in thinking about population. Though (as noted above) historically the issue of human rights – and the impact of high fertility on the well-being of individuals and families – had long been to the fore in the population argument, the decade of the eighties gave a much sharper focus to this issue. A woman's right to bear a child, one of the most fundamental human rights of all, increasingly became linked to a woman's right *not* to bear a child. She was, in other words, to be master (or rather mistress) of her own body. Population policy, in so far as it encompassed information about and programmes for contraception and family planning, was clearly of the greatest relevance here, even though abortion – an area where different human rights appeared to come into direct conflict with each other like ignorant armies clashing by night – has remained a matter of controversy. This was all the more tragic in the light of the evidence that illegal abortions in some parts of the world, particularly in Latin America, represents an enormous human and social problem, a problem that could be substantially reduced if the governments were ready to come forward with enlightened and compassionate legislation in this area.

And if family planning was an integral part of female emancipation, a solid blow struck against the Dark Ages which still prevailed in some regions of the world, for example, in parts of the Middle East, as far as attitudes to women were concerned, so female emancipation (as expressed, for example, in the goals and objectives of the United Nations Women's Decade) was a necessary concomitant of successful family planning programmes. The link between fertility and social patterns extended in both directions. Nothing could be more fundamental. As T.S. Eliot put it in *Sweeney Agonistes*, 'birth, and copulation, and death. That's all the facts, when you come to brass tacks'.

Population and human rights; population and development; population, resources and the environment; population and urbanisation; population and women – all these were themes which have played their part in the process of building the consensus for action which increasingly took shape in the seventies and eighties.

Ultimately, questions of population growth could be linked to the maintenance of world peace itself. The validity of such a linkage has over the years been increasingly explored. It was, for example, specifically mentioned by UN Secretary-General Perez de Cuellar in his own speech to the International Conference on Population in 1984, when he said:

> I consider these (population) activities are directly linked to the first objective of the United Nations, the preservation of peace, since future political stability, like economic development, will depend heavily on the way population policies are handled.

Events of recent years have tended to confirm the wisdom of that observation since population pressures have been at least a contributing factor in local or regional conflicts. The growth in the number of 'environmental refugees', particularly in Africa, bears witness to the potentially explosive disruption that may be caused when the population–resources balance tilts out of kilter.

The three decades of national and international progress in the field of population and family planning chronicled here reflect in different ways and at different times all of the above approaches and concerns. The list is not exhaustive and other rationales will certainly emerge in the future. Or there will be changes of emphasis. The demographic approach may be put on the back burner (for residual Thatcherites or Reaganites the notion of setting population targets or programme objectives may smack of old-fashioned central planning!); the human rights or 'empowerment of women' approach may make the running for a while. This is still an evolving situation.

Whatever the underlying motivations may be, the real question is whether the sum total of all these opinions, beliefs, convictions or whatever will be enough to ensure that the national and international efforts in the field of population and family planning receive a powerful new impetus at the Cairo conference. For the outcome of the International Conference on Population and Development, the final political compromise which is the usual product of these intergovernmental meetings, will of course reflect not only the point of view of the protagonists (of population and family planning programmes) but also of the opposition.

It would indeed be foolish to imagine that the opposition has disappeared. To take just a few examples. The Marxist battalions, opposing population limitation on the grounds that revolution will solve the problems of production, may be much diminished as a result of the world-wide collapse of Communism. But there have been new recruits to the ranks of the sceptical. The feminist movement, for example, which used to be solid in its support of family planning, is now looking a little wobbly. Some northern feminist NGOs are beginning to encourage their southern sisters to resist programmes and approaches which appear to use family planning, not as an end in itself, but as a step to some other male-sponsored or male-decided goal.

Or again, the Roman Catholic Church has certainly not given up the attempt to assert the absolute rightness of its own view of the moral and ethical issues relating to population and family planning questions, particularly those having to do with contraception, abortion and certain other aspects of human sexuality. On the contrary, *Humanae Vitae* has been followed by *Splendor Veritatis*, a document which holds out little hope that any major doctrinal revision is in the offing as far as these matters are concerned. And though in practice, many millions of Catholics around the world apparently ignore the dictates of Rome, the situation is not a happy one. The fact that the present Pope in particular has so much vision and charisma, is in so many ways such an heroic figure, makes it all the more poignant that he is still on the other side of the argument, as it were, while adding to the personal anguish of those who are unable to conform to the Church's prescriptions.

On the whole though, as this book goes to press with the Cairo conference still some months ahead, there seem to be some solid grounds for believing that the historical trends which have emerged over the last several decades will be confirmed rather than confounded. There may still be intellectual and political disagreements at Cairo, as there were in Bucharest in 1974, and Mexico City in 1984, but those disagreements if they occur should be less acute and less disruptive than they were in earlier years. There will certainly be some fireworks over the Nile. But few at this moment predict major explosions or a shattering of the slow but sure progress towards consensus that these last years have witnessed. Barring unforeseen accidents or diversions, at the end of the day one message seems likely to come through loud and clear. *By acting vigorously and effectively to turn back the tide of population growth and to reduce human fertility, mankind is in a very real sense taking back or reasserting its duty and its ability to control its own destiny.*

If such a message does emerge from the Cairo meeting in September 1994, it will on the one hand be a fitting culmination for all that has gone before and, on the other, a beacon lighting the way for the decades which lie ahead.

1

The World Population Situation in 1970

THE DEMOGRAPHIC BACKGROUND

For the purpose of this particular narrative, 1970 is a convenient starting date. Looking back with the benefit of hindsight, it can be argued that many of the threads in the world population tapestry – demographic, political, institutional – had been woven by then even though it would take further decades for the overall picture to emerge with reasonable clarity. The revolution in human fertility, which is the main subject of this book, was already taking shape at the end of the sixties. The political framework, in terms of the way nations and peoples saw the population problem, was evolving rapidly. Institutional structures to respond to population issues were being put in place at both the national and the international level.

Nevertheless, 1970 – as any other starting point would be – is to some extent artificial. The world population situation in 1970 was already determined to a large extent by the demographic events of previous centuries. Though the milestones of the world's demographic history are by now fairly well established, it seems sensible at the beginning of an account such as this, to give a summary description of the evolution of the world's population.

In fact, little is known about world population before the Christian era. The development of ancient city-centred civilizations in the Old World, with the accumulations of relatively large and dense agricultural populations that they required, suggests that the third millennium before Christ may have been a period of comparatively large growth in the population of Asia and North Africa if not of the world as a whole. During the first millennium of the Christian era, the indications are that the pendulum swung again towards slower growth or stagnation. In spite of uncertainties in the estimates, some demographers take the view that population made relatively little gain, if it did not suffer a loss, between AD 0 and 1000 in China, Europe, North Africa and South-west Asia. Population may have increased substantially during the first Christian millennium in Japan, South-east Asia, Tropical Africa and America, but increases in the relatively small populations of these regions would not have carried much weight in the global trend.

Between AD 1000 and 1750, it is clear that a much larger growth in the world population occurred than in the previous 1000 years. Populations expanded between AD 1000 and 1300 in China and Europe and this process continued after the setbacks of the 14th century. (The loss of life which occurred in Europe and neighbouring regions as a result of the Black Death and its sequel of plague epidemics was probably paralleled in Central Asia, China and India.)[1]

By the year 1750, total world population – which had stood at around 250 million at the beginning of the Christian era – had grown to approximately 730 million,

Table 1.1. Population estimates for world regions since the time of Christ, according to Clark (figures in millions, letter codes denote grades of reliability).

Region	AD 14	1000	1200	1500	1750	1900	1975
World total	256	280	384	427	731	1,668	3,967
China[a]	73 B	60 B	123 B	100 C	207 B	500 C	839 B
India-Pakistan-Bangladesh	70 D	70 D	75 D	79 D	100 C	283 A	745 A
Southwestern Asia, total	34	22	21	15	13	38gC	118 B
Asia Minor, Syria and							
Cyprus[b]	14 C	10 D	10 D	8 D	7 D	–	–
Other Southwestern Asia[c]	20 D	12 D	11 D	7 D	6 D	–	–
Japan	2 D	10 C	12 C	16 C	26 A	44 A	111 A
Remainder of Asia, exc. USSR	5 D	10 D	11 D	15 D	32 D	120gB	440 B
Europe, exc. USSR, total	37	32	45	62	102	284 A	476 A
Southern Europe[d]	32 C	24 C	33 C	39 C	60 B	–	–
Northern Europe	5 D	8 C	12 C	23 C	42 B	–	–
USSR, total	8	12	12	12	34	127	255 A
European part	3 D	7 D	6 D	6 C	28 B	110gA	–
Asian part	5 C	5 D	6 D	6 D	6 D	17gB	-
Africa, total	23	50	61	85	100	122	401
Northern Africa[e]	11 C	4 D	4 D	6 D	5 D	27gB	80 A
Remainder of Africa	12 D	46 D	57 D	79 D	95 D	95gC	321 B
America, total	3 D	13 D	23 D	41	15	144	561
Northern America[f]	–	–	–	1 D	2 B	81 A	237 A
Middle and South America	–	–	–	40 D	13 C	63 B	324 A
Oceania	1 D	1 D	1 D	2 D	2 C	6 A	21 A

[a] Present area, including Manchuria, Inner Mongolia, Sinkiang, Tsinghai, Tibet, and Taiwan, as well as historic China Proper.

[b] Asian sector of the Roman Empire in AD 14.

[c] Iran, Iraq, Arabian countries, and other parts of Southwestern Asia outside the borders of the Roman Empire in AD 14 (excluding the European part of Turkey).

[d] Total of estimates for areas corresponding approximately to the territories of the Roman Empire in Europe in AD 14 (France, Belgium, Netherlands, Spain, Portugal, Italy, Greece, and the 'Rest of SE Europe' in the nomenclature of Clark's Table), including the European part of Turkey.

[e] Egypt, Libya, Tunisia, Algeria, and Morocco.

[f] United States, Canada, Greenland, Bermuda, and St. Pierre and Miquelon.

[g] Estimates for regions not shown separately in Clark's tabulation, derived from other sources in such a way as to agree with Clark's totals for broader regions.

[h] In Clark's total estimate of 4 million for Russia in Europe, 'Poland, Czechoslavakia, etc,' and Hungary, 3 million are allocated to Russia in order to complete the regional classification in the form given here.

Source: Article by John D. Durand entitled: 'Historical Estimates of World Population: an Evaluation', published in *Population and Development Review.* Vol. 3, No. 3, September 1977. AD 14–1900, except as noted: Clark (1968), Tables III.1 (p. 64) and III.15 (p. 108). 1975: United Nations *Demographic Yearbook,* 1975.

distributed roughly as follows: China, 207 million; India-Pakistan-Bangladesh, 100 million: South-western Asia, 13 million; Japan, 26 million; remainder of Asia, 32 million; Europe, excluding USSR, 102 million; USSR, 34 million; Africa, 100 million; North America, 2 million; Middle and South America, 13 million; Oceania, 2 million.

Around the middle of the nineteenth century world population passed the 1,000 million mark, an event whose significance was almost certainly not appreciated at the time. If it took all of history, recorded or unrecorded, to reach that first 1,000 million (or billion), it took less than 100 years to reach the second (achieved around 1930); and about 30 years to reach the third (achieved around 1960).

WHAT WERE THE DISTINGUISHING FEATURES OF THE WORLD POPULATION SITUATION AT THE END OF THE 1960s?

The United Nations has over the years produced an invaluable series of summary reports on the world population situation. The first such report, the Concise Summary of the World Population Situation in 1970,[2] spoke in graphic terms of the 'revolutionary change in the reproductive balance of the human species' that had taken place in modern times. The term 'revolutionary change' was used in particular to refer to the *decline in mortality* which had occurred over the previous century.

> It can be stated with certainty, though not with great numerical precision, that *a truly 'revolutionary'[3] change in the reproductive balance of the human species has taken place in modern times.* Never in history had it been possible to reduce human mortality to such an extent as it was in the past hundred years or so. During that period, however, a very sharp distinction has emerged in economic, social and demographic conditions between those areas now regarded as 'more developed' and those that now appear 'less developed'.[4] The 'revolutionary' change attained major importance in the more developed areas from the middle of the nineteenth century onward. More suddenly, and with greater magnitude, it came into prominence in the less developed areas, only in the middle of the present century. (emphasis added)

THE WORLD MORTALITY SITUATION IN 1970

Because a decline in mortality has generally been considered an essential precondition for the onset of the 'demographic transition' (from high mortality/high fertility towards low mortality/low fertility), and because it is in its own right, as the United Nations notes, the evidence of a 'revolutionary' change in human reproductive behaviour, it is worth looking in some detail at the world mortality situation as it appeared at the end of the 1960s.

Separating, somewhat artificially, the more developed from the less developed regions, the UN estimated that, in periods up to about 1850, in both sets of regions there was an average of about 35 deaths and about 40 births per 1,000 inhabitants each year, leaving similarly moderate balances of a natural increase in both sets of regions. But, after 1850, the annual average death rate in the more developed regions decreased to about 28 per 1,000 in 1850–1900, to about 18 per 1,000 in 1900–1950, and to 10 per 1,000 or less since 1950. In the less developed regions the death rate might have averaged 38 per 1,000 during 1850–1900, and

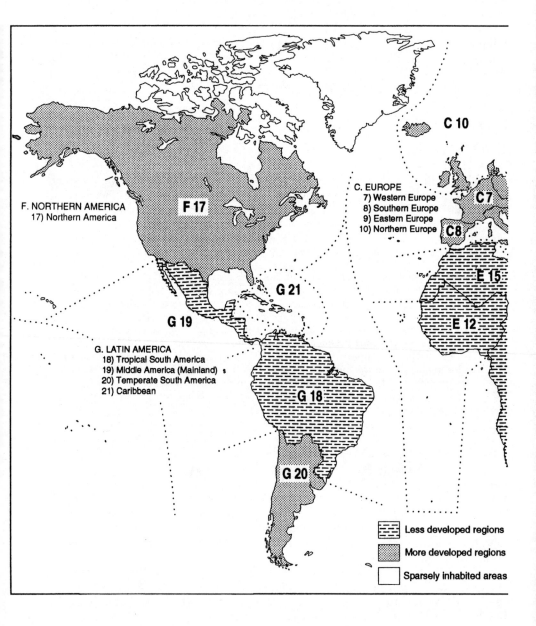

F. NORTHERN AMERICA
17) Northern America

F 17

C. EUROPE
7) Western Europe
8) Southern Europe
9) Eastern Europe
10) Northern Europe

C 10

C 7

C 8

E 15

E 12

G 21

G 19

G. LATIN AMERICA
18) Tropical South America
19) Middle America (Mainland)
20) Temperate South America
21) Caribbean

G 18

G 20

Less developed regions

More developed regions

Sparsely inhabited areas

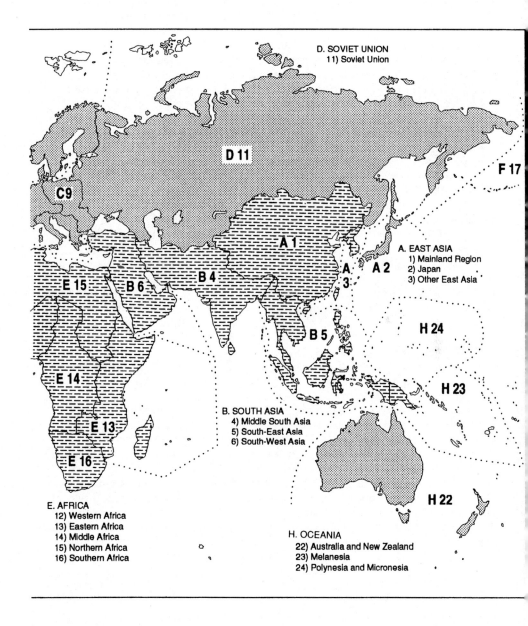

D. SOVIET UNION
11) Soviet Union

D 11

F 17

C 9

A 1

A. EAST ASIA
1) Mainland Region
2) Japan
3) Other East Asia

A 2

A 3

B 4

E 15

B 6

B 5

H 24

E 14

H 23

E 13

B. SOUTH ASIA
4) Middle South Asia
5) South-East Asia
6) South-West Asia

E 16

H 22

E. AFRICA
12) Western Africa
13) Eastern Africa
14) Middle Africa
15) Northern Africa
16) Southern Africa

H. OCEANIA
22) Australia and New Zealand
23) Melanesia
24) Polynesia and Micronesia

Fig. 1.1. Major areas and regions by levels of economic and social development. *Source: UN Concise Summary of the World Population Situation in 1970s,* United Nations.

was still 32 per 1,000 during 1900–1950, as compared with an estimated 21 per 1,000 in 1950–1960, and 17 per 1,000 in 1960–1970. In these regions, as compared with the more developed ones, the modern diminution of mortality was delayed by nearly a century but by the end of the 1960s, the UN observes, it was occurring 'with outstanding speed.'

Severe inequalities in risk of death still persisted between the inhabitants of more developed and less developed regions, but at least it could justifiably be said that the gap, which was at its widest in the first half of our century, was now narrowing considerably. Furthermore, owing to the more youthful structure of their populations, the frequency of death (per 1,000 inhabitants of all ages) in some of the less developed countries had now fallen as low as, or even lower than, that in some of the more developed countries where the proportion of individuals at advanced ages was high.

Exceedingly low crude death rates had recently been recorded in limited areas of East and South-East Asia, Latin America, and islands of the Pacific Ocean and the Caribbean Sea. For example, the fairly accurate data of 1965 included the following crude death rates: 4.8 per 1,000 population in Hong Kong, 5.0 in the Netherlands Antilles, 5.1 in Fiji, 5.3 in the Ryukyu Islands, 5.5 in China (Taiwan), and 5.6 in Singapore. All these were areas of outstanding recent achievements in the field of public health in which, furthermore, only small proportions of the population were of advanced ages. Nevertheless, crude death rates of more than twice this order of magnitude were recorded in the following countries which had some of the best health conditions but also considerable proportions of aged persons in their population: 13.3 per 1,000 in the German Democratic Republic, 13.0 in Austria, 12.3 in Luxembourg, 12.1 in Belgium, and 11.5 in Ireland, Switzerland and the United Kingdom of Great Britain and Northern Ireland. The combination of favourable mortality conditions and, so far, moderate proportions of aged population resulted in 1965 in a crude death rate of 7.2 per 1,000 in Japan, and 7.3 in the USSR. Extreme cases, due to unusual age composition of the population under otherwise comparable health conditions, could also be noted, such as a death rate of 2.9 per 1,000 in the Panama Canal Zone, and 18.0 per 1,000 in West Berlin.

In view of the strong influence of age composition upon the recorded crude death rate, it was necessary also to compare the estimated expectations of life at birth.[5] According to the United Nations in 1965,[6] life expectation at birth was estimated as 69 to 71 years in eight more developed regions, 64 years in temperate South America, and 38 to 60 years in the less developed regions.

The enormous progress in health, medicine and sanitation implicit in these figures was clear, when it was considered that until the second half of the nineteenth century a life expectation greater than 35 years had hardly been attained by any sizeable population. Expectations as low as thirty years, and even lower under adverse conditions, were then common throughout the world. At the beginning of this century, many of the present most advanced regions still had expectations of life no higher than 45 or 50 years.

In the 1950s radical improvements in health conditions led to the inference that, with the exception of some highest and lowest levels, expectations of life tended to advance by as much as five years per decade. As a general rule the population projections based on that inference were also borne out by new census results obtained in and around 1960. More recent observations suggested that gains in expectation of life could be even more rapid in a middle range, notably where current expectations are between, say, 45 and 55 years. At lower expectations it might have to be assumed that continuing geographical, cultural or organizational impediments still caused current gains to be somewhat slower. And when high levels were being approached, a slow-down might again have to be expected, because further improvements would then depend on increased expenditures, if not also on new medical discoveries.

Progress in the prevention of avoidable deaths had been distributed unequally among the population of the two sexes, and very unevenly also among different age groups. The detailed study of mortality according to groups of sex and age drew attention to many particular factors. In most countries the mortality of women is less than that of men but in important areas in South Asia and possibly also in China (mainland), this did not appear to be the case. There were also some other areas, for example in Latin America, where until recently in certain ages (sometimes the childbearing ages and sometimes in adolescence), the mortality of women exceeded that of men. The reasons for differences in the death risks of men and women were many and not easily analysed. On the whole, with recent health improvements greater gains in life expectancy had accrued to women than to men. Various social, environmental and sanitary factors also caused a different incidence of deaths at different ages. Where mortality was low, the chief remaining causes of death at all ages were malignant neoplasms, cardiovascular and nervous diseases, and in addition, among younger age groups, also the incidence of accidents, such as those caused by motor vehicles.

INFANT MORTALITY

An important indicator of social and environmental factors was the level of infant mortality. Unfortunately its accurate statistical measurement was often difficult. The widespread acceptance of the loss of many infant lives had sometimes been attributed to a fatalistic outlook on life; it might also – the UN observes – have been a cause of 'fatalistic attitudes'. Before the introduction of new methods and the development of corresponding attitudes, almost everywhere at least 200 or more out of 1,000 live-born infants died in their first year of life. The loss of many new-born infants had probably long been regarded as unavoidable, and had to be accepted as such, in the history of every human society. In some of the less developed regions this might still be the case.

In the more developed regions, where it was measured accurately, average infant mortality had dropped to about 35 per 1,000 live births by 1960, and to 28 per 1,000 by 1965, with a range from 19 to 44 per 1,000 among particular regions. In some of the smaller, low-income countries with good registration statistics, declines of infant mortality to similarly low levels had also been recorded recently. But since there was probably a high correlation between the conditions permitting public-health work and those facilitating the establishment of reliable vital statistics, it could be assumed that infant mortality had not declined nearly so much in most of the other less developed regions. In those regions, levels in the wide range from 100 to 200 per 1,000 live births were probably still typical. The UN commented:

> Despite often inadequate measurement, this subject has special importance, owing to its probable close connexion with motivated attitudes of parents concerning their progeny and their children's prospect in life.[7]

THE WORLD FERTILITY SITUATION IN 1970

Even if, as noted above, the gap between developed and developing regions as far as mortality was concerned was, in some respects at least, beginning to close, the same could not be said of fertility at the end of the 1960s.

During the nineteenth century, birth rates had fallen very substantially in all the more developed regions. In the present more developed regions combined, the birth rate might have averaged 38 per 1,000 during 1850–1900 and 26 per 1,000 during 1900–1950, the average falling progressively as one region after another underwent this process of change. Post-war 'baby booms' led to an average birth rate of 23 per 1,000 in 1950–1960, subsiding to 19 per 1,000 in 1960–1970.

By contrast, apart from some recent exceptions, birth rates had fallen hardly at all in the less developed regions. In this respect, the gap between developed and developing regions had widened enormously and, with a recently renewed decrease of birth rates in some of the more developed regions, it was still widening. In the UN's view, the difference was so great that *the level of the birth rate could serve as well as any other economic or social indicator to distinguish between more developed and less developed countries*[8] (emphasis added).

Looking at the situation in more detail, the United Nations noted that in eight of the nine more developed regions of the world, birth rates estimated for 1965 ranged from 16 to 20 per 1,000 while in fifteen less developed regions they ranged from 36 to 49 per 1,000. An estimated birth rate of 25 per 1,000 was also to be mentioned for temperate South America, a region of substantial economic development but including some areas of less advanced development. It was noteworthy how similar the birth rates in the more developed regions had become, while among less developed regions the range was still wide. The estimates took into account the assumption that the birth rate in China (mainland) was near the lower limit of the high-fertility group and was gradually declining. Certain circumstantial facts seemed to support this view, but accurate information was lacking.

Elsewhere among less developed regions the birth rate was estimated as 36 per 1,000 in East Asian areas other than China (mainland) or Japan, 38 per 1,000 in the Caribbean, and 40 per 1,000 in tropical South America and the smaller islands of the Pacific. At the other extreme it was estimated as high as 49 per 1,000 in Western Africa, 47 per 1,000 in Northern and Eastern Africa, and 45 per 1,000 in Middle Africa, South Asia and South-East Asia.

The estimates for 1965 reflected some shifts which had occurred in preceding years in more developed regions, notably the subsidence of the baby boom around 1950 in Europe and Japan and by the end of the 1950s in Northern America and Oceania, and also a continuing decrease of the birth rate in the USSR. More recently the birth rates in Europe and Japan had been substantially stabilized and similar levels were discernible also in Northern America, the USSR as well as Australia and New Zealand.

In a few of the less developed regions, the beginnings of a break with previously stable high levels could be noted, such as the decreases which had been observed in East Asian areas as in China (Taiwan), Hong Kong, the Republic of Korea, Singapore, and in many of the Caribbean islands. With less certainty, small decreases in the birth rates of some other parts of Latin America had also been estimated, and a similar trend had been conjectured for China (mainland). No such trend could as yet be discerned among the large populations of most of Africa and South Asia and Latin America.

The United Nations commented:

In a number of high fertility countries, substantial decreases in birth rates have been noted in very recent years. Between 1960 and 1965 the birth rate decreased from 49 to 42 in Brunei, from 43 to 35 in Albania, from 40 to 33 in China (Taiwan), from 39 to 31 in Singapore, and from 36 to 26 in Hong Kong. During the same period, smaller decreases were recorded also in some other countries, notably from 43 to 40 in Guyana, from 42 to 39 in Jamaica, from 41 to 37 in West Malaysia, from 38 to 35 in Mauritius, from 38 to 34 in Guadeloupe, and from 37 to 33 in Ceylon. *But the combined population of these countries is small in comparison with those in which no appreciable change in the high birth rate can as yet be discerned.*[9] (emphasis added)

The interpretation of these varied trends in birth rates was complicated by the large number of interfering factors. Even with similar fertility among women of childbearing ages, crude birth rates could change owing to changes in the age composition of the population. The fertility of women could change also as a result of modifications in their marital condition, such as entry into marriage at an earlier or later age, changes from consensual unions to legal marriage, and a reduced incidence of widowhood owing to decreased mortality and the consequent survival of most husbands to a more advanced age. Health conditions related to sterility or frequent miscarriage could affect fertility and their improvement, other circumstances remaining the same, could cause a rise in the frequency of live-born infants. The mere fact that birth rates in certain regions apparently remained stable might sometimes indicate that circumstances which could have caused their rise had been counter-balanced by others tending towards some restriction of fertility.

Important in this connection was the study of the frequency of childbirth to women of different ages. Various social, cultural, environmental and health conditions accounted for a considerable diversity in the distribution of births among women in the several childbearing age groups. In some populations, childbirth was most concentrated among very young women; in others it was especially frequent among somewhat older women while in others still the frequencies were dispersed among a wider range of ages. The chief factors influencing childbearing patterns could sometimes be identified, such as early marriage, health factors, heterogeneity of the population, or other circumstances. But, so the UN concluded, the complexity of their effects made it difficult to measure the extent of their influence. Nevertheless, it was possible to assess somewhat tentatively whether a given pattern of childbearing was likely to resist strongly or to give way more easily to influences which tended to modify it.

The United Nations went on to observe, in a comment which prefigured the intense debate which would subsequently take place at the World Population Conference, Bucharest, 1974:

Aside from the marital and health factors already mentioned, *the record of all historical and demographic observations indicated that certain developmental features, singly or in combination, exerted a strong influence in the direction of an eventually decisive fertility decline towards the levels now prevailing in the more developed regions.* Among these one may mention the decline of mortality, improved health and education, rises in income, economic transformations, the move from agricultural to other economic activities, urbanization, greater frequency of travel and communications, wider choices for activities on the part of women and so on. But the speed with which these influences make themselves felt and the resistances they may encounter can vary considerably from one area to another, having regard also to a wide variety of culture patterns, traditions, guiding values, and attachments to symbols expressing them. (emphasis added)

The UN also noted:

> *The implementation of family planning policies, official, semi-official, unofficial, or vari-*
> *ously assisted, is a new phenomenon whose possible effect in diverse situations cannot yet be*
> *easily assessed but, with time, may also acquire importance.*[10] (emphasis added)

Given, as we shall argue later, the substantial part played by population and family
planning policies in 'turning the tide' and achieving on a widespread basis important,
and even decisive, declines in fertility, this brief and cautious comment is nonetheless
peculiarly prescient.

YOUTHFULNESS OF THE WORLD'S POPULATION

In the more developed regions, 28 per cent of the population were children and youth
below 15 years of age in 1965; persons aged 65 years and more constituted 9 per cent
in 1965 and might amount to 10 per cent in 1985; consequently the segment in the
most productive ages, between 15 and 64 years, was in the neighbourhood of 63 per
cent of the total. In the less developed regions, owing to their higher fertility, 42 per
cent of the population were aged under 15 years in 1965, and 3 per cent were 65 years
and older, hence 55 per cent were in the ages between 15 and 64. These differences in
age structure, especially between the more developed and less developed regions, had
important implications for priorities in economic and social investment.

NATURAL INCREASE OF WORLD POPULATION IN 1970

As already noted, except in somewhat exceptional areas, both the birth rates and the
death rates were higher in the less developed regions than in the more developed
ones. But the gap in birth rates, between the two sets of regions, was much wider than
the gap in death rates. Towards the end of the sixties, the gap in birth rates had
widened further while that in death rates had diminished. It followed that when the
death rates were subtracted from the birth rates the resulting rates of natural increase
in less developed regions greatly exceeded those in more developed regions, and this
difference had recently become very large.

The combined population of the more developed regions had grown at average
annual rates of 0.7 per cent during 1800–1850, 1.0 per cent during 1850–1900, and 0.8
per cent during 1900–1950, and it was currently growing at a rate close to 1 per cent. In
the less developed regions the combined population had grown at average rates of 0.5
per cent during 1800–1850, 0.4 per cent during 1850–1900, and 0.9 per cent during
1900–1950, and it was (at the end of the sixties) growing at a rate close to 2.4 per cent.

The more developed regions actually constituted two separate groups in the 1950s
and they still did around 1960. Among European regions and in Japan, natural
increase ranged between 7 and 11 per 1,000 in 1960, and also in 1965. In Northern
America, Oceania and the USSR, however, where rates of natural increase were
between 14 and 18 per 1,000 in 1960, they had more recently converged to the level
of 11 per 1,000. At constant annual rates in the range of 7 to 11 per 1,000, populations
would double within sixty to a hundred years.

For all the less developed regions, with their decreasing mortality, it was estimated
that natural increase had risen, except in a portion of East Asia (mainly China
(Taiwan) and the Republic of Korea) where the decrease in birth rates might have

nearly compensated that in death rates. On the low side, among less developed regions, were Middle Africa, the East Asian mainland and Melanesia with rates of natural increase between 18 and 20 per 1,000 in 1960, and between 20 and 25 per 1,000 in 1965. If such rates persisted, populations might double within thirty or thirty-five years. Regions of highest natural increase comprised Northern Africa, South-East Asia, Middle America (mainland) and the Pacific Islands.[11] Here the rates were from 25 to 29 per 1,000 in 1960, and from 26 to 33 per 1,000 in 1965. At such rates, populations could double within twenty-five years or less.

In absolute numbers, natural increase for the world as a whole in 1965 was about 65 million, that is to say, approximately 112 million babies were born, and about 47 million persons died. By comparison, a natural increase of 55 million in 1960 was the result of somewhat fewer births (105 million) and more numerous deaths (50 million). But here the trends again differed between more developed and less developed regions. From 1960 to 1965 the number of births in more developed regions diminished, from just under 21 million to just under 19 million, the number of deaths, which was about 9 million, increased slightly, and the amount of natural increase diminished from 12 million to less than 10 million. Meanwhile in the less developed regions the number of births increased from 84 million to 93 million, the number of deaths diminished from 41 million to 38 million, and the natural increase rose from 43 million to 55 million.

More diverse conditions were obtained when individual countries were considered. In Mexico, for instance, there were 1.6 million births in 1960 and nearly 1.9 million births in 1965, while in both years the number of deaths was almost the same, namely about 400,000. Natural increase, accordingly, rose from 1.2 to nearly 1.5 million. In Sri Lanka (then known as Ceylon), births numbered 362,000 and 369,000 in the two years, and deaths 85,000 and 92,000, leaving natural increase at the level of 277,000.[12]

Table 1.2 and Figure 1.2 show average birth rates, death rates and rates of natural increase in the world's major areas for the period 1965–2000, as projected by the United Nations at the end of the 1960s. The UN admitted that the more detailed estimates were quite tentative and that many figures would no doubt have to be revised when results of the population censuses, to be taken around 1970, became available.

The changing vital rates, both estimated and conjectured, for the period 1750–2000 are depicted in Table 1.3 and Figure 1.3. The growth in population size in the two types of regions is illustrated in Figure 1.4.

Looking ahead, the UN observed that wars, famines and epidemics had occurred in various parts of the world even in modern periods. There was no certainty that large calamities would not occur in the future. Some of the effects of such calamities on past population trends had been assessed and they were considerable in less developed regions in the second half of the nineteenth century and in both the less developed and the more developed regions in the first half of the present one. For instance, there had been the T'ai P'ing Rebellion of 1851–1864, the Indian Mutiny of 1857 and recurrent epidemics, not to mention the more recent two world wars.

The UN was, however, convinced that it would be a fallacy to think that wars in modern times had significantly held population growth in check.

> It can be calculated schematically that all the national and regional disasters on record since 1850, terrible as they have been, have delayed the growth in world population by no more than 10 years. Had there been no war, famine or epidemic since 1850, the world's population might have totalled more than 2,000 million in 1920 instead of in 1930, and more than 3,500 million in 1960 instead of in 1970.

Table 1.2. Birth rates, death rates and rates of natural increase as projected in eight major world areas, 1965–2000 (rates per 1,000 per year).

	Northern America			Europe			USSR			East Asia		
	Birth rate	Death rate	Natural increase	Birth rate	Death rate	Natural increase	Birth rate	Death rate	Natural increase	Birth rate	Death rate	Natural increase
1965–1970	19.3	9.4	9.9	18.0	10.2	7.8	17.9	7.7	10.2	31.5	14.0	17.5
1970–1980	21.0	9.4	11.6	17.9	10.3	7.6	19.1	8.2	10.9	28.1	11.7	16.4
1980–1990	21.2	9.1	12.1	17.8	10.6	7.2	19.9	8.9	11.0	24.0	9.6	14.4
1990–2000	18.7	8.8	9.9	17.0	10.4	6.6	17.8	9.1	8.7	20.2	8.3	11.9

	Latin America			Africa			South Asia			Oceania		
	Birth rate	Death rate	Natural increase	Birth rate	Death rate	Natural increase	Birth rate	Death rate	Natural increase	Birth rate	Death rate	Natural increase
1965–1970	38.5	10.1	28.4	46.7	21..2	25.5	44.3	16.8	27.5	24.5	10.0	14.5
1970–1980	37.1	8.3	28.8	46.3	18.1	28.2	41.4	13.7	27.7	25.7	8.7	17.0
1980–1990	34.8	6.7	28.1	44.3	14.5	29.8	35.3	10.1	25.2	25.6	8.3	17.3
1990–2000	32.0	5.6	26.4	39.5	11.2	28.3	28.3	7.6	20.6	22.6	7.7	14.9

Source: UN Concise Summary of World Population Situation in 1970.

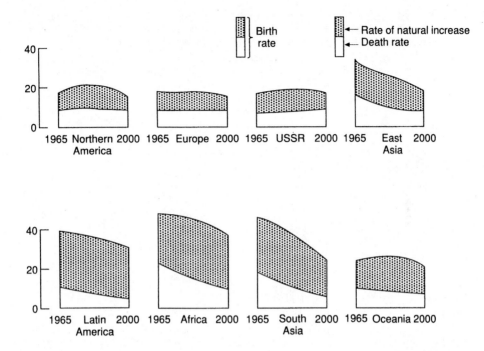

Fig. 1.2. Birth rates, death rates and rates of natural increase as projected in eight major world areas, 1965–2000 (rates per 1,000 per year). *Source: UN Concise Summary of the World Population in 1970.*

In the UN's view, it was generally accepted that death rates everywhere would be brought to the lowest levels which available knowledge, means and other circumstances permitted. A very sudden cut down of birth rates to the levels already reached by the death rates was entirely improbable.

The UN concluded its brief historical perspective with the ominous sentence:

> Enormous future increases in the numbers of mankind are therefore a virtual certainty, unless disasters occur on a hitherto unimaginable scale.[13]

POPULATION PROJECTIONS, 1965–2000

U Thant, the former Secretary-General of the UN, once said: 'The most urgent conflict confronting the world of today is not between nations or ideologies, but between the pace of growth of the human race and the insufficient increase in resources needed to support mankind in peace, prosperity and dignity.'[14] On Human Rights Day, 10 December 1966, he issued a Declaration on Population developed on the initiative of John D. Rockefeller 3rd, Chairman of the Board, Population Council, and signed by the heads of state of twelve countries. A year later, eighteen other heads of state had added their names to the document.[15]

As they made their Declaration, the Heads of State made their own cogent statement about the future growth of the world's population and its implications:

Table 1.3. Estimated and conjectured average annual birth rates, death rates and rates of natural increase for presently more developed and less developed regions, 1960–1967, and selected periods from 1750 to 2000 (rates per 1,000 per year).

Period	More developed regions			Less developed regions		
	Birth rate	Death rate	Natural increase	Birth rate	Death rate	Natural increase
1960–1967[a]	20	9	11	41	18	23
Half centuries						
1750–1800	38	34	4	41	37	4
1800-1850	39	32	7	41	36	5
1850–1900	38	28	10	41	37	4
1900–1950	26	18	8	41	32	9
1950–2000	20	10	10	37	14	23
Decades						
1900–1910	34	21	13	41	34	7
1910–1920	26	23	3	40	37	3
1920–1930	28	16	12	41	31	10
1930–1940	22	14	8	41	29	12
1940–1950	20	15	5	40	28	12
1950–1960	23	10	13	41	21	20
1960–1970[b]	19	9	10	41	17	24
1970–1980	19	9	10	38	13	25
1980–1990	19	10	9	34	10	24
1990–2000	18	10	8	29	8	21

[a] According to *Demographic Yearbook 1967* (United Nations publication, Sales No.: E/F.68.XIII.1)
[b] According to recently revised population projections.
Source: UN Concise Summary of World Population Situation in 1970.

The peace of the world is of paramount importance to the community of nations, and our governments are devoting their best efforts to improving the prospects for peace in this and succeeding generations. *But another great problem threatens the world – a problem less visible but no less immediate. That is the problem of unplanned population growth.* It took mankind all of recorded time until the middle of the last century to achieve a population of one billion. Yet it took less than a hundred years to add the second billion, and only thirty years to add the third. At today's rate of increase, there will be four billion people by 1975 and nearly seven billion people by the year 2000. This unprecedented increase presents us with a situation unique in human affairs and a problem that grows more urgent with each passing day. The numbers themselves are striking, but their implications are of far greater significance. Too rapid population growth seriously hampers efforts to raise living standards, to further education, to improve health and sanitation, to provide better housing and transportation, to forward cultural and recreational opportunities – and even in some countries to assure sufficient food. In short, the human aspiration, common to men everywhere, to live a better life is being frustrated and jeopardized. (emphasis added)

As noted above, the World Leaders stated that there would be 'nearly seven billion' people on this earth by the year 2,000 at 'today's rate of increase.' In fact since 1967,

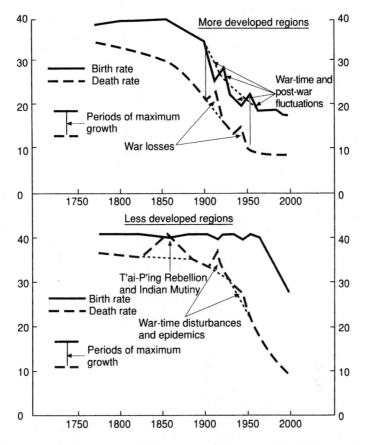

Fig. 1.3. Estimated and conjectured trends in birth rate and death rate, 1750–2000, more developed and less developed regions. *Source: UN Concise Summary of the World Population Situation in 1970.*

when the Declaration on Population was made, the rate of increase had itself accelerated. The United Nations had revised its projections upwards.

Tables 1.6–1.9 present the results of total population estimates and annual rates of growth by regions during the period 1965–2000, according to four variants. The world population of 3,289 million in 1965 was expected, according to the 'medium' variant (Table 1.6), to increase to 6,494 million in 2000. The implied rates of growth indicated that the world population might be growing at almost a constant rate of about 2.0 per cent annually until the middle of the 1980s, and then the rate would gradually decrease until it reached 1.7 per cent by the end of the century. During the period under consideration, the population of the less developed regions was anticipated to increase from 2,252 million to 5,040 million, with a rate of growth which would remain virtually constant and equal to about 2.4 per cent until 1985 and then gradually decrease to 2.0 per cent per annum. On the other hand, the population of the more developed regions might sustain an almost constant annual rate of about 1.0 per cent throughout the remainder of this century, thus increasing from 1,037 million

Table 1.4. World population, 1970 (mid–year estimates).

	Population (in millions)	Rate of increase (per cent)	Birth rate	Death rate
			(per thousand)	
World	3,633	2.0	34	14
Africa	344	2.6	46	20
Western Africa	101	2.5	49	24
Eastern Africa	98	2.5	43	18
Northern Africa	87	3.1	48	17
Middle Africa	36	2.1	45	24
Southern Africa	23	2.4	41	17
America	511	2.1	30	10
North America	228	1.2	18	9
Latin America	283	2.9	39	10
Tropical S. America	151	3.0	41	11
Middle America	67	3.4	44	10
Temperate S. America	39	1.8	26	8
Caribbean	26	2.3	36	13
Asia	2,056	2.3	38	15
Eastern Asia	930	1.8	31	13
Mainland	765	1.8	33	15
Japan	103	1.1	18	7
Other Eastern Asia	61	2.5	34	9
South Asia	1,126	2.8	44	16
Middle S. Asia	762	2.8	45	17
S.E. Asia	286	2.8	43	15
S.W. Asia	77	2.9	43	14
Europe	462	0.8	18	10
Western Europe	149	0.8	17	11
Southern Europe	128	0.9	19	9
Eastern Europe	104	0.8	17	10
North-Eastern Europe	81	0.6	18	11
Oceania	19.4	2.0	24	10
Australia and New Zealand	15.4	1.9	20	9
Melanesia	2.8	2.4	42	18
Polynesia and Micronesia	1.2	3.1	40	9
USSR	242	1.0	18	8

Source: UN Demographic Yearbook 1970.

in 1965 to 1,454 million at the turn of the century. As a result of these differing rates of growth, the projected population of the less developed regions was expected to be about three and a half times the projected figure for the developed regions at the end of the century, while the ratio in 1965 was only a little over two to one.

According to the 'low' and 'high' variants, the range within which the population of the less developed countries would probably fall by the end of the century was from 4,523 to 5,650 million. The 'high' variant implied an acceleration of population

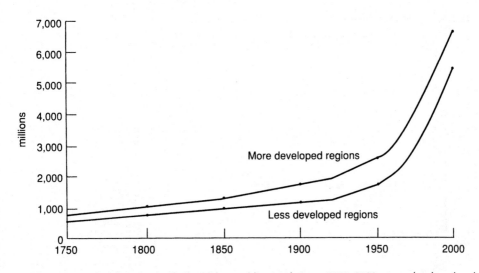

Fig. 1.4. Estimated and conjectured size of the world's population , 1750–2000, more developed and less developed regions. *Source: UN Concise Summary of the World Population Situation in 1970.*

growth at a rate equal to 2.6 or 2.7 per cent per annum until 1985 followed by a gradual decline in the rate of growth to 2.4 per cent per annum during 1995–2000. The 'low' variant envisaged a more moderate rate of population growth which would gradually decrease from 2.3 to 1.6 by the end of the century (Tables 1.7 and 1.8). In the 'constant fertility' variant, the rates of growth given in Table 1.9 indicated that if the population of the less developed regions maintained their 1965 levels of fertility they would have an accelerated increase in their annual rates of growth, from 2.6 in

Table 1.5 World population increase, 1965–70.

	Annual per cent increase		Annual absolute increase (millions)	
	1960–5	1965–70	1960–5	1965–70
World total	1.94	1.98	61.1	68.2
More developed regions	1.15	0.95	11.5	10.0
Less developed regions	2.32	2.45	49.6	58.2
East Asia	1.75	1.75	14.4	15.5
South Asia	2.48	2.75	23.1	28.6
Europe	0.84	1.78	3.7	3.4
Soviet Union	1.52	1.02	3.4	2.4
Africa	2.41	2.55	7.0	8.3
Northern America	1.34	0.98	2.7	2.2
Latin America	2.82	2.84	6.6	7.6
Oceania	1.69	1.45	0.2	0.2

Source: UN Demographic Yearbook 1970.

Table 1.6. Total population estimates (1970) and annual rates of growth by regions, 1965–2000; medium variant.

Regions	Total population (in thousands)					Annual rates of growth (per cent)				
	1965	1970	1980	1990	2000	1965–70	1970–5	1980–5	1990–5	1995–2000
World total	3,289,002	3,631,797	4,456,688	5,438,169	6,493,642	2.0	2.0	2.0	1.8	1.7
More developed regions	1,037,492	1,090,297	1,210,051	1,336,499	1,453,528	1.0	1.0	1.0	0.9	0.8
Less-developed regions	2,251,510	2,541,501	3,246,637	4,101,670	5,040,114	2.4	2.5	2.4	2.1	2.0
East Asia	851,877	929,932	1,095,354	1,265,343	1,424,377	1.8	1.7	1.5	1.2	1.1
Mainland region	700,076	765,386	901,351	1,042,864	1,176,176	1.8	1.7	1.5	1.3	1.1
Japan	97,950	103,499	116,347	125,330	132,760	1.1	1.2	0.8	0.6	0.6
Other East Asia	53,851	61,046	77,656	97,148	115,442	2.5	2.4	2.4	1.8	1.6
South Asia	981,046	1,125,843	1,485,714	1,911,819	2,353,841	2.8	2.8	2.6	2.2	2.0
Middle South Asia	664,868	761,809	1,001,046	1,279,761	1,564,963	2.7	2.8	2.5	2.1	1.9
South-East Asia	249,349	286,925	380,367	491,775	607,709	2.8	2.9	2.7	2.2	2.0
South-West Asia	66,829	77,109	104,302	140,283	181,169	2.9	3.0	3.0	2.7	2.4
Europe	444,642	462,120	497,061	532,636	568,358	0.8	0.7	0.7	0.7	0.6
Western Europe	143,143	148,619	158,214	168,679	179,266	0.8	0.6	0.6	0.6	0.6
Southern Europe	122,750	128,466	140,059	151,605	162,674	0.9	0.9	0.8	0.7	0.7
Eastern Europe	100,060	104,082	112,392	119,607	127,277	0.8	0.8	0.7	0.7	0.6
Northern Europe	78,689	80,953	86,396	92,745	99,141	0.6	0.6	0.7	0.7	0.7
USSR	230,556	242,612	270,634	302,011	329,508	1.0	1.0	1.2	0.9	0.8
Africa	303,150	344,484	456,721	615,826	817,751	2.6	2.8	3.0	2.9	2.8
Western Africa	89,546	101,272	133,406	180,059	240,158	2.5	2.7	3.0	3.0	2.8
Eastern Africa	86,448	97,882	128,757	173,639	233,245	2.5	2.7	2.9	3.0	2.9
Middle Africa	32,318	35,893	45,785	60,449	80,214	2.1	2.4	2.7	2.9	2.8
Northern Africa	74,520	86,606	119,385	163,230	214,404	3.0	3.2	3.2	2.9	2.6
Southern Africa	20,318	22,832	29,387	38,450	49,730	2.3	2.5	2.7	2.6	2.5
Northern America	214,329	227,572	260,651	299,133	333,435	1.2	1.3	1.5	1.1	1.0
Latin America	245,884	283,253	377,172	499,771	652,337	2.8	2.9	2.8	2.7	2.6
Tropical South America	129,854	150,660	203,591	272,495	358,447	3.0	3.0	2.9	2.8	2.7
Middle America (Mainland)	56,961	67,430	94,706	132,387	180,476	3.4	3.4	3.4	3.2	3.0
Temperate South America	36,000	39,378	46,731	54,783	63,266	1.8	1.7	1.6	1.5	1.4
Caribbean	23,068	25,785	32,145	40,107	50,148	2.2	2.2	2.2	2.2	2.2
Oceania	17,520	19,370	24,025	29,639	35,173	2.0	2.1	2.2	1.8	1.6
Australia and New Zealand	14,015	15,374	18,785	22,659	26,214	1.9	2.0	2.0	1.5	1.4
Melanesia	2,452	2,767	3,585	4,743	6,107	2.4	2.6	2.8	2.6	2.4
Polynesia and Micronesia	1,053	1,229	1,657	2,237	2,853	3.1	3.1	3.1	2.6	2.3

Source: UN Population Division: interim revision (1970) of 'World Population Prospects as Assessed in 1963' (*Population Studies*, No. 41, United Nations publication, Sales No.: 66.XIII.2).

Table 1.7. Total population estimates (1970) and annual rates of growth by regions, 1965–2000; high variant, less-developed regions only.

Regions	Total population (in thousands)					Annual rates of growth (per cent)				
	1965	1970	1980	1990	2000	1965–70	1970–5	1980–5	1990–5	1995–2000
Less-developed regions	2,251,510	2,563,561	3,378,768	4,424,950	5,650,426	2.6	2.7	2.7	2.5	2.4
Mainland region	700,076	785,095	983,009	1,183,317	1,369,757	2.3	2.3	2.0	1.5	1.4
Other East Asia	53,851	61,046	78,845	102,115	123,424	2.5	2.5	2.7	2.1	1.7
South Asia	981,046	1,126,115	1,518,153	2,032,456	2,617,382	2.8	2.9	3.0	2.7	2.4
Middle South Asia	664,868	761,993	1,024,890	1,363,525	1,742,573	2.7	2.9	2.9	2.6	2.3
South-East Asia	249,349	286,925	387,315	522,096	677,570	2.8	3.0	3.0	2.7	2.5
South-West Asia	66,829	77,197	105,947	146,835	197,239	2.9	3.1	3.3	3.1	2.8
Africa	303,150	345,818	466,366	648,854	905,702	2.6	2.9	3.3	3.4	3.3
Western Africa	89,546	101,705	136,590	190,624	269,314	2.5	2.8	3.3	3.5	3.4
Eastern Africa	86,448	98,203	131,361	182,218	256,970	2.5	2.8	3.2	3.4	3.5
Middle Africa	32,318	36,013	46,754	63,457	88,626	2.2	2.5	3.0	3.3	3.4
Northern Africa	74,520	87,027	121,883	172,708	236,900	3.1	3.3	3.5	3.3	3.0
Southern Africa	20,318	22,871	29,778	39,847	53,892	2.4	2.6	2.8	3.0	3.0
Tropical South America	129,854	151,266	208,241	288,203	394,822	3.1	3.2	3.3	3.2	3.1
Middle America (Mainland)	56,961	67,498	96,505	138,609	196,659	3.4	3.5	3.7	3.5	3.5
Caribbean	23,068	25,851	32,754	41,915	53,842	2.3	2.3	2.5	2.5	2.5
Melanesia	2,452	2,771	3,645	4,963	6,625	2.4	2.6	3.0	3.0	2.8
Polynesia and Micronesia	1,053	1,230	1,737	2,472	3,337	3.1	3.4	3.6	3.1	2.9

Source: UN Population Division: interim revision (1970) of 'World Population Prospects as Assessed in 1963' (*Population Studies*, No. 41, United Nations publication, Sales No.: 66.XIII.2).

Table 1.8. Total population estimates (1970) and annual rates of growth by regions, 1965–2000; low variant, less-developed regions only.

Regions	Total population (in thousands)					Annual rates of growth (per cent)				
	1965	1970	1980	1990	2000	1965–70	1970–5	1980–5	1990–5	1995–2000
Less-developed regions	2,251,510	2,522,681	3,136,625	3,819,836	4,523,382	2.3	2.2	2.0	1.8	1.6
Mainland region	700,076	752,802	855,508	945,776	1,034,638	1.5	1.4	1.0	0.9	0.9
Other East Asia	53,851	61,046	76,468	92,659	107,712	2.5	2.3	2.0	1.6	1.4
South Asia	981,046	1,121,456	1,438,771	1,785,862	2,119,009	2.7	2.6	2.3	1.8	1.6
Middle South Asia	664,868	758,481	967,173	1,191,467	1,403,391	2.6	2.5	2.2	1.7	1.6
South-East Asia	249,349	286,062	369,499	461,531	550,240	2.7	2.6	2.4	1.9	1.7
South-West Asia	66,829	76,914	102,100	132,864	165,378	2.8	2.8	2.7	2.3	2.1
Africa	303,150	343,596	448,006	582,872	734,159	2.5	2.6	2.7	2.4	2.2
Western Africa	89,546	100,928	130,536	168,751	210,587	2.4	2.5	2.6	2.3	2.1
Eastern Africa	86,448	97,637	126,633	165,633	211,152	2.4	2.6	2.7	2.5	2.3
Middle Africa	32,318	35,766	44,757	57,033	71,306	2.0	2.2	2.4	2.3	2.2
Northern Africa	74,520	86,470	116,964	154,130	194,285	3.0	3.1	2.8	2.4	2.2
Southern Africa	20,318	22,795	29,117	37,325	46,829	2.3	2.4	2.5	2.3	2.2
Tropical South America	129,854	150,035	198,648	257,832	325,152	2.9	2.8	2.7	2.4	2.2
Middle America (Mainland)	56,961	67,136	92,831	127,219	167,641	3.3	3.2	3.2	2.9	2.6
Caribbean	23,068	25,762	31,713	38,814	47,677	2.2	2.1	2.0	2.1	2.0
Melanesia	2,452	2,765	3,533	4,579	5,786	2.4	2.5	2.6	2.5	2.2
Polynesia and Micronesia	1,053	1,213	1,632	2,179	2,733	2.8	3.1	3.0	2.4	2.1

Source: UN Population Division: interim revision (1970) of 'World Population Prospects as Assessed in 1963' (*Population Studies*, No. 41, United Nations publication, Sales No.: 66.XIII.2).

Table 1.9. Total population estimates (1970) and annual rates of growth by regions, 1965–2000; constant fertility variant, less-developed regions only.

Regions	Total population (in thousands)					Annual rates of growth (per cent)				
	1965	1970	1980	1990	2000	1965–70	1970–5	1980–5	1990–5	1995–2000
Less-developed regions	2,251,510	2,559,001	3,381,131	4,583,220	6,638,737	2.6	2.7	3.0	3.2	3.4
Mainland region	700,076	780,941	991,228	1,275,390	1,673,559	2.2	2.3	2.5	2.7	2.8
Other East Asia	53,851	61,573	82,445	113,897	156,700	2.7	2.8	3.2	3.2	3.2
South Asia	981,046	1,126,074	1,515,875	2,100,924	2,988,562	2.8	2.9	3.2	3.5	3.6
Middle South Asia	664,868	761,904	1,023,084	1,414,629	2,012,112	2.7	2.9	3.2	3.5	3.6
South-East Asia	249,349	287,050	387,272	537,323	762,368	2.8	3.0	3.2	3.5	3.5
South-West Asia	66,829	77,121	105,509	148,972	214,081	2.9	3.0	3.4	3.6	3.7
Africa	303,150	344,496	456,620	622,901	872,798	2.6	2.7	3.0	3.3	3.4
Western Africa	89,546	101,272	133,360	180,901	252,231	2.5	2.7	3.0	3.3	3.4
Eastern Africa	86,448	97,882	128,711	174,009	241,750	2.5	2.7	2.9	3.2	3.4
Middle Africa	32,318	35,958	45,603	59,449	79,683	2.1	2.3	2.6	2.9	3.0
Northern Africa	74,520	86,606	119,719	170,143	247,424	3.0	3.2	3.4	3.7	3.8
Southern Africa	20,318	22,779	29,227	38,399	51,710	2.3	2.4	2.7	2.9	3.0
Tropical South America	129,854	151,523	209,966	295,754	420,972	3.1	3.2	3.4	3.5	3.6
Middle America (Mainland)	56,961	67,485	96,413	140,425	206,814	3.4	3.5	3.7	3.8	3.9
Caribbean	23,068	26,041	33,725	44,540	60,115	2.4	2.5	2.7	2.9	3.1
Melanesia	2,452	2,767	3,612	4,886	6,798	2.4	2.6	2.9	3.2	3.4
Polynesia and Micronesia	1,053	1,229	1,733	2,478	3,544	3.1	3.3	3.6	3.6	3.6

Source: UN Population Division: interim revision (1970) of 'World Population Prospects as Assessed in 1963' (*Population Studies*, No. 41, United Nations publication, Sales No.: 66.XIII.2).

Greenland
39

Iceland 21

Faroe Islands
23

Alaska
(USA)

United Kingdom
16

Netherlands
18

Ireland
22

Belgium
15

Luxembourg 13

France
17

Canada
17

Switzerland 16

Spain
20

Portugal 20

United States
18

Bermuda
18

Morocco 49

Algeria
49

Upper
Volta

Bahamas
23

Spanish Sahara 18

Hawaiian Islands (USA)

Mexico
42

Cuba 29

Haiti 44

Senegal

Mauritania
44

Niger
52

Dominican Republic 48

Cape Verde
Islands
41

British Honduras 43

Puerto Rico 25

Honduras 49

Guatemala 43

Jamaica
33

Gambia 42

Mali
55

El Salvador 44

Barbados 30–34

Guinea

Nigeria
50

Nicaragua 46

Trinidad & Tobego 28

Sierra Leone 45

Costa Rica 33

Venezuela

Guyana

Liberia 50

Panama 38

Colombia

Surinam

Ivory Coast

Canal Zone 12

French Guiana

Ghana

Dahomey
50

Ecuador

Togo
51

Cook Island
41

Peru
43

Brazil
37

Bolivia
44

Paraguay

Chile
28

Uruguay

Argentina
21

Falkland Islands
28

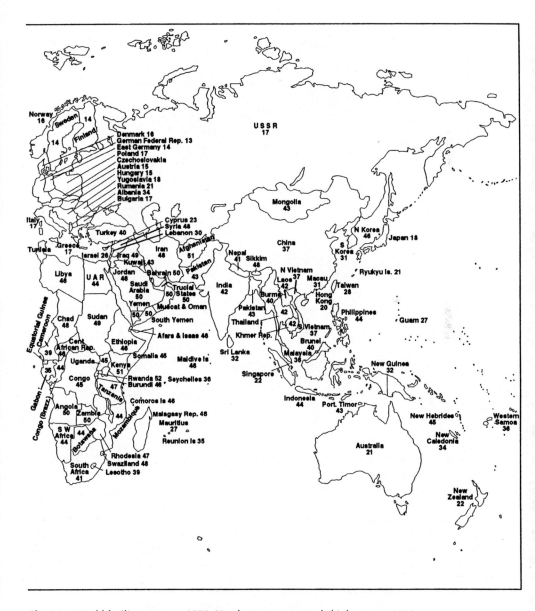

Fig. 1.5.   World fertility patterns c.1970. Numbers represent crude birth rate per 1000.
Source: International Demographic Statistic Center, Bureau of the Census, USA.

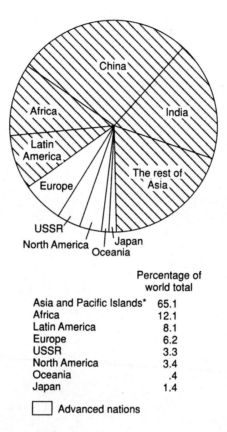

	Percentage of world total
Asia and Pacific Islands*	65.1
Africa	12.1
Latin America	8.1
Europe	6.2
USSR	3.3
North America	3.4
Oceania	.4
Japan	1.4

☐ Advanced nations

Fig. 1.6. World births in percentages by region, 1970. *Source:* Estimates of International Demographic Statistical Center, Census Bureau, supplied by USAID.

1965–70 to probably 3.4 in 1995–2000, and their total population might reach 6,369 million by the end of the century.

Among the world's major areas the largest addition to the population during the 35-year projection period was expected in South Asia, which contained almost one-third of the world's population. As the data in Tables 1.6–1.9 show, the population of this major area was anticipated to increase from 981 million to 2,354 million in the year 2000 according to the 'medium' variant, and it might reach 2,617 million if the assumptions of the 'high' variant materialized. The next major area of importance with respect to addition of population numbers, according to the 'medium' variant, was East Asia where, although the pace of growth was expected to be moderate (from 1.8 per cent per annum in the beginning of the projection period to 1.1 in the end), the absolute increase would be very high. Sizeable increases in total population were also expected in Latin America, from 246 million in 1965 to 652 million in 2000, and in Africa, from 303 million to 818 million during the same period. It was also to be noted that for the year 2000 the 'constant fertility' estimate of total population was higher than the 'medium' estimate by 27 per cent in South Asia, 42 per cent in East Asia (excluding Japan), 17 per cent in Latin America and 7 per cent in Africa.

In making the above projections, the UN noted that the assumption of future mortality trends was 'relatively unproblematical'.[16] It was assumed that governments everywhere would remain committed to the achievement of the best attainable levels of health and that remaining obstacles, still greater in some regions than in others, would be overcome with time. However, it was noted that in countries having the highest expectations of life improvements had recently slowed down suggesting that, with currently known medical techniques, there were limits to what could still be achieved. 'There is no basis now for an assumption that new discoveries will soon be made to push these limits much further.' Accordingly, it was projected that expectation of life at birth would rise with diminishing speed at the higher levels and cease rising when it had attained 74.8 years for both sexes combined (72.5 years for males and 77.5 years for females).

The UN recognized that there was much greater difficulty in drawing up plausible assumptions for future fertility trends. It was considered highly probable that sooner or later fertility would fall low in all regions. The decline from high levels might be provoked by the economic and social development process, and might also 'be assisted by specific programmes designed to promote it.' Since more developed and rapidly developing regions had low or falling fertility, 'the norm of small families can elicit emulation with increasing effect as mass communications penetrate ever further into hitherto remote regions.' But the more detailed timing and speed of such future trends could not be conjectured except within a very wide margin of probable error.

Past observations supported the view that the decline itself, once in progress, was unlikely to be interrupted midway when its momentum was probably the strongest. Uncertainty was greater as regarding the detailed trend while the level was still high, or when it was already fairly low. In regions of generally low fertility, marked fluctuations had been recorded in recent decades, making it uncertain whether the most recent observations indicated a trend or merely another temporary fluctuation.

It was also clear at the beginning of the 1970s that there still remained several regions of high fertility where indications were still lacking as to how soon a decisive

Table 1.10. Expectation of life at birth (both sexes).

World area	Estimated level		Date when assumed to reach 74.8 years
	1970–1975	1995–2000	
Northern America	71.4	72.5	2030
Europe	71.3	74.1	2015
USSR	70.4	73.0	2025
East Asia	62.9	71.2	2040
Latin America	61.9	70.6	2040
Africa	45.2	57.4	2075
South Asia	49.5	61.2	2070
Oceania	68.3	71.4	2035

Source: UN Concise Report on the World Population Situation in 1970–1975, p. 50.

Table 1.11.   Children of either sex born per woman.

World area	Estimated level		Date when assumed to fall to 2.08[a]
	1970–1975	1995–2000	
Northern America	2.19	2.13	2010
Europe	2.28	2.21	2005
USSR	2.42	2.46	2015
East Asia	3.59	2.26	2020
Latin America	5.27	3.90	2035
Africa	6.38	5.43	2070
South Asia	6.13	4.28	2060
Oceania	3.44	2.95	2020

[a]On the 'high' assumption this level will be reached 10 years later and on the 'low' assumption 10 years earlier.
Source: UN Concise Report on the World Population Situation in 1970–1975, p. 51.

decline might begin and how rapidly it might progress once it did begin. While the detail could not be foreseen, all regional fertility assumptions took the form of a decline which at first accelerated and eventually slowed down until fertility approached the net replacement level.

The onset and speed of fertility decline could, of course, be variously assumed in each region. To provide a 'medium' variant for the projections, assumptions were drawn up making reference to known recent levels and trends, past trends observed elsewhere, levels of economic and social development and relevant policies, if any, entertained by the respective governments.

The 'medium' assumption of future fertility trends, as projected by the United Nations,[17] is shown in Table 1.11, which shows the date when fertility is assumed to fall to replacement level (ranging from the year 2005 for Europe, 2020 for East Asia, 2035 for Latin America and 2070 for Africa).

On the 'high' assumption replacement level fertility would be reached 10 years later and on the 'low' assumption 10 years earlier. The 'constant fertility' variant assumed that the population of the less developed countries would maintain 1965 levels of fertility.

Though, for the high, medium and low variants, it was assumed that fertility would fall to net replacement level at certain future dates, it did not follow that population growth would come to an end by the same date. More time was needed until the population age structure was transformed; hence population growth would continue until the age structure resembled that of the eventual stable population.

LONG-RANGE PROJECTIONS, 1950–2075

In 1974, the United Nations, with considerable intellectual enterprise and imagination, published a second Concise Report on the World Population Situation. This document looked at the situation in 1970–1975 in the context of its long-range implications. The UN looked ahead in this case, not to the end of the century which had been the previous bench-mark, but to the year 2075, a hundred years away.

Table 1.11a Birth rates, death rates and rates of natural increase (per 1,000 population) in eight major world areas at the end of each of three phases in the demographic transition according to the "medium" variant of the long-range projections.

Major area	Period	Birth rate	Death rate	Rate of natural increase
End of phase 1 (highest rate of natural increase)				
Northern America[a]	1955–1960	24.9	9.3	15.6
Europe[a]	1950–1955	19.8	11.0	8.8
USSR[a]	1955–1960	25.3	7.6	17.7
East Asia	1960–1965	30.5	12.4	18.1
Latin America	1960–1965	39.1	10.9	28.2
Africa	1985–1990	44.1	14.3	29.8
South Asia	1975–1980	41.1	14.5	26.6
Oceania[a]	1955–1960	27.3	10.8	16.5
End of phase II (lowest death rate)				
Northern America	1970–1975	16.5	9.3	7.2
Europe	1965–1970	17.5	10.2	7.3
USSR	1955–1960	25.3	7.6	17.7
East Asia	1995–2000	15.1	7.7	7.4
Latin America	2010–2015	21.8	5.0	16.8
Africa	2030–2035	21.5	5.7	15.8
South Asia	2020–2025	20.6	6.4	14.2
Oceaniaa	2010–2015	18.1	7.3	10.8
End of phase III (fertility reaches net replacement level)				
Northern America	2010	14.8	9.6	5.2
Europe	2005	14.3	11.0	3.3
USSR	2015	15.2	10.1	5.1
East Asia	2020	14.7	9.0	5.7
Latin America	2035	16.3	6.7	9.6
Africa	2070	14.5	9.4	5.1
South Asia	2060	14.4	9.8	4.6
Oceania	2020	16.4	7.7	8.7

[a] Highest natural disease since 1950. Higher rates of natural increase had already occurred before 1950.
Source: UN Concise Report on the World Population Situation in 1970–1975.

The trends in crude birth rates, death rates and rates of natural increase underlying the medium variant of the UN's (1974) long-range population projections for each of the eight major world areas are plotted in Figure 1.8.

The areas are arranged according to their approximate geographical positions.[1] A horizontal line is drawn in each graph of Figure 1.8 at the level at which the birth rates and death rates would eventually converge when the population becomes stationary, namely 13.4 per 1,000.

[1]For instance, Europe is to the east and Latin America to the south of Northern America; similarly with other world regions.

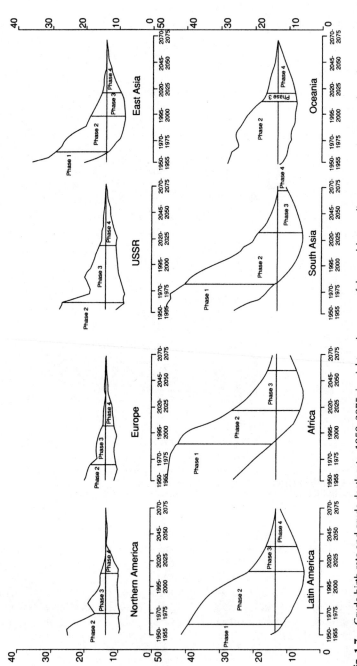

Fig. 1.7. Crude birth rate and crude death rate, 1950–2075, in eight major areas of the world according to past estimates and 'medium' variant of the long-range population projections.

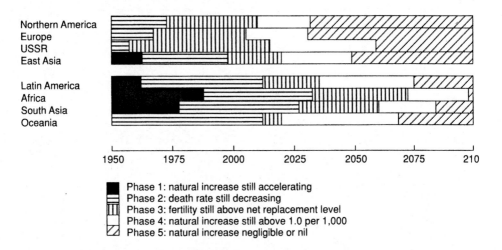

Northern America
Europe
USSR
East Asia

Latin America
Africa
South Asia
Oceania

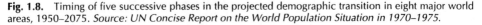

1950   1975   2000   2025   2050   2075   210

■ Phase 1: natural increase still accelerating
≡ Phase 2: death rate still decreasing
Ⅲ Phase 3: fertility still above net replacement level
  Phase 4: natural increase still above 1.0 per 1,000
▧ Phase 5: natural increase negligible or nil

Fig. 1.8. Timing of five successive phases in the projected demographic transition in eight major world areas, 1950–2075. *Source: UN Concise Report on the World Population Situation in 1970–1975.*

In Northern America, Europe, the Soviet Union and Oceania, birth rates had recently fluctuated and might continue to do so in the near future. With these exceptions, birth rates in all world areas were estimated to decline continuously, slowly when the level was still high, faster when it was intermediate and slowly again when it was low.

Death rates were much more dependent on changes in age structure; these declined at first, then levelled off at low figures and thereafter rose again. In accordance with the assumptions, stationary and nearly identical birth rates and death rates might be almost attained by the year 2075 in the northern world areas, namely Northern America, Europe, the Soviet Union and East Asia, whereas in the four southern areas, even by that remote future date, there could still be a significant margin of continuing natural increase. One noteworthy observation was that in all the major world areas birth rates might much sooner approach the stationary level of 13.4 per 1,000 than death rates.

> The eventual cessation of population growth, in the more or less distant future, would then depend on the continued rise in the death rate-caused by a progressive aging of the population-rather than on any further decreases in the birth rate.[18]

The demographic transitions described in these long-range projections could be subdivided into four phases. At first, the death rate decreased faster than the birth rate, with consequent acceleration of the rate of natural increase until this reached a maximum. Subsequently, the birth rate decreased faster than the death rate until the death rate passed through a minimum. Thereafter, the birth rate decreased more and more slowly while the death rate rose. Finally, when fertility had fallen to net replacement level, the birth rate was already near its eventually stationary level, whereas the death rate still had to undergo some further rise before reaching the same level. These four successive phases are marked off by vertical lines in Figure 1.9.

A final phase might be distinguished in which the population was virtually stabilized at a stationary level. Taken very literally, the projections eventually resulted in small fluctuations still persisting over a long time, making it difficult to determine the date of exact stabilization. Perhaps the time after natural increase had fallen below the

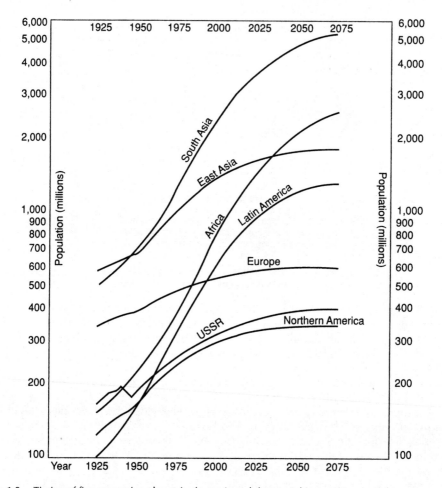

Fig. 1.9. Timing of five successive phases in the projected demographic transition in eight major world areas, 1950–2075. *Source: UN Concise Report on the World Population Situation in 1970–1975.*

annual level of 1.0 per 1,000 should be considered as the final phase. According to the projections, this could occur in the year 2032 in Europe, 2033 in Northern America, 2047 in East Asia, 2058 in the Soviet Union, 2068 in Oceania, 2074 in Latin America, 2085 in South Asia and 2098 in Africa.

The comparative timing of all five phases among the major world areas is also illustrated in Figure 1.9.

POPULATION SIZE, 1925–2075 ('MEDIUM' VARIANT)

Table 1.12 shows estimated and projected populations in the eight world areas, distinguishing a northern and a southern group, for dates from 1925 to 2075 by quarter-centuries.

The import of these numbers is perhaps better visualized from the graphs in Figure 1.9. The figure is drawn on a logarithmic scale so that equal rates of growth are reflected by equal steepness in the respective graphs. The population of South Asia, which until 1945 was smaller than that of East Asia, had since surpassed it because of its greater growth momentum. In fact, the population of South Asia was projected to soar by huge amounts and soon after the year 2030 it might surpass the present world total. However, the population of South Asia grew from a base which was already very large. Speedier growth was likely to occur in Africa and Latin America, where estimated and projected growth rates were higher and might be sustained over longer periods. The populations of Northern America and the Soviet Union had already been surpassed by these two continents, despite their own appreciable rates of growth. In both Northern America and the Soviet Union, growth was calculated to abate in the coming decades and to become slight or negligible later in the next century. Europe had, and probably would have, the slowest growing population, especially in the next century, but even here the population in 2075 might be some 75 per cent greater than it had been in 1925. Because of its comparatively small population Oceania is not included in Figure 1.9, but as can be seen in Table 1.12 its rates of growth, past and future, are quite considerable.

Confining its attention to the future only, the United Nations commented that between 1975 and 2075 the population of Europe might still augment by one quarter, Northern America and the Soviet Union by about one half each, and East Asia by three quarters, while in Oceania growth might be 2.5-fold, in Latin America and South Asia fourfold and in Africa more than fivefold.

Past and anticipated future growth differed so much between the northern and the southern group of major areas that an entire century could be envisaged during which the speed of growth in the south exceeded the maximum ever attained in the north. As shown in Table 1.13, the fastest growth of the north may have already occurred during 1950–1975, when the annual rate averaged 1.3 per cent. The UN commented: 'decidedly higher rates may prevail in the south during all quarter-centuries from 1925 to 2025.'[19]

Table 1.12. Population of the world and eight major areas, at 25-year intervals, 1925–2075 (millions).

Major area	1925	1950	1975	2000	2025	2050	2075
World total	1,960	2,505	3,988	6,406	9,065	11,163	12,210
Northern group	1,203	1,411	1,971	2,530	2,930	3,084	3,107
Northern America	125	166	237	296	332	339	340
Europe	339	392	474	540	580	592	592
USSR	168	180	255	321	368	393	400
East Asia	571	673	1,005	1,373	1,650	1,760	1,775
Southern group	757	1,094	2,017	3,876	6,135	8,079	9,103
Latin America	98	164	3226	625	961	1,202	1,297
Africa	153	219	402	834	1,479	2,112	2,522
South Asia	497	698	1,268	2,384	3,651	4,715	5,232
Oceania	9	13	21	33	44	50	52

Source: UN Concise Report on the World Population Situation in 1970–1975.

Table 1.13. Annual percentage rate of population growth during quarter-centuries from the northern and southern groups of major world areas.

Group of areas	1925–1950	1950–1975	1975–2000	2000–2025	2025–2050	2050–2075
World total	1.0	1.9	1.9	1.4	0.8	0.4
Northern group	0.6	1.3	1.0	0.6	0.2	0.0
Southern group	1.5	2.4	2.6	1.8	1.1	0.5

Source: UN Concise Report on the World Population Situation in 1970–1975.

One consequence of such different rates of growth would be a large displacement southward of the world population's centre of gravity. Three fifths of mankind inhabited the northern group of areas in 1925, and still about one half in 1975; in the coming century, the share of the north might dwindle to no more than one quarter. In 1925, one in every six world citizens was a European, whereas in 2075 it might be only one in every 20. Roughly the opposite would occur in the case of Africa, rising from a small fraction to a considerable proportion of the world's population. Other changes in relative weight could be inferred from the percentage figures of given in Table 1.14.

The UN added:

> If the meteoric rise in the economic needs of the southern portions of humanity is to be met, not only economic development but also the efforts of science and technology will have to address themselves to new problems so as to augment very greatly the efficient use of resources in warm and tropical climates.

Another aspect of population distribution was its relationship to land area. The significance of density measures, relating population to every kind of land surface, was – as the UN admitted – very debatable.[20] Each of the major world areas contained much territory of very limited use for settlement, such as arctic wastes, deserts,

Table 1.14. Percentage of world population in eight major world areas, 1925–2075.

Major area	1925	1950	1975	2000	2025	2050	2075
World total	100.0	100.0	100.0	100.0	100.0	100.0	100.0
Northern group	61.4	56.3	49.4	39.5	32.3	27.6	25.4
Northern America	6.4	6.6	5.9	4.6	3.7	3.0	2.8
Europe	17.3	15.6	11.9	8.4	6.4	5.3	4.8
USSR	8.6	7.2	6.4	5.0	4.1	3.5	3.3
East Asia	29.1	26.9	25.2	21.4	18.2	15.8	14.5
Southern group	38.6	43.7	50.6	60.5	67.7	72.4	74.6
Latin America	5.0	6.5	8.2	9.8	10.6	10.8	10.6
Africa	7.8	8.7	10.1	13.0	16.3	18.9	20.6
South Asia	25.4	27.9	31.8	37.2	40.3	42.2	42.8
Oceania	0.5	0.5	0.5	0.5	0.5	0.4	0.4

Source: UN Concise Report on the World Population Situation in 1970–1975.

jungles and steep mountainsides. Economic organization was also diverse and would change with time. Depending on terms of trade, populations in every region were in part sustained by the resources of other regions, a circumstance which the land areas could reflect. Nevertheless, the trends in average population density shown in Table 1.15 showed such wide differences that they could not be void of meaning.

For instance, in 1975 Europe was still the most densely inhabited major area, with 96 persons per square kilometre of land. In the second half of the coming century density was apt to become nearly as great in Latin America and Africa, while in South Asia as a whole it could rise to almost three times that figure, comparable to present densities in some highly industrialized countries of Western Europe and in Japan. Northern America, the Soviet Union and Oceania would remain regions of comparatively low population density, partly because they contained large portions of land with limited use.

URBAN AND RURAL POPULATION, 1925–2025 ('MEDIUM' VARIANT)

It was clear at the beginning of the 1970s that the increase in the proportion of urban relative to total population had become a world-wide phenomenon and had been progressing so relentlessly that ever greater urbanization would have to be foreseen for many decades ahead. 'Already in many regions, and soon perhaps in many others,' commented the UN 'the majority of the population is that of towns, cities and even larger urban agglomerations. One is tempted to foresee a world that will be totally urban.' But this view of possible future conditions probably had to be modified, the UN added. While cities and urbanized regions grew ever larger, new differentiations of settlement pattern emerged within the urban environment. Perhaps sooner in

Table 1.15. Land area, and inhabitants per square kilometre of land, in the world and eight major world areas, 1925–2075.

Major area	Land area (thousand km²)	Inhabitants per km² 1925	1950	1975	2000	2025	2050	2075
World total	139,450	14	18	29	46	65	80	88
Northern group	60,574	20	23	33	42	48	51	51
Northern America	21,515	6	8	11	14	15	16	16
Europe	4,931	69	79	96	110	118	120	120
USSR	22,402	7	8	11	14	16	18	18
East Asia	11,726	49	57	86	117	141	150	151
Southern Group	78,786	10	14	26	49	78	103	116
Latin America	20,535	5	8	16	30	47	59	63
Africa	30,227	5	7	13	28	49	70	83
South Asia	19,557	25	36	65	122	187	241	268
Oceania	8,557	1	2	3	4	5	6	6

Source: UN Concise Report on the World Population Situation in 1970–1975.

Table 1.16. Percentage of total population in urban localities in the world and eight major areas, 1925–2025.

Major area	1925	1950	1975	2000	2025
World total	21	28	39	50	63
Northern America	54	64	77	86	93
Europe	48	55	67	79	88
USSR	18	39	61	76	87
East Asia	10	15	30	46	63
Latin America	25	41	60	74	85
Africa	8	13	24	37	54
South Asia	9	15	23	35	51
Oceania	54	65	71	77	87

Source: UN Concise Report on the World Population Situation in 1970–1975.

some regions and later in others distinctive forms of settlement would emerge which required new concepts for their description, superceding the historic distinction of 'urban' and 'rural' localities. Even if this did not happen, urbanization might eventually encounter some limits and fail to absorb the remnants of rural population entirely.

A clear grasp of this complicated subject was difficult partly because the statistics which bore on it were not internationally comparable. Countries differed in the selection of features by which they identified 'urban' localities under their diverse circumstances. Dense transport networks in some countries had facilitated the emergence of suburbs, satellite towns, conurbations, urbanized regions, metropolitan areas and megalopoles. At the same time there subsisted a network of minor cities and towns which combined only some but not all the features of urbanism. No less important were changes of settlement pattern within the rural environment which could be variously composed of isolated homesteads, hamlets, villages, service centres and so forth. The simple distinction between 'urban' and 'rural' localities, however defined, failed to reflect many modifications of human geography which could have important implications for economic and social progress.

Because of this elusiveness of the concepts involved and their changing relevance in the course of time, the UN considered that it was unwise to carry projections of urban and rural population very far into the future. However, urbanization at the present rates produced such profound changes in modes of living, thinking, feeling and organizing that it was pertinent to speculate how much farther this change of the human habitat might progress within a more limited future period. The United Nations had ventured to project urban and rural populations as far as the year 2025 but not beyond because of the possibility that in the longer run other changes in the settlement pattern might become more important.

The UN's (1974) estimates and projected levels of urbanization for eight major world areas are brought together in Table 1.16.

As can be seen from these figures, little more than one fifth of the world's population was urban in 1925. Around 1970, the urban proportion in the world total approached two fifths, might attain one half by the century's end and could rise to almost two thirds about 50 years from now. In Northern America, Europe, the Soviet Union, Latin America and Oceania it would then be the overwhelming majority.

Estimated past and future numbers of urban population are shown in Table 1.17.

The world's urban population grew by three quarters between 1925 and 1950, doubled between 1950 and 1975, might double again by the year 2000 and was likely to increase very substantially also beyond that date. In the previous 50 years, the urban population nearly doubled in Europe, grew threefold in Northern America and Oceania, fivefold in the Soviet Union and East Asia, sixfold in South Asia and nearly eightfold in Latin America and Africa. In the next 50 years the urban population of Europe and Northern America might grow by another two-thirds, those of the Soviet Union and Oceania might double, that of East Asia might grow more than threefold, that of Latin America fourfold, South Asia sixfold and Africa eightfold.

The figures were controlled in part by the anticipated growth in total population and in part also by the gradual exhaustion of the rural population as a reservoir supplying additional urban migrants.

In 1925 two-fifths of the world's urban population was still to be found in Europe. Though this had doubled, at the beginning of the 1970s Europe only contained one-fifth of the world's urban population. In the more distant future, one-half of the world's urban population would be shared by East Asia and South Asia. The urban populations of Latin America and of Africa would also eventually surpass that of Europe.

'Such growth in the urban population, past and anticipated,' commented the UN 'is laden with far-reaching consequences requiring much progress in technology, administration, economic and social organization and environmental protection.' Despite this awe-inspiring challenge it would remain necessary to follow with attention concurrent developments in the rural areas. Here, as Table 1.18 shows, tremendous future population increases might yet be seen, especially in the still less urbanized regions of rapid population growth.

As the figures show, in many regions over-all population gains would be so massive that, despite an enormous growth in the size and number of cities, the rural population would continue to augment. This was no longer the case in Northern America, Europe and the Soviet Union, where the rural population had passed its peak, was already declining and might decrease decidedly in the decades to come. For this to happen, two conditions were necessary, namely, that over-all population growth be no longer rapid and that the proportion of urban in the total population be already high.

Table 1.17. Urban population in the world and eight major areas, 1925–2025 (millions).

Major area	1925	1950	1975	2000	2025
World total	405	701	1,548	3,191	5,713
Northern America	68	106	181	256	308
Europe	162	215	318	425	510
USSR	30	71	154	245	318
East Asia	58	99	299	638	1,044
Latin America	25	67	196	464	819
Africa	12	28	96	312	803
South Asia	45	108	288	825	1,873
Oceania	5	8	15	26	38

Source: UN Concise Report on the World Population Situation in 1970–1975.

The long-range projections made it appear likely that in other parts of the world the rural population would also, sooner or later, reach a maximum and then begin to decline. This might occur by 1990 in East Asia and soon after the turn of the century in Latin America, but only in the more remote future in Africa and South Asia. In the last-named area, the rural population in 2025 might be almost 800 million larger than the present one and it was hard to foresee how such an enlarged rural population would then be productively employed. More rapid urbanization might relieve the rural congestion, but the figures for South Asia in Table 1.17 suggested also a huge growth of cities, whose further acceleration would likewise encounter formidable obstacles. Simultaneous pressures on the population in both 'urban' and 'rural' localities might conceivably give rise to new forms of settlement of a character which could no longer be described by traditional concepts.

ALTERNATIVE PROJECTIONS

The UN commented:

> The worried reader may seek solace from the fact that the projections merely result from assumptions made rather arbitrarily. The future will certainly prove that none of the assumptions has been quite correct.[21]

The projections discussed above represented only a 'medium' variant which was perhaps the most probable. But the 'high' and 'low' variants calculated as its companions were still considered to lie within a range which could not be ruled out as improbable. Outside this scheme of three plausible variants some other alternatives had also been computed.

One alternative, namely, the maintenance of fertility levels recently recorded in each region into an indefinite future, the UN ruled out as quite impossible. If mortality diminished as already assumed, but fertility remained unchanged, the total world population would reach 7.2 billion in 2000 and it would exceed 14 billion in 2025, 33 billion in 2050 and 80 billion in 2075. Even then it would continue to grow with breath-taking speed. The UN observed:

Table 1.18. Rural population in the world and eight major areas, 1925–2025 (millions).

Major area	1925	1950	1975	2000	2025
World total	1,555	1,784	2,439	3,215	3,352
Northern America	57	60	56	40	24
Europe	117	177	156	115	70
USSR	138	109	101	76	50
East Asia	513	558	706	735	606
Latin America	73	95	130	161	142
Africa	144	189	305	522	676
South Asia	452	591	980	1,559	1,778
Oceania	4	4	6	8	6

Source: UN Concise Report on the World Population Situation in 1970–1975.

Science-fiction may enable us to envisage some future planet, remote either in time or space, supporting 100,000 million human beings in health, assuming that in the interim there have been carried into effect truly astounding transformations in technology and social organization. Perhaps genetic mutations would be neces-sary for the adaptation of human beings to such a totally altered environment. The year 2075 is decidedly too early for such a cosmic achievement. Constant fertility throughout the next hundred years would certainly provoke disaster.

But it was equally certain that high fertility rates could not be at once reduced to less than half their present levels. A projection had, in fact, been calculated where mortality would decline as already assumed, but where fertility was suddenly cut down to net replacement level, beginning with the year 1970. In this projection, owing to the time needed for the adjustment of age structure, the world's population would still rise to 5.58 billion million by the year 2075, less than one half of the 12.21 billion according to the 'medium' variant already discussed. Despite their lack of realism, it was instructive to compare the results of this projection with those obtained in the 'medium' variant.

The comparison offers the most extreme indication of what might be accomplished if fertility everywhere could be reduced instantly to mere replacement level. In the northern group of world regions, the population in 2075, according to this extreme variant, would be about 80 to 90 per cent that of the 'medium' variant. In the south, this implausible calculation led to results which are only between one quarter and one half as large.

Coming closer to reality, the UN commented, the *'crux of the problem is how to envis-age the timing and speed of those fertility reductions which must inevitably come about.'* There was much pertinent knowledge derived from past trends in at least some parts of the world and from studies of the circumstances under whose influence such down-ward trends had been set into motion. But the area of uncertainty remained wide.

Table 1.19. Population of the world and eight major areas in 1975, and in 2075 according to two projection variants (millions).

		2075		
Area	1975	'Medium' variant (A)	'Instant fertility reduction' variant (B)	Variant (B) as percentage of variant (A)
World total	4,029	12,210	5,615	46
Northern group	1,989	3,107	2,594	83
Northern America	243	340	311	91
Europe	479	592	552	93
USSR	256	400	326	82
East Asia	1,011	1,775	1,405	79
Southern group	2,040	9,103	3,021	33
Latin America	327	1,297	495	38
Africa	395	2,522	617	24
South Asia	1,296	5,232	1,881	36
Oceania	22	52	28	54

Source: UN Concise Report on the World Population Situation in 1970–1975.

Table 1.20.   Population of the world and eight major areas in 1975, and in 2075 according to 'high', 'medium' and 'low' projection variants (millions).

| Area | 1975 | 2075 according to | | | Range between 'high' and 'low' variants |
		'High' variant	'Medium' variant	'Low' variant	
World total	4,029	15,831	12,210	9,462	6,369
Northern group	1,989	3,606	3,107	2,718	888
Northern America	243	488	340	295	193
Europe	479	669	592	533	136
USSR	256	435	400	359	76
East Asia	1,011	2,014	1,775	1,531	481
Southern group	2,040	12,225	9,103	6,744	5,481
Latin America	327	1,796	1,297	1,003	793
Africa	395	3,465	2,522	1,599	1,866
South Asia	1,296	6,898	5,232	4,102	2,796
Oceania	22	66	52	40	26

Source: UN Concise Report on the World Population Situation in 1970–1975.

> It is expected that Government programmes aiming in that direction (fertility reduction) will achieve at least some measure of success. There are also other well established trends, such as more wide-spread education, more frequent survival of children to adolescence, increased circulation of mass communication media, intensifying urbanization and so forth, and these will also play their part.

In the UN's view, the balance of these and other considerations could not be expressed with accuracy but care had been taken to make a reasonable allowance for alternative speeds and timings in the fertility decline of presently less developed regions, resulting in the 'high' and 'low' projection variants presented below. A comparison of results of the 'high', 'medium' and 'low' projection variants for the year 2075 appears in Table 2.20. In the southern world areas, the ranges between the 'high' and 'low' figures in 2075 are much wider than the then current (1975) sizes of the population.

In all the variants discussed the same assumptions were made with respect to mortality. It was evident (to the UN) that a variation of plausible mortality assumptions would have much less effect on the consequent population projections than did the variation of fertility assumptions. It remained justifiable to contemplate also the possibility of severe reversals in the event of major break-downs in international or national organization.

> There is no denying that catastrophic events can happen despite all safeguards to avert them. But no basis can be found to foresee their occurrence or the possible extent of the consequences. Certainly, international efforts will continue to be directed at the preservation of peace, the assertion of human rights, the stimulation of economic and social improvements, the protection of the environment and relief action in disaster-stricken areas.

However, the UN commented with delicately-phrased realism:

> Failure in these undertakings would have to be immense if the consequences were to have a sizable impact on the high rates of population growth which have to be foreseen.

In short, there was no sense in looking to the Four Horsemen for a 'solution' to the world's population problem.

NOTES

1. See John D. Durand 'Historical Estimates of World Population: an evaluation', *Population and Development Review*, Vol. 3, No. 3, September 1977, pp. 253–69
2. ST/SOA/Series A/48. United Nations Publication, Sales No.: E.71.XIII.2
3. The UN notes that the word 'revolutionary' is used here with the connotation of radical change. The changing reproductive balance, furthermore, is not an isolated event, but associated with equally radical changes in the economic, social, environmental, cultural and socio-psychological spheres, all of them having repercussions upon each other. No less 'revolutionary' perhaps than the accelerated growth, is also the increasing urbanization of populations. Economic, social political, and other 'revolutions', and the often cited 'demographic revolution' among them, can be viewed – according to the UN – as so many aspects or events in a much more encompassing change of social and individual awareness presently affecting all mankind.
4. According to then current economic, social and demographic criteria, the following regions have been considered as 'more developed': Europe, Northern America, the Union of Soviet Socialist Republics, Japan, temperate South America, and Australia and New Zealand. With the further subdivision of Europe into four regions, altogether nine 'more developed' regions have been distinguished in the present analysis. For the remainder of the world, fifteen 'less developed' regions have been distinguished. The UN observes that 'the scheme of regionalization is, of course, imperfect and debatable.'
5. The UN notes that these are actuarial measures in which the effects of age composition are eliminated. Expectations of life differ somewhat between males and females. The measures quoted are averages for individuals of both sexes combined.
6. UN, op. cit., p. 14.
7. UN, op. cit., p. 16.
8. This point was empasized in *Population Bulletin of the United Nations No. 7, 1963. With Special Reference to Conditions and Trends of Fertility in the World* (United Nations publication, Sales No.: 64.X11.2).
9. UN, op. cit., p. 2.
10. UN, op. cit., p. 11.
11. Oceania, excluding Australia and New Zealand.
12. The UN observed, op. cit., p. 18, that in a growing population, a constant, or even a rising level in the absolute numbers of increase can be consistent with a diminishing rate of increase. If the annual increase in numbers is also to diminish, the rate of increase would have to decrease rather more rapidly.
13. UN, op. cit., p. 5.
14. cf *The Population Problem*, ed. Stanley Johnson, David and Charles, Newton Abbot, 1973, p. 173.
15. The thirty signatories were: Australia, Barbados, Colombia, Denmark, the Dominican Republic, Finland, Ghana, India, Indonesia, Iran, Japan, Jordan, Malaysia, Morocco, Nepal, the Netherlands, New Zealand, Norway, Pakistan, the Philippines, the Republic of Korea, Singapore, Sweden, Thailand, Trinidad and Tobago, Tunisia, the United Arab Republic, the United Kingdom of Great Britain and Northern Ireland, the United States

of America and Yugoslavia. The Declaration was published, among other places, in *Population Newsletter*, No. 1, April 1968 (United Nations, New York).

16. *Concise Report on the World Population Situation in 1970–1975 and its Long-Range Implications*, Department of Economic and Social Affairs. *Population Studies*, No. 56 ST/ESA/SER.A/56, New York 1974. United Nations Publication. Sales No. E.74.XIII.4, p. 49.

17. op. cit., p. 51.
18. op. cit., p. 54.
19. op. cit., p. 59.
20. op. cit., p. 61.
21. op. cit., p. 66.

2

The Development of
National Population Policies

In the previous chapter, we summarized the world population situation and future prospects, including the long-range projections of future population growth, as these appeared at the end of the 1960s. A brief but cogent picture of the *implications* of these trends was given in 1969 in a report made by the United Nations Association of the United States of America, entitled *World Population: A Challenge to the United Nations and its System of Agencies.*[1]

'High fertility and high rates of population growth,' the UNA Panel wrote, 'impair individual rights, jeopardize national goals and threaten international stability.'

INDIVIDUAL RIGHTS

The International Conference on Human Rights, which took place in Teheran in May 1968, had 'solemnly proclaimed', among other things, that:

> The protection of the family and the child remains the concern of the international community. Parents have a basic right to determine freely and responsibly the number and spacing of their children.[2]

The UNA–USA Panel enlarged on this:

> No woman should conceive an unwanted child. This is emerging as a fundamental human right. In the developed as well as the developing world, unplanned pregnancies can cause or aggravate conditions of social and economic hardship. High rates of infant mortality, permanent mental impairment resulting from malnutrition in the formative years, ignorance and illiteracy – all these, one way or another, bear witness to the problems high fertility can give rise to when household budgets are already at a subsistence level and when the nurture of each additional child must inevitably be at the expense of those already born. But even when economic and social hardships are not immediately apparent, the right of parents to decide on the number and spacing of their children is a natural corollary of belief in an expanded freedom of choice.

NATIONAL GOALS

In the developing world, wrote the Panel, the rate of population growth jeopardized the best efforts of governments for the economic and social development of their peoples. At the most basic level, it was a question of people versus food. Recent increases in agricultural production gave room for hope that governments, temporarily reprieved from the threat of Malthusian catastrophes, might have the time to find more humane solutions to their problems. But many qualifications needed to be made even to this cautious statement. Agronomists were keenly aware of the need for proper husbandry of the new strains of wheat and rice, of the importance of the right application and combination of inputs, of the need for credit and marketing facilities. Many financial and administrative constraints would have to be eliminated before yield-increases which had been achieved over a short time-span in certain parts of the developing world could be sustained, and improved upon, over a wider area. Only continued research could tell what further increases in agricultural production could be expected; only experience could show the dimensions of the political and social problems which would undoubtedly be caused by the 'Green Revolution'.

There was no justification for complacency. Since increases in agricultural production were likely to become ultimately harder to attain, wide-spread famine might return if this precious period of grace (however long or however short it was) was squandered in false optimism.

> But perhaps the choice, in any case, is not between starvation and a subsistence diet. Rather it may be between rapidly improving diets and mass loss of life. For unless rising expectations are gratified – inter alia – by more and better food, political upheaval and disintegration may themselves result in famine and disease.

Food was, of course, only one aspect – though a vital aspect – of the population/ resource equation. The satisfaction of other needs, which might be almost equally important for human dignity and the realization of individual potential, implied far more than a full bowl of rice and a few grams of protein.

> In low-income countries where the size of the population is doubling every 25 years or less, almost intolerable burdens are placed on the educational system. When the proportion of the society under 15 years of age is over 40%, and rising, the absolute number of illiterates is likely to increase rather than diminish, however many schools are built and teachers trained. The strains thrown on the fragile structure of public health facilities may be of similar magnitude. Or again the relentless increase in population in rural areas, taken in conjunction with existing underemployment in agriculture, may accentuate the pressures of rural/urban migration. In the cities, inability to invest in sufficient new jobs combined with the capital intensive bias of industrial technology and the natural increase of urban populations themselves, may lead to the most massive problems of unemployment, squalor and unrest threatening the very foundations of public order. In aggregate terms, the rate of population growth in the developing world renders difficult, if not impossible of attainment, rapid increases in per capita income.

The Panel gave some examples. With a GNP which is growing at an annual rate of 5 per cent and a stationary population it takes 12 years to double per capita income. If population growth is not stationary but is rising, say, at 2.4 per cent a year (the projected average rate for the less developed world), it will take 27 years to achieve a doubling in per capita income. If the annual growth in national income is 4 per cent rather than 5 per cent, doubling of per capita income will take 43 years. And since two-thirds of the world lived in countries where per capita income was less than $300 per annum and often less than $100 per annum, even a doubling in per capita income was hardly likely to represent a satisfactory fulfilment of economic expectations.

In the developed world, the effect of population growth on national goals could be expressed in a rather different way. The ills that industrial civilization was heir to – including pollution, congestion, urban sprawl and a host of psychological ailments – might at least in part be ascribed to the sheer pressure of numbers.

INTERNATIONAL STABILITY

Finally, the UNA report looked at the implications of continued rapid population growth for international stability.

> In the widest sense, the population crisis is the world's concern. It is as important as peace itself. To what extent territorial aggression is a function of population pressures, or military adventurism a smoke screen to hide the real failures of development, cannot be said with certainty. What can be said is that this is an age when the internal stability of countries is constantly threatened by the massive disaffection or disappointment of those whose expectations have not been met; it is an age when the growing polarization between rich and poor nations makes the conduct of orderly external relations increasingly difficult. If it is true that internal stability and external order are influenced, however indirectly, by the rate of population growth, then the commitment of the international community to the cause of peace should be matched by a parallel commitment to population planning.

There were other good reasons for international interest in the population problem. No nation could live in isolation. The world was only just beginning to realize the dangers involved in the changing and complex relationship between man and his environment. Contamination of the streams and oceans, erosion of the soil, destruction of vegetation, the devouring of open space, the rise in the concentration of carbon-dioxide in the atmosphere, in discriminate use of poisonous pesticides and synthetic detergents, the disposal of radio-active waste – these were problems which had vast international implications.

> To deal with effects without dealing also with causes is inadequate and superficial. *One of the causes, perhaps the root cause, of the threat to our environment is the demands made by expanding populations in developed and developing world alike.* The fact that, at the present time, we have only the haziest ideas of the nature of the interrelationships involved should not provide an excuse for inaction. If the present world population of 3.5 billion is allowed to grow to 7 billion or more, our understanding of these things and of possible ways of mitigating their impact may come too late to be of much comfort. (emphasis added)

If we have cited the UNA report at some length here, it is because it was one of the factors which – at the end of the 1960s – led to the strengthening of United Nations activity in the field of population and to the establishment of the United Nations Fund for Population Activities (UNFPA), subsequently to be known as the United Nations Population Fund, a body which was to 'play a leading role in the United Nations system in promoting population programmes.'[3]

In a message on population which President Nixon sent to Congress on July 18, 1969, he wrote:

It is our belief that the United Nations, its specialized agencies, and other international bodies should take the lead in responding to world population growth. The United States will cooperate fully with their programmes. I would note in this connection that I am most impressed by the scope and thrust of the recent report of the panel of the United Nations Association, chaired by John D. Rockefeller 3rd. The report stresses the need for expanded action and greater coordination, concerns which should be high on the agenda of the United Nations.

The position of the United States on the issue of world population growth, and the evolution in US attitudes towards UN activity in this field, is – as we shall see later – of considerable interest and significance. It is important to stress, however, that the growth of international concern with the implications of rapid population growth can in no sense be said to be a US-inspired or US-dominated effort. This is a misconception which needs to be put firmly allayed.[4]

POPULATION POLICIES

Commenting on the situation in 1970, the United Nations writes:

Virtually all Governments appear to design policies, enact laws, and adopt administrative programmes which directly or incidentally influence the components of population growth, the geographical distribution of population and its economic and social characteristics . . .
    The past two decades have brought into the foreground the unprecedented acceleration of population growth in the less developed regions. *Recent observations on implications of this growth have raised international interest in the possibility of formulating policies aimed at reducing the rates of population growth by facilitating the application of methods of fertility regulation.*[5] (emphasis added)

The UN observed that an international consensus had not been reached as to the modes of implementation of such policies. Conditions and problems varied enormously among individual countries, even among those in which population was comparatively small in number, at a low density, or where its rate of increase was relatively low. However, the UN felt able to state:

Considering the world as a whole and the size of population in the respective countries, *a marked shift of opinion can be discerned towards those policies emphasizing the limitation of family size.* More especially this is the case in numerous less developed countries with a substantially reduced mortality, where the continuing of high rates of fertility have caused a large acceleration in rates of population growth. The emphasis on fertility reduction is most pronounced in those countries where population density in relation to natural and capital resources is already high and where, consequently, it is feared that a high rate of population growth can constitute a severe drawback to efforts designed to secure economic and social progress.[6] (emphasis added)

The Governments of less developed countries had given various reasons for initiating and promoting national programmes for family planning. Many had considered that, under conditions of unrestrained population growth, it would be very difficult to generate those savings and investments needed to achieve a satisfactory rate of progress in raising national income and the level of living. No less frequent had been the emphasis on achieving social objectives, since the birth of an unduly large number of children might be detrimental to the mothers' health, social status and freedom to avail themselves of economic opportunities, to the well-being and educational level of the children themselves and to the welfare of the family as a whole. In a number of countries it was felt necessary to combat illegal abortions, frequently resorted to under very hazardous conditions, by making clinical abortions and contraceptive methods more readily available.

The UN observed that the adoption of such policies by many Governments in recent years had also been facilitated by the general climate of increased awareness with regard to population problems, by improvements in contraceptive methods, surveys of knowledge, attitude and practice with respect to methods of family-size limitation, and an increase in the reservoir of technical competence and in resources for bilateral and multilateral technical assistance in this field. 'Recent experience in a few countries, notably in East Asia,' the UN noted 'has also made it apparent that a *rather rapid decline in fertility can become possible*' (emphasis added).

From the stand-point of population growth as a world problem, developments in Asia were indeed of the first importance. In fact the Governments of China (mainland), India, Pakistan and the Republic of Korea were the first on record, as early as the 1950s, with policies aimed to facilitate fertility reductions. In all the Asian countries with a population exceeding 100 million, family planning was being promoted by government agencies. In some other countries, Governments subsidized family-planning programmes or projects undertaken by semiofficial or unofficial agencies, and in still others the Governments permitted, or viewed with favour, projects carried out by unofficial bodies without active official participation.

Government attitudes were more diverse in Africa. Although at least six Governments had committed themselves to national programmes that promoted fertility reduction, there were some African countries in which no governmental attitude could be detected and others in which, rather than favouring fertility reduction, the desire for continuing and rapid population growth had been expressed. In some of the latter countries emphasis had been placed upon problems of low average population density and on policies of internal migration intended to bring about an economically more favourable geographic distribution of the population.

In many Latin American countries, population was also at a low average density, though it was growing at rates which were among the highest in the world. In several of these countries the Government had become concerned with the high frequency of illegal abortion as an important social and health problem and, therefore, favoured family planning activities conducive to an avoidance of this social ill. Economic and social reasons were stated to be the motives behind the policies adopted in some of the more densely settled countries, for instance in the Caribbean region.

In the UN's view, the degree of government involvement had not necessarily been a measure of the effectiveness of family-planning programmes actually implemented. More often than not, direct official involvement, through the enactment of laws or the establishment of official agencies, had been the outcome of activities and programmes already in existence for some time at less official levels, for example through private family planning associations, and which had found support in public opinion. The exact official position was sometimes difficult to determine. Nevertheless, by the end of 1969, the Governments of about thirty less developed countries, comprising almost two thirds of the combined population of the less developed regions, had adopted national family-planning programmes as integral parts of their development policies.

The situation at the end of the 1960s and the beginning of the 1970s is summarised in Table 2.1.

Table 2.1. Number of countries and distribution of the population in the major regions of the developing world, by governmental position on family planning programmes and policies.

Governmental position	All developing countries*	Africa	Latin America†	East Asia‡	Balance of Asia‖
Number of countries					
All positions	*102*	*42*	*23*	*5*	*32*
Official antinatalist policy and a family planning programme	102	42	23	5	32
Support of family planning activities but no official antinatalist policy	23	7	13	1	1
Little or no support of family planning activities and no official antinatalist policy	55	28	5	1	21
Population (in millions)					
All positions	2,542	344	256	820	1,122
Official antinalist policy and a family planning programme	1,838	141	11	786	966
Support of family planning activities but no official policy	213	47	84	4	12
Little or no support of family planning activities and no official antinatalist policy	491	156	161	30	144
Per cent distribution of population					
All positions	100	100	100	100	100
Official antinatalist policy and a family planning programme	72	41	4	96	86
Support of family planning activities but no official policy	9	14	33	0.1	1
Little or no support of family planning activities and no official antinatalist policy	19	45	63	4	13

* Classification primarily on the basis of level of fertility.
† Comprises the Caribbean area and Central and South America, except for Argentina and Uruguay, both of which have low fertility.
‡ Comprises China (Mainland), Hong Kong, North Korea, South Korea, and Taiwan; excludes Japan, which has low fertility. Population for China (Mainland) based on the United Nations estimate of 740 million. A more likely estimate exceeds 850 million.
‖ Excludes Israel, which has low fertility.
Source: Population Council, 1971.[7]

What, at the end of the sixties, was the overall impact of these population policies? The United Nations' view was that despite active policies in numerous countries, substantial decreases in high birth rates had until recently been observed only in relatively few areas of comparatively small populations adjacent to large countries in which the birth rates remained high. In relation to the trend of the world's population, the quantitative effect of fertility decline in these countries, therefore, had been very slight. However, the UN went on to add:

> The long-term significance of declines in birth rates in limited areas should, however, not be underrated . . . *It is quite possible that small areas with decreasing fertility will also be the forerunners in trends towards more decisive fertility limitation that might*

become apparent in the future, in the larger populations of the adjoining countries. Whether this will actually be the case still remains to be seen. (emphasis added)

POPULATION POLICIES AMONG DEVELOPED COUNTRIES

A diversity of official positions concerning matters of family planning could also be discerned among the more developed countries. In these countries, social considerations were most in evidence.

> Rarely is it argued at the present time that an unduly high or low rate of population growth depresses economic conditions in one of the more developed countries. In as much as the social problems differ, in a few of the more developed countries, couples with small families are encouraged to have more children; in other countries the facilitation of fertility reduction is promoted; and there are also some countries where measures of both types exist at the same time, responding to a diversity of social needs, without constituting a contradiction in general policy.[8]

Japan, the USSR and various Eastern European and Scandinavian countries had been prominent in connection with government policies facilitating access to clinically performed abortions. In some instances this was evidently designed as a temporizing policy, pending the wider popular spread of contraceptive methods. In a few instances, however, as in Bulgaria, Hungary and Rumania, where the birth rate had fallen unusually low, new measures had been adopted to counteract the limitation of family size which was believed to be excessive.

In some countries, for example the United Kingdom, the United States and Yugoslavia, enactments had been designed so that means of contraception should not be lacking to any families desiring them, whatever their social stratum. In several other countries, like Canada and France, some old laws concerning the distribution of contraceptive devices, which had long been circumvented in various ways, had been abrogated.

The United Nations went on to add, with considerable circumspection:

> But in some of them no legal concessions have as yet been made to the tendency in many developed countries towards individualism in matters relating to human reproduction.[9]

National policies on various aspects of population, to be useful, had to be implemented in a practical way. The next two chapters look in more detail at the actual implementation of family planning programmes in different countries in those crucial early years. Chapter 3 looks at national population and family planning programmes where the first fruits of success were already apparent. Chapter 4 looks at a number of countries where major family planning efforts had been initiated but where as yet no significant reductions in fertility appeared to have been achieved.

NOTES

1. *World Population: A challenge to the United Nations and its System of Agencies.* A Report of a National Policy Panel established by the United Nations Association of the United States of America (UNA–USA). The panel was chaired by John D. Rockefeller 3rd, Chairman of the Population Council; George D. Woods, former President of the World Bank, served as Vice-Chairman. The author acted as project director.

2. For a discussion of the origins of family planning as a human right, see the author's *World Population and the United Nations*, Cambridge University Press, 1987.

3. See ECOSOC Resolution 1763 (XXVI) of 18 May 1973.

4. Richard Symonds and Michael Carder, in their book *The United Nations and the Population Question*, Chatto & Windus, 1974, stress in particular the efforts made in the 1950s by the representatives of India, Ceylon and the UAR, to encourage the World Health Organization (WHO) to take a more active role in promoting family planning. See especially Chapter 5. See also Stanley P. Johnson, *World Population and the United Nations*, Cambridge University Press, 1987, especially Chapter 1, 'The Rise of Concern'.

5. United Nations, *Concise Summary of World Population Situation in 1970*, p. 29.

6. *A Concise Summary of the World Population Situation in 1970*, United Nations, New York, 1971, p. 30.

7. The source of this table is the Population Council, in Population and Family Planning Programmes: A fact book, by Dorothy Nortman (1971). The difference in totals (the UN says 'almost two-thirds', while the Population Council's figure is nearer three-quarters, for the proportion of developing countries' population covered by official anti-natalist policies) reflects in part the difficulties of categorisation, in part the difference in the dates of the surveys.

8. *UN Concise Summary*, 1970, p. 31.

9. *UN Concise Summary*, 1970, p. 33.

3

National Population and Family Planning Programmes: First Successes

What successes had there been, by the end of the 1960s, in turning the tide of human fertility? In what countries? Were those successes in any way replicable in other countries? This chapter, while in no way seeking to be comprehensive, looks in greater detail at a small number of countries where fertility had fallen, or begun to fall, significantly.

JAPAN

Even as early as the middle and late sixties there were some countries outside the orbit of European cultural traditions where fertility had already fallen to a low level. Probably the most notable among these was Japan. Indeed, the phrase 'demographic miracle' was often used by those who, at the end of the sixties, sought to describe in vivid terms that country's recent demographic history. Though, strictly speaking, this Japanese 'miracle' falls outside the period covered by this book in the sense that the major demographic changes had largely taken place by the end of the sixties, the Japanese experience is nonetheless of some interest.

In the early 1920s birth rates in Japan were as high as 33–36 per thousand. Mortality had begun to decline and stood at a level of 21–25. Since there was no sizable international migration, the rate of natural increase was the gap between the birth and death rates, i.e. around 12 per thousand, or 1.2 per cent.

In 1922 Margaret Sanger, the early pioneer of birth control and family planning, visited Japan at the invitation of a publishing company, Kaizosha. The Japanese government apparently tried to prevent her from landing but finally admitted her on condition that she would give no speech to the general public but only to doctors – an incident which was widely publicized in the press. Margaret Sanger's visit gave an enormous stimulus, particularly to the intellectuals. Socialists and labour leaders promoted the birth control movement. However, looking at the statistics, it is evident that the main influence was political and ideological rather than practical. The Sanger visit did not necessarily result in a sudden emergence of a large number of couples adopting birth control methods on a nationwide basis. Indeed, the use of modern methods of contraception seems to have been rather rare before World War II.

One of Margaret Sanger's supporters was Dr Tenrei Ota who, in the early 1930s, started to experiment with a device to be inserted in the cavity of the uterus for the purpose of contraception. He apparently was inspired in this idea by Grafenburg and tried a series of devices with different shapes and different materials – gold, silver, rubber, etcetera. He himself and some other interested doctors enthusiastically promoted the 'Ota' ring, but the indications are that – from a demographic point of view – the incidence of use was insignificant. Some Japanese authors believe that a small proportion of the population used condoms or spermicidal tablets.

In the late 1930s, however, some decreases in the birth rate were being recorded. The lowest rate of prewar years (26.6 per thousand) is attributable to the Sino–Japanese War, which broke out in 1937, and the subsequent stationing of young males in China and other strategically important areas inside and outside Japan.

As Japan made preparations for war and manpower considerations loomed large, the family planning movement came under severe pressure. After 1935 it was discontinued. The stage was set for the baby boom of the immediate postwar period.

The verdict of scholars is that the sudden and extraordinary upheaval of the birth rate in 1947, 1948 and 1949 was produced by the repatriation and demobilization of some 6.6 million soldiers and the return of overseas migrants to Japan. Some of them immediately rushed into marriage (postponed because of the war); others resumed normal family life. The baby boom ensued.

At the same time, the postwar introduction of DDT and antibiotics gave a strong impetus to a further sharp decline in mortality. There was a great reduction in the death toll from infectious and parasitic diseases such as tuberculosis, pneumonia and enteritis, particularly among infants and young persons. The net result of both trends was that in 1947 the crude birth rate had increased to 34.3 and the death rate had declined to 14.6, with the rate of natural increase at 19.7. In 1948, with further declines in the death rate, the rate of natural increase stood at 21.6 or almost 2.2 per cent per annum.

Compared with the population growth rates experienced in much of the developing world, it might be thought that this rate of 2.2 per cent was not especially high. But demographic trends have to be seen in the context of prevailing economic circumstances. The level of living of the Japanese people was lowered quite viciously after 1945, following their defeat in the war. For the three years 1945 to 1948, they lived on the edge of famine. Here are some of the harsh statistics of defeat:

- 44 per cent loss of territory
- destruction of 82 cities, like Tokyo, Osaka and Nagasaki by air-raid
- level of living in 1946 fell to 52 per cent of the prewar average
- rice and wheat production 30 and 40 per cent below average

The combination of the baby boom with this period of acute economic and social hardship had the effect of focusing a high degree of attention on the problem of overpopulation. Newspapers and radio stations throughout the country reported the critical situation, suggesting that Japan had no productive and economic capacity to support this level of population increase.

On May 10, 1949, the House of Representatives of the Japanese Diet passed a resolution relating to the population problem. The following is an excerpt:

> Today's Japan is extremely overpopulated. This fact prevents the betterment of the level of living of the people and makes it difficult to plan and carry out an economic reconstruction program. Further, it is an obstacle to the development of emancipation of women and maternal civilization. Accordingly, the government should encourage the people to understand the necessity of promoting urgently . . . counter-

measures, and formulate promptly an action program in the meeting of the Population Problem Council which is going to be established in the Cabinet in the near future.

The Population Problem Council had its first meeting on June 15, 1949. Two subcommittees were organized which, on November 29, 1949, made recommendations to the government. The key recommendation regarding the 'Adjustment of Population' read as follows:

> In order to prevent a sharp increase in the population which will have adverse effects on the economic reconstruction and promotion of public health in this country, and to bring a sound and cultural life to realization, it is considered necessary to furnish married couples with necessary information on contraception by teaching reasonable methods and to give guidance of conception control to all classes of our nation so that married couples can regulate the number of births freely and voluntarily by means of conception control.

In November 1951, the Cabinet made a definite decision to promote contraception. The Ministry of Health and Welfare immediately informed the governors of prefectures all over Japan of this decision and in June 1952 sent out a detailed plan of action. The most interesting thing about this plan is that in spite of its pioneering nature – as far as the global family planning movement is concerned – it was in scope remarkably comprehensive. It recognized without any quibble that an almost total involvement of society in the family planning effort was required. It emphasized 'individual guidance' where doctors, midwives, nurses, pharmacists, etcetera, would instruct women in the use of contraceptive devices. It also emphasized 'mass education' for industrial workers, women's associations and other specific groups to be conducted by the 'Eugenic Protection Consultation Offices or Health Centres'. It laid down the special training courses to be offered and facilities to be provided by the Ministry of Health and Welfare and the prefectural governments; specified informational activity to be conducted through radio, newspapers, motion pictures, slides, pamphlets, leaflets, etcetera; authorized for manufacture various contraceptive devices, 'diaphragms, artificial sponges and sea sponges, devices used for applying contraceptive chemicals, irrigators for douche, condoms, etc'.

It is interesting to note that, notwithstanding the existence and limited use of the Ota ring, the intrauterine device had not yet been sanctioned by the government except on an experimental basis. Regulations issued before the war, prohibiting the use of IUD's because of possible harmful effects and uncertain mode of action, were still in force at the end of the sixties. Similarly, conservative opinion in Japan had been worried about possible harmful side effects among long-term users of the Pill. The Pill, like the IUD, had still not been sanctioned by the Japanese government.

In the absence of these two methods, the condom still reigned supreme. It appeared to account for between 50 and 60 per cent of contraceptive practice. The safe period (including the use of basal body temperature) accounted for 30–40 per cent; chemicals (spermicidal jellies and tablets) 15–25 per cent; vaginal diaphragms 5–10 per cent, and the Ota ring 6 per cent. The keen reader may notice that all these add up to well over 100 per cent. The explanation appears to be that many Japanese were 'combined method users'.

Was it the official family planning efforts – based largely on the condom and safe period – which accounted for the spectacular decline in fertility which Japan had experienced by 1957? The answer is very clear: no. The demographic 'miracle' was not achieved through the Cabinet decision of November 1951. Surveys indicate that by 1954 the rate of contraceptive practice throughout the country was hardly more than 30 per cent. What counted in Japan more than any other factor was the passage, in 1948, of the Eugenic Protection Law.

Before and during the last war, the official attitude to induced abortion in Japan was highly restrictive. A National Eugenic Law was in force which was said to copy to a great extent regulations enforced in Nazi Germany. The picture was radically changed in 1948 when the Eugenic Protection Law was introduced, a measure which took a broad liberal approach to induced abortion. The motive for the introduction of this Law appears to be twofold. On the one hand, it was intended to use induced abortion as a countermeasure to the acute problem of overpopulation and the high rate of population growth. On the other hand, it was felt that liberalization of the law would lessen the dangers to health which occurred when the operation was performed illegally.

Article 14 of Eugenic Protection Law read (in part):

> The physician designated by the Medical Association . . . may exercise artificial interruption of pregnancy, at his discretion, to the person who falls under any of the following items, with the consent of the person in question or the spouse.
>
> 1. A person or the spouse who has psychosis, mental deficiency, psychopathology, hereditary bodily disease or hereditary malformation;
> 2. A relative in blood within the fourth degree of consanguinity of the person or the spouse who has hereditary psychosis, hereditary mental deficiency, hereditary psychopathology, hereditary bodily disease or hereditary malformation;
> 3. A person or the spouse who is suffering from leprosy;
> 4. A mother whose health may be affected seriously by continuation of pregnancy or by delivery from the physical or economic viewpoint;
> 5. A person who has conceived by being fornicated by violence or threat, or while incapacitated to resist and refuse.

Before 1952, the physician had to apply to a local committee for authorization. Since that date, as the amended law indicated, it was entirely at the discretion of the physician to decide whether or not the case was eligible. According to the amended law, the designated physician had to report the number of induced abortions he handled in the preceding month to the designated Physicians' Association to which he belonged. Reporting of the age of patient, month of pregnancy and reason for the operation was also required. The number of abortions reported climbed steadily to reach a peak of some 1–2 million in 1955. Since the reported figures were almost certainly underestimates, the figures were adjusted on the basis of various assumptions to give a 'true' peak of some 2 million induced abortions in 1955.

Article 14 of the Eugenic Protection Law, cited above, distinguished five possible reasons for the operation. Statistics issued by the Ministry of Health and Welfare indicated that virtually 100 per cent of the operations were performed under clause 4, for reasons of 'maternal health'. However, the incidence of 'true' health reasons was probably of much less significance than the incidence of reasons which were related to social, economic or psychological conditions ('too poor to have another child', 'if more children, cannot give enough education', etcetera).

Dr Minoru Muramatsu, of the Institute of Public Health, Tokyo, commented that, in the overall reduction of births recorded after the war in Japan, the part played by induced abortion was 'greater than that of any other means'. He estimated that in the postwar period until 1955 at least 70 per cent of the total decrease in the birth rate could be accounted for by induced abortion while the remaining 30 per cent was due to contraception and sterilization; 'if one puts aside the effect of postponement of marriage.' Murumatsu suggested that 'Japanese women as a whole do not necessarily associate induced abortion with the sense of religious sin and they tend to evaluate this particular behaviour in relation to its health hazards or what others may say about it, in addition to their own moral consideration. In short, induced abortion is by no means a commendable thing, but not infrequently pragmatic or realistic consideration outweighs moral or other personal restraints in the ultimate decision on this matter.'[1]

At the same time as it amended the Eugenic Protection Law, the government announced for the first time programmes explicitly designed for the promotion of family planning. The programmes aimed to cover the nation as a whole, the target group being all married persons desiring to practise family planning. Subsidies were given to all prefectures at a rate of one-half to one-third the expected expenditures – in other words, the actual sum spent on official family planning programmes in those years in Japan as a whole was therefore two to three times the amount given by the government.

A certain proportion of the budget was earmarked for preparing audiovisual materials for family planning education, such as leaflets, pamphlets, and slides, but the major portion was for administrative expenses. Until 1954 there were no provisions for the government to subsidize the purchase of contraceptive materials; the main sources of supply were commercial channels, predominantly local drugstores, though in some cases local midwives and women's groups took the initiative in their distribution.

In the actual execution of the programmes the question of personnel naturally came up. Dr Muramatsu wrote:

> Medical doctors, public health nurses, and midwives alike were all regarded as important, especially in relation to the personal consultation on family planning techniques. Viewed from the practical standpoint, however, and particularly from the standpoint of their wide geographical distribution, the government decided to rely heavily on midwives. In order to make village midwives familiar with the principles and techniques of modern family planning, and also to overcome the inherent feeling among some of them that birth control runs counter to their primary mission of helping mothers through childbirth, a number of refresher training courses were initiated throughout the country. A curriculum of 33 hours, including some practical experience in the fitting of the diaphragm in addition to formal didactic lectures, was set up. In the teaching of methods, the general pattern indicated to the trainees was to let the client choose whatever method she liked after an over-all explanation of all methods that the instructor thought appropriate to that particular case. The methods thus advocated included such traditional methods as condoms, diaphragms, tablets, jellies, and the safe period. Upon completion of this official training, graduates were awarded the title of 'family planning instructor,' which authorized the handling and even the sale of contraceptive materials. The instructors were encouraged to seek, on their own, possible clients of family planning in their villages, but no honorarium or the like was provided by the government, at least for the first three years after the initiation of the programmes.[2]

As a result of these measures, the number of induced abortions fell from its 1955 peak. Murumatsu estimated that, compared with the 70 per cent figure for the pre-1955 period, induced abortion since 1955 had probably accounted for 40 to 50 per cent of the fertility control effect. The birth rate itself declined rapidly to a level below 20 and, since 1957, had continued at the low level of about 17.

Muramatsu commented:

Gradually there arose an opinion that the government need not play a large part in the promotion of family planning any longer, except for an effort to reduce further the number of induced abortions, since the understanding of family planning was already well ingrained among the masses. . . . The central government accordingly changed its family planning programmes in 1965. It now has no specific budget allocation for family planning … [3]

By the end of the 1960s it was beginning to seem as though Japan was a victim of its own success. With the country's economic recovery complete there seemed to be a growing preoccupation in official circles that the downward trend in the rate of population growth might have gone too far. The April 1968 number of *Japan Report*, for example, stated that 'The scarcity of young labour has assumed serious proportions in rural areas and the primary industry. Indications are that a similar phenomenon will prevail throughout the country and in all sectors of industry in the not distant future …'

The dearth of young labour, however, was but one aspect of the labour problem stemming from the age structure of the population. Another important aspect was an over-supply of middle-aged and elderly labour, which presented a sharp contrast with the shortage of young people.

The down trend of births since the 1950s is obviously ascribable to birth control. Assuming that for some time to come, Japan's birth-rate will not turn upward with annual births limited to about 1.6 million to 1.7 million, the population pyramid will annually show a 'lean' base with those born in the mid-1950s constituting the broad mid-portion of the structure.... And if the younger generations of the population show a gradual decrease from now on, eventually causing a shrinking of those generations who play a central part in the nation's economic and cultural activities, the most vital issue is how best to establish a comprehensive system for ensuring a constant elevation of economic and cultural standards with even greater efficiency.[4]

This, clearly, is an ambiguous commentary. Official Japan – at the end of the 1960s – had not yet made up its mind what to think. Conventional business wisdom, conventional economic theories of wage inflation and employment, tended to support a mildly pronatalist policy, as distinct from the policy of the postwar period. And yet the last sentence of the commentary suggesting that Japan might come to terms with a low birth rate and rise to even greater cultural and economic heights was of considerable interest. If Japan, far from disavowing its own achievement in 'turning the tide', found a way of building on that success, other countries – particularly the newly-industrializing countries of East Asia (NICS) who seemed destined to follows Japan's economic example – might do the same.

TAIWAN

One such country was Taiwan. The population of Taiwan was slightly over the 6 million in 1946. The birth rate at the end of the war had been quite low because the Japanese drafted all the young men. The bombardment also played a part. After the war, the birth rate rose steadily. It went up from 38 per thousand in 1946 to almost 50 per thousand in 1951. At the same time the death rate came down from 18 per thousand in 1946 to about 11 per thousand in 1951. The rate of natural increase, then, jumped from 2 per cent per annum in 1946 to almost 4 per cent per annum in 1951. And this was not the whole story. The flood of postwar immigration into Taiwan meant that in absolute terms the population grew from 6 million in 1946 to 8 million in 1951. The peak year seems to have been 1949 when, following the Communist victory on the mainland, the rate of population increase was almost 9 per cent.

Dr S.C. Hsu, Chief of the Rural Health Division of the Joint Commission on Rural Reconstruction (JCRR), together with K.T. Li, Minister of Economic Affairs and Vice-Chairman of Taiwan's Council for International Economic Cooperation and Development (CIECD), presented a paper at the Conference on Population Programmes in East Asia which was held in Taipei, the capital of Taiwan, in May 1968. The paper dealt with the 'effect of population pressure on economic development and some solutions'. It discussed the age composition and dependency burden in Taiwan, food and labour supplies, the government's education, health and welfare budget, urbanization, investment etc. On the basis of the evidence presented, the paper concluded that a dollar spent on family planning would save fifty dollars spent on education and job creation, that 'a large and rapidly growing population can be a real deterrent to socio-economic progress', and that 'the centuries-old Chinese tradition in favour of large families is no longer compatible with the process of transformation from a backward agricultural economy to a modern industrial society'.

In the very early days the impetus and rationale behind the family planning programme was somewhat cruder than this analysis by Hsu and Li suggested. Economists and econometrists had not yet come into the picture. Family planning was introduced in Taiwan, in the first instance, as a health measure. It was as a health measure that the programme had received most of its support.

How had the political underpinning of the Taiwan family planning programme expanded beyond the health rationale? It was, so Dr Hsu argued, largely a question of bananas at the outset. Taiwan, at the beginning of the 1950s, used to export bananas to Japan. This trade was an important source of foreign exchange earnings and it was a serious matter when, owing to an outbreak of cholera in Taiwan, it had to be stopped. The authorities investigated the reasons for the cholera and found that the major cause was the very low standard of living in the villages. Going one step further, they came to see that if any single factor could account for this low standard of living, it must be the brutal pressures of Taiwan's extraordinary population growth.

In 1949 and 1950 the JCRR had been involved in the establishment and rehabilitation of waterworks. These were built with funds provided one-third by the benefiting community, one-third by the government and one-third by JCRR. In the early 1950s the JCRR was looking for work in other fields, especially health. In all, it established or strengthened 252 health clinics. There were 361 health centres on the island altogether, one for each of the 361 townships.

The initial emphasis of the JCRR was on sanitation and corrective health education. Dr. Hsu observed that when JCRR started work, 80 per cent of the girls in primary schools had head lice. This was the kind of thing that required urgent attention. With the cholera problem, and the subsequent investigation, those concerned came to see that health activities should – if possible – be broadened to include family planning.

This was easier said than done. JCRR occupied a special place in the hierarchy of government. Its concerns were not necessarily identical with those of officialdom. In the early 1950s – just as in the late 1960s – the need for a 'return to the mainland' was upheld with the force of dogma. Taiwan province had indeed gloriously reverted to Chinese sovereignty – Dr Hsu spoke of the Retrocession of Taiwan, a lovely phrase. But the mainland territory, constituting the rest of the Republic of China, remained under alien domination. There were many who saw family planning as a Communist plot, designed to weaken the forces of Nationalist China and thereby prevent or delay the reunification of the homeland.

Dr Hsu and his colleagues attempted to turn the tables on this argument. They pointed out that the sensible thing for Communists to do in Taiwan would be to oppose rather than to promote family planning. If a lower rate of population increase (through family planning) gave rise to greater productivity, it would help improve the quality and effectiveness of Taiwan's armed forces. Why should the Communists want that? They surely recognized that numerical considerations by themselves were no longer important in modern warfare. What the 700 million Chinese had to fear was not 20 million weak and impoverished Taiwanese but an Israeli-type nation, smaller in numbers but rich in trained men and advanced weapons.

As an additional plea, Hsu and his colleagues pointed out that it would take twenty years for each year's crop of 400,000 babies to be ready to fight the Communists, by which time the return to the mainland would certainly have been achieved. Lastly, it was pointed out that even if by some mischance, reunification was delayed so that 1950s babies still had a fight on their hands in the 1970s, well, even in purely numerical terms it would not be disastrous. Say the birth rate came down to 1.5 per cent a year (or 15 births per thousand population). Then there would still be at least 200,000 births a year. Half of these would be male. After allowing for deaths in infancy and adolescence there would still be enough males around for military service.

Hsu did not leave it at that. The family planning war is not won with a single broadside. He had other weapons – for example, students on bicycles. Armed with a questionnaire and weaving along the narrow roads which link the villages of hill and plain, Hsu's students took a sample of 2,310 mothers. Whether it was a stratified random sample or not, Dr Hsu did not relate. At all events it served the purpose. The survey showed that if a mother had already had three children, infant mortality was 9.9 per cent. If she had between four and six children, it was 17 per cent; between seven and nine, it was 22 to 24 per cent, and if she had over ten children, infant mortality was 54 per cent – i.e., there was less than one chance in two of the additional child surviving. Here was a powerful argument in favour of smaller families.

Finally, Hsu was able to enlist the support – or at any rate the tacit encouragement – of Madame Chiang herself, the revered and powerful wife of Generalissimo Chiang Kai-shek. Madame Chiang, by all accounts, was a dedicated moralist. The eradication of prostitution could be numbered among the goals which she actively pursued. Dr Hsu was able to point out to her that you could not solve the prostitution problem unless you tackled the population problem at the same time. To support this statement, he cited the Taiwanese system for adopting female children out and male children in. The idea behind this seemed to be that if a family could adopt out a daughter or daughters and, either then or later, adopt in a male child or male children who would marry the remaining daughter(s) in the household, the heavy expenses of a proper marriage ceremony could be avoided while, at the same time, there would have been no infraction of laws and customs relating to consanguinity. Hsu showed that there was much more adopting out with large families than with small ones and that the practice itself led to an increase in the number of 'waitresses' and prostitutes.

Gradually, the official attitude to family planning changed. It did not change to the extent that the government was prepared to give any moral or financial support to the programme. The then Minister of the Interior was on record as saying that he thought family planning was a method by which the white race planned to exterminate the yellow one. But it changed enough for Hsu to be able to suggest in 1952 that the China Family Planning Association be formed and for such an association to be officially chartered by the Ministry of the Interior in 1954.

The first real breakthrough seems to have come with the establishment in 1962 of the Taiwan Population Studies Centre in T'ai-chung, a city near the West coast of the island about one hundred and twenty miles south of Taipei. The centre was associated with the Maternal and Child Health Institute of the Taiwan Provincial Health Department. The other Hsu, T.C. Hsu, Commissioner of Health of the province, served as Co-Director, along with Dr Ronald Freedman of the University of Michigan. One of the first things the centre did was to launch what has become known as the T'ai-Chung experiment.

At the end of 1962, when the T'ai-Chung experiment began, the city had a population of about 300,000 people. Its annual per capita income was about one hundred and five dollars, higher than most of Asia outside Japan but comparable with similar areas in Taiwan. There were 36,000 married women aged twenty to thirty-nine. Of these 22,000 had three or more children. The task was to develop an action programme for promoting family planning and to measure the result. In scope and variety it was the largest effort of its kind ever attempted. The objective was to learn whether the birth rate in T'ai-chung could be brought down by a substantial amount and in a short space of time. It was hoped that the lessons learned could be applied on a wider scale to the island as a whole.

The project was divided into two parts. In the first place, there was a broad publicity effort. Since there was still no official approval of family planning, mass communication media – newspapers, radio, television, etcetera – were not exploited. But thousands of posters were distributed throughout the city at street corners, marketplaces, meeting rooms of local associations. Some of these carried detailed information about the services offered; most simply attempted to put the family planning message across. The second and major part of the project involved contact with individual women or individual couples. Since one of the purposes of the experiment was to learn what type of contact was most effective and at what cost, various alternative systems were devised ranging from 'nothing' to 'everything'.

'Nothing' meant you simply relied on the publicity programme to achieve the desired result of a 'contracepted' woman. 'Everything' meant you held special group meetings, made special mailings and topped it all off with special personal visits by trained family planning field workers. As for methods, the programme offered a range of contraceptives – jelly, foam tablets, diaphragm, condom, rhythm, withdrawal, the oral pill, and intrauterine devices.

This is not the place to give a detailed description of the results of the T'ai-chung experiment. What can – and must – be recorded is that the T'ai-chung experiment demonstrated, for the first time ever, that the family planning message could be spread on a wide enough scale for the birth rate of a large population to be affected.

It also demonstrated the overwhelming popularity of the intrauterine device. By June 1,1964, 6,285 couples had accepted family planning guidance through the home visiting and clinical services associated with the Taiwan Action Program. In spite of the variety of choice, 5,000 couples chose the IUD.

With the preliminary data from T'ai-chung tabulated and analyzed, the two Hsus were ready to tackle the next step, the inauguration of an islandwide programme. Health Commissioner T.C. Hsu and his colleagues laboured for some months and finally produced a fat volume of 180 mimeographed pages laying out a ten-year health plan, with family planning an essential part of it. Included were projections of the population if family planning was not undertaken. With the projections went estimates of the tremendous social expenditures, on education and jobs and health etcetera, which would confront the government if the population continued to grow at its present rate. The ten-year health plan made a specific proposal – that 600,000 loops should be inserted within five years. Allowing for expulsions and removals, as well as the age and parity of acceptors, it was estimated that the accumulative reduction in births would be over four hundred thousand by the end of 1970, and that by the end of 1973 the crude birth rate should fall by slightly more than a third, from 36.3 (which is the 1963 figure) to 24 per thousand. The growth rate should fall from 3 per cent to about 1.9 per cent.

The cost of the whole operation was put at $1.5 million over the five years. This worked out – with the couple paying half of the cost of the insertion – at $2.5 per loop, or 2.5 cents per capita per year.

With the plan approved by the authorities, the scorecard for loop insertions at the end of 1968 read as follows:

Through	1964	50,250
	1965	99,253
	1966	111,242
	1967	121,108
	1968	123,670
	Total	505,459

In addition to loop-wearers, there were by the end of 1968 some 63,300 users of the Pill. This did not necessarily represent a net addition to the number of acceptors, since the pills were to be given only to those who had lost their loops or who, the doctors said, should not have loops inserted.

The target, as noted above, was to lower the population growth rate from 3 per cent (in 1963) to about 1.9 per cent by 1973. At the end of 1968, the figure had already fallen to below 2.4 per cent. With an eleven point reduction planned for the decade 1963–73, more than a five point reduction had already been achieved halfway through the decade.

It was difficult, of course, if not impossible to establish precisely what contribution the family planning programme had made to the fall in fertility. A study conducted by Albert I. Hermalin of the Population Studies Centre of the University of Michigan arrived at the following conclusion:

> In summary, we have attempted to determine the effect of IUD acceptance rates and other family planning variables on subsequent fertility by studying their relationship in 282 urban and rural areas of Taiwan. To do this, we have also included a number of socioeconomic and demographic characteristics of the areas which are known to be related to fertility and which may also be related to the family planning program variables . . .
> The results of the analysis indicate that IUD acceptances do have a noticeably negative effect on subsequent fertility. This effect is due not simply to the family planning program's relationship to modernizing trends in Taiwan but rather appears to represent a net contribution to fertility control beyond these other factors.

HONG KONG

Between 1961 and 1966 the birth rate in Hong Kong fell by 27 per cent, from 35.5 per thousand to 25.8. At the end of 1967 it stood at 23 per thousand, with a death rate of 5 per thousand. In Taiwan, we asked the question: how much of the decline in fertility was due to the family planning programme and how much would have occurred in any case ? In Hong Kong, we must go one stage further back and ask: how much of the birth rate decline was due to changes in the age distribution and how much reflected a genuine decrease in fertility?

In January 1968 Professor Ronald Freedman of the University of Michigan and Mr. Arjun L. Adlakha completed their report 'Recent Fertility Declines in Hong Kong'. They pointed out that because of the small number of births and large number of infant deaths during World War II, there was a large decline in the number and percentage of women in the younger child-bearing years (20–29) between 1961 and 1965. The report suggested that the combined effect of changes in the age and marital structure accounted for about 63 per cent, or just under two-thirds, of the 27 per cent decline in fertility noted between 1961 and 1966.

Lest this seem disappointing news to those who wanted to hear about genuine declines in fertility, Professor Freedman looked in detail at the 1965–66 experience. Here the fall in the birth rate was 10 per cent in a single year. Looking at the records Freedman concluded that at least 90 per cent of this 10 per cent was due to real fertility decline. The declines in the birth rate due to age composition were in fact tailing out. Soon there would be a major shift in the pyramid making for higher birth rates. About a fifteen per cent decline in age-specific birth rates would be required if the crude birth rate in 1976 was to be no higher than in 1966. The task confronting the Family Planning Association in the next few years was one of considerable dimensions. Having sailed with the tide for the last few years, the ship now had to encounter currents flowing in the opposite direction.

The authorities were, however, beginning to recognize that the old formula of relying on private charitable efforts with judicious but unspectacular assistance from the government would not be adequate to meet the challenges of the future. In fiscal year 1967–68 the government subvention for the first time reached HK $500,000. This more active posture on the part of the authorities appeared to have paid off. Accurate vital statistics showed that the birth rate in Hong Kong fell from 34.2 per 1,000 in 1960–1964 to 19.4 in 1972.

SINGAPORE

The Republic of Singapore, an island republic of two hundred and twenty-four square miles situated at the southern tip of the Malay Peninsula, had a population of nearly two million in 1969. In 1965 the government of Singapore published a White Paper on Family Planning in which it announced a Five Year National Family Planning Programme, from 1966–1970. This plan aimed to provide a comprehensive family planning service to 180,000 eligible women. Its objective was to bring down the birth rate, which in the preceding year (1964) was 32 per thousand, to below 20 by 1970. The White Paper gave details of the Programme and outlined the manner in which it would be developed. The Singapore Family Planning and Population Board was established by Act of Parliament to implement the plan and act as the national family planning agency.

In his paper 'Preliminary Report on the Results of the National Family Planning Programme and on the Characteristics of New Family Planning Acceptors',[5] Dr K. Kanagaratnam, Deputy Director of Medical Services (Health) and Chairman of Singapore's Family Planning and Population Board noted that the programme had passed its midpoint in June 1968 and that there had been a progressive decline in fertility since

1961. This had, however, become more marked since the end of 1966, one year after the National Programme started in Singapore. What was more, the decline was being achieved at a time when shifts in the age structure of the population (a phenomenon similar to that noted in Hong Kong) was causing large increases in the proportion of fecund women over the plan years.

Kanagaratnam went on to comment on the role of the Singapore Post-partum Programme. (The post-partum concept of family planning is based on the belief that one excellent way of 'motivating' women to adopt contraceptive measures is to approach them shortly after they have had a baby and when they are, physically and psychologically, only too anxious not to 'go through it all again'.)

'In the study of 15,949 new acceptors during the period under review, it was found,' he observed, 'that 13,217 had delivered at the Kandang Kerbau Maternity Hospital during the last pregnancy; of this number 8,243 had delivered within the past three months'.

The government White Paper had placed the major emphasis on the IUD with the contraceptive pill as a preferred alternative. But unfortunately, as the First Annual Report of the Singapore Family Planning and Population Board related, because of a number of factors outside the Board's control, the acceptors of the IUD declined rapidly in the second and third quarters of 1966. 'This was largely the result of ill-founded rumours of the side-effects of this device. A re-orientation of emphasis on methods became necessary; the contraceptive pill has since the middle of 1966 replaced the IUD as the principal method in the national programme; the condom took second place...'

An analysis of the methods prescribed showed that 10,079 were using contraceptive pills, 93 had accepted the IUD, while 5,193 used condoms and 718 adopted miscellaneous methods. The contraceptive pill appeared to be comparatively more popular with Malays (74 per cent) compared to the Indians and Chinese (both 64 per cent). Correspondingly, the condom appeared to be a little more acceptable to the Chinese (16 per cent) compared to the Malays (10 per cent) and Indians (5 per cent). There were possibly social and cultural factors which had resulted in the differential rates of acceptance of these two methods and these were worth further investigation.

The reduction in births had occurred in all three ethnic groups. However, the fall in births began earliest with the Chinese from 1957 onwards. Indian births showed a gradual fall since 1958; this had been marked since 1967. In the case of the Malays, the number of births actually rose from 1957 until 1964, but showed a decline from then until 1966. Since 1967, the fall had been rapid.

Dr Kanagaratnam commented:

> The marked fall in births of all three ethnic groups since 1967 reflects a response
> to the appeal of a national program by all sectors of the population.

Finally, Dr Kanagaratnam dealt with measures which the Singapore government had taken in the way of social and legislative measures going 'beyond' the mere provision of family planning services, measures designed to influence the whole climate of opinion. Obviously, it was difficult to know where to draw the line. Was a large-scale, mass-communications effort, using radio, television, movies, part of family planning proper? Or was it part of 'beyond' ? Though the definitions were not precise, it seemed clear that some aspects of Singapore's efforts were 'beyond family planning', at least in the current sense of the term. Dr Kanagaratnam referred, for example, to recent legislation which denied maternity benefits to women after the third child; it also provided for an increase in hospital fees for the fourth and subsequent pregnancies.

What of the results? The stated objective was to bring the birth rate, which had been 35.6 per 1000 in 1960–1964, in the 1970s to below 20 during the 1970s (assuming that the death rate remained constant at 5.5 per thousand population). This would ensure a net annual increase of population of about 1.5 per cent. By 1969, Singapore was halfway there, and by 1971 the birth rate had fallen to 22.8 per cent so the odds were that Singapore might well achieve – or overachieve – her target.

Any enthusiasm would, of course, need to be tempered by caution. What happened in the tiny island republic of Singapore with its predominantly Chinese population, zealous government and efficient health services might have little or no bearing on what happened in Indonesia, India or Pakistan. Yet it was among these, the most vast and populous nations on earth, that the battle to 'turn the tide' had to be fought and won.

CHINA

At midnight on June 30, 1953, a few days after the first ascent of Everest, the government of China undertook the first systematic census for the whole country. The results, announced on November 1, 1954, revealed that the population of the mainland as of June 30, 1953 (or the twentieth day of the fifth moon of the *kuei-szu* year, lunar calendar) stood at 582.6 million persons. The overall total was given as 602 million, but this included an estimated 7.6 million Taiwanese and 11.7 other Chinese outside the mainland, by custom considered an inseparable part of China. Since the highest working estimate had not exceeded 500 millions, and many had settled for some thing nearer the Kuomintang's 1945 estimate of 450 millions, the census results came as a surprise and as a shock to much of the world. On the basis of the census data, the government announced that the Chinese birth rate was 37 per thousand and the death rate 17 per thousand, the annual rate of population growth being 2 per cent.

At the end of the sixties, the 1953 census was more or less the last beacon the demographer had. Or at least, if there were other guides, they had not been made available to outside observers. What kind of enumeration was made in 1964? What were the results? Had mortality shown the predicted decline, in the absence of major internal disorders and massive famines and given the improved levels of public hygiene and environmental sanitation? Was the population growth rate nearer 2.5 per cent per annum than 2 per cent? We did not know.

Given the uncertainties, economists and demographers had to make their extrapolations, predictions and projections on whatever evidence they had. The United Nations, in its publication World Population Prospects as Assessed in 1963, took as its benchmark the 1953 enumeration. It then developed five alternative projections in which three distinct fertility assumptions were combined with three distinct mortality assumptions. All these alternative projections assumed an eventual decrease in fertility, the differences between them being principally accounted for by the timing, rapidity and extent of the decline.

This anticipated decline, the UN commented:

> ... is related to economic and social changes which will almost certainly occur in a country where the government has taken strong initiatives to overcome long-standing obstacles to progress. *The communal organization of agriculture, the diversi-*

fication of the role of women, the emphasis given to education and acquisition of industrial skills, and other social changes to which mainland China is committed are apt to favour an eventual reduction in the average size of families. (emphasis added).

To conform with estimates made for other parts of the world, the UN used a 1960 population of 650 millions for every variant and classified the projections into high, medium and low alternatives. Even the 'high' alternative assumed a decisive decline in fertility after 1970 to give mainland China a population of 790 million in 1970, 971 million in 1980, 1.67 billion in 1990 and 1.35 billion in the year 2000. The 'medium' variant made still larger assumptions about fertility decline to give a population of 748 million in 1970, 850 million in 1980, 950 million in 1990 and 1.05 billion in the year 2000.

The UN's own comment on the Chinese situation at the end of the sixties was highly instructive. Though the United Nations analysts were not sure exactly what was happening in China as far as fertility was concerned, they suspected that something important was afoot.

The UN commented:

> The case of China would be the most significant one if it were not for the scantiness of relevant information and for the fact that the statistical estimate rests on very limited evidence. Low birth rates and sharp declines in fertility have been reported in a number of cities and districts of China, but it cannot be assessed how representative these data are of conditions in the country as a whole. It is a large country and changes need not occur everywhere with the same speed, despite the known fact that, throughout the country and at all levels, society has undergone much radical change. Official statements do not suggest any concern over the size and rate of growth of the population and express confidence that socially productive labour will suffice to meet the needs and improve the welfare of a growing number of inhabitants. *However, the Government, in co-ordination with organizational bodies at every level, does promote a policy of 'birth planning' regarded as an integral part of the development process. This includes advice to refrain from early marriage and to space births within marriage at suitable time intervals. Quite evidently, traditional or fatalistic attitudes are not condoned and the approach to population reproduction is predominantly rationalistic. Emphasis is placed on the health, welfare, education and social and productive involvement of women whose social equality with men is given stress. It is also made clear that the children of small families enjoy better prospects for adequate care, education and integration into society. A network of medical and para-medical personnel and professional and community associations ensures information on, and distribution of, modern means of fertility regulation. Though an accurate assessment cannot now be made, it is probable that fertility has already been substantially reduced.*[6] (emphasis added).

Commenting generally on demographic events in East Asia, the United Nations observed that the region as a whole had recently undergone much economic and social change and fertility decline might be attributed to that circumstance alone. 'There is also room to argue, however, that a certain type of instrumental rationalism has long been characteristic of East Asian culture, making it particularly responsive to such change.'[7]

In short, economic and social development and 'instrumental rationalism', taken together with the active spread of family planning programmes, seems to have accounted (leaving the special circumstances of Japan aside) for the world's first breakthrough in fertility regulation.

OTHER REGIONS EXPERIENCING REDUCTIONS IN FERTILITY AT THE END OF THE SIXTIES

The next two regions of comparatively moderate fertility, according to Table 3.1, were the Caribbean and Micronesia and Polynesia, both of them composed of islands, a circumstance which the United Nations found 'somewhat puzzling.'[8] Not only in these two regions, but also in the islands of Mauritius, Reunion and Sri Lanka, had there been a marked recent decrease in birth rates.

In the UN's view, an insular situation in itself offered no explanation, unless special conditions accounted for the coincidence. However, some islands were comparatively small and self-contained so that new ideas and attitudes could spread within them rather speedily. Public administration was also comparatively effective as witnessed by the fact, for instance, that they had accurate vital statistics registers. It should be noted that it was also in many cases these same small areas where new health measures, intensified since 1945 and subsequent years, reached their most spectacular success in terms of a rapid and drastic reduction of mortality.

> In the view of many demographers a sharp fall in mortality may be the precursor, or even the pre-requisite, to an equally significant reduction of fertility. If this view is correct, the observations recently made in these comparatively small populations may be a foreshadowing of similar developments to come, perhaps with delay and less speed, in continental countries of much larger population.

Tropical South America is shown in Table 3.1 as another region experiencing – at the beginning of the 1970s – somewhat reduced fertility. In fact, the analysis of census data showed a marked reduction of birth rates especially in the south of Brazil where urbanization and industrialization had progressed to levels characteristic of highly developed countries.[9] In fact the transition to lower fertility was already well under way in Rio de Janeiro and Sao Paulo during the 1950s with total fertility nearly two children per woman lower than the national average (6.32).

The list of countries with recently declining fertility could be extended by another four with fairly accurate birth registration statistics. As shown by the birth rates below, significant fertility reduction had made its appearance also elsewhere in Latin America and in two countries of Arab culture.

With the foregoing observations, evidence of fertility decrease in less developed countries, the UN noted, was 'virtually exhausted'. It could be presumed that in most of South Asia, in Africa south of the Sahara and still in many Latin American countries fertility had continued to be about as high as it had ever been. There was even reason to suppose that in some countries of Africa fertility had risen as a result of increased control over debilitating diseases.

The United Nations final comment on world fertility at the beginning of the seventies is of considerable interest:

> Close associations of fertility levels with indicators of economic and social development have often been observed. *Fertility tends to be lowered with increased education (especially of women), lessened dependence on agriculture, urbanization, the wide availability of mass communication media, improved health and increased access to hospitals. The exact causal relationship between any such factor and fertility has never been clearly established. All these social amenities, it must be supposed, are linked to the entire process of economic and social development. Further, this process itself changes people's outlook from traditions and fatalism towards modern concepts and rationalism. The changed outlook includes an altered attitude towards procreation.* A prominent factor, perhaps, is mor-

tality decline and the consequent experience that most children grow up to make increased demands on their parents and on society for the means needed for their own economic establishment. The observations in certain small populations, mentioned before, point somewhat in that direction. When the public state of mind has matured to a general desire for family limitation, government policies and instruments for their implementation may help substantially in this direction. *On the other hand, evidence is lacking that family planning policy alone, in the absence of other precipitating factors, has ever succeeded in provoking a fertility decline.*[10] (emphasis added)

Over the coming decades, the question raised in the above quotation would be frequently posed. Was economic and social development a necessary precursor of fertility decline? Could fertility decline be in some sense decoupled (for example through

Table 3.1. Gross reproduction rates and net reproduction rates as projected for 1970–1975 in 24 regions.

	Reproduction rate	
Region	Gross[a]	Net[b]
More developed regions	1.13	1.08
Western Europe	1.04	1.00
Japan	1.05	1.02
Eastern Europe	1.07	1.02
Northern America	1.07	1.03
Northern Europe	1.14	1.11
USSR	1.18	1.12
Southern Europe	1.21	1.16
Australia and New Zealand	1.40	1.35
Temperate South America	1.50	1.39
Less developed regions	2.60	2.16
China	1.84	1.65
Other East Asia	2.09	1.89
Micronesia and Polynesia	2.24	2.08
Caribbean	2.37	2.20
Tropical South America	2.63	2.26
Southern Africa	2.76	2.10
Middle Africa	2.92	1.89
Middle South Asia	2.98	2.17
Eastern South Asia	2.98	2.21
Melanesia	3.03	2.19
Northern Africa	3.07	2.29
Western South Asia	3.08	2.42
Middle America	3.11	2.71
Eastern Africa	3.19	2.16
Western Africa	3.25	2.07

[a] Girls born per woman. Since about 1.05 boys are born per each girl born, the numbers of children of either sex born per woman is about 2.05 times the given figures.
[b] Girls born per woman and likely to survive to the ages of their mothers.
Source: Concise Report on The World Population Situation in 1970–1975.

Table 3.2.   Island Birth Rates.

Country	Birth rate	
	1960–1964	1971
Réunion	43.8	31.7
American Samoa	42.2	35.8
Jamaica	39.9	34.8
Fiji	39.2	30.3
Mauritius	38.9	25.2
Trinidad and Tobago	37.1	23.9
Guadeloupe	36.3	30.3
Martinique	35.3	27.1
Sri Lanka	35.1	29.9
Puerto Rico	31.2	25.6

Source: UN Concise Report on the World Population Situation 1970–1975.

Table 3.3.   Significant Fertility Reductions 1960–1970.

Country	Birth rate		
	1960–1964	Recent	(date)
Chile	35.1	29.6	(1970)
Costa Rica	46.1	31.6	(1972)
Egypt	42.6	34.6	(1971)
Tunisia	46.2	37.0	(1972)

Source: UN Concise Report 1970–1975.

vigorous family planning programmes) from economic and social development? Did it make sense to disaggregate the phrase 'economic and social development'? Perhaps certain 'social' developments were more important from the point of view of fertility decline than 'economic' developments so that at least a partial decoupling could be envisaged?

NOTES

1. cf Muramatsu, Minoru, ed. *Japan's Experience in Family Planning.* Tokyo: Family Planning Federation of Japan, 1967.
2. Muramatsu, Minoru. 'Japan: Origins and Operations of Family Planning Programs'. In *Family Planning and Population Programs,* ed. Bernard Berelson and others. Chicago, 1966.
3. Muramatsu, Minoru, in Berelson and others, op. cit., p. 13.
4. *Japan Report,* Vol. 14, No. 7, April 1968. Consulate General of Japan, New York.
5. Dr K. Kanagaratnam, Deputy Director of Medical Services (Health) and Chairman of Singapore's Family Planning and Population Board. Paper delivered at the Fourth Asian Congress on Obstetrics and Gynaecology, Singapore, November 1968.
6. *Concise Report on the World Population Situation in 1970–1975 and Its Long-Range Implications,* United Nations, New York, 1974. ST/ESA/Series A/56. United Nations Sales Publication Sales No. E.74.XIII.4.

  7. United Nations, as above, p. 15.
  8. United Nations, as above, p. 16.
  9. See also: *The Determinants of Brazil's Recent Rapid Decline in Fertility,* Committee on Population and Demography, Report No. 23, National Academy Press, Washington.
10. United Nations, as above, p. 17.

4

National Population and Family Planning Programmes: Early Challenges

The previous chapter recorded some notable first successes in reducing fertility and population growth rates in certain East Asian countries. The United Nations in the Report on the World Population Situation in 1970–1975, which was quoted in that chapter, observed trenchantly – as already indicated:

> It can be presumed that in most of South Asia, in Africa south of the Sahara and still in many Latin American countries, fertility has continued to be about as high as it has ever been ...

It would nevertheless be totally unjust, in a book such as this which aims to record effort as well as achievement, not to spend some time on those major population and family planning programmes which had been launched early on in the Asian subcontinent. We shall in any case have a chance to see later to what extent effort has in fact been translated into achievement.

INDIA

For two thousand years before the British arrived in India, the population seems to have been more or less stationary. The conquest by the Aryans, the incursions of Alexander the Great, the rise of the Mauryans and after them the Guptas and after them the Moguls – all this happened in an India whose population stood at the 100–140 million mark.

The first systematic attempt to collect demographic data was made during the period 1865–1872. It appeared that – under British rule – the population of undivided India had increased to 206 million, which was roughly twice as large as it had been at the beginning of the century.

The growth in population was slower in the last quarter of the nineteenth century and the first twenty years of the twentieth. In the fifty years between 1871 and 1921 it grew only to 250 million, an average increase of less than a million a year over the period. In fact, in the last decade – 1911–1921 – it actually declined by 800,000.

The year 1921 was, however, a watershed. This was when the notion of the 'widening gap' first impinged upon men's minds. Birthrates and death rates were no longer in equilibrium. Whereas in 1921 births stood at 49.2 per thousand and deaths at 48.6, giving a small net increase in population, by 1931 the gap had widened by several points. Births had dropped to 46.4 per thousand, while deaths had dropped to 36.3. Population in 1931 stood at 279 million, an increase of almost 11 per cent on the 1921 figure. During the next decade the increase was 13.5 per cent, with a population of 318 million in 1941, and by 1951, in spite of the separation of Pakistan from India, the population had increased another 14.1 per cent, to 360 million. Even the Bengal famine in 1948 when hundreds of thousands starved to death, could not deflect the rising trend.

Independent India's Planning Commission was set up in March 1950, when the constitution had been in effect about four months. The first five-year plan, submitted to the Prime Minister in September 1952, included this sentence: 'Health is fundamental to national progress in any sphere. In terms of resources for economic development, nothing can be considered of higher importance than the health of the people.' Over the next fifteen years, through three successive five-year plans, the Indians demonstrated that they meant what they said.

In 1941 life expectancy at birth was 32 years for males and just over 31 years for females; girls traditionally appeared to be less well cared for than boys. Only 55 per cent of all males reached 20, and fewer than 13 per cent would live to the age of 60. In 1951 the statistics were more or less the same. By 1966, average life expectancy at birth had increased to 50 and the death rate had fallen to about 16 per thousand. Spectacular successes had been achieved in the campaign against malaria – indeed the almost military efficiency of the spraying teams had become legendary in India. Progress was also made in water supply and sanitation, so that there was at least some hope of a reduction in the incidence of waterborne disease and the slow hideous wasting of whole populations through internal parasites. Recognizing that morbidity was directly linked to adequacy of diet, the government placed increased emphasis on nutritional programmes – skimmed milk powder and other supplements for expectant mothers and children – and health education.

In general, the underlying philosophy veered away from the typical Anglo-Saxon clinic-based, curative approach to medicine towards an extensive preventive approach. The public health concept took precedence over the time-hallowed doctor-patient relationship, a development which – given the relatively modest amounts which India was able to devote to health in the first three plans – was almost inevitable.

The results of all this effort can be seen in the demographic statistics of the first three plan periods. With the death rate declining from 27.4 per thousand to 22.8 between 1951 and 1961, and the birth rate somewhere over 40, India's population grew from 360 millions to 439 millions, an increase of 78 millions or 21.5 per cent over the decade. At the end of the sixties, it was estimated that the population had grown to over 520 millions. With 21 million births a year and 8 million deaths, the annual addition was 13 million, or more than the population of Australia. An Indian baby was born every 1.5 seconds; more than 55,000 were born a day. One in every seven persons, or 14 per cent of the world's population, was Indian, yet India had only 2.4 per cent of the world's land and 1.5 per cent of the world's income.

Whatever hopes there had been for early self-sufficiency in food were soon dashed. Though special attention had been given in the plan to agriculture and various related activities such as irrigation and flood control, and though food production had risen from its tragically low post-independence base of 55 million tons to 72 million tons in

1965, on a per capita basis – with 140 million more mouths to feed – consumption had actually declined – from 12.8 ounces to 12.4.

It was the same story for education and employment. In 1950–51, 23.5 million children went to school. In 1969 the figure was 68 million. But 64 million children were still excluded from the opportunities education could bring. How could it be otherwise in a nation where two-fifths of the population – some 208 millions – were under the age of fifteen?

Official statistics indicated that, in spite of the creation of 31 million additional jobs, unemployment had risen by over 10 million by the end of 1965. The total national income increased from Rs 86 billion in 1948–49 to Rs 149 billion in 1966–67, or 73 per cent over a period of two decades. But per capita income increased during that same period only 20 per cent, from Rs 248 to Rs 297.

The first and second plans assumed a decadal rate of increase of 12.5 per cent while the actual figure was 21.5 per cent. The third plan assumed a population growth of 2.2 per cent per annum, while the rate actually experienced was 2.5 per cent. Looking to the future and assuming that the birth rate remained constant while life expectancy continued to increase, India's population by the time of the next census in 1971 was expected to reach 568 millions.

Gunnar Myrdal, in his book *Asian Drama*,[1] discusses vividly the stultifying effects of colonial rule in India as far as the development of a population policy was concerned. The rapid rise in numbers in the ten years following 1921 was certainly alarming to India's colonial rulers. They had to consider the increasing costs of social services which were a function of population density and growth even if, as Myrdal puts it, 'these were only small-scale and paid by the people of the colony themselves'. They also had to face the disruptive consequences for the *Pax Britannica* of a further pauperization of India.

Even so, they steered clear of any involvement in the propagation of the family planning message. Birth control in the 1930s was still a moral, rather than an economic or social, issue. What was officially reproved in the motherland could not be officially sanctioned in India. In England a typically canny compromise between public disavowal and private tolerance permitted the steady if surreptitious growth of family planning clinics. But the clinic concept, where – with a minimum of publicity – the patient is meant to seek out the doctor rather than vice versa, was hardly relevant to India's problems. It was left to the ubiquitous Mrs Margaret Sanger, visiting India during 1935–36, to make good on the deficiencies of India's rulers.

The Indians, too, bore some of the responsibility for inaction. Though excessive population growth as well as stagnation under imperial rule contributed to her plight, many intellectuals were reluctant to admit this lest the British find an alibi for their failures in the economic sphere. They argued instead, as Marxists would argue later, that with Independence production would be revitalized and the population problem would disappear, a view which Gandhi himself subscribed to.

Gandhi's economic views were reinforced by some strong personal views on contraception. He considered all means of contraception except abstinence immoral. Even abstinence seems to have been tolerated not so much as a contraceptive measure but as a step in his progress towards 'brahmacharya', continence or self-control or, as he wrote, 'the thought and practice which puts you in touch with the Infinite and takes you to his presence'.

Rabindranath Tagore, who won the Nobel Prize for Literature in 1913, spoke of the 'cruel crime, thoughtlessly to bring more children into existence than can properly be taken care of'. The first Indian Population Conference was held in 1936 and a second in 1938. In 1943 Sir Joseph Bhore, who headed the Health Survey and Development Committee, recommended the provision of birth control service. A few clinics were established, and in 1949 the Family Planning Association of India was founded.

But, by and large, the Gandhian view dominated the two decades of the 1930s and 1940s. Even when, in 1951, India became the first government in the world to adopt a comprehensive national family planning policy as an integral part of its development plans, it was a modest enough beginning. Over the period 1951–1956 1.45 million rupees were spent; 147 clinics were established. The method promoted was principally, rhythm, and the impact – so far as can be judged – was negligible.

Not much more progress was achieved in the second five-year plan, from 1956 to 1961. Expenditure increased to 22 million rupees and the number of clinics rose to 4,165. But still Anglo-Saxon attitudes prevailed. There was no thought of a mass-educational campaign nor would the clinic staff, committed to the time-honoured and time-consuming procedures of doctor–patient consultations and overburdened by record keeping, have been able to conduct one in any case. Perhaps the most significant event of the second plan period was that in 1958 the Government of India officially endorsed sterilization as a main method of contraception. In 1960, it began to reimburse the states for the cost of sterilization operations.

The year 1961 was a watershed year. The government realized how badly it had underestimated the rate of population growth in the previous decade; it looked at the future and saw what a gloomy prospect lay ahead unless something could be done to close the 'widening gap'. Clearly what had been achieved in the first two plan periods was nowhere near enough. New approaches were required.

Thus the 'extension' approach was born. The old Anglo-Saxon pattern of specialized birth control clinics was discarded. Family planning was to be incorporated into general health work, becoming a regular part of the activities of health centres, child and maternity clinics and so forth. According to the new philosophy, the services would seek out the people. Systems of mass communication and mass education would be devised to supplement the 'informational' and 'motivational' efforts of medical, paramedical and other personnel engaged in the work. Community participation was to be of paramount importance; there was to be a total mobilization of resources, whereby the energies of the 'panchayats', village councils, 'gram Sewaks', village level workers, 'dais', village midwives, Ayurvedic physicians and other 'practitioners of indigenous systems of medicine', women's organizations, social workers, business and industrial leaders, civil servants, religious bodies and Gandhian 'sarvodaya' workers, would all be harnessed to the task. It was an immense and exciting vision, founded on the belief that the tools now existed to change basic human behaviour on a vast scale and in a most radical way.

The Government's 1962–63 report on the Family Planning Programme set out the 'Basic Goals and Principles'. With the new extension approach, the main objective was to 'accelerate the rate of adoption of family planning so as to reduce the birthrate in India to 25 births per 1,000 population by 1973'.

The 1973 deadline seems to have been lost in the doldrums of the pre-IUD days. Perhaps it was never officially adopted but remained a recommendation of the report. At all events, with the arrival of the intra-uterine device (IUD) and the dawning of the new 'technological era' in the last year of the third plan (1965), the time dimension reemerges with new emphasis. The programme becomes 'timebound and target-oriented'. The goal is to achieve a reduction of the birth rate to 25 per thousand by 1975–76. This overall goal is translated into year by year, method by method subtargets. But once more a shift of emphasis occurs. The programme must have more time to prove itself. The year 1975–76 becomes 1978–79, a movement which can be represented as not so much a retreat as a sidestep, for the family planning authorities announce that their goal by 1978–79 is not 25 but 22.

The commitment by the Government of India to the family planning programme was, at the end of 1968, certainly impressive. Expenditure under the third plan (1961–62 to 1965–66) amounted to Rs 250 million. But in 1966–67 alone Rs 139 million were spent and in 1967–68 Rs 265 million, while Rs 370 million was budgeted for 1968–69. Until the brief but bitter Indo-Pakistan war in the autumn of 1965 and some disastrous harvests upset the even succession of five-year plans, Rs 2,290 million had been allocated in the fourth plan, which was about eight times the allocation of the previous plan. The Government of India had accorded 'top priority' to the programme which had been launched on a 'war footing'.[2]

When, after an interregnum of one-year plans, the five-year cycle was resumed, this 'top priority' was maintained. The Planning Commission stated in its 'Approach to the Fourth Five-Year Plan 1969–74' that 'This programme has already been accepted as a Centrally sponsored scheme for a period of ten years. Whatever can usefully be spent on the programme may be provided....' The programme had been given what, in theory, amounted to a blank cheque. The budget for family planning amounted to 2.1 per cent of total public sector outlays. By comparison, health had 3.0 per cent of public sector outlays, agriculture 15 per cent, power 14 per cent, industry and minerals 21.5 per cent, transport and communications 22 per cent and education 5.6 per cent. (Other minor categories of expenditure accounted for the rest.)

By the end of the 1960s, almost half of all the sterilization operations performed anywhere in the world had been performed in India. Five million operations altogether were performed between 1956 and September 1968. One sterilization was generally assumed to prevent 1.5 births, i.e. had the operation not been performed the man or woman would have had, on average, one and a half more children. An IUD insertion was worth only a third of this, being assumed to prevent 0.5 births. The regular use of the condom scored only one-quarter of the IUD.

There were other more optimistic evaluations. Mr S. Chandrasekhar, India's Minister for Family Planning, suggested for example in an article in Foreign Affairs in October 1968 that 'each sterilization has prevented the arrival of some 3 children who would not otherwise have been born in the next six to ten years. In other words at a conservative estimate, we have prevented the arrival of some 10 to 12 million babies so far. Besides, 2.9 million mothers have accepted the loop and an unestimated number use the condoms. These methods jointly have perhaps prevented the birth of about 15 million babies.'

Dipak Bhatia, Commissioner for Family Planning, provided a heartfelt encore to this when he wrote: 'If progress at the existing rate continues, then by 1976–77, we would be able to prevent about 12.5 million births annually to offset the present annual addition of 13 million.' In other words, Dr. Bhatia was suggesting that instead of the sum reading 21 million births minus 8 million deaths = + 13 million annually = + one Australia, it would read $8\frac{1}{2}$ million births minus 8 million deaths = + $\frac{1}{2}$ million annually = + one Fiji Islands. The family planning programme would, at this point, ease into its 'maintenance' phase merely taking care of new entrants into the target group.

All these calculations were, of course, predictive. Like all predictions they might be wildly inaccurate. Large but unknown numbers of those women who had the IUD inserted did not retain it; had the formulas made sufficient allowance? People kept their tobacco dry in condoms, made catapults out of them, blew them into balloons – as well as using them for the intended purpose. Given the substantial amounts of money involved in the sterilization campaign for incentive and compensation payments; given, too, the inevitable tendency of large bureaucracies to corruption, could analysts be at all sure that the reported sterilization figures were in fact the actual figures?

The only sure way of knowing what is going on was to leave prediction aside and actually measure the birth rate itself. But this was easier said than done. Considerable ambiguity attached to current estimates of the birth rate in India. Was it 41 per thousand, 43, or was it as high as 47?

At the beginning of the 1970s, the Office of the Registrar General of India was developing a network of sample registration areas but it would be some time before these yielded reliable estimates of birth and death rates. There had been a number of localized sample fertility surveys. The Institute of Rural Health and Family Planning in Gandhigram had reported a decline in the birth rate from 43.6 in 1959 to 31.3 in 1966 (in Athoor Block); in Singur in West Bengal a 12 per cent decline in fertility – from 40.2 to 35.4 was observed between 1954–66. A report from the tea-gardens of Assam, where an intensive IUD programme had been under way, showed a reduction from 43.4 in 1960 to 25.6 in 1967. An alternative report on the same programme showed a drop of 16 points (from 53 to 37) in two years, raising considerable doubts about the value of the statistics.

Indeed, no one in general pretended that these scattered sample surveys of fertility could in any sense be taken as representative of the country as a whole. So far, as Govind Narain (Secretary to the Ministry of Health, Family Planning and Urban Development) admitted: 'an evaluation of the programme vis-à-vis the objective of a reduced birth rate has not been made on a uniform basis throughout the country'.

In the circumstances, the omission of India from the United Nations list of countries showing significant fertility declines was understandable and perhaps inevitable. From the point of view of this book, however, those early days of the Indian family planning programme remain of consuming interest.

PAKISTAN

Up to Partition, Pakistan's population problem was India's problem – and vice-versa. The population enumerated in the area now constituting Pakistan had increased from forty-five million at the beginning of the century to about seventy-six million at the time of the 1951 census, despite the Hindu-Muslim bloodbath of 1947–48. In 1953 a group of public-spirited people founded the Family Planning Association of Pakistan and family planning clinics were opened in a few cities. There was no official policy, either for family planning or for population control. The government gave no financial support and the staff involved generally worked on an unpaid part-time basis.

In the first five-year plan, 1955–1960, the government became more conscious of the urgency of the problem. The plan stated:

> The opinion of the educated classes, particularly of medical men, economists and social workers is strongly in favour of extension of family planning facilities. ... The country must appreciate that population growth is a rock on which all hopes of improved conditions of living may founder. It admits of no approach except that the rates of growth must be low.

Notwithstanding this declaration of intent, there was no family planning organization and no programme during the first plan.

With the accession to power of Ayub Khan, after the October Revolution of 1958, the declaration of intent was elaborated into a more formal position. In a speech in March 1959 Ayub Khan announced that he had impressed upon the Minister of Finance 'the need for allocating more and more funds for the movement of family planning'. As the second five-year plan, 1960–65 put it:

> Since population growth can threaten to wipe out the gains of development, the Plan clearly recognizes the paramount need for a conscious population policy and its implementation. A population policy, however, must take into account many implications of population growth for other aspects of planning. The existing pressure of population leads to an intense struggle for the means of life at subsistence levels. Inadequate diet results in a prevalent malnutrition that cannot be cured by public health measures alone. Apathy is the companion of malnutrition and ignorance. Under these conditions people have meagre reserves of energy to strive for wider understanding and improvement....
>
> A gradual decrease in the rate of population growth, with the consequent lightening of the burden on family earnings, and a shrinkage in the amount of unemployment, will have an encouraging effect on the rate of industrialization. An overplentiful supply of cheap labour leads to its wasteful utilization by employers, high turnover and an apathetic response to factory discipline and organization of productive skills ...

The organization and programme during this second five year plan period did not, however, live up to the high promise of the policy. The specific targets set forth in the plan were: to cover 1.2 million families during the plan period or about ten per cent of women of childbearing age; to establish 8,000 family planning centres in existing health facilities and develop a distribution system for conventional contraceptive supplies; to train the required motivational and technical personnel, including 1,200 health personnel – doctors, nurses, midwives and health visitors – each year; and to promote research and administration projects in the field of family planning.

The second five-year plan had stated that population policies must

> take into account the relations between population growth and characteristics on the one hand, and economic development, social change, labour force utilization, health and human welfare on the other. Improvements in the means of communication with the people are necessary if population policies are to be effective.
>
> Education, particularly the education of women, will have far-reaching effects in the modification of attitudes. The spread of literacy and employment opportunities for women, desirable for many reasons, is directly related to the problems of population. Educated women can comprehend the possibilities of family planning more readily; gainfully employed women tend to marry later and to have fewer children ...

The language of the third five-year plan, 1965–70, reflected a new impetus; numerical targets for reduction in the birth rate are specified for the first time:

> It is estimated that in order to have any significant impact on the economic situation the family planning programme must aim to halve the birthrate in the next 25 years. This is a formidable task but it is by no means impossible to accomplish provided an all-out effort is launched in order to effect a break-through during the Third Plan period. The family planning programme included in the Third Plan will need to be implemented with the utmost vigour and single-mindedness if this break-through is to be achieved.

This clearly was the language of a military man. Ayub suited action to the words. With the full authority of martial law behind him, he removed family planning from the health services where it had been such an unwelcome guest, and created instead a semiautonomous organization. Just as India emphasized the IUD in 1965, so the Pakistan third plan, beginning that same year, laid 'primary stress' on the IUD, a 'cheap and effective method which does not require the constant participation of the user'. Just as India used audiovisual vans and all available publicity media, so Pakistan had its film vans and radio talks and hoardings and even a family planning stall at the famous Lahore Horse and Cattle Show.

The principle objective of the third plan programme was to bring down the birth rate from 50 per thousand to 40 per thousand by 1970, a 20 per cent reduction. In order for this to be achieved it was envisaged that 25 per cent or 5 million of the over-all total of 20 million fertile couples would be practising contraception by 1970. By the end of the first year there were 576,000 'contracepting couples', by the end of the second 1,614,000, and by the end of the third the cumulative score stood at 2,944,000. In other words the programme was well on target, at least as far as performance was concerned.[3]

The June 30, 1968 figure of 2.9 million contracepting couples was in turn broken down into 986,000 IUD cases, 817,000 sterilizations and 1,641,000 'conventionals'. The sterilization figures were, in fact, higher than expected owing to a sudden upsurge of interest in East Pakistan. Vasectomies had been running at 60,000 a month compared with only 6,000 in West Pakistan. As the official report on the year 1967–68 put it, 'The coil continued to be our best bet; but, during the year under report, vasectomies caught popular acceptance in East Pakistan like wildfire' – a symptom, many believed, of the greater economic hardships of life in the east wing.

If the programme was on target in terms of performance, the family planning authorities argued that predicted declines in the birth rate must be taking place. As with the Indian programme, the different methods were assigned different 'prevented birth' values. Up till July 1968, a simple formula was used. It was estimated from the 1961 census that on the average 3.49 married women in reproductive ages, fifteen to forty-nine years, give birth to one live-born baby in one year. Thus for each 3.44 married women who wore the IUD for a year, or whose husbands had been sterilized, it was assumed that one birth had been prevented. For conventional contraceptives, owing to their lower efficiency as compared to clinical contraception, the ratio of 4 was used instead of 3.44. (It is interesting to compare these ratios with those used in the Indian programme.)

When the various ratios were applied, the figures (in thousands) for prevented births by mid-1968 looked like this:

	IUD	Sterilization	Conventional	Total
Performance	986	317	1641	2944
Births prevented	287	92	410	789

In other words, where Pakistan might, under constant fertility, have had some 6,254,000 births in 1967–68, she would – thanks to family planning – have had only 5,465,000, or 789,000 fewer. With the death rate assumed to decline linearly by 0.5 per thousand per year so that it reached 18.5 in 1967–68, the figure of 5.46 million births, 43.69 per thousand, implied a population growth rate of 2.52 per cent per annum. In fact according to these calculations, the target decline to 2.5 per cent by the end of the third plan, June 30, 1970, had almost been achieved two years earlier.

Was there any 'independent' evaluation of the 'success' of the Pakistan family planning programme? USAID's Demographic Adviser in Pakistan, while recognizing that the conversion of operation statistics into the probable reduction in the number of births was 'highly conjectural', nevertheless gauged the reduction in births at 500,000 to 600,000 at midpoint in the third plan, or about fifty per cent of the reduction needed to achieve the plan's objective in 1970. He wrote: 'There are ever-increasing indications that Pakistan's ambitious Family Planning target will be achieved. The target may not be surpassed by a significant margin, but the programme would have to suffer serious reverses to fall short of the desired 20 per cent reduction of the birth rate.'

A joint United Nations-World Health Organization Advisory Mission, headed by Sir Roland Walker, the Australian Ambassador to France, was less sanguine. After visiting Pakistan during the first half of 1968, it pointed out that the group known to sociologists as 'early adopters' had been nearly exhausted and that in the future much more resistance would be encountered in persuading people to start practising family planning. It had been suggested that – where the rural masses were concerned – the sole pleasure available to the husband was his sex life and the main interest in life for the wife was the rearing of children, while the prospect of appreciable economic improvement to the individual by forgoing children was by no means apparent in present circumstances. The mission went on to argue that even if the practice of family planning was adopted by a couple, there was the problem of ensuring that it was persisted in systematically and neither followed sporadically nor abandoned on account of various difficulties encountered.

All in all, the mission concluded that 'in our view, it is too early to be certain that the target will be achieved'.

At the beginning of the 1970s, all these judgments about the 'success' of Pakistan's efforts at population control were at best 'guesstimates'. Though the system of reporting and collecting service statistics had been constantly refined; though an immensely complex formula for calculating Couple Years of Protection – involving attrition curves, retention spans, and the constant $e = 2.71828$ – had replaced the cruder conversion ratios for IUDs, sterilizations, etcetera, the harsh truth was that no adequate evaluation of the programme had yet been made.

KENYA

Of the 42 African countries featuring in Table 2.1, only seven are shown as having an official anti-natalist policy and a family planning programme. Kenya, at the beginning of the 1970s, was generally recognized to be in the vanguard of that already highly select band.

Kenya's population at the time of the 1962 census was growing at around three per cent per annum. At that rate it would double, from around 10 million to 20 million, in twenty three years and would – in less than a century – reach 144 million. In fact, a three per cent projection was low. Demographers taking into account continued declines in mortality with fertility remaining constant, foresaw an increase in the average annual rate of growth to about 3.9 per cent by the end of the century, which implied a doubling of the population in eighteen years rather than twenty-three.

When the Union Jack, which had flown over Kenya for sixty-eight years, was lowered at midnight on December 11, 1963, and the black, red and green flag of Kenya raised in its place, the substitution did nothing to alter underlying demographic trends. The leaders of independent Kenya had to face up to a situation which seemed far removed from the difficult but exciting days of the independence struggle, the sudden flights to London, the Lancaster House Conferences, the release and return of Jomo Kenyatta from the forests of Maralal.

That the colonial past left them ill-equipped to deal with these new realities was hardly surprising since Britain herself was signally unaware of and insensitive to the problems which her former dependencies would encounter – in this respect as in so many others.

That Kenya, unlike many other sub-Saharan African countries, grasped so early on the implications of population growth for her future as a proud and independent nation could be ascribed in large measure to the ability, energy and personality of Tom Mboya.

Mboya had been made Minister of State for Constitutional Affairs and Economic Planning in the coalition government that followed the second Lancaster House Conference. After Independence, he retained his position as Minister of Economic Planning, becoming – in the eyes of many observers – the key man in Kenyatta's cabinet, after Kenyatta himself. Like Kenyatta, he saw the need to retain the confidence of the West. Kenya should offer a stable political environment and an expanding market. Legal safeguards, protecting foreign investment, were contained in the constitution, the Foreign Investment Protection Act and in the International Investment Disputes Convention to which Kenya adhered. The government took steps to build up a strong infrastructure and to capitalize on the climatic and other attractions of Nairobi.

This approach could be seen spelled out in the Government White Paper, 'African Socialism and its Application to Planning in Kenya', which Mboya presented on April 27, 1965, as Minister of Economic Planning. As Marshall Macphee said in his book *Kenya*,[4] Mboya's White Paper advocated 'a course half-way between the demands of the Kenya nationalists for undiluted black power and the requirements of the overseas investor for stable economic conditions'.

Especially significant was the fact that Mboya was bold and intelligent enough to refer directly to Kenya's population problem. The passage is worth quoting:

> The Government's capacity to achieve its desired objectives is restricted by our limited resources, which restrain our ability to expand, and by our high rate of population growth, which rapidly increases the size of the task. With population growing in excess of 3 per cent per annum nearly seven million jobs will be needed by the year 2000 and over 230,000 adult males will at that time be added to the labour force each year. A more moderate rate of population growth of 1.7 per cent per annum, approximating the world rate, would mean a male labour force of 4.5 million growing at 60,000 per annum in the year 2000. The effect of slower growth on numbers of children of primary school age is even more pronounced. With present fertility rates universal education would require facilities for over six million children in the year 2000 at an annual recurrent cost of perhaps £49 million. More moderate growth would reduce this cost to £18 million because facilities would be needed for only 2.3 million children. A high rate of population growth means a large dependent population, reduces the money available for development, lowers the rate of growth and makes exceedingly difficult the task of increasing social services. A programme of family planning education will be given high priority....
>
> Immediate steps will be taken towards family planning education, because the present high rate of population growth makes extensive and intensive provision of social services more expensive, the unemployment problem more intractable, and saving for development harder than need be – thus lowering the rate of economic growth.

A few days before the White Paper was published, on April 8, 1965, Mr. T.K. Mbathi – Mboya's Permanent Secretary at the Ministry of Economic Planning and Development – wrote to the Population Council in New York requesting that a team of experts visit Kenya:

to study the population problem in Kenya with a view to making recommendations
on the ideal rate of growth;
to recommend a suitable programme for effecting the ideal rate of growth;
to make recommendations on administration of the programme;
to recommend procedures for obtaining funds and technical assistance for carrying
out the programme.

Two months later the mission arrived in Kenya. It submitted its report in time for
Mboya to incorporate its analysis and principal recommendation in Kenya's Development Plan 1966–1970. The plan stated that: 'The population problem has such a serious impact on the future development of the country that the Government has
decided to place strong emphasis on measures to promote family planning.' These
measures included the establishment of a Family Planning Council to plan and coor-
dinate the activities of the government, the Family Planning Association and other
private agencies in the field of family planning; making available government hospitals and health centres for the establishment of family planning clinics with a directive
to various government ministries asking for full cooperation; preparation by the
Family Planning Council of an educational programme, collection of statistical data,
planning of clinical studies, etcetera.

With the adoption of the plan it seemed that Mboya had scored a remarkable success. In a land whose whole social organization was based on the promotion of fertility; where a woman considered subfertility or sterility the gravest affliction she could
bear; where the production of offspring was accounted to the individual family as a
bulwark against want and to the tribe as a guarantee of its continued existence; where
the brideprice remained an important institution and the phallus the symbol of all
those things that, in African eyes, were lovely and of good report – in this land a man
of courage and conviction, who was incidentally a Catholic, had been able to propose
and have approved a programme aimed at the deliberate control of births.

By how much fertility was to be reduced and in accordance with what timetable, the
plan did not specify. This, after all, was only the beginning.

On December 5, 1966, J.D. Otiende, the Minister of Health, wrote a circular letter
to government medical officers and local authorities, explaining the seriousness of the
population problem and claiming that 'with your full cooperation this can be overcome to the betterment of all the people of Kenya'. Training of medical officers in
different methods of family planning would be started and from a date to be fixed
family planning would become part of medical services. Information and services
would be offered to those desiring it through government hospitals, mission hospitals
and health centres.

On November 13, 1967, J.C. Likimani, Director of Medical Services and Permanent Secretary, wrote a further circular letter which stated that 'the time has come
when it is now possible to provide these (family planning) services aimed at improving
maternal and child health ... Intensive training of medical staff who may not be familiar with the statistical effectiveness and side-effects of the various methods of Family
Planning is to be started and arrangements for their attendance at courses and
seminars will be made.'

However, over the next year or so, the family planning movement clearly suffered a
setback in the sense that the Family Planning Council, proposed in the plan, met two
or three times and then was suddenly and without warning disbanded. The causes of
the setback could be examined at three different but intermingled levels: personal,
national and international.

At the personal level, there appeared to be a good deal of evidence that – in the twenty months or so before his untimely death (gunned down in a Nairobi street in the summer of 1969) – Tom Mboya was backing off a little in his support of the family planning movement. The publication of the Papal Encyclical *Humanae Vitae*, his own Catholicism and the presence of a large Catholic minority – 2 million Catholics out of 5 million Christians out of 10 million Kenyans – undoubtedly had something to do with it. Probably more important, though, were Mboya's relations with Oginga Odinga, who resigned as Vice-President in April 1966, to assume the leadership of the newly formed Kenya People's Union, KPU.

The basis of the conflict between Mboya and Odinga was ideological. Odinga had little patience with Mboya's idiosyncratic approach to African socialism; he saw no need to pander to foreign investors. Communism was what was needed and revolution was the way to attain it. He attracted substantial support from both Russia and China as well as from those elements in the Kikuyu and Luo tribes who felt that they had been excluded from the social and economic benefits of independence.

If President Jomo Kenyatta was conscious of the need to preserve internal unity, he must have been conscious too of Kenya's increasingly delicate international position, vis-à-vis her forty-odd sister states in the Organization of African Unity and especially vis-à-vis her immediate neighbours.

Kenya was special in many ways in sub-Saharan Africa. She had encouraged private enterprise and seemed determined to direct her economy along traditional capitalist lines. This already made her suspect. For to the south, President Nyerere of Tanzania had plunged headlong into his own brand of socialism (Zanzibar having virtually banned capitalism from the island). In both Tanzania and Zambia the Chinese were visible in force (all with blue working suits and blue Mao caps with a red star) as they pressed ahead with the Tanzam railway from Dar es Salaam in Tanzania to Lusaka in Zambia, a project the West had rejected as economically unviable. Guerrilla forces were gathering against the last bastions of white supremacy – Rhodesia, South Africa, Angola and Mozambique – carrying machine guns in one hand and waving in the other the Thoughts of Chairman Mao. Would Kenya join in the great enterprise? Or would she grow fat on American Express and Diners' Club, regarding the terms of the 1967 Treaty of East African Cooperation as the full extent of her obligation to her fellow nations?

For Kenya to adopt a vigorous policy of population control, a 'timebound, target-oriented' programme could be the spark igniting the already smouldering tinder of distrust. Throughout much of black Africa, it is fair to say, family planning at that time was seen as a 'white imperialist plot', a form of neocolonialism designed to ensure the continued subjugation of the black race to Western interests long after the last echoes of Uhuru have died away.

That these fears were ludicrous and unfounded is beside the point. They existed. Suspicion of the white man and of all his works seemed to be ineradicable. If family planning was seen to be promoted by Americans and Englishmen with white faces and bulging briefcases, then by definition it was, or could be made to seem, part of the dastardly Western plot to rob the black man of his virility, suppress his vital forces and leave the continent an easy prey to a new imperialism more hideous and more protracted than the last.

Small wonder, then, that even though Kenya was in the vanguard of those African nations committed to population policies and family planning programmes, the vanguard itself – truth to tell – had not progressed very far.

SUMMARY

In some ways the world population situation at the end of the 1960s appeared as grim as it had ever been. Population growth rates had never been higher. Though governments and private organizations had begun to fund family planning programmes, the results of such programmes – in terms of reduced birth rates – were far from evident. The most significant fertility reductions had occurred in countries such as Hong Kong, Singapore, Taiwan and Thailand which from an overall demographic point of view were not particularly significant. A cloud of unknowing hung over China, India and Pakistan.

Yet seen in historical perspective, the end of the 1960s may in fact have been some kind of a turning point in world demographic trends. If the first truly 'revolutionary' change in the reproductive balance of the human species was the reduction in mortality which took place between 1850 and 1970, to more percipient eyes, the next 'revolutionary' change, namely fertility decline, seemed to be on the horizon.

In August 1965, Ronald Freedman, Director of Population Studies at the University of Michigan, addressed the concluding session of the International Conference on Family Planning Programmes, held in Geneva, Switzerland (August 23–25, 1965). The remarks he delivered on that occasion can be seen as prophetic in many ways.

> In historical perspective, we may be at a turning point in world demographic trends. If we believe what we say about the importance of population trends, the next several decades may mark also an important turning point in world history. Such grandiloquent statements seem a little pompous, but I believe they are justified by the facts today and by what seems plausible, if not probable, for the next five to twenty years.
>
> I base this rather sweeping assertion on two observations. First, there is reason to expect that in the next five years we shall see for the first time in history in at least several small but significant populations really major national fertility declines induced, or at least accelerated, by organized family planning programs. Second, in many other larger countries there are likely to be significant beginnings of fertility decline with new vigorous organized programs, although whether these efforts in other countries will be as successful as needed to accomplish their objectives is still very problematic.[5]

NOTES

1. See pp. 1483–1488. Gunnar Myrdal, *Asian Drama*, published by Allen Lane, London, 1968.
2. Government of India, *India: Family Planning Programme since 1965*, published November 1968; *Population Problem of India*, June 1968.
3. Government of Pakistan, Planning Commission. *The Fourth Five Year Plan (1970–75)*; *Planning in Pakistan*, 1968.
4. Published by Benn, London, 1968.
5. Published in *Population and Family Planning Programmes*, edited by Bernard Berelson, University of Chicago, 1967.

5

The Growth of International Assistance

The growth in national concern over the implications of rapid population growth and the increasing number of official family planning programmes, as outlined in the previous chapters, was reflected in the growth of international assistance in this field during the decade of the seventies. Indeed, international assistance in the field of population, perhaps more than in most other fields, has played a vital role in reinforcing and underpinning national commitments.[1]

THE UNITED NATIONS

The United Nations as early as 1962 in its General Assembly resolution 1838 (XVII) invited Member States to formulate their own population policies. In 1966, the General Assembly re-emphasized the interrelationships between demographic trends and economic and social factors, and recognized 'the sovereignty of nations in formulating and promoting their own population policies, with due regard to the principle that the size of the family should be the free choice of each individual family'. It also requested the Secretary-General to intensify the implementation of the Secretariat's population programme, and called upon the Economic and Social Council and the regional economic commissions, inter alia, to assist, where requested, in further developing and strengthening national regional facilities with due regard to the diverse character of population problems in the world's regions (see General Assembly resolution 2211 (XXI)).[2] These resolutions enabled the Secretary-General to establish in 1967 the United Nations Trust Fund for Population Activities (UNFPA), the resources of which would derive from voluntary contributions of Governments, non-governmental organizations and private individuals.

The purpose of the fund was to assist developing countries with high population growth rates and low national incomes to solve their population problems, to expand the population activities of the United Nations system as a whole, and to pursue new and innovative programmes in this hitherto sadly neglected field. This action was taken in response to resolutions in the Economic and Social Council in July 1965 and the General Assembly in December 1966, the latter being sponsored by some 25 countries including, from the developing world, Ghana, India, Iraq, Iran, Kenya, Libya, Nepal, Nigeria, Pakistan, Syria, UAR, Yugoslavia and several Latin American countries.[3] Governments, institutions and individuals were thus given the opportunity of making voluntary contributions to add international impetus to national population efforts. A few years later, in December 1971, the General Assembly, with 94 votes for, 20 abstentions and no opposition, passed a resolution[4] recognizing the United Nations Fund for Population Activities (UNFPA) or United Nations Population Fund, as it was frequently called, as the focal point of the population efforts of the UN system and giving it a leadership role in promoting and co-ordinating international population programmes.

The interested specialized agencies, namely the International Labour Organisation, the Food and Agriculture Organization of the United Nations, the United Nations Educational, Scientific and Cultural Organization and the World Health Organization, had also received mandates from their governing bodies to deal with population problems and particularly with family planning programmes within the scope of their responsibility and competence.[5]

With the mandate given to the United Nations Children's Fund (Economic and Social Council resolution 1258 (XLIII)) and to the United Nations Development Programme (Council resolution 1347 (XLV)), all the above mentioned competent agencies of the United Nations system interested in population matters were active or were ready to act upon the request of interested Governments. The expertise required to give advice on the feasibility of a population policy, on the evaluation of ongoing family planning programmes, or on other aspects of assistance was both varied and multidisciplinary.

An expanded United Nations programme in the field of population was thus launched in 1967, in co-operation with the specialized agencies concerned. Upon the request of Governments, missions had visited a number of countries giving advice on population matters. Existing regional organizations, such as the regional economic commissions, regional demographic research and training centres and a newly recruited staff of population programming officers at the subregional level had likewise become increasingly engaged in corresponding activities.

In practice, the relationship between population growth and economic and social progress had long been recognized by the United Nations and taken into account by agencies providing assistance to developing countries. The Population Division of the United Nations, in particular, was one of the world's most reliable sources of the demographic information needed by all nations for successful development planning. The advent of the Population Fund, however, not only increased the size and scope of the population work of the United Nations system but also widened its sphere of influence by encouraging greater coordination between United Nations supported activities and those of bilateral, non-governmental and private organizations.

UNFPA assisted national efforts by

– promoting government awareness of social and economic implications of population problems;
– providing systematic and sustained assistance to countries seeking to define and solve population problems;
– helping organizations within the UN system to be more effective and efficient in planning, programming and implementing population projects supported by the Fund;
– assuming a leadership role in developing population strategies.

UNFPA aided all aspects of population work and the projects supported covered a wide range of activities including: collection and analysis of basic demographic data;

provision of demographic research and training facilities; demonstration programmes in family planning connected with maternal and child welfare services; inclusion of courses on population subjects in such educational programmes as adult education, teacher training and agricultural extension; provision of fellowships in the fields of population statistics, census-taking, demography, health education, human reproduction, communications evaluation and public administration; provision of contraceptive supplies and manufacturing materials, if requested, and formulation of population policies and the measures to be taken in accordance with national development objectives.

By mid-1972 the Fund was financing over 500 projects benefitting 74 countries and developing areas.

In Africa, for example, where many countries were virtually without census-based statistics, the first priority was to ascertain population trends and obtain overall demographic information. Under the sponsorship of the Economic Commission for Africa (ECA), an African Census Programme had been launched to provide not only information on the current structure of population but also on the dynamics of population. Twenty out of 41 members of ECA had already started demographic programmes and the rest were preparing to do so. It was estimated that the Fund would provide at least $11 million over a three-year period for censuses and national demographic surveys. The Fund also supported a regional demographic centre in Cameroon for French-speaking nations, and one for English-speaking countries in Ghana.

In Asia and the Far East, where the relationship between population and national advancement was well understood, most countries had already embarked on vigorous population programmes. At the regional level, most of the projects being aided by the Fund were devoted to training, education and research. Among the top-priority activities were a research and action programme concerning population and employment; a project to improve the facilities of the Asian Trade Union College, which was the only trade union workers' education body in Asia; a clearing house and curriculum materials centre in population education; and a medical documentation and production centre with special reference to family planning.

The Asian Press Foundation was receiving assistance to train local journalists in population and development reporting, and to provide a reference system for newspapers. The Population Division of the Economic Commission for Asia and the Far East (ECAFE) in addition to conducting extensive demographic activities also exercised a coordinating function in regard to population activities in the region.

In the Middle East, establishment of a population unit within the United Nations Economic and Social Office in Beirut (UNESOB) marked the beginning of rapidly expanding population programmes. This was the direct result of expert reports and studies made by UNESOB which had revealed urgent needs for help in carrying out comprehensive censuses in many countries, in solving specific problems associated with nomadic societies, in coping with changes brought about by rising rates of urbanization and in determining the underlying causes of the universally high population growth rates in Islamic countries. Among the training and research projects being supported by the Fund were special courses in demography at the Kuwait Institute of Economic and Social Planning, and a Population Study and Research Unit at the National Institute of Social Sciences of the Lebanese University and at the Cairo Demographic Centre.

In Latin America, CELADE, the regional demographic centre located in Santiago, Chile, had provided demographic training, information and advisory services for the benefit of its member countries over a period of years. Fund assistance had been given

to expand the Centre's facilities and to finance such special projects as exchange programmes in teaching and research in the social sciences, as well as training courses in
the evaluation of family planning programmes. As a result of strong religious and cultural attitudes, however, family planning programmes, where they existed at all, had
usually been carried out by private organizations. Only a few countries, mainly in
Central America and the Caribbean, had received aid from the Fund to support government-sponsored programmes. The decision of the Government of Chile in 1972,
to engage in a nation-wide family health programme with assistance from the Fund,
followed by an announcement by the Government of Mexico of the launching of a
major programme, were clear indications of new thinking and policies which might
well affect other countries in the region.

Table 5.1.   Cost of projects approved by the Population Fund (by year, region and sector).

Totals:	
1970.	$6,700,000
1971.	*15,300,000
1972 (estimate)	44,660,000
1972–75 (Four Year Work Plan)	254,000,000
1971 Expenditures by Region	
Africa	$1,800,000
Asia and the Far East	5,800,000
Near and Middle East	2,000,000
Latin America	2,000,000
Inter-regional	3,700,000
	*$15,300,000

* Before year-end adjustments.

Source: United Nations Fund for Population Activities.

An important development in the Fund's programming was the movement away from
small projects handled regionally and inter-regionally to more comprehensive country projects.

MAJOR COUNTRY PROJECTS

In the **Arab Republic of Egypt**, a country covered by vast deserts, 35 million people
had only 2.6 per cent of the land area on which to grow food. With a growth rate of
2.8 per cent per annum, even optimistic projections set the population figure at 70
million in 1995 – unless fertility declined substantially. The Government recognized
the serious problem as far back as 1962 and established a national family planning
programme. The UNFPA stepped in with advisers on population programmes and
contraceptive supplies and, more recently, under an agreement operative since October 1971, the Fund was providing $1.25 million for the first year of a five-year pro-
gramme of support for public information, education, study of population trends,
research, fellowships and further supply of contraceptives through UNICEF.

India, which boasted the oldest government-sponsored family planning programme
in the world, was trying to improve the effectiveness of the programme, which still
reached only a fraction of the population. The aim was to reduce the growth rate

from 25 to 15 per thousand in the next decade. In 1969, India asked the United Nations to evaluate the programme, and the immediate result was a substantial increase in government expenditures and in bilateral support. The Fund, for its part, had agreed to contribute $1 million for an innovative vasectomy campaign; it also had supported a Demographic Training Centre in Bombay as well as educational projects.

Maldistribution of the population in **Indonesia** was a major problem – 60 per cent of the population was concentrated on three small islands, Bali, Java and Madura. The country had a population of 121 million and an annual growth rate of 2.6 per cent. Early in 1972, the Government, aware that a major effort was necessary to change the adverse trend, entered into a unique cooperative agreement with the Fund and the World Bank at a total cost of $33 million. The agreement provided for construction of schools, headquarters and other facilities for family planning services, and for training of personnel and assistance with communications research and evaluation programmes.

Rapidly decreasing water resources in **Iran**, coupled with disproportionate distribution of population, moved the Government to set new targets in an effort to reduce population growth. The Fund became involved at an early stage, providing consultants in demography and also a high-level evaluation mission whose recommendations had been adopted. Under a 17-month agreement signed in 1971, it was providing $1,630,000 in aid of the Iranian family planning programme.

Although the then current population of **Mauritius** was only 800,000, population trends could lead to a doubling of the population by the year 2000 and an intolerable crowding situation. Consequently, the Government in 1970 signed a three-year agreement with the Fund totalling $600,000. It was designed to enable the local Ministry of Health to take over maternal and health services, reorganize and expand them and build in family planning components. Until now, these services had been provided by private organizations. WHO was recruiting advisers to assist the Ministry, and UNICEF was arranging for supply of contraceptives.

Forty million people lived in the **Philippines**, which had one of the highest growth rates (3.4 percent annually) in the world. The spectre of a population of nearly 100 million by the year 2000, with its pressure upon natural resources and social services, had prompted the Government to step up its family planning services. Early in 1972 the Fund increased and consolidated its assistance, committing $3.3 million for a five-year agreement supporting population education, teaching and training programmes in family planning as well as purchase of medical equipment.

A doubled population by 1990 was the prospect for **Thailand**, which currently had 38 million inhabitants. In 1970, the Government launched a voluntary family planning programme which had since expanded to all 71 provinces. The Fund signed an agreement with Thailand, amounting to $3.2 million, to accelerate introduction of maternal and child health services, to support a family planning field workers project, and to develop communications activities and a voluntary sterilization programme. Fund support for Thailand was not new. In recent years, it had funded family planning components in ongoing WHO and UNICEF programmes, involving health clinics, training of midwives, supplies and consultant services.

Chile was the first Latin-American country to conclude an agreement with the Fund, amounting to over $3 million for a four-year period. Under the terms of the agreement, signed in June, 1972, the Fund would support the family health and population programme, for which Chile had allocated $345 million of its own resources. The Fund's aid included $1 million worth of contraceptive materials. The aim of the government programme was to reduce mortality, improve infant care and promote family welfare. An important feature in the Latin-American context was the decision to make birth control information available to all women regardless of marital status. So far, only 10 percent of Chile's women were covered by family planning programmes and the aim was to increase the coverage to 40 percent in the four-year period.

In 1969, when the Population Fund was in its early stages, the Secretary-General entrusted its overall supervision to the Administrator of the United Nations Development Programme (UNDP). Rafael M. Salas, former Cabinet Minister and Executive Secretary of the Philippines, was appointed Executive Director. Close relationship with the UNDP – the world's largest source of pre-investment and technical assistance to low-income countries – enabled the Fund to view the development picture as a whole in determining priorities for population activities and in directing aid to areas where it could do most good.

Resident Representatives, who headed UNDP offices in the developing countries, played a key role in helping the Population Fund to meet its objectives. These officials assisted governments in formulating requests for aid and in co-ordinating the work of all members of the UN family engaged in vital aspects of population programmes. Resident Representatives helped governments identify areas where population activities could best contribute to national development, informed the Fund of

Table 5.2.   UNFPA expenditures by sector, 1972.

	Estimated Costs
Basic population data (Censuses, vital statistics, sample surveys, other statistics)	$ 6,905,000
Population dynamics (Research projects, training & research facilities, population aspects of planning)	5,615,000
Population policy (Policy formulation, including conferences and seminars, and implementation, exclusive of family planning programmes)	1,255,000
Family planning (Delivery systems, programme management, fertility regulation techniques)	20,660,000
Communication and education (For motivation in family planning)	3,960,000
Multi-sector activities (Fellowships, documentation centres, support to non-UN organizations, preparation of World Population Year)	2,230,000
Field staff, infra-structure, overhead	4,035,000
Total	$44,660,000

Source: UNFPA.

the overall pattern of assistance so that resources supplemented, but did not compete with other efforts, and saw that field operations were performed promptly and effectively. Requests for population project assistance from national, non-governmental organizations were also handled by the Resident Representative, who considered the merits of the request and also the standing of the requesting organization. The Fund was seeking to strengthen the Resident Representatives' staff with highly qualified personnel to help monitor and advise on population activities in the field.

UNFPA RESOURCES

The Fund was financed by voluntary contributions from governments as well as private donors. Initially, the programme got under way with a small budget contributed by a few countries. But it grew rapidly. By 1970, 24 countries had contributed $15.4 million, and in 1971 alone pledges had reached $28 million, surpassing the target set for that year by $3 million.

Growth was marked in 1971 by voluntary donations from 21 new contributing nations, bringing the total number of donor countries to 45. The largest donor was the United States with $12.5 million on a matching basis, followed by Sweden with $3 million,

Table 5.3. Trends in development and population assistance, 1961–1977.

	Total official development assistance[1] (in millions of US$)	Population assistance[2]	Population assistance as percentage of total assistance (in per cent)
1977	14,759	345	2.3
1976	13,666	320	2.3
1975	13,588	286	2.1
1974	11,302	257	2.3
1973	9,400	182	2.0
1972	8,700	171	2.0
1971	7,700	155	2.0
1970	6,800	125	1.8
1969	6,600	86	1.3
1968	6,300	58	0.9
1967	6,600	30	0.5
1966	6,000	34	0.6
1965	5,900	18	0.3
1964	6,000	16	0.3
1963	5,800	11	0.2
1962	5,400	5	0.1
1961	5,200	6	0.1

[1] Excluding export credits, private investment, and other commercial transfers.
[2] Net totals excluding double-counting due to transfers between donors. Grants by voluntary organizations are not included for the years 1961–1969. In 1970 these grants amounted to $0.9 million.

Sources: Organization for Economic Co-operation and Development, governments and annual reports of development assistance agencies and organizations. From: *International Population Assistance: The First Decade*, (Salas, R.) Pergamon Press, Oxford, 1979.

Table 5.4. Population assistance by major donors, 1971–1977.[1]

Governments	1971	1972	1973	1974	1975	1976	1977
				(in thousands of US$)			
Australia	–	357	579	639	1,587	967	1,065
Belgium	147	18	75	837	476	934	900
Canada	2,496	2,997	4,159	5,498	7,183	8,989	9,116
Denmark	1,918	2,289	2,035	4,784	3,548	4,978	6,200
Finland	507	892	1,033	2,587	2,026	1,578	1,852
Germany Federal							
Republic of	1,657	2,435	4,392	5,770	13,400	8,739	8,611
Japan	2,090	2,196	2,812	5,293	7,971	12,920	15,400
Netherlands	1,106	2,232	3,718	5,785	6,695	8,954	9,649
New Zealand	–	77	40	580	880	607	573
Norway	3,870	5,539	8,600	10,800	18,500	27,400	36,363
Sweden	7,446	12,739	17,123	21,568	26,169	28,743	31,417
Switzerland	168	191	189	190	200	242	500
United Kingdom	2,311	3,257	3,861	3,032	6,450	6,983	7,168
United States	109,567	121,133	115,106	110,146	106,036	119,027	145,367
Others	1,283	1,592	1,747	2,325	3,580	11,356	12,000
Sub-total	$134,566	157,944	165,469	179,734	204,701	242,417	286,181
Inter-Governmental Organizations							
United Nations	6,995	5,952	8,459	20,786	24,234	28,009	27,952
UNICEF	2,382	2,371	3,711	5,753	6,725	6,611	6,700
UNFPA	8,937	19,840	34,684	57,000	71,213	75,781	78,000
ILO	165	989	2,259	3,827	4,901	6,483	6,775
FAO	607	574	1,370	1,539	2,238	–	–
UNESCO	38	28	2,554	4,130	5,337	4,042	5,034
WHO	2,823	6,374	15,991	18,932	22,979	29,324	34,679
World Bank[2]	1,600	5,700	11,200	18,600	24,900	27,000	28,200
Others	5,200	6,577	1,789	6,225	6,300	6,300	6,500
Sub-total	$28,747	$48,405	$82,017	$139,219	$168,827	$183,550	$195,200
Non-Governmental Organizations							
Ford Foundation	15,221	14,647	12,353	13,774	10,700	10,800	8,900
IPPF	19,294	24,935	33,798	42,910	42,584	45,554	51,198
Population Council	14,084	17,360	16,128	15,582	12,076	11,000	11,338
Rockefeller Foundation	2,864	6,608	6,370	9,007	8,516	8,500	6,178
Others	3,877	4,400	7,400	6,400	6,400	6,400	7,900
Sub-total	$55,340	$67,950	$76,049	$87,673	$80,276	$83,000	$85,514
Total	$218,653	$274,299	$323,535	$406,626	$453,804	$508,967	$566,895
Total excluding double counting[3]							
(a) in current US$	$161,519	$183,785	$208,651	$256,812	$285,663	$320,011	$345,268
(b) in constant US$	$154,860	$170,645	$182,387	$202,214	$206,106	$218,280	$221,179
(1970=100)							

Notes:
[1] Actual expenditures except that some of the 1977 figures are estimates based upon allocations. All figures refer to calendar year.
[2] Annual estimates for the World Bank based upon its commitments according to loan or credit agreements and the planned duration of project execution.
[3] Arrived at by deducting the following from the total.
   Governments' contributions to UNFPA;
   USAID contributions to IPPF, Pathfinder Fund and the Population Council;
   UNFPA contributions to organizations in the United Nations system;
   Contributions from one foundation to another.

Sources: See Table 5.3. In addition, United Nations document E/5673, 'Report of the Administrative Committee on Co-ordination on Expenditue of the United Nations system in relation to programmes,' and U.S. Consumer Price Index, United Nations, *Statistical Yearbook and Monthly Bulletin of Statistics.*
From: *International Population Assistance: The First Decade.* (Salas, R.) Pergamon Press, Oxford, 1979.

Canada and Japan with $2 million each, and the Federal Republic of Germany, Norway and United Kingdom with $1.5 million each.

By mid-1972, the list of donors included: Afghanistan, Barbados, Botswana, Canada, Cyprus, Denmark, Dominican Republic, Egypt, Finland, France, Federal Republic of Germany, Greece, Guatemala, Honduras, Hungary, Iceland, India, Indonesia, Iran, Iraq, Jamaica, Japan, Jordan, Lebanon, Lesotho, Liberia, Madagascar, Mauritius, Morocco, Nepal, Netherlands, New Zealand, Norway, Pakistan, Philippines, Singapore, Somalia, Sri Lanka, Swaziland, Sweden, Switzerland, Thailand, Togo, Trinidad and Tobago, Tunisia, United Kingdom, Republic of Vietnam, Yugoslavia and the United States. Seventy-four nations were receiving aid from UNFPA.

Although funds were increasing rapidly, the urgency of the world's population problems demanded still greater fund-raising efforts. The Fund's planners had already charted a four-year budget for 1972–75 totalling over $250 million. By 1974, the level of annual contribution was expected to surpass $100 million.

TOTAL INTERNATIONAL ASSISTANCE FOR POPULATION

Total international assistance for population activities amounted to only about $2 million in 1960 and $18 million in 1965, but it increased rapidly to $125 million in 1970 and to nearly $350 million by 1977. Between the years 1970 and 1974, the average annual rate of growth in international population assistance was around 20 per cent.

Table 5.3 from shows trends in development and population assistance between 1961 and 1967.

Table 5.4 shows population assistance by major donors. From the early 1950s to the late 1960s four non-governmental agencies – the International Planned Parenthood Federation, the Population Council, the Ford and Rockefeller Foundations were the main sources of assistance for population and related activities. The first government to give assistance for family planning to a developing country was Sweden in 1958. Halvor Gille, a former Deputy Executive Director of UNFPA, writes:

> This was in support of an experimental programme in Sri Lanka and was followed by similar assistance to the government of Pakistan in 1961. The United Kingdom initiated its bilateral population assistance programme on a modest scale in 1964. The U.S. government began to include population activities in its development assistance in 1965. In the early 1970s a number of governments followed the lead

provided by Sweden, the United Kingdom and the United States. These included Canada, Denmark, the Federal Republic of Germany, Japan, the Netherlands and Norway.[6]

By the time of the World Population Conference, 1974, UNFPA had emerged as the largest multilateral source of finance for population activities though, as can be seen from Figure 5.1, support provided in this field by the World Bank and the IPPF remained significant.

THE WORLD BANK

The World Bank's President, Robert S. McNamara, took up his post in April 1968 and lucidly explained why the World Bank was concerned with the population issue.

> We are not lending in the field of population because it is less expensive, or because it is less trouble, or because it constitutes in itself an all-purpose formula for economic progress. Lending for population projects is not development-on-the-cheap. Quite the contrary, lending for population is a premium well worth paying in order to help ensure that a country's entire development effort will have a more reasonable chance to succeed.
>
> It is important to understand why an institution such as the World Bank is concerned with the population problem. The reason is simple. *No other single problem is a greater threat to the prospects for economic and social progress in the developing world.* The World Bank is an international development agency, and for it to be indifferent to the inescapable consequences of rampant population growth in the poorer nations would amount to its being indifferent to the larger goal of development itself.[7] (emphasis added)

During the five-year period ending in fiscal year 1973, the World Bank lent $84 million for population projects in seven developing countries, including two of the largest, India and Indonesia. Based on the experience gained, it envisaged a substantially expanded lending programme for the years 1974–1978: $375 million for projects in twenty-three countries.[8]

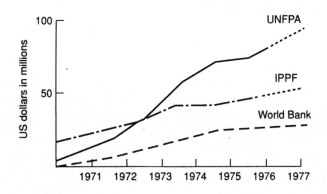

Fig. 5.1. Major multilateral donors, 1971–1977. *Source: International Population Assistance,* (Salas, R.) Pergamon Press, Oxford, 1979.

THE INTERNATIONAL PLANNED PARENTHOOD FEDERATION

In the effort to 'turn the population tide' and to improve knowledge of and access to family planning, the early work of the private sector was often crucial. Volunteers working with local non-governmental family planning associations were often able to create a climate of opinion and build a nucleus of staff and facilities which would later be of great benefit to the public sector programme. Indeed, in some cases the government would in a sense co-opt the private sector as the delivery mechanism for official programmes.

On the non-governmental side, the work of the International Planned Parenthood Federation (IPPF) was of outstanding importance. IPPF was founded in 1952 as an international non-governmental organization dedicated to the belief that knowledge of family planning was a basic human right and that a balance between the population of the world and its natural resources and productivity was a necessary condition of human happiness, prosperity and peace.

The IPPF encouraged the formation of national associations to pioneer family planning services in each country of the world and to bring about a favourable climate of public opinion in which governments could be persuaded to accept responsibility. Family planning associations (FPA's) offered contraceptive services, set and endeavoured to maintained high clinical standards, trained all levels of personnel, and carried out education programmes to inform and teach people about the personal, health, social and economic benefits of family planning.

Where governments had already responded to these initiatives by setting up family planning programmes, IPPF affiliated associations provided a nucleus of experienced staff around which an expanded government programme could be built. As the government gradually developed clinic services, usually based on existing health services, the Association concentrated on education of the general public and training for association and government staff, while often continuing to maintain clinics for both research and training.

With IPPF assistance, many associations were bringing education for responsible parenthood to young people, both in and out of school. They were also reaching industrial and plantation workers and other special groups.

As the IPPF's membership had grown, so too had the demand for resources to support its work. In 1961, the budget of the IPPF was US $30,000. By 1971, only ten years later, the gross budget (including the local income of grant-receiving agencies) had risen to US $20 million, primarily as a result of confidence in the IPPF as a non-governmental body especially qualified to initiate and support the development of family planning services.

The Federation was financed initially by voluntary contributions from foundations and private citizens all over the world and by grants from governments. In 1971, in addition to the assistance which governments gave directly to their national family planning association, grants were made to the IPPF by Britain, Canada, Denmark, Finland, Japan, Norway, Sweden and the United States, as well as by the United Nations Fund for Population Activities.

For administrative purposes, and in recognition of the wide diversity of problems that confronted its members, the IPPF was divided into seven regions. The regional offices in Beirut, Colombo, Kuala Lumpur, London, Nairobi, New York and Tokyo assisted family planning associations in their areas, arranged regional conferences, encouraged the establishment of new organizations, sponsored applications for IPPF membership, and submitted reports and accounts to the IPPF Governing Body, under the direction of their Regional Councils. Technical assistance and advisory services were provided to the associations by both the IPPF Central Office and the Regional Offices.

IPPF had stimulated the growth of indigenous organizations in 15 countries of sub-Saharan Africa to establish pilot clinics and to bring about an awareness of health and economic problems associated with social change and an average population growth rate of 2.5 per cent. Four governments – by the beginning of the 1970s – had begun national family planning programmes and had recognized the pioneering work of the voluntary associations by integrating association activities and government programmes. In the remaining 11 countries, there had been a rapid increase in the number of patients served, in some cases four times greater than in the previous year. Despite a desperate shortage of skilled personnel, volunteers had gradually been supported by salaried professionals while regional seminars and workshops had identified common goals, built confidence, and educated opinion leaders. Educational activities, especially films specifically researched and produced for African societies with differing cultures and traditions, had helped boost the number of family planning acceptors. A unique development in the region had been seven IPPF-supported mobile teams in Kenya which provided over one-third of the total clinic services covering a rural population of 3 million people.

Since governments in the Indian sub-continent were widely involved in clinical services, the family planning associations had increasingly explored new ways of overcoming communications barriers, including the use of mobile units, factory and plantation-based campaigns. Associations had experimented with films and other audio-visual aids, while in India, pioneer work was being carried out to introduce population education into the schools in order to reach the 41 per cent of the population under the age of 15. Because of high illiteracy rates, associations had turned to mass media, especially radio, to motivate the largest possible number of people. Research into past and current work was proving valuable in determining future activities and priorities.

From a new regional base in Beirut, the IPPF, through seminars and meetings, had drawn attention to high abortion and infant mortality rates and had gained growing government recognition of the contribution which family planning could make to the solution of these problems. One result of the IPPF seminars had been to stimulate research never before done on fertility trends and national demographic patterns. Family planning associations in seven countries were building educational and clinical activities as pioneers or in support of government programmes.

Pioneer efforts of IPPF-supported family planning associations in 13 countries had brought several governments, representing more than 200 million people, to the policy and implementation stages of national birth control campaigns. In 1970, most training and family planning services in Indonesia and the Philippines were still being provided by voluntary associations. The quality of their work, especially their ability to recruit and train large numbers of field-workers to carry out massive rural and urban education campaigns, would be vital factors in the success of governmental programmes. In the Pacific islands, Thailand and Laos, IPPF assistance had been directed toward stimulating greater governmental involvement, providing training opportunities for doctors, nurses and field staff, and supporting pilot services.

Recent years had witnessed the increased professionalization of family planning associations in Latin America and the Caribbean. Where most associations were formerly completely dependent on volunteer help from doctors, now the majority also had full-time professional staffs, resulting in more efficient administration, long-range planning and budgeting, and the improvement of information and education programmes.

Some countries of the Western Hemisphere enjoyed a degree of official support but generally governments had been slow to recognize their responsibilities. A number of associations had for the first time initiated local fund-raising campaigns to finance rapidly expanding programmes. Mass media campaigns to motivate women to use family planning were being used in several countries with good results.

The practice of family planning had risen each year and the population growth rate in the Western Pacific region continued to decline. This remarkable achievement had been the result of close co-operation between governments and IPPF-assisted associations. In Hong Kong, the birth rate has declined from 3.6 per cent in 1961 to 2.1 per cent in 1969, while Korea was within sight of its target to reduce population growth to 2 per cent from a 1960 high of 2.9 per cent. The 13 clinics of the Planned Parenthood Federation of Korea served 32,000 patients in 1969 and the total rose to more than 45,000 for 1970. Women were educated through mothers' clubs in 17,000 villages.

THE POPULATION COUNCIL

The Population Council was established in November 1952 'to stimulate, encourage, promote, conduct and support significant activities in the broad field of population'. The Council, a private foundation, sought to advance and apply knowledge by fostering research, training, and technical assistance in the social and biomedical sciences.

Its objectives were:

– to study the problems presented by the increasing population of the world and the relation of that population to material and cultural resources;
– to encourage and support research and to disseminate as appropriate the knowledge resulting from such research;
– to serve generally as a centre for the collection and exchange of facts and information on the significant ideas and developments relating to population questions;
– to co-operate with individuals and institutions in the development of programmes;
– to take initiatives in the broad fields which in the aggregate constitute the population problem.

In 1970, the Population Council's budget was around $16 million. In some countries, it had played an important role in the field, for example in Taiwan. It had sponsored important work in the area of contraceptive development, e.g. the IUD. Its reports, for example, *Studies in Family Planning* and *Population and Development Review* were required reading among practitioners.

THE ROCKEFELLER FOUNDATION

The Rockefeller Foundation started activities in the population field in 1963. Since then, the main part of the $22.2 million population funds (62 per cent) had been used for action programmes, such as supporting the Population Council's technical assistance division, establishing family planning units in medical schools both in the US and in developing countries, integrating family planning in community health services (e.g. in Colombia and India) and supporting Planned Parenthood of America in establishing a Centre for Family Planning Programme Development.

The Rockefeller Foundation was concentrating its population activities increasingly on the interaction of the social, medical and biological sciences. In 1970, 77 per cent of the population allocations was committed to research in reproductive biology and contraceptive development, and 22 per cent to training, research and development in population/family planning. Apart from support for universities in the USA, recent Rockefeller grants had been made to universities in Chile, Colombia, Mexico, Thailand, Turkey and the United Kingdom. The Foundation's commitments in 1970 amounted to $15 million.

The Rockefeller Foundation's Chairman was John D. Rockefeller 3rd. Also Chairman of the Population Council, Mr Rockefeller was keenly aware of the limits, as well as of the potential, of private groups working in the population field.

> Private groups can contribute much in the way of information, specialized knowledge and trained personnel, but population problems are so great, so important, so ramified and often so immediate, that only government, supported and inspired by private initiative, can attack them on the scale required . . . To my mind population growth is second only to the control of atomic weapons as the paramount problem of our day . . ?

THE FORD FOUNDATION

Ford Foundation expenditures in population began modestly in 1952 and had grown to a substantial magnitude ever since. By 1968 the Ford Foundation had devoted US $132 million to work directed to world population problems. However, population expenditures in 1968 only amounted to about six per cent of the Foundation's total commitments. Slightly more than half of the Foundation's population commitments had been directed to research and training in reproductive biology ($72 million), the balance for training and research in other aspects of population and family planning, and for dissemination of information on population problems.

About two-thirds of the Foundation's expenditures in population had gone to American institutions, although the activities supported by these grants were primarily directed toward population problems in developing countries. In population, as in the case of its other development assistance activities, the Foundation was both a grant-making and an operating agency. The Foundation had made substantial funds available to the Population Council ($30 million since 1954) through general support grants, as well as grants for specific technical assistance programmes in such countries as Pakistan and Ceylon. Its commitments in 1970 were $15 million.

OECD

In 1968 the OECD Development Centre was authorised to undertake certain activities in the field of population, in order to :

– draw attention to the importance of the population factor in development;
– promote the exchange of information in the field;
– help the Development Assistance Committee to co-ordinate aid programmes; and
– promote a dialogue between aid donors and recipients on aid problems.

Since its creation, the OECD Population Unit had pursued these objectives by organizing conferences, undertaking a limited amount of applied research, and by building up a network of contacts of international, governmental and nongovernmental organisations working in population.

IUSSP

The International Union for the Scientific Study of Population (IUSSP) was founded in 1928, Paris. Its aims were: to advance the progress of quantitative and qualitative demography as a science, through publications, by organizing congresses, by furthering relationships between demographers of all countries; stimulate interest in demography among countries and among national and international institutions originating in such countries, as well as in the scientific and intellectual world, and the general public.

The IUSSP was thus the principal international association for the demographers of the world. A sound scientific and intellectual understanding of the demographic situation constituted the vital underpinning for successful action programmes to reduce human fertility. IUSSP as a body, and its individual members world-wide acting in their own countries' official statistical bodies, universities or other institutions, helped to provide that basic understanding.

SUMMARY

In summary, by the middle of the seventies, the international community had in a very real sense tried to rise to the population challenge – at least in terms of the resources they were ready to devote to population activities, broadly defined and including the support of family planning programmes around the world.

NOTES

1. The major international donors contributed over $70 million to fertility control programmes in developing countries, excluding the People's Republic of China, in 1971 – roughly one-tenth of the total cost of fertility control. See p. 81 of *Population Policies and Economic Development: A World Bank Staff Report*, published by Johns Hopkins for the World Bank, Baltimore, 1974.
2. For a full account of the origins of United Nations involvement with the population issue, see Richard Symonds and Michael Carder, *The United Nations and the Population Question*, Chatto & Windus, London, 1973. Also, Stanley P. Johnson, *World Population and the United Nations: Challenge and Response*, Cambridge University Press, 1987.
3. See Symonds and Carder, op. cit., p. 146.
4. G.A. Resolution 2815 (XXVI) of 14 December 1971.
5. See, among others, the following resolutions:
    ILO, resolution IV (Resolutions Adopted by the International Labour Conference at its 5Ist Session, 1967);
    FAO, resolution No. 1/67 (Report of the Fourteenth Session of the Conference, p. 12);
    UNESCO, resolution 1.241 (Records of the General Conference, Fifteenth Session, 1968, Resolutions);

    WHO, resolution WHA21.43 (Official Records of the World Health Organization,
    No. 168, Twenty-first World Health Assembly, 1968, part 1, Resolutions and Decisions,
    Annexes).
6. Recent trends in International Population Assistance, by Halvor Gille. Included as Appen-
    dix D in *International Population Assistance: The First Decade*, by Rafael M. Salas, Pergamon
    Press, Oxford, 1979.
7. Cited in *The Population Problem*, ed. Stanley Johnson, published by David and Charles,
    Newton Abbot, 1973, p. 202.
8. See the Introduction by Robert S. McNamara, *Population Policies and Economic Development*,
    Johns Hopkins Press for the World Bank, Baltimore, 1974.
9. Stanley Johnson, *The Population Problem* 1974, p. 210.

6

The World Population Conference, Bucharest 1974

Though two World Population Conferences had been held before under the auspices of the United Nations and with the close collaboration of the IUSSP and interested specialized agencies – the first in Rome in 1954, the second in Belgrade in 1965 – these earlier meetings were not gatherings of official governmental representatives but rather technical and scientific assemblies where experts could examine population trends in different parts of the world and assess their implications. The Third World Population Conference held in 1974 was the first official governmental conference. The conclusions and the recommendations coming out of that meeting had to be seen in an altogether different light from the resolutions emerging from Rome and Belgrade which in the final analysis committed no-one except, perhaps, the individual participants themselves.

The basic building blocks of the Conclusions and Recommendations which were adopted by the meeting held in Bucharest in August 1974, and in particular of the World Population Plan of Action (WPPA) which was the most important text to emerge from that gathering, are to be found in the positions taken at Bucharest by the individual Member States of the United Nations.

In a nutshell, the key issue at Bucharest – and it divided delegations sharply one from the other – was whether population policy or development policy should have primacy where population problems were concerned. Not many other conferences organized by the United Nations can have seen the same level of passionate debate as different national groupings staked out their distinctive points of view on the population issue.

THE US POSITION

The US delegation was among the most forthright. The Honourable Caspar W Weinberger, Secretary of the US Department of Health, Education and Welfare, was leader of the US delegation. In his speech to the Plenary he began by stressing the basic issue of food security. The annual increase of some 80 million people, nearly all in countries which had to import part of their food supply, plus slight improvements in diets for some, would increase world food requirements about 2.5 per cent per year on average. Within many developing countries the annual increase in demand might be closer to 4 per cent. The United Nations Second Development Decade (of the 1970s) called for a 4 per cent annual increase in agricultural production. Unfortunately, in the first three years of the Decade, the increase had only averaged 1 per cent.

Agricultural specialists had indicated that if all went well with weather, soil, water, fuel, fertilizer, and that if incentives were provided to the farmers, the world could produce the food requirements for the UN medium projection for the populations of 1985 and 2000. Unfortunately, even if it worked, much of this food would not be where the people were. The countries with the greatest needs simply would not be able to produce food to meet their needs. In many of these countries, most of the good land with an adequate water supply was already in use. Fuel and fertiliser were scarce, expensive and usually required foreign exchange. In some large regions population growth weakened an already fragile environment in ways that threatened longer term food production. Thus overgrazing, deforestation, land exhaustion, soil erosion and water pollution of many kinds increased in areas that could least afford any of these problems. In addition, the impact of natural or other disasters was greater because more people were trying to exist under marginal and vulnerable conditions.

Most developing countries, he said, would be dependent on continually increasing imports. If their populations grew as projected, their import requirements for basic cereals alone would rise from the 24 million tonnes in 1970 to some 95–112 million tonnes in 2000. The cost of these import requirements would rise from about $2.5 billion in 1970 to $15–$18 billion (1974 prices) in 2000:

> We will be moving toward a debacle described by Dr Norman Borlaug, Nobel Peace Prize Laureate, who has solemnly warned: *'By the green revolution we have only delayed the world food crisis for another 30 years. If the world population continues to increase at the same rate we will destroy the species.'* We all know that many predictions do not come true, but surely there is cause, not only for grave concern – but more important, for specific action in family planning and increasing the world's food supply.

Mr Weinberger then turned his attention to the draft World Population Plan of Action (WPPA). The Plan, he said, quite rightly gave first attention to goals to reduce infant mortality, extend expectation of life and erase the difference in the expectation of life between more developed and less developed regions of the world. The United States firmly supported these goals.

The draft Plan of Action also asserted the basic human right, recognised by repeated United Nations resolutions, of couples to determine freely and responsibly the number and spacing of their children and to have information, education and the means to do so:

> The Plan urges each country to assure that such information, education and means of family planning are made available to all its people by the end of this Second Development Decade or, at the latest, by 1985. This recommendation is the foundation of the Plan. We support it, emphasising the urgency of providing these services by the end of the Second Development Decade as called for by Economic and Social Council (ECOSOC) resolution 1672 (L11) June 2nd 1972, and the Declaration on Population Development of the Second Asian Population Conference. We think it is important also that couples in having children recognise their responsibility to consider the welfare of the children and of their community.

Mr Weinberger said that the United States was glad to find in the Plan of Action recognition that nations, in addition to providing family planning services, should give attention in their development programmes to aspects of development that were desirable in themselves and might also motivate couples towards smaller families. These included the reduction of infant and child mortality; basic education; equality for women; improved status of women, including wider opportunities for employment; the promotion of social justice; improvement of life in rural areas; provision for old age security; education of the rising generation of children as to the desirability of small families; establishment of an appropriate lower limit for age of marriage.

Everyone was aware of the repeated, almost constant argument as to the relative merits of family planning services and of economic and social development for reducing fertility. The United States position was that both were important. Mr Weinberger thought that the draft Plan of Action presented both in a sensible balance. Mr Weinberger commended the Secretary General and all who had been involved in the drafting of the World Population Plan of Action. The United States supported it fully but believed it could be strengthened in a few important aspects.

The most important element in Mr Weinberger's remarks on the draft World Population Plan of Action was his stress on the notion of targets. He did not mince his words. 'My delegation', said the leader of the US delegation, 'will suggest in the working group on the World Population Plan of Action, national goals together with a *world goal of replacement level of fertility by the year 2000*' (emphasis added).

> We believe the Plan should be the commencement of a serious effort by both the developed and developing countries to consider means of arriving at chosen goals. The choice may make the difference between a decent life or early death for hundreds of millions of the next generation and even greater numbers in the following generation. For example, according to the UN medium projection, the world's population will reach about 6.4 billion by 2000 and over 11 billion by 2050. If, however, delegates agree at this conference and are able to persuade their countries to endeavour to attain the practicable goal of a replacement level of fertility – an average of two children per family – by 2000, the world's population in that year will be approximately 5.9 billion. Countries with high fertility will still double or treble their populations, but the world total in 2050 will be about 8.2 billion rather than in excess of 11 billion. The difference is, of course, a half billion people in the year 2000 and over 3 billion in 2050. The quality of life our children enjoy or suffer in 2000 and our grandchildren in 2050 will be deeply affected by the course we take at this conference and later in our countries.

Half a billion extra people by the year 2000. Three billion extra people by the year 2050. The stakes as Mr Weinberger saw them were almost inconceivably large. Attaining replacement level fertility by the year 2000 – as far as one can tell, the first time such a goal had been officially advocated in an intergovernmental forum – might seem to many to be an impossible dream but it was one which the leader of the US delegation offered for the serious consideration of delegates.

No other delegation at Bucharest was ready publicly to follow the United States in this seemingly cold mathematical approach to the population problem. In an anthropocentric world where human life itself was considered the pearl beyond price, there was something deeply heretical for most people in casual talk about 'lopping off' three billion human beings from the world's grand total in the middle of the twenty-first century.

Yet Mr Weinberger pointed convincingly to some of the immediate gains: with this lower population size by 2000, food import requirements of the less developed countries would be reduced by 100 million tonnes of cereals, thereby making self sufficiency in food a real possibility. They would be able to divert enormous funds from food imports to development needs.

Mr Weinberger concluded his remarks by making four undertakings on behalf of the United States:

> First, we will carry out the provisions of the World Population Plan of Action to the best of our ability. Especially we will continue our effort to assure the availability of family planning services to all our people.
>
> Second, we will undertake a collaborative effort with other interested donor countries and UN agencies – especially the World Health Organisation (WHO), the United Nations Fund for Population Activities (UNFPA), the International Bank for Reconstruction and Development (IBRD) and the United Nations Children's Fund (UNICEF) – to assist poorer countries to develop low-cost basic preventative and curative health services, including maternal and child health and family planning services, reaching out into remote rural areas. We have already begun to use our communications satellites for medical consultation and diagnosis. If desired, we could extend these new techniques to family planning organisation and administration.
>
> Third, we will join with other interested countries in a further collaborative effort of national research in human reproduction and fertility control covering bio-medical and socio-economic factors.
>
> Fourth, my government will be glad to join other countries in order to seek increased funds for assistance to bilateral and multilateral health and population programmes in developing countries that desire our help and our voluntary contributions to the UN fund for Population Activities. If other donor countries, especially the newly wealthy countries, indicate an interest in providing a steady increase in funds over the next ten years, my delegation will bring that message home from this conference and, given some evidence of world interest, it is quite possible that our Congress will respond favourably.

'Mr President', Mr Weinberger concluded, 'I believe we all realise the awesome responsibility that falls on us who represent our governments here. We have a unique opportunity to offer guidance by which nations can set their own course towards a brighter future for their people. With the co-operative spirit I feel here, we can achieve success for this conference which will benefit generations to come'.

Mr Weinberger's speech at Bucharest seems with hindsight one of the most positive and categorical statements on the need for action in the population field made by a high official of US Government over the last several decades. He was not, of course, speaking in a vacuum. The Bucharest conference received voluminous documentation dealing with population-development problems which had been worked up by experts before the meeting.[1] These emphasised that rapid population growth had accompanying characteristics (such as the young age distribution) which placed a heavy burden on the economies and resources of developing countries. Increasing concern over population trends and their impact appeared to be fully justified, in view of the clear prospect of having a world population of up to 7,000 million by 2000 – with 3 out of 4 persons living in countries classified as developing. In the developing countries as a whole, the margin of food production over population growth was declining, and in many of the countries food production had lagged behind population growth. The strain on resources created by rapid population growth might be such that traditional policies would no longer be sufficient: 'granted that the most favourable context for fertility decline is rapid and widespread development and modernisation, there is however, no reason to reject the common assumption that family planning and educational programmes as integral parts of development policies may speed up the fall in fertility'.

If Mr Weinberger was able to find the basic conference documentation encouragingly supportive of the official US line, so too were the remarks made by several speakers from the continent of Asia. Historically, Asia had always been in the lead for pushing for rapid action on population. Some of the scruples which had weighed on politicians' minds in other parts of the world seemed not to apply there. Or else the pressures were simply too great for impediments to action to be tolerated.

BANGLADESH

Perhaps the clearest and most unequivocal statement in favour of population control was made by Mr Adbul Mannan, the leader of the Bangladesh delegation. As far as Bangladesh was concerned there was no time for political theorising or for intellectual niceties. The problem was too urgent for that. The conference itself was a recognition of a self evident proposition that *'our finite planet cannot absorb an unlimited growth in the world's population'*.

'The growth of the world's population', he said, 'has taken place at an unprecedented rate in our generation and prospects for its continued increase, for another generation at least, must be viewed as a matter of global concern. All the more so because it is taking place at an alarming rate precisely in those regions which are least able to support them. Unless the world community takes prudent and timely decisions on population leading to the eventual stabilisation, we will have missed an opportunity of assuring material and spiritual well-being for our future generations. The unchecked growth of population might also pose a threat to the stability of the world order. It is of utmost importance, therefore, that we reach a consensus on the solution of the population problems in a constructive and objective manner, free from all ideological and political bias. So it is our hope that no state or ideological grouping should seek to impose its preferences on others at this Conference; but instead strive to find solutions to population problems in a spirit of human solidarity'.

'I come from that region of the world', said Mr Abdul Mannan, *'which is experiencing unprecedented population explosion. But nowhere is it more acute and critical than in Bangladesh – a country with 74 million poverty-stricken people compressed in an area of only 55 thousand square miles of land subject to natural calamities like cyclones and flood. As I am speaking here, millions of people are watching helplessly as the fruits of their labours are being washed away by floods described as the worst in twenty years. But even otherwise floods are now occurring with a frequency not experienced before. It is believed that the pressure of increasing population on available land has led to deforestation of river basins, causing more erosion, more silting and a creeping ecological imbalance characterised by a pattern of almost annual flooding'.* (emphasis added)

The estimated population of Bangladesh was only ten million in 1650 which grew to 40.7 million in 1941 and to 75 million in 1974, showing an accelerating rate of growth estimated now at 3 per cent. With the prospect of a gradual decline in mortality together with an unfavourable age structure of the population, Bangladesh might reach an average density of about 2,600 people per square mile, as compared with 1,350 today, by the end of the century.

The most serious effect of this high rate of population growth in Bangladesh was on its economic growth. With population growing at its present rate Bangladesh was required to save and invest at least 9 per cent of its GNP just to keep the per capita income at par, and to ensure a growth of per capita income of only 2 per cent per

annum the nation would require to save and invest at least 15 per cent of the GNP –
an apparently insurmountable task without some external assistance.

> Our demographic situation leaves us with no alternative but to try to contain and
> curb our population growth by all possible means and as quickly as possible. Under
> the leadership of Prime Minister Shaikh Mujibur Rahman, and with such favoura-
> ble factors as the willing participation of the people, the homogeneity of our popu-
> lation and compactness of area, we have been able to undertake a sizable action
> programme in the field of population. Our nationwide family planning programme
> is field-orientated and has been integrated with the health services to bring infor-
> mation, services and supplies to the doorsteps of the people.

INDONESIA

Another Asian country, Indonesia, took a similar stance by referring in clear and
unambiguous terms to the Government's efforts *'to check its rate of population growth in
order not to hamper the nation's development and nullify the gains made from our development efforts'*. Professor Soenawar Sakowati, Minister of State for People's Welfare,
told the Conference that:

> Indonesia has given high priority to population problems in its development
> efforts . . . the National Family Planning Co-ordinating Board was established
> with a view to co-ordinating and expediting family planning activities. The need is
> felt for an integrated population policy; the recently established National Commis-
> sion of Population is at this stage actively engaged in its formulation . . . We fully
> admit that the primary responsibility for solving population problems lies with
> national governments. At the same time we hold the view that concomitant inter-
> national measures are still required to complement our own efforts in this field.

INDIA AND PAKISTAN

India and Pakistan also spoke out at Bucharest in favour of strong and effective population and family planning policies, though both countries were careful to situate such
policies within the broader context of development.

Dr Karan Singh, India's Minister of Health and Family Planning, stated firmly that
development was 'the best contraceptive'. The path to family planning in every country
lay through the eradication of poverty, which in fact historically had been the main
cause of over-population. It would be difficult for many countries to accept family
limitation as a goal in itself unless it was clearly linked to a more equitable distribution
of the world's resources.

Shaikh Muhammad Rashil, Federal Minister for Health in the Government of
Pakistan and leader of the Pakistan Delegation to the World Population Conference,
spoke in a similar vein

> There is yet another fact of the population situation which deserves recognition by
> this assembly. To those of us who represent developing countries – and we represent
> the majority of the world population – the means to economic betterment were
> denied to us by colonial and neo-colonial forces, who, for such a long time, exploited
> our resources for their own ends. This situation in fact has been mainly responsible
> for preventing the onset of demographic transition in the developing countries
> which had occurred in the early nineteenth century amongst the developed coun-

tries. Had they not been forcibly occupied, they would have achieved the same, if not better, standard of living than the developed countries and would now have the same low population growth rates. That is, however, of the past, and we hold no rancour. We maintain that the developed countries still owe a heavy and long-standing debt to the developing countries which needs to be discharged expeditiously.

In the run-up to the Bucharest Conference, countries like the United States which had, since the middle of the 1960s, taken the lead in pressing for national and international action on population, hoped fervently that what had been referred to as 'the incrementalist' position would prevail. In other words, that the world population conference would lead to a strengthening of the commitment to population and family planning programmes without involving radically new and expensive undertakings in other fields. In practice, Bucharest very nearly failed to reach a consensus on the basic issue of whether current rates of population growth were or were not a 'bad thing'.

AFRICAN COUNTRIES

Most of the participating African countries, for example, appeared to be satisfied with their fertility and population growth rates. The African delegates spoke with the sense – back then in 1974 – that theirs was the continent of wide open spaces, that underpopulation was as much a problem as over-population, that the major need was for rapid economic and social development; and that to achieve this, productive investment generous transfusions of economic assistance were necessary 'to repair the ravages of colonials'.

Zambia portrayed the prevailing attitude: 'It is highly erroneous to jump to the conclusion that Zambia's economic failures were due to rapid population increase'.[2]

However, not all African Countries followed the Zambian line. In Kenya, family planning had long been espoused by the National Government. Nigeria had recently established a National Population Council whose duty as explained by Professor Abediyo Adeji, Federal Commissioner for Economic Development and Construction, was 'watching population trends in the country with a view to recommending policy measures to the Federal Government from time to time'.

LATIN AMERICA

Some of the Latin American delegations at Bucharest also lined up firmly in the pro-natalist camp, most notably Argentina. Indeed, Argentina was possibly the most avowedly pro-natalist country in the world at the time. The Argentine delegate, Juan-Carlos Beltramino, began by saying quite categorically that the Argentine Republic noted with concern that its population was not growing at a sufficient pace to meet the requirements for the exploitation of its wealth and the development of its economy.

The Argentine, with its vast territory of over four million square kilometres, the seventh largest country in the world, had a population of only 25 million, so that much of its land was virtually uninhabited. With a mean continental population density of eight inhabitants per square kilometre, an annual growth rate of 1.5 per cent and 70 per cent of its population concentrated in cities of more than 10,000 inhabitants, Argentina faced the challenge of large areas needing to be populated and wealth awaiting exploitation.

In this unusual situation, his country, said Senor Beltramino, had to increase its population as a fundamental prerequisite for its development and progress.

This prospect, set against the background of the Latin American continent, with a population density per square kilometre lower than anywhere else in the world, with its abundant reserves of natural resources to be exploited and with the unbalanced distribution of its population, had led Argentina to reconsider the terms in which the population/development equation should be stated and to question indiscriminate birth control as a valid instrument for the development of its peoples.

Many arguments were put forward in favour of the indiscriminate control of population growth. However, despite the troubled spectre of over-population and all that was heard of the impossibility of feeding a growing number of human beings, they found that there were countries which did not have enough inhabitants to develop their vast potential for food production.

They also found some countries where the throw-away society predominated while others were starving. Then again, some of the most serious estimates indicated that the earth could perfectly well feed the predicted population over the next few decades with the resources currently available, and these could still be substantially increased by suitable technology.

Finally, they found that even in the countries considered to be over-populated there were minorities who consumed more than they needed and majorities who consumed less than the essential minimum.

'Is population growth', he asked, 'then the real obstacle to ensuring an adequate food supply, or is it rather the failure to exploit resources rationally and the perpetuation of an unjust economic and social order between nations and between men?'

Senor Beltramino did not explicitly mention the Pope or the position of the Roman Catholic Church on birth control but there was no doubt that Argentina and other Latin American countries were profoundly influenced by traditional catholic attitudes and, more to the point, by the ubiquitous presence in Bucharest of the representatives of the Holy See.

THE VATICAN

The immediate question at Bucharest was the stand of the Roman Catholic Church on birth control. Would the Pope take advantage of the occasion Bucharest presented to soften his ban? Would the Encyclical *Humanae Vitae*, whose promulgation in the summer of 1968 had created a worldwide sensation (since at a time when everyone expected Pope Paul VI to follow the majority opinion of his advisers and drop his opposition to 'artificial' methods of contraception, he had instead re-emphasized and reiterated the Church's traditional teaching), be now at last sensibly modified?

In a less immediate sense, the interesting question was where would the Vatican place itself in relation to the debate on the new international economic order? Would it side with the poor against the rich? Or with the rich against the poor?

In the event, in the eyes of the Vatican's delegates to Bucharest, all these questions were linked. As they saw it, to emphasize above all the need for a family to limit the number of its children, was to ignore other important aspects of family life. The Church's position on birth control had to be seen in a moral as well as technical light, (taking 'technical' in the sense of interference with conception or foetal life). In the same way looking at the unit of the nation, the Vatican saw a danger in the too great emphasis on demographic trends and on the advantage to a nation to restricting its birth rate. They wanted to stress their wider vision of a global sharing which gave justice where justice was due.

Monsignor Henri de Reidmatten, the leader of the Holy See's delegation to Bucharest, began by recognising the importance of the problem.

'It is rarely', he said, 'that international gatherings have concentrated on a subject more grave than that of population, such as is posed today. The problem of population touches the primary and fundamental relationship between man and his fellow men, a relationship of vital importance, for it is from man that a man receives his existence and his insertion into the human community. The recommendations which this conference will make will be capable of affecting man in his intimate being and in the exercise of his most sacred rights. Their impact will affect the future of generations and of societies in their life, their culture, their structure and their equilibrium.

We are well aware of the negative effects which are most probably connected with demographic growth; the constant increase in the gap which separates the 'per capita' income of those living in the developed countries and that of countries still in the course of development; the slow progress of productivity in relation to demand, above all in agriculture, the increased cost in certain sectors, notably that of education.

On the other hand we must make known our disappointment at the perspectives put forth in the same report. The imbalance which affects or threatens developing countries seems to be defined as being dependent solely on national potential, as though one were not considering international social justice and solidarity between peoples. We would be the last to deny that often things happen as though these were utopian ideas. However, international cooperation and technical assistance are no longer mere hypotheses, nor have they been for many years. If, to refer to the terms of the Project of a World Plan of Action, we are not to be afraid of envisaging 'vast social, institutional and structural reforms, which can have repercussions on the whole of society', then should we not include in our balance sheet the whole of the international potential, faced as we are with this 'challenge' posed by 'the increasing number of men . . . for the community of peoples and for their governments'? – these are the words which Pope Paul VI addressed to the Secretary-General of our Conference. To proceed in this way is to respect the chronological and ethical priority of our solutions.'

Monsignor Henri de Riedmatten took the opportunity to comment on the draft World Population Plan of Action which had been put before the Conference.

As he saw it, the main concern of the Plan was in relation to the reduction, as rapidly as possible, of the birth rate, while repeatedly affirming the many limitations which were imposed by the sovereignty of States. On many occasions, most recently in the address of the Holy Father to Mr Carrillo Flores[3] and Mr Salas, and the intervention of the Vatican delegation at the Geneva consultation, the Holy See had declared that it shared in the preoccupations which arose from the actual problems of population.

> But it does not think, for all this, that the actions to be taken should be guided by a too exclusive attention to the whole problem of demographic variables. The project of the plan seems to us, in this respect, to be one-sided. We will explain this in more detail in the relevant working group. But we must mention here and now the considerable reservations which would be called forth on our part by the putting into effect of direct and indirect measures to obtain an urgent decrease in the birth rate. The delegation of the Holy See has already said at Geneva:
>
> We fear that to concentrate exclusively on demographic growth, to make it a privileged subject in campaigns on development, to channel huge resources into the solution of this one problem, is to upset the perspectives and only to prepare for mankind new frustrations.

The representative of the Holy See went on to make a specific criticism of the Plan for misinterpreting the passage of the Teheran Conference on Human Rights (1968) which stated that couples 'have a basic right to decide freely and responsibly on the number and spacing of their children and a right to adequate education and information in this respect.'

'This principle', he said, 'is repeated all through the project but is only interpreted as a right to the limitation of birth. The intention of those who were the first to insert this in the international texts was, above all else, to protect the freedom of the married couples against the intrusion of an indiscreet policy for the reduction of fertility.'

Finally, Monsignor Henri de Riedmatten turned to the techniques of contraception themselves. 'We will not pass over the fact that the message of the Plan relative to contraception and the methods of preventing birth are not acceptable to us. They are not acceptable in what concerns contraceptives, in regard to which the Catholic Church has already made her position clear, and is aware of the need to reaffirm and maintain her teaching without ambiguity. Nor are these passages acceptable because we have no guarantee that those who have recourse to abortion and to its legalisation will not appeal to them. The uncertainties expressed during the ' Symposium on Human Rights' do nothing to still our apprehensions.'

Such, he concluded, were the principal positions which the Holy See's Delegation had the task of presenting to the Conference. The Holy See would make an effort in the Commissions to make certain points more explicit and more precise. 'We shall above all apply ourselves to bringing our spirit of complete cooperation to our colleagues in the Conference. We remain convinced that a largely constructive work can be accomplished here and that it will be much better if we do not compromise on the firmness of our principles and do not stint ourselves in the generosity of our commitments. May the Lord, from whom all fatherhood takes its name, help us in all this.'*

MARXIST THEORY

The perspective of the Vatican on the population issue, though not on matters of birth control and abortion, was to some extent similar to that of the socialist countries, particularly the Eastern European countries and the Soviet Union, which took the line that population problems had to do not so much with numbers of people and rates of population growth but with the unfairness of current economic systems and unequal ownership of the means of production.

Marxist dogma held that society properly ordered could confront all challenges. Internationally, the introduction of the new international economic order would ensure that disparities between nations were ironed out, thus ensuring a brighter future for all mankind.

---

*Several weeks after the World Population Conference, the Pope himself addressed the delegates to the World Food Conference meeting in Rome. Here, using less diplomatic language than his representatives had used in Bucharest, he restated his position. He rejected the 'alibi' that birth control ought to be used to keep down the numbers of hungry mouths to feed.

'It is inadmissible that those who have control of the wealth and resources of mankind should try to resolve the problem of hunger by forbidding the poor to be born, or by leaving to die of hunger children whose parents do not fit into the framework of theoretical plans on pure hypothesis about the future of mankind.'

Ironically, the host country, Romania, was one of the most explicit proponents of the classic socialist voice. (Normally at these international gatherings the host country, regardless of its own feelings, feels compelled to exercise wherever possible a bridge-building role between different factions). The Romanian delegation, in the person of Mr Theodore Burghele, the Minister of Health, stated its firm conviction that the continuous growth of population in Romania was necessary to fulfil the targets of the socio-economic plan. As far as the world situation was concerned, Mr Burghele expressed the view that:

> Our Conference should not mark the last stage of our preoccupations concerning demographic policies; thanks to the decisions and the documents which it will adopt, the Conference in Bucharest is to be the prelude of new actions phased out for the future and designed to implement programmes of economic-social development for the benefit of all countries, programmes that should set up a new world economic order for raising living standards of all peoples.

CHINA

Amidst the extraordinary turmoil of conflicting official positions, China – newly emerged as a key player on the stage of the UN – was to be found crying in stentorian tones: ' A plague on both your houses!' The head of the delegation of the Peoples Republic of China, Mr Huang Shu-Tse, the Vice Minister for Health, launched a blistering attack on the two superpowers (the United States of America and the Soviet Union) in general and on their views on population in particular.

> One superpower asserts outright that there is a 'population explosion' in Asia, Africa and Latin America and that a 'catastrophe to mankind' is imminent. The other superpower, pretending at some Conferences to be against Malthusianism, makes the propaganda blast that 'rapid population growth is a millstone around the neck of the developing countries'. Singing a duet, the two superpowers energetically try to describe the Third World's population growth as a great evil. If this fallacy is not refuted, there will be no correct point of departure in any discussion on the world population.

The Chinese delegate then proceeded to refute the fallacy in inimitable language:

> Of all things in the world, people are the most precious. Once the people take their destiny into their own hands, they will be able to perform miracles. Man as worker, as creator and user of tools, is the decisive factor in the social production forces. . . . After prolonged and heroic struggles waged by the people in Asia, Africa and Latin America, a large number of countries in these regions have successively won political independence and achieved marked progress in developing their national economy and culture as compared with the past. Along with this development, the population has grown rather quickly. This is not at all a bad thing but a good thing.
>   In the situation of 'great disorder under heaven', in which the broad masses of the population are increasingly awakening, the large population of the Third World constitutes an important condition for strengthening the struggle against imperialism and hegemonism and accelerating social and economic development. . . . Today, the world population has more than trebled since Malthus' time, but there has been much greater increase in the material wealth of society, thanks to the efforts of the broad masses of the people in surmounting numerous obstacles. In the twenty-odd years since the founding of the People's Republic, China has increased her products manyfold. The creative power of the people is boundless, and, so is man's ability to exploit and utilise natural resources.

The Chinese delegate concluded his rapid review of current attitudes to the world population problem in a typically caustic way:

> The pessimistic views spoken by the superpowers are utterly groundless and are being propagated with ulterior motives.

The Chinese delegate then went on to deal with the true cause of the population problem, as he saw it:

> The claim that 'overpopulation is the reason the have-not countries are poor' is a worn-out tune of the superpowers. What a mass of figures they have calculated in order to prove that the population is too large, the food supply too small and natural resources insufficient! But they never calculate the amount of natural resources they have plundered, the social wealth they have grabbed and the super profits they have extorted from Asia, Africa and Latin America. Should an account be made of their exploitation, the truth with regard to the population problem will at once be out.

As for the solution, he had only to turn to the Chinese experience:

> The deplorable conditions of unemployment and poverty in Old China are universally known. Under the leadership of Chairman Mao Tse-tung and the Chinese Communist Party, the Chinese people, through a long struggle, overthrew imperialism, feudalism and bureaucrat-capitalism which weighed on them like three big mountains, and has since carried out socialist revolution and socialist construction and in a relatively short time succeeded in abolishing unemployment left over from Old China. In the twenty-odd years since the founding of the People's Republic, China's population has increased nearly 60 per cent, from about five hundred million to nearly eight hundred million. Yet in the same period, annual grain output has more than doubled, rising from 110 million to over 250 million tonnes. . . . At present the living standard of our people is still rather low, yet everyone is assured of employment, food and clothing and the livelihood of the people is steadily improving. The broad masses of the Chinese people have never displayed such a high degree of initiative and creativeness. In building socialism, China's vast manpower resources are being used in a planned and rational way. *Facts of China's history have completely exploded the various fallacies spread by the superpowers with regard to the population problem and fully borne out the truth that ' revolution plus production' can solve the problem of feeding the population as set forth by Chairman Mao Tse-tung.* (emphasis added)

All that said, Mr Huang Shu-Tse had some crumbs of comfort to offer when he went on to devote the remainder of his speech to what he described as the 'formulation and implementation of a population policy':

> Our emphasis on combating imperialism and hegemonism and developing the national economy and culture as the primary way of solving the population problem does not imply that in our view population policies are of no consequence. . . . *After overthrowing the rule of the imperialists and their lackeys, we in China secured the prerequisites for the planned development of the national economy as well as the planned regulation of the rate of population growth. On the basis of energetically developing production and raising the living standard of the people, China has developed medical and health services throughout the cities and countryside, strengthened the work of maternity and child care, and, while reducing mortality on the one hand, practised birth planning on the other to regulate the birth rate. Our birth planning is not merely birth control as some people understand it to be, but comprises different measures for different circumstances. In densely populated areas, late marriage and birth control are encouraged on the basis of voluntariness, while active treatment is given in cases of sterility.* (emphasis added)

The Chinese delegate pointed out that in national minority areas and other sparsely populated areas, appropriate measures were taken to facilitate population growth, while birth control advice and help were given to those parents who had too many children and desired birth control.

> Such a policy of planned population growth is in the interest of the thorough emancipation of women and the proper bringing up of future generations as well as of national construction and prosperity.

He admitted that these were but initial achievements.

> We have not yet acquired adequate experience in the work of birth planning, and we must continue our efforts.

Of special interest, particularly to those who favoured an active role for the United Nations in population matters, were the Chinese views on the role of international assistance:

> Any international technical cooperation and assistance in population matters must follow the principles of complete voluntariness of the parties concerned, strict respect for state sovereignty, absence of any strings attached and promotion of the self-reliance of the recipient countries. We are firmly opposed to the superpowers intervening by any means in the population policy of other countries on the pretext of what they call 'population explosion' or 'overpopulation'. We are firmly opposed to the attempt of some international organisations to infringe on the sovereignty of recipient countries by conditioning aid on restricting their population growth rate.

THE MIDDLE WAY

If a compromise eventually emerged at Bucharest, it was because a large number of countries from the developing world saw the need for a middle way. It was not a question of presenting population policy and family planning as an alternative to development. Nor was it enough to state that all problems would be solved by economic and social development (and the implementation of the New International Economic Order) and that there was therefore no need for population policy and family planning. What was needed, they argued, was a combination of both approaches though each individual country had, of course, its own ideas as to the precise balance which would be appropriate.

Thus Dr Karen Singh, India's Minister of Health and Family Planning, made it clear that, even though India had been trying to reduce fertility for over two decades, fertility levels could be effectively lowered only if family planning became an integral part of a broader strategy to deal with the problems of poverty and under-development. He recognized that, 'even with the use of the most advanced technology, we cannot go on raising the population in a finite world indefinitely'. However, the real question was more complex:

> How should policy designed to regulate population growth be effectively woven into plans for economic development and social transformation? . . . We would, therefore, urge that the main question before this Conference should be how to integrate at the international level those instruments of cooperation and common action which aim at promoting development on a global scale, so that those countries which wish to reduce their fertility levels are enabled to do so effectively. (emphasis added)

The Bucharest 'compromise' was nonetheless a fairly fragile plant. There was no clear language about overall or global targets for population growth. Even the language which related to national target setting was fuzzy. Where the draft Plan indicated that 'countries which consider that their present or expected rates of population growth hamper their goals of promoting human welfare are invited, if they have not done so, to consider setting quantitative population growth targets', the Plan as it emerged from the Working Group merely invited countries to 'consider adopting population policies, within the framework of socio-economic development'.

Similarly, there was a proposal in the Draft Plan to 'make available, to all persons who so desire, if possible by the end of the Second United Nations Development Decade, but not later than 1985, the necessary information and education about family planning and the means to practise family planning effectively and in accordance with their cultural values'. The alternative text which the Working Group adopted merely talked of the need to 'encourage appropriate education concerning responsible parenthood and make available to persons who so desire advice on the means of achieving it'. Like so many other amendments whose effect was to pull some of the teeth from the draft Plan, the new sub-paragraph was proposed by Argentina.

Yugoslavia, Mexico and the United States made public protests at the decision. Mr Philander P. Claxton, the American delegate, maintained that it was a step back from the position already taken by the UN through resolutions of the Economic and Social Council. 'It will hurt women and children most', he said. Miss Julia Henderson, Secretary-General of the International Planned Parenthood Federation, also expressed dismay that the decision removed all sense of urgency from the provision of family planning services. 'It virtually amounts to no plan, no action', she said.

The second section of the chapter of the Plan entitled 'Recommendations for Implementation' dealt with the role of international cooperation. To those who had followed the steady evolution of international assistance in the field of population, and in particular United Nations' action in this area, the outcome of the debate on this section was of course of special interest. In the event, it survived unscathed. Though, inevitably, certain amendments were adopted aiming at increasing total flows of development assistance as opposed to specifically population assistance, the final language was consistent with and complementary to the corpus of texts which had over the years established the locus of international assistance in the population field and, more particularly, the role of the United Nations.

> 100. International co-operation, based on the peaceful co-existence of States having different social systems, should play a supportive role in achieving the roles of the Plan of Action. This supportive role could take the form of direct assistance, technical or financial, in response to national and regional requests and be additional to economic development assistance or the form of other activities, such as monitoring progress, undertaking comparative research in the area of population, resources and consumption, and furthering the exchange among countries of information and policy experiences in the field of population and consumption. Assistance should be provided on the basis of respect for Sovereignty of the recipient country and its national policy.

> 101. The General Assembly of the United Nations, the Economic and Social Council, the Governing Council of the United Nations Development Programme/ United Nations Fund for Population Activities and other competent legislative and policy-making bodies of the Specialised Agencies and the various inter-governmental organisations are urged to give careful consideration to this Plan of Action and to ensure an appropriate response to it.

102. Countries sharing similar population conditions and problems are invited to consider jointly this Plan of Action, exchange experiences in relevant fields and elaborate those aspects of the Plan that are of particular relevance to them. The United Nations regional economic commissions and other regional bodies of the United Nations system should play an important role towards this end.

103. There is a special need for training in the field of population. The United Nations system, governments and, as appropriate, non-governmental organisations are urged to give recognition to that need and priority to the measures necessary to meet it, including information, education and services for family planning.

104. Developed countries, and other countries able to assist, are urged to increase their assistance to developing countries in accordance with the goals of the Second United Nations Development Decade and, together with international organisations, make that assistance available in accordance with the national priorities of receiving countries. In this respect, it is recognised, in view of the magnitude of the problems and the consequent national requirements for funds, that considerable expansion of international assistance in the population field is required for the proper implementation of this plan of action.

One small, but significant, amendment occurred on the next paragraph where the coordinating role of the United Nations Fund for Population Activities was stressed. Paragraph 105 read as follows:

105. It is suggested that the expanding, but still insufficient, international assistance in population and developing matters requires increased cooperation; the United Nations Fund for Population Activities is urged, in cooperation with all organisations responsible for national population assistance, to produce a guide for international assistance in population matters which would be made available to recipient countries and institutions and be revised periodically.

In his own speech to the conference, Mr Rafael Salas, who had been appointed in 1969 as the first Executive Director of the UN Fund for Population Activities (UNFPA), referred to the World Population Plan of Action (WPPA) as a milestone of the greatest importance:

It could guide and reinforce the activities of the Fund and at the same time the Fund could play an important role in the realisation of the Plan. The Plan will, of course, only take on its full meaning when it is translated into actual programmes at the international and national levels – programmes appropriate to the needs. . . . The UNFPA, with the cooperation of the United Nations system and other intergovernmental and non-governmental bodies, is ready to offer every possible assistance to enable countries to solve these problems themselves in the long run. We need hardly add that the UNFPA can only discharge this historic task if those members of the international community who have supported us so generously in the past continue to support us even more generously in the future.

The last paragraph of Mr Salas' address to the World Population Conference in Bucharest was a model of eloquence:

I do not believe that it is possible to underestimate the challenge and the significance of this moment. To solve the population problems of countries will require more from us in a shorter time than ever before in the history of mankind. It will require a long-sustained effort without any guarantee that the final aim will be achieved. Yet without the effort, can there be any prospect for a just and peaceful world in the future? The ancient philosophers of Asia in their wisdom stressed the need for a balance and harmony between man and his world. Without a sane and orderly approach to the problems of population, there can be no balance and no harmony.

NOTES

1. E/Conf.60/4.
2. (Cf review of population policies: African Countries, Paulina Makinaai-Adeusoye ESD/d 1194/eg.II/IV).
3. Dr Antonio Carillo Flores, a former Foreign Minister of Mexico, served as Secretary-General of the World Population Conference.

7

Falling Birth Rates – 1974 to 1984

The years which intervened between the first World Population Conference held in Bucharest in 1974 and the International Conference on Population held in Mexico City in August, 1984 were crucial as far as the battle to bring down birth rates was concerned. Whereas at Bucharest a significant number of countries were actively hostile to population policies and programmes, and others were at best indifferent or agnostic, by the time of the Mexico City Conference, ten years later, there had been a clear and discernible shift in the favour of official support of population and family planning programmes.

There were of course important differences in the approach to population policy in different regions of the world during the decade. Population policy was a house in which there were many mansions. In Asia, demographic reasons remained foremost. This was a continent which, more than any other, felt the sheer weight and pressure of human numbers. In Africa and Latin America it was on the whole health or human rights considerations which led countries to support, or tolerate, family planning activities. However, adding the several rationales together, it seemed clear at the beginning of the 1980s that much of the population of the developing world lived in countries which were on the whole not only supportive of population policy in the broad sense, but also of specific programmes, including family planning.

For example, it can be seen from Table 7.1 below that although 25 per cent of the population of French- and Portuguese-speaking sub-Saharan Africa lived in countries not supporting family planning, taking the developing world total as a whole, the proportion of the population living in countries not supporting family planning was only 3.9 per cent. Altogether 52 countries, with a total population of 2.5 billion or 78.6 per cent of the developing world total, supported family planning for demographic reasons; 65 countries, with a population of 569 million or 17.5 per cent of the developing world total, supported family planning for health and human rights reasons while 35, with a population of 128 million, accounting for 3.9 per cent of the developing world's total did not support family planning activities at all.

There also seemed at the beginning of the 1980s to be substantial evidence that progress was being made in achieving actual declines in fertility and in population growth rates.

Table 7.1. Number and population of developing countries by governmental policy position and date[a] of initial governmental support of family planning, by region (1980).

Region	Support: demographic rationale[b]	Support: health and human rights rationale[c]	Nonsupport[d]
South Asia	5	2	0
Population (millions)	882.1	1.4	0
% Regional population	99.8%	0.2%	0

Demographic support: Bangladesh, 1960, India 1951, Nepal 1965, Pakistan 1960, Sri Lanka 1953

Health and human rights support: Bhutan 1979, Maldives 1978

East Asia	4	0	3
Population (millions)	1035.8		19.9
% Regional population	98.1%		1.9%

Demographic support: China 1956, Hong Kong 1955, South Korea 1961, Taiwan 1959

Nonsupport: North Korea, Macao, Mongolia

Southeast Asia and Oceania	14	4	7
Population (millions)	311.1	3.3	44.4
% Regional population	86.7%	0.9%	12.4%

Demographic support: Indonesia 1967, Malaysia 1964, Philippines 1969, Singapore 1959, Thailand 1967, Vietnam 1962 (South Vietnam 1968), Cook Islands 1974, Fiji 1962, Kiribati 1970, New Hebrides 1972, Samoa 1970, Solomon Islands 1970, Tonga 1958, Tuvalu 1970

Health and human rights support: Papua New Guinea 1968, American Samoa 1973, Guam 1967, St Helena 1975

Nonsupport: Brunei, Burma, Kampuchea (support 1971–7), Laos (support 1971–6), Nauru, Tahiti, Tokelau Island

Latin America and the Caribbean	15	22	6
Population (millions)	120.4	203.9	6.1
% Regional population	36.4%	61.7%	1.8%

Demographic support: Colombia 1967, Dominican Republic 1968, El Salvador 1968, Guatemala 1969, Mexico 1972, Puerto Rico 1967, Barbados 1955, Grenada 1974, Guadeloupe 1968, Jamaica 1966, Martinique c. 1976, St Kitts-Nevis 1971, St Lucia 1975, St Vincent 1972, Trinidad & Tobago 1967.

Health and human rights support: Brazil 1974, Chile 1962, Costa Rica 1967, Cuba early 1960s, Ecuador 1968, Haiti 1971, Honduras 1966, Nicaragua 1967, Panama 1969, Paraguay 1972, Peru 1976, Venezuela 1965, Anguilla 1979, Antigua 1973, Bermuda 1937, Cayman Islands 1977, Dominica 1970, Guyana 1977, Montserrat 1976, Netherlands Antilles 1965, Br. Virgin Islands 1979, US Virgin Islands 1970

Nonsupport: Bolivia (support 1968–76), Bahamas, Belize, French Guiana, Suriname, Turks and Caicos

Middle East	5	11	10
Population (millions)	153.6	93.3	19.5
% Regional population	57.7%	35.0%	7.3%

Demographic support: Iran 1967, Turkey 1965, Egypt 1965, Morocco 1965, Tunisia 1964

Health and human rights support: Afghanistan, 1970, Bahrain 1974, Iraq 1971, Jordan 1976, Lebanon 1970, Syria 1974, North Yemen 1975, South Yemen 1973, Algeria 1971, Somalia 1977, Sudan 1970

Nonsupport: Kuwait, Oman, Palestine (Gaza), Qatar, Saudi Arabia, United Arab Emirates, Djibouti, Libya, Mauritania, Albania

Table 7.1. *Contd*

Region	Support: demographic rationale[b]	Support: health and human rights rationale[c]	Nonsupport[d]
English-speaking			
Sub-Saharan Africa	810	1	
Population (millions)	45.0	176.9	6.1
% Regional population	19.7%	77.6%	2.7%

Demographic support: Botswana 1970, Ghana 1968, Kenya 1966, Lesotho 1974, Mauritius 1964, Seychelles 1975, Swaziland 1971, Uganda 1971

Health and human rights support: Ethiopia 1972, Gambia 1968, Liberia 1973, Namibia 1972, Nigeria 1970, Sierra Leone 1976, South Africa 1966, Tasmania 1970, Zambia 1974, Zimbabwe 1968

Nonsupport: Malawi

French and Portuguese-speaking			
Sub-Saharan Africa	1	16	8
Population (millions)	5.7	90.1	32.2
% Regional population	4.5%	70.4%	25.2%

Demographic support: Senegal 1976

Health and human rights support: Benin 1969, Burundi 1979, Cameroon 1975, Cape Verde 1978, Central African Republic 1978, Comoros 1979, Congo 1976, Guinea-Bissau 1976, Madagascar 1976, Mali 1971, Mozambique 1977, Niger 1977, Réunion 1966, Rwanda 1977, Togo 1974, Zaire 1972

Nonsupport: Angola, Chad, Equatorial Guinea (Spanish-speaking), Gabon, Guinea, Ivory Coast, Sáo Tomé & Principe, Upper Volta

Developing world total			
Countries	52	65	35
Population (millions)	2553.7	569.0	128.2
% Regional population	78.6%	17.5%	3.9%

[a] Earliest date with reasonable evidence of *governmental* commitment to family planning (e.g. by formal programmatic effort, by initial *governmental* budgetary or facilities support of family-planning association, or by *governmental* agreement with or submission of request to UNFPA for family planning support.)

[b] Countries supporting family planning to reduce threat of rapid population growth to development or for related demographic reasons usually also support it for health and human rights.

[c] Some countries supporting family planning for health and human rights reasons recognize that a programme may have demographic consequences and thus affect development.

[d] Position of some countries unclear; several seem to be moving toward support.

Source: International Encyclopedia of Population, 1982. From: World Population and the United Nations – Challenge and Response. (Johnson, S.P. 1987) Cambridge University Press.

In its *Concise Report on the World Population Situation in 1983*, the United Nations summarises this trend in the following terms:

> During the periods between 1950–1955 and 1975–1980, the developed countries were nearing the end of a long transition towards lower fertility which began more than a century ago, while many less developed countries had just begun to experience a marked downward trend. The result was that there has been a *spectacular*

Table 7.2.   Relationship Between Views of Governments on Desirability of Higher or Lower Rates of Natural Increase, 1980, and Actual Rate of Natural Increase 1975–1980: World and More Developed and Less Developed Regions (Number of governments).

Views of governments	Total	Rate of natural increase 1975–1980 (percentage)			
		Under 1.0	1.0–1.9	2.0–2.9	3.0 or higher
World					
Total number of countries	165	35	31	66	33
Higher rate desirable	35	12	7	10	6
Lower rate desirable	55	–	16	23	16
Neither higher nor lower rate desirable	75	23	8	33	11
More developed regions					
Total number of countries	39	34	4	1	–
Higher rate desirable	11	11	–	–	–
Lower rate desirable	–	–	–	–	–
Neither higher nor lower rate desirable	28	23	4	1	–
Less developed regions					
Total number of countries	126	1	27	65	33
Higher rate desirable	24	1	7	10	6
Lower rate desirable	55	–	16	23	16
Niether higher nor lower rate desirable	47	–	4	32	11

Source: Concise report on The World Population Situation in 1983. (1984) UN.

decline (emphasis added) in the birth rate for the world and its more developed and less developed components according to estimates prepared by the United Nations. In 1950–1955, the birth rate for the world as a whole was 38.0 per 1000 persons. The corresponding figures for the more developed and less developed regions were 22.7 and 45.4. By 1975–1980, the birth rate for the world had fallen to 28.9 and, for the more developed and less developed regions, to 15.8 and 33.5 per 1000, respectively. Over a 25 year period the birth rate had fallen by 7 points in the developed countries and by 12 points in the developing countries.

Because birth rate trends are influenced by changes in the age structure, they are often studied in terms of the total fertility rate (which is expressed in terms of the number of children per woman). During the periods between 1950–1955 and 1975–1980, the total fertility rate for the world as a whole declined from 5.0 to 3.9; the rate declined from 2.8 to 2.05 in the developed countries and from 6.2 to 4.6 in the developing countries.

Greater confidence, the UN observed, could be placed in assessments of fertility levels and trends than in those of mortality. This was particularly true in developing countries, where there were often substantial year-to-year fluctuations in mortality owing to epidemics, disruptions of the political order and natural catastrophes. Such events tended to distort our perception of mortality levels and trends in these countries, while birth rates were likely to be relatively stable, diverging only slightly from their trend values.

Many less developed countries had assessed their level of fertility by means of a survey. In some cases, especially in Africa, the only estimates dated from the early 1960s, and occasionally from the 1950s. Unfortunately, these early estimates of fertility were often based on weak data. Furthermore, levels of fertility in these countries might have changed over time. For example, many countries in Asia and Latin America appeared to have undergone persistent nuptiality changes, while in other countries the traditional birth-spacing mechanisms (prolonged breast-feeding or taboos on sexual intercourse for some period after birth) had lost their force.

When fertility started to decline, the need for timely estimates of fertility trends became greater. Fortunately, there appeared to be a strong correlation between the improvement of statistics and the decline in fertility. Table 7.3 presents available information on the birth rate per 1,000 population in selected less developed countries which – during the period 1970–1981 – had relatively complete birth registration data. Although areas of the world in which fertility had declined tended to be over-represented, the data showed that a significant and widespread decline in fertility was in progress.[1]

In all world regions except sub-Saharan Africa, there had been substantial declines in fertility. The picture was mixed in the case of Asia, the most populous and, demographically, the most heterogeneous continent. Fertility remained high in most countries of Western South Asia while declines in fertility had been recorded in many countries elsewhere in Asia. Not only had fertility declines been observed in city States, such as Singapore, and islands, such as Sri Lanka, but they had also been observed in parts of some of the largest countries of the region: India, Indonesia and the Philippines. China, which comprised approximately one-third of the total population of all developing countries, had experienced a particularly rapid fertility decline. Its birth rate was much below the average for the developing countries of Asia. However, little or no change in fertility appeared to have taken place in Bangladesh, Pakistan or the Islamic Republic of Iran.

There was also diversity in Latin America, but the decline in fertility was not limited, as it was a few years previously, to the countries of Temperate South America and the Caribbean. There was evidence of decline in the largest countries in the region, including Brazil, Mexico, Colombia and Venezuela.

According to the United Nations,[2] Africa exhibited the highest levels of fertility world-wide. Nowhere in that region were there sustained indications of fertility decline except in Mauritius and Reunion. North of the Sahara, the birth rate had declined since the 1960s in Tunisia and Egypt, but recent estimates showed no further declines and it was possible that much of the earlier drop in fertility was due as much to nuptiality changes as to the adoption of family limitation. The crude birth rate was below 45 per 1,000 in only 14 of the 50 African countries and areas shown in United Nations estimates for 1975–1980. *Although the statistical bases of these estimates were particularly weak, it was less likely that sustained fertility declines had occurred in this region than that fertility had increased.* Furthermore, there was evidence that the high rates of sterility observed earlier in Zaire and other Central African countries had been reduced.

· In all but a few of the developed countries, fertility was lower in 1980 than a decade earlier, and variation among the developed countries had decreased. In some cases, fertility fell throughout the 1970s and early 1980s. In some countries, most notably in Western Europe, birth rates rose slightly during the late 1970s, although these increases

Table 7.3. Crude Birth Rate for Selected Developing Countries with Relatively Complete Birth Registration Data,[a] 1970–1981.[b]

Major area, region and country	Crude birth rate (per 1,000 population)							
	1970	1975	1976	1977	1978	1979	1980	1981
AFRICA								
Eastern Africa								
Mauritius	26.8	25.1	25.7	25.7	27.0	27.6	26.4	25.1[c]
Réunion	30.2	27.7	26.7	25.5	23.9	25.3	25.1	...
Northern Africa								
Egypt	34.8	36.0	36.4	37.4	37.1	...	...	37.6[c]
Tunisia	36.4	36.5	36.0	37.2	34.1	34.8	34.9	34.1
LATIN AMERICA								
Caribbean								
Cuba	27.6	20.7	19.8	17.6	15.3	14.7	14.0	13.9[c]
Guadeloupe	28.7	25.0	21.0	19.8	17.6	18.2	20.1c	...
Jamaica	34.4	30.1	29.3	28.8	27.4	27.1	27.0	...
Martinique	27.5	20.8	18.3	16.9	15.8	17.0	17.4	17.4[c]
Puerto Rico	24.8	23.8	24.1	24.4	24.1	23.3	22.8	...
Trinidad and Tobago	24.4	23.7	24.7	24.9	25.7	24.6	...	...
Middle America								
Costa Rica	33.4	29.5	29.8	31.0	29.8	30.2	29.4	...
El Salvador	40.0	39.9	40.2	41.7	39.7	39.2	35.8	...
Guatemala	40.3	39.9	41.5	42.9	41.5	41.9	41.8	...
Panama	37.1	33.2	31.9	31.0	30.3	29.6	28.6	...
Temperate South America								
Chile	26.8	24.6	23.3	21.6	21.4	21.5	22.2	...
Uruguay	19.0	20.9	20.8	20.3	19.9	19.7	18.6	18.3
EAST ASIA								
Hong Kong	20.0	18.2	17.7	17.7	17.6	16.8	16.9	16.9
Eastern South Asia								
Malaysia	34.0	31.3	31.6	30.7	30.1	30.5	...	...
Singapore	22.1	17.6	18.8	16.6	16.9	17.3	17.2	17.0
Middle South Asia								
Sri Lanka	29.4	27.7	27.8	27.9	28.5	28.7	27.6	...
Western South Asia Non-Arab countries								
Cyprus	19.5	16.0	18.7	18.4	19.3	20.5	21.7	20.6
Israel	27.2	27.7	28.0	26.4	25.1	24.7	24.3	23.6[c]
OCEANIA								
Micronesia–Polynesia								
Fiji	29.9	29.0	28.2	27.0	28.3	29.8	29.4	...

[a] Relatively good birth registration data means at least 90 per cent coverage.
[b] Countries with less than 300,000 population are excluded.
[c] Provisional

Source: *Concise report on The World Population Situation in 1983*. (1984) UN.

Table 7.4. Crude Birth Rate for More Developed Countries, 1970–1981 (per 1,000 population).[a]

Major area, region and country	1970	1975	1976	1977	1978	1979	1980	1981
NORTHERN AMERICA								
Canada	17.4	15.8	15.6	15.5	15.3	15.4	15.4	...
United States	18.3	14.6	14.5	15.1	15.0	15.5	15.8	15.9
EAST ASIA								
Japan	18.8	17.0	16.2	15.4	14.9	14.2	13.5	13.0
EUROPE								
Eastern Europe								
Bulgaria	16.3	16.6	16.5	16.1	15.5	15.3	14.5	14.1[b]
Czechoslovakia	15.9	19.6	19.2	18.7	18.4	17.9	16.2	15.5[b]
German Democratic Republic	13.9	10.8	11.6	13.3	13.9	14.0	14.6	14.2[b]
Hungary	14.7	18.4	17.5	16.7	15.7	15.0	13.9	13.3
Poland	16.8	18.9	19.5	19.1	19.0	19.5	19.5	18.9
Romania	21.1	19.7	19.5	19.6	19.1	18.6	18.0	...
Northern Europe								
Denmark	14.4	14.2	12.9	12.2	12.2	11.6	11.2	10.4[b]
Finland	14.0	13.9	14.1	13.9	13.5	13.3	13.2	13.2[b]
Ireland	21.7	21.1	21.0	21.1	21.1	21.5	21.9	...
Norway	16.6	14.1	13.3	12.6	12.8	12.7	12.5	12.8
Sweden	13.7	12.6	12.0	11.6	11.3	11.6	11.7	11.3
United Kingdom								
England and Wales	16.1	12.3	11.9	11.6	12.1	13.0	13.3	...
Northern Ireland	21.1	17.0	17.1	16.5	17.0	18.2	17.6	...
Scotland	16.8	13.0	12.5	12.4	13.2	13.4	...	
Southern Europe								
Albania	32.5	...	...	...	30.3	...	...	...
Greece	16.5	15.7	16.0	15.5	15.7	15.7	15.4	...
Italy	16.8	14.8	13.9	13.1	12.5	11.8	11.2	10.9[b]
Malta	16.3	18.3	18.0	17.9	17.3	17.4	16.0	15.0
Portugal	19.4	19.0	19.3	18.6	17.1	16.3	16.3	...
Spain	19.6	18.8	18.8	18.2	17.2	16.1	15.1	14.1
Yugoslavia	17.8	18.2	18.2	17.7	17.4	17.2	17.0	16.7
Western Europe								
Austria	15.1	12.5	11.6	11.4	11.4	11.5	12.1	12.4[b]
Belgium	14.8	12.2	12.3	12.4	12.5	12.6	12.7	12.6[b]
France	16.8	14.1	13.6	14.0	13.8	14.2	14.9	14.9[b]
Germany, Federal Republic of	13.4	9.7	9.8	9.5	9.4	9.5	10.1	10.1[b]
Luxembourg	13.0	11.2	10.9	11.2	11.2	11.2	11.5	12.0
Netherlands	18.3	13.0	12.9	12.5	12.6	12.5	12.8	12.5
Switzerland	15.8	12.2	11.7	11.5	11.3	11.3	11.6	...
OCEANIA								
Australia–New Zealand								
Australia	20.6	16.9	16.4	16.1	15.7	15.5	15.3	15.8[b]
New Zealand	22.1	18.4	17.7	17.4	16.4	16.8	16.2	16.3
USSR	17.4	18.1	18.4	18.1	18.2	18.2	18.3	18.7[b]

[a] Countries with less than 300,000 population are excluded.
[b] Provisional.

Source: Concise report on The World Population Situation in 1983. (1984) UN.

were not sufficient to return fertility to the level of 1970. In most of Eastern Europe, fertility rose during the late 1970s but then reassumed an earlier decline. The United Nations commented that the temporary increases may have been the result of national policies that combined incentives to increased fertility, such as family allowances, with restrictions on access to contraception and abortion. The subsequent decreases in fertility in most of Eastern Europe testified to the difficulty of reversing strong fertility trends through policy action, although it should be noted that fertility in most of Eastern Europe remained higher than for the developed countries as a whole.

In 1980, all developed countries except Albania and Ireland had crude birth rates below 20 per 1,000 population and in most of Northern and Western Europe the rate was below 15 per 1,000. In the Federal Republic of Germany the provisional crude birth rate of 10.1 per 1,000 for 1981 was well below the death rate of 11.7 per 1,000 for the same year. Denmark and Hungary also had death rates that exceeded the birth rate as of the early 1980s.

Fertility, the UN noted, could also be expressed in terms of the number of children born to the average woman throughout her life. At the levels of mortality then prevailing in developed countries, a total fertility rate (TFR) of exactly two children per woman implied that the couples of that country were not quite reproducing themselves. In fact, the TFR was 2.0 or less, as of 1980 or 1981, in all of Western and Northern Europe (with the exception of Ireland and Northern Ireland) and in developed countries outside Europe (with the exception of New Zealand and the USSR). Several nations of Eastern and Southern Europe also had a TFR of 2.0 or less: the German Democratic Republic, Hungary, Italy, Spain and Yugoslavia. Apart from the three countries mentioned earlier, the countries with a low TFR still had an annual excess of births over deaths, since the age distribution of most developed countries was still favourable to growth. Specifically, the proportion of persons in the reproductive ages was quite large as a result of previous regimes of higher fertility. Nevertheless, many countries of Europe had a TFR only slightly higher than the 1.4 children per woman observed in Denmark and the Federal Republic of Germany in 1981 and, unless fertility rose, the number of countries experiencing natural decreases of the population would soon grow.

While current fertility trends in the more developed countries might provide some indications as to the future course of fertility in the developing countries, it was the course of the Western countries' fertility in the nineteenth century that was usually used to explain current fertility trends in the less developed countries. This pattern had given rise to the theory of demographic transition which postulated that the decline in fertility was the result of social and economic development. Thus, a central recommendation of the World Population Plan of Action, adopted at the 1974 World Population Conference, was that 'countries wishing to affect fertility levels give priority to implementing developmental programmes and educational and health strategies which, while contributing to economic growth and higher standards of living, have a decisive impact upon demographic trends, including fertility'.

Development was likely to influence fertility in a variety of ways. The decline in mortality, an important result of development, should reduce fertility since parents could obtain the same completed family size with fewer births. In addition, the cost of child-rearing and education increased with development, while at the same time parents could expect less from their children as labourers in a familial production process or as providers of security in old age. Furthermore, as development proceeded, women gained status and increased their participation in the paid labour force, thus raising the cost of bearing and rearing children. Thus, it was postulated that during the process of modernization there occurred a reversal in the direction of intergenerational wealth flows and at some stage parents perceived that the costs of a large family exceeded its benefits.

Stated in such general terms, these arguments underlying the theory of demographic transition were widely accepted. The UN pointed out, however, that they did not provide an explicit guide to policy. The theory in this form did not identify a necessary level of development (a threshold) that must be attained before fertility could be reduced and, therefore, did not rule out the possibility that fertility could decline even in countries that were in the early stages of economic development. In fact, it was becoming increasingly clear that there were great disparities in the socio-economic and demographic conditions of various European countries when they entered their periods of fertility decline.

> There is also cause to question whether the experience of European countries in the nineteenth century is even relevant to the situation of the developing countries. At that time, the governments of European countries favoured large populations and high birth rates. In contrast, many governments in the developing world now perceive rapid population growth to be an obstacle to achieving their socio-economic goals. *In nineteenth-century Europe, the Church and the State were hostile to the practice of family limitation, while many governments in the developing world now support family planning resolutely. These governments possess powerful means to inform and persuade the public and thus can provide an effective counter to the weight of tradition and individual assessments of the gains from a large family. Furthermore, these governments can diffuse modern methods of contraception through public health networks. Thus, it is not surprising that recent studies suggest that programmatic efforts have made significant contributions to current reductions in fertility.*[3] (emphasis added)

Although the debate on the prospects of a deliberate policy of fertility reduction, independent of broadly based socio-economic progress, continued, a great deal of recent statistical material bearing on this issue was becoming available. Knowledge of fertility trends and their determinants had been recently expanded by the World Fertility Survey, a series of national inquiries using a comparable methodology in a large number of countries. This had been hailed as one of the largest and most ambitious social science studies ever undertaken.

The results of the World Fertility Survey indicated that, in most developing countries of Latin America, Asia and Oceania, preferences were for moderate-sized rather than large families. In all but 7 of 25 countries, over half of the women with 3 living children wanted no more, and in all but 4 countries, at least 40 per cent of all married fecund women wanted no more children. The average number of children desired ranged from 3.0 (Turkey) to 6.2 (Jordan), with a typical value of 4.3 children for all 25 countries. In sub-Saharan Africa, large families were desired – averages of 6 to 9 children were reported in the surveys as the preferred family size, and typically less than 20 per cent of married fecund women wished to have no more children.

It was often the case that stated preferences for family size were not matched by behaviour. In most countries older women had, on average, exceeded the number of children stated as desired. In 14 countries in which women were asked whether they had wanted the last child, between 14 and 48 per cent said they had not, with the average being 35 per cent. Furthermore, in 22 of 29 countries at least 40 per cent of the women who said they did not want more children were not using contraception.

The UN commented:

> The respondents' resignation to continued child-bearing might be explained by fatalism, by the weight of tradition or by pressure from the husband or other

family members. *However, in many instances, women reported that they had no access to modern methods of contraception, or that they knew of no source of information on supplies, an indication that there may be a large unmet need for family planning services.*[4] (emphasis added)

The findings of the Survey indicated that the problem facing women who desired to limit family size was not so much an absence of theoretical knowledge about how to prevent births as an absence of practical knowledge of how to gain access to contraceptive implements. For example, in Nepal, Pakistan and Kenya, 22, 75 and 88 per cent, respectively, of the married women surveyed knew of at least one modern method of contraception but only 6, 32 and 42 per cent, respectively, knew of an outlet where contraceptives could be obtained. While improved access to contraceptives would certainly cause some increase in their use in these countries, it was not known which levels of use would be attained without further socio-economic advance.

The view that large numbers of unwanted births would be prevented if contraceptive methods were made more widely accessible had been challenged by an appeal to Western experience in the past century. The decline in fertility in the more developed countries began before the advent of modern contraceptive techniques, such as sterilization, the pill and the intra-uterine device (IUD), when it was often forbidden to advertise or sell the contraceptive implements that did exist. Thus, folk methods of contraception, such as coitus interruptus, were largely responsible for the decline in birth rates. It was thus argued that, if couples in developing countries had truly preferred to have fewer children, folk methods of proved effectiveness were available to them.

It might be, however, that some women did not know of these folk methods or were unable to distinguish between effective and ineffective ones. Other women (or their partners) might have chosen not to use folk methods of contraception that would cause inconvenience or would decrease sexual pleasure. This view was consistent with observations of a rapid increase in the level of contraceptive usage in recent times, coinciding with the diffusion of modern methods. With the exception of Peru and the Philippines, where the rhythm and withdrawal methods accounted for about one half of all contraceptive activity, *the survey indicated that modern and relatively effective methods were chiefly responsible for declining birth rates. Rather than simply replacing traditional methods of contraception, as might have happened in the more developed countries, these newer methods met an existing demand that had hitherto been unsatisfied.* (emphasis added)

Modern methods of contraception were used for spacing, as well as limiting, family size. In Latin American countries, for example, the use of contraception by women exposed to the risk of pregnancy and who wanted more children ranged from 19 per cent in Haiti to 71 per cent in Costa Rica. It was also noteworthy that its use for spacing births seemed to be most prevalent in countries in which the period of breast-feeding was the shortest, suggesting that contraception was used to ameliorate the fertility consequences of changing customs. The evidence thus tended to indicate that there might be a significant demand for contraceptive methods in developing countries even before couples perceived a need to reduce their eventual family size.

The World Fertility Survey was due to end during 1984, but further analysis of these data, and data from additional surveys which had already been conducted in a number of countries, would continue to provide information on the circumstances attending the introduction of birth control in the less developed countries. The UN added succinctly:

Although the exact nature of the factors that determine the acceptance and diffusion of family limitation in a given culture is still poorly understood, the data indicate that modern methods of contraception find at least some users in every country studied and that, *when effective governmental policies favour their use, contraceptive methods can spread quite rapidly and accelerate the decline in fertility.* (emphasis added)

The United Nations did not, however, wish to appear one-sided in the population-versus-development debate.

At the same time, it appears unlikely that a large and sustained decline in marital fertility can be expected in the poorest countries without some improvement in the material well-being and health of the population. Furthermore, underdevelopment itself generally implies poor communications, irregular supplies and a shortage of trained personnel, all of which make it difficult to provide an adequate network of family planning services.

The improved access to effective contraception might help to explain the very rapid drop in fertility in many developing countries during the past decade. In the run-up to the Mexico City Conference, the UN felt constrained to comment:

How fast fertility will decline in the future remains an important but unresolved question, the answer to which will profoundly influence the future size of the world population.

Another question that would profoundly affect the world's demographic future was how far the incipient fertility declines in the less developed countries would proceed before they levelled off.

There is nothing inevitable about an average of two surviving children per woman, nor the eventual reduction in the rate of natural increase of national populations to zero (as is assumed by many population projections, including those of the United Nations). Fertility may stabilize at a higher level, resulting in substantial long-term growth, or levels of fertility may fall into a pattern of alternating high and low birth rates.

An examination of recent fertility trends in developed countries might provide some indication of what the future held in store for those nations just entering a period of fertility decline.

The birth rates of many Western countries were very low during the 1930s and, as a result, many projections made at that time foresaw population declines. Instead, much higher levels of fertility were reached after the Second World War (although they were followed by a precipitous fall after 1964). A striking example was provided by the Federal Republic of Germany. In 1933, at the height of the pre-War depression, the total fertility rate was 1.58 children per woman, well below the level required to ensure reproduction. By 1966, however, the total fertility rate had climbed back to 2.53. Subsequently, the number of births dropped by almost half between 1966 and 1978 and the total fertility rate fell to 1.4 – the lowest level so far recorded by a country in time of peace. The baby boom in the United States peaked in 1957, with a crude birth rate of 25.3 per 1,000 population, well above the low point of 18.4 reached in 1936. However, the total fertility rate was halved in the subsequent 20 years, from 3.8 in 1957 to 1.8 in 1977.

Several writers, the UN pointed out, had argued that a cyclical alternation of high and low birth rates was a natural feature of countries in the final stages of the demographic transition. They postulated that the generations depleted by the preceding fertility decline tended to have economic advantages; conversely, larger generations must compete for scarce educational resources and jobs. Thus, the difference in the size of successive cohorts generated fluctuations in fertility since those born in small cohorts were more optimistic about the future of their children and therefore chose to have larger families than those born in large cohorts. Given this view, the present low fertility exhibited by the baby boom cohorts of the 1950s was but a transient episode.

Other authors had argued that the low birth rates reached in many developed countries were inseparable from other social and economic transformations inherent in mature urban, post-industrial societies, where powerful cultural changes were leading to a change in familial values and functions. In Western Europe, the pro-natalist attitudes of governments had weakened and legal restrictions against contraception and abortion had been relaxed. Furthermore, the attitude of some churches in regard to sexual matters had changed radically. Social and economic forces had contributed to making female labour force participation more attractive and child-bearing and rearing more expensive. It might therefore be that below-replacement fertility levels would continue to prevail in the more developed countries unless the continuing deficit of births in relation to deaths provoked strong action by governments to support and encourage higher fertility.

PROGRESS MADE BY 1984

By 1984, it was clear that already considerable progress had been made in lowering birth rates. At a global level declines in fertility had been recorded which were at least consistent with the assumptions made in the United Nations medium projections. In fact, the rate of world population growth which it was assumed (under the medium projections shown in Table 1.6) would remain constant at around 2.0 per cent until the middle of the 1980s had already fallen by the time of the Mexico Conference to 1.67 per cent per year.

Table 7.5 shows the total world population in 1984 by country or area in the world, according to the major areas or regions. It also shows birth rates, death rates, gross reproduction rates, expectation of life, percentage of urban population, and annual growth rates.

A comparison with Table 1.4 (p. 28) shows that the main declines in the birth rate, contributing substantially to the decline in the world population growth rate, had occurred in Asia, although there had also been significant declines in some other regions. It also shows that the world population growth rate would have declined still further between 1970 and 1984 but for the fall in mortality recorded, especially in Africa and Latin America.

ASIA

In 1975, two out of every four persons in the world lived in Asia. Excluding those in Soviet Asia and Western South Asia (or the Middle East) there were more than 2 billion Asians in the total world population of 3.9 billion. The region had the world's two most populated countries, India and China – which together accounted for 36 per cent of the world total. According to the United Nations' figures, China's population

Table 7.5. Demographic indicators (1984) by country or area in the world, major areas and regions.[a]

Country or area	Population (thousands)		Annual growth			Age distribution of population 1980			Crude vital rates 1980–5 (per 1000 population)		Gross reproduction rate 1980–5	Expectation of life. 1980–5 (years)	Percentage of urban population 1980
	1984	2000	1950–5	1980–5	1995–2000	0–14	15–64	65+	Births	Deaths			
World total	4,763,085	6,123,278	1.8	1.7	1.5	35.6	58.6	5.7	27.3	10.6	1.73	58.9	40.9
More-developed regions[b]	1,165,789	1,272,194	1.3	0.6	0.5	23.0	65.6	11.4	15.5	9.5	0.96	73.1	71.0
Less-developed regions[c]	3,597,297	4,851,083	2.1	2.0	1.8	40.0	56.2	3.8	31.2	11.0	2.00	56.6	30.6
A. Africa	536,589	877,061	2.1	3.0	3.1	45.2	51.7	3.1	46.4	16.5	3.16	49.7	28.5
1. *Eastern Africa*[d]	155,447	266,238	2.2	3.2	3.4	46.8	50.6	2.6	49.1	17.0	3.35	48.8	16.0
Burundi	4,503	6,951	1.7	2.7	2.7	43.4	53.4	3.3	47.6	20.9	3.17	44.0	2.4
Comoros	443	715	2.3	3.0	2.8	45.8	51.3	2.8	46.3	15.9	3.10	50.0	10.5
Ethiopia	35,420	58,407	2.0	2.6	3.1	45.5	51.9	2.6	49.2	21.5	3.30	42.9	14.2
Kenya	19,761	38,534	2.9	4.1	4.1	52.2	45.9	1.9	55.1	14.0	4.00	52.9	13.5
Madagascar	9,731	15,552	1.8	2.8	3.0	43.4	53.2	3.4	44.4	16.5	3.00	49.6	18.5
Malawi	6,788	11,669	1.9	3.2	3.4	47.7	50.1	2.2	52.1	19.9	3.45	45.0	34.7
Mauritius[e]	1,031	1,298	2.9	1.9	1.2	34.1	62.9	3.0	25.5	6.0	1.35	66.7	52.5
Mozambique	13,693	21,779	1.2	3.0	2.9	44.3	52.4	3.3	44.1	16.5	3.00	49.4	7.5
Réunion	555	685	3.1	1.4	1.2	35.0	61.3	3.7	20.5	6.5	1.10	66.4	54.9
Rwanda	5,903	10,565	2.3	3.5	3.7	48.2	49.2	2.6	51.1	16.6	3.60	49.5	4.0
Somalia	5,423	7,079	1.6	3.7	2.5	43.2	53.3	3.5	46.5	21.3	3.00	42.9	30.3
Uganda	15,150	26,774	3.1	3.5	3.5	48.0	49.4	2.5	49.9	14.7	3.40	52.0	11.9
United Republic of Tanzania	21,710	39,129	2.2	3.5	3.7	48.4	49.3	2.3	50.4	15.3	3.50	51.0	11.9
Zambia	6,445	11,237	2.4	3.3	3.5	46.9	50.4	2.6	48.1	15.1	3.33	51.3	38.8
Zimbabwe	8,461	15,132	4.0	3.5	3.6	47.2	50.0	2.7	47.2	12.3	3.25	55.7	23.1

Table 7.5. *contd*

Country or area	Population (thousands) 1984	Population (thousands) 2000	Annual growth 1950–5	Annual growth 1980–5	Annual growth 1995–2000	Age distribution of population 1980 0–14	15–64	65+	Crude vital rates 1980–5 (per 1000 population) Births	Deaths	Gross reproductive rate 1980–5	Expectation of life 1980–5 (years)	Percentage of urban population 1980
2. *Middle Africa*^f	60,723	95,693	1.8	2.7	2.9	43.6	53.2	3.2	44.9	18.1	2.97	47.2	33.6
Angola	8,540	13,234	1.4	2.5	2.8	44.2	52.9	3.0	47.3	22.2	3.15	42.0	19.**
Central African Republic	2,508	3,736	1.2	2.3	2.6	41.5	54.6	3.9	44.7	21.8	2.90	43.0	40.9
Chad	4,901	7,304	1.3	2.3	2.6	41.9	54.5	3.6	44.2	21.4	2.90	43.0	17.**
Congo	1,695	2,646	1.7	2.6	2.9	43.2	53.5	3.3	44.5	18.6	2.95	46.5	37.**
Equatorial Guinea	383	559	1.1	2.2	2.4	40.7	55.1	4.2	42.5	21.0	2.79	44.0	55.**
Gabon	1,146	1,611	0.6	1.6	2.4	34.0	59.9	6.1	34.6	18.1	2.30	49.0	18.**
United Republic of Cameroon	9,371	14,045	1.9	2.4	2.6	41.9	54.3	3.8	43.6	19.2	2.85	46.0	34
Zaire	32,084	52,410	2.2	2.9	3.1	44.8	52.3	2.9	45.2	15.8	3.00	50.0	39.**
3. *Northern Africa*^g	121,386	185,671	2.2	2.9	2.4	43.2	53.0	3.8	41.9	12.9	2.93	55.9	44.**
Algeria	21,272	35,194	2.1	3.3	2.9	46.6	49.4	3.9	45.1	12.3	3.40	57.8	61.**
Egypt	45,657	65,200	2.4	2.5	2.0	39.5	55.9	4.5	38.4	12.5	2.55	57.3	46.**
Libyan Arab Jamahiriya	3,471	6,072	1.8	3.8	3.3	46.7	51.1	2.2	45.6	10.9	3.50	57.9	52.**
Morocco	22,848	36,325	2.5	3.3	2.6	46.0	50.9	3.1	44.0	11.5	3.14	57.9	41.**
Sudan	20,945	32,926	2.0	2.9	2.7	44.9	52.4	2.7	45.9	17.4	3.22	47.7	24.**
Tunisia	7,042	9,725	1.8	2.4	1.7	42.0	53.7	4.3	34.1	10.1	2.40	60.6	51.**
4. *Southern Africa*	36,246	54,456	1.7	2.5	2.5	41.7	54.3	4.0	39.6	14.2	2.57	53.0	46.**
Botswana	1,042	1,865	2.1	3.5	3.7	49.7	48.4	2.0	50.0	12.7	3.20	54.5	26.**
Lesotho	1,481	2,251	1.6	2.5	2.6	42.0	54.5	3.6	41.7	16.4	2.85	49.3	4.**
Namibia	1,507	2,382	2.0	2.8	2.9	44.0	52.8	3.2	45.1	17.3	3.00	48.2	34.**
South Africa	31,586	46,918	1.7	2.5	2.4	41.3	54.7	4.1	38.7	13.9	2.50	53.5	50.**
Swaziland	630	1,041	1.9	3.0	3.2	45.4	51.6	3.0	47.5	17.2	3.20	48.6	8.**

Table 7.5. *contd*

Country or area	Population (thousands) 1984	Population (thousands) 2000	Annual growth 1950–5	Annual growth 1980–5	Annual growth 1995–2000	Age distribution of population 1980 0–14	Age distribution of population 1980 15–64	Age distribution of population 1980 65+	Crude vital rates 1980–5 (per 1000 population) Births	Crude vital rates 1980–5 (per 1000 population) Deaths	Gross reproduct-rate 1980–5	Expectation of life 1980–5 (years)	Percentage of urban population 1980
5 *Western Africa*^h	162,787	275,002	2.1	3.1	3.3	46.6	50.7	2.7	49.3	18.5	3.38	46.8	22.**
Benin	3,890	6,381	0.7	2.9	3.2	45.8	51.2	3.0	51.0	22.5	3.45	42.5	31.**
Cape Verde	317	382	2.7	1.4	1.0	35.4	61.1	3.5	23.9	10.3	1.30	57.0	6.**
Gambia	630	898	1.1	1.9	2.3	42.1	54.9	3.1	48.4	29.0	3.15	35.0	19.**
Ghana	13,044	21,923	4.8	3.2	3.2	46.3	50.9	2.8	47.0	14.6	3.20	52.0	36.**
Guinea	5,301	7,935	1.0	2.3	2.6	42.9	54.2	2.9	46.8	23.5	3.05	40.2	19.**
Guinea-Bissau	875	1,241	0.6	1.9	2.3	40.1	55.6	4.3	40.7	21.7	2.65	43.0	16
Ivory Coast	9,474	15,581	1.2	3.4	3.0	44.6	52.4	2.9	46.0	18.0	3.30	47.0	36.**
Liberia	2,123	3,564	1.9	3.2	3.3	45.6	51.3	3.1	48.7	17.2	3.40	49.0	34.**
Mali	7,825	12,363	1.7	2.8	2.8	45.9	51.4	2.8	50.2	22.4	3.30	42.0	19.**
Mauritania	1,832	2,999	2.0	2.9	3.1	45.7	51.5	2.8	50.1	20.9	3.40	44.0	35.**
Niger	5,940	9,750	1.0	2.8	3.2	45.9	50.3	3.8	51.0	22.9	3.50	42.5	12.**
Nigeria	92,037	161,930	2.4	3.3	3.6	48.1	49.5	2.4	50.4	17.1	3.50	48.5	19.**
Senegal	6,352	10,036	1.9	2.7	2.9	44.5	52.6	2.9	47.7	21.2	3.29	43.3	25.**
Sierra Leone	3,536	4,868	1.1	1.8	2.1	40.9	56.1	3.0	47.4	29.7	3.02	34.0	25.**
Togo	2,838	4,599	1.2	2.9	3.1	44.2	52.7	3.2	45.4	16.9	3.00	48.7	18.**
Upper Volta	6,768	10,542	1.4	2.3	2.8	44.1	53.1	2.8	47.8	22.2	3.20	42.0	9.**
B. Latin America	397,138	549,971	2.7	2.3	1.9	39.4	56.3	4.3	31.8	8.2	2.01	64.1	65.5
6. *Caribbean*	31,364	40,833	1.8	1.5	1.6	37.2	57.3	5.5	27.1	8.4	1.64	64.0	52.5
Barbados	262	307	1.5	0.8	1.0	29.5	61.2	9.3	19.9	8.6	1.10	71.6	40.6
Cuba	9,966	11,718	1.9	0.6	1.0	31.3	61.4	7.3	16.9	6.4	0.96	73.4	65.4
Dominican Republic	6,101	8,407	2.7	2.3	1.7	43.9	53.2	2.9	33.1	8.0	2.04	62.6	54.5
Guadaloupe	319	338	2.3	0.1	0.5	35.8	57.5	6.7	19.5	7.3	1.25	70.4	45.0
Haiti	6,419	9,860	1.7	2.5	2.7	43.6	52.9	3.6	41.3	14.2	2.80	52.7	24.9
Jamaica	2,290	2,849	1.9	1.4	1.3	40.6	53.6	5.8	28.3	6.7	1.65	70.3	41.6
Martinique	312	338	2.1	0.0	0.7	33.6	59.1	7.3	18.8	7.6	1.15	70.9	69.2
Puerto Rico	3,404	4,212	0.3	1.5	1.2	31.6	60.5	7.9	22.4	6.9	1.28	73.9	81.0
Trinidad and Tobago	1,105	1,321	2.5	0.9	1.0	34.2	60.8	4.9	24.6	6.2	1.40	70.1	23.5
Winward Islands^i	418	525	2.0	1.2	1.4	41.2	54.3	4.5	30.4	6.2	1.75	69.1	0.0
Other Caribbean^j	769	958	1.8	1.3	1.3	34.8	60.0	5.2	24.8	6.1	1.40	70.6	61.9

Table 7.5. *contd*

Country or area	Population (thousands)		Annual growth			Age distribution of population 1980			Crude vital rates 1980–5 (per 1000 population)		Gross reproduct- rate 1980–5	Expecta- tion of life. 1980–5 (years)	Percent- age of urban population 1980
	1984	2000	1950–5	1980–5	1995–2000	0–14	15–64	65+	Births	Deaths			
7. *Middle America*[k]	102,811	149,557	2.9	2.7	2.1	44.6	51.9	3.4	35.1	7.4	2.32	65.0	60.9
Costa Rica	2,534	3,596	3.5	2.6	1.9	38.5	58.0	3.6	30.5	4.2	1.71	73.0	42.1
El Salvador	5,388	8,708	2.7	2.9	2.9	45.2	51.4	3.4	40.2	8.1	2.71	64.8	41.4
Guatemala	8,165	12,739	2.9	2.9	2.7	44.1	53.1	2.9	38.4	9.3	2.52	60.7	38.9
Honduras	4,232	6,978	3.2	3.4	3.2	47.8	49.4	2.7	43.9	10.1	3.17	59.9	36.0
Mexico	77,040	109,180	2.9	2.6	1.9	44.7	51.8	3.6	33.9	7.1	2.25	65.7	67.0
Nicaragua	3,162	5,261	3.0	3.3	3.0	47.4	50.1	2.4	44.2	2.90	59.8	52.6	
Panama	2,134	2,893	2.5	2.2	1.7	40.5	55.4	4.1	28.0	5.4	1.69	71.0	52.7
8. *Temperate South America*[l]	44,964	55,496	1.9	1.5	1.2	30.5	61.9	7.6	24.3	8.6	1.57	69.0	79.9
Argentina	30,094	37,197	2.0	1.6	1.2	30.0	61.8	8.2	24.6	8.7	1.66	69.7	78.9
Chile	11,878	14,934	2.0	1.7	1.3	32.5	62.0	5.5	24.8	7.7	1.42	67.0	81.1
Uruguay	2,990	3,364	1.2	0.7	0.7	27.1	62.5	10.4	19.5	10.2	1.35	70.3	84.5
9. *Tropical South America*[m]	217,999	304,085	3.0	2.4	1.9	39.2	57.0	3.8	32.4	8.5	2.01	62.9	66.6
Bolivia	6,200	9,724	2.1	2.7	2.9	43.5	53.3	3.3	44.0	15.9	3.05	50.7	32.9
Brazil	132,648	179,487	3.2	2.2	1.7	37.7	58.2	4.0	30.6	8.4	1.86	63.4	67.5
Colombia	28,110	37,999	2.9	2.1	1.7	39.4	57.1	3.5	31.0	7.7	1.92	63.6	70.2
Ecuador	9,090	14,596	2.8	3.1	2.8	44.4	52.0	3.5	40.6	8.9	2.93	62.6	44.6
Guyana	936	1,196	2.8	2.0	1.3	39.4	56.8	3.7	28.5	5.9	1.59	68.2	22.3
Paraguay	3,576	5,405	2.7	3.0	2.3	42.7	53.9	3.4	36.0	7.2	2.37	65.1	39.4
Peru	19,197	27,952	2.6	2.6	2.1	41.8	54.6	3.6	36.7	10.7	2.44	58.6	68.7
Suriname	352	423	3.0	0.1	1.6	46.4	49.1	4.5	29.5	6.1	2.00	69.4	49.4
Venezuela	17,819	27,207	3.8	3.3	2.3	42.2	55.1	2.8	35.2	5.6	2.11	67.8	83.3
C. 10. *Northern America*[n]	261,190	298,006	1.8	0.9	0.7	22.6	66.3	11.1	16.0	9.0	0.90	74.3	75.6
Canada	25,289	29,393	2.7	1.2	0.8	23.2	67.9	8.9	16.2	7.3	0.88	74.5	76.8
United States of America	235,764	268,443	1.7	0.9	0.7	22.5	66.2	11.3	16.0	9.2	0.90	74.2	75.5

Table 7.5. *contd*

Country or area	Population (thousands) 1984	Population (thousands) 2000	Annual growth 1950–5	Annual growth 1980–5	Annual growth 1995–2000	Age distribution of population 1980 0–14	Age distribution of population 1980 15–64	Age distribution of population 1980 65+	Crude vital rates 1980–5 (per 1000 population) Births	Crude vital rates 1980–5 (per 1000 population) Deaths	Gross reproduction rate 1980–5	Expectation of life 1980–5 (years)	Percentage of urban population 1980
D. East Asia	1,238,640	1,470,036	2.0	1.1	1.1	35.5	59.5	5.1	18.2	6.8	1.12	68.0	32.5
11. China	1,051,551	1,255,656	2.2	1.2	1.2	36.9	58.4	4.7	18.5	6.8	1.14	67.4	25.5
12. Japan	119,492	127,683	1.4	0.6	0.4	23.6	67.4	9.0	12.4	6.7	0.83	76.6	78.2
13. *Other East Asia*[o]	67,597	86,697	0.6	1.8	1.4	34.9	61.1	4.0	23.8	6.6	1.42	66.7	59.5
Hong Kong	5,498	6,894	4.6	2.1	1.0	25.5	68.0	6.5	17.9	5.9	1.00	73.9	91.5
Korea	59,939	76,742	0.3	1.7	1.4	35.5	60.6	3.8	24.1	6.7	1.43	66.3	56.7
Korea, Democratic People's Republic of	19,630	27,256	-1.4	2.3	1.8	40.0	56.3	3.7	30.5	7.4	1.95	64.6	59.7
Korea, Republic of	40,309	49,485	1.0	1.4	1.1	33.4	62.7	3.9	21.0	6.3	1.20	67.5	55.3
Mongolia	1,851	22,673	1.9	2.7	2.0	43.0	53.8	3.2	33.8	7.2	2.35	64.6	50.6
E. South Asia	1,538,745	2,073,657	2.0	2.2	1.7	40.8	55.9	3.3	34.9	12.9	2.27	53.6	24.7
14. *Eastern South Asia*[p]	393,082	519,707	2.0	2.1	1.6	40.7	56.0	3.3	31.7	10.9	2.01	56.8	22.8
Burma	38,513	55,186	1.7	2.5	2.0	41.3	55.0	3.7	37.9	12.7	2.60	55.0	27.5
Democratic Kampuchea	7,149	9,918	2.2	2.9	1.4	32.9	64.6	2.5	45.5	19.6	2.50	43.4	14.7
East Timor	638	876	1.3	2.5	1.5	34.2	63.4	2.4	48.0	23.0	2.85	39.9	14.1
Indonesia	162,167	204,486	1.7	1.8	1.3	41.0	55.6	3.3	30.7	13.0	1.90	52.5	19.8
Lao People's Democratic Republic	4,315	6,213	2.1	2.5	2.1	43.4	53.7	2.9	40.6	15.5	2.85	49.7	12.8
Malaysia	15,204	20,615	2.5	2.3	1.6	39.1	57.2	3.7	29.2	6.4	1.80	66.9	29.8
Philippines	53,395	74,810	3.0	2.5	1.8	40.6	56.6	2.9	32.3	6.9	2.05	64.5	36.9
Singapore	2,540	2,976	4.9	1.3	0.7	27.1	68.2	4.7	18.0	5.3	0.84	72.2	73.3
Thailand	50,584	66,115	2.7	2.1	1.6	40.2	56.6	3.1	28.6	7.7	1.75	62.7	14.6
Viet Nam	58,307	78,129	1.7	2.0	1.7	41.7	54.6	3.6	31.2	10.1	2.10	58.8	19.8

Table 7.5. *contd*

Country or area	Population (thousands)		Annual growth			Age distribution of population 1980			Crude vital rates 1980–5 (per 1000 population)		Gross reproduct. rate 1980–5	Expectation of life 1980–5 (years)	Percentage of urban population 1980
	1984	2000	1950–5	1980–5	1995–2000	0–14	15–64	65+	Births	Deaths			
15. *Middle South Asia*[q]	1,036,011	1,385,652	1.9	2.2	1.6	40.7	56.1	3.2	35.8	33.9	2.33	51.8	22.4
Afghanistan	14,292	24,180	1.6	0.0	2.2	44.2	53.3	2.4	49.6	27.3	3.35	37.0	16.8
Bangladesh	98,464	145,800	1.6	2.7	2.2	46.2	50.4	3.4	44.8	17.5	3.00	47.8	11.2
Bhutan	1,388	1,893	1.6	2.0	1.8	40.4	56.4	3.2	38.4	18.1	2.70	45.9	4.0
India	746,742	961,531	1.9	2.0	1.3	39.2	57.6	3.2	33.2	13.3	2.15	52.5	22.1
Iran, Islamic Republic of	43,799	65,549	3.7	3.0	2.2	44.2	52.4	3.4	40.5	10.4	2.75	60.2	49.1
Nepal	16,107	23,048	1.2	2.3	2.2	43.5	53.5	3.0	41.7	18.4	3.05	45.9	4.8
Pakistan	98,971	142,554	2.1	3.1	2.2	45.0	52.1	2.8	42.6	15.2	2.85	50.0	28.1
Sri Lanka	16,076	20,843	2.6	2.0	1.4	36.9	59.0	4.2	27.0	6.7	1.65	67.5	26.6
16. *Western South Asia*	109,651	168,298	2.7	2.9	2.5	41.6	54.4	4.0	37.8	10.1	2.67	60.6	54.0
Arab Countries[R]	55,964	93,695	2.4	3.4	3.0	45.2	51.8	3.0	43.8	11.3	3.27	58.4	56.5
Bahrain	414	688	2.9	4.3	2.6	34.7	63.3	2.1	32.3	5.3	2.26	68.2	70.3
Democratic Yemen	2,066	3,309	1.8	2.7	2.9	46.1	51.3	2.7	47.6	18.8	3.35	46.5	36.9
Iraq	15,158	24,926	2.7	3.4	2.9	46.8	50.7	2.6	44.9	10.7	3.25	59.0	70.9
Jordan	3,375	6,400	3.1	3.7	4.0	49.4	47.5	3.1	44.9	8.4	3.60	64.2	62.5
Kuwait	1,703	2,969	5.4	5.3	2.8	42.6	55.9	1.4	36.8	3.5	3.00	71.2	87.1
Lebanon	2,644	3,617	2.2	-0.0	1.9	40.1	54.5	5.4	29.3	8.8	1.85	65.0	75.5
Oman	1,181	1,909	1.9	4.5	2.8	44.0	53.4	2.6	47.3	15.9	3.45	49.7	6.6
Qatar	291	469	6.7	4.0	2.7	32.6	65.1	2.2	30.1	4.6	3.30	70.6	82.9
Saudi Arabia	10,824	18,864	2.3	3.9	3.2	43.3	53.9	2.8	43.0	12.1	3.45	56.0	64.9
Syrian Arab Republic	10,189	18,102	2.5	3.7	3.3	47.5	49.3	3.2	46.5	7.2	3.50	67.0	51.3
United Arab Emirates	1,255	1,916	2.5	5.8	1.9	29.0	69.0	2.0	27.0	4.0	2.90	70.6	53.3
Yemen	6,386	9,859	1.8	2.4	2.8	45.8	51.0	3.3	48.5	21.6	3.30	44.0	10.2
Non-Arab Countries	53,686	74,602	2.9	2.3	1.8	38.0	57.0	5.0	31.7	8.8	2.10	63.8	51.5
Cyprus	659	759	1.4	1.1	0.8	24.3	65.4	10.3	19.7	8.2	1.12	74.3	45.6
Israel	4,216	5,376	6.6	2.1	1.3	33.2	58.4	8.4	23.6	6.8	1.50	74.0	90.5
Turkey	48,811	68,466	2.7	2.3	1.9	38.6	56.7	4.6	32.5	.0	2.17	63.0	48.2

Table 7.5.　*contd*

Country or area	Population (thousands)		Annual growth			Age distribution of population 1980			Crude vital rates 1980–5 (per 1000 population)		Gross reproduction rate 1980–5	Expectation of life 1980–5 (years)	Percentage of urban population 1980
	1984	2000	1950–5	1980–5	1995–2000	0–14	15–64	65+	Births	Deaths			
F. Europe	490,259	510,197	0.8	0.3	0.2	22.3	64.7	13.0	14.0	10.9	0.93	72.9	70.4
17. *Eastern Europe*	112,285	120,393	1.0	0.6	0.4	23.5	64.6	11.9	16.4	10.9	1.05	71.5	59.3
Bulgaria	9,184	9,685	0.7	0.5	0.3	22.2	65.8	12.0	15.4	10.7	1.09	72.4	4.0
Czechoslovakia	15,575	16,679	1.1	0.4	0.5	24.0	63.3	12.7	16.1	12.0	1.07	71.3	63.0
German Democratic Republic[5]	16,647	16,459	-0.5	-0.1	-0.0	19.5	64.2	16.3	12.5	13.9	0.80	72.4	77.3
Hungary	10,772	10,816	1.0	0.1	0.1	21.5	65.0	13.5	14.4	13.1	1.00	70.6	54.6
Poland	37,216	41,222	1.9	0.9	0.6	24.1	65.9	10.0	18.5	9.1	1.09	71.8	56.6
Romania	22,891	25,531	1.4	0.8	0.7	26.5	63.1	10.4	17.4	9.8	1.19	70.8	48.1
18. *Northern Europe*	82,054	82,929	0.4	0.1	0.0	21.4	64.1	14.6	12.8	12.0	0.87	73.7	85.1
Denmark	5,138	5,091	0.8	0.1	-0.1	20.9	64.9	14.2	11.1	11.1	0.74	74.6	84.2
Finland	4,861	4,947	1.1	0.4	0.0	20.1	67.9	12.0	12.7	10.2	0.78	73.4	63.1
Iceland	240	269	2.0	1.0	0.6	27.0	63.5	9.6	17.0	6.9	0.99	76.5	88.7
Ireland	3,553	4,228	-0.3	1.1	1.1	31.0	57.9	11.1	20.9	10.0	1.55	72.7	56.2
Norway	4,137	4,204	1.0	0.3	0.0	22.2	63.2	14.6	12.3	10.7	0.82	75.5	52.4
Sweden	8,286	8,081	0.7	0.0	-0.2	19.6	64.3	16.2	10.5	11.5	0.75	75.9	87.2
United Kingdom	55,592	55,849	0.2	-0.0	0.0	21.1	64.1	14.8	12.9	12.6	0.87	73.4	91.2
19. *Southern Europe*	141,822	152,262	0.8	0.6	0.4	24.0	64.3	11.7	15.4	9.7	1.03	73.0	62.7
Albania	2,984	4,089	2.4	2.2	1.7	37.3	57.9	4.8	27.8	5.9	1.75	70.7	36.8
Greece	9,900	10,752	1.0	0.6	0.5	22.9	63.9	13.3	15.8	9.5	1.12	75.0	59.9
Italy	56,644	57,635	0.6	0.2	0.0	21.8	64.7	13.5	12.8	10.8	0.88	73.6	70.3
Malta	380	418	0.1	0.7	0.5	23.0	67.1	9.9	17.3	10.4	0.95	71.9	77.5
Portugal	10,005	10,949	0.5	0.7	0.5	26.1	63.5	10.4	17.8	10.0	1.11	70.5	30.9
Spain	38,700	43,217	0.8	0.8	0.6	25.9	63.2	10.9	17.0	8.9	1.17	74.0	74.1
Yugoslavia	23,022	25,103	1.4	0.8	0.5	24.4	66.4	9.2	16.4	8.9	1.00	71.0	42.3

Table 7.5. *contd*

Country or area	Population (thousands)		Annual growth			Age distribution of population 1980			Crude vital rates 1980-5 (per 1000 population)		Gross reproduction rate 1980-5	Expectation of life 1980-5 (years)	Percentage of urban population 1980
	1984	2000	1950-5	1980-5	1995-2000	0-14	15-64	65+	Births	Deaths			
20.　Western Europe^y	154,198	154,613	0.8	0.1	-0.0	20.4	65.4	14.2	11.7	11.3	0.77	7.39	77.5
Austria	7,484	7,454	0.0	-0.1	-0.0	20.4	64.1	15.5	12.1	12.8	0.79	72.7	54.0
Belgium	9,872	9,867	0.5	0.0	0.0	20.1	65.6	14.3	12.1	12.3	0.78	73.1	72.2
France	54,453	56,588	0.8	0.3	0.2	22.2	64.0	13.7	13.8	10.7	0.89	74.1	77.5
Germany, Republic of^8	61,212	59,456	0.9	-0.2	-0.2	18.6	66.3	15.0	10.2	12.0	0.69	73.3	83.7
Luxembourg	363	356	0.6	-0.1	-0.1	19.7	66.3	14.0	10.1	12.0	0.67	72.6	76.7
Netherlands	14,452	14,957	1.2	0.4	0.1	22.1	66.4	11.5	11.6	8.7	0.70	75.7	75.5
Switzerland	6,309	5,871	1.2	-0.3	-0.5	18.1	67.1	14.8	8.1	10.7	0.65	75.8	58.9
G. Oceania	24,458	30,410	2.2	1.5	1.3	29.5	62.6	7.9	21.1	8.4	1.32	67.6	74.9
21.　Australia–New Zealand	18,781	22,368	2.3	1.2	1.0	25.9	64.8	9.3	16.1	7.8	0.96	74.1	87.4
Australia	15,518	18,675	2.3	1.3	1.1	25.6	65.1	9.3	16.2	7.7	0.97	74.3	87.4
New Zealand	3,263	3,693	2.3	0.8	0.7	27.1	63.6	9.3	15.6	8.1	0.90	73.4	87.4
22.　Melanesia	4,158	6,165	1.6	2.8	2.2	42.8	54.1	3.2	40.4	12.7	2.92	55.0	27.5
Papua New Guinea	3,601	5,292	1.6	2.7	2.2	42.4	54.3	3.2	40.4	13.6	2.92	53.3	27.3
Other Melanesia^w	557	873	2.0	3.2	2.5	45.0	52.2	2.8	39.9	6.6	2.90	66.8	28.7
23.　Micronesia-Polynesia	1,519	1,877	2.8	1.7	1.1	40.7	56.1	3.1	32.1	5.4	2.08	69.3	40.9
Micronesia^x	348	437	2.7	1.7	1.3	41.1	55.6	3.3	34.9	8.5	2.43	62.7	39.1
Polynesia	1,171	1,440	2.8	1.7	1.0	40.6	56.3	3.1	31.3	4.4	1.98	71.6	41.5
Fiji	674	821	3.0	1.7	1.0	36.9	60.0	3.1	27.2	4.1	1.55	72.5	42.2
Other Polynesia^y	498	619	2.5	1.7	1.1	45.6	51.3	3.1	36.8	4.9	2.70	70.6	40.6
H.　24.　USSR	276,066	313,940	1.7	1.0	0.7	24.3	65.6	10.0	18.8	9.0	1.15	71.3	63.2

Source: Data compiled by the population division of the Department of International Economic and Social Affairs of the United Nations Secretariat. This table is published as an Annex to the *United Nations Concise Report on The World Population Situation in 1983:* ST/ESA/SER.A/85, Department of International Economic and Social Affairs, No. 85, United Nations, New York, 1984.

Notes: Crude vital rates are average annual births and deaths per 1,000 population at the middle of the period. Gross reproduction rates are sums of average rates of female births to women by age during the period indicated. Expectation of life is average of expectations for males and females at birth, based on average death rates by age during the period indicated. Population totals may not agree with sums of figures for component areas because of rounding or omission of small populations.

a Data for small countries or areas, generally those with a population of 300,000 or less in 1975, are not given separately in this table but have been included in the regional population figures.

b More developed regions include Northern America, Japan, all regions of Europe, Australia–New Zealand and the union of Soviet Socialist Republics.

c Less-developed regions include all regions of Africa, all regions of Latin America, China, other East Asia, all regions of South Asia, Melanesia and Micronesia–Polynesia.

d Including British Indian Ocean Territory, Djibouti and Seychelles.

e Including Agalesa, Rodrigues and St. Brandon.

f Including São Tomé and Principe.

g Including Western Sahara.

h Including St. Helena.

i Including Dominica, Grenada, Saint Lucia and Saint Vincent and the Grenadines.

j Including Antigua, Bahamas, British Virgin Islands, Cayman Islands, Montserrat, Netherlands Antilles, St. Kitts-Nevis-Anguilla, Turks and Calcos Islands and United States Virgin Islands.

k Including Belize and Panama Canal Zone.

l Including Falkland Islands (Malvinas).

m Including French Guiana.

n Including Bermuda, Greenland and St. Pierre and Miquelon.

o Including Macau.

p Including Brunei.

q Including Maldives.

r Including Gaza Strip (Palestine).

s The data which relate to the Federal Republic of Germany and the German Democratic Republic include the relevant data relating to Berlin for which separate data have not been supplied. This is without prejudice to any question of status which may be involved.

t Including Channel Islands, Faeroe Islands and Isle of Man.

u Including Andorra, Gibraltar, Holy See and San Marino.

v Including Liechtenstein and Monaco.

w Including New Caledonia, Norfolk Island, Solomon Islands and Vanuatu.

x Including Canton and Enderbury Islands, Christmas Island, Cocos (Keeling) Islands, Johnston Island, Midway Islands, Pitcairn Island, Tokelau and Wake Islands, Kiribati, Guam, Nauru, Niue, Pacific Islands and Tuvalu.

y Including American Samoa, Cook Islands, French Polynesia, Samba, Tonga and Wallis and Futuna Islands.

at the end of 1975 stood at 838.8 million and India's at 613.2 million. Each was considerably bigger than Europe's 473 million, Latin America's 324 million, the Soviet Union's 255 million, North America's 236 million, and Oceania's 21.3 million. Indonesia and Japan had over 100 million each, and outside Asia their populations were exceeded only by those of the Soviet Union and the United States. Despite their separation in 1971, Pakistan with 70.5 million people and Bangladesh with 73.7 million still counted among the world's ten most populated countries. Three Asian countries – re-unified Vietnam, Thailand and the Philippines – had each gone past the 40 million mark and were experiencing an annual population increase of 1 million or more.

A prominent feature of the region's population was its rapid growth. In the first half of the decade (1970–75) that growth averaged 2.3 per cent growth annually, higher than the world average of 1.8 per cent for the same period and exceeded only by Africa's 2.6 per cent and Latin America's 2.7 per cent. Other regions had far lower growth rates. Europe averaged only 0.6 per cent, the Soviet Union 0.9 per cent and the United States of America 0.8 per cent. A notable exception in Asia was Japan which, after a long, almost imperceptible, process spanning a century, completed its demographic transition in the 1950s. In 1975, Japan had low birth rates and low death rates, a fairly stable age structure and a low net reproduction rate – factors which pointed to eventual cessation of growth. A few other countries, like China and other areas in East Asia, seemed to be moving in the same direction, but paucity of data (as in China's case) and the presence of many variables, made it difficult to predict how soon their transition would be completed.

The most rapid population growth was being experienced in Middle South, Eastern South, and Western South Asia, where growth rates had gone up to 2.4–2.8 per cent annually, compared to just 2 per cent for all Asia in the 1950s and less than 1 per cent in the first half of this century.

In numerical terms, the dimensions of such growth seemed even starker. In 1800 Asia's population was only about 600 million. It took a century to grow to 925 million – a gain of slightly over 50 per cent. By 1920, the figure had exceeded 1 billion. Net additions had grown progressively larger ever since. The population doubled only 50 years after reaching the billion mark. The third billion was expected by 1990 and, if growth rates remained at their current high levels, Asia in the year 2000 would have had 3.6 billion people – exceeding the earth's total population in 1970.

In its World Development Report 1984, the World Bank observed that the 930 million people of Bangladesh, India, Nepal, Pakistan and Sri Lanka comprised between one-fifth and one-quarter of the population of developing countries. Although incomes in South Asia were among the lowest in the world, the region's fertility had already fallen substantially. In Sri Lanka, for example, the total fertility rate fell from 5.5 in 1960 to 3.5 in 1974; in India, it dropped from 6.5 in the 1950s to 4.8 in 1982. The Bank noted that progress in South Asia had not been uniform and rapid population growth was a source of continuing concern. The experience in Sri Lanka and in some Indian states suggested that much more could be done to bring about fertility decline. In every country there was considerable scope for reducing infant mortality, raising the legal marriage age and increasing female education – all of which would have a profound effect on fertility. To satisfy unmet needs, family planning programmes must resolve important issues of access and quality.

Turning to East Asia, the Bank noted that countries there had experienced marked declines in fertility in the last decade. Total fertility (less than 3) and rates of natural increase (about 1.5 per cent a year, 2.2 per cent excluding China) were the lowest of any developing region. *For the most part, the Bank observed, recent declines in fertility had occurred in countries where fertility was already lower than would be expected, given the region's income.* The most dramatic reductions had been in China: total fertility dropped from 7.5 to 2.3 over the past two decades, despite a per capita income of only $310 in 1982. Indonesia, the Philippines and Thailand had also experienced remarkably rapid falls in fertility with only modest increases in income. However, the Bank noted that replacement level fertility was still a long way off for Burma, Indonesia, Malaysia, the Philippines, Thailand and Vietnam with total fertility rates of at least 3.6; total fertility in Korea, at 2.7, was also still above replacement level.

Though contraceptive use was higher in East Asia than in most other developing regions, the Bank noted there was still considerable unmet need for contraception. Low and high estimates of unmet need were 19–49 per cent of married women of child bearing age in the Philippines (1978); 20–31 per cent in Indonesia (1976), 15–26 per cent in Thailand (1981), and as much as 30 per cent in Korea (1979).

Some countries had overlooked potentially important methods of family planning (for example, the Indonesian programme did not offer sterilisation). The Bank

Table 7.6.   Birth-rates and change, 1965–70 and 1975–80, ESCAP region (Asia and the Pacific).

Country or area	Crude birth rate (per 1000 population)		Percentage change 1965–70 to 1975–80	General fertility rate (per 1000 women aged 15–49)		Percentage change 1965–70 to 1975–80
	1965–70	1975–80		1965–70	1975–80	
ESCAP region	37	29	–20	164	124	–24
East Asia	31	21	–32	137	87	–36
China	32	21	–34	149	90	–40
Hong Kong	24	19	–21	104	74	–29
Japan	18	15	–15	63	56	–11
Mongolia	42	37	–11	182	162	–11
Republic of Korea	32	25	–21	138	100	–28
South East Asia	42	35	–16	180	147	–18
Burma	40	39	–4	166	164	–1
Democratic Kampuchea	44	31	–30	189	123	–35
Indonesia	43	34	–22	183	139	–24
Lao People's Democratic Republic	45	44	–2	190	190	0
Malaysia	39	33	–15	181	140	–23
Philippines	41	36	–11	183	153	–16
Singapore	25	17	–31	109	63	–42
Thailand	42	32	–23	187	137	–27
Vietnam	41	40	–3	173	168	–3
Middle South Asia	43	38	–13	194	164	–15
Afghanistan	50	48	–3	219	219	0
Bangladesh	50	47	–6	233	217	–7
Bhutan	45	43	–4	192	187	–3
India	42	35	–16	186	151	–19
Iran	45	44	–2	213	202	–5
Nepal	46	44	–4	191	194	2
Pakistan	47	43	–8	224	199	–11
Sri Lanka	32	28	–12	141	115	–18
Oceania	24	22	–11	106	91	–14
Australia	20	17	–16	84	68	–19
Fiji	32	29	–11	140	111	–21
New Zealand	23	18	–21	100	74	–26
Papua New Guinea	42	42	0	191	193	1

Source: Selected papers; Third Asian and Pacific Population Conference (Colombo, September 1982). *Asian Population Studies Series* No. 58, Economic and Social Commission for Asia and the Pacific, Bangkok, Thailand. Published by the United Nations, New York, 1984.

observed also that, given the relatively advanced state of population policies, more use could be made of incentives and disincentives.

Among the countries of East Asia, China, Singapore and, to a lesser extent, Korea, had made greatest use of measures to promote small families. The Bank noted that most governments had not chosen to promote such drastic measures as those in China with its complex structure of incentives, disincentives, and birth quotas to promote a one-child family. And few had the administrative control necessary to implement national schemes of deferred payments or social security to promote smaller families.

In China the one-child policy had been challenged by an apparent preference for sons. The same bias in favour of sons existed in Korea and had been partly responsible for keeping total fertility, now at 2.7, from declining to replacement level. 'To counteract this bias,' the Bank suggested, 'governments need public information campaigns and legal reforms of inheritance, property rights and employment. Incentives might also be offered to one- or two-child families with girls such as lower educational and medical costs or preferred access to schooling.'

These comments by the World Bank in its 1984 Report are instructive. They make it clear that much more remained to be done in Asia if fertility rates were to be brought down towards replacement levels for the continent as a whole.

At the same time, it was plain that Asia had much to offer the rest of the world. Asia had longer experience than any other developing region with interventions to modify reproductive behaviour. As already noted, the region had witnessed the adoption of family planning as a national policy by India in the 1950s and in a few other countries, such as Pakistan (which then included Bangladesh) and Malaysia in the 1960s. By the time of the World Population Conference in Bucharest in 1974, 17 Asian countries had population policies and almost all countries had family planning programmes. As Dr Nafis Sadik, who would later succeed Rafael Salas as Executive Director of UNFPA, commented:

> In general, Asian countries have had the least problems in legitimising family planning as a means of achieving smaller family size and, consequently, lower fertility rates. The first United Nations meeting on family planning in the region, sponsored by ESCAP (then ECAFE) in 1966, was on the management of family planning rather than on the justification for family planning.[5]

In the run-up to the Mexico City Conference, it seemed that it would be easier perhaps for the United Nations than for other (less obviously neutral or impartial) organisations to draw on this Asian experience in the formulation and implementation of population policy so as to deploy Asian expertise both within and outside the region.

LATIN AMERICA

From a demographic point of view, Latin America was commonly divided into three sub-regions: Temperate (Argentina, Chile and Uruguay); Central or Middle America (Mexico, Panama, Nicaragua, Costa Rica, Guatemala, Honduras and El Salvador); and Tropical which includes the other nations of South America, along with the Caribbean Islands of Cuba, the Dominican Republic and Haiti.[6]

The three temperate-zone countries were fairly homogeneous. These populations were characterised by large proportions of European migrants, high educational levels, low rates of population growth, small proportions engaged in agriculture, and low fertility and mortality. With a total population of approximately 45 million (1984) and an average density of 16 persons per square kilometre, their annual growth rate, on average, was 1.6 per cent and life expectancy at birth was – in the early eighties – around 68 years.[7]

In contrast, the regions of Middle America and tropical South America showed markedly higher growth rates, 2.7 per cent and 2.4 per cent respectively per annum. With fertility levels of 4.8 per woman and 4.1 per woman as well as a lower expectation of life – about 65 and 63 years respectively, those regions had much in common with other developing areas of the world.

According to estimates made by CELADE (the UN's Latin American Centre for Demographic Studies, based in Santiago, Chile), for the latter half of the 1950s, birth rates were 45 or more in 14 of the 20 Latin American countries. In a number of them birth rates seemed to be rising and, with few exceptions, the high and possibly rising rates were sustained in the face of low death rates, high urbanisation, moderately high literacy, and rising per capita product. According to J. Mayone Stycos:

> Impressive post-World War II economic gains and moderate social progress in the ten largest countries appeared to have no impact on overall fertility levels, leading to speculation that Roman Catholic resistance to birth control and a Luso-Espanic culture favouring large families make Latin America an exception to the theory that economic modernisation eventually leads to low fertility.[8]

Stycos noted that there had been other ideological streams as important as Catholicism in inhibiting family planning programmes. Nationalism, coupled with the belief that a nation's economic and military power was enhanced by a large and rapidly growing population, had been characteristic of the political right, while the Marxists' traditional opposition to Malthusian doctrines had been salted with the notion that population pressures were a useful precipitant of revolution:

> Both left and right have been vociferous in identifying family planning with North American Imperialism. US President Lyndon Johnson's dictum that five dollars invested in population control is worth a hundred dollars in economic growth was widely interpreted as proof that pills at worst were being substituted for Imperialist bullets, or at the very best were to be a cheap substitute for economic assistance.

In such an atmosphere, Stycos suggested, the pioneering efforts of private family planning organisations were critical. Spearheaded by organisers from the International Planned Parenthood's Western Hemisphere branch, local footholds were established before 1960 only in the English-speaking Caribbean and Puerto Rico, but by the mid-1960s they were in nearly all the Latin American nations. The later private programmes met much less opposition from governments than the earlier ones, for the international climate had become favourable to family planning. Also, policy makers had available, in many instances for the first time, two consecutive decennial censuses that conclusively demonstrated extraordinary rates of population growth.

By the early 1970s most governments had added family planning to Social Security and Health Ministries' services, usually rationalised as anti-abortion or maternal and child health programmes. By the mid-1970s some countries were evidencing case loads of a magnitude sufficient to effect substantial reductions in birth rates.

Towards the mid-1970s, most governments had come to accept the view that demographic factors played a significant role in the process of socio-economic planning. By the early eighties, seven Latin American countries – Costa Rica, the Dominican Republic, El Salvador, Guatemala, Mexico, Nicaragua and Peru – perceived their rates of growth as being too high, and pursued policies to alter spatial distribution and international migration patterns, and directly or indirectly to lower fertility. Brazil, Colombia, Cuba, Ecuador, Haiti, Honduras, Panama and Venezuela perceived their rates of growth and fertility rates as satisfactory. Nonetheless, they all provided some form of government support for family planning, sometimes directly through the public health structure or, less frequently, by tacit endorsement of a non-governmental group.

According to their official statements, Argentina, Bolivia and Chile desired high rates of growth. Argentina and Bolivia did not limit access to family planning services but did not provide government-subsidised services, whereas Chile provided some direct support for family planning.

Most Caribbean governments had at least an implicit policy to slow down the rate of population growth and many had enacted measures to achieve this objective. Barbados, Dominica, Grenada, Jamaica and Trinidad and Tobago had implemented a family planning programme. Although the Bahamas, St Lucia and St Vincent did not have government support and interventions for this purpose, access to contraceptives was not restricted. Guyana and Surinam regarded their growth rate and fertility rates as acceptable.

In its World Development Report 1984, the World Bank pointed out that almost all of the countries in Latin America and in the Caribbean were middle-income, but with great demographic diversity. In four countries with per capita incomes exceeding US $2,500 – Argentina, Chile, Trinidad and Tobago, and Uruguay – population growth had slowed to below 2 per cent a year and total fertility was nearing replacement level. The highest fertility in the region was in six lower-middle-income countries: Bolivia, Ecuador, El Salvador, Guatemala, Honduras, and Nicaragua. Total fertility in these countries exceeded five and population growth ranged from 2.5 to 3.4 per cent. Fertility was high in the Caribbean, with the exception of Cuba, but emigration moderated population growth.

The Bank commented that in three countries, Brazil, Colombia and Mexico (which accounted for almost two-thirds of Latin America's population), fertility was consistently and inversely related to household income and to education. Surveys in Brazil indicated that poor rural women bore twice as many children as did women from the upper 40 per cent of urban households. Brazilian women who neither had paid jobs nor had completed primary school had more than twice as many children as working women who completed secondary school. Similar differentials occurred in Mexico and Colombia. The well-to-do were able to spend more per child than were the poor and they had fewer children. But the Bank went on to say:

> Population policies have helped to reduce fertility in Latin America. In 1966 Colombia's Ministry of Health signed an agreement with a private medical association to provide a programme of training and research that included family planning. By combining low-key public support with private family planning programmes, the Colombian Government has helped facilitate a rapid fertility decline.

> The Mexican Government adopted a population policy to reduce fertility in 1973 and began providing family planning services in 1974. By 1976 contraceptive use had doubled, almost entirely because of public programmes. Between 1970 and 1980 fertility fell in both Mexico and Colombia by about one third: in contrast, it declined by less than 20 per cent in Brazil, a country in which the national Government had not committed itself to a population policy or programme.

> This contrast becomes even sharper when it is noted that per capita real incomes nearly doubled in Brazil but were up only 50 per cent in Colombia and Mexico. Whereas Colombia and Mexico managed a sharp decline in fertility in relation to income growth. Brazil's fertility decline was more modest. If Brazil had followed the pattern of Colombia and Mexico, its total fertility rate would have fallen to 3.0 by 1982 given its income growth; in fact it was 3.9. With a population policy no more vigorous than that of Colombia and Mexico during the 1970s, Brazilian fertility might now be one quarter lower than it is. Most of the difference would come from lower fertility among the poor, since it is they who would be assisted most by a public policy.[9]

NORTH AFRICA AND MIDDLE EAST

Karol J. Krotki, in his regional survey of North Africa and the Middle East, writes that the area has an ideological unity, having become Muslim within a few decades of the Hegira (AD 622) and having remained so ever since.

> The religious, cultural, political and economic explosion of the seventh century is the last of the three mono-theistic movements of this area, after Judaism and Christianity. The population of the area, more than 200 million by 1980, is a minor although central part of the Islamic populations of the world. Religious uniformity is paralleled by an ethnic and linguistic unity, for 19 of the 23 units are predominantly Arabic (the exceptions are Cyprus, Israel, Sudan, and Turkey).[10]

Population size in the Arab countries differed substantially from one country to another. At one extreme was Egypt with a population of about 46 million in 1984, and on the other Qatar with around 290,000.

Population size and growth rates in the Arab countries are shown in Table 7.7.

Table 7.7. Population and growth rates – Arab countries (in thousands).

Country	Official population based on census		Population 1975		Growth rate 1970–5 % per year	Years for population to double	Population 1980*
	Year	Population	UNESCO	UN			
Morocco	1971	15,380	17,540	17,504	2.92	24	20,255
Mauritania	1972	1,180	–	1,283	1.99	35	1,417
Algeria	1966	12,000	16,908	16,792	3.35	21	19,854
Tunisia	1975	5,810	5,810	5,810	2.24	33	6,502
Libya	1973	2,291	2,255	2,255	3.50	20	2,686
Egypt	1976	38,000	37,140	37,543	2.38	29	42,278
Sudan	1973	14,900	18,268	18,268	3.04	23	18,312
Somalia	1972	2,941	–	3,170	2.56	27	3,603
Syria	1970	6,303	7,606	7,259	3.30	21	8,561
Lebanon	1970	2,126	2,720	2,869	2.50	27	3,251
Jordan	1970	2,320	–	2,688	3.29	21	3,169
Iraq	1965	8,262	11,124	11,067	3.36	21	13,092
Kuwait	1975	995	1,188	1,085	7.13	10	1,550
Bahrain	1971	216	262	251	7.10	10	358
Qatar	1976	180	163	92	7.10	10	232
Emirates	1971	217	345	222	7.10	10	492
Oman	no census		700	766	3.50	20	912
Saudi Arabia	1974	7,013	–	8,966[†]	2.94	24	8,124
Yemen, A.	1975	5,300	5,300	6,668	2.90	24	6,127
Yemen, D.	1973	1,590	1,695	1,660	2.90	24	1,959

*Based on 1970–5 annual growth rate.
[†]Overestimate.

Source: Cairo Demographic Centre, 1970; UNESCO 1977; UN Secretariat, 1975; UN Statistical Office, 1974. Table given in *Population in the Arab World: Problems and Prospects* by Abdel-Rahim Omran, published by Croom Helm, London 1980.

During the period 1970 to 1975, the rate of population growth in the Arab countries was generally high with some variation between countries. The highest rate was registered for Kuwait (7.13 per cent per year), due to high fertility, decline in mortality, and substantial immigration. Among other countries, Saudi Arabia had high fertility but its mortality rate was high enough to offset the population growth rate somewhat, keeping it at a level of 2.9 per cent per year. High population growth rates were shared by Algeria, Jordan, Morocco, Oman, Sudan, Syria and the Yemens. Mauritania had the lowest growth rate, probably due to the high mortality rate of 25 per 1000. In Lebanon, the high growth rate was attributed to declining mortality.

The demography of each country was almost the same throughout the region: early marriage of females, high proportions of the population marrying, no illegitimacy, high marital fertility, high remarriage rates of males, with simultaneous or consecutive polygamy taking up the remaining females.

With the exceptions of Cyprus and Israel, and to a lesser extent Egypt, Lebanon, Tunisia and Turkey, the countries of North Africa and the Middle East were – at the beginning of the 1980s – still experiencing high fertility. Krotki commented: 'It is seldom that such high rates are reliably reported for large human populations.'[11] And Omran remarked that there was no doubt that the fertility level of the Arab populations was probably the highest in the world.

> Over the five year period 1970–1975 the average birth rate for the Arab World was 45 per 1000 population, with several countries reaching 50 births per 1000 population. These figures can be compared with 32 in the world as a whole and 17 in the more developed countries . . . in general, fertility is higher in the Asian than in the African regions of the Arab World. It is also relatively high in the oil-rich countries, both Asian and African, than in other countries. Fertility is moderate only in Tunisia, Egypt, and possibly certain areas of Lebanon.[12]

Omran went on to say:

> Reproductive behaviour among Arab women in different countries has some common features. In most countries, fertility is high with child bearing starting early and continuing throughout the reproductive span. The age at marriage is generally low with marriage being universal. There is a traditional preference for sons and large families. Fertility in the Arab World is still viewed as a major basis for determining the wife's status in the family and community and a sign of virility for men.

Omran did not, however, conclude that the situation was without hope. He believed there was convincing evidence from at least three Arab countries – Tunisia, Lebanon and Egypt – that fertility could decline in response to family planning efforts without drastic changes in societal values and beliefs and without substantial socio-economic development comparable to the Western model.

SUB-SAHARAN AFRICA

In its 1986 survey of population growth and policies in sub-Saharan Africa, the World Bank noted that sub-Saharan Africa had about 9 per cent of the world's population and about one-fifth of its land, divided into some 48 countries with over 800 ethnic groups. By world standards, nearly all African countries had small populations. Only six (Nigeria, Ethiopia, Sudan, Tanzania, Kenya and Zaire) exceeded 20 million in 1984; except for Nigeria and Ethiopia with about 94 and 44 million respectively, none exceeded 35 million. Three quarters of sub-Saharan countries had fewer than 10 million people and nearly half had fewer than 5 million.

The rate of population growth in sub-Saharan Africa was extraordinarily rapid. Africa was the only region that had not had a fall in population growth rates. Apart from a brief baby boom after World War II, growth rates in the industrial countries had been declining for decades and in some countries were at or below zero. The population growth rate for Latin America peaked at 2.9 per cent a year in the early 1960s and had fallen to 2.3 per cent in the early eighties. *But in sub-Saharan Africa growth rates were continuing to rise, from 2.5 per cent a year in 1960 to 3 per cent a year in 1983.* If these rates were to continue, sub-Saharan Africa's population of 459 million (1985) would double in just 22 years.

The World Bank noted that Africa's rapid population growth resulted from a steady fall in death rates and no fall – indeed, in some countries an increase – in birth rates. In the previous 20 years the average crude death rate for all of sub-Saharan Africa fell by one third to 15.9 per thousand – in itself a success. Yet the average crude birth rate

Table 7.8. Birth-rates, death-rates, and rates of natural increase: Sub-Saharan Africa and selected other developing countries.

Region and country	Crude birth-rate per thousand population 1983	Crude death-rate per thousand population 1983	Growth rates 1983 (per cent)
Sub-Saharan Africa			
Cameroon	46	15	3.2
Ethiopia	41	20	2.1[a]
Ghana	49	10	3.9
Ivory Coast	46	14	4.2
Kenya	55	12	4.3
Mali	48	21	2.3
Nigeria	50	17	3.3
Senegal	46	19	2.8
Sudan	46	17	2.8
Tanzania	50	16	3.4
Uganda	50	19	3.3
Zaire	46	16	3.1
Zambia	50	16	3.4
Zimbabwe	53	13	4.0
Other regions			
Bangladesh	42	16	2.6
China	19	7	1.2
Colombia	28	7	1.9
India	34	13	2.2
Indonesia	34	13	2.1
Mexico	34	7	2.5
Philippines	31	7	2.3
Peru	34	11	2.3
Thailand	27	8	1.9

[a] This unusually low rate for Ethiopia reflects the famine in 1983.
Source: World Bank: *World Development Report 1985*, p. 212.

changed hardly at all. (By contrast, birth rates as well as death rates were declining in all other continents.) Table 7.8 shows 1983 levels for African and other selected countries: in Africa, birth rates were almost all very high; death rates varied more but, compared to non-African countries, were not particularly low. Indeed, they could be expected to fall further in the decade ahead.

Over the previous 40 years life expectancy had risen substantially in Africa, to average about 50 years at birth. In the 1950s life expectancy of under 40 years, with corresponding infant mortality rates of 200 or more, was common; life expectancy over 50 was rare. By the 1980s, however, few countries had life expectancies below 45. Some had climbed above 55, with corresponding infant mortality rates of less than 100. Although the average level of mortality in Africa was still the highest in the world, some countries in eastern and southern Africa had achieved life expectancies comparable to countries in other developing regions.

By contrast, fertility in Africa was extremely high by world standards. In most African countries, total fertility rates were over 6. Several were over 7, with rates in Eastern Africa generally higher than in Western Africa. Most rates below 6 reflected involuntary pathological sterility. Meanwhile total fertility rates in China, Thailand and Indonesia had fallen from the peak of 5–6 to 2–4. In other areas such as Central America, the Middle East and North Africa, and the Muslim parts of the Indian subcontinent, total fertility rates of up to 7 could be found. But the rates of 7–8 in Eastern and Southern Africa and occasionally in West Africa were almost unparalleled elsewhere. The Bank summarised the situation as follows:

> Other developing regions have achieved a demographic transition: both death rates and birth rates have declined from high levels. Africa has begun its demographic transition with death rate declines but has yet to achieve the second stage of falling birth rates. With the exception of Zimbabwe, no documented cases of national fertility decline has occurred in Africa.

In November 1985, Mr Robert McNamara, former president of the World Bank, delivered the Sir John Crawford Memorial lecture in Washington DC, on 'the Challenges for sub-Saharan Africa.'[13]

> The most important long-term issue is the rampant growth of population. For most countries in Africa that issue constitutes a ticking time-bomb.

Table 7.9 was used by McNamara to illustrate the possible course of African demographic development. The assumptions concerning the future tempo of fertility decline in the African countries, incorporated in the projections, reflected the judgement – or the hope – that the high fertility rates, which were still increasing in some countries, would start to decline well before the century's end, and that then the downward trend would be precipitous and sustained until replacement-level fertility was achieved. These were, McNamara said,

> heroic assumptions. They require that the move from high fertility to replacement-level fertility – which took about a century and a half in the United States – be completed within a drastically shorter time span in Africa. They envisage no possibility of temporary reversals or pauses on the downward course of fertility. They allow for no 'baby booms' such as the West experienced once replacement fertility had been attained.

He continued:

> And yet the populations that must conform to these demanding assumptions are largely poor and rural. They are populations in which security and old age is still

Table 7.9. African population projections, 1980–2100 (population in millions).

Selected Countries	1950	1980	2000	2025	2050	2100	Total fertility rate, 1983	Year in which NRR = 1[a]
Cameroon	4.6	8.7	17	30	42	50	6.5	2030
Ethiopia	18.0	37.7	64	106	142	173	5.5	2035
Ghana	4.4	11.5	23	40	53	62	7.0	2025
Kenya	5.8	16.6	37	69	97	116	8.0	2030
Malawi	2.9	6.0	11	21	29	36	7.6	2040
Mozambique	6.5	12.1	22	39	54	67	6.5	2035
Niger	2.9	5.5	11	20	29	38	7.0	2040
Nigeria	40.6	84.7	163	295	412	509	6.9	2035
Tanzania	7.9	18.8	37	69	96	120	7.0	2035
Uganda	4.8	12.6	25	46	64	80	7.0	2035
Zaire	14.2	27.1	50	86	116	139	6.3	2030
Other Sub-Sahara	59.8	121.7	218	381	524	651	6.5	2040
Total Sub-Sahara	172.4	363.0	678	1,202	1,658	2,041	6.7	2040
Other Africa	42.6	89.6	148	225	282	319	5.5	2025
Total Africa	215.0	452.6	826	1,427	1,940	2,360	6.5	2040

[a] NRR refers to net reproduction rate. When NRR = 1, fertility is at replacement level.

Source: Sir John Crawford memorial lecture, *The Challenges for Sub-Saharan Africa* by Robert S. McNamara, November 1, 1985, published by the World Bank.

derived primarily from the support of one's children. Many are populations with religious and cultural values that place a high premium on fertility.

And even if such heroic assumptions proved to be borne out by events, by the year 2025 Kenya would be four times the size it was in 1980; Nigeria and Ghana would have grown more than three-fold; all of the other countries would have at least tripled; and the population of sub-Saharan Africa as a whole would have risen from 363 million to 1201 million.

Looking at the implications of rapid population growth for sub-Saharan Africa, McNamara noted that countries 'will find it increasingly difficult to reverse the 20-year decline in per capita food production'. Sub-Saharan Africa would almost certainly find it impossible to achieve and maintain a rate of growth in food production that exceeded its current population growth rate of 3.2 per cent. Agricultural growth rates that high had been achieved by very few countries, and only then under the most favourable conditions. 'The reality is that agriculture in sub-Saharan Africa is unlikely to grow at more than 2.5 per cent per year for at least the next two decades. Thus, the already high levels of malnutrition will grow even worse, and punishing years of famine will become even more frequent.'

Another serious consequence of the runaway population growth rate would be mounting unemployment. By the end of the century, industry and agriculture combined would be able to absorb only about half of the projected increase in the labour force.

The present population explosion would also aggravate the ecological vulnerabilities of the continent. Already the pressures had led to a significant decline in wood resources. The demand for firewood had increased so intensely that it had resulted in widespread deforestation. This in turn had brought on severe fuel shortages.

> In many countries of West Africa families that traditionally cooked two meals a day now have fuel for only one hot meal a day, or one every other day. Thus deforestation is beginning to lead to an accelerated degradation of the basic life-support system. . . . The population problem in Africa is clearly related to its growing ecological difficulties.

High population growth rates would also put heavy strains on already overburdened educational and health care systems. Countries such as Kenya faced a doubling or tripling of their school-age population within the next 15 years. Growth rates such as these would immensely exacerbate the problems of expanding these services to anything approaching required levels.

The high fertility rate – an average of 6.7 children per woman in 1983 – was the result of a broad mix of economic, social and cultural forces. These included such factors as the early age of marriage for African girls; the diminishing practice of prolonged breastfeeding, and of sexual abstinence after childbirth; and the very limited use of modern contraception. Fewer than 5 per cent of couples used contraceptives in sub-Saharan Africa, as compared with some 30 per cent in India and some 70 per cent in China.

The high fertility rates, McNamara suggested, were due in part also to the low relative status that women had in African societies. Though both males and females derived benefits from children, it was generally the women who bore most of the costs. In addition to the health risks of bearing children women often had the major financial responsibility for raising them. This was particularly true in polygamous households where each wife had primary responsibility for her own children.

> Men, on the other hand, enjoy the benefits of children at a much lower cost. They are less involved in their day-to-day care, less concerned with their health, educational and emotional needs, and hence less conscious of the costs to the children of having many siblings. Thus, to the extent that males continually dominate the decision to have another child, fertility is likely to remain high.

McNamara pointed out, however, that recent surveys of a number of African countries had indicated that women too expressed a very high demand for children. The surveys showed that even though most married women already had six children, more than 80 per cent wanted still more. In six of the countries surveyed, women said they wanted between six and nine offspring.

McNamara noted that until quite recently many African leaders regarded population growth as a distinct asset, rather than a potential hazard. They had not fully realised the inevitable consequences of runaway growth rates. 'Population control', furthermore, was often a sensitive political issue in Africa, particularly when different groups in a society competed for power and resources.

> The perception, moreover, that much of the pressure for small families comes from western aid donors leads to resentment and inaction on the part of the officials. Government commitment is further constrained by the lack of recent and reliable demographic data. Many countries do not have a history of census-taking, and even when censuses have been taken, political controversy has often prevented them from being public. The result is that the size of the population and its rate of

growth in countries such as Guinea, Nigeria and Zaire are not known with any degree of certainty.

McNamara noted that as recently as 1974 – the year of the United Nations World Population Conference held in Bucharest – only two countries, Kenya and Ghana, had adopted policies to moderate their population growth. However, there are signs that 'at least on the surface, the attitudes of sub-Saharan African Governments are beginning to change.' He cited the Kilimanjaro Programme of Action on Population, a document adopted in January 1984, when representatives from most African Governments met at the Second African Population Conference, sponsored by the United Nations in Arusha, Tanzania. The Conference recommended, among other things, that *'population should be seen as a central component in formulating and implementing policies and programmes for accelerated socio-economic development plans'*, and that *'Governments should ensure the availability and accessibility of family planning services to all couples or individuals seeking such services freely or at subsidised prices.'*

If McNamara's memorial lecture has been quoted at some length, it is because he summarised in stark terms the demographic situation in Africa in the middle of the 1980s and the dimensions of the task which confronted most countries in Africa if they were to bring their birth rates down. That task involved:

First, improving understanding in African countries as to the nature of the problems posed by population growth and promoting greater support and political commitment to the solution of those problems;

Second, implementing development strategies and information and education programmes that build demand for smaller families;

Third, supplying safe, effective and affordable family planning and other basic health services targeted particularly at the reduction of high infant and childhood mortality and focused on the poor in rural and urban settings.

REVIEW AND APPRAISAL OF THE WORLD POPULATION PLAN OF ACTION

With the approach of the tenth anniversary of the World Population Conference, the United Nations undertook a substantive Review and Appraisal of progress made in implementing the World Population Plan of Action (WPPA) adopted at Bucharest in 1974. The Review and Appraisal noted that, in the decade since Bucharest, world population had grown from 4 billion to 4.8 billion, or roughly by one-fifth. Of the increase, 90 per cent occurred in the less developed regions of the world. During the ten year period, it was estimated that the annual rate of growth of the world population had declined from 2.0 per cent to 1.7 per cent. Declines had occurred in the developed as well as in the developing countries. Among the latter group, the decline observed in China was of the most significance. Birth rates in that country had dropped to around 20 per thousand with the rate of natural increase around 1.3 per cent per annum. Since 1971, birth planning in China had been considered as an integral part of other social and economic planning. If China was excluded from the group of developing countries, the decline in the rate of growth of this group, although still noticeable, was far less significant (from 2.5 to 2.1 per cent per year). This was due to the fact that the fertility decline in developing countries, a decline of about 15 per cent in terms of the total fertility rate, was almost offset by a corresponding decline in mortality.

The deceleration did not occur evenly among the various regions. For the developing countries as a whole, the decline in the rate of growth was from 2.5 per cent per annum in 1970–5 to 2 per cent in 1980–5: the corresponding decline for the developed countries was from 0.9 to 0.6 per cent. The declines were most marked in Asia, which reduced its rate of growth by 50 per cent (from 2.4 to 1.2 per cent per annum) and least in Africa, where the rate probably rose (from 2.7 to 3.0 per cent per annum).

There was evidence that an increasing number of countries had formulated policies concerned with population growth as such. As of mid-1983, about two thirds of all countries indicated that they had formulated an explicit policy with respect to population growth. *The most important change that was observed over the decade was a decline in the number of countries that viewed their rate of population growth as too low. It was estimated that one country in five held that position in 1974, whereas a survey among governments showed that it had declined to one in ten by 1983.*

The latest population projections (Tables 7.10, 7.11 and 7.12) indicated that the growth rate of the world population would decline much slower than during the previous ten years or it might even turn to increase between 1984 and the end of this century. During this period, the growth rate was projected to reach 1.5 or 1.8 per cent (from the present 1.7 per cent) according to the medium and high variant of the United Nations projections, respectively. The major reasons why the growth rate was expected to decrease more slowly or even turn to increase in the future were:

(a)   because of the already low level of fertility in East Asia and the effects of a less favourable age composition, a further reduction of the growth rate in this region would become more and more difficult in the near future;

(b)   the very low fertility rates in the developed countries were expected to remain near the current levels;

(c)   a moderate rise of growth rate could continue in Africa for the rest of this century owing to the persistently high level of fertility levels and the slow but continuing improvement in life expectancy for the region.

These projections suggested that world population growth would continue to be sustained during the rest of this century *unless further actions significantly altered the projected trends.* For the world as a whole, the current annual increment of 78 million was projected to increase to 89 million by 1995–2000, which was more than the current population of Mexico. In the 16 years from 1984 to 2000, the world population was expected to increase by 1.3 billion, from 4.8 billion in 1984 to 6.1 billion in 2000, an increment greater than the combined current populations of Africa and Latin America. Of this increase, 56 per cent would occur in Asia, 25 per cent in Africa and 11 per cent in Latin America.

Uncertainty about the future course of demographic changes, which depended in part on the future paths of social and economic development and on the intensity of Governments' actions in the field of population, was reflected in the high and low variants of projections. It was noted that the range of possible outcomes was by no means trivial. For example, the difference between the high and low variants for the world population in the year 2000 was 500 million (6.4 and 5.9 billion, respectively), which was approximately the current size of the population of Africa.

Table 7.10. Projected (1983) population and percentage increase according to three variants: world, more-developed and less-developed regions, 1975–2100.

	Population (millions)				Percentage increase		
Year	Medium variant	High variant	Low variant	Period	Medium variant	High variant	Low variant
World							
1975	4,076	4,076	4,076	1975–2000	50.2	56.1	44.6
2000	6,123	6,363	5,895	2000–25	33.3	44.1	23.2
2025	8,162	9,171	7,263	2025–50	16.6	26.8	5.8
2050[a]	9,513	11,629	7,687	2050–75	6.1	14.8	−0.3
2075[a]	10,097	13,355	7,662	2075–2100	0.9	6.3	−1.8
2100[a]	10,185	14,199	7,524				
More-developed regions							
1975	1,095	1,095	1,095	1975–2000	16.2	19.9	12.8
2000	1,272	1,313	1,235	2000–25	8.6	15.8	2.1
2025	1,382	1,521	1,261	2025–50	1.4	5.8	−5.3
2050[a]	1,402	1,610	1,194	2050–75	1.2	5.6	−3.6
2075[a]	1,419	1,701	1,151	2075–2100	0.1	1.9	−1.2
2100[a]	1,421	1,733	1,137				
Less-developed regions							
1975	2,981	2,981	2,981	1975–2000	62.7	69.4	56.3
2000	4,851	5,050	4,660	2000–25	39.7	51.5	28.8
2025	6,779	7,649	6,002	2025–50	19.6	31.0	8.2
2050[a]	8,111	10,018	6,493	2050–75	7.0	16.3	0.3
2075[a]	8,677	11,654	6,511	2075–2100	1.0	7.0	−1.9
2100[a]	8,764	12,466	6,387				

[a] The long-range projections, 2050–2100, are taken from: United Nations Secretariat. Long-range global population projections, as assessed in 1980, *Population Bulletin of the United Nations*, No. 14–1982 (United Nations publication. Sales No. E.82.XIII.6).

Source: Results of United Nations demographic estimates and projections as assessed in 1982. Table printed in *United Nations Concise Report on the World Population Situation in 1983*: ST/ESA/SER.A/85,

Since the present unprecedented rapid growth of world population was likely to continue for quite a while, it was only natural to ask what would eventually happen to the size and structure of the world population. In the United Nations, experimental calculations had been attempted, assuming that life expectancy at birth in all parts of the world would eventually reach the level currently considered as maximum (78.7 years for both sexes), and that fertility levels would eventually converge to, or fluctuate around, the replacement level (net reproduction rate of one).

According to these long-range projections (medium variant), the world population would reach 8.2 billion by 2025, exceed 9.5 billion by 2050, and ultimately stabilise at 10.2 billion near the end of the twenty-first century. The expected maximum size of the world population would be slightly more than twice the current one. By then, the proportion of the world population living in the currently developing countries would have risen from the present 74 per cent to 86 per cent. The average annual increment

Table 7.11. Population and annual rate of increase: world and major areas (medium variant) 1980–2025.

Area	Population (millions)							
	1980	1985	1990	1995	2000	2010	2020	2025
World	4,453	4,842	5,249	5,677	6,123	6,987	7,793	8,162
Africa	476	553	645	753	877	1,170	1,488	1,642
Latin America	362	406	453	501	550	647	742	787
North America	252	263	275	287	298	319	339	348
East Asia	1,182	1,252	1,317	1,390	1,470	1,589	1,662	1,696
South Asia	1,408	1,572	1,740	1,909	2,074	2,379	2,654	2,771
Europe	484	492	499	505	510	515	518	518
Oceania	23	25	27	29	30	34	38	40
USSR	265	279	291	303	314	334	352	361

Area	Annual rate of increase (percentage)							
	1975–80	1980–5	1985–90	1990–5	1995–2000	2000–5	2010–15	2020–5
World	1.77	1.68	1.61	1.57	1.51	1.38	1.15	0.93
Africa	2.99	3.00	3.08	3.09	3.05	2.96	2.56	1.96
Latin America	2.37	2.30	2.19	2.02	1.85	1.69	1.43	1.17
North America	1.07	0.90	0.88	0.83	0.75	0.68	0.66	0.49
East Asia	1.42	1.14	1.02	1.08	1.11	0.91	0.48	0.40
South Asia	2.30	2.20	2.03	1.85	1.65	1.44	1.17	0.86
Europe	0.40	0.32	0.28	0.24	0.22	0.13	0.05	0.02
Oceania	1.65	1.50	1.43	1.37	1.28	1.20	1.08	0.90
USSR	0.93	0.97	0.90	0.76	0.72	0.64	0.55	0.52

Source: Results of United Nations demographic estimates and projections as assessed in 1982. Table printed in *United Nations Concise Report on the World Population Situation in 1983*: ST/ESA/SER.A/85, Department of International Economic and Social Affairs, No. 85, United Nations, New York, 1984.

to the world total during the first quarter of the next century would be over 80 million. In the second and third quarters, there would be significant reductions in the annual increment, down to 53 and 23 million per year, respectively. The average annual increment was expected to become minimal only in the last quarter of the twenty-first century.

In the low variant, it was calculated that the total population of the world would peak at 7.7 billion in 2060, but in the high variant it would exceed 14 billion in the 22nd century (it would be even higher under the 'constant fertility' assumption). The difference between the high and low variant estimates, which was more than six billion, was mainly caused by the differing fertility assumptions. The year in which the replacement level is reached in all the regions of the world (Africa happens to be the last region to do so) was assumed to be 2065 in the high variant, 2010 in the low variant, and 2035 in the medium variant.

Figure 7.1 shows the past and projected evolution of fertility for the world as published by the UN in 1983. It covers the more developed and less developed countries and major areas for the period between 1950–1955 and 2020–2025. The figure depicts fertility estimates and projections in terms of the gross reproduction rate which represents the average number of daughters that would be born to a cohort of

Table 7.12. Population of the 12 most populous countries, 1980, and annual rate of increase (medium variant) 1980–2025.

Country	Population (millions)							
	1980	1985	1990	1995	2000	2010	2020	2025
China	1,003	1,063	1,120	1,184	1,256	1,362	1,429	1,460
India	689	761	832	899	962	1,113	1,154	1,189
USSR	265	279	292	303	314	334	352	361
United States of America	228	238	248	259	268	287	306	313
Indonesia	151	165	178	192	204	228	248	255
Brazil	121	136	150	165	179	207	234	246
Japan	117	120	123	125	127	130	129	128
Bangladesh	88	101	115	130	146	177	206	219
Pakistan	87	102	113	128	143	173	201	213
Nigeria	81	95	113	135	162	228	302	338
Mexico	69	79	89	99	109	128	146	154
Germany, Federal Republic of	62	61	61	60	59	57	54	53

Country	Annual rate of increase (percentage)							
	1975–80	1980–5	1985–90	1990–5	1995–2000	2000–5	2010–15	2020–5
China	1.44	1.17	1.04	1.12	1.17	0.95	0.51	0.43
India	2.15	1.99	1.78	1.55	1.34	1.09	0.87	0.58
USSR	0.93	0.97	0.90	0.76	0.72	0.64	0.55	0.52
United States of America	1.05	0.87	0.86	0.82	0.75	0.68	0.65	0.49
Indonesia	2.14	1.77	1.57	1.46	1.27	1.15	0.89	0.62
Brazil	2.31	2.23	2.07	1.87	1.67	1.51	1.26	1.00
Japan	0.91	0.57	0.43	0.40	0.40	0.29	−0.09	−0.15
Bangladesh	2.83	2.73	2.61	2.46	2.24	2.04	1.61	1.26
Pakistan	2.96	3.08	2.16	2.44	2.16	2.02	1.63	1.17
Nigeria	3.49	3.34	3.49	3.56	3.57	3.49	3.01	2.27
Mexico	2.86	2.59	2.39	2.16	1.92	1.70	1.36	1.08
Germany, Federal Republic of	−0.06	−0.18	−0.15	−0.17	−0.22	−0.39	−0.49	−0.50

Source: Results of United Nations demographic estimates and projections as assessed in 1982. Table printed in *United Nations Concise Report on the World Population Situation in 1983*: ST/ESA/SER.A/85, Department of International Economic and Social Affairs, No. 85, United Nations, New York, 1984.

women during their reproductive ages, assuming no mortality and a fixed schedule of age-specific fertility rates. The UN projected that, for the world as a whole, this rate would decline from 1.91 in 1975–1980 to 1.38 in 1995–2000 and to 1.13 in 2020–2025. During the latter part of the century, the decline would accrue mainly to the less developed regions, falling from 2.26 to 1.47 between 1975–1980 and 2000–2005. By 2025, the gross reproduction rates of the more developed and less developed regions would be, respectively, 1.04 and 1.15.

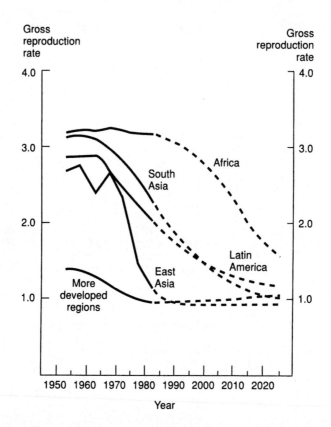

Fig. 7.1. Gross reproduction rate by region, medium variant, 1950–2025, as assessed in 1982.

Notwithstanding the progress made over the previous decade or so, the projections published by the United Nations in 1983 in the run-up to the International Conference on Population that would be held in Mexico City in August 1984 illustrated dramatically the magnitude of the tasks which still lay ahead.

NOTES

1. The discussion that follows is based both on these relatively reliable statistics and on United Nations estimates for other countries.
2. United Nations, Concise Report on the World Population Situation in 1983, United Nations New York, 1984.ST/ESA/SER.A/85. Sales No. E.83.XIII.6.
3. United Nations, op. cit., p. 30.
4. United Nations, World Population Situation in 1983, p. 31.
5. Sadik, op. cit., p. 34.
6. Article by J. Mayone Stycos on Latin American Demography. International Encyclopedia of Population, p. 405.
7. Sadik, op. cit., p. 61.
8. Stycos, op. cit.
9. World Bank, World Development Report, 1984.
10. *International Encyclopaedia of Population.* Article by Karol J. Krotki p. 477.

11. op. cit.
12. Abdel-Rahim Omram. Population in the Arab World, Problems and Prospects, published by Croom Helm Ltd, London, 1980, p. 77.
13. Published by the World Bank, Washington DC.

8

The International Conference on Population, 1984

In 1981, in a report addressed to the Economic and Social Council, the United Nations Population Commission recommended 'the convening of a new population conference'. In the light of that report and of other considerations, the Council adopted Resolution 1981/87 of 20 November 1981 by which it decided, inter alia

> to convene in 1984, under the auspices of the United Nations, an International Conference on Population open to all States as full members and to the specialised agencies, bearing in mind that it should be conducted with the utmost economy in size, duration and other cost factors and the need to utilise extrabudgetary resources for its financing to the maximum extent possible.

The Council further decided the Conference should 'be devoted to the discussion of selected issues of the highest priority', and made certain recommendations concerning preparations for the Conference. By the same resolution the Council designated the Population Commission as the Preparatory Committee for the Conference and requested the Secretary General to appoint the Executive Director of the United Nations Fund for Population Activities to serve as Secretary-General of the Conference and the Director of the Population Division of the Department of International Economic and Social Affairs as Deputy Secretary-General.

The Government of Mexico offered to act as host to the Conference, an offer which was accepted by the Economic and Social Council with gratitude in its resolution of 27 July 1982.[1]

The Mexico City Conference could in a sense be seen as the culmination of a remarkable decade. As we have seen in the previous chapter, official support of population and family planning programmes had strengthened in many parts of the world and at the same time there had been dramatic falls in fertility. As delegates left their home countries for Mexico City in that summer of 1984, it seemed reasonable to expect that a new international consensus would be forged, one built on a far more solid basis than had been available at Bucharest, ten years earlier where, truth to tell, the plaster had barely covered the cracks in the agreement.

THE US POSITION

In the event, hopes of a trouble-free meeting were rudely torpedoed right at the start of the Mexico City Conference by – of all countries – the United States of America. On 8 August, James L. Buckley, a former Conservative Senator and head of the United States delegation to the Conference, elaborated on the themes already advanced in a US policy paper. Blithely ignoring the fact that it had been largely US influence and US pressure which had contributed to the major expansion of population activities at the international level over the last two decades, Buckley assured the conference that:

> First, and foremost, population growth is, of itself, neither good nor bad. It becomes an asset or a problem in conjunction with other factors, such as economic policy, social constraints, and the ability to put additional men and women to useful work. People, after all, are producers as well as consumers.

He went on to refer to the experience of Hong Kong and South Korea.

> They have few natural resources, and over the past 20 years they have experienced major increases in population, yet few nations have experienced such rapid economic growth. We believe it is no coincidence that each of these societies placed its reliance on the creativity of private individuals working within a free economy.

The second main theme of Buckley's speech was its clear statement of US policy on abortion. He said that, over the past decade, the United States had not allowed its population assistance contribution to be used to finance or promote abortion. The present policy tightened this existing restraint in three ways.

> First, where US funds are attributed to nations which support abortion with other funds, the US contribution will be placed into the segregated accounts which cannot be used for abortion; second, the US will no longer contribute to separate nongovernmental organisations which perform or actively promote abortion as a method of family planning in other nations; and third, before the US will contribute funds to the United Nations Fund for Population Activities, it will first require concrete assurances that the UNFPA is not engaged in, and does not provide funding for, abortion or coercive family planning programmes. Should such assurances not be possible, and in order to maintain the level of its overall contribution to the international effort, the United States will redirect the amount of its intended contribution to other, non-UNFPA family planning programmes.
>   When efforts to lower population growth are deemed advisable, US policy considers it imperative that such efforts respect the right of couples to determine the size of their own families. Accordingly, the United States will not provide family planning funds to any nation which engages in forcible coercion to achieve population goals.

To what extent the US position at Mexico, as set out in the position paper and Buckley's speech, was simply a reflection of domestic politics was a matter of speculation. Writing in the London *Sunday Times*, Rosemary Righter clearly took the view that internal political considerations were a determining factor.

> The Reagan administration's team, headed by the Conservative ex-Senator James Buckley, a Roman Catholic, will arrive with speeches and policies which pander to the phobias of the anti-abortion Moral Majority and the arch-conservative lobbies in the US, and which also plainly have an eye on the Republican Party convention the following week.[2]

The same newspaper commented in its lead editorial:

> Two immensely powerful leaders, the Pope and President Reagan, are combining to do mankind a profound disservice. Even though human fertility has diminished in the past ten years, the prospect is still that today's 4.8 billion people will grow to something between 10 billion and 12 billion before the numbers finally stabilise. Even attaining the lower figure will require an unprecedentedly determined mobilisation of the world's social resources. Yet the Vatican with its grim opposition to any 'artificial' form of birth control, and the White House, with its decision to withhold funding from anybody that even countenances abortion, are sabotaging much of the necessary effort before it can even begin.[3]

If the US statements amazed journalists and leader-writers around the world, it disturbed the delegates at Mexico even more. Leon Tabah, the former director of the Population Division of the United Nations and a member of the French delegation to the International Conference on Population, commented:

> the developing countries gave the impression they were living in a baffling world and attending a no less baffling Conference. After being to some extent upset by the impatience and the excessive eagerness of rich countries to obtain prompt results on the family-planning front, they heard at Mexico, voiced by the most activist, that population was a mere 'neutral factor' at a moment when they, the developing countries were finally ready to accept the idea of curbing their population growth. At a working group dealing with redrafting a proposed American amendment on population and development trends over the last decade which took a generally 'rosy' view of things, I was struck by the attitude of African delegates. They were insisting that development in Africa had proceeded at a slower rate than stated by the American draft. They said that poverty was growing in Africa while population growth was continuing at a high pace, mortality levels were falling short of the objectives set by the Bucharest Conference, and food availability was declining.[4]

CHINA'S RESPONSE

The US bombshell rocked the consensus which had been so hardly won at Bucharest, but it did not destroy it. Counter-attacking in measured tones, China's delegate, Mr Wang Wei, stressed that China 'as a developing socialist country' had been making unremitting efforts to develop her economy while controlling rapid population growth. The natural population growth rate had dropped to 1.154 per cent in 1983 from 2.089 per cent in 1973. 'All this has proved that the policy decision of promoting family planning to control population growth along with planned economic development is a correct one.'

And he defended not only the decision itself but also the programme methods.

> Since 1979, the Chinese Government has advocated the practice of '1 couple, 1 child'. This, however, does not mean that one couple should have one child only in every case. The Government gives guidance for the implementation of family planning programmes in the light of specific conditions such as economic developments, cultural background, population structure and the masses' wishes in different localities. The requirements are more flexible in rural areas than in urban areas and more so among the people of national minorities than among the people of the Han nationality. In rural areas, those couples who have actual difficulty and wish to

have two children may have a second birth with planned spacing. At present, the women with single-children account for only 21.2 per cent of all the married women of reproductive age who have children. The advocacy of the practice of '1 couple, 1 child' is a policy of a specific historical period in China. Our family planning policy is based upon actual conditions and is reasonable, and thus has gained the masses' support.

Mr Wang Wei did not, in this Plenary speech, speak directly about abortion. He affirmed that in carrying out its family planning programme, China had consistently adhered to the principle of 'integrating state guidance with the masses' voluntariness'.

The Government has always emphasised the importance of encouraging the people's own initiatives, through publicity and education, which is the key link in implementing the family planning programme. We rely upon hundreds of thousands of full-time and part-time family planning workers, masses' organizations and other social potentials in disseminating constantly and extensively family planning policies and the knowledge about contraception and prevention of genetic and birth defects. We have maintained the principle of taking contraception as the main method, providing multiple services, free of charge, for the users to choose from.

And as though he intended deliberately to indicate China's view of the threats and warnings contained in the stated US position, the Chinese delegate addressed himself deliberately to the area of international collaboration.

In the past decade, the relevant organizations of the United Nations, especially the UNFPA headed by Dr Salas, have exerted fruitful efforts and made important contributions to the implementation to the World Population Plan of Action and so did some international non-governmental population and family planning organizations. In seeking the solution to its population problem, China mainly relies upon its own efforts. At the same time, it also attaches great importance to the development of friendly international co-operation with the United Nations population agencies and some non-governmental organizations in the population and family planning field; it has also established bi-lateral relations of co-operation with some countries. We wish to make further efforts to strength such friendly co-operation.

As a counter-balance to the United States, the position of China was crucial. Actions spoke louder than words. China's demographic achievements were plain for all to see. Privately there were several even among the United States delegation (which included veteran 'populationists' like Philander P. Claxton) who were ready to admit that those achievements were not all brought about by the unfettered operation of the 'free-market economy'.

But quite apart from China's conversion, since Bucharest, into a wholehearted protagonist of population policies, it was clear to anybody who heard the speeches in the Plenary or read the texts that the basis of the consensus (leaving the United States' quixotic intervention aside) was a good deal stronger at Mexico than it had been at Bucharest. Some countries, whose enthusiasm for population policy and family planning had in 1974 been at best lukewarm, were far more positive ten years later. Other countries which at Bucharest had been actively hostile had, by the time the Mexico Conference came round, modified their views even to the point of adopting a position of guarded neutrality. Brazil was a case in point.

BRAZIL

It was symbolic perhaps of the new atmosphere that the leader of the Brazilian delegation, Dr Walyr Mendes Arcoverde, Minister of State for Health, was the first to speak in the Plenary debate after the formalities of the opening session were over.

Dr Arcoverde reminded delegates that Brazil was firmly convinced that the deliberations of the 1984 International Conference on Population must be based, as in 1974, on two premises: (a) strict respect of states' sovereignty with regard to the definition and implementation of their national population policies; and (b) the recognition that social and economic development is the central factor in the solution of demographic problems.

Brazil rejected the 'apocalyptic perspective which preceded both the convening of the Bucharest Conference and the 1972 Stockholm Conference on the Human Environment'.

> We cannot accept the simplistic diagnosis which blames demographic growth as the source of the developing countries' ills. Moreover, we cannot admit that the population control prescription be one more magic solution for the problems of poverty, hunger and disease which affect the greater part of humanity. The seriousness of our subject does not allow the uncritical acceptance of imported demographic models, nor does it lend itself to pious exhortations of the 'put your own house in order' type, a kind of advice that can certainly be applied both ways. In short, my delegation understands that population policies must not be considered as a replacement for development policies, nor can they constitute a form of escapism from the responsibilities of international cooperation.

Dr Arcoverde referred in particular to the debt crisis among developing nations, and especially in Latin America. 'The world goes today through an economic crisis of unprecedented proportions. Nevertheless, contrary to the conservationists' diagnosis, this did not come about as a result of an exhaustion of resources or of a demographic explosion.'

Having thus established his credentials as it were, the Brazilian delegate went on to deal with the population situation in his own country. Brazil had the world's sixth largest population: 120 million inhabitants according to the 1980 census. For more than a century, the Brazilian population had been doubling practically every 30 years. Approximately 3.1 million individuals were being added each year to the country's population. Though, since 1960, the rate of total growth of the population, which was at 2.48 per cent per annum between 1970 and 1980, had been declining, the relatively young age of the Brazilian people would lead to an absolute increase in the population for many years, with a probable duplication of the present stock in little more than four decades.

> The Brazilian Government is wholly conscious of the challenge presented by the growth of its population. The acuteness of this challenge is particularly noticeable in a time of economic crisis induced by factors which are largely beyond national control and in a situation where the levels of consumption and employment are being compressed.

Dr Arcoverde went on to explain in very clear terms the present position of the Brazilian Government as far as population policy and family planning were concerned:

> The Government is aware of the fact that today the Brazilian people increasingly demands knowledge and adequate means for planning its reproduction. As I have already stressed, my Government's answer to this demand is ethically grounded: it

is based on the recognition that the planning of the number of offspring is one of the fundamental rights of the human being. As the Brazilian Government sees it, this matter must not be subject to goals which are established beforehand; on the contrary, it should be the result of a social consensus. According to this view, the legitimate growth-rate for Brazil is that which corresponds to the sum total of the free and well-informed decisions of these couples and individuals who aim at planning their reproductive life.

For these reasons Dr Arcoverde explained, Governmental interference in birth control was not to be found in Brazil. However, the state played a decisive role, namely that of assuring everyone's right to health care, whether or not the population was on the increase.

As the Minister of Health for my country, I wish to lay particular stress on this point. In fact, since the 1970s, the Brazilian Government has been willing to incorporate into the field of health care those activities related to family planning. The President of the Republic has just approved a set of guidelines, according to which family planning will be considered as an integral part of public health activities.

NIGERIA

If Brazil was an example of one major country which was moving, however cautiously, in the right direction along the spectrum of demographic policies, Nigeria was another. The Nigerian delegate told the meeting that, at the Bucharest Conference, his country's position was that the capacity of the Nigerian economy, which was then growing at the rate of 12 per cent per annum (during a period of economic boom) to cope with a population growth rate of 2.5 per cent per annum was not in doubt. However, two national development plans had been launched since the 1974 conference in Bucharest and there had been a certain evolution in thinking. The crude birth rate was about 50 per 1000 while the crude death rate was about 17 per 1000, resulting in an annual growth rate of 3.3 per cent. Average family size was about six children. The estimated population for 1984 was slightly over 90 million and by the year 2000, the population was expected to increase to well over 150 million.

The Government now recognises, more than ever before, the fact that the overall rate of growth has to be brought down to the level which will not impose excessive burdens on the economy in the long run. The Government plans to achieve this through an integrated approach to population planning. The Government is not only concerned about the rate of growth of the population but also the spatial distribution and the effects of early and frequent childbearing on mothers and their children. The primary concern is with the wellbeing of the family as a social unit and of the nation in general. The issue of fertility regulation and child-spacing is being viewed within the context of national goals and objectives, as well as the aspirations of the people. These goals and objectives include the provision of basic health care for the entire population by the year 2000 through the Nigerian Primary Health Care System and active support for family planning activities during the current Plan period as part of the basic health care system, so such families willing to take advantage of such services may have easy access to them.

Given the importance of Nigeria in the context of African demography, this shift of position was highly significant, even if any practical effect in terms of fertility reductions had yet to be realised.

KENYA

Kenya, on the other side of the African Continent, was another example of a country where there had been an evolution since Bucharest, though in Kenya's case the significant developments were more at the level of practical implementation of a long-agreed programme than of basic policy formulation. (The Kenyan Government adopted an official population policy and family planning programme as early as 1965 – the first sub-Saharan country to do so.)[5]

Mr Mwai Kibaki in his speech outlined the basic demographic facts. Population growth in Kenya had been rapid. The population grew from 5.4 million in 1948 to 8.6 million in 1962, a 59 per cent increase in 14 years. It increased from 10.9 million in 1969 to 15.3 million in 1979, an increase of 78 per cent in only ten years. In the period before 1962 the population grew by less than 3.0 per cent per annum, between 1962 and 1969 by about 3.3 per cent per annum, and between 1969 and 1979 by just over 3.5 per cent per annum. Data from the 1977–1978 Kenya Fertility Survey recorded a rate of 4.1 per cent per annum and it was evident from these data that the rate of population growth had been increasing since around 1962.

The Government had established the National Council for Population and Development in December 1982. This Council, which brought together all the Governmental and non-Governmental agencies dealing with family planning matters, had the primary responsibility of developing national policies. The Council was also charged with the responsibility for introducing information and education programmes towards the establishment of a small family norm.

Mr Kibaki went on to outline the steps that Kenya was actually taking to put its population policy into practice:

> Kenya has realised that rapid population growth frustrates her efforts to provide the population with the basic-needs services of education, health, housing, food and employment. For this reason we have given a lot of thought on how to mount an effective family planning programme while at the same time realising that family planning is not the panacea of all population issues. The strategies that are going to be enacted will basically involve recruiting a large force of family planning acceptors through:

(a)   making contraceptives accessible to all clients by increasing service delivery points from 400 now to 800 by 1986;
(b)   using medical practitioners to dispense contraceptives freely to suitable clients;
(c)   using rural and urban shops to sell certain types of contraceptives through an organised 'social marketing';
(d)   using community-based delivery systems.

> Kenya has realised that satisfied clients are the best recruiters. For instance, in agriculture, introduction of hybrid maize or high grade dairy cattle has been very successful because neighbours have been able to observe the benefits enjoyed by the participating farmers in the form of higher yields. Kenya will be using local and satisfied family planners as educators, informants, recruiters and promoters.

Higher yields in terms of maize, lower yields in terms of babies – two facets of the same problem!

TURKEY

Progress was also to be noted in the Middle East.

Mr Mehmet Aydin, Turkey's Minister of Health and Social Assistance, told the Conference that Turkey believed that by adopting effective population policies she would be able to maintain a rate of population growth which was in harmony with her economic and development goals. He drew attention to a pronouncement about family planning in the Muslim scriptures:

> the Holy Koran in its Surah Enfal set out the family edict 14 centuries ago: 'Beware that you will be examined and put to test on account of your children and property'. This edict imposes on the parents the responsibility of proper upbringing of their children. Should they be unable to fulfil this duty because of their economic and social position they would suffer divine responsibility. For this reason parents should have no more children than they can appropriately care for. The rationale for all this is a self-imposed discipline which encompasses flexibility of choice.

He said that the fall in Turkey's rate of population increase had been sustained during the past decade. While the percentage increase was 2.50 per annum in the 1970s, in the 1980s it had been brought down to 2.06 per annum. Measures were now being taken so that family planning services could be made available to those requesting them throughout the country, as affirmed by the Turkish Constitution. 'With the new measures' Mr Aydin said, 'we are hoping to bring the population growth rate down to 1.76 per cent by the year 2000'.

INDONESIA

As at Bucharest, some of the most powerful advocates of population policies and programmes came from the Asian countries. Emil Salim, Indonesia's Minister of State for Population and Environment, told the Conference that achievements since Bucharest were 'significant, but not sufficient'. The annual rate of world population growth had declined from 2.03 per cent in 1974 to 1.67 per cent in 1984. This reduction, however, had been influenced mainly by the achievements of China and the industrialised countries.

> The world is already facing today the problem of poverty, heart-rending and spirit-killing poverty in most developing countries. Population growth in many developing countries already outstrips the rate of development. Population pressure already threatens to deplete resources beyond our capabilities for sustaining the environment. Employment opportunities are already inadequate and unevenly distributed between and within countries, leading towards higher unequal distribution of income between and within countries. Population growth has raised population density and increased population mobility. If the total population of 4.8 billion persons today is already overburdened by these broad range of social problems which are undermining social solidarity among nations of the globe, then the impact of a rapidly increasing number of people under these circumstances may well lead towards a global social upheaval.

'Global social upheaval' – this was strong language but it was used deliberately. To avoid such upheaval, Salim told the Conference, it was 'imperative to launch a two-prong approach to development; first, a population-centred development policy. i.e. a development policy aimed at solving population problems; second, a development-oriented population policy, i.e. a population policy which stimulates development.'

He spoke of Indonesia's own commitments and argued strongly for concerted global action.

> We have passed the journey from Bucharest to Mexico City. Let us now move forward for the next journey from Mexico City to the goal of life with quality for all by the year 2000.

INDIA

Similarly, Mr B. Shankarananda, India's Minister of Health and Family Welfare, left the Conference in no doubt about India's determination to carry on with its family planning programme.

> India is the first country in the world to have adopted an official family planning programme as early as 1952. Since then increasing emphasis is being laid on this programme in our successive Five Year Plans. Family planning is an important component of our Prime Minister's new twenty-point Programme of socio-economic development. Recent trends in the Programme have raised hopes that we may be able to reach the goal we have set for ourselves of achieving a net reproduction rate of 1 by the year 2000. Our greatest hope is that a vast majority of people wish to limit the size of their families. We intend to cover 60 per cent of all eligible couples with effective contraception and achieve a crude birth rate of 21 per 1000, a crude death rate of 9 per 1000 and infant mortality rate of less than 60 per 1000 live births by the year 2000. This is a stupendous task. But we are confident that the goals are attainable. While we have spent over RS 14.5 billions in the Sixth Five Year Plan, we plan to spend RS 64 billion in the Seventh Five Year Plan. This is an indication of the growing resource needs of the population programme for developing countries in an atmosphere of resource constraints.

Mr Shankarananda warned the Conference that although the interplay between population and development was increasingly being recognised, the slogan 'development is the best contraception' had yet to move from the realm of rhetoric to something more serious. Poverty and rapid population growth reinforced each other in a vicious cycle. In breaking this cycle the donors and the developing countries had to cooperate with each other.

THE DEVELOPED WORLD

What then was the position of the donors at Mexico City in August 1984? Had there been any evolution in attitudes since Bucharest, any strengthening or weakening of commitment? Leaving aside the initial reservations that had been expressed by some of the industrialised countries at the idea of holding another World Population conference, as well as the particular circumstances of the United States discussed above, the answer on the whole is: yes.

The Scandinavian countries stood four-square behind the recommendations which emerged from the Mexico Conference, just as they had at Bucharest ten years earlier. The delegate from Sweden indicated that the Government would extend a 'substantial share' of Swedish official development assistance to population, family planning and related programmes. The delegate from Norway told the meeting that Norwegian development assistance was at present 1.15 per cent of the gross national product (GNP). Norway had decided in 1971 that 10 per cent of those allocations should be earmarked for population activities. In 1983, the Norwegian Parliament had stressed that '10 per cent should be considered as the lower limit for such allocations'. The delegate from Denmark spoke of his Government's 'high priority to continue to support developing countries in their efforts to implement population policies'.

Lord Glenarthur, leader of the United Kingdom delegation and parliamentary secretary of the Ministry of Health and Social Security, confirmed that the British Government was 'committed to continuing our development efforts and within them, our support for population-related activities'. He announced that in 1985, subject to Parliamentary approval, the United Kingdom Government intended to increase its overall contribution to multilateral organisations working in the population field by £1.5 million, bringing total contributions from the United Kingdom to such organisations to £9.5 million, a 50 per cent increase over the level of support provided in 1982.

The delegate of France, though not committed to massive support of family planning activities, nevertheless indicated that his Government was ready to extend considerable assistance in the field of demographic studies and spoke of the renowned and venerable institutions in France for whom the science of demography was meat and drink.

Most of the donors indicated that not only were they committed to increasing their support for population assistance, they also intended to increase the proportion of their aid given through multilateral channels. The United Nations Fund for Population Activities (UNFPA) and the International Planned Parenthood Federation (IPPF) were usually singled out for special mention in this connection. The delegate of the Federal Republic of Germany, for example, stated that his Government considered population policy to be an important component of its development aid strategy, believed that this was an area which, as much as any other, demanded the respect of national sovereignty, and concluded that 'an international organisation is thus particularly suitable to act as impartial counsellor and helper in this delicate field'. The Federal Republic of Germany would therefore continue its support through such international organisations as UNFPA and IPPF.

In view of the trouble which loomed on the not-so-distant horizon regarding the United States' contribution to UNFPA and IPPF, this announced readiness on the part of other donors to maintain or even increase their assistance for population activities was specially significant. Indeed, it might spell the difference between life and death as far as the continuation of viable international programmes was concerned.

What, precisely, were the areas where the Mexico City Conference could be regarded as an advance on Bucharest?

STATUS OF WOMEN

Without doubt, Mexico represented a net advance on Bucharest in the treatment it gave to the status and role of women.

On the opening day of the Conference, Queen Noor of Jordan had set the tone:

> The woman of the family is the single most effective agent for improving the socio-economic welfare of a community. Improving women's status might be the most cost-effective and efficient investment possible in the long run.

Queen Noor pointed out that of the 700 million illiterate people in the world, two-thirds were female; that women were generally in poorer health than men and that wage-earning women in industrialized countries worked longer hours, earned less money, had less free time and enjoyed fewer hours of sleep than men. If women's lot was improved, women would pass on their knowledge to their families, dramatically improve their welfare with an awareness of family planning and nutrition, and increase the family's standards of living with their extra income from work.

In its own Conclusions, the Mexico City Conference recalled that the World Population Plan of Action as well as other important international instruments – in particular the 1975 Mexico City Plan of Action, the 1980 Copenhagen Programme of Action for the United Nations Decade for Women and the Convention on the Elimination of all Forms of Discrimination Against Women – stressed the urgency of achieving the full integration of women in society on an equal basis with man and of abolishing any form of discrimination against women. Comprehensive strategies to address these concerns would be formulated at the 1985 Nairobi Conference which was being convened to review and appraise the achievements of the United Nations Decade for Women. The Conference observed that the ability of women to control their own fertility formed an important basis for the enjoyment of other rights; likewise, the assurance of socio-economic opportunities on an equal basis with men and the provision of the necessary services and facilities enabled women to take greater responsibility for their reproductive lives. The Conference therefore made several recommendations aimed at ensuring that women could effectively exercise rights equal to those of men and in all spheres of economic, social, cultural and political life, and in particular those rights which pertained most directly to population concerns.

These recommendations were also reflected in the Mexico City Declaration on Population and Development which stated:

> Improving the status of women and enhancing their role is an important goal in itself and will also influence family life and size in a positive way. Community support is essential to bring about the full integration and participation of women into all phases and functions of the development process. Institutional, economic and cultural barriers must be removed and broad and swift action taken to assist women in attaining full equality with men in the social, political and economic life of their communities. To achieve this goal, it is necessary for men and women to share jointly responsibilities in areas such as family life, child-caring and family planning. Governments should formulate and implement concrete policies which would enhance the status and role of women.

Access to Family Planning

Of special interest were the 11 recommendations which the Conference adopted on reproduction and the family. Though the World Population Plan of Action had recognized the basic human right of all couples and individuals to decide freely and responsibly the number and spacing of their children, many couples and individuals had been unable to exercise that right effectively, either because they lacked access to information, education and/or services or because, although some services were available, an appropriate range of methods and follow-up services was not. Data from the World Fertility Survey for developing countries indicated that, on average, over one-fourth of births in the year prior to the survey had not been desired. The Conference therefore recommended inter alia (Recommendation 25):

Governments should, as a matter of urgency, make universally available information, education and the means to assist couples and individuals to achieve their desired number of children. Family planning information, education and means should include all medically approved and appropriate methods of family planning, including natural family planning, to ensure a voluntary and free choice in accordance with changing individual and cultural values. Particular attention should be given to those segments of the population which are most vulnerable and difficult to reach.

This emphasis was also reflected in the Declaration on Population and Development which was adopted by acclamation at the 12th (closing) plenary meeting on 14 August 1984. Paragraph 13 of that Declaration read:

Although considerable progress has been made since Bucharest, millions of people still lack access to safe and effective family planning methods. By the year 2000 some 1.6 billion women will be of child bearing age, 1.3 billion of them in developing countries. Major efforts must be made now to ensure that all couples and individuals can exercise the basic human right to decide freely, responsibly and without coercion, the number and spacing of their children and to have the information, education and means to do so. In exercising this right, the best interests of their living and future children as well as the responsibility towards the community should be taken into account.

STRENGTHENING INTERNATIONAL CO-OPERATION

It would have been ironic, to say the least, if the Mexico City Conference had produced a less ringing endorsement of the need for international cooperation in the population field than had been the case at Bucharest ten years earlier. Yet, as the Conference opened, there seemed a real risk that this might indeed prove to be the situation. The United States had after all for almost 20 years been the leading proponent of international population assistance. Now it was precisely the United States which appeared to have the gravest doubts about the wisdom of such activities. Had that country's delegation pressed its new-found philosophy to a logical conclusion, tabling dozens of amendments as Argentina had done at Bucharest, a worthwhile consensus – certainly a consensus that represented an advance on Bucharest – would probably have been impossible to achieve. So the last state would have been worse than the first.

In the event, wiser counsels prevailed. The recommendations for the further implementation of the World Population Plan of Action contained a substantial section on the role of international co-operation (Recommendations 79 to 87). Governments, for example, were urged to 'increase their level of assistance for population activities'; the 'international community should play an important role; organs, organizations and bodies of the United Nations system and donor countries . . . are urged to assist governments at their request'; the importance of non-governmental organizations and activities was stressed. In all this, the co-ordinating and catalytic role of UNFPA in particular was firmly recognized. Whereas the recommendations of Bucharest were somewhat hesitant in recognizing the place of UNFPA in the population field, the delegates at Mexico knew no such inhibitions, Recommendation 83 stated unambiguously:

In view of the leading role of the United Nations Fund for Population Activities in population matters, the Conference urges that the Fund should be strengthened further so as to ensure the more effective delivery of population assistance, taking into account the growing needs in this field. The Secretary-General of the United Nations is invited to examine this Recommendation, and submit a report to the General Assembly on its implementation as soon as possible but not later than 1986.

When the United Nations General Assembly came to deal with the results of the Mexico Conference at its 39th session, the importance of international co-operation and of the role of UNFPA was confirmed.

The General Assembly Resolution adopted on 10 December 1984:

> Emphasises that international co-operation in the field of population is essential for the implementation of recommendations adopted at the Conference, and in that context calls upon the international community to provide adequate and substantial international support and assistance for population activities, particularly through the United Nations Fund for Population Activities, in order to ensure more effective delivery of population assistance in the light of growing needs in the field and the increasing efforts being made by developing countries.

All of this certainly represented solid progress. However, one area where Mexico City could *not* be seen as an advance on Bucharest was in the setting of targets for population growth.

TARGETS FOR POPULATION GROWTH

In his own speech at the Conference's inaugural ceremony, Mr Salas speaking not only as Executive Director of UNFPA, but also as Secretary-General of the Conference set out in clear and unambiguous language, his own views of what, as T. S. Eliot put it, might be called 'the goal of all our striving'.

The passage is worth quoting in full because it was possibly the most explicit statement on the subject so far made by a high official of the United Nations, speaking in an official capacity and in the most public way. Salas said:

> *Our goal is the stabilization of global population within the shortest period possible before the end of the next century.* The combination of rapid population growth, slowly growing incomes and inadequate level of technology continue to widen the disparities in international levels of living and frustrate the efforts of developing countries to improve the quality of life of their people. Even a high growth rate of 5 to 6 per cent in national income of the developing countries between 1985 and 2000 would still leave over 600 million persons below the poverty line. *Population stabilization will make it less difficult for the developing countries to improve their levels of living. Voluntary family planning is a vital means of reaching this global goal provided it is in accord with individual human rights, religious beliefs and cultural values. It is essential that population programmes be maintained until the promise of stabilization is within sight.* (emphasis added)
>
> Only the determined, rational and humane national population policies of countries can bring about a more satisfying future for the forthcoming generations. Governments must plan and work to bring about a global society that is secure and viable, one in which individuals can develop their full potential free from the capricious inequalities of development and threats of environmental degradation. This should be done without violating the dignity and freedom of the human person and by giving all people the knowledge and the means to bring forth only the children for whom they can provide the fullest opportunities for growth. . .

To what extent did the Mexico Conference heed the appeal of its Secretary-General? Was there in any sense in Mexico City in August 1984 an international commitment to the concept of 'population stabilization'? In purely formal terms, the answer is: no or not much. Recommendation 8 of the draft 'Recommendations for the further implementation of the World Population Plan of Action'[6] attempted to reintroduce the notion of quantitative targets which, as we have seen, was lost at Bucharest. It read:

> Countries which consider their population growth rate detrimental to their national purposes are invited to consider setting *quantitative population growth targets*, within the framework of socio-economic developments.

The attempt failed in the final recommendations as adopted by the Mexico Conference. Draft Recommendation 8 became Recommendation 13 and read:

> Countries which consider their population growth rates hinder the attainment of national goals are invited to consider pursuing *relevant demographic policies*, within the framework of socio-economic development. Such policies should respect human rights, the religious beliefs, philosophical convictions, cultural values and fundamental rights of each individual and couple, to determine the size of its own family.

By dropping the reference to 'quantitative population growth targets' in favour of the more neutral expression 'relevant demographic policies' the Conference could hardly be said to have improved upon the language agreed at Bucharest.[7]

A fortiori, there was no mention in the final Mexico recommendation of a global target for reducing population growth or attaining population stabilization. The United Nations' own official account of this aspect records in typically neutral tones:

> Many delegations stressed that, while it would be useful for the Conference to approve broad general guidelines, it was in the final analysis the responsibility of Governments in the exercise of their sovereign authority, to formulate the population policies which they considered most appropriate and consistent with national social, economic and cultural conditions and factors. Several delegations considered that it was utopian to aspire to the formulation of global policies, in view of the diversity of national situations. It was generally recognised, however, that conscious efforts had to be made by Governments to frame coherent population policies adapted to the conditions in their countries and consistent with plans or programmes relating to social and economic development as a whole. It was also stressed that population policies were integral parts of the long-range socio-economic development policies of each country.[8]

In spite of the fact that there was no explicit commitment to the goal of world population stabilization, there was nonetheless an underlying current of interest in such an idea. R.P. Kapoor, who was a member of the Indian delegation to the Conference, wrote:

> Even though it has not been specifically stated, it was clear in Mexico that, in the long term, global population policies should aim at a stabilised population size in a limited time-frame and at a level of around 8 billion people. Bucharest made the world conscious of the need to slow down population growth; Mexico has brought about an awareness regarding the urgency of *halting* the population growth.[9] (emphasis added)

Though, as noted above, it is doubtful whether the actual text adopted at Mexico would allow of such a bullish interpretation, it is certainly true to say that other speakers besides Mr Salas specifically advocated the goal of World Population Stabilization in the statements they made to the Plenary. Thus His Excellency the Honourable Mwai Kibaki, MP, vice-president of the Government of Kenya, after describing Kenya's own objectives ('the projections indicate that if we do not curb the population increase now an incredible total of 160 million people will be reached by the year 2050'), went on to exhort the Conference: 'let us commit ourselves to the goal of stabilization of World Population within the next 50 years'.

Coming from an African such a statement was especially significant. Nor was Mr Kibaki alone in using such explicit language. The delegate from Mauritius spoke of a 'race against time' and said that 'the challenge is ours – not for the past nor for the future generations'. The delegate from Pakistan told the Conference that 'the good news is that population planners have not failed the world; globally there is an overall decline in fertility'. But he added that 'ours is an expanding world, and population growth rates continue to deny a quality of life and macro socio-economic development which mankind is worthy of'.

The delegate from the Philippines indicated that the Commission on Population in his country had 'established a strategy that should make it possible to reach replacement levels of fertility by the year 2000'. And the delegate from the Republic of Korea indicated that: 'Korea hopes to achieve its population replacement level by 1988.'

The delegate from Turkey spoke of 'hopes that the world population may eventually be stabilized' if the trend towards lower population growth in the developing countries continued. And the delegate from Nepal told the Conference that: 'It has become all too clear that the World at large must accelerate efforts to control population growth if the citizens of the Third World are to enjoy a reasonable level of living.'

Among the developed countries, Sweden, Norway and New Zealand spoke in the most emphatic terms about the need for global population planning. The Swedish Delegate told the Conference that the review and appraisal of the World Population Plan of Action showed that, in absolute terms, the population growth figures were still 'staggering'. 'The global population could increase by 1.3 billion to reach 6.1 billion by the year 2000 – only 16 years from now.'

> Most of this tremendous increase will take place in countries which already have difficulties providing their people with a decent quality of life. Population growth will result in major strains on the already limited availability of food, clean water, shelter, energy, education, health services and job opportunities. It will also increase the strains on fragile environments and speed up desertification, deforestation and soil erosion. This will negatively affect food and agricultural production on which the survival of millions of human beings depends. It will also affect our climate. Furthermore, population growth may cause tensions which can lead to war and unrest. All this underscores the importance of the links between population, resources, environment and development and of unfair consumption patterns which were recognised already in Bucharest, and the need for action now.
>
> What is urgently needed are effective measures to promote economic and social development and to increase the productive resources available to the developing countries to combat poverty, starvation and disease. But this is not enough. Measures to slow down rapid population growth are also imperative. If such measures are not taken the future will look bleak. Mortality rates will increase and Governments may feel forced to take drastic measures to halt the population growth, measures that will infringe on human rights. Do we want this to happen?

Norway took a similar position. Norway's delegate told the Conference

> The World Population Conference in Bucharest agreed on a World Population Plan of Action, which became a landmark in our joint task of coming to grips with

a threat of over-population of our planet. Despite the achievements reached in Bucharest, my Government feels that the population problems we face today are as serious as they were ten years ago, even though their nature is different. Whereas some countries have demonstrated that it is indeed possible to bring population growth under control through determined policies, other countries, accounting for about one-fourth of the world population, have not yet experienced any significant decline in their fertility rate. At the current growth rate the population in these areas will double in twenty-five years. Unless a reduction of fertility is brought about, the growth of the population may be checked by a tragic increase in mortality, especially among the poor, infants and children. It will seriously affect political and social stability, human rights, economic development and the possibilities of orderly change.

The delegate from Norway added that it was:

imperative that this Conference generate a new powerful momentum at the national and international levels in the struggle to curb the growth of the world population.

Finally, from the other side of the world, the New Zealand delegate told the meeting:

ultimately, in a finite world with finite resources only a dramatic decline in population growth can assure the majority of the world's people of adequate food and shelter and access to other basic human requirements.

ABORTION

The other area where Mexico represented more of a retreat than an advance in comparison with Bucharest was abortion. If the Chinese defence of abortion was implicit rather than explicit in the speech of that country's delegate to the International Conference on Population, Sweden's Minister of Health and Social Affairs, Mrs Sigurdsen, was more forthright.

Effective contraception liberates women from unwanted pregnancies and induced abortion, and improves considerably the health of both mothers and children. Prevention of unwanted pregnancies must always be our aim. I note, however, that illegal abortion, performed under unsafe medical conditions, is a very serious health problem in many countries today. Therefore I would like that all women in the world have access to legal and safe abortions.

In draft recommendation number 13, governments were urged, inter alia:

to take appropriate steps to help women avoid abortions and, whenever possible, to provide for the humane treatment and counselling of women who have had recourse to illegal abortion.

Sweden fought hard, but unsuccessfully, to have that paragraph maintained in the final recommendations. In the event, the final text adopted by the conference read:

Governments are urged . . . to take appropriate steps to help women avoid abortion, which in no case should be promoted as a method of family planning, and whenever possible, provide for the humane treatment and counselling of women who have had recourse to abortion. (Paragraph 18e)

Sweden, in the explanation of its vote on the whole report, regretted that the paragraph which dealt with 'steps to help women avoid abortion' did not refer to illegal abortion, thereby implying that all abortions are illegal and should be avoided without mentioning the use of legal abortion.

The addition of the words to paragraph 18e 'which in no case should be promoted as a method of family planning' was accepted by a consensus. However, the fact that the amendment was proposed by the French delegation was another revealing example of the way in which even as late as 1984 the 'Old Guard' – namely the Catholic countries of Western Europe – were still ready to be mischievous, fighting and sometimes, as on this occasion, winning small rearguard victories even though they had essentially lost the main battle almost 20 years before, when the United Nations adopted those historic resolutions of the 1960s.[10]

THE HOLY SEE

None of this, however, went far enough for the delegate of the Holy See. Bishop Jan Schotte, speaking on the morning of August 8, 1984, expressed the Vatican's 'concern about the setting of quantitative population growth targets. There is always' he said, 'the danger that the achievement of such targets, especially in terms of declines in population growth and/or fertility rates, will be used as a condition for economic assistance.' And he also expressed the Church's opposition, on moral grounds, to abortion, sterilization and contraception.

> Despite affirmations to the contrary, and often contrary to the explicit formulations of national legislation, abortion is more and more used as an integral part of family planning programmes, financed even by governments and international organizations.

As far as sterilization was concerned, Bishop Schotte told the Conference that, in the ten years since Bucharest, sterilization had 'become more and more widely used in family-planning programmes in many nations'.

> The Holy See has constantly opposed the practice of sterilization because of the finality with which it destroys one of the person's prerogatives, the ability to procreate, and because as a demographic measure it can be too easily used in violation of human rights, especially among the poor and the uninformed.

Not surprisingly, the Holy See disassociated itself, as it had done at Bucharest, from the adoption by the Conference of the recommendations of the Main Committee 'by consensus and by acclamation' being, as at Bucharest, the only delegation to do so. Though it recognized that the recommendations contained some valuable proposals with regard to development, the important role of the family, migration and ageing, the Holy See could not agree with or give approval to those sections that 'asserted for individuals, including unmarried adolescents, the prerogatives that belonged to married couples in regard to sexual intimacy and parenthood'. Furthermore, the recommendations endorsed and encouraged methods of family planning that the Catholic Church considered morally unacceptable.

The Holy See's problems with the reference to 'individuals' as well as 'couples' were not new, but they had been compounded since Bucharest. Whereas the World Population Plan of Action referred to the basic right of 'all couples and individuals to decide freely and responsibly the number and spacing of their children and to have the information, education and means to do so' the recommendations for the further implementation of the World Population Plan of Action, adopted in Mexico City went further. Recommendation 25 read:

> Governments should, as a matter of urgency, make universally available information, education and the means to assist couples and individuals to achieve their desired number of children.

While under Recommendation 30:

> Governments are urged to ensure that all couples and individuals have a basic right to decide freely and responsibly the number and spacing of their children and to have the information, education and the means to do so.

In other words, while Bucharest had stated a 'basic right', Mexico not only restated that right but also urged governments to ensure that it was respected. A nuance, perhaps, but an important nuance, nevertheless.

Looking back at the Mexico City Conference a few months later, Rafael Salas described it as 'one of the shortest, one of the most economical and one of the best attended, among recent United Nations Conferences'. The results of the Conference provided 'definitive guidelines for population policies and programmes to be undertaken by governments and the international community in the next decade'.

There were 147 delegations at the Conference (including Namibia), as compared with 136 countries represented at Bucharest. The number of official participants exceeded 1000, including more than 200 women. Twenty-two delegations were headed by women. All UN agencies and organizations concerned with population were represented, as well as 154 non-governmental organizations with 367 representatives. Sixteen NGOs were given their opportunity to speak at the plenary sessions. Forty-one papers prepared by NGOs were distributed as background documents.

No separate secretariat was established for the Conference. The responsibility for substantive preparations was assigned to the Population Division of the Department of International Economic and Social Affairs, which worked in close co-operation with UNFPA and the UN's Department for Technical Cooperation for Development (DTCD). The preparatory meetings as well as the Conference itself were serviced by existing units and organizations in the United Nations system. The total amount budgeted for the Conference was approximately US \$2.3 million (\$1.5 million from extra budgetary sources, with up to US \$800,000 from the regular budget.) In fact, conference expenditures remained well within the budget established.

Mr Salas concluded his review of the Mexico City Conference by writing:

> The task before us now is to sustain the momentum generated by the Conference. This will require a concerted effort by national governments to implement the recommendations of the Conference, in the framework of their own national needs and requirements; and a redoubled effort by the international community to keep population developments and issues in focus and to provide increasing support for population activities.[11]

Salas's article appeared towards the end of 1984. In September 1985, the Administrator of USAID announced that the United States Government would not pay US \$10 million of its pledged contribution of US \$46 million to the UNFPA because of the alleged participation of UNFPA in the 'management' of the China Population Programme which in its judgement included coercive abortions. The Administrator of the USAID laid down conditions for its 1986 contribution: a drastic change in China's population policies or the reduction of UNFPAs multi-sector assistance to China so as to limit it solely to the supply of contraceptives. In the judgement of the management of the Fund, both of these conditions were difficult for UNFPA to fulfil because of the principle of the national sovereignty which it observed strictly, and because of

UNFPA's inability to alter unilaterally agreements which had been previously approved by its Governing Council. Similar strictures were to be applied to IPPF.

UNFPA's management recognized that a total United States withdrawal of its 1986 contribution would mean a 25 per cent reduction of UNFPA assistance to the 134 developing countries. However, it would not stop UNFPA from operating. Including increases from pledges, the organization could still operate with a budget of about US $120 million in 1986. But withdrawal of US funding was certain to disrupt current programmes, diminish the Fund's ability to support new and needed projects and stall the momentum generated by UNFPA in developing countries.

For many, the final outcome of the International Conference on Population which was held in Mexico City in August 1984 was – in retrospect – difficult to interpret. Should it be seen as the consolidation of the Bucharest consensus, setting the stage for new commitments by developing countries and by the international community? Or should it in the end be registered as a setback, if only because in Mexico the major supporter of international population programmes, certainly the major supporter of United Nations efforts in this field, was seen to waver in its dedication to these goals?

It was only with the coming of the Clinton Administration in 1993 that the United States finally signalled its intention to reverse the 'Mexico City' policy and restore full funding to UNFPA and IPPF. Given the role of Congress in approving allocations, it remained to be seen how that decision would be reflected in practical terms in the US aid programme.

NOTES

1. 1982/42.
2. *Sunday Times*, London, August 5, 1984.
3. August 5, 1984.
4. *Populi*, Vol. II, No. 4, 1984; article by Leon Tabah.
5. See p. 89.
6. E/Conf.76/5, 6 June 1984.
7. See p. 124. Also Paragraph 17 of the *World Population Plan of Action*, contained in the Report of the World Population Conference 1974. E/CONF.60/19.
8. E/CONF.76/19, Paragraphs 43 and 44.
9. *Populi*, Vol.12, No. 4, 1985.
10. See Chapter 6.
11. *Populi*, Vol. II, No. 4, 1984, article by Rafael Salas.

9

Evolving Perceptions

Without in any way seeking to be exhaustive, this Chapter looks at some of the highlights in the population debate which emerged during the latter part of the seventies and the eighties and which, to a greater or lesser extent, influenced the practical agenda.

POST-BUCHAREST

In its own way, Bucharest 1974 was a major landmark on the path towards the acceptance by the nations of the world that the population problem was of real and vital concern and that it was a legitimate subject for concerted action at all appropriate levels ranging from the humblest village hut with barefoot doctor at the door to the loftiest podium of the United Nations. Though, as noted, the debate at Bucharest was long and at times anguished, what finally precipitated the awkward consensus was the sense that something had to be done and a way found of reconciling the views of opposing camps.

In the quinquennium which followed Bucharest, more and more countries began to realise that no development effort could afford to ignore the question of population. Its interrelationship with policies on education, food and agriculture, industrialisation, urbanisation, employment, health facilities, the improvement of the status of women and other disadvantaged sectors and with numerous other areas of development was increasingly acknowledged as a pivotal consideration for all societies irrespective of their differences in political creed or economic standing. By 1978, 18 countries in Asia, 18 in Africa, 16 in Latin America and 2 in the Middle East – comprising 82 per cent of the population in the developing world – indicated in response to an enquiry by the United Nations that they considered their fertility levels 'too high'.

Not all these countries, of course, had developed effective population policies and programmes. Deeds had not always followed words. But already, five years or so after Bucharest, it could be said that a deeper and more lasting consensus than had been possible to attain at that time was rapidly being built. That new consensus was based on the premise, increasingly validated by real experiences in real countries, that population policy was not a substitute for social and economic development, nor was development an alternative to population policy but that both were inextricably linked sides of a single coin and, taken together, the vital ingredients of change.

THE COLOMBO CONFERENCE OF PARLIAMENTARIANS

Nor was this new consensus confined to official circles, or restricted to the rarefied domain of planners or economists. One meeting which took place in Colombo, Sri Lanka, in August 1979 was of special interest. Co-sponsored by UNFPA and the Inter-Parliamentary Union, it brought together parliamentarians from 58 countries to proclaim their commitment to the goal of linking Population and Development. The Colombo Declaration stated:

> Today most countries have recognised that population and development are inextricably bound together and that no population programme should be considered in isolation from policies and plans on health, housing, education, employment, the environment and the use of resources. Equally, there is increasing recognition that development programmes should reflect population policies.

The Colombo Declaration referred to the first United Nations review and appraisal of the effectiveness of the World population Plan of Action (WPPA), which had just been carried out and stressed that such progress as had been achieved did not go far enough:

> In the 25 years up to 1975 the total world population increased from just under 2,500 million to over 4,000 million; by the year 2000 it is expected to reach 6,200 million, of which four fifths will be in the developing countries, with a substantial majority living in desperate poverty.
>
> The implications of such increases are staggering. In the developing countries, between now and the end of the century, 800 million additional jobs will need to be created. This is more than the entire actively employed population of the developed world at the present time. Problems of similar magnitude will be posed as far as the provision of food, water and shelter is concerned.

Though its primary focus was on the link between population and development, the Conference did not ignore other themes.

> In the developed countries, per capita consumption of resources – so much higher than in the developing world – has been a cause of much pollution, waste and environmental degradation. It has also contributed to worldwide shortages in key resources. Other questions such as the ageing of the population and internal and international migration are becoming important. At the global level, continuously expanding human demands have created intolerable pressures on resources, particularly energy. The pressures on biological resources – fisheries, forests, grasslands and croplands – are mounting steadily and will continue to do so. Human needs have already begun to outstrip the productive capacity of many local biological systems as currently managed.

The Conference then addressed itself explicitly to the link between population and development.

> Peace itself, which is the precondition of development, will be put in jeopardy. For one of the principal threats to peace is the social unrest caused by the accumulation of human fear and hopelessness.

POPULATION AND THE URBAN FUTURE

Another important step in the evolution of perceptions about the nature of the population problem was marked by the International Conference held in Rome in September

1980 on Population and the Urban Future. Imaginatively, the Conference, organised by UNFPA with the cooperation of the Italian Government and the City of Rome, brought together mayors, administrators and planners from 41 cities whose populations were projected to be five million or more by the year 2000, as well as national planners from the 31 countries in which these cities were located. The Conference was not only opened by the Mayor of Rome amid the splendours of the ancient Capitoline Palace; it was also addressed – if in somewhat guarded tones – by His Holiness Pope John Paul II.

The Rome Declaration on Population and the Urban Future began by noting that in 1950 there were only six cities with populations of 5 million or more, and their combined population was only 44 million. By 1980, this had risen to 26 such cities with a combined population of 252 million.

By the year 2000, the indications were that this number would rise to approximately 60 cities, with an estimated population of nearly 650 million. Whereas in 1950 there was only one city, Shanghai, with a population of 5 million or more in the less developed countries, by the year 2000 there would be 45 such cities in the Third World, and most of these would be in Asia.

The Declaration recognised that, historically, the city had been 'the engine of development and the forge of human creative energies. In fact the city has often been the place in which civilisation has blossomed'. The process of urbanisation could be harnessed to achieve mankind's goal of just, peaceful and lasting progress. But if this were to happen, urbanisation must take place under 'planned and orderly conditions'.

The eminent delegates to the Rome Conference took a look at the world around them and concluded that:

> planned and orderly conditions for urbanisation for the most part do not exist. We find that the problems confronting urban settlements are in fact already acute in many parts of the world. They include shortages in virtually every service, amenity and support required for tolerable urban living. Housing and shelter, basic health services, sanitation, clean air and potable water, education, transport, energy supplies, open spaces and recreational facilities – all these are lacking in many parts of the world. Moreover, under conditions of unplanned urbanisation, the situation is becoming worse rather than better.

Economic problems – such as unemployment and underemployment – loomed large. It was estimated that, during the next two decades, over 600 million people would be added to the labour force in the less developed countries alone, and many of these would be flocking to the cities in search of jobs. Social problems – crime, delinquency, social segregation and the exploitation of certain groups, e.g. migrants and urban-squatters – were becoming increasingly acute, as were environmental problems such as congestion and pollution.

> Unplanned urbanisation may generate tension between groups and classes within the city itself: it may also generate tension between urban and rural areas within national boundaries.

The Conference recalled the language of the Colombo Declaration on Population and Development when it concluded that 'peace itself, which is the precondition for development, may be put in jeopardy'. It re-affirmed that:

> one of the principal threats to peace is the social unrest caused by the accumulation of human fear and hopelessness. Fear and hopelessness can accumulate both quickly and enduringly in the hearts of the urban poor when their aspirations are not realised.

Table 9.1. Twenty largest agglomerations in the world, ranked by size, 1950–2000 (population in millions).

Rank	1950	Population	1970	Population	1980	Population	1990	Population	2000	Population
1	New York/north-eastern New Jersey	12.4	New York/north-eastern New Jersey	16.3	Tokyo/Yokohama	17.0	Mexico City	21.3	Mexico City	26.3
2	London	10.4	Tokyo/Yokohama	14.9	New York/north-eastern New Jersey	15.6	Sao Paulo	18.8	Sao Paulo	24.0
3	Shanghai	10.3	Shanghai	11.4	Mexico City	15.0	Tokyo/Yokohama	17.2	Tokyo/Yokohama	17.1
4	Rhein-Ruhr	6.9	London	10.6	Sao Paulo	12.8	New York/north-eastern New Jersey	15.3	Calcutta	16.6
5	Tokyo-Yokohama	6.7	Shanghai	10.3	Shanghai	11.8	Calcutta	12.6	Bombay	16.0
6	Beijing	6.7	Mexico City	6.7	Greater Buenos Aires	10.1	Shanghai	12.0	New York/north-eastern new Jersey	15.5
7	Paris	5.5	Greater Buenos Aires	8.5	London	10.0	Bombay	11.9	Seoul	13.5
8	Tianjin	5.4	Los Angeles/Long Beach	8.4	Calcutta	9.5	Greater Buenos Aires	11.7	Shanghai	13.5
9	Greater Buenos Aires	5.3	Paris	8.3	Los Angeles/Long Beach	9.5	Seoul	11.5	Rio de Janeiro	13.3
10	Chicago/north-western Indiana	5.0	Beijing	8.3	Rhein-Ruhr	9.3	Rio de Janeiro	11.4	Delhi	13.3
11	Moscow	4.8	Sao Paulo	8.2	Rio de Janeiro	9.2	Los Angeles/Long Beach	10.5	Greater Buenos Aires	13.3
12	Calcutta	4.4	Osaka/Kobe	7.6	Beijing	9.1	Cairo/Giza/Imbaba	10.0	Cairo/Giza/Imbaba	13.2
13	Los Angeles/Long Beach	4.1	Rio de Janeiro	7.2	Paris	8.8	London	9.5	Jakarta	12.8
14	Osaka/Kobe	3.8	Moscow	7.1	Bombay	8.5	Beijing	9.5	Baghdad	12.8
15	Milan	3.6	Calcutta	7.1	Seoul	8.5	Jakarta	9.3	Teheran	12.7
16	Rio de Janeiro	3.5	Tianjin	6.9	Moscow	8.2	Moscow	9.2	Karachi	12.2
17	Mexico City	3.1	Chicago/north-western Indiana	6.8	Osaka/Kobe	8.0	Delhi	9.2	Istanbul	11.9
18	Philadelphia/New Jersey	3.0	Bombay	5.9	Tianjin	7.7	Rhein-Ruhr	9.1	Los Angeles/Long Beach	11.3
19	Bombay	2.9	Milan	5.6	Cairo/Giza/Imbaba	7.3	Teheran	9.0	Dhaka	11.2
20	Detroit	2.8	Seoul	5.4	Chicago/north-western Indiana	6.8	Paris	9.0	Manila	11.1

Source: Results of United Nations demographic estimates and projections as assessed in 1982. Table printed in *Population, the UNFPA Experience*, edited by Nafis Sadik and published for the United Nations for Population Activities by New York University Press, 1984.

The pace and pattern of urbanisation, and the nature of the economic and social development that took place, was crucially influenced by demographic trends. In the less developed countries, migration from rural areas formerly contributed the major part of urban growth. By the time of the Rome Conference, natural increase – the excess of births over deaths – generally contributed 60 per cent of urban growth.

The Conference believed that:

> the process of urbanisation can only be managed where the demographic factors contributing to this process are themselves managed through economic, social, political and cultural measures. We must seek to match population with resources in cities, in regions, in countries and – ultimately – in the world itself.

The Conference called on countries to develop a strategy for national planning for the urban future. Such strategies, supported by appropriate legislation and funding, should include the formulation of comprehensive national population policies, policies for balanced development between urban and rural areas and between small, intermediate and large cities; and policies for the improvement of urban areas.

THE BRANDT REPORT

The Rome Declaration on Population and the Urban Future stands as a precursor to the equally powerful conclusions of the Brandt Report published in early 1980 under the title 'North-South: A Programme for Survival'.[1] The Commission's 18 regular members included several former prime ministers, and ten persons from the developing countries, though none from the Communist world. The Report noted that:

> the present staggering growth of world population will continue for some considerable time. It will be one of the strongest forces shaping the future of human society. . . .Depending on whether the decline in fertility accelerates or slows down, world population could, as projections show, stabilise – or possibly turn down – at levels anywhere between 8 and 15 billion in the course of the next century. Even on the assumption of continued fertility decline, the populations of most countries in the developing world are likely to reach at least twice their present size. Nigeria and Bangladesh are projected to have as many people as the United States and the USSR today, and India will have at least 1.2 billion inhabitants. The cities of the Third World are growing even faster than the total populations. and the biggest of them are likely to exceed 30 million by the end of this century.

The Brandt Commission observed, in a passage which is as striking as any in the Report, that:

> It is easy to feel a sense of helplessness at these prospects. The growth of population at rates between 2 and 3 per cent per annum will produce a doubling of population in 25 to 35 years. This compounds the task of providing food, jobs, shelter, education and health services, of mitigating absolute poverty and of meeting the colossal financial and administrative needs of rapid urbanisation.

Like the parliamentarians who met in Colombo in 1979, the Brandt Commission saw the vital link between population, development, environment and peace. Would the ecological system itself suffice to meet the needs of a greatly increased world population at the economic standard that was hoped for? Could sustainable development take place where biological systems were taxed beyond the limit?

Population growth in some parts of the Third World is already a source of alarming ecological changes, and its industrialisation is bound to lead to greater pressure on resources and environment.

In effect, the Brandt Commission expanded the population–development relationship to incorporate explicitly the dimension of environmental management. The Brandt Commission did not argue that population growth was the only, or even (necessarily) the major, factor in environmental overload. But it was seen as an important contributory factor, leading – via ecological degradation – to important constraints on growth. Thus, the impact of population on development could be seen in the classic terms of demand (numbers to be fed, housed, clothed and watered) and also in terms of its impact on supply in terms of resource availabilities – forests and fisheries, croplands and water catchment areas, etc. These environmental and resource constraints would sometimes have a local or regional impact, to be felt primarily in those developing countries where the resource pressures were most acute. But sometimes, as in the case for example of climatic change induced through deforestation, the consequences might be wider and even global, adding new north-south tensions to those that already existed.

Looking ahead, the Brandt Commission found it:

> *difficult to avoid the conclusion that a world of 15 billion people would be marked by a host of potentially devastating economic, social and political conflicts. Whether the nightmarish vision of a hopelessly overcrowded planet in the next century can be averted depends gravely on what is done now to hasten the stabilisation of population.* (emphasis added)

GLOBAL 2000

The decade of the 1980s, which had begun with the publication of the Brandt Report, saw other landmarks in the process of building an integrated view of the interrelationships between population, development and environment. The Global 2000 Report to the President, which was prepared by the Council on Environmental Quality and the United States Department of State, and published in 1980, came to the conclusion that:

> already the populations in sub-Saharan Africa and in the Himalayan hills of Asia have exceeded the carrying capacity of the immediate area, triggering an erosion of the land's capacity to support life . . . yet there is reason for hope. It must be emphasised that the Global 2000 Study's projections are based on the assumption that national policies regarding population stabilisation, resource conservation and environmental protection will remain essentially unchanged through the end of the century. But, in fact, policies are beginning to change. In some areas forests are being replanted after cutting. Some nations are taking steps to reduce soil losses and desertification. Interest in energy conservation is growing and large sums are being invested in exploring alternatives to petroleum dependence. *The need for family planning is slowly becoming better understood.* Water supplies are being improved and waste treatment systems built. High-yield seeds are widely available and seed banks are being expanded. Some wild lands with their genetic resources are being protected. Natural predators and selective pesticides are being substituted for persistent and destructive pesticides. (emphasis added)

The Report concluded that, though these developments were encouraging, they were far from adequate to meet the global challenges projected in the Study.

Vigorous, determined new initiatives are needed if worsening poverty and human suffering, environmental degradation and international tension and conflicts are to be prevented. There are no quick fixes. The only solutions to the problems of population, resources and environment are complex and long term. These problems are inextricably linked to some of the most perplexing and persistent problems in the world – poverty, injustice and social conflict.

THE WORLD CONSERVATION STRATEGY

Another landmark study, the World Conservation Strategy (WCS) launched in June 1981, was prepared by the International Union for the Conservation of Nature and Natural Resources (IUCN) with the advice, cooperation and financial assistance of the United Nations Environment Programme (UNEP) and the World Wildlife Fund (WWF) with the collaboration of FAO and UNESCO. The Strategy had three main objectives:

> to maintain essential ecological processes and life-support systems; to preserve genetic diversity; to ensure the sustainable utilisation of species and ecosystems.

These objectives, according to WCS, had to be achieved as a matter of urgency because the planet's capacity to support people was being irreversibly reduced in both developing and developed countries. Thousands of millions of tonnes of soil were lost each year as a result of deforestation and poor land management; at least 3000 square kilometres of prime farmland disappeared annually under buildings and roads in developed countries alone. Hundreds of millions of rural people in developing countries, including 500 million malnourished and 800 million destitute, were compelled to destroy the resources necessary to free them from starvation and poverty. The rural poor were stripping the land of trees and shrubs for fuel in widening swathes around their villages, so that many communities did not have enough food to cook or to keep warm. The rural poor were also obliged to burn every year 400 million tonnes of dung and crop residues badly needed to regenerate soils.

The energy, financial and other costs of providing goods and services were growing. Throughout the world, but especially in developing countries, siltation was cutting the lifetime of reservoirs supplying water and hydro-electricity, often by as much as half. Floods were devastating settlements and crops (in India the annual cost of floods ranged from $140 to $150 million). At the same time, the resource base of major industries was shrinking. Tropical forests were contracting so rapidly that by the end of the century the remaining area of unlogged productive forest would have been halved. The coastal support system of many fisheries were being destroyed or polluted.

WCS addressed itself explicitly to the links between population, development and conservation, arguing that much habitat destruction and overexploitation of living resources by individuals, communities and nations in the developing world was a response to relative poverty, caused or exacerbated by a combination of population growth and inequities within and among nations.

> Peasant communities, for example, may be forced to cultivate steep, unstable slopes because their growing numbers exceed the capacity of the land and because the fertile, easily managed valley bottoms have been taken over by large landowners. Similarly, many developing countries have so few natural resources and operate under such unfavourable conditions of international trade that they often have

very little choice but to exploit forests, fisheries and other living resources unsustainably. In many parts of the world population pressures are making demands on resources beyond the capacity of those resources to sustain.

The WCS concluded that:

> every country should have a conscious population policy to avoid as far as possible the spread of such situations, and eventually to achieve a balance between numbers and the environment.

At the same time it was essential that the affluent constrain their demands on resources, and preferably reduce them, shifting some of their wealth to assisting the deprived. 'To a significant extent the survival and future of the poor depends on conservation and sharing by the rich.'

POPULATION AND PEACE

Over the previous ten or fifteen years, there had been a growing realisation that the population issue was not only central to development and environment but also that it was linked, both directly and indirectly, to the maintenance of peace itself.

On the occasion of the International Conference on Population, which took place in Mexico City in August 1984 (see previous chapter), 92 Heads of State or Heads of Government though not attending the Conference in person nevertheless transmitted brief statements of their views on population.[2] A review of these statements indicates a growing concern with the relationship between demographic factors and situations which can or do give rise to tensions, instabilities and conflicts whether within nations or between nations. To cite just one example, Turgut Ozal, Prime Minister of Turkey, wrote:

> Population issues cannot be confined within national boundaries. They are closely related to the attainment of our ideals for peace, security and stability in the world.

The relationship could be presented positively or negatively. Where it was evident, for example, that population planning contributed to economic and social development and where – as presumably it should – economic and social development contributed to national and individual well-being, and therefore to stability (both internal and external), there was a virtuous cycle. On the other hand, it could be argued that an absence of population planning and other appropriate demographic policies could make orderly development more difficult to achieve. Where the prospects for improvement were low or non-existent, fear and hopelessness tended to accumulate (to use the language of the Rome and Colombo Declarations) and, under such conditions, tensions and instabilities might be caused which themselves might impact negatively on the development process, either by causing a diversion of scarce resources towards military or security expenditures or through other forms of disruption. Here there was a vicious cycle.

Among its Recommendations for the Further Implementation of the World Population Plan of Action, the International Conference on Population held in Mexico City in August 1984 included a section on Peace, Security and Population. It stressed that it was:

> of great importance for the world community to work ceaselessly to promote, among nations, peace, security, disarmament and co-operation, which are indispensable for the achievement of the goals of humane population policies and for economic and social development.

Without peace there could be no orderly development, and therefore no orderly approach to population planning now recognised to be an integral part of development.

But the reverse might apply as well. As Mr Salas, Executive Director of UNFPA and Secretary General of the 1984 Conference, pointed out in his speech on the opening day:

> Population policies and programmes by looking towards a moderation of popula-tion growth and a rational spatial distribution of population thus represent humane efforts to reduce imbalances and disparities that lead to crises.

In saying this, Mr Salas reiterated, in explicit terms, a theme which had been devel-oped over the years in different fora, such as the Colombo meeting of Parliamentar-ians on Population and Development, the Rome Conference on Population Growth and the Urban Future and the UNA-USA Panel Report, previously quoted, on World Population.[3]

As noted in Chapter 2, this latter report had stated with considerable cogency:

> If it is true that internal stability and external order are influenced, however indi-rectly, by the rate of population growth, then the commitment of the international community to the cause of peace should be matched by a parallel commitment to population planning.

As the eighties progressed, it was becoming increasingly apparent that – in addition to the destabilising effects caused by the 'accumulation of human fear and hopelessness' as development objectives were vitiated by demographic pressures – environmental degradation and the wastage of renewable natural resources caused, in part at least, by population pressures, were playing important and growing roles in causing wars regional and national insecurity, internal strife and bloodshed.

The UN Environment Programme's *State of the Environment, 1984* report noted that 'the processes of environmental despoliation constitute a threat to the future of humankind' no less insidious than nuclear war. But 'at present this threat lies hidden – obscured by a preoccupation with an economic, social and political analysis that pays little or no heed to the environmental destabiliser'.

According to an Earthscan document published in November 1984, it was possible to distinguish at least three types of environmental factors, often linked to demo-graphic pressures and associated with recent and current strife:

> The accelerating trends in forest and soil degradation, combined with growing populations and a stagnant world economy, are rapidly marginalising hundreds of millions of Third World people – especially in ecological zones already troubled by deep social and political unrest: the Andes, the Himalayas, the Sahel region of Africa.

> As water needs increase (for irrigation, electricity and simply to supply growing populations), the year-round yield of many shared rivers decreases because defor-estation and soil erosion have reduced the 'sponge effect' of the land to rapidly absorb and slowly release water. Rivers now tend to flood after the rains and run low in the dry season, making it impossible for governments to realise their needs from theses rivers.

> Many shared marine fisheries are declining in yield due to over fishing, at the same time as demand and exploitation are increasing.

In states where governments give little priority to ordering their rural sectors, but where large proportions of the people (in many cases the vast majority) live on the land, the result was often profound disorder. People seeking livelihoods were leaving the land in uncontrolled waves to:

> move across national boundaries as refugees or migrant workers, creating tension between states:

> move into regions of better agricultural land, creating conflicts with people already settled there: convert forests to fields, disrupting the societies of and often fighting with forest peoples; move into swollen cities, which can offer few opportunities and which are often already stretched far beyond what their infrastructures can support. Large numbers of new arrivals can have a deep effect on urban political stability of cities.

The Earthscan survey restricted itself to cases where significant bloodshed had been caused – riots, guerrilla movements, revolutions and wars – or where significant interstate conflict had occurred short of war (the Soviet–Japan fisheries dispute and the tension between Brazil and Argentina over shared rivers). It did not argue that all the security problems it examined had led, or were likely to lead, to wars between states. The violence between indigenous peoples and settlers in forest lands, though it resulted in thousands of deaths a year, was almost always a purely internal affair.

The survey did, however, examine cases in which a government's neglect of its resources base had led to 'internal' strife which had resulted in the fall of that government. Often the new government was of a radically different political persuasion than the previous regime – and this could affect governments of almost any political colour. Regional security might be seen to be threatened, and the attention of larger powers drawn to the scene of instability. Examples included Nicaragua, Ethiopia, Iran, Afghanistan and Poland.

The possibility of escalation could be ruled out in any of these conflicts. Thus, what might begin, in Harold Macmillan's immortal words, as a 'little local difficulty', fundamentally caused by the imbalance between population and resources in one particular country or region, might grow and spread like a forest fire until the flames of that fire might one day truly engulf the world.[4]

Looking at matters from this perspective we could argue that Professor Richard Gardner even understated the case when he wrote 'a really effective response by the UN to the challenge of population growth. . . might prove to be the Organisation's most vital contribution to human welfare second only to keeping the peace'.[5] The United Nations' population activities could in fact be seen as an essential part of its primary mandate: the maintenance of peace itself.

BRUNDTLAND

Probably the most influential report to be published in the development–environment field during the 1980s was that of the World Commission on Environment and Development, entitled *Our Common Future*. Chaired by Mrs Gro Harlem Brundtland, Prime Minister of Norway, the Commission's Report was possibly the most important single intellectual influence on the whole UNCED process. The members of the Commission sat in their personal capacities but the eminence of the participants combined with the quality and coherence of the document which they produced effectively ensured that the report had a far-reaching impact.

One of the most lucid chapters in the Commission's Report was entitled *Population and Human Resources*. The Commission summarized the situation:

> In 1985, some 80 million people were added to a world population of 4.8 billion. Each year the number of human beings increases, but the amount of natural resources with which to sustain this population, to improve the quality of human lives, and to eliminate mass poverty remains finite. On the other hand, expanding knowledge increases the productivity of resources.
>
> Present rates of population growth cannot continue. They already compromise many governments' abilities to provide education, health care, and food security for people, much less their abilities to raise living standards. This gap between numbers and resources is all the more compelling because so much of the population growth is concentrated in low-income countries, ecologically disadvantaged regions, and poor households.

Yet the population issue was not solely about numbers. And poverty and resource degradation could exist on thinly populated lands, such as the dry lands and the tropical forests. People were the ultimate resource. Improvements in education, health, and nutrition allowed them to better use the resources they command, to stretch them further. In addition, threats to the sustainable use of resources came as much from inequalities in people's access to resources and from the ways in which they used them as from the sheer numbers of people. Thus, concern over the 'population problem' also called forth concern for human progress and human equality.

> Thus many governments must work on several fronts – to limit population growth; to control the impact of such growth on resources and, with increasing knowledge, enlarge their range and improve their productivity; to realize human potential so that people can better husband and use resources; and to provide people with forms of social security other than large numbers of children. The means of accomplishing these goals will vary from country to country, but all should keep in mind that sustainable economic growth and equitable access to resources are two of the more certain routes towards lower fertility rates.
>
> Giving people the means to choose the size of their families is not just a method of keeping population in balance with resources; it is a way of assuring – especially for women – the basic human right of self-determination. *The extent to which facilities for exercising such choices are made available is itself a measure of a nation's development.* In the same way, enhancing human potential not only promotes development but helps to ensure the right of all to a full and dignified life. (emphasis added)

In addition to the need for industrial countries to attend seriously to the impact of their own patterns of consumption on world resources, the Commission pointed out perceptively that:

> *Industrial countries seriously concerned with high population growth rates in other parts of the world have obligations beyond simply supplying aid packages of family planning hardware. Economic development, through its indirect impact on social and cultural factors, lowers fertility rates. International policies that interfere with economic development thus interfere with a developing nation's ability to manage its population growth. A concern for population growth must therefore be a part of a broader concern for a more rapid rate of economic and social development in the developing countries.* (emphasis added)

The Commission pointed out that the processes of population growth were changing in most developing countries as birth and death rates fell. In the early 1950s, practically all

developing countries had birth rates over 40 and death rates over 20, the major exception being the low death rates in Latin America.

Today the situation is quite different:

- Thirty-two per cent of the people in the Third World live in countries –
  such as China and the Republic of Korea – with birth rates below 25 per
  thousand and death rates below 10.
- Forty-one per cent are in countries where birth rates have fallen, but not as
  much as death rates, and their populations are growing at around 2 per cent
  – doubling, in other words, every 34 years. Such countries include Brazil,
  India, Indonesia, and Mexico.
- The remaining 27 per cent live in countries, such as Algeria, Bangladesh,
  Iran, and Nigeria, where death rates have fallen slightly but birth rates
  remain high. Overall population growth is in the range of 2.5 to 3 per cent
  (doubling every 28 to 23 years), with even higher growth rates in some
  countries, such as Kenya.

The Commission commented pungently on the 'real choices' that the world could
make. Reflecting the 'momentum' of population growth, long-term UN projections
showed that at the global level:

> if replacement-level fertility was reached in 2010, global population would stabilize
> at 7.7 billion by 2060;
> if this rate was reached in 2035, population would stablilize at 10.2 billion by 2095;
> if, however, the rate was reached only in 2065, global population in 2100 would be
> 14.2 billion.

'These projections' the Commission argued 'show that the world has real choices.
*Policies to bring down fertility rates could make a difference of billions to the global population
next century'.* (emphasis added) And the Commission added that since the greater part
of the differences between the three variants was accounted for by South Asia, Africa,
and Latin America, much depended on the effectiveness of population policies in
these regions.

Though, as we shall see later, the final outcome of UNCED, and in particular
Agenda 21, did not fully reflect the analysis and the prescriptions of the World Commission on Environment and Development as far as population was concerned (as
well as in some other important respects), the Commission's treatment of the population issue was in many ways exemplary. It was comprehensive; it was forthright; but at
the same time it showed great tact and sensitivity. Curbing population growth, limiting human fertility, was central to the whole business of pursuing and attaining sustainable development in the developing countries. But it was not the only central issue
– far from it.

The key paragraph in the Commission's report was entitled: 'Managing Population
Growth':

> Progress in population policies is uneven. Some countries with serious population
> problems have comprehensive policies. Some go no further than the promotion of
> family planning. Some do not do even that.
>
> *A population policy should set out and pursue broad national demographic goals in rela-
> tion to other socio-economic objectives. Social and cultural factors dominate all others in
> affecting fertility. The most important of these is the roles women play in the family, the
> economy, and the society at large. Fertility rates fall as women's employment opportunities
> outside the home and farm, their access to education, and their age at marriage all rise.
> Hence, policies meant to lower fertility rates not only must include economic incentives and*

disincentives, but must aim to improve the position of women in society. Such policies should essentially promote women's rights. (emphasis added)

Poverty breeds high rates of population growth: families poor in income, employment, and social security need children first to work and later to sustain elderly parents. Measures to provide an adequate livelihood for poor households, to establish and enforce minimum-age child labour laws, and to provide publicly financed social security will all lower fertility rates. Improved public health and child nutrition programmes that bring down infant mortality rates – so parents do not need 'extra' children as insurance against child death – can also help to reduce fertility levels.

All these programmes are effective in bringing down birth rates only when their benefits are shared by the majority. Societies that attempt to spread the benefits of economic growth to a wider segment of the population may do better at lowering birth rates than societies with both faster and higher levels of economic growth but a less even sharing of the benefits of that growth.

Thus developing-country population strategies must deal not only with the population variable as such but also with the underlying social and economic conditions of under-development. They must be multifaceted campaigns: to strengthen social, cultural, and economic motivations for couples to have small families and, through family planning programmes, to provide to all who want them the education, technological means, and services required to control family size.[6]

It was both intriguing and impressive that the Brundtland and Commission did not hesitate to delve into the detail of implementation of family planning programmes. In this respect, as well as in others, it represented a real advance on previous reports which, while being eloquent on the subject of the population problem, were usually short of insights as far as the 'solutions' were concerned. The Commission observed cogently:

Family planning services in many developing countries suffer by being isolated from other programmes that reduce fertility and even from those that increase motivation to use such services. They remain separate both in design and implementation from such fertility-related programmes as nutrition, public health, mother and child care, and preschool education that take place in the same area and that are often funded by the same agency.

Such services must therefore be integrated with other efforts to improve access to health care and education. The clinical support needed for most modern contraceptive methods makes family planning services heavily dependent on the health system. Some governments have successfully combined population programmes with health, education, and rural development projects, and implemented them as part of major socio-economic programmes in villages or regions. This integration increases motivation, improves access, and raises the effectiveness of investments in family planning.

Only about 1.5 per cent of official development aid now goes for population assistance. Regrettably, some donor countries have cut back on their assistance for multilateral population programmes and so weakened them; this must be reversed.

The Commission also pointed out that the population in North America, Europe, the (then) USSR and Oceania was expected to increase by 230 million by the year 2025. It was not enough to seek to limit fertility in the developing countries:

Nor are population growth rates the challenge solely of those nations with high rates of increase. An additional person in an industrial country consumes far more and places far greater pressure on natural resources than an additional person in the Third World. Consumption patterns and preferences are as important as numbers of consumers in the conservation of resources.

Five years after the Brundtland Commission reported, UNCED would adopt Chapter 4 of Agenda 21, entitled Changing Consumption Patterns. It was no coincidence that the chapter immediately preceded Agenda 21's Chapter 5, on Demographic Dynamics and Sustainability. On the international agenda, reducing fertility in the developing world and changing consumptions patterns in the developed world were becoming increasingly linked.

THE INTERNATIONAL FORUM ON POPULATION IN THE TWENTY-FIRST CENTURY

A major highlight of the decade of the eighties as far as the great debate on population was concerned was the International Forum on Population in the Twenty-First Century which was held in Amsterdam in the Netherlands 6–9 November, 1989. The Forum took place at the mid-point of the decade between the International Conference on Population, held in Mexico City in 1984, and the International Conference on Population and Development, to be held in Cairo in 1994. The primary purpose of the Forum, which was organized by UNFPA in co-operation with the Government of the Netherlands, was to bring together ministers, senior government officials and population experts from around the world to discuss openly and frankly the most important population issues of the 1990s and beyond.

In many ways, the conclusions of the Forum and the Amsterdam Declaration which resulted from it were of crucial importance for the whole population debate. The Amsterdam meeting was probably the first meeting of an intergovernmental character to view the population issue through the Brundtland prism.

The Amsterdam Declaration contained the following general statement on the subject of:

> POPULATION AND SUSTAINABLE DEVELOPMENT: Recognizing that balancing population and resources as well as protecting the environment are key elements to quality of life and sustainable development, we emphasize the following:
>
> To be effective, a development strategy must reflect population concerns among its primary objectives. Similarly, a population strategy must reflect development concerns. It must link population programmes to programmes on health, education, housing and employment, among others. Indeed, it is only through such linkages that sustained and sustainable development can be achieved.
>
> The attainment of population goals and objectives should rest on seven main pillars:
>
> Strengthening of political commitment;
> Development of national strategies and programmes;
> Acceleration and expansion of resource mobilization;
> Strengthening of the role and status of women;
> Strengthening of the quality, effectiveness and outreach of family planning and maternal and child health programmes and services in both the public and the private sector;
> Heightening of community awareness and participation at all levels in the formulation and implementation of programmes and projects based on priorities and needs expressed by the women and men involved;

> Intensification of international co-operation in the sphere of population activities, specially directed and adapted to the specific conditions, particularly socio–cultural conditions, of recipient countries.

The Amsterdam Declaration went on to set some specific population goals and objectives. In view of the inability of both the Bucharest and the Mexico meetings to agree on any hard-hitting language in this area, it was of outstanding interest that the Amsterdam meeting managed to agree that:

> At the very least, national population goals and objectives for the coming decade and beyond should include:

> A reduction in the average number of children born per woman commensurate with achieving, as a minimum, the medium variant population projections of the United Nations;
> A major reduction in the proportion of women and men who are not currently using reliable methods of family planning, but who want to postpone, delay or limit childbearing;
> A substantial reduction in very early marriage and in teen-age pregnancy;
> An increase in contraceptive prevalence in developing countries so as to reach at least 56 per cent of women of reproductive age by the year 2000 in view of the considerable unmet needs in family planning, thereby expanding the currently estimated 326 million user couples to 535 million user couples.

The first of these national goals and objectives, namely the aim of attaining fertility rates consistent with the United Nations medium variant projections, could be seen as an endorsement – probably for the first time at intergovernmental level – of the idea that countries should be aiming to attain replacement level fertility by specific target dates, since that is the basis of UN medium variant projection projections (as, of course, for the 'high' and 'low' variant projections, the difference being that the date for the attainment of replacement-level fertility is assumed to be either later or earlier).

The objective of attaining an increase in contraceptive prevalence in the developing countries to 56 per cent of women of reproductive age (expanding the number of user couples from 326 million to 536 million) was also path-breaking. Nothing as specific as this was to be found in the Bucharest or Mexico conclusions.

> The Amsterdam Declaration went on to call for:

> A reduction of the 1980 rate of infant mortality to rates of at most 50 per 1000 live births by the year 2000 in all countries and major sub-groups within countries;
> A reduction in maternal mortality from all causes, including illegal abortion, by at least 50 per cent by the year 2000, particularly in regions where this figure currently exceeds 100 per 100,000 births;
> An increase in the average life expectancy at birth to 62 years or more for men and women in countries with high mortality by the end of the century;
> A better geographical distribution of the population within national territories in balance with the proper use of resources.

The participants recognized that expanding contraceptive use was not by itself enough. A wider approach was necessary, one which situated family planning within the broader social framework, particularly female education and employment, and which emphasised the quality of care.

> A reconsideration of programme priorities and approaches should, in particular, be sensitive to and aware of:

The effects of education on demographic behaviour and the critical importance for development of increasing female literacy and achieving universal enrolment of girls in primary school by the year 2000;

The need to raise the social and economic value of girl children in the family, community and national development;

The need to increase women's participation in decision making and management of population policies and programmes and special programmes for the economic development of women, with the aim of achieving equality of representation;

The need to improve coverage and quality of maternal and child health and family planning programmes wherever possible within the context of primary health care and, where circumstances make it necessary, through other approaches;

The health benefits of birth spacing and breast-feeding to mothers and infants, such as: the importance of spacing births two or more years apart; the avoidance of pregnancy tool early or too late in a woman's reproductive period; and, the encouragement of breast-feeding for nutritional and family planning reasons;

The value of information, education and communication activities in developmental work in general and in population programmes in particular; and the need to direct information activities to both women and men;

The impact of rural development and investment on regional employment opportunities for both sexes and, by implication, on the magnitude of rural-to-urban migration and the needs of slum dwellers;

The need to train adequate numbers of staff, including programme managers, so as to enable them to become self sufficient in carrying out expanded population programmes;

The close relationship between activities dealing with sexually transmitted diseases, including AIDS, and maternal and child health, family planning, and population education and information;

The need to recognize that some problems that seriously affect developed countries are also beginning to affect the developing world, in particular in regard to international migration and to the aging of populations in countries with low fertility.

The Forum recognized that the population issue was an intrinsic part of general economic and social development. Changes in population both influenced and responded to changes in other areas, including income levels, economic growth, education, employment, health and status of women. This Forum was dealing with the core of population activities, i.e., family planning; information, education and communication; basic data collection; population dynamics; and population policy. At the same time participants fully realized that these were all closely related to efforts in other areas. For example, the success of family planning efforts was closely linked to the quality of health programmes in general, particularly maternal and child health programmes. These in turn were an integral part of overall development.

Population goals and objectives were not easily translated into cost estimates. For one thing, countries were generally at different stages in the development of their population programmes. Some required substantial financial support to develop the capacity to carry out their programmes; others with programmes at a more advanced level had been able to devise ways to improve cost effectiveness. It was extremely difficult, therefore, to accurately project costs as programmes progressed from one stage to another.

A balanced, comprehensive population programme encompasses several important activities. These include family planning information and services; data collection; biomedical, demographic, socio-economic and operations research; policy development and evaluation; and information, education and communications activities. The estimated minimum annual cost in the year 2000 to support such activities is in the order of US$9 billion, distributed in accordance with the specific needs of individual countries.

   Programmes will have to be developed and funds made available for participation of women and men at the community level and their needs and priorities addressed, since this is essential for development of sustainable population activities. Considerable funds have to be set aside for education programmes, in particular for women and girls, and for maternal and child health care, including meeting the needs for family planning.

The Forum noted that total national and international expenditures for family planning and other major population activities in all developing countries in 1987 amounted to about US$4.5 billion.

   How to mobilize the additional US$4.5 billion needed annually by the year 2000 is thus a central challenge facing all of us today, both as members of the international community and as individuals seeking to realize the vision of sustainable development throughout the world.

In summary, the International Forum on Population in the Twenty-first Century, coming as it did right at the end of the decade of the eighties:

   established some clear population targets
   indicated clear programme priorities
   gave a realistic assessment of programme costs.

The challenge which lay ahead was to incorporate the Amsterdam conclusions firmly into the international agenda. In December 1989, the United Nations General Assembly adopted a Resolution on 'Future needs in the field of population, including the development of resource requirements for international population assistance.' This resolution 'took note with appreciation' of the Amsterdam Declaration and 'stressed the importance' of taking it into account in further international conferences etc.[7] The most notable of these, of course, would be the United Nations Conference on Environment and Development (UNCED), to be held in Rio de Janeiro in June 1992 and the International Conference on Population and Development, to be held in Cairo in September 1994.

THE SOUTH COMMISSION

Family, mention must be made of the South Commission. Plans to establish the South Commission were first announced at the eighth Meeting of the Heads of State and Government of the Non-Aligned Countries, held in Harare, Zimbabwe, in September 1986 by Dr Mahathir bin Mohammed, Prime Minister of Malaysia. He also announced that Julius K. Nyerere, former President of Tanzania, had accepted the invitation to be the Commission's Chairman. Its term was set for three years and its work was supported by financial contributions from the developing countries and the Government of Switzerland which made a contribution to the operational costs of the secretariat based in Geneva.

   Like the World Commission on Environment and Development, the South Commission functioned as an independent body, with its members and with a distinguished membership drawn entirely from developing countries. Like the World Commission, it was concerned to place development in the widest possible perspective. Its main recommendations were aimed at domestic policy within the national setting, calling for better economic performance by the developing countries but also for action to spread the benefits of economic growth more widely among the people. It linked genuine development to popular participation, democracy, public accountability, and respect for human rights.

The Commission urged developing nations to be increasingly self-reliant and to make greater use of their own resources, national and collective. It also stressed the role of united action by the countries of the South in increasing their strength as a group and in securing global reforms through negotiations with the countries of the North.

Within this context, the South Commission's recommendations on population were especially pertinent:

> Rapid population growth rates present a formidable problem for most developing countries. Action to reduce them through integrated population and human resource planning can ease the pressures on the economy to provide jobs and lead to more benefits from investment in human resources. Developing countries should devise effective population policies, giving priority to improving child survival rates, expanding female education, and raising the social and economic status of women along with a rapid extension of family planning services. While the impact of these measures will be felt only in the long run, they must be taken now to ensure the well-being of future generations.

The Report of the South Commission was published in October 1990, some twenty months before UNCED.[8] It could be seen as another important step in the direction of the broader and deeper international consensus which, both in the months which led up to the Rio meeting and during UNCED itself, was still being sought.

NOTES

1. The Brandt Commission on Population, 1980.
2. *Perspectives*, published by UNFPA 1984.
3. See Chapter 3.
4. See Nazil Choucri, op. cit; also *Population and Conflict* by the same author, UNFPA, 1983.
5. *The Global Partnership: International Agencies and Economic Development*, edited by Richard N. Gardner and Max F. Millikan, Praeger, New York.
6. *Our Common Future*, The Report of the World Commission on Enviroment and Development, Oxford University Press, 1987.
7. United Nations General Assembly Resolution 44/210, adopted 22 December 1989.
8. *The Challenge to the South*, An Overview and Summary of the South Commission Report, The South Commission, Geneva, 1990.

10

Population at the Earth Summit: The United Nations Conference on Environment and Development (UNCED), June 1992

It was billed, inevitably, as the 'Earth Summit'. Twenty years earlier, in June 1972, when the United Nations had organised the first world conference on the human environment in Stockholm, Sweden, only one head of state or government had participated apart from the Prime Minister of the host country, Mr Olaf Palme. The sole 'Summiteer' then had been Mrs Indira Gandhi, Prime Minister of India, who had made her impassioned plea: 'Are not poverty and need the greatest polluters?'.[1] Two decades later, it was a very different matter. In the run-up to the United Nations Conference on Environment and Development – or UNCED as it was commonly known – which was to be held in Rio de Janeiro, Brazil, in June 1992, over one hundred of the world's leading statesmen and stateswomen signalled their intention to be present in person.

The heads of state or of government were not, of course, expected to attend for the whole of the two weeks which UNCED would last. But a 'Summit Segment' had conveniently been reserved towards the end of the two-week period. Time had been allotted in the Plenary sessions at the conference for the 'Summiteers' to make their statements and President Collor de Mello of Brazil, who was to preside, was urged by the conference organisers to impose a rigid limit on speaking time.

This, on the whole, he succeeded in doing. While, elsewhere in the huge conference complex situated on the outskirts of Rio, governmental delegates went about the business of agreeing UNCED's decisions and recommendations, the Plenary witnessed a succession of short, and often surprisingly inspiring, speeches. It was as though the moment – the first Earth Summit – became the men and women who took the floor. Individually and collectively they rose to the challenge. They had something important to say and they made the most of their opportunity. Some of them were resplendent in their national costumes or military uniforms; some were sombre-suited, almost bureaucratic in aspect. But, notwithstanding the difference in attire, the vast majority of the speakers pursued a single theme. The problems of the environment would not be solved unless the problems of development were addressed as well because development 'impacted' (a favourite word) on the environment, often with adverse effects. And if the problems of development were to be adequately handled, the environment and natural resources had to be safeguarded because these were the basis, the raw material as it were, of development.

LEADERS FROM THE DEVELOPING WORLD

Not all the heads of state or government addressed themselves at Rio to the question of population as the vital third leg in a development–environment–population tripod. The constraints of time alone would have made such an outcome improbable. And, as we shall see later, the inclusion of population as the third leg of the tripod, or third side of the triangle, was not yet part of received international wisdom. Nevertheless, a significant number of Rio's high-level participants did touch on this theme, directly or indirectly, and often in terms that were both vivid and moving.

For example, Fidel Castro, the long-serving President of Cuba, strode to the podium in the green guerrilla fatigues which he had worn for the last thirty years, held up an outspread palm to indicate that he would keep his remarks to an unprecedented five minutes and told an audience which included the then President of the United States, George Bush, that:

> Forests disappear, deserts grow, thousands of millions of tons of fertile soil end up in the oceans every year. Numerous species face extinction. *Overpopulation and poverty lead to desperate efforts for survival even at the expense of nature.*

Of the Latin American 'Summiteers', President Castro was perhaps the most explicit in addressing the issue of population. But leaders from other parts of the world did not mince their words either. President Soeharto of Indonesia proclaimed that:

> *To us, the interaction among development, environment and population is a cornerstone of national policy.*

Mr Ato Tamrat Layne, the Prime Minister of Ethiopia, a country whose tragedy had been played almost nightly on the world's television screens over the previous decade, said:

> *The population spiral juxtaposed with economic under-development is equally a major threat to environmentally – sound sustained development.* Consequently farmers are pressed up against the limits of cultivation which has lead to the use of marginal lands for no other than subsistence agricultural production. This, coupled with the use of wood for fuel, has accelerated the rate of deforestation. Such deforested areas in fragile eco-systems do not sustain production but rather promote soil degradation and deforestation. Consequently, the highlands are exposed to severe erosion which further accelerates desertification and drought.

For the francophone participants in the 'Earth Summit' from the developing world, the phrase 'démographie galopante' ('runaway population') seemed to be inescapable. Thus Mr Blaise Compaore, President of Burkina Faso announced:

> *La crise que voilà est encore aggravée par un démographie galopante et une urbanisation accélérée. . . .*

Mr Compaore pointed out that Burkina Faso's population was doubling every 25 years thanks to a population growth rate of 3 per cent per annum while the towns were 'literally exploding'.

His Royal Highness Side Mohammed, the Prince Royal of the Kingdom of Morocco, spoke in similar terms:

> Il est cependant une autre menace qui pèse sur notre planète, *celle d'une démographie galopante*, d'une pauvreté absolue en croissance. . . .

Speakers from Asia were no less explicit. Mr Mohammad Nawaz Sharif, Prime Minister of Pakistan, observed:

> In this endeavour, developing countries must assume their full share of responsibility in *limiting population growth to manageable levels. Although over-population is a symptom and not the root cause of poverty a meaningful effort must be made to control it.*

Mr Suleyman Demirel, Prime Minister of Pakistan's close neighbour, Turkey, added:

> *Furthermore no real progress is possible until and unless we are able to control the strains placed on natural resources by rapid population growth. The rate of increase of population has reached alarming levels. Addition of a quarter of a million new souls each day to our planet hinders efforts to eliminate poverty and maintain a decent level of economic development.* On the other hand the careless, irrational utilisation of earth's limited resources needs to be avoided.

It is, of course, important not to exaggerate the significance of these and other similar quotations. Not all the heads of state or of government who attended the Earth Summit in Rio in June 1992 took the view that population growth was a problem, let alone the vital third element in an development–environment–population triangle or tripod or whatever. Some, like Dr Mahathir Mohammed, Prime Minister of Malaysia, explicitly rejected the link between population growth and environmental degradation. Dr Mahathir protested:

> It is claimed that one of the causes of environmental degradation is the size of the population of developing countries. We dispute this assumption.

Dr Mahathir went on to add:

> We know that the 25 percent of the world population who are rich consume 80 per cent of its wealth and produce 90 percent of its waste. Mathematically speaking, if the rich reduce their wasteful consumption by 25 percent, worldwide pollution will be reduced by 22.5 percent. But if the poor 70 percent reduce consumption totally and disappear from this earth altogether the reduction in pollution will only be by 10 per cent.

Of course, Malaysia in general – and Dr Mahathir in particular – had throughout the preparations for UNCED taken a highly articulate stance on the need for the Rio conference to address fairly and squarely the fundamental concerns of the developing countries, including debt, technology transfer, trade and aid. Leaving Malaysia aside and looking primarily at the speeches delivered in the UNCED Plenary in June 1992, it is probably fair to say that on the whole Third World heads of state or government from developing countries were definitely concerned by the implications of demographic trends for the attainment of national goals in the field of environment and development.

HEADS OF DELEGATION – THE DEVELOPING WORLD

If we move beyond the 'Summit Segment' of Rio to analyze the overall package of speeches made by heads of delegations from the developing countries in the Plenary, we have – again – a sense of the deliberate emphasis given by many speakers to these questions.

Taking the speeches not in the order of delivery, but in the alphabetical order of the countries represented, we find Botswana's Assistant Minister for Local Government and Lands and Housing, Mr B. Mokgothu, stating:

> *Effective population policies are becoming crucial although economic betterment can in itself promote smaller families.* There is a dire need for a·re-direction of available resources and a better use of bi-lateral debt not only to regenerate economic growth but to eradicate poverty, *to reduce high rates of population growth* and to rehabilitate and conserve our natural resources.

Dr Song Jian, Minister in charge of the China's Science and Technology Commission in China and Chairman of the Environmental Protection Commission of China's State Council, said:

> As a big developing country, China is keenly aware of its responsibility and the important role incumbent on it in the protection of the global environment. Despite the financial, technological and other difficulties, we have made unremitting efforts over the years with a strong sense of responsibility for the whole of mankind, especially for the future generations, to maintain an ecological balance and protect the environment and eradicate poverty, improve peoples's living conditions and curb *population growth.*

Señor Luís Donaldo Colosio, Mexico's State Secretary for Social Development, said:

> All countries must work together to conserve the world's biodiversity, to preserve our woods, our seas, our animal species, to control the excessive waste of energy... to eliminate hunger, poverty, *to stabilize the growth of the world's population...*

Mr Ruhumuliza Gaspard, Rwanda's Minister of the Environment and Tourism, admitted:

> *It is, preeminently, demographic pressure on natural resources which is the root cause of the numerous handicaps which restrict the country's general development....*

And Tunisia's Minister for the Environment and Planning, Mr Salah Jebala, asked his audience the question:

> Stockholm 1972 – Rio 1992: two great rendez-vous with history. But the big questions are always there: *Have we dealt more satisfactorily with our population growth?*

In fact, if we look at the whole range of speeches made in the Plenary sessions of the UNCED conference (i.e. both in the Summit Segment and in the other Plenary meetings), we find that well over a third of the developing countries present explicitly addressed the issue of population in the context of development and environment.

LEADERS FROM THE MORE DEVELOPED COUNTRIES

The strike-rate increases dramatically, moreover, if we look at the speeches made by the representatives of the *developed* countries, heads of state or of government on the one hand or heads of delegation on the other. Not only do almost all the developed world participants address the population issue; the views expressed, and the standpoint from which such views are delivered, are virtually identical. A handful of quotations makes the point.

Mr Jean-Luc Dehaene, Prime Minister of Belgium, spoke of the 'acquis essentiel' of the conference as being the *'reconnaissance du principe qu'une démographie gallopante figure parmi les causes principales de la pression exercée par l'homme sur l'environnement'*.

Mr John Major, Prime Minister of the United Kingdom and possibly the first head of state or government to indicate a firm commitment to attend the Rio Summit, observed:

> If the emerging generation of young people is to have a chance in life at least as good as my generation, then the Rio Process must succeed. *But it has no chance of success if we do not do much better in our efforts to slow the growth of population.* Britain has long supported action which enables all women to have children by choice. We shall continue to improve access to family planning. We must improve health education more generally.

Mr Major spoke explicitly of the need to 'do much better in our efforts to slow the growth of population'. He was joined in this by Mr R.F.M. Lubbers, Prime Minister of the Netherlands. Mr Lubbers said:

> Sustainable development is not just about environment and development, but also about development at *a tenable level of population growth.*

And Mrs Gro Harlem Brundtland, who as both Prime Minister of Norway and Chairman of the World Commission of Environment and Development (usually known as the Brundtland Commission) occupied a very special place in the hearts and minds of Rio delegates, proclaimed in her speech to the Plenary:

> *We must curb population growth by more effective means than we are able to agree upon here and which recognise and reinforce the links to poverty and the rights of women.*

She spoke of the principles which had guided the Norwegian Programme for Development Cooperation. 'Our development assistance has always had an Agenda 21. It has always been poverty-orientated. It has focused on health, on basic needs, women, children, education, family planning, and – increasingly – the environment.'

Felipe González, President of Spain (a country at the heart of Old Catholic Europe) was no less emphatic:

> *The world's population will double by the middle of the next century. For that reason, the decrease of population growth is a key element to make development and environmental protection compatible.* Otherwise, food, health, water supply and urban development problems and many others, will dramatically increase. To halt this process it is necessary to defeat poverty which is at the same time the cause and effect of the population boom and constitutes, as Indira Gandhi said twenty years ago, the worst form of pollution.

Looking back over the Plenary speeches as the Rio Conference came to an end, one was struck by the way in which the population issue was being nudged from the wings more towards the centre of the stage. Kings and Queens, Princes, Presidents and Prime Minsters were talking about it and, moreover, talking about it as though they meant what they said. Population was not the main thrust of their discourse. That would have been too much to expect. But it was certainly more than a casual aside.

There was, nevertheless, a strange paradox in the workings of the Rio Conference. What the Heads of State or Government said in the Plenary sessions of the Conference did not in the end seem to matter very much. For the real business of the conference did not take place in the Plenary. It took place in the Main Committee and in the various working groups which the conference had established. This was where the hard negotiations were held. This was were the detailed page by page, paragraph by paragraph, line by line scrutiny of Agenda 21 was carried out.

Two years earlier, in his speech to the first meeting of UNCED's Preparatory Committee, held in Nairobi in August 1990, Mr Maurice Strong, UNCED's Secretary-General,[2] had explained what Agenda 21 was meant to be. He had indicated that:

> Agenda 21 would go well beyong the kind of 'action plans' which have traditionally emerged from UN conferences. It should provide the basic framework and instrumentality which will guide the world community on an ongoing basis in its decisions on the goals, targets, priorities, allocations of responsibilities and resources in respect of the many environmental issues which will determine the future of our planet.

Given such a description of the purposes and scope of Agenda 21, given moreover the clear priority which so many of the heads of state or government or heads of delegation from both developed and developing world appeared to attach to the population issue, one might have reasonably supposed that the population issue would – right from the start – have been a central part of Agenda 21.

NATIONAL REPORTS

It was not, after all, just a question of the rhetoric of the conference chamber. The detailed reports which the UNCED Secretariat had, by 1 July 1992, received from 150 countries provided striking evidence of the importance which countries themselves attached to the population issue. In an analysis completed before UNCED opened, the Conference secretariat arrived at the conclusion that 'concerns for national population dynamics are mentioned in 82 per cent reports from developing countries ... Population growth or the potential for it, is a major concern for 60 per cent of developing countries.'[3]

The figures cited may appear at first sight to be strikingly high. If so many governments were expressing concern in their own national reports, how could it be that the actual results of Rio were not more positive as far as population issues were concerned? One explanation is that the UNCED national reports in many cases arrived too late to have a meaningful impact on UNCED's deliberations. Another is that countries for one reason or another failed to take the necessary steps in the context of UNCED's cumbersome international negotiating process to convert national statements and convictions into a new international consensus.

It is illuminating in this context to go back to the original source material which the secretariat analyzed. Even a casual perusal of the national reports submitted to UNCED tends to confirm the observation that the vast majority of countries placed population high up on the list of their national priorities.

The following excerpts taken, in alphabetical order, from the collection of UNCED national reports, make the point:

> **Algeria.** 'Estimated at 10.2 million in 1962, the Algerian population rose to 16.9 million in the census of 1977 and to 23 million in the census of 1987 posing the problem of how to satisfy the needs of an important young population as far as education, health, housing, employment etc are concerned.... With a forecast of 33 million inhabitants in the year 2000 and 57 million by 2025, Algeria will be con-

fronted with the problems of the pressure on water resources and on good agricultural land, by an increasing dependence on outside sources of food and *by the absorption through population increase of the gains of economic growth'*.

Antigua and Barbuda. 'the relationship between population, common resources and environment is well documented. Given the fragile nature of insular Caribbean environments, their finite land area and limited absorptive capacity, *the question of future population growth and distribution must emerge as a top priority for policy makers in the 1990s...'*

Bangladesh. 'Bangladesh faces serious problems of over-population, extreme poverty, illiteracy and environmental degradation with natural resource depletion. These factors combine to multiply the scale of constant socio-economic setbacks, imposed by recurring natural hazards, often of exceptional magnitude. *The single most important factor that will hamper devvelopment in Bangladesh, if not addressed properly, is the size and rate of growth of an already overwhelmingly large population... In view of Bangladesh's limited resources, it is essential to focus parallel efforts to slow down population growth, on the one hand,* and adequately address the problems of depletion of forest, loss of inland wetlands, over-exploitation of fisheries, destruction of fish habitat and larvae, and poor land and soil management on the other.'

Benin. 'Because of *galloping population growth,* the global performance of the Beninese economy is much less than it ought to be in order to maintain the present standard of living.... In densely populated areas, the problem of land tenure is becoming crucial as it aggravates the degradation and the quality of life to such an extent that known methods of detection provide no relief.'

Bhutan. *'The population is growing rapidly,* and will be further accelerated by better health programmes resulting in lower child mortality and longer life expectancy. This increase cannot easily be absorbed by the existing rural or urban communities. The future socio-economic balance depends on a strictly enforced population planning policy and or new means of livelihood dependent on the land.'

'The royal Government of Bhutan is preparing a comprehensive family planning policy, including a social security scheme for elderly childless citizens...'

Turning to countries ranged in the middle of the alphabet, we find the following:

Ghana. 'The impact of these demographic trends and characteristics on the environment mirrors a number of issues. *The fast momentum of population growth continues to exert tremendous pressure on natural resource systems in the country.* Without sound and sustainable environmental management, pressure of population leads to land degradation, impoverishment of the soil, outright loss of arable land and decline in the crop yields especially in the rural area of the country.

In the urban areas, features of population concentration have generated some environmental problems such as vehicular emissions, industrial pollution and slums.'

Iran. 'Iran at present, with 57 million people, is the 20th most populated country in the world. *If the trend of population growth (3.15 per cent) continues over the next thirty years, Iran will become the 10th most populated country.* Three million Afghani and Iraqi refugees in recent years have increased the real population to over 60 million. The reasons for such growth are multifaceted: The population under 15 years old comprises 45.5 per cent of the total, while those over 65 years account for

35. With such a young population, it is anticipated that the country's population will double in thirty years, further affecting natural resources use. Thus the consequence will be a more degraded environment, unless some vigorous measures are taken. As a result, family planning is considered one of the main challenges of the country over the next decade, aimed at decreasing the rate of population growth from 3.2 per cent to 2.3 per cent by the year 2010.'

Jordan. *'There is no doubt that high and rapid population increase has great effects on the development processes on the one hand, and the disturbance of population distribution on the other.* In Jordan, the population increase has had negative effects on the environment in terms of concentration around urban areas and the main cities where demand on social and security services and the public facilities such as the sewage system increases. That leads to decreasing capacity of these facilities to meet all demands resulting from the rapid population increase and the emergence of unplanned slum and squatter areas which lack most services and basic facilities. All that leads to the emergence of environmental pollution due to dumping waste in the alleys and open yards or burning waste in an unhealthy way, emitting smoke and gases which pollute the air into the area. This is reflected in the emergence of large and numerous population settlements at the expense of agricultural lands (thus decreasing agricultural productivity), on the one hand, and increasing unhealthy practices by the population on the other.'

Korea. 'Korea is a country which has successfully implemented birth control. In 1970, the increase of population per year was 2.04 per cent.'

In 1990, the rate was 0.98 per cent. *As over-population is a major reason for environmental disruption, the success in birth control is regarded as a success for sustainable development.* Though much of the success should be credited to the economic planners of the government, the important role of women should be recognised. In a society where the Confucian tradition has been strong, the voluntary participation of women in the national effort to curtail the population increase is impressive. Without such voluntary movement among the women, Korea's social structure could have been quite different today.'

Lebanon. *'Demography constitutes the basic element of any analysis on the environment and development. The equilibrium between population numbers and their distribution and available resources constitutes a major objective of development – environment policies and distinctly influences the well-being of the population.* Any demographic pressure leading to an over-exploitation of resources constitutes a danger to the very safeguard of such resources. Demographic tendencies, the protection of the environment and a lasting economic development are closely connected and policies must aim at creating balanced objectives among these three fields.'

However, although no accurate statistics are known, demographic pressure is manifest in urban concentrations which group about 60 per cent of the total population with all that this implies in problems relating to the environment and infrastructure problems (distribution of drinking water, evacuation of used waters, household rubbish, transport etc.).'

Lesotho. 'Lesotho's population is currently estimated at around 1.7 million, but considering land area, Lesotho is somewhat more densely populated than many low income countries. *The relatively small population, and by African standards the modest 2.6 per cent annual increase, is of major concern when related to available resources.* The largest settlement is Maseru, the capital city which was enumerated in 1986 at 106,000 but is increasing at a rate of 7 per cent per annum.'

Mauritius. 'Mauritius also shows that scientific studies concerning the future, such as the Mead and Titmuss reports, did have a significant impact on national population policies, and that international support through the International Planned Parenthood Federation (IPPF) and UNFPA was instrumental for implementing family planning successfully on a larger scale. *But above all, it was the understanding of the Mauritian people that, for a sustainable development on the limited space and resources given by the Island, the population cannot grow indefinitely.*'

Myanmar. 'Although Myanmar has relatively low population density compared to most countries of South East Asia, the forest resources have come *under growing population pressure, resulting in certain amount of deforestation and a decline in wildlife populations through overhunting and habitat destruction.*'

Finally, we may turn to countries appearing at the end of the alphabet. Once again, we find that there is a striking emphasis on demographic issues.

Swaziland. *'The rapid growth of the population is one of the most important development issues that concerns Government.* In 1986 the population of Swaziland was 681,000 people indicating an average population growth of 3.2 per cent per annum for the inter-census period 1976–1986. The high population growth rate has resulted in increasing pressure on the natural resources such as the depletion of natural forests which are heavily used in the provision of shelter and fuel, soil erosion due to over-utilisation of land, poor conservation methods and overgrazing by livestock.'

Tanzania. 'Between 1978 and 1988, the mainland experienced an annual population growth rate of 2.8 per cent and Zanzibar 3 per cent. Due to rural–urban migration, the mainland urban population has jumped from 12.2 per cent in 1978 to 20 per cent in 1990. On Zanzibar over 40 per cent of the population now live in urban areas.

The fast growing population is posing new challenges to sustainable utilization of natural resources. More intensive human activities and denser settlement patterns exacerbate environmental degradation.

This perception of the impact of rapid growth on development and the environment is recasting the role of population in planning; hence the need to influence population trends both qualitatively and quantitatively.'

Vietnam. *'While formulating policies on environment and sustainable development, Vietnam pays special attention to the relationship between population and socio-economic situation; as population grows, human basic needs to be met from various eco-systems would also increase and consequently it is inevitable that the environment and natural resources will be further damaged as shown by experiences from many countries in the world and in the region.* Greater efforts should be made to carry out family planning programmes in order to reduce the natural population growth rate, alleviate poverty, rapidly expand the national economy with a view to breaking up the vicious circle of poverty – rapid population growth – environment damage and further poverty. Facts of life indicate clearly that effective protection of environment and development also mean concerns for the living conditions and benefits of local people; apart from the income generation, schooling problems should be solved to raise people's intellect, and attention should be given to health service, water supply and sanitation.

The rapid increase in population and the growing needs for food will surely go hand in hand with the abusive use of chemical fertilizers, insecticides and greater demand for water. The increasing uses of chemical fertilizers and water will cause damages to land resources, water pollution and in long term perspective, it will seriously threaten food security. Vietnam is endeavouring to step up the use of fertilizers in the forms of tree leaves, dungs, azalea, and other organic sources, to improve the use of water for irrigation by using techniques and technology that could safeguard the fertility of land.

Fresh water sources which vitally link to human life are now becoming depleted as the demand is getting bigger due to *increasing population pressure*, and at the same time water quality is getting worse due to pollution. Climatic changes could result in a re-distribution of fresh water sources.'

Zaire. '*Realizing the need of a controlled population growth for the proper implementation of integrated rural and urban development*, it is necessary that the following measures are undertaken.

Country strategies and recommendations.

1. Ensure the preparation and adoption of a national urbanization plan through the provision of basic infrastructure.

2. *Promote and enhance the adoption of a comprehensive policy on population control.*

3. *Provide education on family planning to both men and women.'*

Zimbabwe. 'The 1969 census gave a crude birth rate of 48 per thousand and a crude death rate of 15 per thousand, which provided a rate of natural increase of 3.33 per cent. The 1982 data for the same parameters were 39.5 and 10.8, giving a rare of natural increase of 2.9 per cent. Whatever the actual figure is, *the country's population growth rate is high and has a bearing on the nature of development planning. Also this rate threatens the sustainability of development particularly in the Communal Areas where population pressure on limited resources is already having negative impacts on the environment.'*[4]

In addition to their general concern with the implications of population growth for sustainable development, the Conference secretariat further calculated that around 40 per cent of the countries submitting national reports to UNCED saw *urbanisation* trends as threatening their development prospects and as a major constraint in their fight against poverty. Around 30 per cent recognised that the spatial distribution of their population posed problems and should be modified. One out of four countries was faced with *migration* and/or *refugee* problems.[5]

As noted above, it might have been expected that the content of these national reports with their striking emphasis on population issues (taken together with the speeches delivered at UNCED itself by heads of state or government, or heads of delegation) would have had a major impact on the final outcome. In fact that does not appear to have been the case. On the whole, the comments about the importance of population issues for environment and development which occur in the national reports, as well as in the speeches made in Plenary, give a largely misleading impression of the priority accorded to population issues in the final outcome of UNCED.

The reality is that UNCED, *judged by the texts actually adopted at the Conference*, notably Agenda 21, did not handle the population issue satisfactorily. Indeed, this is preeminently an area where UNCED failed to live up to expectations. Because the issue is so tremendously important for so many countries and for so many people, as indicated by all the reports and speeches cited above, it is instructive to look at the negotiating record.

POPULATION WITHIN THE UNCED PROCESS

For practical purposes, UNCED owed its origin to a resolution of the United Nations adopted on 22nd December 1989 (GA resolution 44/228). UNCED's purpose, as set out in the General Assembly resolution, was nothing less than 'to elaborate strategies and measures to halt and reverse the environmental degradation of the planet'. Neither the original resolution of the UN General Assembly calling for the conference, nor the early planning documents, made any reference to the extraordinary increase in human numbers or to the rapid changes in their distribution which were taking place. These texts also failed to mention the complex links between these factors and the earth's resources, its environment and efforts to achieve sustainable development.[6]

However, in the months which followed the first General Assembly Resolution, a great deal of work was done within the UNCED Secretariat and outside to make good these omissions. By the time the fourth UNCED preparatory meeting was convened in New York in March 1992, the draft text of Agenda 21 contained a balanced treatment of population in relation to issues such as consumption, poverty, education, human settlements, fragile ecosystems, agriculture, oceans and fresh water.[7]

The draft of Agenda 21 also included at this stage carefully developed proposals on how to deal with the population issue. There was clear specific language in Chapter 5 dealing with 'Demographic Dynamics and Sustainability' urging governments to provide 'integrated health care, including universal access to family planning and the provision of safe contraceptives.' It also called for an increase in population funding from the then funding levels of US $5 billion to a year 2000 level of about US $9 billion – or an average of US $7.5 billion over the next eight years. To achieve this, donor support would have to rise from less than US $1 billion to over US $4 billion by the year 2000.

An article published in *Rio Reviews, 1992* (a collection of essays looking back at UNCED published in the autumn of 1992 by the Centre for Our Common Future) described what happened in practice:

> In the event, both this language and the proposals for funding suffered in the final preparatory meeting where the Holy See succeeded in finding political support to weaken the language on population and remove any references to 'family planning' as such. The Vatican which opposes all form of contraception other than 'natural methods' claimed that the draft language in Agenda 21 undermined family values and personal dignity and encouraged contraceptive use without adequate attention to safety. The Vatican representatives also argued that the relationship between population and development is both 'complex and tenuous, and took the position that 'Population growth in and of itself is seldom the primary cause of environmental problems'.

The 'political support' which the Holy See found in New York in April 1992 at the fourth and crucial meeting of the UNCED PrepCom did not materialize purely as a result of last-minute divine intervention. If the lobbying efforts undertaking by the representatives of the Holy See in the corridors of the United Nations during those few weeks of PrepCom IV were successful it was in the end because there was as yet no rock-solid consensus within UNCED on the vital place of population policies and programmes as part of the environment – development – population triad. In a sense, the Holy See was pushing at a door which, if not fully open, was at least ajar. (Besides being able through its membership of the United Nations to table amendments in its own right, the Vatican could usually rely confidently on some delegations, for example the Philippines, to act as surrogates when required and to give aid and comfort in Committee sessions, drafting groups, caucuses and so on.)

Not surprisingly, a few weeks before Rio, there was a small flurry of articles in the media claiming that UNCED was signally failing to address the issue of population growth and the linkages between demographic factors and the environment. The United Kingdom's Prince Charles, never a stranger to intellectual controversy, addressed a specially reconvened session of the World Commission on Environment and Development in forthright terms on April 22, 1992.

> I do not want to add to the controversy over cause and effect with respect to the Third World's problems. Suffice it to say that I don't, in all logic, see how any society can expect to improve its lot when population growth regularly exceeds economic growth. The factors which will reduce population growth are, by now, easily identified: a standard of health care that makes family planning viable, increased female literacy, reduced infant mortality and access to clean water. Achieving them, of course, is more difficult – but perhaps two simple truths need to be writ large over the portals of every international gathering about the environment: we will not slow the birth rate until we address poverty. And we will not protect the environment until we address the issue of poverty and population growth in the same breath.[8]

Prince Charles went to say that he wished that 'these simple and incontestable truths could find greater prominence on the Rio agenda. Sadly, it seems that certain delegations are determined to prevent discussion of population growth. In so doing, of course, they deny everyone else the opportunity for constructive discussion of policies which would address the environment, poverty and population growth together, rather than in isolation.'

Perhaps mindful of Prince Charles' criticism, Maurice Strong himself, in his opening statement to the Conference on 3 June, 1992, pointedly referred to 'the explosive increase in population, largely in the developing world, that is adding a quarter of a million people daily. Since 1972 world population has grown by 1.7 billion people, equivalent to almost the entire population at the beginning of this century. 1.5 billion of these live in developing countries which are least able to support them. This cannot continue. Population must be stabilized, and rapidly. If we do not do it, nature will, and much more brutally.'

In her own remarks to the Conference, Dr Nafis Sadik, the Executive Director of the United Nations Population Fund (UNFPA), reminded the gathering that nine out of ten developing countries which had reported to UNCED referred to population growth and distribution as being among their major concerns. She referred in particular to a recent statement by President Collor of Brazil. Population, according to President Collor, did not stabilize through authoritarian 'population control'. 'On the contrary' said Dr Sadik, 'it emerges naturally through education, health and welfare policies. Development plans must therefore give priority to social investment – to education, especially for women, health and welfare; and to the other measures which will encourage slower population growth.'[9]

HEADS OF UN AGENCIES' SPEECHES

In addition to Maurice Strong and Dr Nafis Sadik, almost all the other heads of the international organisations represented at Rio referred explicitly to the population question.

Dr Mostafa Tolba, Executive Director of the United Nations Environment Programme (UNEP), said:

> The world population of 5.4 billion is expected to increase by 1.7 billion in the next two decades, by far the largest increase in human history. Population equilibrium

may be reached at 10.5 billion by the year 2110, or it may surge to approximately 14 billion. This is a matter of deep concern as it will be coupled with more dwindling of the world's resources, carrying capacity and pollution assimilative capacity.

For decades, we have recognised the urgent need to design and fund family planning programmes which reflect and respect cultural, religious, ethical and traditional values; which recognise the vital role of women in development, education, environmental management and family health; and which are designed to empower people. We all know what must be done. What we need, is the courage, leadership and resources to do it.

James P. Grant, Executive Director of UNICEF, spoke in moving terms of the necessary links between population policy and investment in human development.

Nowhere is the linkage between environment and development more tangible and dramatic than in the issue of population. The present global pattern of human activity at current population levels is rapidly depleting resources and placing natural systems under extraordinary stress. No-one knows exactly what our Earth's carrying capacity is, but there is no question that growth rates that are now doubling the world's population in the space of only 35 years present a challenge which needs action at the global, national and household level. Stabilizing the Earth's population is possible – the experience of the industrial world and a number of developing countries attests to this – but the sharp reductions that will have to take place in the developing world will require a massive assault on poverty's worst consequences, a major improvement in the basic health care, education and the status of women, a revolution in social values and reproductive behaviour.

Mr William Draper, the then Administrator of the United Nations Development Programme (UNDP), spoke in similar terms:

We must recognise that environment is not an isolated problem, and cannot be addressed as such. Explosive population growth, poverty and environmental degradation are part of the same vicious circle. In developing countries, the choices that people make which harm the environment, such as chopping down forests for fuelwood and farmland, are for reasons of survival – not lack of concern. We can't force people to stop cutting down trees, but we can help people develop alternative livelihoods. Similarly, we can lower population growth by making education and economic opportunities available to women. World population has doubled between 1950 and 1990 and is likely to double again by the year 2050. For the outcome and follow-up to this crucial conference to be meaningful, the linkages between population, poverty and the environment must be addressed by the whole world. The population issue must not be pushed to the sidelines.

Finally, Mr Lewis T. Preston, President of the World Bank, stressed the Bank's own concern with the population issue:

Today, over a billion people live in acute poverty. Within the next forty years, the world's population will grow by about 4 billion people, most of them in poor countries. To meet their needs, food production will have to double. Industrial output and energy use will triple worldwide, and increase five-fold in the developing countries. This will place great strains on the environment.

Policies which make economic sense, as well as environmental sense, are the most important positive links. For example: promoting the role of women, so often the principle managers of resources, and implementing programs aimed at slowing the population growth rate which is placing unsustainable pressure on natural resource use.

The Bank will expand its work in areas where urgent action is required, such as water supply and sanitation, agricultural research and extension, energy conversation, reforestation, family planning, health and education – particularly education for girls.

CLEAR MESSAGE – DISAPPOINTING OUTCOME

The message, surely, could not have been clearer. Yet it has to be said that as far as the detailed drafting of the relevant chapter of Agenda 21 is concerned these appeals in the Plenary from the 'great and the good', from the bright stars in the firmament of United Nations organizations, were of no more effect that those earlier appeals, during UNCED's Summit Segment, of the various heads of state or government. Looked at coldly and objectively, the language of Agenda 21 on population was a big disappointment – at least to those who came to Rio hoping that here at last, after so many years of passionate, often anguished debate, an international consensus, both practical and political, would at last be achieved.

Why, among the 'practitioners' was the language of Agenda 21's Chapter 5 on 'Demographic Dynamics and Sustainability' regarded as unsatisfactory? There seem to be a number of reasons.

In the first place, the treatment given to population issues in Agenda 21 clearly was not conclusive. It did not define, incontestably, a new international consensus on population, elevating population to its rightful place in the new trinity. Secondly, after Rio there was considerable debate as to whether the language actually agreed at UNCED as far as population and family planning was concerned was in any sense to be considered an advance when set against previously agreed texts, or whether on the contrary it was to be seen as a set-back.

Take, for example, the question of global or national population targets. Agenda 21, in paragraph 5.3 recognized that 'the growth of world population and production combined with unsustainable consumption patterns places increasingly severe stress on the life-supporting capacities of our planet.' It accepted, in paragraph 5.4, that 'there is a need to develop strategies to mitigate both the adverse effect on the environment of human activities and the adverse impact of environmental change on human populations.' It called for better understanding of, and more research into the relationships between population, environment and development. But nowhere did Agenda 21 suggest clearly and unambiguously that the world as a whole should try to limit its rate of population growth, with a view ultimately to stabilizing world population. Nor did it invite individual countries to do so.

On any analysis, this was disappointing. It can even be argued that it represented a retreat vis-à-vis the somewhat muddy language on the subject of global and national targets which is to be found in the conclusions and recommendations of the Bucharest, 19774 and Mexico City, 1984, world population conferences (see Chapters 6 and 8).

What kind of global and national demographic targets might UNCED have adopted? At the very least, the language of the Amsterdam Declaration could have been included which, as noted in Chapter 9, calls for:

> A reduction in the average number of children born per woman commensurate with achieving, as a minimum, the medium variant population projections of the United Nations.

What would such a target have meant in numerical terms? In an article entitled 'A New Development Agenda' published soon after the conclusion of the Rio Conference, UNFPA's Executive Director, Dr Nafis Sadik, wrote:

> in population, the internationally agreed aim should be to keep overall population growth within or slightly below the medium projection – that is to say 6.2 billion by the end of the century, 10 billion by the middle of the next century and eventually about 11 billion.[10]

As we shall see in the final chapter of this book, Dr Sadik, as Secretary General of the International Conference on Population and Development to be held in Cairo in September 1994, made a determined effort at the May 1993 meeting of the ICPD's Preparatory Committee, to persuade delegates to put forward a whole series of goals for the Cairo meeting, including – amongst others – goals for world population stabilization at an early date.

Another disappointment, where population is concerned, is to be found in the description, under Programme Area C, of 'supporting programmes that promote changes in demographic trends and factors towards sustainability.' Take, to give another example, the crucial question of official support for family planning programmes which are at the core of efforts to control fertility. The language in paragraph 5.50 of Agenda 21 about 'women and men' having 'the same right to decide freely and responsibly on the number and spacing of their children' appears at first sight to echo the language of the World Population Plan of Action (WPPA) agreed at the World Population Conference, 1974. There are clear references in the WPPA to the right of couples to decide 'in a free, informed and responsible manner, the number and spacing of their children.'[11]

However, para 5.50 also talks about 'freedom, dignity and personally-held values taking into account ethical and cultural considerations.' This phraseology resulted from a controversial discussion which had taken place in New York during the final meeting of the Preparatory Committee in April 1992, and in particular from a set of amendments introduced by the Holy See both in Chapter 5 of Agenda 21 on 'Demographic Dynamics and Sustainability' and in Chapter 6 of Agenda 21 which dealt with the 'Protection and Promotion of Human Health'. Though the language of the 'Recommendations for the further implementation of the World Population Plan of Action' which were adopted at Mexico City in August 1984, ten years after the Bucharest meeting, on the occasion of the International Conference on Population, nuanced to some extent the Bucharest affirmation by referring to 'changing individual and cultural values' (Recommendation 25), the victory which the Vatican gained at PrepCom IV was seen by many as introducing an unnecessary qualification to a previously unambiguous statement.

Equally, para 5.51 talks about 'responsible planning of family size'. Here, we again find the Vatican formula 'in keeping with freedom, dignity and personally held values and taking into account ethical and cultural considerations'. It has also been pointed out, for example by Dr Nafis Sadik,[12] that Agenda 21 does not mention family planning as such.

'This is disappointing' says Sadik. 'The phrase used in Agenda 21, 'responsible planning of family size', is less comprehensive than the language we are used to; family planning refers to the well-being of the whole family, not just the question of size.'
She goes on to argue that:

> targets for the end of the century should include raising the number of couples using family planning by 50 per cent, raising age of marriage while reducing teenage pregnancy and maternal and infant mortality.

'We hope that these targets,' writes Dr Sadik, 'will be further strengthened by decisions taken at the International Conference and Development in Cairo in 1994, which should embody firm and precise global agreement on action.'

One last area where the outcome of Rio was disappointing was on the question of resources for population and family planning programmes.

The UNCED Secretariat estimated the average total cost of implementing the Agenda 21 programme for Chapter 5 ('Demographic Dynamics and Sustainability') at around US$7 billion annually. In 1992 total national and international expenditures for family planning and other major population activities in all developing countries amounted to about US$4.6 billion annually, with around 80 per cent coming from the developing countries themselves. There was thus a shortfall of around $3 billion.[13] No solid commitments were made at Rio by the industrialized countries with a view to bridging the gap. To that extent, Rio failed to deliver what was needed.

Of course, not all of the extra funding, the missing US $3 billion or whatever would necessarily have to be provided by the rich industrialised countries. As noted above, in the population field, as in most other sectors of activity, resources generated domestically in the developing countries underpin the bulk of national expenditures. The UNCED secretariat calculated nevertheless that some $3.5 billion annually should be provided by the international community on grant or concessional terms. Dr Sadik has argued that the target should be:

> to increase the proportion of assistance (in the population field) to 50 per cent. For the industrialized countries, this will mean increasing their population assistance to four per cent of their aid budgets.[14]

UNCED's shortcomings on the financial resources front were not limited to the field of population. Indeed, there were very few sectors of activity where it was possible to identify 'new and additional financial resources' as having been specifically committed towards the implementation of Agenda 21.[15] This challenge still lay on the table of the international community in the months which followed the Rio Conference. In a general sense, it would be taken up by the Commission for Sustainable Development, the body set up by the United Nations General Assembly after Rio to be responsible for the follow-up to UNCED. And as far as population and family planning is concerned, it was certain that the question of resources would have to be faced fairly and squarely in Cairo in August 1994. We return to this question in the penultimate chapter.

UNCED AS A POINTER TO THE FUTURE

Even if the Rio meeting, in the area of population, failed in the final analysis to deliver crucial commitments, notably on demographic targets, support of family planning programmes and increased resources, it was nevertheless a valuable exercise. In the article already quoted,[16] Lassonde and Rowley state their belief that:

> Behind all the noise and confusion over population at Rio, UNCED will we believe, prove to be something of a turning point in the manner in which population issues are seen in international fora.

They distinguish at least four major changes.

First of all, a series of analytical breakthroughs have taken place. Population dynamics is now more widely recognised as one of the major driving forces of environmental change, and as a major component of any sound development policy.

Second, UNCED contributed to the dismantling of the strong pernicious and long-lasting stereotype of the North imposing fertility reduction methods on the South in exchange for financial and technical assistance. Lassonde and Rowley comment:

> At first, the group of 77 fell into this trap, using population programmes as a 'bargaining chip' but soon realised that it was in their own interest to support the inclusion of population activities in Agenda 21 .... They are now more aware of the huge development benefits of family planning especially when provided alongside other programmes to improve the lives of women and children.

Third, UNCED has motivated a new sense of urgency. Identification of irreversible trends driven by population dynamics has created the awareness of the need to act immediately. Land degradation in Africa (and South–North migrations resulting from this) is but one example of the interdependence of population, economic and social factors, that affect the world community.

Lastly, UNCED greatly revived interest and concern for population issues. Those people who thought that the demographic transition was taking place smoothly in all regions discovered, through national analysis, that this was not the case. Urbanisation, migration, movement of refugees and displacement of people because of environmental disruption were examples of the realities that were directly linked to population.

> One other pointer, or potential pointer, was thrown up not in the Conference centre but in the Global Forum (a non-governmental event which took place in downtown Rio, some twenty or thirty miles from the UNCED proceedings). Lassonde and Rowley note that discussions on population at the women's tent *Planeta Femea* were marked by harsh criticism of 'top down' population control programmes which in the opinion of many speakers put an emphasis on demographic targets which 'too often lead to insensitive and coercive services.' An Alternative Treaty on Population, Environment, and Development, negotiated and agreed by several NGOs, stressed that women's empowerment to control their own lives is a foundation for all action linking these ares. The Alternative Treaty denounced 'abusive population control programmes and called for 'women-centred, women-managed and women-controlled' comprehensive reproductive health care ... including safe and legal voluntary contraceptives and abortion facilities.'[17]

Lassonde and Rowley pointed out that such views, strongly held as they were by feminist groups in various parts of the world, were perhaps more a result of insensitive policies of the past than of the present when there was much emphasis on integrated approaches and quality family planning services. They believe it was now widely understood that such services – defined in terms of real care and concern for the user – were essential for the success of any programme.

The Global Forum was, of course, a special example of the participation of non-governmental organizations (NGOs) in the whole UNCED process. More generally, NGOs were made to feel welcome both during the preparatory phases of UNCED and during the Conference itself. Their active contribution was sought and the Conference organizers, in particular Mr Maurice Strong – the UNCED Secretary-General – went out of his way to assure NGOs that their input was valuable, even essential.

The lessons learned from UNCED, as far as the participation of NGOs are concerned, have not been forgotten. The Rio formula has been adopted for other meetings, including the forthcoming Cairo Conference on Population and Development, One may argue that, though Rio failed to deliver all that had been hoped as far as population was concerned and though the final output failed to match the initial rhetoric; it was nevertheless, on the question of NGO participation a truly path-breaking event. For that reason, if for no other, Rio must be considered as more than just a way-station on the long road from Bucharest to Cairo.

NOTES

1. See p. 65 *The Population Problem*, ed. Stanley Johnson, David and Charles, Newton Abbot 1973.
2. Maurice Strong, a Canadian businessman, also served as the Secretary-General of the first United Nations Conference on the Human Environment, held in Stockholm in June 1972.
3. Mimeograph text. Population issues in the United Nations Conference on Environment and Development. Final Report, Louise Lassonde, July 1992. Mrs Lassonde was loaned to UNCED staff by the United Nations Population Fund (UNFPA). After the Rio Conference, she resumed her post with UNFPA as the Fund's representative in Geneva.
4. These UNCED national reports are in some ways the most interesting – and most revealing – of all the UNCED documentation, though they remain relatively inaccessible for the present. A two-volume summary of the national reports submitted to UNCED has been published by the United Nations. In addition, the full texts of the national reports are available on CD-ROM, which can be obtained through the United Nations Publication Office.
5. Lassonde, op. cit.
6. cf Louise Lassonde's and John Rowley's essay 'Population: an emerging factor' published in *Rio Reviews 1992*, The Centre for Our Common Future. John Rowley, a former head of the publications programme of the International Planned Parenthood Federation, is now editor of the magazine *People and the Planet*.
7. Lassonde and Rowley, op. cit., p. 27.
8. Cited in *The Earth Summit: The United Nations Conference on Environment and Development*, ed. Stanley P. Johnson, Graham and Trotman/Martinus Nijhoff, London/Dordrecht 1993. See p. 157.
9. Earth Summit, as cited, p. 157.
10. *People and the Planet*, Vol. 1, No. 4, 1992, p. 7.
11. World Population Plan of Action, para. 29 (a). Report of the United Nations World Population Conference, 1974. E/CONF.60/19. United Nations publications sales No. E. 75. XIII. 3.
12. Article reviewing outcome of UNCED, as far as population questions were concerned, by Dr Nafis Sadik, Executive Director of UNFPA, published in *People and the Planet*, Vol. 1. No. 4, 1992, p. 7.
13. For newer calculations concerning the cost of population and family planning programmes, see Chapter 15. These calculations, without adjusting for inflation, show the cost of population and family planning expenditures rising to around $10.7 billion by the year 2000, with some $4.1 billion or 38 per cent coming from the DAC countries – countries which are members of the Development Assistance Committee of the Organization for Economic Co-operation and Development (OECD).
14. Sadik, op. cit.
15. The first substantive meeting of the Commission for Sustainable Development (CSD) established as a result of UNCED was held in New York in June 1993 with the issue of financial resources for the implementation of Agenda 21 high on its agenda.
16. 1992 Rio Reviews, Population: An emerging factor.
17. Alternative Treaties: Synergistic Processes for Sustainable Communities and Global Responsibility, International NGO Forum, Rio de Janeiro, June 1992. Edited by Robert Pollard, Ruth West and Will Sutherland. Published by Ideas for Tomorrow Today and International Synergy Institute.

11

World Population Situation in 1989

In 1990, the Population Division of the United Nations Department of International Economic and Social Affairs published the seventh in its series of periodic reviews of world and regional developments in the field of population.[1] The UN reported that the 1988 revision of the United Nations population estimates and projections estimated the total population of the world in mid-1988 to be 5.1 billion. Between mid-1986 and mid-1987 the population of the world increased by 86 million, and from mid-1987 to mid-1988 by another 88 million. After a period of deceleration from its historic peak (2 per cent) in the late 1960s, the rate of population growth for 1987–1988 had levelled off at around 1.7 per cent – the rate maintained during the period 1975–1980 and 1980–1985. It was expected that the rate would continue at that level through the decade 1985–1995.

The developing regions had a population of about 3.68 billion as of mid-1985, three-quarters of the world's total population and were estimated to be growing at 2.1 per cent a year. The developed regions had a population of 1.17 billion in mid-1985 and were increasing at 0.65 per cent annually in the early eighties.

There were considerable differences between both the developed and the developing regions in terms of trends and patterns of population growth. Africa, which had 11.5 per cent of the world's population, was currently growing the most rapidly, at 3 per cent per year. Moreover, the rate of population growth there did not give any indication of having yet reached its peak. Latin America, with 8.3 per cent of the world's population, grew at 2.2 per cent per year between 1980 and 1985. Population growth in Asia, with 58 per cent of the world's population, slowed to 1.9 per cent per year during the first half of the 1980s and was projected to remain at about the same rate during 1985–1990.

In the developed regions, Europe grew by about one third of 1 per cent per year during the first half of the 1980s and was continuing to decelerate. Northern America grew at 2 per cent annually and was also decelerating.

In the closing years of the 1980s, 76 countries out of 170 viewed their rate of growth as satisfactory. The proportion of countries holding such a view had remained quite steady for a decade and a half. On the other hand, there had been a continuing decline in the number of countries that viewed their population growth as too low, and a corresponding increase in the number that considered it to be too high.

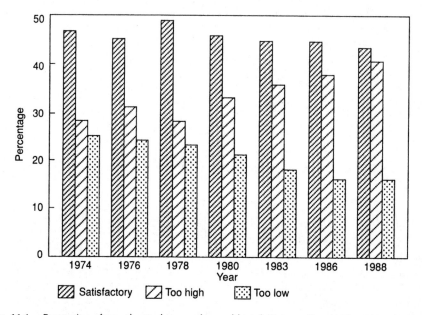

Fig. 11.1.   Perception of growth rate, by year, for world total. *Source: Concise Report on the World Population Situation in 1989.* (1990) United Nations.

As of 1988, 68 countries considered their rate of growth to be too high and 26 saw it as too low. 31 per cent of the world's population lived in a country where the Government viewed the rate of population growth as satisfactory, 63 per cent where it was viewed as too high, and 6 per cent where it was viewed as too low.

Among the less developed countries, just over one third of the Governments considered the rate of growth to be satisfactory; 52 per cent viewed it as too high and 14 per cent as too low. Over the previous decade and a half, the marked trend had been for an increasing proportion of the Governments to perceive the rate as too high, with corresponding declines in the proportion viewing it as either too low or satisfactory. The United Nations commented:

> *83.5 per cent of the population of the developing countries live where the Government viewed the rate as too high.* The 18 countries where the rate is viewed as too low tended to be very small in absolute size of population: in total, they account for just 3 per cent of the population of all developing countries. (emphasis added)

In the developed regions, Governments were divided between those that considered the rate of growth too low (21 per cent, with 14 per cent of the population) and those that considered it to be satisfactory (79 per cent, with 86 per cent of the population). During the previous decade and a half there had been a steady increase in the number of developed countries viewing their rate as satisfactory and a corresponding decrease in those that viewed it as too low. (In 1974, more than two out of five Governments reported that they considered the rate to be too low; by 1988 the fraction had fallen to one in five.) This change had occurred during a period when the rate of growth itself had fallen from around 0.6 to about 0.4 per cent per year.

Ninety-nine countries reported that they intervened to influence the rate of growth, while the remaining 71 indicated that they did not. Some 61 per cent of the world's population lived in countries where the Government intervened to lower the rate of population growth; virtually all of them were developing countries.

The UN reported that, in general, the world's population continued its overall trend towards demographic aging. As of 1985, the median age of all human beings was 23.4 years, nearly two years older than a decade and a half earlier, when the global median age reached its lowest point since the middle of the century. Only in Africa had there as yet been no indication of the beginning of a demographic aging process; the median age for the population of Africa declined to 17.3 years as of 1985.

Despite the trend towards demographic aging, children (conventionally defined as persons aged 0–14 years) remained the largest group of dependants nearly everywhere in the world. In 1985, there were some 1.6 billion children in the world. About 16 per cent of them lived in the developed regions and 84 per cent in the developing regions. Sixty-one per cent of all children – nearly 1 billion – lived in Asia. What was most striking, however, was that the population of children was growing at less than half the rate of the world's population at all ages. Moreover, except for Africa and the somewhat special case of the Union of Soviet Socialist Republics, the population of children in every region was growing more slowly than the total population. In Europe, the population of children had entered a decline in absolute numbers; there were just over 6 million fewer children in Europe in 1985 than in 1980.

The elderly population (defined as those aged 65 years and over) numbered some 290 million in 1985, 6 per cent of the total at all ages. Continuing reductions in mortality and fertility were raising the proportion of the elderly in all regions of the world; the rate of growth among them was higher than it was for the total population. For the world as a whole, the elderly were increasing at about a 40-per-cent-higher rate.[2]

In the developed regions, the elderly comprised some 11.5 per cent of the total population. They were slightly over 4.2 per cent in the developing regions, where their rate of growth was 3.1 per cent per year, twice that in the developed regions (1.5 per cent per year). The comparatively higher rate of growth of the elderly in the developing regions was projected to continue at least through the first quarter of the next century.

In general, children and the elderly were the dependent members of a population, with those in the years between providing the main productive force. For the world as a whole, the number of persons in the dependent ages relative to those in the productive ages had been steadily declining since it peaked in the mid-1960s. The decline was chiefly the result of the widespread fall in fertility, moderately offset by the progressive improvements in mortality. The burden of dependency was about 40 per cent higher in the developing than in the developed countries, reflecting the higher fertility of the former. However, the dependency ratio for the less developed regions was projected to continue to fall through the first quarter of the next century, when it would reach the same level as that currently found in the developed regions. The dependency ratio in the developed countries was expected to remain at its present level until early in the next century, when it would begin to rise as the larger birth cohorts of the post-Second World War baby boom reached the older ages. Thus, the current levels and trends of dependency ratios were neutral-to-favourable for development in all regions and were projected to remain so beyond the end of the century. However, the UN pointed out

> a stationary or declining dependency ratio will not reflect declines in one dependent age group which are offset by increases in another, although such a shift may impose substantial social and economic costs.[3]

The UN further commented that in the Sixth Population Inquiry,[4] questions on national policy perspectives with respect to changes in population structure were posed for the first time. In the responses of 82 Governments in all regions of the world, 52 per cent indicated that they viewed their current age distribution as to some degree unsatisfactory or problematic. Twelve per cent saw it as satisfactory, while the remaining third reported no official position on the matter. Concern about the age distribution was more frequently reported by developing countries: 60 per cent expressed some degree of dissatisfaction, while only 30 per cent of the developed countries did so. Not surprisingly, the main concern of the developing countries was that the proportion under age 15 was too high. 'For countries in both regions, no more than one country in five reports that it views the proportion of the population who are elderly to be a matter of concern.'

MORTALITY

As of 1980–1985 the expectation of life was 58.2 years for men and 61.1 for women. The estimated global infant mortality rate for the first half of the 1980s was 79 deaths per 1,000 live births.

For the developing countries as a whole, the expectation of life at birth was 57.6 years for the period 1980–1985 – 56.6 years for men and 58.7 years for women. The gain in expected years of life over the preceding decade for both sexes combined was 3.4 years – 3 years for men and 3.8 years for women. The infant mortality rate for 1980–1985 was estimated to be 89 per 1,000 live births, a reduction from the level of 106 per 1,000 of 10 years earlier.

In the regions of the developing world, mortality conditions in Africa continued to be the worst. For the continent as a whole, expectation of life at birth in 1980–1985 was 49.9 for both sexes, nearly eight years less than in the developing regions as a whole. Life expectancy was 48.3 for men and 51.5 for women. For 29 of the 51 countries in Africa, life expectancy was still below 50 years, the target for 1985 set by the World Population Plan of Action for countries with the highest mortality. Moreover, only five of the 29 were projected to reach 50 by the period 1985–1990. Mortality conditions were considerably better in Asia, which had reached a life expectancy of 59.3 years in 1980–1985, 58.6 for men and 60.0 for women. Conditions were better still in Latin America, where life expectancy reached 64.5 years for that period. The infant mortality rates for Africa, Asia and Latin America for 1980–1985 were 116, 83 and 63 per 1,000, respectively. Thirty-two high-mortality countries failed to reach the World Population Plan of Action's 1985 target of an infant mortality rate below 120 per 1000. Twenty-one of those countries were in Africa, nine in Asia and two in Latin America.

In the developed countries, expectation of life at birth was estimated to be 68.5 years for men and 76.3 years for women. The values ranged from 64 to 75 years for men and from 72 to nearly 81 years for women.

Infant mortality in the more developed regions was estimated to be 16 per 1,000 live births in 1980–1985. Two out of 3 developed countries had rates below 10; the lowest level was that of Japan (5.2), and infant mortality rates below 7 were reported for Finland, Sweden and Switzerland. In more than half of all developing countries, infant mortality rates declined by more than 20 per cent between 1980 and 1985.

The increasing availability of survey data from developing countries had recently made apparent the importance of complications of childbirth as a cause of death in those regions. Among all indicators of public health, maternal mortality showed the widest disparities between developed and developing countries. In developed countries, pregnancy-related deaths were now rare, with registered rates for individual countries typically showing less than 10 deaths per 100,000 births. On the other hand, in the developing countries, estimates of maternal mortality rates prepared by WHO were much higher, 640 maternal deaths per 100,000 births in Africa, 270 in Latin America and 420 in Asia. Moreover, since fertility levels were much higher in many less developed countries, a woman there was exposed to the risk of dying in childbirth more often and over a longer period of her life.

One of the most alarming developments during the 1980s, the UN reported, had been the emergence of AIDS. Up through 1988, the number of cases of AIDS estimated by WHO was about 250,000. The number of deaths due to AIDS was as yet a minuscule proportion of all deaths. However, the disease was a global issue of unknown but deeply threatening dimensions. Between 5 million and 10 million persons were estimated to have been infected by the virus that causes AIDS, the human immuno-deficiency virus (HIV). WHO projected that cumulative deaths from AIDS would exceed 1 million by the early 1990s and some 3 million by the late 1990s. The victims of HIV/AIDS were most often young and middle-aged adults, but the number of infants born with HIV was increasing, especially in developing countries. Costs for dealing with the disease were already very high and were rising. At present, there is no known cure, and the mortality consequences are very difficult to predict – there was no similar virus infection in humans to provide an analogy.

FERTILITY

The United Nations' 1988 assessment indicated a global decline of 6 per cent in total fertility rate over the period 1975–1980 to 1980–1985, as the TFR fell from 3.6 to 3.4. For the developing countries as a whole during the period, the decline was estimated at 8 per cent (from 4.5 to 4.2 births per woman). For the developed countries, the decline was 5 per cent as the average TFR fell to 1.9 births. That drop reflected *a deceleration in fertility decline* from the pace estimated for a five-year period a decade previously (1970–1975 to 1975–1980), when the TFR dropped by 8 per cent in the more developed regions and by 16 per cent in the less developed regions.

While, on balance, fertility levels in the more developed countries continued to become increasingly homogenous at below replacement level fertility, the distribution of countries of the world was no longer as prominently bimodal as was the case some 20 or even 10 years previously. At that time, the distinction between high and low TFRs closely mirrored the distinction between more and less developed countries. The UN reported:

> With the advent of substantial fertility declines in a number of developing countries of East and South Asia and Latin America and persisting high fertility in most of sub-Saharan Africa and Western Asia, the range of fertility levels currently observed within the developing world has become wider than that found between Europe and Africa at the time of the 1974 World Population Conference.[5]

In the developing countries, the distribution across broad stages of fertility transition showed the following picture: 27 countries with a combined population of 288 million were still at the pre-transitional stage, with a total TFR of 6.5 or more. Most of those countries were in sub-Saharan Africa. Whereas 48 per cent of the population of

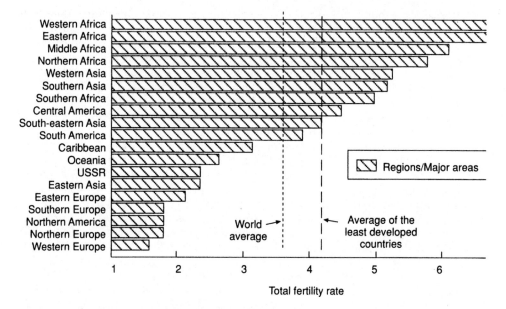

Fig. 11.2. Total fertility rates for world regions, 1980–1985. *Source: Concise Report on the World Population Situation in 1989. (1990) United Nations.*

sub-Saharan Africa lived in a country where the average fertility was pre-transitional, the proportion dropped to 26 per cent in northern Africa, 1 per cent in South Asia and Melanesia and to nil in eastern Asia and Latin America.

Thirty-seven developing countries, with a total population of 807 million, were in the early stage of fertility transition, with a TFR of 4.5–6.5. They were relatively more evenly distributed, with all regions but Eastern Asia represented. Slightly more than half of the population of sub-Saharan Africa lived in 12 countries of that type; in Northern Africa and Western Asia, the figures were 47 per cent in eight countries; for South Asia and Melanesia, 30 per cent in 11 countries; and for Latin America, 8 per cent in six countries.

Twenty-seven developing countries had TFRs of 2.5–4.5, in the advanced stage of fertility transition. They included one small country of sub-Saharan Africa, and three countries of northern Africa/western Asia, in which were concentrated 27 per cent of the population of that region. In Latin America and South Asia/Melanesia, 86 and 65 per cent of regional populations, respectively, had fertility levels typical of the advanced stage.

Ninety-six per cent of the population of eastern Asia might be classified as low fertility, having a TFR of 2.5 or lower. In addition, three countries in Latin America, two in South Asia, one in Western Asia and one in sub-Saharan Africa had TFRs of 2.5 or lower. Most of them were small in population size: their shares of regional populations ranged from near 0 in sub-Saharan Africa to 6 per cent in Latin America.

The United Nations felt able to state with confidence:

> *The most rapid fertility declines had occurred in those developing countries that were characterized by the combination of substantial improvements in child survival, rapid increases in educational levels (especially of women) and widespread access to family planning services.*

Table 11.1.   Distribution of developing countries or areas, by stages of fertility transition in the 1980s.

	Pretransitional[a]	Early transition[b]	Advanced transition[c]	Low fertility[d]
		Sub-Saharan Africa		
Africa and Western Asia	Rwanda	Senegal	Réunion	Mauritius
	Malawi	Guinea		
	Kenya	Nigeria (Ondo)		
	Côte d'Ivoire	Cameroon		
	Zambia	Zaire		
	Niger	Togo		
	United Republic of Tanzania	Ethiopia		
		Chad		
	Mali	Central African Republic		
	Benin			
	Burundi	South Africa		
	Uganda	Congo		
	Liberia	Cape Verde		
	Botswana			
	Djibouti			
	Madagascar			
	Somalia			
	Sudan			
	Zimbabwe			
		Northern Africa and Western Asia		
	Yemen[e]	Algeria	Turkey	Cyprus
	Saudi Arabia	Qatar	Lebanon	
	Libyan Arab Jamahiriya	United Arab Emirates	Israel	
	Syrian Arab Republic	Kuwait		
		Tunisia		
	Oman	Morocco		
	Democratic Yemen[e]	Bahrain		
		Egypt		
	Iraq			
	Jordan			
		Southeastern Asia and Oceania		
South and Eastern Asia	Afghanistan	Lao People's Democratic Republic	India	Thailand
			Malaysia	Singapore
		Nepal	Indonesia	
		Pakistan	Fiji	
		Bhutan	Sri Lanka	
		East Timor		
		Bangladesh		
		Papua New Guinea		
		Iran (Islamic Republic of)		
		Democratic Kampuchea		

Table 11.1.   *contd*

	Pretransitional[a]	Early transition[b]	Advanced transition[c]	Low fertility[d]
		Viet Nam Myanmar		
		Eastern Asia		

			Mongolia
			Democratic
			People's
			  Republic of
			  Korea
				China
				Hong Kong
				Korea,
				  Republic of

Latin America		Guatemala
		Honduras
		Haiti
		Bolivia
		Nicaragua
		Paraguay
			Ecuador
			El Salvador
			Peru
			Mexico
			Venezuela
			Dominican
			  Republic
			Brazil
			Costa Rica
			Suriname
			Colombia
			Panama
			Argentina
			Trinidad and
			  Tobago
			Uruguay
			Guadeloupe
			Puerto Rico
				Chile
				Martinique
				Cuba

Source: World Population Prospects, 1988 (United Nations publication, Sales No. E.88.XII.7), table 32.

[a] Total fertility rate = 6.5 or more
[b] Total fertility rate = 4.5–6.5
[c] Total fertility rate = 2.5–4.5
[d] Total fertility rate is below 2.5
[e] On 22 May 1990, Democratic Yemen and Yemen merged to form a single state.

Where infant and child mortality rates remained well above 150, both female and gross enrolment ratios for secondary education and proportions of married women currently using contraception were typically around 10 per cent, and total fertility rates averaged six or seven children and showed few indications of decline. Such conditions were widespread in sub-Saharan Africa and in the northern tier of countries of South Asia.

Around 1983, 45 per cent of couples in the developing countries with the wife in the reproductive ages were using contraception: 74 per cent in East Asia, 56 per cent in Latin America, 34 per cent in southern Asia and 14 per cent in Africa. The United Nations went on to observe that since no society had reached a low level of fertility without extensive use of contraception within marriage, substantial further increase in contraceptive use in developing regions was implicit in any continuing reduction in the rate of population growth (barring, of course, a massive rise in mortality).

To achieve the UN's medium variant projections (which as we have seen was one of the goals of the Amsterdam Declaration) the total fertility rate would have to decline in the developing regions from a current 4.1 children per woman to 3.2 children in 2000–2005 and to 2.3 in 2020–2025; in order for the projection to be borne out, it was estimated that contraceptive prevalence would have to rise to 56 per cent in the year 2000 (a figure also to be found in the Amsterdam Declaration) and 73 per cent in 2025. In particular, the current projections for Africa that total fertility would fall to 3.1 children per woman implied that the *increase in the numbers of contraceptive users would have to be more than tenfold by the year 2025.*[6]

Among the developed countries, there were – at the end of the 1980s – just six where fertility in the current period was at or just slightly above replacement level. As a group, they had a total population of some 366 million, or 31 per cent of all developed countries. In the rest of the developed countries, current fertility was well below replacement. In 13 developed countries with a combined population of 358 million (30.5 per cent of the total for all developed), the total fertility rate was at least 20 per cent below replacement; in all but one of those countries, the rate had been below 2.1 for more than 10 of the years since 1965. In eight other developed countries, with a combined population of 413 million (35 per cent of all developed), the current total fertility rates were 10–19 per cent less than 2.1 and, again, in all but one, below-replacement had persisted for more than a decade.

As of 1988, over half of the world's Governments (57 per cent) found their levels of fertility to be unsatisfactory. Within the group there were 22 countries that viewed their rates as too low, and 75 countries, with 64 per cent of the world's population, which saw them as too high. The other 73 countries considered their levels to be satisfactory. Among the 131 developing countries, 10 viewed their fertility as too low, 75 (with 84 per cent of the population of the developing regions) viewed it as too high, and the remaining 46 viewed it as satisfactory. Of the 39 developed countries, 12 reported that fertility was too low, and 27 reported it to be satisfactory.

Only seven countries in 1988 indicated that they restricted access to modern methods of fertility control in general. Seventeen countries provide no support, 21 countries supported access to fertility control indirectly, and 125 provided direct support. In both the developed and the developing regions, the majority of countries provided direct support for the provision of modern methods of fertility regulation.

During the previous two years, some 25 countries had shown major changes in the nature of their policies and programmes concerned with fertility levels. There was an increase in the number of countries in Africa and Latin America that expressed increasing concern about how high their fertility was (six in Africa and seven in Latin America), and there was a smaller increase in the number of countries in Europe and Latin America (three in each region) where fertility had already fallen and where the concern was for how low it was.

An important area of change in sub-Saharan Africa was the relaxation of legislation and regulations that had limited access to contraception and abortion. Moreover, one out of four African Governments reported increasing concern with adolescent fertility.

In Europe, measures intended to reduce obstacles to child-bearing and to reinforce the family were strengthened. Typical steps were increased maternity/paternity leave, maternity and child allowances, housing and medical benefits, tax benefits and opportunities for employment for mothers.

In Latin America, support for family planning activities by Governments was generally being extended and strengthened. The main thrust of new measures in Asia and Oceania was to improve the effectiveness of already existing programmes. In general, the UN reported, the 'salience of policies concerned with fertility remains comparatively low for the Arab countries.'

INTERNAL DISTRIBUTION

The urban population of the world was estimated to be slightly less than 2 billion as of 1985. Thus, some 42 per cent of the world's population lived in an urban area. Each year nearly 50 million people were added to the world's urban population and about 35 million to the rural population. The urban population was growing at nearly 2.5 per cent per year, twice the rate of growth of the rural population. The rate of growth of the world's urban population had not changed appreciably in over a decade and was projected to remain at about the present level through the end of the century. The world's rural population had entered a period of decelerating growth.

In the developed countries, over 71 per cent of the population lived in an urban area. The rate of urbanization had largely stabilized at a low level, and the rural population had begun to decline in numbers. The less developed regions were considerably more diverse in patterns of urbanization.

Latin America showed a level of urbanization that was well within the range of the developed countries. (Indeed, the percentage urban in South America was slightly more than that in Europe.) However, the urban populations of Latin America were currently growing at more than three times the rate of the urban populations of the developed regions, chiefly as a reflection of the higher rate of growth of the total population. The rural populations of the countries of Latin America had commenced a decline in numbers, the first time such a phenomenon had been observed in a major developing region.

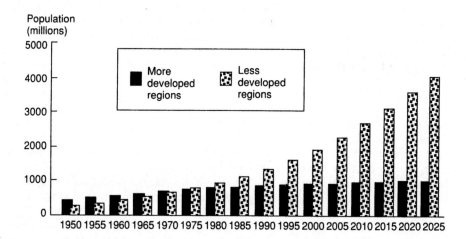

Fig. 11.3. Urban population in the more developed and the less developed regions. *Source: Concise Report on the World Population Situation in 1989.* (1990) United Nations.

Currently, about 55 per cent of the population of Western Asia lived in an urban area. Reflecting the very high rates of total population growth, both the urban and the rural populations of the subregion were growing more rapidly than the corresponding populations of all developing regions.

The rest of Asia and most of Africa were between 20 and 40 per cent urban. In Africa, the urban populations were growing at over 5 per cent per year in the eastern, middle and Western subregions, somewhat more slowly (between 3.5 and 3.9 per cent per year) in Northern and Southern Africa. The rate of growth of the urban population of Eastern Asia had moderated to less than 2 per cent per year, largely because of the decline in the overall rate of population growth. In South-eastern and Southern Asia the urban populations were growing at about 4 per cent per year. The rural populations of Africa and Asia continued to grow, most commonly between 1.5 and 2 per cent per year.

The UN reported that an extremely important part of all urban growth took place in the large urban agglomerations.[7] As of 1985, there were 100 agglomerations in the world with a population greater than 2 million, 30 with more than 5 million (comprising 5.8 per cent of the world's population), and 11 agglomerations with more than 10 million each (having a combined population of 141 million). In general, the large agglomerations of the developed world were growing more slowly, most of them at less than 1.5 per cent per year. On the other hand, most of the agglomerations of the developing regions were growing at substantially more than 2 per cent per year.

Currently, only 14 per cent of 170 Governments, with 11 per cent of the world's population, considered their patterns of population distribution to be satisfactory. More than half of those countries were developed countries.

Forty-one per cent of all Governments felt that their patterns of population distribution required minor change; 45 per cent felt that they required major change. The desire for major change was expressed by 71 per cent of Governments in Africa, 70 per cent in Latin America, 34 per cent of those in Asia and only 8 per cent of those in the Middle East.

With respect to overall policies designed to modify population distribution, at the world level, more than 70 per cent of Governments had formulated explicit population distribution policies. Governments had adopted a variety of strategies and instruments designed to influence population distribution and migration trends. Strategies included slowing primate city (or metropolitan) growth, promoting small towns and intermediate cities, and fostering rural development so as to retain or attract rural population. Other strategies were relocation of the national capital city, counter-magnets (i.e. diverting migrants from the primate city by promoting one or two other major cities), development of growth centres (i.e. promoting industrial poles with subsequent spread effects into the hinterland), establishment of new towns, development of lagging regions and/or border regions, and land colonization in sparsely occupied territory.

Policy instruments included public infrastructure subsidies, development grants, loans and tax incentives to new industries and relocatees; controls on transportation costs; decentralization of governmental administrative or educational activities; provision of housing and social services to migrants; human resource investment and job training; and direct residential controls.

Development assistance to lagging regions was so common as to be nearly the norm; it was reported by 133 developing and developed countries. Rural development strategies were very widely used, except by the countries of the Economic Commission for Europe (ECE). Currently, 12 countries (including seven in Africa and three in South America) had reported plans or programmes to relocate the national capital, in line with population distribution policies.

INTERNATIONAL MIGRATION

The UN reported that, during the 1980s, migration trends in those regions of the world having reliable statistics held few surprises. During the 1980–1985 period, the intake of permanent immigrants by the traditional countries of immigration – Australia, Canada, New Zealand and the United States – amounted to nearly 3.8 million persons, the highest level recorded since the early 1960s. The aggregate increase was largely the result of increased flows of migrants to the United States. Australian and Canadian immigration in general remained stable at levels below the peaks reached in the 1960s and 1970s. New Zealand maintained a very small positive net migration level. For all four countries, the migration flows increasingly originated in countries of the developing regions.

In the European countries of immigration, the foreign populations essentially stabilized in number during the first half of the 1980s. As of about 1985, there were approximately 3.7 million nationals of Turkey and of countries of North Africa living in Western Europe, along with an estimated 5.6 million nationals of other countries of Europe. During recent years, the overall stabilization of numbers of foreign-born in European countries had been the result of a reduction in the foreign populations of European origin which was balanced by increases in the numbers originating outside the region. The change in the distribution of migrants by country of origin had almost certainly been a major factor in the host countries' growing concern about the integration issues that such foreign communities raised.

In the labour-importing countries of Western Asia, the available evidence indicated that the aggregate immigrant stocks entered a period of 'stabilization' analogous to that of Western Europe during the first half of the 1980s. There was very probably some further increase over the estimated 3.5 million that had been reached in the mid-1970s, possibly followed by a decline beginning after the mid-1980s. Asian migration to the labour-importing countries of Western Asia might have remained stable during the early 1980s and then probably started to decline towards 1984–1985. There had been numerous reports of return flows of Arab migrants, but reliable statistical evidence was not yet available.

Sizeable migration flows were known to occur in Africa, usually between neighbouring countries, but in general they remained the least documented in the world. One subregional flow that had historically been highly significant was the movement of workers from nearby countries into South Africa. During the first half of the 1980s, the number of foreign workers employed in the gold and coal mines of South Africa rose very slightly (to just over 200,000 as of 1985), while foreign workers as a proportion of all workers in the mines changed little, remaining at slightly over 40 per cent.

During recent years, Latin America had experienced significant flows between countries in the region as well as a substantial net movement to Northern America. Within Latin America, three countries had been the destination of most of the migrants: Argentina, Brazil and Venezuela. The migration streams had originated largely in neighbouring countries. However, the main destination of Latin American international migrants in recent years had been the United States. As of 1980, the United States received some 4.4 million persons from Latin America and the Caribbean; slightly less than half were from Mexico. As of about the same date, among the

4.8 million migrants present in the countries of Latin America, 41 per cent originated within the region, and most of the rest originated in Europe.

Probably the most notable change in international migration during recent years had been the rapid increase in the number of refugees. There were estimated to be some 8.5 million refugees in the world in 1980; by early 1987 the number had risen to 12.3 million. Most of the recorded increase took place in developing countries, which received slightly more than 10 million refugees in early 1987. About 28 per cent of the world's refugees were of African origin and had found asylum in another African country. The largest concentration was in the Horn of Africa. However, the most important recent refugee movement was the massive outflow of over 500,000 persons from Mozambique which started in late 1985 as a result of conflict exacerbated by sporadic drought. The region receiving the largest number of refugees continued to be Asia, with nearly 51 per cent of the total. During the 1980–1987 period, the growth of the refugee population in Asia was mostly attributable to the outflow of Afghan refugees, nearly 5.1 million of whom were present in the Islamic Republic of Iran and Pakistan as of early 1987. In addition, according to the registers of the United Nations Relief and Works Agency for Palestine Refugees in the Near East (UNRWA), the region continued to harbour some 2.2 million Palestinian refugees as of 1987. In Latin America, only moderate changes in the numbers of refugees were reported. The number reached 335,000 in 1987; half were living in Mexico. There were 710,000 refugees in Europe, approximately 1 million in the United States, and 353,000 in Canada. In the United States, the numbers of refugees who changed their legal status to that of immigrant was about 100,000 per year as of the mid-1980s.

Echoing the comparative stability in trends, there had also been few major changes in the overall policy goals in international migration. More than three-quarters of all Governments considered their current level of immigration to be satisfactory; 56 per cent had policies designed to maintain the current levels, while 28 per cent had policies to decrease immigration, and 5 per cent to increase it; 12 per cent did not intervene to influence migration flows. In general, there were not marked differences between the developed and developing countries in the range of policy goals adopted. The United Nations commented:

> The only notable difference is that in the developed countries, there are disproportionately more Governments that report that they view the level of immigration as satisfactory but nevertheless intervene to lower it.[8]

* * * *

This, then, was the World Population Situation at the end of the decade of the 1980s, as viewed by the United Nations. The data used by the United Nations to review the current situation served also as the basis for future projections, both for the medium-term future, i.e. up to the year 2025, and for the longer-term, as far ahead in fact as the year 2150. These medium and long-range projections are summarized in the following chapter.

NOTES

1. *Concise Report on the World Population Situation in 1989*, United Nations, New York, 1991. United Nations Publication. Sales No.E.90.XIII. 32.

2. See United Nations, op. cit. p. 14.
3. Para 56, *Concise Report on World Population Situation in 1989*, ST/ESA/SER.A/118, United Nations New York, 1991 United Nations Publication, Sales No. E.90.XIII. 32.
4. The United Nations has at regular intervals conducted enquiries among governments on the subject of population, the first such being held in 1962.
5. United Nations, op. cit., p. 17.
6. United Nations, op. cit., p. 19.
7. United Nations, op. cit., p. 23.
8. United Nations, op. cit., p. 26.

12

Projecting Future Populations

WORLD POPULATION PROSPECTS – 1990

The total population of the world was 5.3 billion persons at mid-year 1990, according to the medium variant of the 1990 revision of the United Nations population estimates and projections.[1] During the previous 12 months, the world population had grown by 91 million persons; during the next 12 months, it was expected to grow by 93 million persons.

Table 12.1. World population (billions).

Year	Population
1950	2.5
1990	5.3
2000	6.3
2025	8.5

Source: World Population Prospects 1990.
(1991) UN.

The world population was growing at around 1.7 per cent per year. This growth rate had remained nearly unchanged since 1975, although it was still significantly lower than the historical peak of 2.1 per cent which occurred between 1965 and 1970.

The medium-variant projections indicated that the population growth rate would remain around 1.7 per cent per year for five more years until 1995, after which it would resume its downward trend, reaching 1.6 per cent in 1995–2000, 1.5 per cent in 2000–2005, 1.2 in 2010–2015 and 1.0 in 2020–2025. Correspondingly, the world population was projected to reach 6.3 billion in 2000 and 8.5 billion in 2025. Hence, the annual increment to the world population, which grew from an average of 47 million between 1950 and 1955 to an average of 88 million between 1985 and 1990, was expected to continue increasing until it reached a high of 98 million between 1995 and 2000. The annual increment was not expected to start declining until after 2000; it would reach an average of 83 million between 2020 and 2025, which was about the level that existed in 1985.

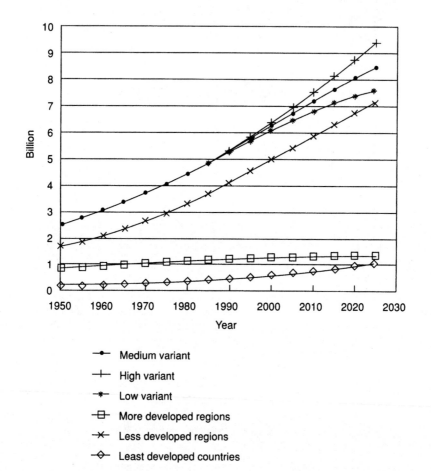

Fig. 12.1. World population: medium, high and low variants; medium variant for the more and less developed regions and the least developed countries. *Source: World Population Prospects 1990.* (1991) UN.

The figures presented in Tables 12.1 and 12.2 are the results of the medium variant of population projections. In the high variant, which assumed a slower fertility decline, the annual average growth rate would increase to 1.9 per cent per year in 1990–1995 and then decline slowly to 1.4 per cent in 2020–2025, resulting in a world population of 9.4 billion in 2025. Under this variant, the annual increments to the world population keep increasing and would reach an average of 128 million per year during the period 2020–2025.

In the low variant, which assumed a faster fertility decline, the average annual growth rate would have resumed its decline after 1985 and would reach 0.6 per cent in 2020–2025, resulting in a world population of 7.6 billion in 2025. The annual increments to the world population in the low variant increase until reaching a high of 84 million during 1990–1995 and then decrease monotonically to an average of 43 million persons per year between 2020 and 2025. In 2025, according to the UN's 1990 projections, the difference in the annual increment to the world's population between the high and the low variant would be 85 million people at year; between the

Table 12.2. World population growth (medium variant).

	Annual increment (millions)	Annual growth rate (percentage)
1950–1955	47	1.8
1965–1970	72	2.1
1975–1980	74	1.7
1985–1990	88	1.7
1995–2000	98	1.6
2020–2025	83	1.0

Source: World Population Prospects 1990. (1991) UN.

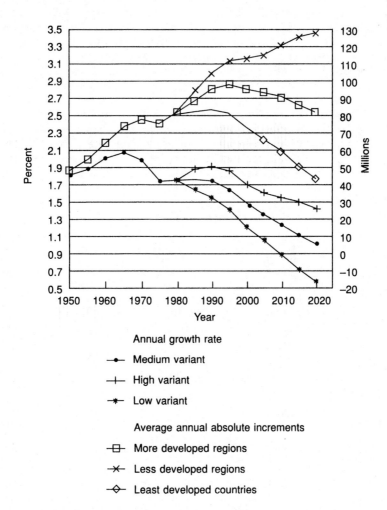

Annual growth rate

—•— Medium variant

—+— High variant

—*— Low variant

Average annual absolute increments

—☐— More developed regions

—✕— Less developed regions

—◇— Least developed countries

Fig. 12.2. World population growth; annual growth rates and average annual absolute increments. *Source: World Population Prospects 1990.* (1991) UN.

high and the medium variant, the difference would be 45 million a year; and the difference between the medium and the low variant would be 40 million a year.

As can be seen from Table 12.11, the difference in total world population between medium and low projections would be half a billion people in the year 2015 (7.66 as against 7.12 billion), rising to almost a billion in 2025 (8.5 as against 7.6 billion), while the difference between the high and the low projections would be over a billion in 2015 (8.16 against 7.12 billion) and 1.85 billion in 2025 (9.44 against 7.59).

In making its projections, the United Nations distinguished three phases of world population growth since the Second World War: (i) a rapid increase in the rate of population growth from 1950 to 1970; (ii) a steep decline in the population growth rate during the decade of the 1970s; and (iii) a relatively constant population growth rate from the late 1970s to the present.

The first phase was associated with the rapid population expansion of the two decades following the Second World War. This rapid population growth was often referred to as 'mortality-induced'. The increase in the population growth rate from 1.8 per cent per year in 1950–1955 to 2.1 per cent in 1965–1970 resulted from the combination of a rapid decrease in mortality (the crude death rate declined from 20 to 13 deaths per 1,000 persons, with life expectancy at birth increasing from 48 to 57 years) and a stagnation in fertility (the total fertility rate declined only from 5.0 to 4.9, but, as an effect of changes in age structure, the crude birth rate declined three points – from 37 to 34 births per 1,000).

The rapid decline in the rate of population growth during the second phase could, in a parallel fashion, be described as 'fertility-driven'.[2] After 1970, fertility declined fast, from 4.9 to 3.8 children per woman and the crude birth rate fell to 28 births per 1,000 population by 1975–1980; meanwhile, mortality declines slowed down and the crude death rate was still 11 deaths per 1,000 population in 1975–1980.

Table 12.3.   Phases of population growth (medium variant).

	Crude birth rate (per thousand)	Crude death rate (per thousand)	Population growth rate (percentage)
Phase I: 1950–1955 to 1965–1970			
1950–1955	37.5	19.7	1.79
1965–1970	33.9	13.3	2.06
Change	–3.6	–6.4	+0.27
Phase II: 1965–1970 to 1975–1980			
1965–1970	33.9	13.3	2.06
1975–1980	28.3	11.1	1.73
Change	–5.6	–2.2	–0.33
Phase III: 1975–1980 to 1990–1995			
1975–1980	28.3	11.1	1.73
1990–1995	26.4	9.2	1.73
Change	–1.9	–1.9	0.0

Source: World Population Prospects 1990. (1991) UN.

Since 1975, the population growth rate had been relatively constant, and was anticipated to remain so during the third phase, until 1995, according to the United Nations medium-variant projections. Between 1975–1980 and 1990–1995, fertility would decline at a slower pace, decreasing by 14 per cent, from 3.8 children per woman to 3.3 children; however, the crude birth rate would only decline by 7 per cent, from 28 to 26 births per 1,000. This divergence resulted from a change in the age-structure of the population, which was itself the result of the past decrease in fertility, with the number of women in the reproductive ages being relatively large compared to the decreasing proportion of children. The slowdown in the decline of the crude birth rate explained the stagnation of the growth rate between 1975–1980 and 1990–1995, as the crude death rate declined by two points also – from 11 to 9 per 1,000 – during this period.

The United Nations went on to identify a fourth phase – **a rapid decrease in the population growth rate** as a result of declining fertility – which was projected to begin after 1995 and would result in a return to a **fast decrease in the rate of growth**, from 1.7 per cent in 1990–1995 to 1.0 in 2020–2025.

REGIONAL POPULATION GROWTH

Between 1950 and 1990, the population of the more developed regions increased by 45 per cent, compared to an increase of 143 per cent for the population of the less developed regions. Within the less developed regions, the increase was 162 per cent among the least developed countries and 140 per cent among the other less developed countries. More recently, between 1985 and 1990, the average annual rate of growth was, for the medium variant, 0.5 per cent for the more developed regions and 2.1 per cent for the less developed regions. Among the less developed regions, the growth rate was 2.8 per cent for the least developed countries and 2.0 per cent for the other less developed countries.

The medium-variant projections of the United Nations anticipated that the population of the more developed regions would increase by 12 per cent between 1990 and 2025, while the population of the less developed regions would increase by 75 per cent during the same period. Within the latter group the population of the **least** developed countries would increase by 143 per cent and the population of the other less developed countries would increase by 68 per cent. In 2020–2025, the annual rate of growth was expected to be 0.2 per cent in the more developed regions and 1.15 per cent in the less developed regions. However, among the less developed regions, the least developed countries would be increasing at 1.7 per cent per year in comparison to 1.0 per cent in the other less developed countries. That is, in 2025 the least developed

Table 12.4.   Average annual rate of population growth – (percentage).

	1985–1990	2020–2025
More developed regions	0.5	0.2
Less developed regions	2.1	1.2
Least developed countries	2.8	1.7
Other countries	2.0	1.0

Source: World Population Prospects 1990. (1991) UN.

countries, on average, would still be about 20 to 25 years behind the other less developed countries in their demographic transition.

The United Nations illustrated the differences by the relative evolutions of the average annual increments to the total population.[3] In 1950–1955, out of a total increment to the world population of 47 million, 23 per cent originated in the more developed regions and 77 per cent in the less developed regions (7 per cent in the least developed countries and 70 per cent in the other less developed countries). During the period 1985–1990, the world gained an average of 88 million persons per year. However, the share from the more developed regions was only 7 per cent. Ninety-three per cent of the world population growth occurred in the less developed regions (13 per cent in the least developed countries and 80 per cent in the other less developed countries). In 2020–2025, it was expected that, out of an average annual increment

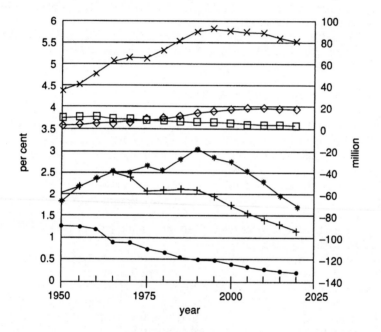

Annual growth rate

—•— More developed regions

—+— Less developed regions

—*— Least developed countries

Average annual absolute increments

—▱— More developed regions

—✕— Less developed regions

—◇— Least developed countries

Fig. 12.3. Population growth in the more and less developed regions and the least developed countries; annual growth rates and average annual absolute increments. *Source: World Population Prospects 1990.* (1991) UN.

Table 12.5.   Vital rates within the regions of Europe.

Region of Europe	1980–1985				1985–1990			
	Growth rate (%)	Birth rate	Death rate	Migration rate	Growth rate (%)	Birth rate	Death rate	Migration rate
		(per thousand)				(per thousand)		
Eastern	0.41	16.1	11.2	−0.8	0.27	14.6	11.3	−0.6
Northern	0.17	12.9	11.2	0.0	0.25	13.4	11.5	0.6
Southern	0.51	13.2	8.9	0.8	0.24	12.0	9.5	−0.1
Western	0.16	12.1	11.1	0.6	0.24	12.2	11.1	1.3

Source: World Population Prospects 1990. (1991) UN.

of 83 million for the world, only 3 per cent would originate in the more developed regions and 97 per cent in the less developed regions (21 per cent in the least developed countries and 76 per cent in the other less developed countries).

There were also differences in growth rates within each of the two groups of more developed and less developed regions. Among the more developed regions, for the period 1985–1990, population growth was fastest in Australia–New Zealand (1.3 per cent), followed by Northern America and the USSR (0.8 per cent each).

The four regions of Europe had nearly identical growth rates during the period 1985–1990, between 0.24 and 0.27 per cent. This change from the earlier patterns of higher growth rates in Eastern and Southern Europe than in Northern and Western Europe resulted from increases in the lower growth rate regions and decreases in the higher rate regions.

The increase in growth rates for Northern and Western Europe, from 0.17 and 0.16 per cent, respectively, in 1980–1985 to 0.25 and 0.24 per cent in 1985–1990, resulted principally from an increase in international migration. The decrease in the growth rate from 0.41 to 0.27 in Eastern Europe resulted from a decrease in the birth rate, while the decrease in Southern Europe from 0.51 to 0.24 resulted from the combined effects of a decrease in the birth rate, an increase in the death rate (caused by the aging of the population), and a decrease in international migration.

In the future, the medium-variant projections indicated that the population of Western Europe would grow very slowly and start declining after the year 2005 and that the population of Southern Europe would start declining after 2010. In both cases, the age structure would result in higher death rates and lower birth rates. The other regions of Europe would continue increasing very slowly. Australia–New Zealand, the (then) Union of Soviet Socialist Republics and Northern America were projected to continue growing slowly, at rates of 0.6, 0.5 and 0.3 per cent, respectively, during the period 2020–2025. Migration would account for half of the growth rate in the case of Australia–New Zealand and Northern America.

LESS DEVELOPED REGIONS

The major areas of the less developed regions had historically exhibited a greater range of population growth rates than the more developed regions had. One of the largest differences within the less developed regions was between the least developed

Table 12.6.   Vital rates within the less developed regions, 1985–1990.

	Mortality		Fertility	
	Life expectancy at birth (years)	Crude death rate (per thousand)	Total fertility rate (no. of births per woman)	Crude birth rate (per thousand)
Least developed countries	49	17	6.2	45
Other countries	63	9	3.7	29

Source: World Population Prospects 1990 (1991) UN.

countries and the other less developed countries. This difference resulted from very large differences in both fertility and mortality levels.

For the period 1985–1990, the *least* developed countries exhibited a crude birth rate of 45 births per 1,000 population and a total fertility rate of 6.2, and a crude death rate of 17 deaths per 1,000 population and a life expectancy at birth of 49 years. The other less developed countries had a crude birth rate of 29.3 for a total fertility rate of 3.7, and a crude death rate of 9.0 for a life expectancy of 63 years.

The United Nations pointed out, significantly:

> In demographic terms, the least developed countries in 1985–1990 were at the same stage as all the less developed regions were in 1950–1955 with respect to fertility, and in 1955–1960 with respect to mortality.

During the period 1950–1955, the earliest date for which the United Nations provided demographic estimates on a regular basis, population growth rates ranged from 2.7 per cent per year in Latin America to 2.2 per cent in Africa and 1.9 per cent in Asia. The high Latin American population growth rate was primarily explained by the region's earlier start of mortality reduction. Life expectancy at birth in the major area was 10 years greater than in Africa and Asia and the crude death rate about 10 deaths per 1,000 lower. Africa and Asia exhibited similar life expectancies at birth and similar crude death rates but African women, on average, exhibited about 0.7 more births per woman than their Asian counterparts; the African population growth rate was hence higher.

Table 12.7.   Vital rates of Africa, Asia and Latin America.

	Growth rate (percentage)			Birth rate (per thousand)			Death rate (per thousand)		
	Africa	Asia	Latin America	Africa	Asia	Latin America	Africa	Asia	Latin America
1950–1955	2.2	1.9	2.7	49	43	43	27	24	15
1965–1970	2.6	2.4	2.6	47	38	38	21	14	11
1985–1990	3.0	1.9	2.1	45	28	29	15	9	7

Source: World Population Prospects 1990 (1991) UN.

A temporary convergence in growth rates occurred during the period 1965–1970. Africa, Asia and Latin America had similar growth rates, varying only from 2.4 to 2.6 per cent per year. The population growth rate had risen sharply from the earlier period in Africa and Asia owing to falling mortality rates and little or moderate fertility change. The Latin American population growth rate held steady, as crude birth and death rates fell by similar amounts. In recent years, population growth rates had diverged again. The African population growth rate had risen to 3 per cent per year owing to falling mortality and little fertility change; whereas, Asian and Latin American population growth rates fell to 1.9 per cent and 2.1 per cent, respectively.

Population growth rate variations were even more pronounced for regions within the major areas. The lowest growth rates in 1985–1990, below 1.5 per cent, were found in Eastern Asia (1.3 per cent) and the Caribbean (1.5 per cent). Trends in Eastern Asia mainly reflected patterns in China, whose population made up 85 per cent of the population of the region. Other regions exhibited growth rates greater than 2.0 per cent. Moderately high growth rates, between 2.0 and 2.5 per cent, were found in South America (2.0), South-eastern Asia (2.1), Southern Asia and Central America (2.3) and Southern Africa (2.4). High growth rates, between 2.5 and 3.0 per cent, were found in Northern Africa (2.7) and Western Asia (2.8). Very high growth rates, more than 3.0 per cent, characterized Middle Africa (3.0) and Eastern and Western Africa (3.2).

Table 12.8. Population growth rates of the less developed regions (percentage).

	1950–1955	1985–1990	2020–2025
Africa			
Eastern Africa	2.3	3.2	2.1
MiddleAfrica	1.8	3.0	2.2
Northern Africa	2.3	2.7	1.3
Southern Africa	2.3	2.4	1.4
Western Africa	2.3	3.2	2.0
Latin America			
Caribbean	1.8	1.5	1.0
Central America	2.9	2.3	1.3
South America	2.8	2.0	1.1
Asia			
Eastern Asia	1.8	1.3	0.4
South-eastern Asia	1.9	2.1	1.0
Southern Asia	2.0	2.3	1.1
Western Asia	2.7	2.8	1.7

Source: World Population Prospects 1990. (1991) UN.

Such differences were expected to continue in the future. During the period 2020–2025, the medium-variant projections indicated a regional growth rate of 1.1 per cent in Latin America and 0.9 per cent in Asia. The growth rate of Eastern Asia (0.4 per cent) was projected to be similar to that of some of the more developed regions, whereas Western Asia (1.7 per cent) might exhibit a growth rate not far from that of Africa. A population growth rate of 1.9 per cent was projected for Africa, with growth exceeding 2 per cent per year for Middle, Eastern and Western Africa, but below 1.5 per cent for Southern and Northern Africa.

The distribution of population increments had also been changing and would continue changing. During the period 1950–1955, China accounted for 23 per cent of the population increment of the world, India for 16 per cent, the remainder of Asia for 19 per cent, Africa for 11 per cent and Latin America for 10 per cent. During the period

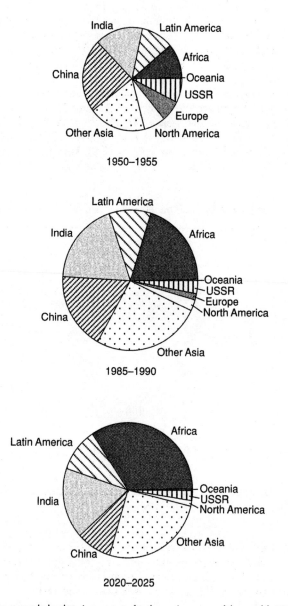

Fig. 12.4. Average annual absolute increments for the major areas of the world, 1950–1955, 1985–1990 and 2020–2025. *Source: World Population Prospects 1990.* (1991) UN.

1985–1990, China contributed 18 per cent of the population increment of the world, India 16 per cent, the remainder of Asia 26 per cent, Africa 20 per cent and Latin America 10 per cent. It was expected that during the period 2020–2025, Africa would contribute 35 per cent of the population increment of the world, China only 9 per cent, India 17 per cent, the remainder of Asia 26 per cent and Latin America 10 per cent.

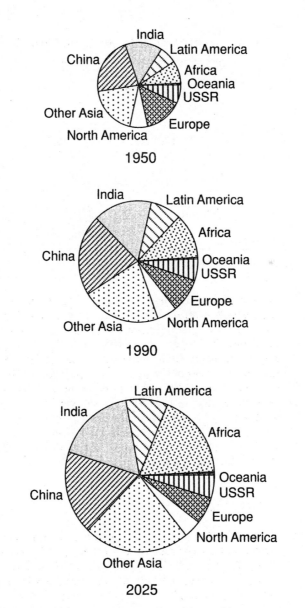

Fig. 12.5. Distribution of population among major areas of the world, 1950, 1990 and 2025. *Source: World Population Prospects 1990.* (1991) UN.

DISTRIBUTION OF THE WORLD'S POPULATION

As a result of differences in the projected rates of growth, the distribution of the population between the different regions of the world was expected to continue changing.
The share of Europe, which declined from 16 to 9 per cent of the population of the
world between 1950 and 1990, was projected to decline further, to 6 per cent in 2025.
Northern America and the USSR would follow a nearly identical course, each of their
shares declining from 7 per cent in 1950 to 5 per cent in 1990 and 4 per cent in 2025.

Table 12.9.   Percentage distribution of the population of the world medium variant.

	1950		1990		2025	
Africa	8.8		12.1		18.8	
Latin America	6.6		8.5		8.9	
Asia	54.7		58.8		57.0	
China		22.1		21.5		17.8
India		14.2		16.1		17.0
Other Asia		18.4		21.2		23.0
Northern America	6.6		5.2		3.9	
Europe	15.6		9.4		6.1	
Oceania	0.5		0.5		0.5	
USSR	7.2		5.4		4.1	
World	100.0		100.0		100.0	

Source: World Population Prospects 1990. (1991) UN.

The UN projected that, among the less developed regions, the share of Africa in
total world population, which increased from 9 to 12 per cent between 1950 and
1990, might reach 19 per cent in 2025. The share of the world's population residing
in Asia remained nearly stable at 55 per cent in 1950 and 59 per cent in 1990 and was
projected to still be 58 per cent in 2025. However, within Asia, the share of China
would continue to decline, from 40 per cent of the population of Asia in 1950 to 37
per cent in 1990 and 31 per cent in 2025. The population of India, which accounted
for 26 per cent of Asia's population in 1950 and 27 per cent in 1990, was projected to
reach 29 per cent in 2025. The population of the remaining countries of Asia would
increase from 36 per cent in 1990 to 40 per cent in 2025. The share of Latin America,
having increased from 7 per cent in 1950 to 9 per cent in 1990, would remain nearly
constant at that level until the year 2025.

COUNTRY-LEVEL ANALYSIS

The United Nations observed that in 1990, 169 countries had population sizes ranging from 1,000 for the Holy See and 9,000 each for Nauru and Tuvalu to 853 million
for India and 1.1 billion for China.[4] The population of these latter two countries
combined made up 38 per cent of the total population of the world. The 19 next largest countries, all of which had a population size of more than 50 million and among
which eight had over 100 million, accounted for an additional 38 per cent of the
world's population. Of these 21 largest countries, 11 were in Asia, 4 in Europe, 3 in

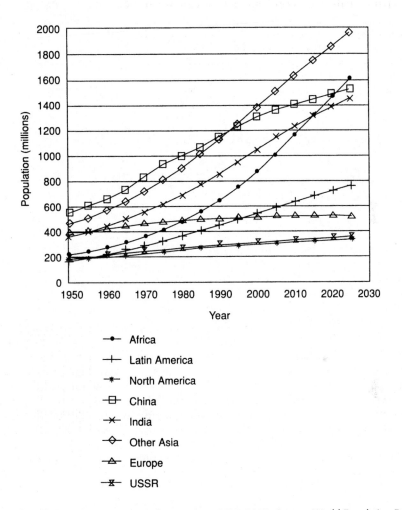

Fig. 12.6. Population of major areas medium variant, 1950–2025. *Source: World Population Prospects 1990.* (1991) UN.

Northern or Latin America, 2 in Africa, plus the USSR. At the other end of the scale, there were 49 countries with populations of less than 2 million, with a combined population of 25 million.

In 1950, including China and India, there were nine countries with populations of 50 million or over, among which four were over 100 million. Thirty-eight per cent of the population of the world lived in China and India, and 26 per cent in the other seven countries. It was expected that in 2025, in addition to China and India, there would be 30 countries with a population of over 50 million, among which 13 would be over 100 million; 46 per cent of the world would live in those 30 countries, in addition to the 35 per cent living in China and India.

Table 12.10.   Distribution of countries according to the size of their population in 1990.

Size of country (millions)	Africa	America	Asia	Europe	Oceania	USSR	Total
Number of countries							
Over 300	–	–	2	–	–	–	2
50–300	2	3	9	4	–	1	19
10–50	15	8	10	10	1	–	44
2–10	21	12	10	10	2	–	55
Under 2	14	12	8	7	8	–	49
Total	52	35	40	31	11	1	169
Population (millions)							
Over 300	–	–	1 992	–	–	–	1 992
50–300	161	488	841	232	–	289	2 011
10–50	342	168	223	203	17	–	952
2–10	127	60	42	63	7	–	299
Under 2	12	4	7	1	2	–	25
Total	642	719	3 105	498	26	289	5 279

Source: World Population Prospects 1990. (1991) UN.

Among the 32 countries with the largest population in 1950, 4 were in Africa, 5 in America, 13 in Asia, 9 in Europe, plus the USSR. In 1990, among the 32 most populous countries, 6 were in Africa, 6 in America, 13 in Asia, 6 in Europe, plus the USSR. It was expected that in 2025, the 32 most populous countries, that is all the countries having a population of more than 50 million at that time, would include 10 in Africa, 4 in America, 13 in Asia, 4 in Europe, plus the USSR. Europe would gradually be replaced by Africa as the second most populous continent.

Among the largest countries of the world, the fastest population increase during the 75 years between 1950 and 2025 would be for Kenya, whose population would grow to 13 times its size in 1950, and for the United Republic of Tanzania, whose population would increase to 11 times its size in 1950.

FERTILITY

The total fertility rate for the world as a whole, the UN commented, did not change considerably during the 1950s and 1960s and remained around the level of nearly five children per woman.[5] A significant decline in the total fertility rate started in the 1970s; it fell to 4.5 children per woman during the period 1970–1975 and fell further to 3.6 in 1980–1985 and to 3.45 in 1985–1990. The medium, high and low variants projected total fertility rates of 3.0, 3.3 and 2.5 children per woman for the period 2000–2005, and 2.3, 2.8 and 1.8 for the period 2020–2025.

The total fertility rate in the more developed regions had declined continuously from 2.8 in 1950–1955 to 1.9 in 1985–1990.

The United Nations commented:

> Currently, the fertility rate in these regions (except for the Soviet Union), ranging from 1.6 to 2.0 births per woman is below the replacement level (around 2.1 births

Table 12.11. World population and average annual growth rate, medium, high and low variants, 1950–2025.

	Population (millions)				Average annual growth rate (percentage)			
Year	Medium	High	Low	Period	Medium	High	Low
1950	2 516	–	–	1950–1955	1.79	–	–
1955	2 752	–	–	1955–1960	1.86	–	–
1960	3 020	–	–	1960–1965	1.99	–	–
1965	3 336	–	–	1965–1970	2.06	–	–
1970	3 698	–	–	1970–1975	1.96	–	–
1975	4 079	–	–	1975–1980	1.73	–	–
1980	4 448	–	–	1980–1985	1.74	–	–
1985	4 851	–	–	1985–1990	1.74	1.87	1.62
1990	5 292	5 327	5 262	1990–1995	1.73	1.90	1.54
1995	5 770	5 857	5 682	1995–2000	1.63	1.83	1.40
2000	6 261	6 420	6 093	2000–2005	1.47	1.69	1.20
2005	6 739	6 986	6 469	2005–2010	1.33	1.59	1.04
2010	7 204	7 564	6 813	2010–2015	1.23	1.54	0.88
2015	7 660	8 169	7 120	2015–2020	1.10	1.49	0.71
2020	8 092	8 802	7 376	2020–2025	0.99	1.41	0.57
2025	8 504	9 444	7 591				

Source: World Population Prospects 1990. (1991) UN.

per woman) and the continuation of the fertility and mortality levels of the 1980s would result in 'negative population growth' in the long run.

It was notable that in Southern Europe (where fertility declines started later and proceeded more slowly than in the other more developed regions), fertility declined very steeply and to very low levels in the 1980s. In Italy, for example, traditionally a country of large families, the total fertility rate went down to 1.3 in 1987, the lowest in the world. In Eastern Europe, fertility declined slower than in Southern Europe. At the same time, in countries of Northern Europe and Western Europe there was a stabilization of fertility levels in 1985–1990 and even a rise in fertility in such countries as Denmark, Sweden and the United Kingdom. This reversed the previous pattern of international variation in fertility (lower Northern European than Southern European fertility). There was a stabilization of fertility level and some increase in Northern America and the USSR, while in Australia–New Zealand and Japan it continued to decline.

Table 12.12.   Population size and rate of increase for the world, more developed regions, less developed regions and least developed countries, medium variant, 1950–2025.

Year	Population (millions)				Period	Average annual growth rate (percentage)			
	World	More developed regions[a]	Less developed regions[b]	Least developed countries[c]		World	More developed regions[a]	Less developed regions[b]	Least developed countries[c]
1950	2 516	832	1 684	169	1950–1955	1.79	1.28	2.04	1.82
1955	2 752	887	1 865	186	1955–1960	1.86	1.25	2.14	2.18
1960	3 020	945	2 075	207	1960–1965	1.99	1.19	2.35	2.35
1965	3 363	1 003	2 333	233	1965–1970	2.06	0.90	2.54	2.48
1970	3 698	1 049	2 649	263	1970–1975	1.96	0.86	2.38	2.50
1975	4 079	1 095	2 984	299	1975–1980	1.73	0.74	2.08	2.62
1980	4 448	1 137	3 311	340	1980–1985	1.74	0.66	2.09	2.52
1985	4 851	1 174	3 677	386	1985–1990	1.74	0.54	2.11	2.80
1990	5 292	1 207	4 086	444	1990–1995	1.73	0.48	2.08	3.03
1995	5 770	1 236	4 534	517	1995–2000	1.63	0.45	1.94	2.83
2000	6 261	1 264	4 997	595	2000–2005	1.47	0.38	1.74	2.71
2005	6 739	1 289	5 451	681	2005–2010	1.33	0.32	1.57	2.49
2010	7 204	1 310	5 895	772	2010–2015	1.23	0.27	1.43	2.25
2015	7 660	1 327	6 332	864	2015–2020	1.10	0.22	1.28	1.97
2020	8 092	1 342	6 750	953	2020–2025	0.99	0.18	1.15	1.73
2025	8 504	1 354	7 150	1 039					

[a] Including Northern America, all regions of Europe, Australia–New Zealand, Japan and the Union of Soviet Socialist Republics.
[b] Including all regions of Africa, Latin America, East and South Asia and Oceania (excluding Australia–New Zealand and Japan).
[c] Including those countries of the less developed regions which have been officially designated as least developed.
Source: World Population Prospects 1990. (1991) UN.

The medium, high and low variants projected different paths of fertility for the more developed regions. According to the medium variant, the total fertility rate for the developed regions would remain at about 1.9 between 1990 and 2025. The high variant projected a slow increase to 2.25 for 2020–2025. In the low variant, it was assumed that the total fertility rate would decline further, to slightly below 1.6 in 2025.

Fertility levels and trends in the less developed regions would vary considerably more. Taking the less developed regions as a whole, the TFR would – on the medium

Table 12.13. Average annual population increment for the world, more developed and less developed regions and least developed countries, medium, high and low variants, 1950–2025 (in millions).

Area	1950–1955	1955–1960	1960–1965	1965–1970	1970–1975	1975–1980	1980–1985	1985–1990	1990–1995	1995–2000	2000–2005	2005–2010	2010–2015	2015–2020	2020–2025
World total															
Medium	47.1	53.5	63.3	72.3	76.2	73.8	80.7	88.2	95.6	98.1	95.7	93.0	91.1	86.4	82.5
High								95.2	105.9	112.5	113.2	115.5	121.0	126.7	128.4
Low								82.1	84.1	82.1	75.1	68.7	61.3	51.2	43.0
More developed regions															
Medium	11.0	11.5	11.6	9.2	9.3	8.3	7.6	6.4	5.9	5.6	4.9	4.2	3.6	2.9	2.4
High								7.1	7.4	7.7	7.6	7.2	7.1	7.1	7.1
Low								5.8	4.7	3.8	2.6	1.5	0.4	-0.9	-2.0
Less developed regions															
Medium	36.1	42.0	51.7	63.1	67.0	65.5	73.1	81.7	89.7	92.5	90.8	88.8	87.5	83.4	80.1
High								88.0	98.5	104.8	105.7	108.2	113.9	119.7	121.3
Low								76.3	79.3	78.3	72.6	67.2	60.9	52.0	45.0
Least developed countries															
Medium	3.2	4.3	5.2	6.2	7.0	8.4	9.2	11.6	14.5	15.7	17.3	18.1	18.4	17.9	17.2
High								12.4	15.8	17.5	19.8	22.3	24.7	26.2	25.8
Low								11.1	13.5	14.1	14.6	14.3	13.5	12.5	11.7

Source: World Population Prospects 1990. (1991) UN.

Table 12.14. Size, percentage distribution, annual rate of increase and increment of population by major areas of the world, medium variant, 1950–2025.

	World	Africa	Latin America	Northern America	Asia	Europe	Oceania	USSR
Population (millions)								
Year								
1950	2 516	222	166	166	1 378	393	13	180
1970	3 698	362	286	226	2 102	460	19	243
1990	5 292	642	448	276	3 113	499	26	289
2010	7 204	1 148	629	311	4 240	516	34	327
2025	8 504	1 597	757	332	4 912	515	38	352
Percentage distribution								
Year								
1950	100	8.8	6.6	6.6	54.7	15.6	0.5	7.2
1970	100	9.8	7.7	6.1	56.8	12.5	0.5	6.5
1990	100	12.1	8.5	5.2	58.8	9.4	0.5	5.4
2010	100	15.9	8.7	4.3	58.9	7.2	0.5	4.5
2025	100	18.8	8.9	3.9	57.8	6.1	0.5	4.1
Annual rate of increase (percentage)								
Period								
1950–1955	1.79	2.21	2.73	1.80	1.89	0.79	2.25	1.71
1965–1970	2.06	2.64	2.60	1.13	2.44	0.66	1.97	1.00
1985–1990	1.74	2.99	2.06	0.82	1.87	0.25	1.48	0.78
2000–2005	1.47	2.89	1.62	0.55	1.43	0.15	1.13	0.61
2020–2025	0.99	1.90	1.12	0.34	0.89	−0.05	0.76	0.47
Average annual increment (millions)								
Period								
1950–1955	47.1	5.2	4.9	3.1	27.3	3.2	0.3	3.2
1965–1970	72.3	8.9	7.0	2.5	48.2	3.0	0.4	2.4
1985–1990	88.2	17.8	8.8	2.2	55.5	1.2	0.4	2.2
2000–2005	95.7	27.0	9.1	1.6	55.0	0.7	0.3	1.9
2020–2025	82.6	29.0	8.2	1.1	42.5	−0.2	0.3	1.6

Source: World Population Prospects 1990. (1991) UN.

variant – decline from 3.71 for the period 1990–95, to 2.71 for the period 2010–2015 and 2.32 for 2020–25. On the low variant, the TFR for the developing regions as a whole would decline from 3.38 for the period 1990–95 to 2.19 in the period 2010–15 and 1.83 for the period 2020–25.

In Africa, the total fertility rate remained in the range of 6.5 to 6.8 children per woman from 1950–1955 to 1975–1980. It declined slightly, to 6.2 children per woman, in 1985–1990. The small decline was mostly attributable to the downward fertility trends in the Northern African region. In the rest of Africa, with only a few

Table 12.15. The 32 most populous countries, ranked by size, medium variant, 1950, 1990 and 2025 (in millions).

1950		1990		2025	
Country	Population	Country	Population	Country	Population
1. China	555	1. China	1 139	1. China	1 513
2. India	358	2. India	853	2. India	1 442
3. USSR	180	3. USSR	289	3. USSR	352
4. USA	152	4. USA	249	4. USA	300
5. Japan	84	5. Indonesia	184	5. Indonesia	286
6. Indonesia	80	6. Brazil	150	6. Nigeria	281
7. Brazil	53	7. Japan	123	7. Pakistan	267
8. United Kingdom	51	8. Pakistan	123	8. Brazil	246
9. Germany,Fed. Rep. of [a]	50	9. Bangladesh	116	9. Bangladesh	235
10. Italy	47	10. Nigeria	109	10. Mexico	150
11. France	42	11. Mexico	89	11. Japan	127
12. Bangladesh	42	12. Viet Nam	67	12. Ethiopia	127
13. Pakistan	40	13. Philippines	62	13. Viet Nam	117
14. Nigeria	33	14. Germany, Fed. Rep. of [a]	61	14. Iran (Islamic Republic of)	114
15. Viet Nam	30	15. United Kingdom	57	15. Philippines	112
16. Mexico	28	16. Italy	57	16. Zaire	99
17. Spain	28	17. France	56	17. Egypt	90
18. Poland	25	18. Turkey	56	18. Turkey	88
19. Philippines	21	19. Thailand	56	19. United Republic of Tanzania	85
20. Turkey	21	20. Iran (Islamic Rep. of)	55	20. Thailand	81
21. Republic of Korea	20	21. Egypt	52	21. Kenya	79
22. Egypt	20	22. Ethiopia	49	22. Myanmar	73
23. Thailand	20	23. Rep. of Korea	43	23. South Africa	65
24. Ethiopia	20	24. Myanmar	42	24. France	60
25. Germany, Dem. Rep. [a]	18	25. Spain	39	25. United Kingdom	60
26. Myanmar	18	26. Poland	38	26. Sudan	60
27. Argentina	17	27. South Africa	35	27. Germany, Fed. Rep. of [a]	55
28. Iran (Islamic Republic of)	17	28. Colombia	33	28. Colombia	54
29. Yugoslavia	16	29. Argentina	32	29. Uganda	53
30. Romania	16	30. United Rep. of Tanzania	27	30. Italy	53
31. Canada	14	31. Canada	27	31. Algeria	52
32. South Africa	14	32. Sudan	25	32. Republic of Korea	52

[a] Through accession of the German Democratic Republic to the Federal Republic of Germany with effect from 3 October 1990, the two German States have united to form one sovereign State. As from the date of unification, the Federal Republic of Germany acts in the United Nations under the designation "Germany". The data are reported separately here since the report was completed prior to unification.

Source: World Population Prospects 1990. (1991) UN.

Table 12.16.   Crude birth rate and total fertility rate for the world and major areas, medium variant, 1950–2025.

Period	World	More developed regions	Less developed regions	Africa	Latin America	Northern America	Asia	Europe	Oceania	USSR
				Crude birth rate (per thousand)						
1950–1955	37.4	22.6	44.6	49.2	42.5	24.6	42.9	19.8	27.6	26.3
1975–1980	28.3	15.6	32.8	46.1	32.4	15.1	29.7	14.4	20.9	18.3
1985–1990	27.1	14.5	31.0	44.7	28.7	15.0	27.8	12.9	19.4	18.4
1995–2000	24.9	13.4	27.9	41.6	24.8	13.1	24.7	12.4	17.9	15.9
2020–2025	17.5	11.9	18.6	26.0	18.4	11.7	16.1	10.9	14.0	14.1
				Total fertility rate (number or births per woman)						
1950–1955	5.00	2.84	6.19	6.65	5.87	3.47	5.92	2.59	3.83	2.82
1975–1980	3.84	2.03	4.54	6.54	4.36	1.91	4.06	1.98	2.79	2.34
1985–1990	3.45	1.89	3.94	6.24	3.55	1.81	3.48	1.72	2.51	2.38
1995–2000	3.14	1.90	3.47	5.70	3.00	1.86	3.02	1.74	2.34	2.25
2020–2025	2.27	1.94	2.32	3.04	2.39	1.94	2.06	1.85	2.02	2.10

Source: World Population Prospects 1990. (1991) UN.

exceptions (Cape Verde, Kenya, Mauritius, Reunion, Senegal, South Africa and Zimbabwe), most countries showed no sign of noticeable fertility decline. According to the medium variant, the TFR for Africa would decline to 5.31 for 2000–2005 and to 3.04 for 2020–25. Under the low variant, the TFR in Africa would decline to 4.61 for 2000–05, 3.26 in 2010–15 and 2.31 in 2020–25.

In Latin America, a noticeable fertility decline appeared to have begun in the mid-1960s. The total fertility rate there remained at about 5.9 between 1950 and 1965, fell to 5.5 in 1965–1970 and fell further, to 3.9 in 1980–1985 and 3.5 in 1985–1990. The past trend in the most populous Latin American country, Brazil, fitted the pattern: the total fertility rate remained at approximately 6.2 during the period 1950–1965, then declined to 3.5 in 1985–1990. Fertility decline in Mexico, the second most populous country in the region, started slightly later: the total fertility rate stayed at about 6.7 in the 1950s and 1960s, then fell during the 1970s, to reach 3.6 in 1985–1990. According to the medium variant, the TFR for Latin America would decline to 2.81 in 2000–05 and 2.39 in 2020–25. (Low variant, TFR 2.40 for 2000–05, and 2.11 for 2020–25)

A marked fertility decline in the 1970s characterized fertility trends in Eastern Asia. In China, the total fertility rate in the 1950s and 1960s was estimated to have been approximately 6.0. The fertility decline in the 1970s was 'spectacular' and the fertility rate was believed to have been around 2.4 in the 1980s. According to the medium variant, the total fertility rate was projected to fall under 2.0 after the year 2000 and to stabilize at 1.8 until 2025. (In the low variant, fertility in East Asia would fall to 1.51 by 2000–05).

Fertility decline in South-eastern Asia was also remarkable but somewhat slower than that in Eastern Asia. The total fertility rate before 1970 was approximately 6.0; it then began to fall, reaching 3.7 in 1985–1990. The gradual decline was projected to continue to below 3.0 around the year 2000 (low variant 2.6) and to 2.1 by 2020–2025 (low variant 1.53). In Southern Asia and Western Asia, the decline was much smaller, with a total fertility rate of about 4.7 and 5.1, respectively, in 1985–1990. The decline was projected to accelerate in Southern Asia, the total fertility rate falling to 4.0 in 1995–2000 (low variant 3.09) and further to 2.2 in 2020–2025 (low variant 1.69). The decline was projected to be slower in Western Asia, the total fertility rate declining from 4.74 in 1990–95, to 3.96 in 2000–05 (low variant 3.24) and reaching 2.7 in 2020–2025 (low variant 2.00)

The recent decline in the crude birth rate for the total world population, from 37 in 1950–1955 to 27 in 1985–1990, was expected to continue in the future, and the projected rate for 2020–2025 was 17.

The estimated crude birth rate for the more developed regions followed a downward trend, from 23 in 1950–1955 through 14 in 1985–1990 to 12 in 2020–2025. The corresponding rates for the less developed regions followed a steeper curve, from 45 in 1950–1955 through 31 in 1985–1990 to 19 in 2020–2025.

Table 12.17. Crude death rate, life expectancy and infant mortality rate for the world and major areas, medium variant, 1950–2025.

Period	World	More developed regions	Less developed regions	Africa	Latin America	Northern America	Asia	Europe	Oceania	USSR
			Crude death rate (per thousand)							
1950–1955	17.9	10.1	24.3	26.9	15.4	9.4	24.1	11.0	12.4	9.2
1975–1980	11.1	9.4	11.7	17.6	8.6	8.5	10.7	10.4	8.8	10.0
1985–1990	9.8	9.8	9.8	14.7	7.4	8.7	9.0	10.7	8.1	10.6
1995–2000	8.6	9.5	8.4	11.9	6.6	8.8	7.8	10.3	7.9	9.5
2020–2025	7.6	10.6	7.1	7.0	7.0	9.9	7.2	11.5	8.3	9.4
			Life expectancy at birth (both sexes; years)							
1950–1955	47.5	66.0	42.2	37.7	51.9	69.0	42.0	65.8	60.8	64.1
1975–1980	60.4	72.0	57.4	47.9	63.3	73.3	58.3	72.6	68.2	67.9
1985–1990	63.9	74.0	61.4	52.0	66.7	75.6	62.7	74.4	71.3	70.0
1995–2000	67.0	75.8	65.0	56.1	69.4	77.1	66.5	76.1	73.5	72.5
2020–2025	72.9	79.0	71.6	65.6	73.2	79.8	73.4	79.2	77.9	76.9
			Infant mortality rate (per thousand live births)							
1950–1955	155	56	180	188	126	29	181	62	68	73
1975–1980	86	19	97	126	70	14	91	19	35	28
1985–1990	70	15	78	103	54	10	72	13	26	24
1995–2000	57	11	63	85	42	7	56	9	21	17
2020–2025	30	6	33	48	25	5	27	6	11	8

Source: World Population Prospects 1990. (1991) UN.

Table 12.17a.   Estimated and projected total fertility rates 1985–2025; world and major regions (low variant) 1985–2025.

	1985–1990	1990–1995	1995–2000	2000–2005	2005–2010	2010–2015	2015–2020	2020–2025
World	3.29	3.03	2.78	2.52	2.30	2.10	1.90	1.79
More Developed Areas	1.85	1.78	1.73	1.68	1.65	1.52	1.58	1.56
Less Developed Areas	3.75	3.38	3.06	2.71	2.44	2.19	1.95	1.83
Africa	6.08	5.72	5.23	4.61	3.91	3.26	2.70	2.31
Latin America	3.32	2.87	2.58	2.40	2.28	2.20	2.15	2.11
North America	1.75	1.69	1.63	1.59	1.58	1.58	1.58	1.58
Asia	3.29	2.94	2.63	2.31	2.08	1.88	1.69	1.63
East Asia	2.17	1.95	1.73	1.51	1.51	1.51	1.51	1.51
South East Asia	3.44	3.02	2.60	2.18	1.86	1.69	1.55	1.53
South Asia	4.53	4.01	3.56	3.09	2.64	2.22	1.83	1.69
Western Asia	4.87	4.33	3.79	3.24	2.76	2.42	2.17	2.00
Europe	1.67	1.62	1.59	1.56	1.54	1.53	1.52	1.52

Source: World Population Prospects 1990. (1991) UN.

WORLD POPULATION PROJECTIONS 1950–2150

Every two years, the United Nations prepares revised estimates and projections of world, regional and national population size and growth and demographic indicators. The 1990 revision was published in 1991 and has been summarized in the previous section. These biennial projections refer to the period 1950–2025.

The United Nations, also prepares, as warranted, supplementary world population projections, extending the regular projections past 2025 into the 'long term'. In 1992, the United Nations updated the long-range population projections it had published in 1982, providing long-range projections of the population of the world and nine major areas to the year 2150.[6] The UN pointed out that such projections, 160 years into the future, were in no way a forecast of the future trend of population in the world. They did illustrate, however, the evolution of population size and its character-istics under possible – and very hypothetical – scenarios of future levels of fertility and mortality.

The long-range projections presented extended the 1990 revision of the United Nations global population estimates and projections for an additional 125 years (to the year 2150), using as a base the population size and characteristics for 2025 from one of the four variants of the 1990 revision. Seven such extensions of the 1990 revi-sion were prepared, each extension differing according to the assumed future trend of fertility. The seven extensions presented in the publication were in one sense arbi-trary, in that there was an unlimited set of future scenarios that could be hypothe-sized. However, in practical terms, they were established a priori, since they were designed to be consistent with the fertility assumptions underlying the four variants of projections in the 1990 revision.

According to the medium-fertility extension, which assumed that fertility would ultimately stabilize at the replacement level, the population of the world would be multiplied by 4.6 between the years 1950 and 2150, growing from 2.5 billion to 11.5 billion. As already noted, population growth was very fast during the period 1950–

Table 12.18. Estimated and projected population of the world (in millions), major extension, 1990–2150.

Year	Medium	High	Medium/ high	Medium/ low	Low
1990	5 292	5 327	5 327	5 262	5 262
2000	6 261	6 420	6 420	6 093	6 093
2025	8 504	9 444	9 444	7 591	7 591
2050	10 019	12 506	12 495	7 817	7 813
2075	10 841	15 708	15 328	7 199	7 082
2100	11 186	19 156	17 592	6 415	6 009
2125	11 390	23 191	19 358	5 913	5 071
2150	11 543	28 025	20 772	5 633	4 299

Source: World Population Prospects 1990. (1991) UN.

1990, with an average annual increase of 1.9 per cent resulting in a multiplication by 2.1 of the initial population, to 5.3 billion. The growth of the world population was projected in the medium-fertility extension to slow gradually thereafter, with increases of 89 per cent between the years 1990 and 2050 (to 10.0 billion), 12 per cent between 2050 and 2100 (to 11.2 billion), and 3 per cent between 2100 and 2150 (to 11.5 billion). At stabilization, the crude death rate and the crude birth rate would both equal to about 12 events per 1,000 population.

The other fertility extensions produced a wide range of results. In the medium/ high extension, where fertility stabilizes at 2.17 children (5 per cent higher than replacement level), the world population would reach 12.5 billion in 2050, 17.6 billion in 2100 and 20.8 billion in 2150. In the high-fertility extension, where fertility stabilizes at 2.5 children, the world population would reach 12.5 billion in 2050, 19.2 billion in 2100 and 28.0 billion in 2150. In the medium/low extension, where fertility stabilizes at 1.96 children (5 per cent below replacement level), the world population would reach 7.8 billion in 2050, and decline to 6.4 billion in 2100 and 5.6 billion in 2150.

LOW-FERTILITY EXTENSION

In the low-fertility extension, the total fertility rate assumed for 2020–2025 in the low-variant projection of the 1990 revision continues. It is assumed that fertility will stabilize for every major area at an average of 1.7 children per woman. As with the other extensions, the time-path to reach the 1.7 mark is partially determined by the pace and direction of fertility change that had been assumed for the periods prior to 2020–2025 in the low variant of the 1990 revision.

For Africa, it is assumed that fertility will decline from the level of 2.31 children per woman indicated in the low-variant projection for 2020–2025 and reach the stabilized level of 1.7 during 2035–2040. It is assumed that the total fertility rate for China will reach 1.5 by 2020–2025; according to the long-range projections, it will remain at that level until 2045–2050 before increasing to 1.7 in 2100–2105. Similar assumptions were made for India, wherein it is assumed that fertility will decline from 1.56

children per woman in 2020–2025 to 1.50 children in 2025–2030, and remain at that level until 2045–2050, before increasing to 1.7 in 2095–2100. In Other Asia it is assumed that a time-path similar to that of China and India will be followed, but with a lag. It is assumed that the total fertility rate will decrease from 1.76 in 2020–2025 to 1.50 in 2040–2045, followed by an increase to 1.7 during 2095–2100. It is assumed that the total fertility rate for Latin America will decline continuously from 2.11 in 2020–2025 to the 1.7 mark in 2095–2100.

The projected total fertility rates in the low variant for all the group-I major areas (Europe, Northern America, the USSR and Oceania) are between 1.5 and 1.6 for 2020–2025. It is assumed that fertility will remain constant (or in the case of Oceania, decline slightly) through 2045–2050, and then increase and stabilize at 1.7 during 2100–2105.

In the low-fertility extension, where fertility stabilizes at 1.7 children, the world population would reach 7.8 billion in 2050 and decline to 6.0 billion in 2100 and 4.3 billion in 2150.

The United Nations also elaborated two other 'illustrative extensions'. One was called the *'constant-fertility' extension*. The UN recognized that for fertility levels to remain unchanged from their 1990 level through 2150 was certainly not a plausible assumption, but was useful as an analytical tool and a standard for comparison with the other extensions. In the constant-fertility extension, the total fertility rate remains constant for each major area at the level exhibited for 2020–2025 in the constant-fertility variant of the 1990 revision. These total fertility rates are 6.48 for Africa, 2.45 for China, 4.41 for India, 4.98 for Other Asia, 4.06 for Latin America, 1.81 for Europe, 1.79 for Northern America, 2.41 for the USSR and 3.17 for Oceania. The UN notes that even though it is assumed that fertility will remain constant, the aggregated total fertility rate for the world rises from 4.3 during 2020–2025 to 5.7 for 2145–2150. This results from the continuously increasing share of the world which belongs to the major areas having the highest fertility levels.

With such a projection, the population of the world would reach 18 billion inhabitants in 2050, 109 billion in 2100 and 694 billion in 2150! The UN comments:

> To many, these data would show very clearly that it is impossible for world fertility levels to remain at current level for a long time in the future, particularly under assumptions of continuing mortality improvement.[7]

The other 'illustrative extension' is the *instant-replacement-level-fertility extension*.

Like the constant-fertility extension, the instant-replacement-level extension was, the UN commented, 'not a likely picture of the world's population future but a useful point of comparison in the analysis of results.'[8] It assumed that, for each major area, total fertility reaches the replacement level in 1990 and stays at that level thereafter. This extension shows that, even under the assumption of world fertility levels immediately falling to replacement level, world population size would rise for 200 more years before stabilizing at 8.4 billion persons in 2150. This total increase of 58 per cent from the world population size in 1990 is the result of the momentum for population growth built into the existing 1990 age structure and the continuation of mortality decline for 85 years or more (depending upon major area) after 1990.

According to this extension, the population of the world would increase from 5.3 billion persons in 1990 to 7.1 billion in 2025, 7.7 billion in 2050, 8.1 billion in 2100 and 8.4 billion in 2150, after which it would stabilize at the 8.4 billion level. According to the instant-replacement-level-fertility extension, the world would reach 90 per

Table 12.19.   Fertility assumptions for the major areas of the world, all extensions.

Area	Target fertility period	Total fertility rate	
		Target period	2020–2025
Medium-fertility extension			
Group I			
Europe	2100–2105	2.06	1.85
Northern America	2100–2105	2.06	1.94
Oceania	2100–2105	2.06	2.02
USSR	2030–2035	2.06	2.10
Group II			
Africa	2045–2050	2.04	3.04
Latin America	2045–2050	2.06	2.39
China	2100–2105	2.07	1.80
India	2025–2030	2.06	2.07
Other Asia	2040–2045	2.06	2.25
World aggregate	2100–2105	2.06	2.27
High-fertility extension			
Group I			
Europe	2100–2105	2.50	2.17
Northern America	2100–2105	2.50	2.25
Oceania	2100–2105	2.50	2.39
USSR	2045–2050	2.50	2.41
Group II			
Africa	2045–2050	2.50	4.01
Latin America	2045–2050	2.50	2.81
China	2100–2105	2.50	2.10
India	2040–2045	2.50	2.58
Other Asia	2040–2045	2.50	2.73
World aggregate	2100–2105	2.50	2.78
Medium/high-fertility extension			
Group I			
Europe	2100–2105	2.17	2.17
Northern America	2100–2105	2.17	2.25
Oceania	2100–2105	2.17	2.39
USSR	2100–2105	2.17	2.41
Group II			
Africa	2095–2100	2.17	4.01
Latin America	2095–2100	2.17	2.81
China	2075–2080	2.17	2.10
India	2095–2100	2.17	2.58
Other Asia	2095–2100	2.17	2.73
World aggregate	2100–2105	2.17	2.78

Table 12.19. (continued)

Area	Target fertility period	Total fertility rate	
		Target period	2020–2025

Low-fertility extension

Group I

Europe	2100–2105	1.70	1.52
Northern America	2100–2105	1.70	1.58
Oceania	2100–2105	1.70	1.62
USSR	2100–2105	1.70	1.60

Group II

Africa	2035–2040	1.70	2.31
Latin America	2095–2100	1.70	2.11
China	2100–2105	1.70	1.50
India	2095–2100	1.70	1.56
Other Asia	2095–2100	1.70	1.76
World aggregate	2100–2105	1.70	1.79

Medium/low-fertility extension

Group I

Europe	2100–2105	1.96	1.52
Northern America	2100–2105	1.96	1.58
Oceania	2100–2105	1.96	1.62
USSR	2100–2105	1.96	1.60

Group II

Africa	2095–2100	1.96	2.31
Latin America	2075–2080	1.96	2.11
China	2100–2105	1.96	1.50
India	2095–2100	1.96	1.56
Other Asia	2095–2100	1.96	1.76
World aggregate	2100–2105	1.96	1.79

Constant-fertility extension

Group I

Europe	2020–2025	1.81	1.81
Northern America	2020–2025	1.79	1.79
Oceania	2020–2025	3.17	3.17
USSR	2020–2025	2.41	2.41

Group II

Africa	2020–2025	6.48	6.48
China	2020–2025	2.45	2.45
India	2020–2025	4.41	4.41
Latin America	2020–2025	4.06	4.06
Other Asia	2020–2025	4.98	4.98
World aggregate	…	…	4.30

Table 12.19. (continued)

Area	Target fertility period	Total fertility rate	
		Target period	2020–2025

Instant-replacement-fertility extension

Area	Target fertility period	Target period	2020–2025
Group I			
Europe	1990–1995	2.06	2.06
North America	1990–1995	2.06	2.06
Oceania	1990–1995	2.06	2.06
USSR	1990–1995	2.06	2.06
Group II			
Africa	1990–1995	2.04	2.04
Latin America	1990–1995	2.06	2.06
China	1990–1995	2.07	2.07
India	1990–1995	2.06	2.06
Other Asia	1990–1995	2.06	2.06
World aggregate	*1990–1995*	*2.06*	*2.06*

Source: Long-range World Population Projections – Two Centuries Growth 1950–2150. (1992) UN.

Table 12.19a. Life expectancy at birth for the major areas of the world: estimates for 1985–1990 and assumptions for 2020–2025 and 2145–2150.

Area	1985–1990	2020–2025	2145–2150
World	63.9	72.9	84.7
Group I	73.2	78.7	84.9
Europe	74.4	79.2	84.9
Northern America	76.6	79.8	84.9
Oceania	71.3	77.9	84.9
USSR	70.2	76.9	84.9
Group II	61.2	71.7	84.6
Africa	52.0	65.6	83.9
Latin America	66.7	73.2	84.9
China	69.4	76.8	84.9
India	57.9	71.5	84.9
Other Asia	62.7	73.3	84.9

Source: Long-range World Population Projections - Two Centuries Growth 1950–2150 (1992) UN.

cent of its ultimate population size within 50 years and would reach 99 per cent in an additional 95 years.

The medium-fertility extension also assumed that replacement-level fertility will be ultimately reached; however, current fertility levels would move towards replacement level in a plausible fashion rather than instantly. The medium-fertility extension exhibits an ultimate world population size which is 3.2 billion persons more (38 per cent greater) than the instant-replacement extension, which is the consequence of the length of time needed before fertility reaches replacement level.

POPULATION EVOLUTION AMONG THE MAJOR AREAS

The growth of the populations of the major areas of the world from 1950 to 2150, according to the medium-fertility extension, is shown in Table 12.20 and in figure 12.7. For the convenience of analysis, the major areas have been consolidated into two groups. Group I is comprised of Northern America, Europe, Oceania and the USSR; group II consists of Asia, Latin America and Africa.

Although the major areas of group I currently include about 20 per cent of the population of the world, they will contribute less than 2 per cent of the increase in the world population between 1990 and 2150 – that is, 98 per cent of future world population growth will take place in the group II major areas of Africa, Asia and Latin America.

After increasing by 45 per cent between 1950 and 1990, the population of group I is projected to increase by only a further 13 per cent between 1990 and 2050 and then to decline by 3 per cent between 2050 and 2150. The total increase in the population of group I during the two centuries between 1950 and 2150 is projected to be less than 60 per cent.

The ultimate population size for Europe is projected to be smaller than its current size: 425 million persons, compared to 498 million persons in 1990. All other major areas within group I exhibit projected ultimate populations larger than their current 1990 size. Northern America is projected to increase from 276 million persons in 1990 to 332 million in 2025, before declining to a stabilized population size of 308 million, 12 per cent greater than its 1990 level. The populations of the USSR and Oceania are projected to increase continually: from 289 million in 1990 to 416 million in the case of the USSR, and from 26 million to 41 million for Oceania. These projections do not assume any migration beyond the year 2025; the picture could be modified if significant migrations occurred.

The share of the world's population living in group I declined from 30 per cent in 1950 to 21 per cent in 1990 (see Table 12.21 and Figure 12.8). Their share is projected to continue declining, to 12 per cent in 2050 and 10 per cent in 2150. Europe's population share decreased the most between 1950 and 1990 (from 15.6 to 9.4 per cent of the world's population) and is projected to decrease the most in the future. Europe's share of world population is projected to fall to 4.9 per cent in 2050 and 3.7 per cent in 2150.

Northern America's share of world population declined from 6.6 per cent in 1950 to 5.2 per cent in 1990 and is projected to decrease further, to 3.3 per cent in 2050 and 2.7 per cent in 2150. The percentage of the world population residing in the (former) USSR fell from 7.2 per cent in 1950 to 5.4 per cent in 1990 and may decrease further, to 3.8 per cent in 2050 and 3.6 per cent in 2150.

Table 12.20. Estimated and projected population of the major areas of the world, medium-fertility extension, 1950–2150 (in millions).

Area	1950	1990	2000	2025	2050	2075	2100	2125	2150
World	2 518	5 292	6 261	8 504	10 019	10 840	11 186	11 391	11 543
Group I	752	1 089	1 143	1 237	1 233	1 211	1 202	1 195	1 191
Europe	393	498	510	515	486	456	440	430	426
Northern America	166	276	295	332	326	319	314	310	308
Oceania	13	26	30	38	41	41	41	41	41
USSR	180	289	308	352	380	395	407	414	416
Group II	1 766	4 203	5 118	7 267	8 786	9 629	69 984	10 196	10 352
Africa	222	642	867	1 597	2 265	2 727	2 931	3 021	3 090
Latin America	166	448	538	757	922	1 024	1 075	1 102	1 117
China	555	1 139	1 299	1 513	1 521	1 451	1 405	1 395	1 389
India	358	853	1 042	1 442	1 699	1 820	1 870	1 913	1 949
Other Asia	465	1 121	1 372	1 958	2 379	2 607	2 703	2 765	2 807

Source: Long-range World Population Projections – Two Centuries of Growth 1950–2150. (1992) UN.

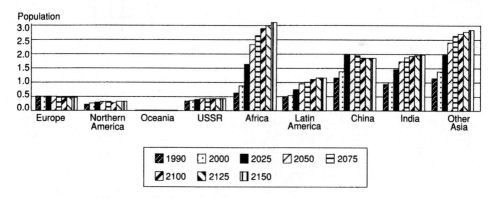

Fig. 12.7. Population of the major areas of the world, medium-fertility extension, 1990–2150 (in billions). *Source: Long-range World Population Projections – Two Centuries of Growth 1950–2150.* (1992) UN.

The growth of the world's population will mainly take place in the major areas of group II. Group II's share of the world's population increased from 70 per cent in 1950 to 79 per cent in 1990. This share is projected to increase further, to 88 per cent in 2050 and 90 per cent in 2150. However, this increase will vary among the major areas.

Africa has been and will continue to be the fastest growing major area. *According to the medium-fertility extension, the population of Africa will stabilize at 3.2 billion persons, nearly five times its 1990 population size and 14 times its 1950 population size.* It will take

Table 12.21.   Percentage distribution of the world's population, by major area, 1950–2150.

Area	1950	1990	2050	2150
World	100.0	100.0	100.0	100.0
Group I	29.9	20.5	12.4	10.4
Europe	15.6	9.4	4.9	3.7
Northern America	6.6	5.2	3.3	2.7
Oceania	0.5	0.5	0.4	0.4
USSR	7.2	5.4	3.8	3.6
Group II	70.1	79.5	87.6	89.6
Africa	8.8	12.1	22.6	26.8
Latin America	6.6	8.5	9.2	9.7
China	22.1	21.5	15.2	12.0
India	14.2	16.1	17.0	16.9
Other Asia	18.4	21.2	23.7	24.3

Source: Long-range World Population Projections – Two Centuries of Growth 1950–2150. (1992) UN

Table 12.22.   Estimated and projected population of the world, all extensions, 1950–2150 (in millions).

Year	Medium	High	Medium/ high	Medium/ low	Low	Instant replacement	Constant
1950	2 516	2 516	2 516	2 516	2 516	2 516	2 516
1975	4 079	4 079	4 079	4 079	4 079	4 079	4 079
1990	5 292	5 327	5 327	5 262	5 262	5 292	5 311
2000	6 261	6 420	6 420	6 093	6 093	5 792	6 463
2025	8 504	9 444	9 444	7 591	7 591	7 069	10 978
2050	10 019	12 506	12 495	7 817	7 813	7 697	21 161
2075	10 841	15 708	15 328	7 199	7 082	7 883	46 261
2100	11 186	19 156	17 592	6 415	6 009	8 087	109 405
2125	11 390	23 191	19 358	5 913	5 071	8 251	271 138
2150	11 543	28 025	20 772	5 633	4 299	8 351	694 213

Source: Long-range World Population Projections – Two Centuries of Growth 1950–2150. (1992) UN.

95 years, to 2085, for Africa to reach 90 per cent of this ultimate population size. As a consequence of this more rapid growth, *Africa's share of world population, which increased from 9 per cent in 1950 to 12 per cent in 1990, is projected to reach 23 per cent in 2050 and 27 per cent in 2150.*

Latin America, India and Other Asia have relatively similar growth patterns. According to the medium-fertility-extension projections, their ultimate population sizes will be between five and seven times their 1950 sizes. The populations of these major areas will more than double between 1990 and stabilization, increasing from 448 million to 1.1 billion in Latin America, from 853 million to nearly 2 billion in

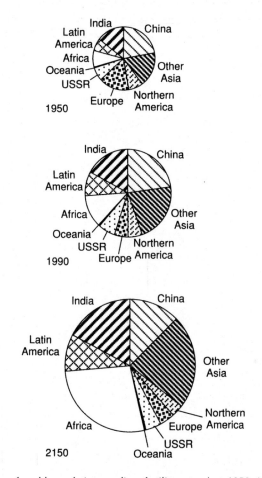

Fig. 12.8. Distribution of world population, medium-fertility extension, 1950, 1990 and 2150. *Source: Long-range World Population Projections – Two Centuries of Growth 1950–2150.* (1992) UN.

India, and from 1.1 billion to 2.8 billion in Other Asia. These major areas will reach 90 per cent of their ultimate population size in 80 years or less.

The population of China doubled between 1950 and 1990, a trend similar to that of Other Asia. However, after 1990 the population of China is projected to follow a trend similar to that of the major areas of group I. China's population is projected to peak in 2035 at 1.54 billion, an increase of 35 per cent from 1990. It is then projected to decline and stabilize at just under 1.4 billion, just 21 per cent over its 1990 size.

Sixteen per cent of the world's population resided in India in 1990; this share is projected to rise to 17.0 per cent in 2050, before decreasing slightly, to 16.9 per cent in 2150. However, China's share of world population, which remained at about 22 per cent between 1950 and 1990, is projected to decline to 15 per cent in 2050 and to 12 per cent in 2150. The share of the world's population residing in Other Asia is projected to

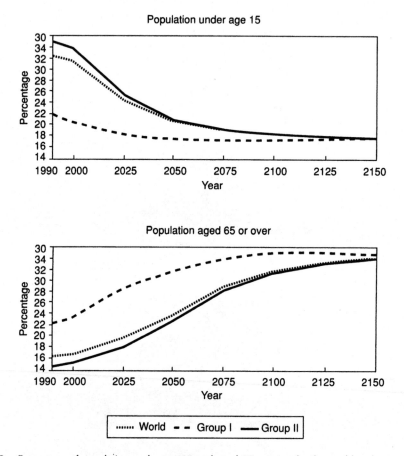

Fig. 12.9. Percentage of population under age 15 and aged 65 or over, for the world and two groups, medium-fertility extension, 1990–2150. Group I comprises the major areas of Northern America, Europe, Oceania and the USSR. Group II comprises the major areas of Africa, Latin America and Asia. *Source: Long-range World Population Projections – Two Centuries of Growth 1950–2150.* (1992) UN.

increase from 21.2 per cent in 1990 to 23.7 per cent in 2050 and 24.3 per cent in 2150. Latin America contained 8.5 per cent of the world's population in 1990; this share is projected to increase further, to 9.2 per cent in 2050 and 9.7 per cent in 2150.

The medium-fertility extension indicates dramatic changes in the future age structure of the world's population. By the year 2150 the world population will have aged considerably. The median will have risen to 42 years, from 24 years in 1990. In 2150, 18 per cent of the world's population will be under age 15 (having declined from 32 per cent in 1990), and 24 per cent will be aged 65 or over (having risen from 6 per cent in 1990). An extremely dramatic change is projected among the very old, those aged 80 or over. Their proportion is projected to increase ninefold, from 1 per cent in 1990 to 9 per cent in 2150.

In summary, the long-range projections of future world population outlined above serve to illustrate several different possible scenarios for the world population situ-

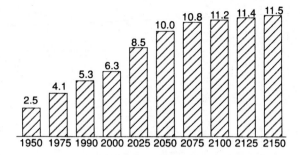

Fig. 12.10. World population, medium-fertility extension, 1950–2150 (in billions).

ation in the coming century and beyond. Though the United Nations rules out as implausible both the 'instant replacement' and the 'constant fertility' scenarios, the differences between the results of the other projections are remarkable enough. As can be seen from Table 12.22 the total world population in the year 2150 (a date which could certainly fall within the life-time of this generation's grand-children or great grand-children) could vary between 28 billion, the high projection and 4.3 billion, the low projection, the difference between the two projections being over 23 billion or more than four times the current world population. The difference between the high and the medium projections would be 16.5 billion people, and the difference between the medium and the low projections almost 7 billion people.

Both the medium-term and the long-range population projections discussed above serve as a useful framework against which to assess the progress which has currently been made in reducing human fertility rates as well as the challenges which lie ahead.

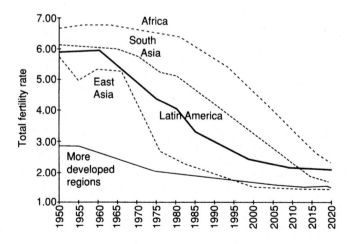

Fig. 12.11. Total fertility rate – actual and projected (1950–2025) United Nations 'low' projection. *Source: United Nations World Population Prospects 1990 (1991) UN.*

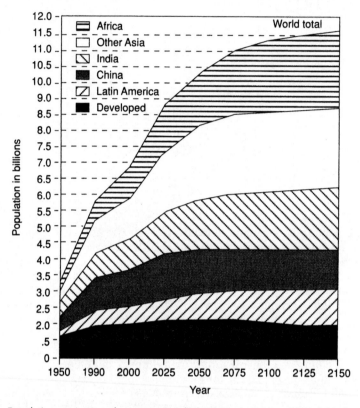

Fig. 12.12. Population projections by region (medium variant). *Source: United Nations Population Division.*

NOTES

1. *World Population Prospects 1990*, United Nations, New York, 1991. United Nations Publication, Sales No.E.91.XIII.4.
2. United Nations, op. cit., p. 8.
3. United Nations, op. cit., p. 10.
4. United Nations, op. cit., p. 17.
5. United Nations, op. cit., p. 24.
6. *Long-Range World Population Projections: Two Centuries of Population Growth 1950–2150,* United Nations, ST/ESA/SER.A/125, United Nations Publication Sales No. E.92.XIII.3.
7. *Long-Range World Population Projections*, p. 22.
8. United Nations, op. cit., p. 13.

13

The Unfinished
Reproductive Revolution

In December 1992, a report of enormous significance to all those concerned with population trends and their implications was published by the Population Information Program of Johns Hopkins University, Baltimore. That report, entitled *The Reproductive Revolution: New Survey Findings*, was based on the findings of the Demographic and Health Surveys (DHS) and Family Planning Surveys (FPS), two large-scale survey programmes which had interviewed nationally representative samples of more than 300,000 women of reproductive age in 44 developing countries since 1984. They continued a series of comparable surveys begun 20 years previously with the World Fertility Survey in 1972. The DHS and FPS results were considered to be broadly representative of developing regions, except Asia, where recent independent national surveys had also revealed rising use of contraception and falling fertility.

The Johns Hopkins report stated unambiguously:

> *In much of the developing world, fertility has declined so rapidly that the trend has been called 'extraordinary', reflecting 'fundamental changes in reproductive attitudes and behaviour'.* Although in most of sub-Saharan Africa couples still have large families, surveys show that fertility decline may be starting even in several sub-Saharan countries. There are, of course, large differences in family size among countries within each region and, within countries, among different areas and population groups. Still, *outside Africa fertility is declining nearly everywhere.* (emphasis added)

Looking at the results of the surveys in detail, the report noted that family size had been declining steadily for several decades in most of Latin America and the Caribbean, the Near East and North Africa, and Asia, as comparisons of recent survey data with earlier data from the World Fertility Survey (WFS) and other surveys showed. In the developing world as a whole, fertility had declined by about one-third since the mid-1960s, from an average of about six children per woman to an average to about four.

In 8 of 11 Latin American and Caribbean countries where surveys were conducted both in the 1970s and in either the 1980s or 1990s, fertility had fallen by at least one child per woman since the 1970s. In a few countries fertility had fallen even more dramatically. For example, in Colombia the total fertility rate (TFR) had declined from 3.7 children per woman in 1976 to 2.8 in 1990, a decline of 40 per cent. In Jamaica the TFR had fallen from 5.0 children per woman in 1975–76 to 2.9 in 1989, also a decline of about 40 per cent.

Table 13.1. Total fertility rate (TFR). The average number of children that would be born to a woman by the end of her childbearing years if she conformed to the current age-specific fertility rates.

Region, Country, year	TFR	Region, Country, year	TFR	Region, Country, year	TFR
AFRICA		LATIN AMERICA & CARIBBEAN		NEAR EAST & NORTH AFRICA	
Botswana 1984	6.5	Belize 1991	4.5	Egypt 1980	5.3
1988	4.8	Bolivia 1989	4.9	1988–89	4.6
Burundi 1987	6.5	Brazil 1986	3.6	Jordan 1976	7.5
Cameroon 1978	6.4	Colombia 1976	4.7	1983	6.6
1991	5.9	1980	3.6	1990	5.5
Ghana 1979–80	6.5	1986	3.2	Morocco 1979–80	5.8
1988	6.1	1990	2.8	1987	4.6
Kenya 1977–78	8.3	Costa Rica 1981	3.8	1992	4.0
1989	6.5	1986	3.6	Tunisia 1978	6.0
Liberia 1986	6.4	Dominican Republic 1975	5.7	1988	4.3
Mali 1987	6.8	1983	4.1	Turkey 1978	4.3
Mauritius 1985	2.0	1986	3.7	1988	3.4
1991	2.2	1991	3.3	Yemen 1991–92	7.0
Niger 1992	7.3	Ecuador 1979	5.3		
Nigeria 1981–82	6.3	1987	4.1		
1990	5.7	1989	3.8		
Senegal 1978	7.2	El Salvador 1978	6.3	ASIA & PACIFIC	
1986	6.4	1985	4.4	Bangladesh 1975–76	6.1
Sudan 1978–79	6.0	1988	4.6	1991	5.5
1989–90		Guatemala 1978	6.1	China 1988	2.5
Swaziland 1988		1983	5.8	India 1988	4.3
Tanzania 1991–92	4.8	1987	5.6	Indonesia 1987	3.2
Togo 1988	5.0	Haiti 1977	5.5	1991	3.0
Uganda 1988–89	6.1	1983	5.9	Korea, Rep. of 1988	1.7
Zambia 1992	6.1	1989	6.0	Pakistan 1975	6.3
Zimbabwe 1984	7.2	Jamaica 1975–76	5.0	1990–91	5.2
1988–89	6.3	1983	3.5	Philippines 1988	4.3
	6.5	1989	2.9	Sri Lanka 1975	3.8
	5.3	Mexico 1976–77	6.2	1987	2.7
		1978	5.2	Thailand 1975	4.6
		1979	4.6	1987	2.3
		1987	4.0	Vietnam 1988	3.9
		Panama 1984	4.0		
		Paraguay 1977	6.8		
		1979	5.0		
		1987	5.4		
		1990	4.6		
		Peru 1977–78	6.6		
		1981	5.2		
		1986	4.2		
		1991–92	3.5		
		Trinidad & Tobago 1977	3.3		
		1987	3.1		

All TFRs calculated for women ages 15–44 except Bangladesh 1991 and China 1988, ages 15–49.
Source: Population Reports. (Johns Hopkins University) Vol. XX, No. 4, December 1992.

In the Near East and North Africa, family size had fallen in all five countries with more than one survey – Egypt, Jordan, Morocco, Tunisia, and Turkey. In Morocco, for example, fertility had declined from 5.8 children per woman in 1979–80 to 4.0 in 1992. In Egypt fertility had declined from 5.3 children per woman in 1980 to 4.6 in 1988–89 (see Table 13.1).

In Asia, family size had fallen substantially in Sri Lanka and Thailand since the mid-1970s, based on comparisons of DHS and WFS data. In Thailand the TFR had fallen from 4.6 children per woman in the 1975 WFS to 2.3 in the 1987 WFS, a decline of 50 per cent. In Sri Lanka fertility had fallen almost 30 per cent, from 3.8 in the 1975 WFS to 2.7, in the 1987 DHS. Also, in Indonesia fertility had fallen from 5.6 children per woman, estimated from the 1971 census, to 3.0 in the 1991 DHS, a decline of 46 per cent.

Fertility had fallen less in Pakistan – from 6.3 children per woman in the 1975 WFS to 6.0 in the 1984–85 Pakistan Contraceptive Prevalence Survey (CPS) and, further, to 5.2 in the 1990–91 DHS. Because the DHS might underestimate Pakistan's actual fertility to some extent, the exact magnitude of the change in Pakistan was disputed and was the subject of further analysis. Independent national surveys confirmed that family size had declined substantially in some other Asian countries.

Fertility remained high in sub-Saharan Africa but had declined 26 per cent in Botswana, 22 per cent in Kenya, and 18 per cent in Zimbabwe based on a comparison of DHS and WFS data. Such declines, the report argued, could signal the start of a sustained transition to lower fertility. In other sub-Saharan countries with DHS surveys, however, declines had been negligible.

FERTILITY DIFFERENCES

Surveys pointed to large differences in fertility among countries and regions. Surveys also showed that fertility differed among women in the same country depending on where they lived – whether in an urban or a rural area – and how much education they had had.

Among all recently surveyed countries, fertility was lowest in South Korea, at 1.7 children per woman. This level was below the 2.1 replacement level – the number of children per couple that over the long run leads to zero population growth because each couple has just enough children to replace themselves in the population. Fertility in Mauritius was at about replacement level, at 2.2 children per woman recorded in the 1991 survey and 2.0 in 1985. Fertility was highest in Niger, at 7.3 children per woman, and Uganda, at 7.2.

In Asia, fertility ranged widely, from 2.5 children per woman or less in China, South Korea, and Thailand to more than five children per woman in Bangladesh and Pakistan.

In Latin America and the Caribbean, where fertility averaged between three and four children per woman, the TFR was lowest in Colombia, at 2.8 children per woman in the 1990 DHS, and highest in Haiti, at 6.0 children per woman in the 1989 FPS.

Among the six surveyed countries in the Near East and North Africa, the TFR ranged from a low of 3.4 children per woman in Turkey to a high of 7.0 in Yemen.

In sub-Saharan Africa the TFR averaged six to seven children per woman. In particular, fertility was much higher than elsewhere at ages under 20 and over 35. *'In most sub-Saharan countries women start childbearing at younger ages than women in other regions, have larger families, and make much less use of family planning to limit childbearing when they are older.'* Among sub-Saharan countries surveyed, fertility was lowest in Botswana, at 4.8 children per woman.

By comparison, fertility was much lower in the developed world, estimated at about two children per woman. The TFR was 1.7 children per woman in Japan, 1.8 in the United Kingdom, and 1.9 in the US.

In countries where the fertility transition was just beginning, or had yet to begin at all, fertility was high among all groups. Among the surveyed countries Mali and Uganda belonged in this group. In Uganda, for example, according to the 1988–89 DHS, women with no education averaged almost eight children, and the fertility of women who had some primary schooling and of women with some secondary education was nearly as high.

As the fertility transition progressed, and some women reduced their fertility before other women did, the differences in fertility by education levels often became wide. Most surveyed developing countries were in this stage. Bolivia was an example. According to the 1989 DHS, women with no education or with some primary school had about six children compared with only about three among women with some secondary schooling.

Differences in fertility shrunk again as the whole society approached a small-family norm. In such countries as Costa Rica, Sri Lanka, and Thailand, fertility was low or moderate among less educated women as well as more educated women. In Thailand, for example, women with no education averaged less than four children compared

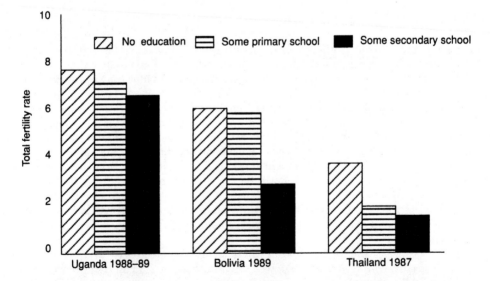

Fig. 13.1.   Total fertility rates by women's education in three countries. Three steps in broad national fertility decline: Before fertility rates start to fall, fertility is high among all groups (Uganda). As educated women reduce their fertility first, differences widen among groups (Bolivia). Eventually, fertility is low among all groups of women (Thailand). *Source:* Demographic and health Surveys in Bolivia (7), Thailand (11) and Uganda (26). *Population Reports.* (Johns Hopkins University) Vol. XX, No. 4, December 1992.

with about two for women with secondary education. The Johns Hopkins report observed:

> Policies that promote the small-family norm and widely provide family planning services can speed the adoption of new reproductive attitudes and the use of contraception, thus lowering fertility sooner among the groups. In Indonesia, for example, the government family planning programme from the beginning has tried to reach all couples rural as well as urban, less educated as well as more educated. As a result, fertility has fallen more equally across the country than it would have without such a programme.[1]

FERTILITY DETERMINANTS

The DHS and FPS helped explain why fertility was declining, so the Johns Hopkins report argued. The surveys measured the factors that influenced fertility directly and also factors that influenced fertility indirectly.[2] The factors that influence fertility directly, termed the proximate determinants of fertility,[3] were: (1) the use of effective contraception; (2) the age at first marriage, reflecting the start of regular sexual relations; (3) postpartum infecundability (because of breastfeeding or sexual abstinence following childbirth); and (4) induced abortion. Other proximate determinants of fertility included infertility levels, the frequency of intercourse, and spontaneous abortion.

The Johns Hopkins report stated categorically:

> *The most important proximate determinant of fertility is the use of family planning.* In country after country, surveys reveal that, where few couples use contraceptives, fertility is high. Where contraceptive use is widespread, fertility is low. Differences in levels of contraceptive use explain 92 per cent of the variation in fertility among the 50 countries in Figure 13.2.
>
> *In the past two decades changes in the use of family planning have largely determined national fertility trends. Fertility levels have dropped in countries where there have been increases in the percentage of married women of reproductive age currently using contraception. On average, among countries surveyed by the DHS, an increase of approximately 15 percentage points in contraceptive prevalence has accounted for a decrease of one birth in the total fertility rate (TFR).* (emphasis added)[4]

National surveys suggested that many programmes still had far to go in making family planning widely known and widely available. The surveys showed that knowledge and use of contraceptive method and access to family planning services varied substantially among countries and population groups. Also, surveys reported that many women who began using a contraceptive method abandoned it because of concerns about side effects, supply problems, misinformation, fears, or other reasons. Often they did not switch immediately to another method.

CURRENT USE OF FAMILY PLANNING

Excluding China, 38 per cent of all women of reproductive age in the developing world who were married or living in consensual unions were currently using family planning.[5] This level was well below the contraceptive prevalence of over 70 per cent estimated for the developed world, ranging from 58 per cent in Japan through 74 per

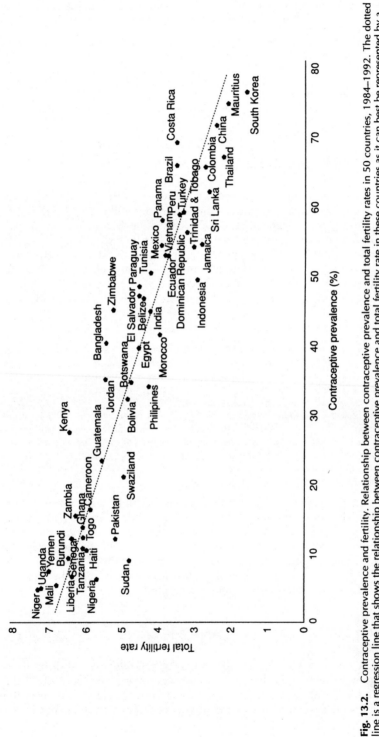
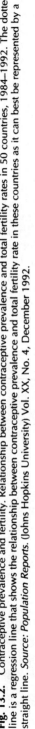

Fig. 13.2. Contraceptive prevalence and fertility. Relationship between contraceptive prevalence and total fertility rates in 50 countries, 1984–1992. The dotted line is a regression line that shows the relationship between contraceptive prevalence and total fertility rate in these countries as it can best be represented by a straight line. *Source: Population Reports.* (Johns Hopkins University) Vol. XX, No. 4, December 1992.

Table 13.2. Family planning methods currently used by married women of reproductive age (per cent).

Region, country and year	Any method	Any traditional method[a]	Any modern method[b]	Voluntary sterilization female	Voluntary sterilization male	OCs	IUDs	Condoms	Injectables	Vaginal methods	Periodic abstinence	Withdrawal	Other[c]
AFRICA													
Botswana 1988	35	1	33	4	0	16	6	1	6	0	0	0	1
Burundi 1987	9	6	1	0	0	0	0	0	1	0	5	1	2
Cameroon 1991	16	8	4	1	0	1	0	1	0	0	7	2	0
Ghana 1988	13	7	4	1	0	2	1	0	0	0	7	1	2
Kenya 1989	27	8	18	4	0	6	4	1	4	0	8	0	1
Liberia 1986	6	1	5	0	0	4	1	0	0	0	1	0	0
Mali 1987	5	2	1	0	0	1	0	0	0	0	1	0	2
Mauritius 1985	75	30	45	5	0	21	2	10	6	1	17	13	1
1991	75	25	49	7	0	21	3	13	4	0	9	16	1
Niger 1992	4	0	2	0	0	2	0	0	1	0	0	0	2
Nigeria 1990	6	2	4	0	0	1	1	0	1	0	1	1	1
Senegal 1986	12	1	2	1	0	1	1	0	0	0	1	0	8
Sudan 1989–90	9	3	6	1	0	4	1	0	0	0	2	0	1
Swaziland 1988	21	3	17	5	0	5	2	1	4	0	1	2	0
Tanzania 1991–92	10	3	7	2	0	3	0	1	0	0	1	2	1
Togo 1988	12	9	3	1	0	1	1	1	0	1	7	2	0
Uganda 1988–89	5	2	3	1	0	1	0	0	0	0	2	0	0
Zambia 1992	15	4	9	2	0	4	0	2	0	0	1	3	2
Zimbabwe 1988–89	45	6	38	2	0	33	1	1	0	0	0	5	2
ASIA & PACIFIC													
Bangladesh 1991	40	3	31	9	1	14	2	3	3	0	1	2	0
China 1988	72	NA	71	28	8	3	30	2	<1	<1	NA	<1	<1
India 1988	45	5	40	— 31 —		1	2	5	NA	NA	— 5 —		0
Indonesia 1987	51	3	47	3	0	18	14	2	10	0	1	1	2
1991	50	2	47	3	1	15	13	1	12	NA	1	1	2
Korea, Rep. of 1988	77	NA	70	37	11	3	7	10	NA	2	NA	NA	7
Pakistan 1990–91	12	3	9	4	0	1	1	3	1	0	1	1	0

Table 13.2. *contd*

Region, country and year	Any method	Any traditional method[a]	Any modern method[b]	Voluntary sterilization female	Voluntary sterilization male	OCs	IUDs	Condoms	Injectables	Vaginal methods	Periodic abstinence	Withdrawal	Other[c]
ASIA & PACIFIC (contd)													
Philippines 1988	34	13	21	11	<1	6	2	1	<1	NA	8	5	2
Sri Lanka 1987	62	19	41	25	5	5	2	2	3	0	15	4	2
Thailand 1987	68	2	66	22	6	20	7	1	9	0	1	1	0
Vietnam 1988	53	15	38	3	<1	<1	33	1	0	0	8	7	<1
LATIN AMERICA & CARIBBEAN													
Belize 1991	47	3[d]	42[e]	19	f	15	2	2	4	1	3	1	3
Bolivia 1989	32	18	13	4	0	2	5	0	1	0	17	1	1
Brazil 1986	66	9	57	27	1	25	1	2	1	1	4	5	1
Colombia 1986	67	11	54	18	0	18	12	2	1	2	6	5	1
1990	66	11	55	21	1	14	12	3	2	2	6	5	1
Costa Rica 1986	70	11[g]	58	14	1	21	8	13	1	1	8[g]	3	0
Dominican Rep. 1986	51	3	47	32	0	10	3	2	0	0	1	2	1
1991	56	4	52	39	0	10	2	1	0	0	2	2	0
Ecuador 1987	46	8	37	14	0	9	11	1	1	1	6	2	0
1989	53	11	42	19		9	12	1	0	0	9	3	0
El Salvador 1985	49	3	45	32	1	7	4	1	1	0	2	2	0
1988	47	3	44	30	1	8	2	2	1	0	2	1	0
Guatemala 1987	23	4	19	10	1	4	2	1	1	0	3	1	0
Haiti 1989	10	1[g]	9	3	0	4	1	1	2	0	0[g]	0	0
Jamaica 1989	55	3[g]	51	14		20	2	9	8	h	1[g]	2	0
Mexico 1987	55	8	46	18	1	11	11	2	8	1	5	4	0
Panama 1984	58	4	53	32	0	12	6	2	1	1	2	1	0
Paraguay 1987	38	9	29	4		14	5	2	4	1	6	3	0
1990	48	8	35	7	0	14	6	3	5	1	5	3	1
Peru 1986	48	23	24	6	0	7	8	1	2	1	19	4	1
1991–92	59	25	33	8	0	6	13	3	2	1	21	4	1
Trinidad & Tobago 1987	54	8	46	7	0	15	5	12	1	5	2	6	0

Table 13.2. *contd*

Region, country and year	Any method	Any traditional method[a]	Any modern method[b]	Voluntary sterilization female	male	OCs	IUDs	Condoms	Injectables	Vaginal methods	Periodic abstinence	Withdrawal	Other[c]
NEAR EAST & NORTH AFRICA													
Egypt 1988–89	40	1	37	1	0	16	17	3	0	0	1	0	1
Jordan 1990	35	8	27	6	0	5	15	1	0	1	4	4	0
Morocco 1987	37	5	30	2	0	24	3	1	0	0	2	3	2
1992	42	6	36	3	0	28	3	1	0	0	3	3	0
Tunisia 1988	51	9	41	10	0	9	18	1	1	1	7	3	1
Turkey 1988	60	29	31	2	0	6	14	7	0	2	4	26	1
Yemen 1991–92	7	1	6	1	0	3	1	0	1	0	1	1	0

[a] Includes only periodic abstinence and withdrawal: excludes folk methods

[b] Includes voluntary sterilization, oral contraceptives (OCs), intrauterine devices (IUDs), condoms, injectables and vaginal methods (spermicides, diaphragms, and cervical caps). DHS include Norplant where available.

[c] Includes all other methods mentioned: excludes douche or folk methods where available. FPS include Norplant.

[d] Includes only periodic abstinence

[e] Includes female sterilization, OCs, injectables, condoms, and IUDs

[f] Included in 'other' category

[g] Includes Billings method

[h] Included in IUDs

Source: Population Reports. (Johns Hopkins University) Vol. XX, No. 4, December 1992.

cent in the United States and 81 per cent in the United Kingdom to 84 per cent in Norway.

The averages concealed wide variation. Among surveyed countries contraceptive prevalence ranged from below 10 per cent, in seven sub-Saharan African countries and in Yemen to 70 per cent or more in China, Costa Rica, Mauritius, and South Korea. It was nearly 70 per cent in three other countries – Brazil, Colombia, and Thailand

In Latin America and the Caribbean as a whole, contraceptive prevalence was 57 per cent. Prevalence exceeded 50 per cent in 10 Latin American and Caribbean countries – Brazil, Colombia, Costa Rica, the Dominican Republic, Ecuador, Jamaica, Mexico, Panama, Peru, and Trinidad and Tobago. Among all surveyed Latin American and Caribbean countries, contraceptive prevalence was below the 38 per cent average for the developing world only in Bolivia, Guatemala, and Haiti (see Table 13.2).

In five of the six surveyed countries of the Near East and North Africa, contraceptive prevalence was near or above the developing-world average – for example, in Jordan, 35 per cent, and in Tunisia, 51 per cent.

Contraceptive prevalence was well above average in three of the four Asian countries surveyed by the DHS: Indonesia, at 50 per cent; Sri Lanka, at 62 per cent; and Thailand, at 68 per cent. In Pakistan, however, only 12 per cent of married women used contraception, according to the 1990–91 DHS. Among countries with independent surveys, contraceptive prevalence in Bangladesh was 40 per cent; in India 45 per cent; in the Philippines, 34 per cent; and in Vietnam, 53 per cent.

Contraceptive prevalence was lowest in sub-Saharan Africa, where prevalence exceeded the average for the developing world only in Zimbabwe, at 45 per cent. In only two other sub-Saharan countries did prevalence exceed 25 per cent – Botswana, at 35 per cent, and Kenya, at 27 per cent. Prevalence was below 10 per cent in Burundi, Liberia, Mali, Niger, Nigeria, Sudan, and Uganda.

TRENDS IN USE OF FAMILY PLANNING

As contraceptive use had become more common in developing countries, the use of modern methods – voluntary sterilization, oral contraceptives, intrauterine devices (IUDs), condoms, injectables, and vaginal methods – had grown much more than the use of traditional methods – chiefly periodic abstinence (rhythm) and withdrawal. In fact, in some countries the use of traditional methods had declined. Recent surveys confirmed that the dramatic increase in contraceptive prevalence was due almost entirely to rising use of modern methods. The prevalence of modern contraceptive method use in the developing world, excluding China, was 32 per cent.[6]

The availability of effective contraceptive supplies and services gave developing countries an advantage over European societies that experienced the fertility transition earlier. Before modern, effective methods existed, most European societies managed to reduce their fertility through widespread use of less effective methods such as sexual abstinence and withdrawal and through abortions. In some countries, primarily in Eastern Europe, couples still relied on such practices rather than effective contraception, which was in short supply.

The advent of modern methods, however, had enabled couples in developing countries to control their fertility much more effectively than couples in nineteenth century Europe. Eight of every 10 women in the developing world who practised family planning used a modern clinical

or supply method. More than 50 per cent of married women were currently using modern methods in Brazil, China, Colombia, Costa Rica, the Dominican Republic, Jamaica, Panama, South Korea, and Thailand. In only three countries – Peru, Mauritius, and Turkey – did as many as 20 per cent of married women use traditional methods – primarily periodic abstinence in Peru and withdrawal in Mauritius and Turkey. Traditional methods accounted for a majority of contraceptive use only in four African countries, all of which had low contraceptive prevalence and high fertility – Burundi, Cameroon, Ghana, and Togo – and in Bolivia, where 17 per cent of married women relied on the rhythm method for family planning (see Table 13.2).

The Johns Hopkins Report commented:

> *The growing use of effective family planning methods is a major reason that the recent fertility declines in developing nations have been so rapid,* according to Naomi Rutenberg and colleagues, who studied data from 19 countries that participated in the WFS or CPS as well as in the DHS. For example, in three surveyed sub-Saharan African countries in which fertility has fallen substantially – Kenya, Botswana, and Zimbabwe – the use of modern contraceptive methods rose sharply during the 1980s, while the use of traditional methods fell.[7] Even in Peru and Turkey, where traditional methods comprise a substantial percentage of total prevalence, a rising proportion of all contraceptive users rely on modern methods.[8] (emphasis added)

CONTRACEPTIVE METHOD MIX

In virtually every surveyed country some combination of three methods – female sterilization, oral contraceptives, and IUDs – accounted for most use of modern methods.

Voluntary female sterilization was the most widely used method in the world as a whole. It was particularly prevalent throughout most of Latin America and in parts of Asia. In contrast, sterilization was uncommon throughout Africa and the Near East.

Among the 50 surveyed countries in Table 13.2, voluntary female sterilization was the most widely used family planning method in 15 – Belize, Brazil, Colombia, the Dominican Republic, Ecuador, El Salvador, Guatemala, India, Mexico, Pakistan, Panama, the Philippines, South Korea, Sri Lanka and Thailand. The prevalence of female sterilisation was highest in the Dominican Republic at 39 per cent and South Korea at 37 per cent. India's 1988 contraceptive prevalence survey, which reported contraceptive use by couples and did not distinguish between male and female sterilization in its statistics, indicated that 31 per cent of couples rely on sterilization. An independent estimate based on programme statistics as well as survey data[9] indicated that about 24 per cent of married women in India were protected by female sterilization.

Oral contraceptives were the leading modern method in Bangladesh, Costa Rica, Haiti, Indonesia, Jamaica, Mauritius, Morocco, Paraguay, Trinidad and Tobago, Yemen, and every sub-Saharan country except Burundi, Cameroon, and Togo. In Zimbabwe, 33 per cent of married women used oral contraception – the highest prevalence of any surveyed country – accounting for 86 per cent of all use of modern methods. In Morocco, 28 per cent of married women used oral contraceptives, accounting for 79 per cent of use of modern methods. In Brazil, 25 per cent of married women used oral contraceptives, accounting for 45 per cent of modern contraceptive use – nearly as much as female sterilization.

The IUD also was an important method in some surveyed countries. It was the leading modern method in Vietnam, at 33 per cent; China, at 30 per cent; Tunisia, at 18 per cent; Egypt, at 17 per cent; Jordan, at 15 per cent; Turkey, at 14 per cent; and

Peru at 13 per cent. In Vietnam the IUD was virtually the only modern method available, accounting for 87 per cent of all modern method use. In Jordan the IUD accounted for more than half of the use of modern contraceptives, and in Egypt and Tunisia, for nearly half. Also, in Colombia, Ecuador, Indonesia, and Mexico, the IUD was used by at least 10 per cent of married women.

Injectables were less widely used in the surveyed countries as a whole, but in Indonesia they were the third most popular method, used by 12 per cent of married women and accounting for about one-fourth of all modern contraceptive use. Elsewhere, injectables were an important method in Botswana and Kenya, where they accounted for about one-fifth of modern contraceptive use, and in Jamaica and Thailand, where they accounted for about 15 per cent of use of modern methods.

Only a small portion of married couples in the surveyed countries used condoms as a family planning method. The prevalence of condom use exceeded 5 per cent only in Costa Rica, at 13 per cent; Trinidad and Tobago, at 12 per cent; Mauritius, at 11 per cent; South Korea, at 10 per cent; Jamaica, at 9 per cent; and Turkey, at 7 per cent.

Two other methods, male sterilization and vaginal barrier methods – diaphragms or spermicides – were used much less than any of the other modern methods in the surveyed countries. Surveys reported the highest prevalence of male sterilization, or vasectomy, in South Korea, at 11 per cent. In China the prevalence of vasectomy was 8 per cent. An estimate of the prevalence of vasectomy in India was 7 per cent. In Thailand the prevalence of vasectomy was 6 per cent; in Sri Lanka, 5 per cent; and in other surveyed countries, 1 per cent or less. As for vaginal methods, only in Colombia, South Korea, Trinidad and Tobago, and Turkey did more than 1 per cent of married women use them.

CHARACTERISTICS OF CONTRACEPTIVE USERS

Contraceptive use varied by women's characteristics, including age, number of children, education, and urban or rural residence.

Women's Age

In most countries contraceptive prevalence was lowest among young women, reached a peak among women in their thirties, and declined among older women. For example, in the 1988–89 Egypt DHS 24 per cent of married women ages 20–24 used family planning, rising to 53 per cent among women ages 35–39, then declining to 48 per cent in the 40–44 age group. This pattern reflected the desire for childbearing among young women, then growing interest in, at first, spacing births and, later, ending childbearing. Also, the contraceptive method mix varied according to age, as some women changed from using temporary methods for spacing births to permanent methods for preventing births.

Prevalence declined somewhat among older women because some believed that they were no longer at risk of becoming pregnant, held traditional views that favoured large families, or did not want to use contraceptives for other reasons.

Each new generation of women was more likely than the previous one to use contraception at each stage of the childbearing years. This fact reflected both the increasing availability of modern contraceptive methods in many countries and the growing interest in family planning among younger women.[10]

Table 13.3. Use of family planning by characteristics of women – current use among married women of reproductive age, by age, number of children, residence, and education.

Region, country and year	% Using any method	Current age						Number of living children			Residence		Education			
		15-19	20-24	25-29	30-34	35-39	40-44	0-1	2-3	4+	urban	rural	No education	Some primary school	Primary completed	More than primary
AFRICA																
Botswana 1988	35	17	26	37	36	38	36	19	41	36	42	31	21	33	39	52
Burundi 1987	9	4	9	10	10	7	8	5	11	10	27	8	8	12	12	30
Cameroon 1991	16	18	17	17	14	17	17	15	15	18	25	11	5	—19—		43
Ghana 1988	13	5	11	13	14	15	18	8	13	17	20	10	13	12	13	29
Kenya 1989	27	13	20	26	32	34	31	13	27	32	30	27	19	26	31	40
Liberia 1986	6	2	5	8	8	5	8	3	6	10	11	3	3	5	10	27
Mali 1987	5	9	5	5	6	3	2	6	4	5	12	3	3	9	43	53
Mauritius 1985	75	55	72	78	84	85	77	57	85	78	74	76	—74—		80	73
1991	75	NA	NA	NA	NA	NA	NA	64	85	82	78	72	—79—		75	74
Niger 1992	4	2	5	6	5	5	3	2	5	6	16	3	4	—16—		24
Nigeria 1990	6	1	5	6	7	9	8	4	5	10	15	4	2	8	11	33
Senegal 1986	12	10	11	13	13	13	8	7	14	14	15	11	10	14	17	23
Sudan 1989-90	9	4	8	7	12	10	11	5	10	10	17	4	3	13	12	24
Swaziland 1988	21	6	19	21	23	21	16	10	23	20	28	13	10	—13—		42
Tanzania 1991-92	10	5	10	10	13	13	11	7	11	12	18	8	4	—14—		32
Togo 1988	12	5	13	14	13	12	12	10	14	13	19	10	9	12	24	17
Uganda 1988-89	5	2	3	4	6	8	8	2	4	7	18	3	2	5	9	59
Zambia 1992	15	9	13	15	18	22	17	8	16	20	21	10	8	13	27	55
Zimbabwe 1988-89	45	30	46	50	51	42	37	31	49	50	53	42	35	43	47	55
ASIA & PACIFIC																
Bangladesh 1991	40	19	33	46	53	57	46	NA	NA	NA	48	39	37	NA	41	NA
India 1988	45	9	23	44	58	66	61	NA	NA	NA	56	39	37	—54—		NA
Indonesia 1987	51	26	47	54	59	56	43	32	61	56	57	48	38	49	54	65
1991	50	30	51	54	57	58	48	36	59	52	56	47	37	47	54	59

Table 13.3. *contd*

Region, country and year	% Using any method	Current age						Number of living children			Residence		Education			
		15–19	20–24	25–29	30–34	35–39	40–44	0–1	2–3	4+	urban	rural	No education	Some primary school	Primary completed	More than primary
ASIA & PACIFIC contd																
Korea, Rep. of 1988	77	— 14 —		65	87	90	82	48	90	87	78	76	79	NA	NA	NA
Pakistan 1990–91	12	3	6	10	13	20	16	2	11	18	26	6	8	— 18 —		35
Sri Lanka 1987	62	20	42	57	67	74	72	32	71	80	65	62	55	63	68	62
Thailand 1987	68	43	57	69	75	73	69	47	81	73	69	67	60	69	70	66
Vietnam 1988	53	5	32	52	60	69	55	50	63	58	67	50	NA	NA	NA	NA
LATIN AMERICA & CARIBBEAN																
Belize 1991	47	27	37	45	53	55	56	27	52	53	55	33	40	39	49	56
Bolivia 1989	32	16	23	34	39	36	28	23	37	32	41	21	14	25	38	50
Brazil 1986	66	48	55	68	74	70	67	50	78	66	70	57	47	66	78	73
Colombia 1986	67	29	57	69	74	76	70	47	77	71	72	56	51	63	68	73
1990	66	37	54	67	75	77	74	51	75	75	71	60	57	63	67	72
Costa Rica 1986	70	51	60	65	74	84	78	53	63	74	74	65		— 66 —	69	85
Dom. Rep. 1986	51	25	38	51	61	65	55	26	57	66	53	47	36	50	45	56
1991	56	17	43	55	66	71	69	30	66	68	60	50	42	55	58	61
Ecuador 1987	46	16	34	46	54	54	51	29	53	49	54	34	18	38	47	57
1989	53	25	39	55	63	61	59	36	62	54	62	40	25	— 48-	63	58
El Salvador 1985	49	22	35	54	63	57	52	25	60	54	59	36	38	47	54	58
1988	47	17	37	51	57	59	53	27	58	49	60	34	34	44	51	60
Guatemala 1987	23	5	16	21	31	31	28	27	29	24	43	14	10	24	47	60
Haiti 1989	10	5	7	16	14	11	7	10	NA	NA	22	8	8	11	12	19
Jamaica 1989	55	48	53	57	58	59	57	40	63	55	52	56		— 66 —		56
Mexico 1987	55	30	47	54	62	62	60	31	67	55	34	54	24	46	63	70
Panama 1984	58	23	43	57	65	74	72	31	67	68	36	48		— 25 —	53	62
Paraguay 1987	38	23	37	43	39	39	32	30	51	31	52	32		— 26 —	38	61
1990	48	35	42	52	54	55	50	36	59	46	57	39	NA	NA	50	62

Table 13.3. *contd*

Region, country and year	% Using any method	Current age						Number of living children			Residence		Education			
		15–19	20–24	25–29	30–34	35–39	40–44	0–1	2–3	4+	urban	rural	No education	Some primary school	Primary completed	More than primary
LATIN AMERICA & CARIBBEAN contd																
Peru 1986	48	23	40	50	55	54	48	36	59	45	62	25	22	36	50	64
1991–92	59	29	49	60	67	70	64	52	68	59	69	42	59	47	58	67
Trin. & Tob. 1987	54	42	55	54	57	56	53	42	62	61	56	53	33	52	52	58
NEAR EAST & NORTH AFRICA																
Egypt 1988–89	40	6	24	37	47	53	48	14	47	48	54	26	29	45	54	53
Jordan 1990	35	8	22	30	42	47	49	9	35	43	44	34	30	36	42	37
Morocco 1987	37	17	26	36	43	42	41	21	39	45	53	25	31	54	61	65
1992	42	24	35	40	45	48	48	24	48	47	54	32	36	57		65
Tunisia 1988	51	11	35	44	55	59	61	22	58	59	62	34	42	51	63	67
Turkey 1988	60	23	50	68	73	73	60	42	71	60	66	53	47	56	64	74
Yemen 1991–92	7	1	5	9	8	10	8	3	7	9	23	4	5	17		34

Source: Population Reports. (Johns Hopkins University) Vol. XX, No. 4, December 1992.

Number of Children

Use of contraception increased sharply with the number of children a woman had up to the third child, as many women who had reached their desired family size sought to stop having more children. In some surveyed countries, however, the increase in contraceptive use slowed once women had had three children and even declined among women with four or more children. For example, in the 1990 Paraguay DHS 36 per cent of women with one child or none used family planning, rising to 59 per cent of women with two or three children but falling to 46 per cent of women with four or more children (see Table 13.3). While some women with many children might not use contraception because they wanted to have large families, some might have had more children than they wanted because they lacked access to contraception. Also, many women with more children were older and might not be using contraception for reasons associated with their age.

Urban and Rural Residence

Surveys in almost all countries found that urban women were more likely to use contraception than rural women. The differences were largest in countries with low contraception prevalence and smallest where prevalence was highest. For example, in Cameroon, where the 1991 DHS reported contraceptive prevalence of 16 per cent, prevalence was 15 per cent among urban woman compared with 11 per cent among rural women. In South Korea, however, where total contraceptive prevalence was 77 per cent, 78 per cent of urban women and 76 per cent of rural women used family planning.

There were several reasons that urban couples were more likely than rural couples to use contraception. More were educated and had 'modern' attitudes that included wanting smaller families; it was more expensive to raise children in the cities; conditions were more crowded; and urban couples had less need for children's labour than couples in agricultural areas. Also, family planning was often much more available in cities and towns than in villages.

In sub-Saharan Africa the urban–rural gap in contraceptive prevalence was much wider when only modern family planning methods are considered. This was because, except in Botswana, Kenya and Zimbabwe, both access to modern methods and interest in having small families were confined to a small percentage of couples who lived in cities. In contrast, in most of Latin America the urban–rural gap shrank when only modern methods were considered because family planning programmes that began in the cities had been extended to many rural areas. Also, in Indonesia and Thailand, where governments had invested heavily in rural family planning programmes and services from the beginning, urban–rural differences in the use of modern methods had always been small.

Education

The Johns Hopkins survey affirmed: 'In most countries the better educated a woman is, the more likely she is to use family planning.' Generally, women with a primary education were much more likely to use a contraceptive method than women with no education but not as likely as women with a secondary education or more. For example, in Botswana, where contraceptive prevalence was 35 per cent, near the average for the developing world, the 1988 DHS reported that 21 per cent of women with no education used family planning compared with 33 per cent of women with some primary school, 39 per cent of women who completed primary school, and 52 per cent of women with education beyond primary school (see Table 13.3).

In countries where the fertility transition was well advanced, however, many poorly educated women used family planning. Among surveyed countries, for example, there was little difference in contraceptive prevalence by women's level of education in Mauritius, Sri Lanka, or Thailand. In most of the developing world, contraceptive prevalence had risen among all education groups. Also, the gaps in use of family planning by education level had narrowed in some countries as family planning services and interest in having smaller families had become more widespread.

KNOWLEDGE OF FAMILY PLANNING

In most developing countries surveyed by the DHS, more than three-quarters of women could name at least one modern method of contraception spontaneously – that is, without prompting. In seven African countries, however – Burundi, Ghana, Liberia, Mali, Niger, Senegal, and Uganda – fewer than 40 per cent of married women were able to name any modern family planning method spontaneously.[11]

After being prompted with names and descriptions of the methods, a large majority of surveyed women in all regions recognized at least one modern family planning method (see Table 13.4). In fact, with prompting, nearly as many women were able to name two family planning methods as were able to name a single method. By these measures, awareness of modern family planning had become nearly universal. Still, in Bolivia, Guatemala, and several sub-Saharan countries, many married women were not able to name any modern family planning method after prompting. In Nigeria, for example, the 1990 DHS reported that only 44 per cent of married women recognized any family planning method, modern or traditional, even after being prompted (see Table 13.4).

In all surveyed countries except Mali, Niger, Senegal, and Togo, awareness of modern methods exceeded awareness of traditional methods, often by a wide margin. For example, in Pakistan 77 per cent of married woman recognized a modern method compared with 26 per cent who recognized a traditional method; in Mexico 93 per cent knew of a modern method compared with 72 per cent who knew of a traditional method. Among all surveyed countries oral contraceptives and female sterilization were most widely recognized, followed by injections and the IUD. Male sterilization was least known (see Table 13.4).

Knowledge by Women's Characteristics

Like contraceptive use itself, recognition of contraceptive methods varied according to women's education and other socio-economic characteristics, but it did not vary as much. In every country, for example, nearly all women with more than a primary education knew of at least one family planning method. Except in Bolivia and Mali, however, most women with no education also knew of at least one method.

In some countries less educated women were just as likely to recognize some contraceptive methods as were more educated women. For example, in Egypt 96 per cent of women with no education recognized the pill, as did virtually all women with a secondary education. In other countries, however, there were wide gaps in knowledge of

Table 13.4. Knowledge of contraceptive methods among currently married women of reproductive age (per cent):[a]

Region, country and year	Any method	Any traditional method[b]	Any modern method[c]	Voluntary sterilization female	Voluntary sterilization male	OCs	IUDs	Condoms	Injectables	Vaginal methods	Periodic abstinence	Withdrawal
AFRICA												
Botswana 1988	96	46	96	67	25	95	91	88	91	53	24	30
Burundi 1987	79	64	65	15	4	43	25	15	58	7	48	26
Cameroon 1991	70	58	63	51	7	46	30	40	40	15	39	36
Ghana 1988	80	53	77	58	11	65	40	51	48	40	42	34
Kenya 1989	93	57	92	73	22	89	68	57	93	28	52	19
Liberia 1986	70	28	68	41	6	62	32	27	43	10	13	14
Mali 1987	44	38	30	15	5	23	16	9	18	6	8	5
Mauritius 1985	NA	95	100	98	50	100	94	98	96	58[d]	88[e]	81
1991	100	92	100	92	24	99	88	95	94	NA	92	75
Niger 1992	77	67	58	40	11	45	25	23	39	11	10	10
Nigeria 1990	44	26	42	19	7	35	20	22	34	13	15	13
Senegal 1986	92	89	68	56	3	51	29	27	27	9	16	14
Sudan 1989–90	71	39	71	44	5	70	39	18	46	8	36	19
Swaziland 1988[f]	NA	NA	NA	45	8	80	62	56	75	20[g]	18	24
Tanzania 1991–92	74	44	72	50	10	69	31	51	40	20	1	24
Togo 1988	96	93	82	69	14	47	48	37	61	27	52	41
Uganda 1988–89	85	63	79	63	9	68	21	32	41	12	45	22
Zambia 1992	94	67	87	64	18	78	43	72	38	24	36	48
Zimbabwe 1988–89	99	87	98	55	18	97	60	82	73	15	27	79
ASIA & PACIFIC												
Indonesia 1987												
1991	95	41	95[h]	54	27	92	83	67	86	4	22	16
	94	28	94	54	29	90	82	63	87	6	21	14
Pakistan 1990–91	78	26	77	70	20	62	52	35	62	13	18	14
Sri Lanka 1987	99	69	99	98	92	94	84	75	85	15	62	40
Thailand 1987	100	46	100	98	96	99	95	91	98	17	30	29

Table 13.4. *contd*

Region, country and year	Any method	Any traditional method[b]	Any modern method[c]	Voluntary sterilization female	male	OCs	IUDs	Condoms	Injectables	Vaginal methods	Periodic abstinence	Withdrawal
LATIN AMERICA & CARIBBEAN												
Belize 1991	NA	NA	NA	88	50	93	71	82	86	46	53[i]	35
Bolivia 1989	77	62	69	53	16	54	56	30	44	24	56	28
Brazil 1986	100	89	100	95	56	100	67	87	58	36	77	70
Colombia 1986	100	81	100	96	52	99	94	72	91	86	65	60
1990	100	80	100	95	65	99	94	88	92	84	71	60
Costa Rica 1986	NA	NA	NA	95	65	99	95	97	90	77	91[i]	62
Dominican Rep. 1986	99	74	99	98	47	98	91	89	36	69	54	62
1991	100	79	100	99	57	99	88	96	57	57	67	63
Ecuador 1987	91	60	91	78	19	86	80	52	66	58	51	39
1989	NA	NA	92	77	24	83	80	61	72	52	58[i]	22
El Salvador 1985	93	59	93	87	65	89	80	79	67	37	40	22
1988[k]	NA	NA	NA	95	76	94	83	90	81	64	46[i]	15
Guatemala 1987	72	42	72	62	41	64	44	37	46	22	25	14
Haiti 1989[l]	88	NA	NA	45	18	82	34	38	61	13[g]	15[i]	25
Jamaica 1989[k]	NA	NA	NA	92	56	99	83	99	96	61[m]	35[i]	59
Mexico 1987	93	72	93	86	68	91	87	67	87	65	64	52
Panama 1984	NA	NA	NA	92	70	95	86	83	86	39[m]	47[i]	41
Paraguay 1987[k]	NA	NA	NA	67	20	92	80	60	82	35	54[i]	35
1990	98	91	98	70	16	94	85	67	89	46	55	53
Peru 1986	90	80	88	76	27	78	73	53	69	48	75	51
1991–92	97	90	95	83	51	89	87	78	82	65	86	58
Trinidad & Tobago 1987	99	85	99	93	61	97	90	97	80	81	48	78

Table 13.4. *contd*

Region, country and year	Any method	Any traditional method[b]	Any modern method[c]	Voluntary sterilization female	Voluntary sterilization male	OCs	IUDs	Condoms	Injectables	Vaginal methods	Periodic abstinence	Withdrawal
NEAR EAST & NORTH AFRICA												
Egypt 1988–89	99	69	98	55	10	98	94	46	63	42	23	14
Jordan 1990	99	86	99	95	26	98	98	55	51	58	78	70
Morocco 1987	98	76	98	77	4	97	80	61	56	25	53	48
1992	99	73	99	85	7	99	87	72	63	31	61	54
Tunisia 1988	99	92	99	96	17	96	95	67	60	62	56	52
Turkey 1988	NA	NA	NA	65	28	94	94	76	5	6[m]	38	85
Yemen 1991–92	53	15	53	24	13	51	34	10	32	7	13	9

a Both spontaneous and prompted responses
b Includes withdrawal and (not shown separately) douche, prolonged abstinence, and 'other'
c Includes voluntary sterilization, oral contraceptives (OCs), intrauterine devices (IUDs), condoms, injectables, and vaginal methods (spermicides, diaphragms, and cervical caps). DHS include Norplant where available.
d Foam jelly only
e Temperature method only
f Married by Swazi custom only (excludes civil marriages, which account for 16 per cent of all marriages)
g Vaginal tablets only
h 66 per cent of women had heard of Norplant includes Billings method
i Includes Billings method
j 75 per cent of women had heard of Norplant
k Includes all women regardless of marital status
l Excludes consensual unions
m Diaphragm only

Source: Population Reports. (Johns Hopkins University) Vol. XX, No. 4, December 1992.

some methods. In Peru, for example, knowledge of the pill was widespread among women with a secondary education, at 95 per cent, but only 42 per cent of women with no education knew of the pill.

Also, urban women were somewhat more likely than rural women to recognize family planning methods, although there was little difference by residence in about half of the surveyed countries. There was little difference in awareness of family planning methods according to the number of children a woman had or according to her age.

Broad Knowledge of Family Planning

The Johns Hopkins report commented:

> Awareness of a range of effective contraceptive methods, not just one or two methods, is essential to informed choice. The more methods that women know, and the more that they know about them, the better they will be able to choose an appropriate method. Couples who know of several effective methods are less likely to become dissatisfied and to discontinue use without immediately switching to another effective method. . . .[12]

In some countries many women knew about most of the modern methods. Contraceptives were particularly well known in Costa Rica, where at least 90 per cent of currently married women recognized oral contraceptives, condoms, IUDs, female sterilization, and injections. In 8 of 25 countries for which Rutenberg and colleagues had analyzed DHS data – Brazil, Colombia, the Dominican Republic, Mexico, Sri Lanka, Thailand, Tunisia, and Trinidad and Tobago – 80 per cent or more of women recognized five or more family planning methods. In most countries of North Africa, Latin America, and Asia, a majority of women recognized at least five methods. In many other countries, however, knowledge of family planning appeared limited. For example, in all surveyed sub-Saharan African countries except Botswana, Kenya, Togo, and Zimbabwe, only a minority of women recognized five or more family planning methods, whether modern or traditional. The same was true in two Latin American countries – Bolivia and Guatemala – where large indigenous populations were separated from the Spanish speaking population by culture and language.

Promoting Family Planning in the Mass Media

Promoting family planning on radio and television could be an important means of raising awareness, improving knowledge, and stimulating use of modern contraceptive methods. Johns Hopkins reported that recent studies of survey data had demonstrated that family planning messages broadcast in the mass media had increased the use of contraception.

In virtually every surveyed country a majority of married women of reproductive age considered mass-media messages about family planning acceptable. The highest percentages were in Colombia and Zimbabwe, at 96 per cent; the lowest were in Nigeria, at 56 per cent, and Pakistan, at 48 per cent. In 19 of 24 countries with comparable survey data, at least three-fourths of married women considered it acceptable to broadcast family planning messages.

Radio and television reached potentially vast audiences. In 22 of 28 countries with survey data, a majority of married women of reproductive age had radios in their households. The percentage with radios ranged from 18 per cent in Burundi to 93 per

Table 13.5. Family planning messages in the mass media – access, exposure, and acceptability among currently married women ages 15–44.

| Region, country and year | Have radio | Have television | % of women who: | |
			Have heard family planning messages on radio[a]	Consider mass-media family planning messages acceptable
AFRICA				
Botswana 1988	69	9	NA	78
Burundi 1987	18	1	NA	91
Ghana 1988	40	8	NA	76
Kenya 1989	61	4	66	89
Liberia 1986	57	NA	NA	NA
Mali 1987	52	3	NA	75
Nigeria 1990[b]	55	19	25[c]	56
Senegal 1986	78	12	NA	NA
Sudan 1989–90	56	25	NA	73
Togo 1988	49	9	NA	80
Uganda 1988–89	28	1	NA	68
Zimbabwe 1988–89	44	12	9	96
ASIA & PACIFIC				
Indonesia 1987	61	29	28	NA
Pakistan 1990–91[d]	35	27	21[c]	48
Sri Lanka 1987	76	20	NA	89
Thailand 1987	75	50	29	88
LATIN AMERICA & CARIBBEAN				
Bolivia 1989	NA	NA	39	80
Brazil 1986	81	70	NA	NA
Colombia 1986	87	69	46	97
1991[b]	86	76	39[c]	96
Dominican Rep. 1986	67	51	14[c]	88
1991[b]	59	57	31	94
Ecuador 1987	84	63	74	91
El Salvador 1985	79	40	NA	NA
Guatemala 1987	66	30	54	66
Paraguay 1990[b]	88	61	29[c]	91
Peru 1986	84	57	60	94
1991–92	85	64	59[c]	NA
Trinidad & Tobago 1987	93	90	NA	95
NEAR EAST & NORTH AFRICA				
Egypt 1988–89	NA	77	32 (69[e])	NA
Jordan 1990[d]	88	91	NA	84
Morocco 1987	83	43	26	79
Tunisia 1988	76	73	64	90

[a] In last month.

[b] All women.

[c] Heard messages on radio or TV.

[d] Ever-married women.

[e] 69 per cent heard messages on TV.

Source: Population Reports. (Johns Hopkins University) Vol. XX, No. 4, December 1992.

cent in Trinidad and Tobago. Although not as widespread as radio, television also reached a large percentage of households except in sub-Saharan Africa. In 11 surveyed countries a majority of women had television in their households, and in Colombia, Egypt, Jordan, and Trinidad and Tobago, at least 75 per cent had television (see Table 13.5). The more urban the country, the greater the exposure to all mass media.

The reach of family planning messages broadcast on radio varied substantially by country. Differences in findings reflected the communication strategies of family planning programmes as well as the timing of media campaigns in relation to the date of the survey. The often large gap between the percentage of women with access to radio and television and the smaller percentage who had received information about family planning via these media suggested opportunities for more use of the mass media. This was particularly true in urban areas, where surveys showed that acceptance of family planning typically started and where broadcasts reached large numbers of people.

The rising influence of television and its importance to family planning promotion were apparent in survey data from Egypt. In Egypt family planning messages reached more women through television than through radio. More than two of every three women reported seeing a family planning message on television in the month before the DHS compared with about one of every three, who had heard a family planning message on radio.

AVAILABILITY OF FAMILY PLANNING

In the surveys cited in the Johns Hopkins report almost all women who reported that they knew about a contraceptive method said that they also knew where to obtain it. Thus lack of knowledge about sources of modern contraceptive methods did not appear to be a major barrier to using family planning.

There did, however, appear to be large differences in the availability of family planning. For example, in Egypt, a densely populated country with a strong national family planning programme and many private providers, the median distance to the nearest family planning outlet in rural areas was less than 1km, and virtually all women lived within 5km of a facility. In Uganda, however, which was less well served with family planning, the median distance to the nearest facility in rural areas was more than 19km, and only about one of every five rural women lived within 5km of a family planning facility.

As might be expected, women in urban areas had a much better access to a range of family planning sources than women in rural areas. In Tunisia, for example, more than two-thirds of urban women lived within 5km of a health centre, a clinic, a pharmacy, and a private doctor providing family planning services. In contrast, health centres were the only type of facility within 5km of more than half of rural women. These data showed that in some countries family planning programmes had far to go in extending services to rural areas.

In most of the surveyed countries governments were the most important source of family planning methods and services. Governments served a majority of family planning users in 25 of 42 surveyed countries. In 10 of 15 surveyed Latin American and Caribbean countries, however, governments served a minority of users.

Private, for-profit suppliers also were an important source of contraceptives in many surveyed countries, particularly in Latin America. In Egypt private suppliers

Table 13.6.   Family planning accessibility in rural areas percentage distribution of rural currently married women ages 15–49 by distance to nearest facility where family planning is available, and median distance to nearest facility.

Region, country and year	Distance to Nearest Facility				Median distance (km)
	0–4 km	5–14 km	15 or more km	Other*	
AFRICA					
Togo 1988	45	25	21	9	7
Uganda 1988–89	22	18	23	37	19
Zimbabwe 1988–89	48	40	10	2	5
ASIA					
Thailand 1987	67	26	7	0	3
NORTH AFRICA					
Egypt 1988–89	96	4	0	0	1
Tunisia 1988	60	30	8	0	4
LATIN AMERICA & CARIBBEAN					
Colombia 1990	54	37	9	0	4
Dominican Rep. 1991	60	28	8	3	3
Ecuador 1987	63	33	4	0	3
Guatemala 1987	56	25	12	2	3

*Togo: nearest identified facility did not in fact provide family planning; Uganda: no facility with family planning was known, or information was missing; other countries: information missing. Note: If the facility was in the woman's village, no distance estimate was recorded; such facilities were included in the 0–4 km category. Percentages may not total 100 per cent because some sample clusters were not surveyed for service availability data.

Source: Population Reports. (Johns Hopkins University) Vol. XX, No. 4, December 1992.

served 71 per cent of all users of family planning, the highest percentage of any surveyed country, followed closely by Brazil at 68 per cent and Paraguay at 67 per cent. For-profit sources included retailers, such as pharmacies and dispensaries, and private clinical and medical service providers, such as hospitals, clinics, physicians, and midwives.

Although the private sector charged fees for services and sold contraceptive supplies, it sometimes did so at prices subsidized by governments or donor agencies as part of social marketing programmes. In Egypt, for example, where 87 per cent of oral contraceptive users obtained their supplies from pharmacies, some of these customers bought social marketing brands at low, subsidized prices.

The private sector typically played a greater role in providing supply methods (oral contraceptives, injectables, and barrier methods) than clinical methods (IUDs and voluntary sterilization) – probably because the private sector charged much higher fees for clinical methods than did the public sector. In the 1987 Mexico DHS, for example, 67 per cent of women reported obtaining supply methods from private sources compared with just 20 per cent for clinical methods. In contrast, the Mexican government was the source of 78 per cent of clinical methods compared with only 32 per cent of supply methods.[13]

In some countries private nongovernmental organizations (NGOs) also provided family planning methods and services. Nonprofit organizations supplied more than

Table 13.7. Sources of contraception for currently married women of reproductive age who are using modern methods.

Region, Country and Year	Government[a]	Private for-profit[b]	Nonprofit/NGOs	Other[c]
		% of contraceptive users served by:		
AFRICA				
Botswana 1988	92	————————8————————		1
Burundi 1987	87	————————2————————		11
Cameroon 1991[d]	30	————————61————————		5[e]
Ghana 1988	39	25	20	16
Kenya 1989	73	9	17	1
Liberia 1986	37	17	46	1
Mali 1987	76	2	8	15
Mauritius 1985	71	6	19	4
1991	66	9	23	2
Niger 1992	93	————————6————————		0
Nigeria 1990[d]	37	47	4	9
Senegal 1986[g]	47	————————43————————		10
Sudan 1989–90	58	————————35————————		6[h]
Swaziland 1988	78	7	14	2
Tanzania 1991–92[d]	73	7	14	2
Togo 1988	51	26	12	11
Uganda 1988–89	56	10	31	3
Zambia 1992[d]	67	24	3	6
Zimbabwe 1988–89	88	4	2	6
ASIA & PACIFIC				
Indonesia 1987	81	12	NA	7
1991[j]	76	————————22————————		2
Pakistan 1990–91	56	————————30————————		4[k]
Sri Lanka 1987	86	10	0	3
Thailand 1987	83	15	1	1
LATIN AMERICA & CARIBBEAN				
Belize 1991	38	41	10	11
Bolivia 1989	34	62	1	3
Brazil 1986	29	68	1	2
Colombia 1986	18	44	37	2
1990	19	40	38	2[h]
Costa Rica 1986	74	————————24————————		2
Dominican Rep. 1986	49	47	1	4
1991	33	53	12	2
Ecuador 1987	41	45	14	1
1989	41	43	15	1
El Salvador 1988	75	10	13	2
Guatemala 1987	31	28	39	3
Haiti 1989	70	————————29————————		1
Jamaica 1989	70	28	1	1
Mexico 1987	62	————————36————————		2
Peru 1986	48	49	3	1
1991–92	48	45	6	1
Paraguay 1987	46	32	10	12
1990	19	67	10	5
Trinidad & Tobago 1987	38	46	15	1

Table 13.7. *contd*

Region, Country and Year	% of contraceptive users served by:			
	Government[a]	Private for-profit[b]	Nonprofit/NGOs	Other[c]
NEAR EAST & NORTH AFRICA				
Egypt 1988–89	26	71	1	2
Jordan 1990	24	44	30	1
Morocco 1987	62	20	1	17
1992	63	33	3	1
Tunisia 1988	77	————23————		1
Yemen 1991–92	57	————35————		3[j]

NGOs = Nongovernmental organizations
[a] Public hospitals, clinics, and other services.
[b] Private hospitals, clinics, pharmacies, doctors, nurses, and midwives.
[c] Includes friends, relatives, traditional healers.
[d] All women.
[e] An additional 4 per cent don't know/missing.
[f] An additional 3 per cent don't know/missing.
[g] Oral contraceptives and IUD only.
[h] An additional 1 per cent don't know/missing.
[i] An additional 5 per cent don't know/missing.
[j] Ever-married women.
[k] An additional 10 per cent don't know/missing.
Data are for married women ages 15–44. Exceptions are Cameroon 1991, Colombia 1990, Indonesia 1991, Jordan 1990, Morocco 1992, Niger 1992, Tanzania 1991–92, and Zambia 1992, married women ages 15–19.

Source: Population Reports. (Johns Hopkins University) Vol. XX, No. 4, December 1992.

25 per cent of contraceptive users in Colombia, Guatemala, Jordan, Liberia, and Uganda (see Table 13.7). In most surveyed countries, however, NGOs supplied only a small percentage of all users. NGOs included such organizations as religiously affiliated medical centres and nonprofit family planning associations, some of which were affiliates of the International Planned Parenthood Federation (IPPF).

POTENTIAL DEMAND FOR FAMILY PLANNING

The Johns Hopkins survey reported that about 375 million married women in developing countries were using family planning. *But at least 120 million more were not using family planning even though they wanted to avoid becoming pregnant.* Meeting all of this large potential demand for contraception was one of the top priorities of family planning programmes.

> Westoff has used the data on desired number of children to calculate a 'desired total fertility rate' (DTFR) – the TFR if women were to bear exactly the number of children that they desired.[14] *By this measure, in virtually every country outside sub-Saharan Africa, desired fertility is below three children per woman.* For example, in Thailand the DTFR is 1.8; in Colombia, 2.1. In contrast, in sub-Saharan Africa the DTFR is above five children per woman in all surveyed countries except Botswana, Kenya, and Zimbabwe. (emphasis added)

Table 13.8. Fertility intentions among currently married women ages 15–44.

Region, country and year	Are pregnant	Want more now[a]	Want more later[b]	Want no more
		% of women who:		
AFRICA				
Botswana 1988	10	25	33	32
Burundi 1987	15	15	52	18
Ghana 1988	14	20	47	19
Kenya 1989	13	13	28	46
Liberia 1986	17	33	36	14
Mali 1987	16	34	36	13
Mauritius 1985[c]	8	——— 22 ———		70
Nigeria 1990	16	34	37	13
Senegal 1986	22	14	44	21
Sudan 1989–90	16	32	32	21
Togo 1988	14	19	48	20
Uganda 1988–89	17	36	32	15
Zimbabwe 1988–89	14	22	37	28
ASIA & PACIFIC				
Indonesia 1987	8	11	31	50
Pakistan 1990–91	16	24	19	42
Sri Lanka 1987	7	13	20	60
Thailand 1987	7	12	19	62
LATIN AMERICA & CARIBBEAN				
Belize 1991[c]	11	——— 40 ———		49
Bolivia 1989	13	10	10	68
Brazil 1986	10	13	15	62
Colombia 1986	10	13	15	63
1990	9	14	17	60
Costa Rica 1986[c]	12	——— 35 ———		51
Dominican Republic 1986	12	17	16	56
1991	10	14	16	60
Ecuador 1987	11	11	20	59
1989[c]	10	——— 28 ———		62
El Salvador 1985	11	10	22	57
1988[c]	12	——— 24 ———		64
Guatemala 1987	15	12	27	46
Haiti 1989[c]	12	——— 33 ———		55
Mexico 1987	13	5	16	67
Paraguay 1987[c]	13	——— 50 ———		37
1990	11	20	26	48
Peru 1986	11	9	14	67
1991–92	10	8	14	69
Trinidad & Tobago 1987	8	17	22	53
NEAR EAST & NORTH AFRICA				
Egypt 1988–89	14	13	13	61
Jordan 1990	16	14	23	48
Morocco 1987	14	20	24	42
Tunisia 1988	12	12	23	53

[a] Want more children within two years.
[b] Want more children after two years or later.
[c] Survey asked nonpregnant women whether or not they want another child but not when they wanted to have another child.

Source: Population Reports. (Johns Hopkins University) Vol. XX, No. 4, December 1992.

The gap between desired fertility and actual fertility suggested the extent of unwanted births. The gap was smallest in sub-Saharan African countries because most African women want large families. The gap was greatest in Latin American countries, where, even though contraceptive use was rising, nearly one-third of women already had more children than they said was ideal. In Brazil, for example, the DTFR was 2.2 children per woman compared with the TFR of 3.6. In Bolivia the DTFR was 2.8 compared with the TFR of 4.9.

In most surveyed countries between 20 per cent and 30 per cent of married women had an unmet need for family planning. Of 38 surveyed countries reported in Tables 13.9 and 13.10, unmet need was less than 20 per cent only in 12 – Brazil, Colombia, Costa Rica, the Dominican Republic, Indonesia, Mauritius, Panama, Peru, Sri Lanka, Thailand, Trinidad and Tobago, and Turkey. It was more than 30 per cent in seven – Bolivia, Ghana, Kenya, Liberia, Paraguay, Swaziland, and Togo. Among countries with DHS data, unmet need for family planning ranged from 11 per cent of married women in Thailand to 38 per cent in Kenya and 40 per cent in Togo. Among countries surveyed by the FPS, unmet need ranged from 3 per cent in Costa Rica and Mauritius to 44 per cent in Swaziland.

In most countries surveyed by the DHS, unmet need for spacing births and unmet need for limiting births were roughly equal. In Bolivia, Mexico, and Peru, however, unmet need for limiting was more than twice unmet need for spacing, while in all surveyed countries of sub-Saharan Africa except Nigeria and Zimbabwe, the unmet need for spacing births exceeded the unmet need for limiting (see Table 13.9).

Total Potential Demand for Family Planning

The concept of total potential demand defined the 'market' for family planning. It recognized not only that family planning providers must serve current contraceptive users but also that many other couples who wanted to control their fertility would use contraception if it were more available or better promoted or if other barriers to use were removed.

Most developing countries faced large potential demand for family planning. Outside sub-Saharan Africa a majority of women in every surveyed country except Pakistan and Haiti either already used family planning or had an unmet need for family planning. Outside sub-Saharan Africa most potential demand for family planning was to limit childbearing. In all sub-Saharan countries with survey data, however, potential demand was greater for spacing than for limiting births except in Kenya, where the two were about equal (see Table 13.9).

In Asian and Latin American countries surveyed, much of the potential demand for family planning was being met. For example, in Brazil, Colombia, Costa Rica, Mauritius, Panama, Sri Lanka, and Thailand, more than 80 per cent of the potential demand for family planning was satisfied. In 14 of 38 countries surveyed, however, less than half of the total potential demand was satisfied. In most sub-Saharan countries less than one-third of the potential demand was satisfied and less than one-fifth in Liberia, Mali and Uganda.

Even in countries with extensive family planning programmes, where much of the potential demand for family planning was being met, women in rural areas and less educated women were at a disadvantage. In Egypt, for example, 72 per cent of the potential demand in urban areas was met compared with only 43 per cent in rural areas; in Colombia 85 per cent in urban areas compared with 71 per cent in rural areas; and in Botswana 64 per cent in urban areas compared with 49 per cent in rural areas.

Table 13.9. Unmet need and potential demand for family planning, demographic and health surveys (DHS) – percentages of currently married women ages 15–49.

Region, country and year	Unmet need[a]			Current use			Potential demand[b]			% of potential demand satisfied[c]		
	total	for spacing	for limiting	total	for spacing	for limiting	total	for spacing	for limiting	total	for spacing	for limiting
AFRICA												
Botswana 1988	27	19	7	33	18	15	62	39	23	54	46	66
Burundi 1987	25	18	7	9	6	3	34	24	10	26	25	28
Ghana 1979–80	35	26	9	13	8	5	48	34	14	27	23	35
Kenya 1989	38	22	16	27	9	18	65	31	34	42	28	54
Liberia 1986	33	20	13	6	4	3	39	23	16	16	15	18
Mali 1987	23	17	6	5	4	1	28	21	6	17	19	11
Nigeria 1990	21	9	12	6	3	3	27	15	12	22	23	23
Sudan 1989–90	26	18	9	9	5	4	35	22	13	25	21	33
Togo 1988	40	29	12	12	8	4	52	36	16	23	22	26
Uganda 1988–89	27	20	7	5	2	3	32	22	10	15	10	28
Zimbabwe 1988–89	22	10	12	43	28	16	65	38	27	67	73	57
ASIA & PACIFIC												
Indonesia 1987	16	10	6	48	18	30	65	29	36	74	63	83
Sri Lanka 1987	12	7	5	62	13	49	76	22	54	81	61	89
Pakistan 1990–91	28	11	17	12	2	10	40	13	27	30	17	36
Thailand 1987	11	6	6	66	16	50	77	22	55	85	73	90
LATIN AMERICA & CARIBBEAN												
Bolivia 1989	36	10	26	30	7	24	70	18	52	43	37	46
Brazil 1986	13	5	8	66	18	48	81	24	57	82	74	85
Colombia 1986	14	5	8	65	15	49	81	22	59	80	70	84
1990	15	3	12	66	20	46	81	23	58	81	87	79
Dominican Rep. 1986	19	10	9	50	10	40	71	21	50	70	46	80
1991	17	8	9	56	11	45	75	20	55	75	55	82

Table 13.9. *contd*

Region, country and year	Unmet need[a]			Current use			Potential demand[b]			% of potential demand satisfied[c]		
	total	for spacing	for limiting	total	for spacing	for limiting	total	for spacing	for limiting	total	for spacing	for limiting
Ecuador 1987	24	11	13	44	12	33	71	24	47	63	49	70
El Salvador 1985	29	16	13	47	8	39	74	22	52	64	36	76
Guatemala 1987	24	11	13	53	14	39	79	26	53	43	23	58
Mexico 1987	28	8	20	46	11	35	78	22	56	67	52	74
Paraguay 1990	20	8	12	48	24	24	68	32	36	71	75	67
Peru 1986	26	14	12	47	8	39	74	22	52	59	52	62
1991–92	16	4	12	59	14	45	82	22	60	72	64	75
Trinidad & Tobago 1987	16	8	8	53	19	34	71	29	48	74	66	80
NEAR EAST & NORTH AFRICA												
Egypt 1988–89	25	10	15	38	6	32	65	17	48	58	36	66
Jordan 1990	22	8	14	40	12	28	66	22	44	61	55	64
Morocco 1987	22	13	10	36	13	23	61	26	34	59	48	67
Tunisia 1988	20	11	9	50	14	36	71	25	46	70	54	79

Unmet need in the DHS = per cent of fecund, sexually active married women who are not using contraception even though they do not currently want to become pregnant.
Potential demand = current use + unmet need + method failures among currently pregnant or postpartum amenorrheic women (method failures not shown separately)
Per cent of potential demand satified = current use divided by potential demand

Source: Population Reports. (Johns Hopkins University) Vol. XX, No. 4, December 1992.

Table 13.10. Unmet need and potential demand for family planning, family planning surveys (FPS) – percentages of women ages 15–44.

Region, country and year	Unmet need[a]	Current use	Potential demand[b]	% of Potential demand satisfied[c]
AFRICA				
Mauritius 1985	3	75	78	96
Swaziland 1988	44	21	65	32
LATIN AMERICA & CARIBBEAN				
Belize 1991	26	47	73	64
Costa Rica 1986	3	70	73	96
Ecuador 1989	25	53	78	68
El Salvador 1988	30	47	77	61
Haiti 1989	27	10	37	27
Jamaica 1989	20	55	75	73
Panama 1985	13	58	71	82
Paraguay 1987	33	38	71	54
NEAR EAST & NORTH AFRICA				
Turkey 1988	19	60	79	76

[a] Unmet need in the FPS = per cent of fecund, sexually active women regardless of marital status who are not using contraception even though they do not currently want to become pregnant.

[b] Potential demand = unmet need + current use.

[c] Per cent of potential demand satified = current use divided by potential demand.

Source: Population Reports. (Johns Hopkins University) Vol. XX, No. 4, December 1992.

Policy Implications

The Johns Hopkins analysis of the results of the surveys showed that millions of women wanted family planning but were not using it. *If family planning programmes could meet all of the existing potential demand – including the estimated 120 million women with an unmet need as well as the 375 million currently using contraception – contraceptive prevalence would rise substantially. From the current level of 51 per cent in developing countries, including China, prevalence could rise to over 60 per cent.*

The Johns Hopkins report concluded, crucially:

> *Such an increase could lower fertility about halfway to replacement level.*

The Johns Hopkins report cited conservative estimates that meeting the current unmet need for family planning with high-quality services would reduce fertility levels from an average of four children per woman in developing countries to about three.[15] The decline would be even greater in the future if the percentage of women wanting smaller families continued to grow.

Even if the percentage of women wanting to use contraception were not increasing, however, the number of women to be served by family planning programmes in developing countries would continue to increase because of past rapid population growth. The Johns Hopkins survey cited estimates made by W. Parker Maudlin, a former President of the Population Council, that, even with no increase in contraceptive prevalence, an additional 100 million married couples would need family planning in the year 2000 compared with 1990 just because of the rising number of women of reproductive age.[16]

Similar estimates were made by the World Bank in February 1993.

> The numbers of people who will need contraception in the future are large and rising. Estimates of the market for contraception suggest no lack of future customers and a significant potential for eventually completing the fertility transition. Merely to maintain current levels of contraceptive prevalence, the number of contraceptive users in developing countries would have to rise 20 percent – from 365 million in 1990 to 436 million in 2000 – because of the increasing numbers of people of reproductive age. Current projections are that the increase during the decade will be double this figure (assuming that services are available), bringing the total to 514 million by 2000. Even that increase will still leave total fertility at about 3.2 children per woman.[17]

World Bank estimates shown in Table 13.11 indicate that the number of contraceptive users in the developing world would have to rise still further to 673 million in the year 2010 if a total fertility rate for the developing regions as a whole of 2.8 were to be attained by the latter date. An average figure of 2.8 for the TFR in developing regions is approximately what would be needed if the UN's medium variant for the year 2010 is to be attained, though attaining the low variant would require a TFR of 2.4 by the quinquennium 2005–2010.

Table 13.11. Current and projected fertility, contraceptive prevalence, and number of users, by region.

Region	Total fertility			Contraceptive prevalence rate			Contraceptive users (millions)		
	1990	2000	2010	1990	2000	2010	1990	2000	2010
Developing countries	3.8	3.2	2.8	51	58	63	365	514	673
West Africa	6.2	5.6	4.5	14	22	36	6	13	28
East Africa	6.5	6.0	5.0	15	21	33	7	14	30
North Africa	4.8	3.7	2.9	36	50	60	8	14	22
Southwest Asia	5.0	4.3	3.6	44	52	60	10	16	24
South Asia	4.4	3.4	2.8	41	53	61	91	149	213
East and Southeast Asia and the Pacific	2.7	2.3	2.1	67	72	74	201	246	280
Latin America and the Caribbean	3.3	2.6	2.2	59	69	73	42	62	77
Industrial countries[a]	2.0	1.9	2.0	70	70	69	127	131	127

Total fertility rates (TFRs) are World Bank projections. Contraceptive prevalence rates (CPRs) are calculated from these using an equation estimated from survey data: CPR = 94.8 −12.7 × TFR (R^2 = 0.83). Numbers of users (actually numbers of couples using contraception) assume that marriage rates are constant over time and include unmarried users when data are available.

[a] Europe, the former U.S.S.R., Japan, Australia, New Zealand, Canada, and the United States.

Source: Effective Family Planning Programs. (1993) The World Bank.

The World Bank observed that the projections shown in Table 13.11, derived from fertility trends, appeared 'reasonable.'[18] Studies of the potential market for contraception showed that substantial proportions of women wanted to avoid pregnancy and were not protected by sterility or other involuntary factors but were not using contraception. The World Bank's estimates of 'unmet need' echoed those of the Johns Hopkins report cited above. According to the World Bank, the 'unmet need' for family planning was experienced by at least 10 per cent of reproductive-age women and as much as 40 per cent in such countries as Kenya and Togo. Across countries, unmet need was highest where contraceptive prevalence was around 15 per cent. At prevalence

Table 13.12   The market for contraception as a percentage of married women of reproductive age, selected countries, 1985–89.

Region and country	Total market for contraception	Potential market/ unmet need	Percentage of market served
Sub-Sahara Africa			
Botswana	62	27	54
Burundi	34	25	26
Ghana	48	35	27
Kenya	65	38	41
Liberia	39	33	16
Mali	28	23	17
Togo	52	40	23
Uganda	32	27	15
Zimbabwe	65	22	67
North Africa			
Egypt	65	25	58
Morocco	61	22	59
Tunisia	71	20	70
Asia			
Indonesia	65	16	74
Sri Lanka	76	12	81
Thailand	77	11	85
Latin America and the Caribbean			
Bolivia	70	36	43
Brazil	81	13	82
Colombia	81	13	80
Dominican Republic	71	19	70
Ecuador	71	24	63
El Salvador	74	26	64
Guatemala	53	29	43
Mexico	79	24	67
Peru	78	28	59
Trinidad and Tobago	71	16	74

The total market for contraception includes actual users, those whose method failed, and those with unmet need for both spacing and limiting births. Only actual users are counted as being served.

Source: Effective Family Planning Programs. (1993) The World Bank.

levels above 15 per cent, unmet need tended to be concentrated among rural, less educated women.

The World Bank commented:

> Many of the reasons for unmet need can be addressed by better services that respond to client preferences and by effective promotion among the relevant groups.[19]

> *In most countries outside Sub-Saharan Africa, if all current unmet need were filled, contraceptive use would rise to industrial country levels of 70–80 per cent, bringing fertility close to replacement.* Filling unmet need would not be enough for such countries as Burundi and Mali, where the total market for contraceptives is still small. Good services, however, can themselves be expected to expand the market[20] particularly if they are linked with social development. (emphasis added)

According to the World Bank, the '*central observable event in the reproductive revolution is a substantial, irreversible decline in human fertility*'. The reproductive revolution 'alters the rhythm of women's lives, raising their consumption aspirations and the value they set on their time and transforming the institution of the family. Falling fertility partly releases women's lives from regular punctuation by pregnancy, childbearing, and childcare.'[21]

The main mechanism for fertility transition was increased fertility regulation within marriage, through the use of contraception or abortion. Average fertility levels of about 15 children would be attained if all women married early, limited their breastfeeding (and therefore became able to conceive quickly after a previous birth), entirely avoided deliberate fertility regulation, and were subject to other conditions that maximized fertility.

Like the Johns Hopkins Survey, the World Bank report argued that:

> *organized family planning programmes have contributed significantly to contraceptive availability and acceptability and therefore to fertility reduction. Their demographic impact to date appears to have been large. Their effectiveness has often depended critically on government support* . . .

> *Family planning has already significantly altered world population size and its future prospects. Without the programmes, total fertility for developing countries in 1980–5 would have been 5.4 instead of 4.2 children per woman* . . . As of 1990, family planning programmes had averted more than 400 million births. At a rough estimate, they have also reduced infant mortality rates in developing countries by 10 points per thousand.[22] (emphasis added)

Government commitment to family planning had been essential to fertility decline in various developing countries, enabling programmes to obtain the necessary leadership, publicity, and resources to provide essential services.

> *Fertility decline would undoubtedly have begun even without organized programmes, but it would have been a much more lengthy process, posing great difficulties for individuals.* Commercial contraceptives are beyond the financial reach of many couples around the world. Even were they affordable, many couples would not have sufficient access to them or to the necessary information about the importance of family planning.[23] (emphasis added)

The World Bank pointed out, however, that despite the changes that had already taken place in human reproduction in developing countries, the revolution was far from complete. Many of the benefits of the fertility transition were still denied to large portions of the developing world. Population growth remained substantial;

infant, child, and maternal mortality were several times as high as in industrial countries; many women's lives were still burdened by uncontrolled and unplanned childbearing; and some social groups had barely begun to feel the effects of the reproductive revolution.

NOTES

1. Johns Hopkins, op. cit., p. 6.
2. The Johns Hopkins Report cites in footnote 279 Davis K. and Blake J. *Social Structure and Fertility. Economic Development and Cultural Change* 4 (3): 211–235, April 1956.
3. Citing in footnote 258 Bongaarts J. A framework for analysing the proximate determinants of fertility. *Population and Development Review* 4 (1): 105–132. Mar. 1978, and in footnote 259 Bongaarts J. The fertility-inhibiting effects of the intermediate fertility variables, *Studies in Family Planning*, 13 (6–7): 179–189, June–July 1982.
4. Johns Hopkins, op. cit., p. 9.
5. According to an estimate by Mary Beth Weinberger based on survey data. Johns Hopkins, op. cit., p. 11.
6. Op. cit., footnote 244.
7. Op. cit., footnote 111.
8. Op. cit., footnotes 35, 45.
9. Op. cit., footnote 267.
10. Op. cit., p. 12.
11. The Johns Hopkins report (p.15) indicates that in the DHS, after giving each respondent an opportunity to name family planning methods spontaneously, the interviewer probes by reading the name and a brief description of each of nine methods, both modern and traditional, that the woman did not mention spontaneously and asking if she has heard of these methods. For example, interviewers read, 'Female sterilization: Women can have an operation to avoid having any more children.' In addition, the DHS questionnaire contains the open-ended question, 'Have you heard of any other ways or methods that women or men can use to avoid pregnancy?' In the FPS interviewers go directly to probing with a description of each method, without first asking women to name methods spontaneously. It is argued that such detailed, prompted questioning about each method helps to ensure accurate responses to questions that follow concerning the use of specific methods. Because the surveys ask only if the respondent has 'heard of' each method, however, a positive response indicates awareness of the method but not necessarily an understanding of how to use it correctly.
12. Op. cit., footnote 111.
13. Op. cit., p. 18.
14. The Johns Hopkins survey cites Westoff, C.F. *Reproductive Preferences: A comparative view,* Maryland, Institute for Resource Development, Feb 1991. DHS Comparative Studies No. 3.
15. The Johns Hopkins report cites a paper by S.W. Sinding. *Getting to replacement: Bridging the gap between individual rights and demographic goals.* Presented at the IPPF Family Planning Congress, New Delhi. Oct 23–25, 1992.
16. The Johns Hopkins report cites Mauldin, W.P. *Contraceptive Use in the Year 2000.* In DHS World Conference Proceedings, Vol. 3, p. 1373–1394.
17. *Effective Family Planning Programs,* World Bank, Washington DC, 1993.
18. World Bank, op. cit., p. 15.
19. World Bank, op. cit., p. 16.
20. Cochrane, Susan H., and David K. Guilkey. 1991. 'Fertility Intentions and Access to Services as Constraints on Contraceptive Use in Colombia', pp. 1305–28, Proceedings of the DHS World Conference, Washington DC, 1991, Vol. 2.

21. Between 1975 and 1987, the number of months that the average Thai woman spent preg-
    nant during her lifetime fell from 40 to 20, and by 1987 she could expect to spend only ten
    years with a child under the age of six. In Kenya in 1977–78, by contrast, the average
    woman could expect to spend 23 years – two-thirds of her reproductive life – with a child
    under the age of six. See World Bank, Effective Family Planning, February 1993, p. 9.
22. World Bank, op. cit., p. 11.
23. World Bank, op. cit., p. 11.

14

Effective Family Planning

If family planning programmes met all of the existing potential demand, they would have a dramatic impact on contraceptive prevalence in the developing world and hence on fertility levels. That was the clear message of the documents cited in the previous chapter. The Johns Hopkins survey in particular, was based on the findings of some of the most comprehensive sociological enquiries ever undertaken which, as noted in the previous chapter, involved interviews with more than 300,000 women of reproductive age in 44 developing countries. These enquiries indicated that with an increase in contraceptive prevalence from the current level of 51 per cent to over 60 per cent, fertility would fall from an average of about four children per woman to about three, or halfway to replacement level, and the UN medium projection of population growth in the year 2000 would be met. The World Bank report went even further, stating: 'In most countries outside Sub-Saharan Africa, if all current unmet needs were filled, contraceptive use would rise to industrial country levels of 70–80 per cent, bringing fertility close to replacement.'[1]

The urgent questions therefore were: Can the supply of family planning catch up, and keep up, with the demand? Will women who want family planning now – and throughout this decade – find the services that they need to achieve their desired family size?

In attempting to answer these questions, the World Bank in 1993 undertook a thoughtful review of the record of family planning programmes, focusing first on the more mature programmes in East Asia and Latin America and then on programmes in South Asia and Africa that had faced greater difficulties. Without seeking to be comprehensive, it attempted to illustrate the variety of obstacles family planning had faced and continued to face and the ways in which programmes had been effective.

Clearly, no single institution, no individual scholar or group of scholars has a monopoly of insight into what is happening in the field of population and family planning. This is now a vast subject, engaging the attention of thousands, perhaps tens of thousands, of demographers, economists, sociologists and other specialists. In this area, as in most others, opinions and perspectives vary. Nevertheless, the World Bank's slim volume *Effective Family Planning* provides an enormously useful and up-to-date guide to present-day realities. It outlines succinctly the challenges which have to be confronted if family planning programmes are to be made more effective and if national and international resources are to be better targeted.

The results of the World Bank review are summarized below.

EAST ASIA

East Asia (defined to include Southeast Asia), which had some of the earliest family planning programmes, had shown rapid increases in contraceptive prevalence and consequent declines in fertility. Figure 14.1 shows the dates when national family planning programmes started, which are not necessarily identical with the dates when population policies were adopted. The Republic of Korea, Thailand, and Indonesia showed steady increases in contraceptive prevalence of about 3 percentage points a year – which would allow a country to complete the fertility transition in 25 years. Prevalence was now close to or above 70 per cent in the first two countries and was approaching 50 per cent in Indonesia. Prevalence had increased much more slowly in the Philippines, by only 1.7 points a year on average, and even more slowly or hardly at all in some other countries not shown.

The World Bank argued that the initial socio-economic and cultural conditions in these East Asian countries were not particularly favourable to fertility transition. Table 14.1 provides some indicators of levels of development for these and other selected countries at the start of their national family planning programmes, as well as at the time fertility transition is estimated to have begun. Overall, socio-economic conditions in these East Asian countries at these initial points were roughly comparable to conditions in the average low-income economy today. The cultural barriers to reducing fertility included, for example, Confucian traditions in Korea that stressed the centrality of the family. The extended household was common, and the patrilineal family structure allowed parents to influence their children's reproductive decisions. 'Political opposition to family planning also appeared in various places, often based on religion – Islamic fundamentalism in Indonesia and Roman Catholicism in the Philippines, for example.'[2]

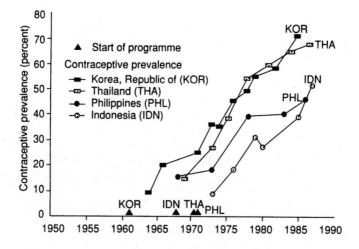

Fig. 14.1. Starting dates of family planning programmes and contraceptive prevalence trends, selected East Asian countries. *Source: Effective Family Planning Programs.* (1993) The World Bank.

Table 14.1. Socio-economic indicators at the start of a population programme and at the start of fertility transition, and annual rates of change from programme start to 1990, selected countries.

Region and country	At start of population program					At start of fertility transition					Annual rate of change, start of program to 1990a			
	Date	GNP per capitab	Infant mortality rate	Female secondary enrollment	Percentage urban	Date	GNP per capitab	Infant mortality rate	Female secondary enrollment	Percentage urban	GNP per capitab	Infant mortality rate	Female secondary enrollment	Percentage urban
East Asia														
Indonesia	1968	189	122	9	17	1975	253	109	15	19	4.3	-3.1	1.7	0.6
Korea, Republic of	1961	563	70	16	29	1960	550	70	14	28	6.7	-3.9	2.4	1.5
Philippines	1970	488	66	50	33	1970	488	66	50	33	1.4	-2.4	1.2	0.5
Thailand	1970	471	73	15	13	1970	471	73	15	13	4.7	-4.8	1.3	0.5
South Asia														
Bangladesh	1971	155	140	8	8	1975	138	138	11	9	0.4	-1.5	0.2	0.4
India	1952	203	190	8	17	1965	218	150	13	19	1.5	-1.9	0.6	0.3
Pakistan	1960	147	155	3	22	1985	304	113	8	30	2.8	-1.3	0.3	0.3
Sri Lanka	1965	216	63	35	20	1965	216	63	35	20	2.8	-4.6	1.8	0.1
Latin America														
Brazil	1974	1,656	86	28	60	1965	889	104	16	50	0.9	-2.5	1.3	0.9
Colombia	1970	780	77	24	57	1965	676	86	16	54	2.1	-3.5	2.0	0.6
Costa Rica	1968	1,247	60	27	39	1965	1,109	72	25	38	1.5	-5.7	0.8	0.4
Mexico	1974	1,467	66	26	62	1975	1,504	64	28	63	1.0	-3.2	1.9	0.7
Sub-Sahara Africa														
Botswana	1971	287	98	8	9	1980	721	63	22	15	8.3	-4.9	1.6	1.0
Ghana	1969	469	112	8	28	—c	–	–	–	–	-1.0	-1.3	1.2	0.2
Kenya	1967	235	108	3	9	1980	358	83	16	16	1.9	-2.1	0.8	0.6
Rwanda	1981	366	134	3	5	—c	–	–	–	–	-3.0	-1.5	0.4	0.3

Table 14.1. *contd*

	At start of population program					At start of fertility transition					Annual rate of change, start of program to 1990a			
Region and country	Date	GNP per capita[b]	Infant mortality rate	Female secondary enrollment	Percentage urban	Date	GNP per capita[b]	Infant mortality rate	Female secondary enrollment	Percentage urban	GNP per capita[b]	Infant mortality rate	Female secondary enrollment	Percentage urban
Zaire	1973	329	125	6	31	—c	—	—	—	—	-3.0	-1.8	0.6	0.5
Zimbabwe	1968	440	99	6	16	1970	544	96	6	17	1.4	-3.8	1.8	0.5
Comparative data by income group[d]														
All low-income economies (excluding China and India)						1989	300	94	20	25	1.4	-1.8	0.6	0.5
All low-middle-income economies						1989	1,360	51	54	53	2.0	-2.9	1.3	0.5
All upper-middle-income economies						1989	3,150	50	58	66	2.6	-2.3	1.4	0.9

Not applicable; GNP, gross national product.

[a] Rates given are exponential change in per capita GNP, percentage change in infant mortality, and mean increase in the other two variables.

[b] Constant 1987 U.S. dollars.

[c] Fertility transition has not started.

[d] Female secondary enrollment estimates are for 1988. Rates of change are for 1965–89.

Sources: Program dates follow World Bank (1984). Fertility transitions are dated from initial declines of at least 0.7 points in total fertility over a quinquennium, following Bulatao and Elwan (1985). Data are from World Bank files, with comparative data from World Bank (1991). Some figures are interpolations. *Effective Family Planning Programs.* (1993) The World Bank.

Despite the barriers, some desire for smaller families did exist, and it increased over time. Near the start of fertility transition in Korea, Thailand, and Indonesia, ideal family size was recorded at about four children. Over the next decade or two it fell an average of about 0.08 points a year in each country. As ideal family size declined, socio-economic conditions were improving. Table 14.1 shows annual rates of change for the socio-economic indicators, from the year a population programme started up to 1990. Rapid improvement in the East Asian countries was evident, especially in gross national product (GNP) per capita – except in the Philippines – and infant mortality.

> *Family planning programmes succeeded in these countries by taking advantage of opportunities to mobilize political support, exploiting the existing demand for contraception, and developing innovative ways to deliver contraceptive services.* Relative political stability and strong governments created conditions in which such social programmes could be effectively run, but political upheaval sometimes provided an initial impetus.[3] (emphasis added)

In Korea the programme began in the context of a massive reconstruction effort launched by a new administration a decade after the end of the Korean War. In Indonesia a pronatalist population policy under President Sukarno was promptly replaced by an antinatalist policy after his overthrow. Existing demand was exploited in pilot projects that demonstrated widespread desire for contraception, such as the Jakarta pilot project in Indonesia, and by private voluntary organizations, such as the Planned Parenthood Federation of Korea, which was instrumental in preparing the ground for the government programme. Delivery systems for family planning underwent extensive experimentation. Thailand tested optimal delivery systems in the Potharam project, and Korea experimented with urban programmes in Sungdong Gu and with rural programmes in Koyang.

The contribution of programmes to the rise in contraceptive prevalence was substantial. For example, programme-supplied contraceptives accounted for 40 per cent of Korea's fertility decline in 1963–73.

The World Bank observed that fertility transition was far from complete in East Asia, however. A number of countries, including the Philippines and Vietnam, remain mired in slow fertility transitions. Even in the more successful countries, significant numbers of people still lacked adequate access to contraception. In Indonesia the Outer Islands were well behind Java and Bali. Provincial total fertility rates ranged from 2.4 in Bali to as high as 5.3 in Southeast Sulawesi and Irian Jaya.

LATIN AMERICA

Latin America developed national family planning programmes later than East Asia, but private voluntary organizations had been active for some time, and demand for contraception was high. As Figure 14.2 shows, substantial use of contraception appeared to predate the start of national programmes. Prevalence was now 70 per cent in three of these countries, and for the region as a whole, it was close to 55 per cent.

The World Bank noted that, at the start of their programmes, as well as at the start of fertility transition, socio-economic conditions in these countries were more favourable for fertility transition than had been the case in East Asia and were roughly comparable to conditions in the average lower-middle-income economy today. The Bank went on to add:

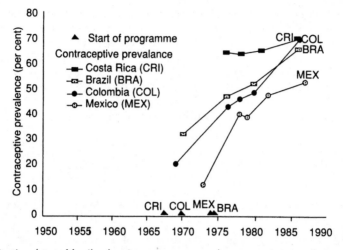

Fig. 14.2. Starting dates of family planning programmes and contraceptive prevalence trends, selected Latin American countries. *Source: Effective Family Planning Programs.* (1993) The World Bank.

Cultural barriers to contraception existed, but political obstacles were more significant. The predominant Catholicism of these countries did not deter individuals from adopting contraception but provided arguments against it that had political impact.[4]

The demand for contraception in the early years of fertility transition appeared to have been substantial; it probably exceeded the capacity of programmes, and it increased with socio-economic development. Some analysts had identified gains in female education as a particularly important factor in this demand and in fertility decline in the region. Demonstration of the demand was critical for the eventual institution of public services.

The World Bank argued *that relatively high levels of socio-economic development did not lead to fertility transition until services – initially private and later public as well – were provided*. Public services eventually eclipsed organized private services in Mexico, but in Colombia private services continued to be more important. Public services were estimated to have accounted for 42 to 48 per cent of births averted in Mexico around 1978. The contributions of public services included wide promotion of family planning and the extension of access to the large rural and less privileged classes, which were specifically targeted. In Costa Rica, for example, an initial fertility decline was observed between 1960 and 1970, but it mainly affected the more privileged classes. A second wave of decline occurred after the government programme (which started in 1968) began to improve services in more remote areas.

As in East Asia, several countries still had a considerable way to go in the fertility transition, and even in the more advanced countries some sectors of the population were poorly served. Contraceptive prevalence was only 30 per cent in Bolivia and only 10 per cent in Haiti. Where prevalence was already high, contraceptive failure might be common. Brazilian women had failure rates of 10–12 per cent a year. That the higher rates appeared among the more educated suggested a serious lack of information and counselling. Another indication of the considerable continuing problems was the widespread practice of induced abortion, which was illegal in most countries and was therefore clandestine and dangerous. 'More effective contraception would reduce this problem,' the World Bank argued.

SOUTH ASIA

South Asian countries started family planning programmes early and then generally had to wait a long time for fertility transition to begin. As Figure 14.3 shows, contraceptive prevalence rose 2.3 points a year in Sri Lanka, the most successful case among these countries. In India prevalence rose 1.7 points annually between 1970 and 1988, but for the entire period from the start of the programme in 1952, the rate at best was only 1.2 points a year.

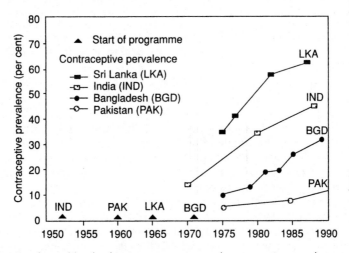

Fig. 14.3. Starting dates of family planning programmes and contraceptive prevalence trends, selected South Asian countries. *Source: Effective Family Planning Programs.* (1993) The World Bank.

Socio-economic and cultural conditions were distinctly unfavourable for fertility transition in these countries (see Table 14.1). Whether one focused on the starting date of the programme or the date fertility transition began, these countries were less developed than the average low-income economy today. As a group, they did not differ greatly in GNP per capita and urbanization from Indonesia at the start of its programme, although they did have higher infant mortality. Cultural barriers to lower fertility in South Asia had received much attention; they included traditional family structures, the subordinate social position of women, and some continuing dependence on child labour. Political barriers were largely insignificant at the national level.

Demand for contraception was weak to begin with in South Asia, the World Bank argued, and slow social development did little to advance it. Although over the entire period from programme start GNP per capita grew at roughly the same pace as low- and middle-income economies as a whole, improvements in infant mortality and especially in female enrolment were painfully slow. Sri Lanka stood out as having improvements in these social indicators that were comparable to improvements in the East Asian and Latin American countries.

In the World Bank's view, the spread of contraception was retarded *not only by unfavourable socio-economic conditions but also by programme limitations*. The government programmes were heavily bureaucratic and were largely administered from the top. This was especially true in Pakistan, where little attempt was made to gauge client demand or to meet the needs of front-line staff. The Indian programme was harder to characterize because of its diversity and the control exercised by individual states, but in general, it failed to capitalize on demand from all sources. Targets were set high up in the hierarchy, and officials at the top were largely out of touch with village life.

> A comparison between India and Sri Lanka – which had the most successful programme – highlights the effect of failure to be sensitive to clients' needs. Although Sri Lanka's success is partly attributable to more favourable social indicators, differences in programmes also played a role. The Sri Lankan programme provided a greater range of methods, including such temporary methods as pills and intrauterine devices (IUDs), and used community-based distributors in rural areas. The Indian programme relied largely on sterilization and avoided community distribution of other methods. The Indian programme enjoyed more public statements of support and better advertising, but the Sri Lankan programme delivered the contraceptives.[5]

Some other examples of successful programmes in South Asia, on a smaller scale than national programmes, illustrated the importance of an orientation toward client needs. The family planning programme in the Kerala state of India was more effective than other state programmes partly because of the state's higher educational levels and lower mortality but also because the programme provided better access through a greater number of service delivery points. The Matlab family planning project in Bangladesh raised contraceptive prevalence in a poor region through a strong client orientation. It offered more choice of contraceptive methods, emphasized counselling and follow-up of acceptors, and provided ancillary care. The Kundam project in India, which covered 65 villages in a hilly area with a predominantly tribal population, raised contraceptive prevalence from 20 to 68 per cent in five years, using a high degree of community participation that enabled it to orient itself toward clients' needs.

SUB-SAHARAN AFRICA

A few African programmes started in the late 1960s and early 1970s, eventually producing slow increases in contraceptive use. These programmes were theoretically about the same age as some Latin American programmes, but they faced a substantially weaker demand for contraception. Prevalence was flat for a decade and did not rise above 10 per cent until the 1980s. Contraceptive prevalence increased at widely divergent rates: in Zimbabwe at 3.1 percentage points a year, in Botswana at 2.1 points a year, in Kenya at 1.7 points a year, and in Ghana at 0.9 points a year. (No national data were available for Zaire and Rwanda.)

Socio-economic conditions in these countries at the time programmes started fell roughly between those in the East Asian and in the South Asian countries. In Botswana, Kenya, and Zimbabwe at the time fertility transition is assumed to have started, socio-economic indicators were essentially at the level East Asia had attained when transition began there and were slightly better, especially for GNP per capita, than the average for low-income economies today.

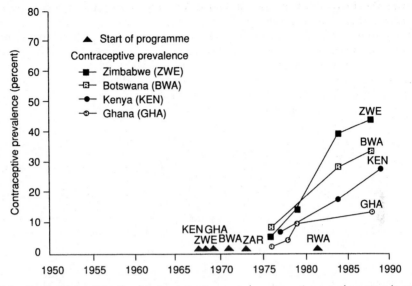

Fig. 14.4. Starting dates of family planning programmes and contraceptive prevalence trends, selected sub-Saharan African countries. *Source: Effective Family Planning Programs.* (1993) The World Bank.

The World Bank observed:

> The cultural barriers to family planning in Africa are significant but not insurmountable. Researchers have argued that children are important assets to the older generation and provide security for the future and that deciding to limit childbearing is difficult because of the influence of the extended family. Nevertheless, fertility has declined in these three countries, and similar barriers have been faced and overcome in other regions.[6]

What demand for contraception existed in Botswana, Kenya, and Zimbabwe was largely for spacing births. Socio-economic development, which should have affected this demand, proceeded unevenly across countries. In comparison with all the other countries in Table 14.1 in which prevalence grew at least 2 points a year, Kenya had slower and Zimbabwe substantially slower income growth. However, their social indicators improved at rates comparable to those for East Asia.

The programmes in Botswana, Zimbabwe, and Kenya attempted to address existing demand by emphasizing the benefits of child spacing and providing temporary methods, often the pill. However, the three countries had used quite different delivery systems. Botswana, with presumably stronger demand because of socio-economic factors, as well as a public health system that covered the country fairly evenly, had relied so far on health posts and health centres to provide contraceptives. Zimbabwe had placed primary emphasis on community-based distribution to the rural population. Kenya had also emphasized outreach but had relied to a much greater extent than Zimbabwe on private voluntary organizations to complement public services.

Initial socio-economic conditions in Ghana, Rwanda, and Zaire – the three African countries shown in Table 14.1 that had not started fertility transition – were not much different from those in the first three countries; indeed, GNP per capita was slightly higher. But these countries had had negative economic growth since their programmes began and had recorded the smallest improvements in social indicators of all the countries listed. Despite such unfavourable socio-economic trends, family planning programmes had had some effect in small areas.

The World Bank recognized that its review of effective family planning programmes left out many countries and even some regions. Nevertheless it believed the review illustrated the significant impact that family planning had had and the complex factors that modulated its effects. In some countries, increases in contraceptive use had brought fertility down to replacement levels within one generation. In other countries, contraceptive use spread at a much slower pace or barely rose at all.

The World Bank concluded:

> The speed at which contraception has spread bears little relation to initial socio-economic conditions, but it does depend on their improvement. *A few countries with initial GNP per capita as low as $200 (below the average for low-income economies today) demonstrated as rapid increases in contraceptive prevalence as countries with several times that income level.* Some countries with initial female secondary enrolment ratios of 15 or so (also below the average for low-income economies today) demonstrated more rapid increases in prevalence than countries with twice that ratio. (emphasis added)

Nevertheless, for the selection of countries covered in the World Bank review, *more rapid improvement in each of these indicators was related to more rapid spread of contraception.* The relationship was strongest for female secondary enrolment, as illustrated in Figure 14.5. The effectiveness of the family planning programme also affected the rapidity of increases in contraceptive use. Figure 14.6 illustrates a substantial relationship across countries, using family planning effort scores for 1982.

In summary, the World Bank review noted a number of elements that had made some programmes more effective than others: sensitivity to existing demand for con-

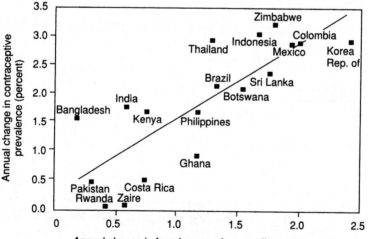

Fig. 14.5.   Annual changes in female secondary enrolment and contraceptive prevalence, from starting date of family planning programs, selected countries. *Source: Effective Family Planning.* (1993) The World Bank.

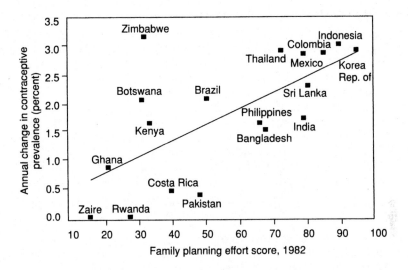

Fig. 14.6. Family planning effort score, 1982, and annual change in contraceptive prevalence, from starting date of family planning program, selected countries. *Source: Effective Family Programs.* (1993) The World Bank.

traception, provision of good access to the methods people wanted, and responsiveness to client needs. Strategic use of pilot projects and other means of building public support had been critical in some cases. A variety of strategies for delivering contraceptives and dealing with barriers to their use had been applied in different areas. Private sector delivery systems made significant contributions in Latin America and in some other places, such as Kenya. The importance of providing information and otherwise promoting services was clear. Finally, it was essential to have political and financial support from governments and donors.

GOVERNMENT AND DONOR ROLES

In the World Bank's opinion, national policy-makers and international donors would, as in the past, play critical roles in the further development of family planning. A long menu of suggestions for making family planning programmes more effective emerged from the World Bank's review.

Programmes, the Bank believed, should expand method choice, strengthen counselling, assess and improve client relations, reorient programmes to deal with other client needs, measure quality, nurture political support, involve communities, provide community-based distributors, improve supervision, strengthen logistics, apply operations research, provide assistance to voluntary organizations, utilize social marketing, revise regulations that limited the private sector, test other ways of involving the private sector, raise user charges, integrate promotional activities into programmes, and improve media materials.

The most significant areas of weakness were twofold:

- The services clients received were inadequate. Clients received too few choices of method, too little counselling, and an insufficient range of options for obtaining services. Additional resources would undoubtedly be needed to deal with these limitations, but the returns could be high with regard to attracting new clients and encouraging more continuity in contraceptive use.
- The support front-line staff received was inadequate. These staff were poorly supervised, and the logistics chain did not provide them with the essential products they needed. The limitations had little to do with the availability of supplies or facilities. They had much more to do with the way systems were organized and with how people were trained or not trained. Programmes had to be fundamentally oriented toward providing support for front-line staff.

The review also suggested two broad areas that offered significant opportunities for programmes.

- Options for involving the private sector, both the nonprofit and the for-profit segments, had multiplied. National programmes needed to be actively engaged in working with the private sector and should seek to extend the most promising forms of collaboration.
- Techniques for reaching potential clients through the media had improved but had not been fully exploited. Some programmes had made effective use of media appeals, in conjunction with interpersonal means of reaching people. As programmes focused on broader populations, they would have to become more sophisticated in using the media.

Appropriate government policies in several areas were needed if the main weaknesses in family planning programmes were to be addressed and opportunities exploited.

Strong political support was critical for programme success, but by itself it was not enough; it needed to be translated into adequate resources and budgets. *The World Bank argued that if governments that were not doing so committed as little as 0.5 per cent of their budgets to population programmes, a considerable expansion in services would be possible.* In 1989 governments in 125 developing countries provided support for contraception for demographic, health, and human rights reasons and as part of poverty alleviation efforts. This was twice the number that expressed concern about population growth or supported fertility reduction. However, the depth of support was hard to measure and was probably quite variable. And 16 of the 131 countries that responded to a United Nations questionnaire still provided no support for family planning.

Laws and regulations could have symbolic value in reinforcing national commitment to family planning. More important, a variety of regulations affected the availability, distribution, and advertising of contraceptive methods and abortion, limiting the potential of private sector programmes and hampering public programmes. Import licenses for contraceptives were required in the majority of countries in each region except Sub-Saharan Africa, and import duties were imposed in 40 per cent of all countries. These duties could be high; in Colombia in 1987 duties of 57 per cent were imposed on all the contraceptives imported by PROFAMILIA, the main provider.

Many governments also limited access to fertility regulation procedures by restricting who could prescribe contraceptives or perform procedures (although these regulations were not always enforced). Studies had shown that family planning fieldworkers could safely distribute pills and that properly trained paramedics could safely insert IUDs and perform sterilizations. Nevertheless, the World Bank pointed

Table 14.2. Percentage of developing countries imposing limitations on the sale and use of contraception and on abortion, by region.

Limitation	All regions	Sub-Saharan Africa	Middle East and North Africa	Asia	Latin America and the Caribbean
Import license required	68	36	100	83	79
Import duties imposed	39	29	33	40	55
Physician required for					
Pill	34	20	50	42	31
IUD	62	42	67	58	80
Female sterilization	80	77	80	77	85
Male sterilization	77	71	67	73	90
Status of female sterilization[a]					
Illegal	9	22	14	0	0
Spouse approval needed	71	69	80	85	57
Legal conditions for abortion					
Only to save mother's life[b]	50	54	44	36	58
For life or health only[b]	86	92	87	68	87
Number of countries[c]	45	13	5	12	13

[a] Restrictions on male sterilization also exist but are less widespread. Other requirements besides spouse approval may be imposed on female sterilization, such as minimum ages and parities. (In Lesotho trhe minimum number of children for sterilization is twelve, except after two caesarean sections.)

[b] In some cases abortion may also be legal after rape or incest or because of genetic defect.

[c] Each percentage may be based on a different number of countries. The mode is given. The abortion data tend to cover twice as many countries as the mode.

Source: Effective Family Planning Programs. (1993) The World Bank.

out, only physicians were allowed to prescribe pills in one-third of reporting countries, to insert IUDs in 60 per cent of countries and to perform sterilizations in 80 per cent of countries. In addition, a few countries had legislation that completely prohibited sterilization, and 70 per cent of all countries required the spouse's approval.

> In most developing countries, abortion is legally restricted to situations in which the woman's life or health is endangered, effectively endangering the lives of many more.[7]

When governments were successful in promoting social and economic development, contraceptive use increased more rapidly and fertility fell faster. As noted earlier, the expansion of female education made an important contribution to increases in contraceptive prevalence. Some steps for promoting female education that had proved effective include provision of culturally appropriate facilities, special scholarships, flexible and convenient schedules, and assistance to relieve older siblings of childcare responsibilities; programmes to delay pregnancy and marriage; and measures to counteract wage and employment discrimination. A judicious selection of such policies could have a direct effect on the status of women and also contribute to fertility decline. Development in other areas, such as improvements in health and the reduction of mortality, was also important.

THE COST OF FAMILY PLANNING

Public Expenditures

The World Bank estimated that total expenditures on family planning in 1990 were at least $4 billion and probably higher; estimates ranged up to $5 billion. (This was equivalent to $1 to $1.25 per capita for developing country populations).[8]

Donor expenditures for population were not large as a proportion of official development assistance (ODA) and had barely kept pace with population growth in the recipient countries. Donors provided $802 million in grant funds and $169 million in loans in 1990, the last year for which data had been compiled. For the eighteen leading donors, population assistance constituted 1.2 per cent of ODA in 1990 – roughly typical for the 1980s but lower than the proportion for the 1970s, which was just under 2 per cent of ODA.[9] In constant dollars, population assistance in 1990 was 13 per cent above the amount in 1985 and 1986, after several years when it had fallen as much as 18 per cent below the level of those years. Population assistance in 1990 was equivalent to $0.24 per capita for the developing world, an increase of less than 2 per cent in constant dollars over 1985.

Developing country governments funded variable proportions of their programmes – in general, substantially greater proportions than those covered by donors. In the aggregate, government funding for family planning might be double or triple that provided by donors; estimates ranged from 50 to 200 per cent more. China and India paid for 85 per cent of their programme costs, but most other countries contributed a smaller proportion.[10] For countries with data from the mid-1980s, the proportion of government health and total central budgets going to family planning ranged between 0.3 and almost 30 per cent of health budgets and between 0.01 and just over 1 per cent of total budgets. Some successful programmes, such as Korea's, had received a relatively large proportion of the government health budget, but less successful programmes, such as some in South Asia, had also received relatively large shares of 15 per cent or more.

User Expenditures

What individuals spent on family planning was very roughly estimated at between 35 and 55 per cent of what governments spent, or about equal to what donors spent. Estimates did not include spending on abortion, the amount of which was unknown but could raise the total considerably. What individuals would have to spend if there were no public provision or subsidy was substantial. The retail price of an annual supply of contraceptive pills exceeded $100 in half a dozen developing countries, as did the retail price of an annual supply of condoms. To pay for pills, users in 15 out of 24 Sub-Saharan African countries would need 5 per cent or more of average annual income, and users in 6 of these countries would pay 20 per cent or more. In Asia users in Laos, Myanmar, and the Philippines would have to pay more than 5 per cent of average annual income for a year's supply of pills. Incomes in Latin America were higher, but users in Bolivia, the Dominican Republic, Ecuador, and Guatemala would all have to pay more than 5 per cent of average annual income. In Lebanon, Morocco, and Yemen, for example, an annual supply of either pills or condoms would require more than 4 per cent of average income.

Table 14.3.   Average cost of contraceptives from commercial sources, by region.

Method and region	Number of countries	Price of annual supply (dollars)	Cost as percentage of GNP per capita
Pills (13 cycles)			
Developing countries	71	36	3.7
Sub-Saharan Africa	24	27	9.3
Middle East and North Africa	14	43	1.9
Asia	14	14	1.6
Latin America and the Caribbean	19	48	3.1
Industrial countries	22	65	0.5
Condoms (100 pieces)			
Developing countries	69	27	3.0
Sub-Saharan Africa	23	27	8.4
Middle East and North Africa	12	36	2.8
Asia	15	16	2.0
Latin America and the Caribbean	19	29	2.0
Industrial countries	23	66	0.6

Source: Effective Family Planning Programs. (1993) The World Bank.

In industrial countries, contraceptives seldom cost more than 1 per cent of average annual income (even at prices double those in developing countries). In four out of five developing countries contraceptive pills cost more than this. Consumers were sensitive to price: high programme fees discouraged use, and price decreases stimulated demand. High costs were less of a factor once demand for contraception was firmly established because prices declined as the number of users increased and because users already habituated to contraception were less likely to discontinue after a price increase.

FUTURE RESOURCE NEEDS

Estimates of future budgetary requirements for family planning in developing countries covered a broad range, but studies largely agreed on expected rates of growth. The World Bank calculated that, assuming that prevalence increased at about 0.8 percentage points a year (from 51 per cent in 1990 to 58 per cent in 2000), annual expenditures would have to grow about 4.6 per cent a year.[11] Over the decade a 55–60 per cent increase in expenditures could be expected, but per capita expenditures, including user payments, should remain modest at $1.25–1.50.

The World Bank estimates cited above would lead to a total annual requirement for family planning programmes of between around $7.25 billion and $7.50 billion in 1990 dollars (based as noted above on a per capita cost for family planning in the less developed regions of between $1.25 and $1.50 per person and assuming that the population of the less developed regions was 5 billion in 2000 – the medium variant).

Working on the actual numbers of couples using contraception in the developing countries (514 million couples if the medium variant target of an average TFR of 3.2 for the developing countries is to be achieved by that date), the cost per user couple per year would be between $14.10 and $14.59.

Alternative assumptions could raise or lower expenditures. For example, if fertility declined faster than assumed – say, as rapidly as in the developing countries with the fastest fertility declines – public expenditures in 2000 would be 36 per cent higher. If, by 2000, 3 per cent of users switched to Norplant, a five-year implant with high up-front costs (but the total number of users stayed the same), costs in that year would be 2.7 per cent higher.

Most of the projections assumed that costs per user for a given method remained constant. As programmes expanded, costs might be expected to fall as a result of economies of scale (unless facilities were near saturation), and because staff members learned to do their jobs more efficiently. Costs might be expected to rise if programme extension or elaboration was needed to reach less accessible populations. Across countries, programmes with higher contraceptive prevalence had lower per-user costs. But in Asian countries the trend in per-user costs over time had been sometimes upward and sometimes downward after the first three years or so, when the trend was steeply downward.

The actual trend in costs per user as programmes expanded was therefore, the World Bank pointed out, still undetermined and probably varied, but some potential for reducing costs did exist. For example, a time-use and costs survey of 17 ambulatory health facilities in Morocco showed that 34 per cent of labour costs were for time spent waiting for patients. Reducing inefficiencies of this sort by reallocating resources or increasing their use could, in principle, reduce future costs per user.

None of the estimates of future costs cited by the World Bank made provision for an increase in the proportion of costs paid by users. A substantial increase in user payments (currently 20–25 per cent of the total) would be needed to reduce the (otherwise required) growth in public expenditures. For example, to cut the required rate of growth of public expenditures in half, from 4.6 to 2.3 per cent, user payments would have to grow 10 per cent a year over the decade, and the increase could hold down the demand for contraception.[12]

The World Bank estimate, cited above, of $7.25–$7.50 billion for total annual costs of effective population and family planning in the developing countries was broadly in line with that given in UNCED's Agenda 21, although, as noted in Chapter 10, Agenda 21 did not contain any precise goals or targets as regards population growth or fertility reduction. It is worth pointing out, however, that the Amsterdam Forum on Population in the Twenty-First Century, held in November 1989, recommended somewhat higher figures. The Amsterdam Forum, as pointed out in Chapter 9, concluded that in order to achieve the medium variant population projection by the year 2000, total national and international expenditures for family planning should increase from the level of $4.5 billion annually to around $9 billion.

In April 1993, Population Action International (PAI), a US-based charity, taking the cost of family planning at $16 per user per year (as against the current cost of around $12 per user), and calculating the number of users necessary (685 million) to achieve a total fertility rate of *2.1 or replacement level by the year 2000* (as compared with the medium variant TFR target of 3.2 and a low variant TFR target of 2.7) estimated that $10.8 billion in constant 1990 US dollars would be needed from all sources (i.e. national and international) for family planning programmes.

It might be questioned whether assuming a TFR of 2.1 by the year 2000 (virtually equivalent to the 'instant replacement' extension discussed in Chapter 11), was realistic. It was nonetheless revealing that very large gains, in terms of births averted, appeared to be achievable with relatively small sums of money. $10 billion a year represented around one per cent of total military spending and somewhat less than one per cent of outstanding Third World debt. That same amount spent on family planning between now and the end of the century could, if the money was well targeted, set the world firmly and possibly irreversibly on the path to replacement level fertility.

DONOR ASSISTANCE

At the beginning of the 1990s, most donor assistance in population came from 18 countries, 10 of which provided 96 per cent of the funds. In descending order of their 1990 contributions, the ten were the United States, Japan, Norway, Germany, Canada, Sweden, the United Kingdom, the Netherlands, Finland, and Denmark.[13] About a third of this population assistance was provided directly to recipient countries, with one agency, the US Agency for International Development (USAID), providing three-quarters of bilateral assistance. About a third of population assistance flowed through multilateral channels, mainly the United Nations Population Fund (UNFPA). The remaining third went through nongovernmental organizations, chief among them the International Planned Parenthood Federation (IPPF), whose confederation now included 150 national family planning associations. Additional assistance provided by the World Bank (in the form of loans, often at concessional rates, rather than grants) was somewhat less than the amount of direct bilateral population assistance. The United Nations also provided a small amount of additional assistance out of funds not earmarked for population, and international nongovernmental organizations provided another small amount.

The World Bank commented:

> Each of the bilateral and multilateral agencies has particular strengths and weaknesses, and specific agencies can, in appropriate circumstances, largely complement each other. Staffs in the area of population vary in size and expertise. Staffs of bilateral donors are quite limited, with the notable exception of USAID, which can, in addition, draw on a large network of US-based contractors, including nonprofit agencies, universities, and companies. Some donors have inadequate field staff and so maintain an arm's-length approach to implementing projects. Because the political constraints affecting agencies vary, particular donors are present in some settings and not others and lean toward specific approaches or activities. The effect of having fewer such constraints is apparent in the history of IPPF, which has been able to take risks. IPPF pioneered work on community-based distribution, some new contraceptive methods, and women's reproductive health, and it continues to conduct research on abortion and to stress post-abortion family planning counselling. The agencies also vary in the breadth of their population interests, from a narrow concern with family planning to wider interests in such areas as censuses and migration.[14]

THE ADEQUACY OF DONOR FINANCING

'Adequacy has often been a matter of the quality of assistance,' the World Bank commented,[15] 'but the quantity is now increasingly problematic.' Total assistance available probably exceeded the absorptive capacity of developing country governments in the 1960s and 1970s and roughly matched the demand in the 1980s. The amounts available had risen slightly in constant terms but hardly at all in per capita terms for the recipient countries. Prospects for the 1990s and the early part of the next century were uncertain, and trends did not allow optimism. On the demand side, the substantially larger cohorts coming along would require a growing volume of services, as already indicated. Many country programmes, especially in Sub-Saharan Africa, were new and would need substantial funding as they expanded. New programmes were being started faster than mature programmes were graduating, as the latter faced continuing problems of ensuring supplies for large numbers of users and of reaching the poorest and the most disadvantaged segments of the population.

On the supply side, about half of the ten leading donors were enthusiastic about increasing population assistance. Whether increases would actually materialize was uncertain, given internal political pressures and the overwhelming requirements for aid for other purposes. 'Since total population expenditures will have to grow 4.6 per cent a year over this decade to keep pace with the need, the uncertainty of future donor financing has to be confronted.'

The World Bank pointed out that Asia had received the largest share of population assistance so far because of its large population and receptive governments. Aid for Sub-Saharan Africa had grown rapidly; between 1982 and 1990 its share more than doubled, reaching 25 per cent. Assistance for the Middle East and North Africa was only 9 per cent of the total, which was probably inadequate, but politically these countries had often been unreceptive. Some countries had received quite substantial amounts of aid, and Bangladesh, Brazil, Indonesia, Kenya, Mexico, and Thailand had brought down fertility with this assistance – in some cases after considerable delays. Egypt and Pakistan had so far shown little progress. Other countries, such as Algeria, Vietnam, Zaire, Burundi, and Yemen, badly needed assistance but were not receiving enough. Through most of the 1980s the first three of these countries received less than $0.10 per capita each year in population assistance. The last two received somewhat more, but they were smaller countries, and programmes consistently cost more per capita in smaller countries.

Donor support was probably adequate overall in some functional areas but less than adequate in others. Despite heavy support for delivery systems, meeting their recurrent costs was often difficult. Covering the costs of commodities was an emerging problem. USAID, for years the main buyer and distributor of commodities, was increasingly attempting to have other agencies take a greater role in this area. Some shortages, especially of condoms, were apparent, and shortages were in prospect for newer injectables and implants. Contraceptive research was seriously underfunded. Given the withdrawal of international drug companies from research, only a handful of institutions did any work in this area. On the other hand, the World Bank added: 'substantial amounts have been poorly spent on inadequately conceptualized and unevaluated educational and promotional activities instead of more promising marketing approaches.'

The World Bank argued that, given possible resource shortfalls, it would be useful if donors became increasingly selective in extending support. Better means of assessing project impact would help maximize the gain from donor investments. A strong emphasis on project sustainability – on projects that could demonstrate effectiveness, were well integrated into administrative structures, and obtained substantial local funding – would help ensure longlasting impact. Focusing on factors that were critical for programme success would help rationalize expenditures; among such factors, as noted above, were the quality of services, field supervision, contraceptive logistics, and sophisticated promotional campaigns. Cost-effective approaches, such as social marketing, required emphasis and greater development so that quality was not sacrificed. Support for greater involvement of the private sector could eventually pay dividends. Increasingly, also, in more mature programmes, government services needed to be targeted to those in need, and in other programmes more emphasis should be placed on cost recovery.

DONOR COORDINATION

Donor coordination had generally been better at the country level than at the headquarters level. Donors funding specific projects were often able to work together in the field. Coordination depended heavily on the host government's capacity to manage the donors. Some countries, such as Thailand and Indonesia, had done well in this respect, but others had failed to assign adequate, trained staff to the full-time task of coordinating external assistance. Coordination problems could also arise, at the country level, when donors themselves had inadequate field staff or could make decisions on the ground. At the global level the absence of coordination was more common, as tasks were less specific and each organization had its own mandate and preoccupations. Consistent messages and advice from donors and compatible forms and requirements would simplify the burden on many recipients but would require much effort to achieve.

Strengthening coordination, and optimizing donor contributions generally, required improvement in both the quantity and quality of population staff. More adequate staffing would mean that donor resources would be better spent.

*   *   *   *   *   *   *

As noted above, the World Bank's report on *Effective Family Programmes* was published at the beginning of 1993. Its message was clear. So too was the message of the Johns Hopkins survey cited in the previous chapter. Ambitious goals could be set; and they could be achieved. Just meeting unmet needs for family planning would by itself represent a huge stride in the right direction; the benefits would be felt by individuals and couples, by nations and even by the world as a whole.

But the question to be faced was whether the strong message of hope was being understood. Was the right action being taken? Were the right preparations being made to nail down a new international consensus on population and development? What would the International Conference on Population and Development (ICPD) achieve? How would Cairo, 1994, compare with Rio, 1992? Or Mexico, 1984? Or Bucharest, 1974?

As this book was being prepared for publication, preparations for Cairo were well in hand. These preparations and the prospects of a new international consensus on population emerging from the Cairo Conference are the subject of the last two chapters.

NOTES

1. World Bank, op. cit., p. 16.
2. World Bank, *Effective Family Planning Programs*, Washington DC 1993, p. 18.
3. World Bank, op. cit., p. 19.
4. World Bank, op. cit., p. 22.
5. World Bank, op. cit., p. 25.
6. World Bank, op. cit., p. 26.
7. World Bank, op. cit., p. 83.
8. World Bank, op. cit., p. 31.
9. World Bank cites *UNFPA Global Population Assistance Report*, 1990; New York, 1992.
10. World Bank cites Sadik, Nafis, ed. 1991a. *Population Policies and Programmes: Lessons learned from two decades of Experience*, New York: New York University Press; and 1991b, *The State of the World Population*: 1991, New York: United Nations Population Fund.
11. World Bank, op. cit., p. 35.
12. World Bank, op. cit., p. 36.
13. World Bank, op. cit., p. 84, citing UNFPA, *Global Population Assistance Report*, 1990.
14. World Bank, op. cit., p. 84.
15. World Bank, op. cit., p. 85.

15

Towards a New World Population Plan of Action

Bucharest, 1974. Mexico City, 1984. Rio de Janeiro, 1992. At least three mega-conferences and a host of lesser gatherings over the years had, as we have seen, failed to say the last word on population. True, agreement of a kind had been reached at some of these meetings and in this field as in so many others some agreement was usually better than no agreement. But the paper over the cracks was fairly transparent. In Bucharest in 1974, the population–versus–development dispute lay like a submerged iceberg beneath the surface, threatening careless mariners with instant shipwreck. In Mexico City in 1984, the controversy over abortion and the role of the free market ensured that the United States – a key player – effectively distanced itself from any consensus. In Rio de Janeiro in 1992, the search for a durable international accord on population had to take second place to UNCED's other objectives in the field of development and environment.

Yet each one of the events mentioned, as well as others described in this book, could be seen as a useful building-block for that 'final and definitive consensus on population and development' which many expected to emerge at the International Conference on Population and Development to be held in Cairo in September 1994. Indeed, if ever a moment seemed to favour the emergence of such a consensus, this was that moment.

The 'reproductive revolution' discussed in earlier chapters had thrown the population–versus–development debate into a wholly new perspective; the ending of the Cold War had taken the sting out of the ideological controversies which had bedevilled earlier efforts to reach international agreements on population; the Republican 'free-market' administration of President Bush had been replaced by the more pragmatic Democratic administration of President Clinton; China with its unique experience in population planning was rapidly emerging as the dominant power, both politically and economically, in Asia if not the world.

True, the Vatican had not noticeably changed its tune (the 1993 Encyclical *Splendor Veritatis* was clearly from the same stable as 1968's *Humanae Vitae*) but the power of the Vatican to destroy, deflect or dilute an international consensus on population and family planning had in the past often resided in the Catholic Church's ability to make common cause with the most unlikely allies (for example, Marxists or militarists), and those allies, as 1994 approached, seemed increasingly thin on the ground.

BACKGROUND

The United Nations Economic and Social Council (ECOSOC) adopted on 26 July 1989 resolution 1989/91 which called for the convening in 1994 of an 'international meeting on population.' ECOSOC adopted on 26 July 1991 resolution 1991/93, in which it decided to call the meeting the International Conference on Population and Development, and further defined the objectives and the themes of the Conference. Resolution 1992/37, adopted by the Council on 30 July 1992, accepted with gratitude the offer of the Government of Egypt to host the Conference in Cairo in September 1994.

The objectives of the Conference were set out in Council resolution 1991/93 as follows:

(a) To contribute to the review and appraisal of the progress made in reaching the objectives, goals and recommendations of the World Population Plan of Action and to identify the obstacles encountered;
(b) To identify instruments and mechanisms in order to ensure the operational implementation of the recommendations;
(c) To maintain and strengthen the level of awareness of population issues on the international agenda and their linkage to development;
(d) To consider the desired focus of intensified action at the global, regional and national levels, as well as all necessary ways and means of treating population issues in their proper development perspective during the forthcoming decade and beyond;
(e) To adopt a set of recommendations for the next decade in order to respond to the above-mentioned population and development issues of high priority;
(f) To enhance the mobilization of resources needed, especially in developing countries, for the implementation of the results of the Conference; resources should be mobilized at the international and national levels by each country according to its capacity.

In the same resolution, the Council emphasized that the overall theme of the Conference would be population, sustained economic growth and sustainable development. Within that theme it identified six groups of issues (not listed in any order of priority) as those requiring the greatest attention during the forthcoming decade:

(a) Population growth, changes in demographic structure, including ageing of the population, and the regional diversity of such changes, with particular emphasis on the interaction between demographic variables and socio-economic development;
(b) Population policies and programmes, with emphasis on the mobilization of resources for developing countries, at the international and national levels by each country according to its capacity;
(c) The interrelationships between population, development, environment and related matters;
(d) Changes in the distribution of population, including socio-economic determinants of internal migration and the consequences for urban and rural development, as well as determinants and consequences of all types of international migration;

(e)   Linkages between enhancing the roles and socio-economic status of women and population dynamics, including adolescent motherhood, maternal and child health, education and employment, with particular reference to the access of women to resources and the provision of services;

(f)   Family planning programmes, health and family well-being.

THE SIX EXPERT GROUP MEETINGS

ECOSOC, in resolution 1991/93, authorized the Secretary-General of the Conference to convene six expert group meetings corresponding to the six groups of issues defined above. The Expert Group Meetings were organized by the Population Division of the Department of Economic and Social Development of the United Nations Secretariat, in consultation with the United Nations Population Fund (UNFPA). Each Expert Group included 15 experts, invited in their personal capacities, along with representatives of relevant units, bodies and organizations of the United Nations system and selected intergovernmental and nongovernmental organizations. Efforts were made to have a full range of relevant scientific disciplines and geographical regions represented. Each Expert Group Meeting lasted five days. The standard documentation for each Meeting included a substantive background paper prepared by the Population Division in consultation with UNFPA, technical papers prepared by each of the experts and technical contributions provided by the participating United Nations regional commissions, specialized agencies and other organizations and bodies of the United Nations system, as well as intergovernmental and nongovernmental organizations. At the conclusion of each Meeting, a set of recommendations was adopted to be submitted to the Preparatory Committee of the Conference at its second session, in May 1993. The number of recommendations in each set varied between 18 and 37, adding up to a total of 162 recommendations.

The first Expert Group Meeting, on population, environment and development, was held at United Nations Headquarters from 20 to 24 January 1992. The second, on population policies and programmes, was hosted by the Government of Egypt in Cairo, from 12 to 16 April 1992. The third, on population and women, was hosted by the Government of Botswana in Gaborone, from 22 to 26 June 1992 and financed by a contribution from the Government of the Netherlands. The fourth, on family planning, health and family well-being, was hosted by the Government of India in Bangalore, from 26 to 29 October 1992. The fifth, on population growth and demographic structure, was hosted by the Government of France in Paris, from 16 to 20 November 1992. The sixth, on population distribution and migration, was hosted by the Government of Bolivia in Santa Cruz, from 18 to 23 January 1993.

At the second session of the Preparatory Committee (PrepCom) for the International Conference on Population and Development, held in New York in May 1993, delegates were provided with a synthesis of the expert group meetings as well as the full reports of the Meetings.

In addition to the six expert group meetings, several round tables were organized following PrepCom II. The round table on Women's Perspectives on Family Planning, Reproductive Rights and Reproductive Health was held in Ottawa, Canada on 26–27 August 1993; and the round table on Population Policies and Programmes; the Impact of HIV/AIDS was held in Berlin, Germany from 28 September to 1 October, 1993. Other round tables took place during the first months of 1994.

REGIONAL CONFERENCES

Another key element in the preparations for the International Conference on Population and Development to be held in Cairo in September 1994 was the series of regional conferences held during 1992 and 1993 in accordance with ECOSOC resolution 1991/93.

The first of these regional conferences, the Fourth Asian and Pacific Population Conference, jointly sponsored by the Economic and Social Commission for Asia and the Pacific (ESCAP) and UNFPA, was held in Denpasar, Indonesia from 19 to 27 August 1992. The conclusions of that conferences, enshrined in the Bali Declaration on Population and Sustainable Development, served once again to underline the Asia and Pacific region's 'pole position' as far as the population policy and family planning programmes were concerned.

The Bali Declaration recognized that fertility, as measured by the total fertility rate, currently averaged 3.1 per woman in the Asia and Pacific region. However, there were substantial differences between and within the sub-regions of Asia and the Pacific. Fertility, at 2.1 per woman, was currently lowest in East Asia. It was highest, at 4.3 per woman, in South Asia. Similar marked disparities were exhibited in sub-regional levels of mortality. Thus, for example, infant mortality at 90 per 1000 births, in South Asia, was more than three times the level of the corresponding rate in East Asia where it was 26.

In the Bali Declaration,[1] the countries of the ESCAP region set themselves the ambitious target of attaining replacement level fertility by the year 2010.

> In order to help reduce high rates of population growth, countries and areas should adopt suitable strategies to attain replacement level fertility, equivalent to around 2.2 children per woman, by the year 2010 or sooner.

The ESCAP countries also fixed the objective of reducing the level of infant mortality to 40 per 1000 births or lower during the same period and, in those countries and areas where maternal mortality was high, of reducing it at least by half by the year 2010.

The Third African Population Conference, jointly organized by the Economic Commission for Africa (ECA), the Organization of African Unity (OAU) and UNFPA, in collaboration with the African Development Bank (ADB) and the Union for African Population Studies (UAPS), was held in Dakar from 7 to 12 December 1992.

The Conference adopted the Dakar/Ngor Declaration on Population, Family and Sustainable Development[2] which included a commitment by the participating governments to:

> Integrate population policies and programmes in development strategies, focusing on strengthening social sectors with a view to influencing human development and work towards the solution of population problems by setting *quantified national objectives for the reduction of population growth with a view to bringing down the regional natural growth rate from 3 per cent to 2.5 per cent by the year 2000 and 2 per cent by 2010.*[3] (emphasis added)

The Dakar/Ngor Declaration, in a section on *'Fertility and the Family'* declared that African governments should:

> (a) Create a conducive socio-economic climate and sustained political will for the pursuit of such effective fertility policies as make for (i) setting fertility and family

planning (FP) targets for all people of reproductive age and takes measures to reduce infertility where needed; (ii) implementing legal measures to improve the status of women and their reproductive health; (iii) establish strong maternal and child health (MCH) programmes; (iv) ensuring strong management and close collaboration between private and public sectors and communities in the implementation of their MCH and national FP programmes; (v) decentralizing health care delivery systems for urban and rural areas; (vi) strengthening information, education and communication (IEC) in MCH and FP programmes; (vii) strengthening family institutions; (viii) addressing unmet family planning needs of adolescents and others; and (ix) promoting the education of men and women on joint responsible parenthood.

The Dakar/Ngor Declaration went further than generalities where family planning was concerned (useful though the generalities listed above were in view of the African continent's very special demographic situation). The Declaration committed African governments to:

> Ensure the availability and promote the use of all tested available contraceptive and fertility regulation methods, including traditional and natural family planning methods ensuring choice of methods with a view to doubling the regional contraceptive prevalence rate (CPR) from about 10 to about 20 per cent by the year 2000 and 40 per cent by the year 2010.[4]

The Economic and Social Commission for Western Asia (ESCWA), the League of Arab States and UNFPA jointly sponsored the Arab Population Conference in Amman, Jordan from 4–8 April 1993. Though less forthright than their Asian and Pacific counterparts, the Arab delegates adopted as one of their objectives:

> Achieving appropriate population growth rates through provision of the services needed to attain national policy goals. In the case of countries wishing to reduce their population growth rates, this requires provision of the services needed to develop and enhance family planning and family protection services, including maternal and child health care, and the formulation of economic, social, health and education policies to help create the requisite climate in which couples will accept and react to these objectives.[5]

The last of the developing world's regional conferences, the Latin America and Caribbean Population and Development Conference, jointly sponsored by the Economic Commission for Latin America and the Caribbean (ECLAC) and UNFPA, was held in Mexico City from 29 April to 4 May 1993.[6] The Conference adopted the Latin American and Caribbean Consensus, which, like the declarations from the other regional gatherings, viewed its subject-matter not through narrowly-focused spectacles but in the larger framework of social and economic priorities. In the Latin American and Caribbean case, the key was the search for 'equity.' This, by itself, was not surprising since social inequalities within the Latin American nations were certainly as high, if not higher, than those obtaining in other regions of the world. An analysis prepared by the ECLAC and Latin American Demographic Centre[7] and presented to the Conference argued that achieving greater equity within Latin American societies was an important and possibly essential element in the control of fertility. The rich, as the old saying had it, got richer while the poor got children.

The search for equity between nations was no less important than the search for equity within nations. The region's external indebtedness accounted for a more than disproportionate share (almost a quarter) of overall Third World debt. The Consensus stated:

External debt and its servicing place a heavy burden on Latin American and Caribbean countries that prevents resources being allocated for development; specifically, it prevents those countries from giving priority to social programmes aimed
at raising the population's standard of living. Consequently, regional consensus-
building mechanisms must be created to release resources now used to repay and
service debt for the implementation of social development programmes, including
those related to population and development.

Debt servicing could force structural adjustment programmes with their difficult consequences for social expenditures (including family planning programmes) no less
surely than the International Monetary Fund.

The Latin American and Caribbean Consensus on Population and Development
recognized that:

One of the most outstanding demographic changes in Latin America and the
Caribbean in the past 25 years is the pronounced decline in fertility, from 6 to 3.5
children per woman. . .[8]

However, there were wide disparities between the countries in the region, evidenced
not only by differences in basic demographic indicators, such as fertility and life
expectancy, but also in discrimination directed against women. Special efforts had to
be made to 'prevent any lack of equity with respect to women's education and
employment status' and to reduce the high morbidity and mortality rates associated
with child-birth.

Given that this was an official governmental conference, and given the fact that the
Conference was being held in a Latin American country with a majority of the delegates being Latin American (and probably Catholic), it was not surprising that the
meeting failed to address the abortion issue as directly as had some of the Expert
Groups referred to earlier. However, Jyoti Singh, a senior UNFPA official who served
as Executive Coordinator for the International Conference on Population and Development (ICPD), did allude forcefully to the topic of abortion in his opening speech in
Mexico City, as did some of the Caribbean delegates.

UNFPA circulated a paper which stated that throughout the region 'abortion is
pervasive and carried out in vast numbers'. In the early 1980s, it was estimated that
3.4 million women had resorted to induced abortion, with a rate of 45 abortions for
each 1000 women of childbearing age. (UNFPA estimated that each year throughout
the world nearly 55 million unwanted pregnancies were terminated through
abortion.[9])

The upshot of it all was that a grammatically opaque but nonetheless helpful reference was included in the final Consensus document:

Considering that abortion is a major public health issue in the countries of the
region and that, while various views are held in this regard, none of them accepts
abortion as a method of regulating fertility, it is recommended that Governments
devote greater attention to the study and follow-up of this issue, with a view to
evaluating how prevalent abortion really is and its impact on the health of women
and their families; Governments should also promote universal access to proper
guidance on how to prevent unwanted pregnancies.

On the family planning front, the Consensus stressed the need for quality and for a
variety of choice of contraceptive methods, and sounded a note of caution about the
use of female sterilization, reported to be the most widely used method of birth control in the world (it was estimated that nearly one-third of the women who controlled
their fertility had undergone this treatment).[10] The Consensus asked for more attention

to be given to the rhythm method of family planning 'taking into account that some population groups show a preference for methods based on periodic abstinence.' It also recommended that governments, though it might be 'desirable to set targets as to either the number of users or fertility rates' refrain from 'establishing quotas for the number of persons that may use the services provided.' Targets – *si*; quotas – *non*!

Participants in the European Population Conference, which was jointly convened by the Economic Commission for Europe (ECE), the Council of Europe and UNFPA and held in Geneva, from 23 to 26 March 1993, included the major donors from Europe and North America. It was therefore a matter of particular interest that the Conference made a strong plea for strengthened international cooperation in the population field. Recommendation 51 stated:

> Cooperation with developing countries should be built upon a strengthened part-nership based on the recognition of sovereign equality, mutual interest and shared responsibility with mutual commitments. While developing countries have a pri-mary responsibility for their own economic and social development, including the formulation and implementation of appropriate national policies relating to popu-lation and development, *developed countries have a special responsibility to help create a favourable international economic environment and to increase the quantity and quality of their assistance, particularly in the field of population.* (emphasis added)

In its Recommendation 53, the European Conference referred to the 'large, and growing, unmet demand in developing countries for family planning services' and to UNFPA's estimates that 300 million women lacked access to such services.

> Efforts should thus be intensified to ensure the availability of family planning ser-vices to all who wish to make use of them. Such efforts can be expected to help in achieving population growth rates which contribute to a sustainable use of natural resources.

As one of the basic principles of cooperation, the European Conference attached 'par-ticular importance to gender perspectives, to the full involvement of both women and men in reproductive health programmes' and to improving the status of women who should be 'free to make responsible decisions affecting their lives and those of their families, including decisions on reproduction.'

The Recommendations of the European Conference called on the governments of the region 'to be aware that poverty, population growth and environmental degrada-tion are closely interrelated. While population growth and poverty result in certain kinds of environmental stress, the major causes of the continued deterioration of the global environment are the unsustainable patterns of production and consumption, particularly in industrialized countries.'

The Conference recommended that 'common targets should be the promotion of patterns of consumption and production that reduce environmental stress, and the encouragement of social and economic development that meets basic needs and allows for better living conditions and appropriate fertility rates'.

The call to change consumption patterns in the rich, industrialized world had, as we saw in Chapter 10, been a feature of the United Nations Conference on Environ-ment and Development (UNCED) held in Rio in June 1992. UNCED's recommen-dations as to just how such consumption patterns were to be changed had been on the thin side, inviting much further study but little specific action.[11] The recommenda-tions of the European Conference in this respect were, if anything, pitched at an even higher level of generality. There was little, if any, talk in Geneva in March 1993 of a 'global bargain' under which the West would change its life-styles, and the South would change (or further change) its patterns of fertility. That kind of a deal was not on the table in Geneva, nor – by all indications – would it be on the table in Cairo in September 1994. There were undoubtedly many good reasons for the West to change its life-styles, just as there were many good reasons for the South to reduce rapid rates of population growth but the two issues would not, and probably could not, be linked as part of an international negotiating process.

ICPD PrepCOM II, MAY 1993

As already noted, the participants in the expert groups attended in a personal capacity, while the series of regional population conferences took place at the official governmental level. Already in 1992 and 1993, national positions on key issues were being worked out and the framework for subsequent negotiations established. However, it was not until the second meeting of the Preparatory Committee of the ICPD, held in New York in May 1993, that the main elements of a new action plan for world population began to emerge.

GOALS FOR 2015

In her speech to the Preparatory Committee on 14 May, 1993, Dr Nafis Sadik – the ICPD's Secretary-General, invited delegates to consider a set of goals for inclusion in the new World Population Plan of Action.

> I propose that all countries commit themselves to reach or assist others to reach the average of the developing countries in such areas as maternal mortality, infant mortality, life expectancy, education especially for women and girls, gender equality and availability of and access to a full range of modern, safe and effective family planning services to enable the exercise of choice.
>
> Such an approach should be seen as a challenge for the whole international community rather than an imposition on any part of it. Setting goals for the international community is not an attempt to impose a rigid formula, or to over-simplify a complex problem, but rather a way to address the basic components of an acceptable quality of life for all members of our global family. The proposed 20 year time-frame offers the necessary flexibility of response by individual countries and the wider community.

Dr Sadik went on to say :'A call for quantifiable, reachable goals is unusual for a conference such as ours, but not unprecedented. Optimism as well as commitment will be needed for success.'

TOTAL SIZE OF THE HUMAN FAMILY

Dr Sadik addressed herself first to the 'total size of the human family'. Looking forward to 2025, three scenarios were proposed by the United Nation's Secretariat's Population Division, based on different assumptions about fertility. The projections ranged from a high of 7.92 billion in 2015 to a low of 7.27 billion. The difference in world population between high and low projections was 660 million. The difference between the medium and low scenarios was 338 million. Of these, 266 million would be in today's developing countries and only 71 million in the developed regions.

Though, as noted in Chapter 10, Dr Sadik had suggested after the UNCED Conference that attaining the medium projection should be the overall policy goal objective, in her speech to the PrepCom in May 1993, she was able to advise delegates of an important evolution in her (and UNFPA's) thinking and of the reasons for it.

> The needs and the impact of a population of 7.27 billion in 2015, the low projection, are very different from the high projection of 7.92 billion, or even 7.16 billion, the medium projection. *I believe that we must strive for the low projection. I believe that it can be achieved with sufficient commitment at the local, national and international level. There is ample evidence that the currently unmet needs of couples and individuals make up the difference between the medium and the low population scenario.* As many as 300 million people have no access to contraception, and there are many more who now that information and services are available but in fact have no access to them. (emphasis added)

In formal terms, the Secretary-General of the ICPD circulated a paper to delegates under the heading *Goals for 2015* which contained the following paragraph:

> The Secretary-General of the Conference believes that the low population projection can be reached by 2015, if family planning information and services are provided to all couples and individuals who need them and if policies are formulated and implemented to empower women to participate fully in socio-economic development. *She therefore urges the Conference to set the goal of attaining the low variant population projection of 7.27 billion for 2015.* (italics added)

The last sentence, especially, was a clear and unambiguous statement. Dr Sadik did not mince her words; she did not duck and weave. She did not urge the Conference to 'consider the possibility of setting the goal. . .' or even to 'envisage considering the possibility of setting the goal etc.' As Secretary-General of the Conference, and as Executive-Director of UNFPA, she had a right and a duty to show leadership. In proposing to PrepCom II to adopt the 'low variant' with all that that implied in terms of further falls in fertility, particularly in sub-Saharan Africa, South and West Asia, North Africa, and some parts of Latin America, Dr Nafis Sadik set the stage for a final immense effort in the international endeavour, now decades old, to 'turn the tide' of human fertility.

Dr Sadik also proposed other specific targets. She suggested that *infant mortality* in the developing countries, which had dropped from 92 per 1000 births in 1970–75 to 62 over the period 1990–95 should be reduced to the developed country levels (12 deaths per 1000 in 1990–95)

> Is it realistic to believe that infant mortality could be so dramatically reduced in 20 years? The answer must be yes. We know why these infants are dying. The remedies are affordable if the resources are available.

She proposed that *maternal mortality* be reduced in the developing countries to 30 per 100,000 live births (the level of the developed countries) from the present 450 per 100,000 live births.

> It is estimated that half a million women die each year as a consequence of pregnancy. Almost all these deaths are preventable. As many as half result from unsafe and illegal abortions.

The issue of *abortion* had to be addressed, as a health issue not as a means of family planning. 'The international community is expecting us to turn our attention to this subject. We must not shy away from it.'

She proposed that the gap in *life-expectancy* between developed and developing regions should be closed (aiming at 75 years for developing countries by 2015, as against the projected 77.5 years for the developed countries.)

The Conference should also adopt the goal of *'universal access to and completion of primary education' by 2015*. To achieve this, access to quality education must be assured for girls and women, and obstacles removed that hampered their active participation.

Finally, Dr Sadik turned to the question of targets for access to family planning information and services. *'In no other area'* she said *'has such dramatic progress been achieved. In 1970–75, contraceptive prevalence in developed regions was between 65–70 per cent compared with 20–25 per cent in developing regions. In 1990 virtually no change had been recorded in developed regions while developing regions had doubled to 51 per cent.'* However, there was still a very large measure of unmet demand in developing countries.

> Clear evidence is found in the 50 million abortions that take place each year. All of these women would surely have preferred to have prevented rather than interrupted their pregnancies. This especially applies to adolescents, for whom pregnancy carries special risks.

The paper on *Goals for 2015* circulated to delegates proposed a target of *71 per cent for contraceptive prevalence by the year 2015*.

What in practice did this imply for fertility? Dr Sadik pointed out that there had been a steady decline in total fertility from 4.46 (in 1970–75) to around 3.26. 'If steps are taken to meet unmet demand among couples and individuals for family planning information and services, this rate could well decline to 2.62 by the year 2015.'[12]

GENERAL DISCUSSION AT PrepCOM II

Throughout the four days of debate at PrepCom II, governments, UN agencies and NGOs made a number of concrete recommendations on the structure, format and contents of what became known succinctly as 'the Cairo Document.' The highlights of the debate were captured by the journalists from the Bulletin.

> Colombia, on behalf of the Group of 77, recommended a chapter on finance for international cooperation for population activities and suggested that more emphasis be placed on issues such as education, empowerment of women, the role of men in family planning, and migration. Denmark, on behalf of the EC, identified four key areas for organizing the proposed section on guiding principles: Human Rights and Population; Human Development and Population; Sustainable Development and Population; and Partnership and Population.
>
> Egypt proposed that the principles section be merged into the section on choices and responsibilities and that the preamble be expanded to include the right to development, national sovereignty, mutual responsibility and global partnership. Sweden, on behalf of the Nordic countries, stated that the draft outline must be better articulated with regard to the interrelationships and dynamics between population, sustained economic growth and sustainable development. Sweden also urged that the document should address follow-up measures, and suggested that Part II of the draft outline should give special emphasis to a limited number of

issues or clusters such as: integrating population concerns into development; the role and status of women; and reproductive rights, reproductive health and family planning.

Australia urged that over-consumption and inequitable distribution of wealth be addressed and that additional resources are needed to improve both the quality and the availability of reproductive health services. Zimbabwe said that the document needs to consider financial provisions. Canada suggested that the Commission on Sustainable Development should participate in the monitoring of the results of the ICPD and that the Conference should focus more on the causes, rather than the effects, of international migration. Poland and the Russian Federation called for distinctions to be maintained between regional and global recommendations, especially in light of the special socio-economic problems of countries in transition.[13]

Of particular interest given the position taken by the United States at the Mexico City Conference was the US delegate's intervention. Speaking on behalf of the United States, Timothy Wirth, a former US Senator, stressed the changes in US policy since President Clinton took office. He mentioned that the US was developing a comprehensive new approach to international population issues, including: freedom of choice regarding family size; access to quality reproductive health care; the empowerment of women; preservation of the natural environment; and sustainable development. He mentioned three major concerns to be addressed by the Conference: women's health and status; population and the environment; and migration. Finally, he said that the US '*supported reproductive choice, including access to safe abortion.*' This last comment, according to the Bulletin, 'generated a round of applause.'

Another interesting – and possibly courageous intervention – was made by India which stated that the Cairo Conference should not become an umbrella conference that crowded the agenda with important issues that were not directly related to population and development, such as the environment and women. India also made a number of specific recommendations for the restructuring of the conceptual framework to focus more on population.

The position of the Holy See was of particular concern. As we have seen, the Holy See at the Bucharest and Mexico Conferences had, at the end of the day, refused to join the consensus even though in certain cases the text of key documents had been sensibly modified or weakened in order to accommodate its objections. In Rio, at UNCED, the Vatican had again sought, on the whole successfully, to dilute the recommendations on population. Would Cairo be a repetition of Bucharest, Mexico and Rio?

Though no doubt there was still scope for the Vatican to fight some rearguard actions over terminology ('couples', as opposed to 'individuals and couples' or – worst of all from the Vatican's point of view – 'individuals' *tout court*), the key issue for the Holy See looking towards Cairo 1994 was perhaps not so much contraception, as abortion.

ABORTION

Most of the Expert Groups had clearly recommended that women should have legal access to abortion counselling and services. The need for safe legal abortion had been stressed in the context of the various regional population conferences, including in that most Catholic of regions, Latin America. The Secretary-General of the Conference, who spoke with the authority of gender as well as position, had – as noted above – urged delegates not to shrink from the issue. As noted in the previous chapter, her deputy, Jyoti Singh, had used similar terms at the opening of the Latin America and Caribbean regional population conference in Mexico in May 1993. Any new World Population Plan of Action worth its salt would surely have to address this issue head on.

At the time this book was being written, it was too early to predict the final outcome of this particular contest. During the debate on the Conceptual Framework, Archbishop Renato R. Martino, speaking for the Holy See, stated that voluntary abortion under the guise of other perceived rights 'violates the most fundamental right of any human being to life.' He said that the Catholic Church did not propose procreation at any cost, but rather it opposed 'demographic policies and family planning that are contrary to the liberty, dignity and conscience of the human being.'

According to the Bulletin,[14] at the conclusion of the Holy See's intervention, Dr. Sai, PrepCom's Chairman 'welcomed the introduction of moral and ethical issues into the discussion. He then asked why the Vatican could support the blessings of modern medicine but could not make modern contraceptives available, saying that morals and ethics are a two-way street.' Though not even the Bulletin recorded the fact, anecdotal evidence suggests that Dr Sai's well-aimed thrust met with applause from several, perhaps many, of the delegations present. Certainly in the debate which followed, several delegations, including Sweden and the US, urged that attention should be given to this issue, above all in the health context. Argentina, predictably, expressed its opposition to any mention of abortion in the context of family planning.

A key paragraph on the subject of abortion was included in the 'Chairman's Summary on the Conceptual Framework'. Though it could not be considered as an agreed record of the meeting (pressures of time ruled that option out), the Chairman's summary, presented by Dr Sai on the last day of PrepCom II, could safely be deemed to reflect the general tendency of the meeting. The text of paragraph 37 of the Chairman's Summary read as follows:

> It was pointed out that among the issues that the Conference needed to address were unacceptably high levels of maternal mortality and morbidity in many developing countries. *Unsafe and illegal abortion, which in many countries was an important cause of maternal morbidity and mortality, constituted one of the most neglected problems affecting women's lives. It was seen by most delegations as a major public health issue which the Conference needed to recognize and address as such. While many delegations suggested that all women should have access to safe abortion, others suggested that the best way to eliminate abortions was provision of effective, modern contraception information and services; a few delegations reiterated that abortion should not be promoted as a method of family planning.*[15] (emphasis added)

QUANTITATIVE GOALS

Encouragingly, the Chairman's summary indicated that:

> there was general support for the proposal of the Secretary-General of the Conference to include a set of quantitative goals in the Cairo document. Such goals must take into account regional and national variations. Some delegations suggested that the proposed time-frame of 20 years could be segmented into 5- and 10-year frames. Progress towards achieving the goals should be monitored.

The point was made by many delegations that the goals must be consistent with each other and with those set at other international forums. There must be no coercion of any kind in the programmes formulated to achieve those goals. Some delegations suggested the possibility of including other social and economic goals.[16]

RESOURCES FOR THE NEW WORLD POPULATION PLAN OF ACTION

On the question of resources for population activities, another issue which was unlikely to be finally resolved until the last minute of the Cairo meeting (if then) the Chairman's summary stated[17] that 'the Amsterdam Declaration on a Better Life for Future Generations . . . should be refined in this respect, so as to provide the Cairo Conference with more precise estimates of the resources required over the next decade.'

Reference was also made in the Chairman's summary to the proceedings of the European Population Conference. A paper presented to that conference by Mr Halvor Gille, former Deputy Executive Director of UNFPA, had pointed out that the $9 billion estimate was in 1989 dollars; after adjustment for inflation it would be around $13 billion in the year 2000 if a similar change in purchasing power should apply as experienced in the 1980s.[18] Mr Gille argued, moreover, that if the goals set by the Amsterdam Forum as regards the reduction of infant and maternal mortality were to be achieved, core population activities would not be sufficient; improved maternal and child health care such as ante-natal and post-natal care, health education, promotion of breast-feeding and the immunization of infants would also be needed, requiring an additional amount of between $4 and $7.6 billion annually.

A few weeks after the second session of the ICPD Preparatory Committee ended, Population Action International (PAI) published estimates of the resource requirements involved in stabilizing world population below the 10 billion level.[19] As noted in Chapter 14, PAI calculated that if the world was to reach an average family size of two children early in the twenty-first century, 70 to 80 per cent of all couples would need to use contraception by the year 2000 requiring a doubling of family planning users from about 350 million in 1990 to roughly 700 million by the end of the decade. Assuming that the cost of providing high quality family planning information and services was about $16 per couple, annual expenditures on family planning would need to more than double to about $11 billion in constant 1990 dollars, or, adjusted for inflation, to an estimated $15 billion.

The goals put forward by PAI were obviously more ambitious, at least in terms of target dates, than those proposed by ICPD's Secretary-General – and those proposals were in themselves as noted above bold enough. The new calculations were nevertheless of interest in providing, or attempting to provide, an answer to the question: how much would 'going for broke' (i.e. attaining replacement level fertility by the end of the century, cost?

PAI also addressed itself very directly to the question of donor contributions. They pointed out that at the Amsterdam Forum the international community agreed that 4 per cent of overall development assistance should be allocated to population programmes. In 1991, however, the industrialized countries contributed an average of slightly more than one per cent of total foreign aid to population assistance. Overall,

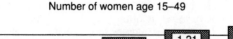

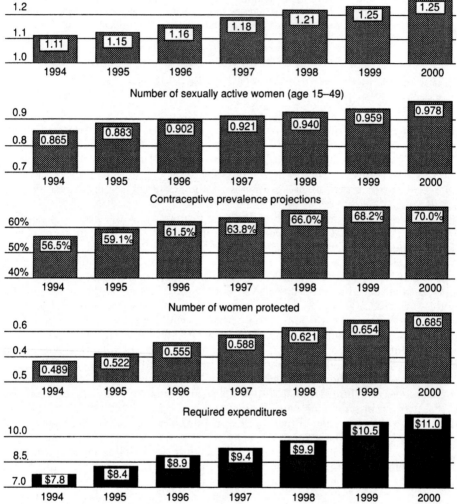

Fig. 15.1. Cost implications for achieving universal access to family-planning by the year 2000 – Goals for the 1994 International Conference on Population and Development for Developing Countries only.

–The number of sexually active women (based on data provided by the U.N. Population Division) is used instead of couples in union.

–Contraceptive prevalence projections assume gradual increases in contraceptive use to 70 percent by the year 2000 – a level of contraceptive use consonant with an average family size of just over two children, key to stabilizing world population by midcentury.

–The "number of women protected" refers to women protected from unintended pregnancy.

–Required expenditures are based on an average per person cost of $16.00 per year for family planning services, in constant 1990 dollars. Actual costs vary widely. The $16.00 average takes into account costs for multi-year methods, such as male or female sterilization, and the need to improve the quality of services, including the provision of safe abortion services.

Source: Global Population Assistance: A Report Card on the Major Donor Countries. (Conly, S.R. and Speidel, J.J., 1993) Population Action International.

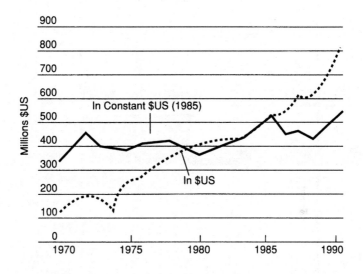

Fig. 15.2. Trends in donor contributions for population assistance, 1970–1990. Figures do not include World Bank assistance. *Source: Global Population Assistance – A Report Card on the Major Donor Countries.* (Conly, S.R. and Speidel, J.J., 1993) Population Action International.

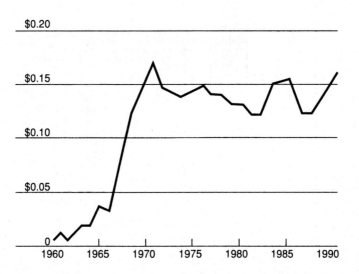

Fig. 15.3. Donor population commitments for each person in the developing countries, 1960–1990 (Constant 1985 $US). *Source: Global Population Assistance – A Report Card on the Major Donor Countries.* (Conly, S.R. and Speidel, J.J., 1993) Population Action International.

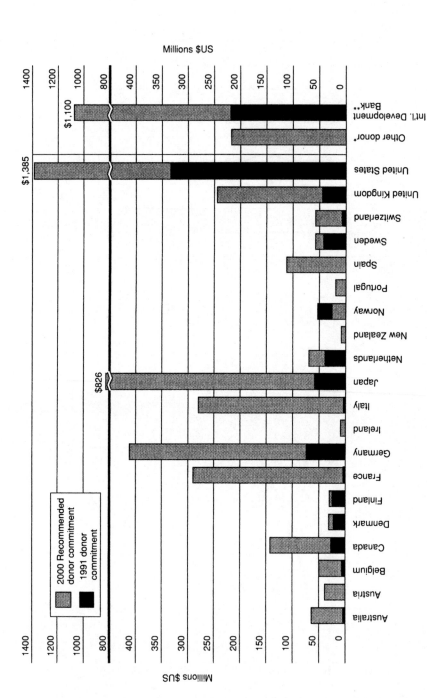

Fig. 15.4 Donor commitments for family planning in developing countries, by source (constant 1990 $US). *Source: Global Population Assistance – A Report Card on the Major Donor Countries.* (Conly, S.R. and Speidel, J.J., 1993) Population Action International. *Other donors include non-DAC donor countries and philanthropic organizations – no 1991 data available. **1991 figure reflects three-year average (1989–1991) of World Bank commitments only. †Norway is the only donor whose 1991 commitment exceeded the recommended amount for the year 2000.

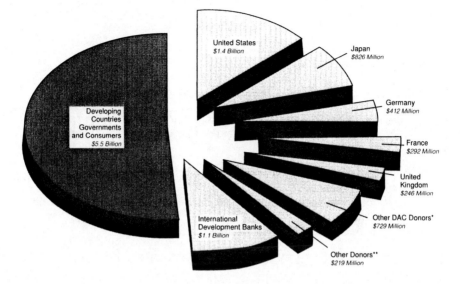

Fig. 15.5. Year 2000 model family planning budget, by source (constant 1990 $US). *Source: Global Population Assistance – A Report Card on the Major Donor Countries.* (Conly, S.R. and Speidel, J.J., 1993) Population Action International. *Other DAC donors: Australia, Austria, Belgium, Canada, Denmark, Finland, Ireland, Netherlands, New Zealand, Norway, Portugal, Spain, Sweden, Switzerland. **Other donors include non-DAC donor countries and philanthropic organizations.

the share of development assistance allocated to population activities increased only marginally between 1982 and 1991.

Some donors did more than others. Norway had led the way by consistently committing four to five per cent of economic assistance to population. Finland, the United States, Denmark, Sweden and Canada had also contributed well above the donor average. Other countries making a significant effort included the Netherlands, the United Kingdom and Germany.

'Many rich countries, however,' Population Action International commented 'are still not doing their fair share to make family planning more widely available in poorer countries.' Japan, while a major donor in absolute terms, had consistently contributed under one per cent of official development assistance to population. France and Italy provided negligible levels of population assistance relative to their large aid programmes and to the effort made by the United Kingdom and Germany.

THE UN GENERAL ASSEMBLY, NOVEMBER 1993

On November 4–5 1993, the UN General Assembly considered a number of documents relating to the ICPD, including the Report of the Secretary-General on the implementation of General Assembly resolution 47/167 and ECOSOC resolution 1991/93 (A/48/430) and the annotated outline of the final document of the Conference (A/48/430/Add.1) which covered the following main headings:

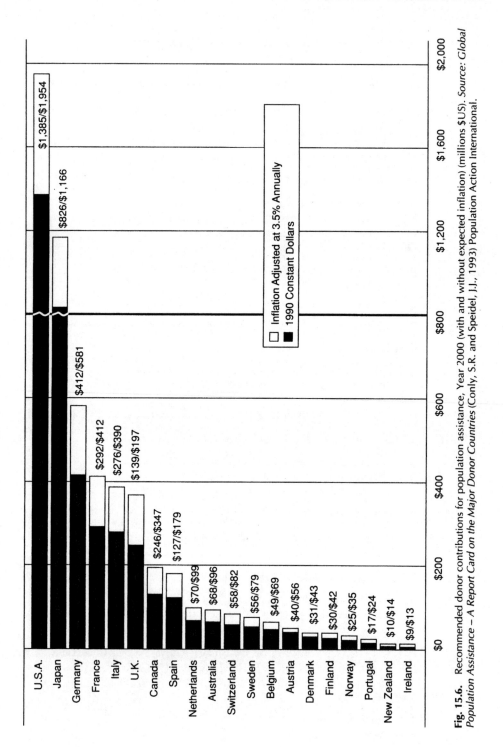

Fig. 15.6. Recommended donor contributions for population assistance, Year 2000 (with and without expected inflation) (millions $US). *Source: Global Population Assistance – A Report Card on the Major Donor Countries* (Conly, S.R. and Speidel, J.J., 1993) Population Action International.

The annotated outline was the focus of many statements during the Second Committee debate. These were summarized by Dr. Sadik in her closing statement as follows:

The 'centrality of population' must be maintained in the deliberations and in the final document, while at the same time the interrelationships between population, sustained economic growth and sustainable development was to be stressed –

The recommendations should be action-oriented, clear and concise;
There should be an emphasis on implementable activities, not just recommendations;
The interests and rights of the individual must be central in all population and development efforts;
Personal integrity, the particular needs of women, and freedom of choice must be extended in all population programmes;
The empowerment of women in society must be championed in its own right;
The document should give more attention to sexuality and the family planning needs of youth and adolescents;

With regard to *goals*, Dr Sadik observed:

> I am pleased to note your strong support for the inclusion of a set of 20-year goals in the draft Cairo document. I should like to reiterate here that we are *not* proposing the setting of demographic targets or quotas. The attainment of these goals, which focus on the needs of the individual and the responsibility of society to protect them, will result, in the opinion of the experts, in demographic consequences, i.e. a decline in population growth rates. *The optimistic estimates indicate that population levels could stabilize at the low population projection level of the United Nations.* The goals we are proposing relate to infant, child and maternal mortality; universal access to and completion of primary school education; and *universal access to family planning information and services with emphasis on meeting all unmet demand.* (emphasis added)

This then was the skeleton of the new World Population Plan of Action as it was presented to the United Nations General Assembly in November 1993. With the Second Committee's debate on the International Conference on Population and Development at an end, the next step could begin. Delegates would meet in informal session to negotiate a resolution that would likely elevate the status of the ICPD Preparatory Committee to a subsidiary body of the General Assembly, and determine the 1994 budgetary implications for the Preparatory Committee and the Conference. That resolution would be procedural in nature. It was expected to be adopted by the Second Committee in mid-December and then forwarded to the Plenary before the General Assembly concluded for the year.

As far as the *substance* was concerned – the business of putting flesh on the skeleton – the preparatory process would be pursued with ever-increasing intensity through the first half of 1994 with the third session of the preparatory committee formally scheduled to take place at UN Headquarters in New York from 4 to 22 April 1994. With the active participation of non-governmental organizations envisaged for every stage of the process (including at the Cairo Conference itself where some 10,000 NGOs were anticipated), it would at the end of the day be up to the nations and peoples of the world to ensure that the document which finally went to, and emerged from, Cairo in September 1994 was the best that could possibly be achieved.

NOTES

1. E/CONF.84/PC/14, 29th April 1993.
2. E/CONF.84/PC/13, 27 April 1993.
3. Dakar/Ngor Declaration, Para 1.
4. Op. cit. para 3b.
5. E/CONF.84/PC.16, para. 19.
6. E/CONF.84/PC/17, 10 May 1993.
7. *Population, Social Equity and Changing Consumption Patterns,* ECLAC and CELADE, Santiago, Chile, 1993.
8. Op. cit., para 6.
9. *Experiences in Population in Latin America and the Caribbean: Historical Perspective and Current Challenges,* UNFPA, 1993.
10. *Population, Social Equity and Changing Production Patterns,* as cited, p. 61.
11. See especially Agenda 21, Chapter 4, Changing consumption patterns.
12. As can be seen from Table 12.17, even a TFR of 2.62 for developing countries as a whole by 2015 is still above the required TFR of 2.19 (for the quinquennium 2010-2015) if the low variant is to be attained.
13. *Earth Negotiations Bulletin,* Vol.6, No.11, 2 June 1993.
14. Op. cit., Vol. 6, No. 11, p. 3.
15. E/CONF.84/PC/L.9 of 20 May 1993.
16. Op. cit., para 62.
17. Op. cit., para 59.
18. See *International Cooperation in the Field of Population,* by Halvor Gille, Former Deputy Executive Director, UNFPA, E/CONF84.RM.EUR.WP.5, of 15 December 1992.
19. *Global Population Assistance: A Report Card on the Major Donor Countries,* Shanti R. Conly, and J. Joseph Speidel, Population Action International, Washington, June 1993.

16

Turning the Tide – Cairo, September 1994 and Beyond

On 24 January, 1994, the United Nations circulated to the Preparatory Committee for the International Conference on Population and Development (ICPD) a document for discussion at the Committee's third session, to be held in New York in April 1994. The document was called: 'Draft final document of the Conference: Draft Programme of Action.'[1]

The ICPD Preparatory Committee, like the forthcoming Cairo conference itself, would of course be sovereign in its deliberations and therefore not necessarily bound by the text prepared by the Secretariat (even though that text followed closely the outline shown in the previous chapter); it is nonetheless worth looking fairly closely at the Draft Programme of Action in so far as it represented at the time of going to press the most comprehensive statement to date of a possible new international consensus on population and development.

The ICPD's Draft Programme of Action was not a short document. With its 83 pages, it exceeded in length the World Population Plan of Action adopted at the first World Population Conference held at Bucharest in August 1974 (23 pages),[2] as well the Recommendations for the Further Implementation of the World Population Plan of Action adopted at the International Conference on Population held in Mexico City in August 1984 (36 pages).[3] For *aficionados* of the international conference circuit, some comfort could be taken from the fact that the draft Cairo document was substantially shorter than the 600-page draft of 'Agenda 21' submitted to the United Nations Conference on Environment and Development (UNCED) held in Rio de Janeiro in June 1992.[4]

Within those 83 pages of the ICPD's Draft Programme of Action, what were the key elements of the possible new consensus? There is, inevitably, an element of subjectiveness in producing an answer to that question. People tend to look first for the things they expect or wish to see. Feminists and their increasingly numerous supporters (aren't we all feminists now?) may, for example, focus on the document's treatment of 'gender' issues. Environmentalists may look for evidence that the Draft Programme has something new to say about the thorny issue of 'changing consumption patterns.' The priority accorded to the role of 'indigenous peoples' will be a primary interest of several non-governmental organizations (NGOs). NGOs as a whole will probably focus on the way in which the Draft Programme recognizes NGO concerns and provides for their active involvement and participation.

That said, given the particular perspectives of this book and given the limitations of space, what are the most noteworthy features of the Draft Programme?

POPULATION GROWTH

As we have seen,[5] the objective of *world population stabilization* has not so far been formally retained by an official intergovernmental conference organized under the auspices of the United Nations. The Cairo Draft Programme points out that in 1985–1990, 44 per cent of the world's population were living in the 114 countries that had population growth rates of more than 2 per cent per annum. Those countries included nearly all countries in Africa, whose population doubling times average about 24 years, two-thirds of those in Asia and one-third of those in Latin America. On the other hand, 66 countries comprising 23 per cent of the world population, the majority of them in Europe, had growth rates of less than one per cent per annum. The first *objective* proposed in the Draft Programme's section on Population Growth and Structure,[6] is:

> To reduce disparities in national and regional population growth and *achieve stabilization of the world population as soon as possible*, fully respecting individual rights, aspirations and responsibilities, in order to create conditions for developmental sustainability at the community, national and global level. (emphasis added)

The Draft Programme's section on The Interrelationships Between Population, Sustained Economic Growth and Sustainable Development, argues[7] that indiscriminate pursuit of economic growth in nearly all countries 'with little or no regard for conserving natural resources or protecting the environment' is threatening or undermining the basis for progress by future generations. 'Substantial research also indicates that demographic pressures often exacerbate problems of environmental degradation and resource depletion and thus inhibit sustainable development.' The Draft Programme proposes as an *objective*:[8]

> To achieve and maintain *a harmonious balance between population, resources, food supplies, the environment, and development*, in order not to constrain the prospects for future generations to attain a decent quality of life. This implies reassessing and changing agricultural, industrial and energy policies, reducing excessive resource consumption, and *curbing unsustainable population growth and distribution.* (emphasis added)

How soon is population stabilization to be achieved? The Draft Programme does not tackle this issue head on, but rather suggests that, if the measures proposed in the Programme are taken, the result would be world population growth 'close to the United Nations low variant.' Paragraph 1.20 of the Draft Programme is worth quoting in full:

> During the remaining six years of this critical decade the world's nations by their actions or inactions will choose from among a range of alternative demographic futures. The most likely of these alternatives are foreseen in the low, medium and high variants of the United Nations populations projections. Looking ahead 20 years, these alternate projections range from a low of 7.27 billion people in 2015 to a high of 7.92 billion. The difference of 660 million people in the short span of 20 years is nearly equivalent to the current population of the African continent. By the year 2050, the United Nations low projection shows a world population of 7.8 billion, and the high projection a population of 12.5 billion. *Implementation of the goals*

and objectives contained in this 20-year Programme of Action, which address many of the fundamental population, health, education and development challenges facing the entire human community, would result in world population growth during this period and beyond at levels close to the United Nations low variant. (emphasis added)

SOME KEY ELEMENTS OF THE PROGRAMME OF ACTION

What are some of the specific elements of the proposed Programme of Action which, if implemented, could result in the attainment of the 'low variant' population levels (as indicated in Table 12.22, this would see world population peak at about 7.8 billion around the middle of the next century and decline thereafter)?

The draft put forward for the consideration of the Cairo Conference would commit the international community to quantitative goals in three areas that are described as 'mutually supporting and of critical importance to the achievement of other population and development objectives.' These areas are: education, especially for girls; infant, child and mortality reduction; and the provision of universal access to family planning and reproductive health services.

Education

The draft points out that in spite of notable efforts by countries around the globe that have appreciably expanded access to basic education, there are approximately 960 million illiterate adults in the world, of whom two-thirds are women. More than one-third of the world's adults, most of them women, have no access to printed knowledge, to new skills and technologies that would improve the quality of their lives and help them shape and adapt to social and economic change. One hundred and thirty million children are not enrolled in primary school and 70 per cent are girls.

> Beyond the achievement of the goal of universal primary education in all countries before 2015, all countries are urged to ensure the widest and earliest possible access by girls and women to secondary and higher levels of education, bearing in mind the need to improve the quality and relevance of that education.[9]

Infant and Maternal Mortality

In the last half century, expectation of life at birth in the world as a whole has increased by about 20 years and the risk of dying in the first year of life has been reduced by nearly two-thirds. The draft points out that there nevertheless remain entire national populations and sizeable population groups within many countries that are still subject to very high rates of morbidity and mortality, particularly among infants and young children and women in their child-bearing years. The draft proposes that:

> Countries should aim to achieve by 2015 a life expectancy at birth greater than 75 years; countries with the highest levels of mortality should aim to achieve by 2015 a life expectancy at birth greater than 70 years ...[10]

The draft points out that the number of infant deaths per 1,000 live births at the world level declined from 92 in 1970–1975 to about 62 in 1990–1995. For developed regions, the decline was from 22 to 12 deaths of children under one per 1,000 births, and for developing regions from 105 to 69 deaths per 1,000 births. The draft proposes that, over the next 20 years, the gap between average infant and child mortality rates should be 'substantially lowered', and major differences among socio-economic and ethnic groups should be eliminated.

> Countries should strive to reduce their infant and under-five mortality rates by one-third or to 50 and 70 per 1,000 live births, respectively, whichever is less, by 2000, with appropriate adaptation to the particular situation of each country: countries with the highest levels of mortality should aim in any case to achieve these levels by 2015. Countries with intermediate levels of mortality should aim to achieve by 2015 an infant mortality rate below 35 per 1,000 live births and an under-five mortality rate below 45 per 1,000. Countries which achieve these levels should strive to further lower them.

As far as maternal mortality was concerned, the draft points out that, at the global level, half a million women each year die from pregnancy-related causes, 99 per cent of them in developing countries. Rates of maternal mortality range from 700 per 100,000 live births in the least developed countries to about 26 per 100,000 live births in the developed regions. The draft proposes as an objective:

> To achieve a rapid and substantial reduction of maternal morbidity and mortality, reducing the differences observed between developing and developed countries, and eliminate all deaths from unsafe abortion.

The draft proposes that countries with intermediate levels of mortality should aim to achieve by the year 2015 a maternal mortality rate below 60 per 100,000 live births. Countries with the highest levels of mortality should aim to achieve by 2015 a maternal mortality rate below 75% per 100,000 live births.

The draft's treatment of the still controversial issue of abortion is clear and concise. It is estimated[11] that 50 million abortions occur each year, many of them unsafe. Mortality resulting from complications of poorly performed abortions accounts for a significant proportion of the annual 500,000 maternal deaths 'particularly in countries where abortions are unsafe and illegal.'[12]

> All governments, intergovernmental and non-governmental organizations are urged to deal openly and forthrightly with unsafe abortion as a major health concern. Governments are urged to assess the health impact of unsafe abortion, to reduce the need for abortion through expanded and improved family-planning services and to frame abortion laws and policies on the basis of a commitment to women's health and well being rather than on criminal codes and punitive measures. Prevention of unwanted pregnancies must always be given the highest priority and all attempts should be made to eliminate the need for abortion. In the case of rape and incest, women should have access to safe abortion services. Women who wish to terminate their pregnancies should have ready access to reliable information, compassionate counselling and services for the management of unsafe abortions.

As we shall see later, at the time of going to press it remained an open question whether this brave language would survive the April 1994 meeting of the ICPD's Preparatory Committee and the subsequent debate during the Cairo Conference itself. While the draft stops short of calling for the general legalization of abortion, there is no question that a new orientation, a new approach is being proposed, in particular with the reference to the need to frame abortion laws on the basis of a commitment to women's health rather than from a criminal or punitive perspective.

Family Planning

The draft Cairo document clearly states that the aim of family planning programmes must be to establish the widest possible freedom of choice in matters of procreation.[13] At the present time, about 55 per cent of couples in developing regions use some method of family-planning, a figure which represents a nearly five-fold increase since the 1960s. However, the full range of modern family-planning methods still remains unavailable to at least 350 million couples worldwide, many of whom say that they wish to space their children or prevent another pregnancy. Another 120 million additional women are potential users of a modern family-planning method given better information or more supportive husbands. The draft proposes as an *objective*:

> To help couples and individuals meet their reproductive goals in a framework that promotes good health and respects the dignity of all persons and their right to bear and raise children. To eliminate unwanted pregnancies and reduce the incidence of high-risk pregnancies. To make family-planning services available to all who need and want them. To improve the quality of family-planning services. To increase the participation of men in family-planning.

The draft proposes the target date of 2015 for all countries to provide 'universal access to the full range of safe and reliable family planning methods and to related reproductive health services.' The draft goes on to state:

> If all expressed unmet need for family planning were to be met over the next two decades, along with efforts to improve the status of women and reduce child mortality, it is expected that average contraceptive use would rise to an average of 69 per cent in the developing world, close to the levels seen in developed countries.[14]

Significant efforts would need to be made to improve the quality of care. Programmes should 'recognize that no one method is appropriate for all individuals and couples and ensure that women and men have information on and access to the widest possible range of safe and effective family planning methods ...'

POPULATION INFORMATION, EDUCATION AND COMMUNICATION (IEC)

The draft proposes as an *objective*

> To increase awareness, understanding and commitment at all levels of society so that individuals, groups, nations and the international community will take those actions necessary to address population issues within the context of sustainable development. To alter attitudes in favour of responsible behaviour in family life; to encourage individuals and couples to make informed choices and to take advantage of family-planning and reproductive health services.[15]

TECHNOLOGY, RESEARCH AND DEVELOPMENT

The draft also calls, predictably but – in this case – wholly justifiably, for more research. 'The international community must mobilize the full spectrum of basic, bio-medical, social and behavioural and programme related research on reproductive health and sexuality.'

Special priority should be given to the development and introduction of new fertility regulation methods that are safe, effective, affordable, suitable for different age groups and designed in response to users' needs. High priority should also be given to the development of new contraceptives for men …'[16]

RESOURCE MOBILIZATION AND ALLOCATION

The draft programme spells out in some detail the resource implications of implementing the measures outlined above.

–   Meeting unmet needs for family-planning information and services implies that the number of couples using contraceptives in the developing countries and countries in economic transition (countries of Eastern Europe and the former Soviet Union) will rise from some 550 million in 1995 to nearly 640 million in the year 2000 and 880 million in 2015. In 1993 US dollars, this would cost $10.2 billion in 2000, $11.5 billion in 2005, $12.6 billion in 2010 and $13.8 billion in 2105.

–   Adding an expanded package of activities for reproductive health care going beyond the usual components of family-planning programmes but still executable in a primary health care setting would cost an additional $1.2 billion in 2000, approximately $1.3 billion in both 2005 and 2010 and $1.4 billion in 2015. Similar amounts would be needed for a package of activities relating to the prevention of sexually transmitted diseases (including HIV infection).

–   An additional package of activities to meet expanded population data collection, analysis and dissemination, and policy formulation needs would add between $220 million and $670 million per year.

Overall, the Cairo Draft Programme of Action estimates that the projected resource requirements of national population programmes (in 1993 US dollars) would total: $13.2 billion in 2000, $14.4 billion in 2005, $16.1 billion in 2010 and $17.0 billion in 2015. The draft indicates: 'The savings in other sectoral costs and the benefits to be derived from these programmes far exceed these modest investments.'

The draft submitted to the April 1994 meeting of the ICPD's Preparatory Committee confidently expects that two-thirds of the costs of national population programmes will continue to be met by the countries themselves. But it also recognizes that developing countries are faced with increasing difficulties in allocating sufficient funds for their population programmes. Additional resources are urgently required, not only to satisfy the already large unmet need for reproductive health care including family-planning information and services, but also to respond to future increases in demand, to keep pace with the growing populations that need to be served, and to improve the quality and scope of the programmes. The draft estimates that the need for 'complementary' resource flows from donor countries would be (in 1993 US dollars): $4.4 billion in 2000, $4.8 billion in 2005, $5.3 billion in 2010 and $5.7 billion in 2015.

A BOLD, VISIONARY DOCUMENT

In sum, the draft Programme of Action circulated in early 1994 was a bold, even visionary document, setting out clear goals and commitments in a number of fields and stressing consistently two main themes: the need to integrate population and development issues and the need to emphasize what Dr Nafis Sadik, UNFPA's Executive Director and the Secretary-General of the ICPD, frequently referred to as the 'centrality of the individual'.

These two main themes were themselves increasingly interrelated, the intellectual synthesis being attained in phrases such as 'people-centred development' or the 'human development index' (first devised by the United Nations Development Programme) which, in addition to the classical macro-economic indicators such as GNP, GNP per capita etc., included social factors such as education, health and other forms of social infrastructure.

As far as the subject matter of this book is concerned, namely the progress made at national and international level in turning the tide of human fertility and bringing down *birth rates*, it is impossible to exaggerate the importance of the new approaches. Development programmes which emphasize health and education, especially female education, may not only be a useful adjunct to family planning programmes; they may actually be *the vital concomitant* if such programmes are to be successful quite apart from the other objectives which they are designed to meet.

Equally, stressing the 'centrality of the individual' is much more than a slogan. The enormous emphasis placed in the draft Programme of Action on individual rights and choices, particularly on what have come to be referred to as 'gender issues', has been one of the unique features in the preparation of the Cairo Conference and, as much as any other factor, has served to distinguish Cairo, 1994 from the previous world population conferences.

As delegates met in New York in April 1994 at the final meeting of the ICPD's Preparatory Committee (PrepCom) they had before them a new document which made it clear that, despite many expected modifications, the draft that would be sent to Cairo was certain to contain dozens of issues, actions and approaches never approved by earlier population conferences. The document, compiled by the ICPD secretariat, cross-referenced sections of the current draft of the programme of action with the World Population Plan of Action approved in Bucharest in 1974 and the recommendations of the Mexico City population conference in 1984. According to the secretariat's own count, the current draft contained 40 'new issues' and 22 'new specific actions' that had no precedent in the Bucharest or Mexico City documents. In addition, the current draft contained 78 'new approaches' that 'bring a distinctly innovative perspective' to issues previously considered.

In the introduction to the document, the secretariat said it was compiled in response to requests for highlighting what was described as 'the value added' of the ICPD draft programme of action. Most of the 'new issues' cited deal with gender issues, including: Exploitation of and violence against women (paragraph 4.7); women's time (4.8); preference for sons (4.14); female genital mutilation (4.19, 7.33); responsibility of men in sexual behaviour and family life (4.24); high-risk sexual behaviour of men (8.23).

Many of the 'new issues' in the ICPD draft expanded on the question of violence and exploitation of women and children. They deal specifically with: domestic violence, drugs and alcohol and sexual and child abuse and neglect (5.9); child exploitation and abuse, prostitution and child labour (6.8); protecting women and children from sexual exploitation and violence (7.32).

Related 'new specific actions' called for by the ICPD draft include: meeting the nutritional, reproductive health, educational and social needs of girls and young women (4.17); and ensuring that fathers meet their financial responsibilities (4.25).

Most of the remaining 'new issues' raised in the ICPD draft deal with sustainable development and the environment, reproductive health issues, and the needs of specific groups such as migrants, adolescents, the urban poor, indigenous peoples and people with disabilities.

New issues covered by the draft in the area of health care include: reproductive health needs of countries in transition (7.8); reproductive health care needs of migrants (7.9); sexually transmitted diseases (7.24, 7.25, 7.26); the need to base policies on a better understanding of sexuality and sexual behaviour (7.30); the reproductive health care needs of adolescents (7.38); the role of women as primary custodians of family health (8.6); HIV/AIDS (8.26, 8.27, 8.28); the need for ethical and technical standards in reproductive health research (12.12); and the need to involve the for-profit sector in contraceptive research (15,15, 15.16, 15.17).

Many of the 'new specific actions' called for in the ICPD draft also deal with research. They include: research on specific population and environmental issues (3.33); monitoring the impact of governmental policies on families (5.8); compiling comprehensive statistical databases (12.5); research on the linkages between population, the environment and economic development (12.16); research on ecosystems beset by population pressures (12.18); research on specific aspects of sexuality and gender (12.21); research on the causes of differentials in mortality rates of various groups (12.22).

The secretariat's analysis of the Cairo draft also showed dramatically increased emphasis on education, on the equitable representation of women in population policy-making, the elimination of gender stereotypes in society, and strict enforcement of laws setting a minimum age for marriage. New approaches in the current draft also called for focusing on the poorest families and increasing the earning power of poor women, and enforcing laws against child labour and child abuse. The draft called for establishment of a global facility for the procurement of contraceptives, for considering unsafe abortion as a major public health concern, and for making condoms more widely available.

CHILDREN BY CHOICE NOT CHANCE

By any yardstick this is an impressive inventory. It was a demonstration, in very practical terms, of what 'putting people first' or the 'centrality of the individual' could mean. All of these were, moreover, 'win–win' or 'no regret' actions or activities in the sense that they were not only of outstanding value and importance in and of themselves and likely to enhance the potential and capabilities of the individual and of his or her position in society; they were also likely to improve dramatically the prospects for achieving the goals of safe motherhood, responsible parenthood, family planning, fertility regulation, population stabilization or whatever. The point was made perhaps most succinctly by Baroness Chalker of Wallasey, the British Minister for Overseas Development, when she stressed that the underlying philosophy of the British aid programme in the field of population was 'children by choice not chance'. The achievement of demographic goals, whatever they may be, is inextricably linked to issues of gender empowerment, personal responsibility and expanded freedom of choice by individuals and couples. 'Countries whose governments establish a climate within which couples can exercise reproductive choice should eventually attain population growth rates that are in balance with their economic and natural resources.'[18]

THE THIRD PREPCOM

Looking back at the third PrepCom, it is satisfying to be able to report that many of the programmes and activities and actions put forward in the draft Programme of Action appear to have survived more or less intact. Take, for example, Section IV. As submitted to PrepCom, this section was entitled: Gender Equity and Empowerment of Women. It contained three sub-sections on (A) Empowerment and status of women; (B) The girl child; and (C) Male responsibilities and participation. Each of these sub-sections contained a range of commitments. Under sub-section A, para 4.4 read:

> countries should empower women and close the gender gap as soon as possible by:
>
> – encouraging women's participation at all levels of the political process in each community and society;
> – promoting the fulfilment of their potential through education and skill development, paying urgent attention to the elimination of illiteracy among adult women;
> – eliminating all legal, political and social barriers against women; assisting women to establish and realize their rights, particularly those that relate to sexual and reproductive health;
> – adopting concrete measures to improve women's ability to earn income, achieve economic self-reliance, inherit, own and dispose of property and have access to credit.[19]

There then followed a number of specific actions to be undertaken by those concerned (governments, employers etc.) to meet those objectives. A similar pattern was followed for the other programme areas in Section IV.

It might have been supposed, given the fact that in many countries women are as far from 'empowerment' as they ever were, that this section of the draft programme would emerge from the PrepCom, if it emerged at all, littered with square brackets denoting serious disagreements to be resolved (hopefully) at a later date. In practice this was not the case. The Earth Negotiations Bulletin of 7 April 1994 gives an illuminating summary of the debate which took place in PrepCom's Working Group II, the previous day. (The *Earth Negotiations Bulletin* appeared at regular intervals during the meetings of the Preparatory Committee for the ICPD both in written form and on various electronic information exchange networks. Though not an official publication of the United Nations, the Bulletin's concise and prompt summaries of debates were much appreciated by delegates–all the more so since United Nations verbatim records had long since been curtailed for budgetary reasons.)

IV. Gender Equality, Equity and Empowerment of Women:

> *A.* Empowerment and status of women: In the paragraph on objectives, Australia suggested making explicit reference to women's decision-making. In paragraph 4.4 (gender gap), New Zealand, the US and Australia called for a stronger statement on closing the gender gap. Indonesia suggested that literacy and development of skills are imperative for both men and women. Norway asked to make the issue of child care more central. The Holy See objected because of problems in the French and Spanish translations. Peru agreed with the text itself, but asked that translation problems be dealt with separately. Benin disagreed. Peru and US asked to strengthen the sub-paragraph on women's property rights.

In 4.5 (discrimination and sexual harassment), Australia suggested a more encompassing definition of sexual harassment. Switzerland called for an exclusive section on disaggregated gender data. Senegal asked for reference to the enforcement of anti-discrimination laws. Sweden proposed deleting the unrealistic deadline of 2015. Bolivia and Peru asked for a statement against discrimination based on proof of pregnancy. In 4.7 (violence against women), the US, Australia, Peru, New Zealand and Malaysia asked for stronger wording, including domestic violence against women, girls and boys. Croatia, Pakistan and Norway called for a phrase on war violence against women. In 4.8 (burden of women's work), Mexico and Australia wanted a statement on men's responsibility in domestic labour. In 4.9 (grassroots support for women), Nigeria and Mexico asked for clarity on the role of government.

B. The girl child: Venezuela objected to the title and asked that it include women. In paragraph 4.13 (objectives), the US called for more emphasis on the role of poverty in gender discrimination. Norway said that poverty does not always lead to gender preference. In 4.14 (gender discrimination), Switzerland, the US and Egypt added 'inheritance' to the list of gender inequalities. In 4.15 (education for girls), Switzerland and Sweden asked to delete the target date for education for all. Bangladesh asked to include vocational training for women. In 4.16 (school stereotypes), Switzerland and Norway asked to include sex selection as a form of discrimination. The US asked for a statement on change in teachers' attitudes and curricula. In 4.18 (minimum age of consent), the US, Madagascar and Switzerland asked for an increase in the minimum age of marriage. Norway and Cuba asked for reference to child pornography. In 4.19 (female genital mutilation), Indonesia and India objected to forcing any policy on a country. Bolivia called for a statement on the active prevention of genital mutilation. In 4.20 (education for girls), Sweden, Norway, Bangladesh and Bolivia called for reference opposing expulsion of pregnant girls from school. Burkina Faso and Morocco asked for international financial contribution to building schools.

C. Male Responsibilities and participation: In the objectives (4.22), Australia and Holy See asked to include women in the section on fertility and parental responsibility. In 4.23 (family responsibility), Bangladesh and India asked for a more emphatic statement on men's participation. In 4.25 (child support), numerous countries asked for mechanisms to enforce child support payments.

The above extract gives something of the flavour of the debate on this Section. The generally positive tone was on the whole maintained during later discussions. On April 13, for example, at a further meeting of Working Group II, Malaysia and most Muslim delegations objected to 'equal inheritance for women'. However, after informal deliberation with the Vice-Chair of Working Group II, they eventually agreed that women could 'receive' property on an equal basis with men.[20]

In the final outcome, Section IV was renamed 'Gender Equality, Equity and Empowerment of Women.' At the request of the European Union (formerly the European Community), the reference to the goal of achieving universal primary education for all by the year 2015 (para 4.15) remains in square brackets (for discussion at Cairo) pending the discussion of goals. The only other brackets in this chapter are around the terms 'reproductive and sexual health', at the request of the Holy See. This particular difficulty, as we shall see, was part of the Vatican's general concern with the preparations for the ICPD and should not be construed as an attack on the overall objectives of Section IV which the Vatican, as most other delegations, appeared to endorse warmly.

A FUNNY THING HAPPENED ON THE WAY TO CAIRO

The Earth Times, a newspaper produced by the Earth Times Foundation, ran the following editorial by Robert S. Hirschfield on April 21 as the PrepCom finally wound down after a long and exhausting session.

> A funny thing has happened on the way to Cairo. During PrepCom3 for the International Conference on Population and Development, the scope of this world meeting has metamorphosed to include the subject of women's rights. The addition of this third element was unplanned but not accidental. It has come about quite naturally, indeed inevitably, as the PrepCom's mostly female participants have gotten more deeply involved in fashioning an Action Programme. For in this process it has become increasingly apparent that the way to attain population stabilization is not just providing more information, services and devices related to family planning. What is needed, rather, is a basic global change in the status of women. Thus issues like guaranteeing that girls are accorded the same educational opportunities as boys, that legal or cultural barriers to female ownership of property are removed, and that other similar areas of inequity which relegate women to an inferior position are addressed, become matters of world attention.
>
> Interestingly, the initial stimulus for this new approach at PrepCom 3 came from a man – the head of the American delegation, State Department Counsellor Timothy Wirth – who outlined a seven-point agenda designed to achieve the empowerment, employment and involvement of women, at the beginning of the session. With women present in unprecedented numbers at the PrepCom, serving on national delegations as well as representing a record number of nongovernmental organizations, this call for change has been answered enthusiastically. Moreover, it has been aided by the actions of Secretary General Nafis Sadik and Chairman Fred Sai in opening PrepCom proceedings to allow for significant participation by eager NGOs. The result has been an expansion of scope and a change of focus that has had the effect of relating population problems to both women's rights and social development, thus linking the Cairo conference to last year's Vienna meeting on Human Rights and to next year's Copenhagen Social Summit. It also sets the stage for making Cairo itself an historic event.
>
> How much of this new approach to the way the world works will be reflected in the final document for ICPD remains to be seen.

The *Earth Times* Editorial cited above goes on to say:

> If family planning and population stabilization are placed in the context of achieving gender equality, and if effective programmes to attain that goal can be approved in Cairo, the International Conference on Population and Development will be a landmark in global affairs.

HOW IMPORTANT ARE THE 'IFS'?

Just how big and important are the 'ifs?'

On the positive side, it is clear from the meetings of the Preparatory Committee that the United States is once again ready to play a leading role in the population field and that it has firmly put behind it the doldrums of the 'Mexico' years. Over the last two years the United States has increased its overseas population budget by US $152 million to a total of $502 million. The Clinton Administration has asked Congress for

$585 million for population assistance in 1995 and plans to reach $1.2 billion by the year 2000. Japan has announced that it will expand its funding of population and AIDS-related programmes to US $3 billion over the next seven years. Germany has also announced a substantial increase in its population assistance and other nations, such as Norway – a traditional high donor of development aid, including population assistance – have indicated that they will maintain the priority accorded to such programmes.

The fact that 'new and additional money' is clearly on the table is psychologically extremely important. Though the bulk of the resources for population, family-planning and related activities will continue to come from the developing countries themselves, the perceived readiness of donor nations to contribute to this effort – *and to announce this in good time*–will make a major difference to the climate in which the final Cairo text is negotiated. And while for some countries, such as China, external assistance may be a very small proportion of total spending (some $15 million out of an annual total of $1.1 billion), for others the question of extra financial resources may be crucial. As the delegate of Bangla Desh put it in his statement to the Preparatory Committee on April 5th:

> Mobilization of new and additional resources at international level is crucial in order to achieve the goals set forth in the Programme of Action. The less-developed countries (LDCs) should receive increased technical and financial support. The seriousness with which we approach the Programme of Action will have to be matched by equal seriousness for new and additional resources mobilization and its allocation.

It remains to be seen whether other donor nations, particularly those of the European Union, will be ready to match the United States, Japan, Germany and Norway etc. with a clear commitment to increased funding. Judging by the performance of the European Union at PrepCom, where EU delegates sprinkled square brackets like confetti whenever the question of financial resources was discussed, there is still some way to go before this issue is resolved. This is all the more disappointing – and ironic – in view of the fact that it has often been EU delegations who have pushed for a steady expansion in the very concept of population activities to include the wider notions of reproductive health, female education and even women's rights in general. Seen from the perspective of the developing countries, this is a situation where either the existing butter will be spread more thinly or there will have to be more butter.

THE POSITION OF THE VATICAN

As this book goes to press, one other major question mark hangs over the forthcoming Cairo Conference: the position of the Vatican.

Two weeks before PrepCom began Dr Nafis Sadik had an interview with Pope John Paul II in the Vatican. Unusually, the Vatican issued a statement on that occasion recapitulating the message which His Holiness had conveyed to his visitor. Ironically, the points of departure for the Vatican on the one hand and for UNFPA on the other are not a million miles apart. The Pope told Dr Sadik:

> Today, the duty to safeguard the family demands that particular attention be given to securing for husband and wife the liberty to decide responsibly, free from all social or legal coercion, the number of children they will have and the spacing of their births. It should not be the intent of governments or other agencies to decide

for couples but, rather, to create the social conditions which will enable them to make appropriate decisions in the light of their responsibilities to God, to themselves, to the society of which they are a part, and to the objective moral order. What the Church calls 'responsible parenthood' is not a question of unlimited procreation or lack of awareness of what is involved in rearing children, but rather the empowerment of couples to use their inviolable liberty wisely and responsibly, taking into account social and demographic realities as well as their own situation and legitimate desires, in the light of objective moral criteria. All propaganda and misinformation directed at persuading couples that they must limit their family to one or two children should be steadfastly avoided, and couples that generously choose to have large families are to be supported.

Give or take a nuance here or there it is not impossible to imagine such a paragraph being penned in the offices of the International Planned Parenthood Federation. However, though the starting points may be more or less the same, the tracks soon begin to differ. The Pope went on to tell Dr Sadik:

In defense of the human person, the Church stands opposed to the imposition of limits on family size, and to the promotion of methods of limiting births which separate the unitive and procreative dimensions of marital intercourse, which are contrary to the moral law inscribed in the human heart, or which constitute an assault on the sacredness of life. Thus, sterilization, which is more and more promoted as a method of family planning, because of its finality and its potential for the violation of human rights, especially of women, is clearly unacceptable; it poses a most grave threat to human dignity and liberty when promoted as part of a population policy. Abortion, which destroys existing human life, is a heinous evil, and it is never an acceptable method of family planning, as was recognized by consensus at the Mexico City United Nations International Conference on Population (1984).

The Pope emphasized his unease with regard to the preparations for the Cairo. It was not just a question of the references to abortion and to fertility regulation. 'Marriage is ignored, as if it were something of the past. An institution as natural, universal and fundamental as the family cannot be manipulated without causing serious damage to the fabric and stability of society.'

HOW MANY DIVISIONS HAS THE POPE?

The Pope's powerful restatement of his position just before PrepCom was not the most auspicious sign – hardly a benediction – though those who knew the man and his record probably expected no less. Pope John Paul II has never been afraid to stand up for what he sees as the truth. What did, however, take many people by surprise was the energy, even the ferocity, with which the Vatican defended its position at PrepCom 3. Nor was the Holy See alone. Honduras, Nicaragua, Malta, Benin, Morocco, Guatemala and Argentina all lined up at various times and in various ways in support of the Vatican's stance. Terms like 'family planning' and 'reproductive health' which few thought were still contentious given national and international developments over the past twenty or thirty years were suddenly questioned, challenged and – when disagreement persisted – placed in square brackets. Though it is true that the Vatican had officially disassociated itself from the Bucharest and Mexico consensus, other Catholic countries had not. It began to seem possible, even probable that not only would the Holy See refuse to sign up to the Cairo Final Document; this time round at least a handful of other countries might join it in abstaining.

In UN terms, a consensus exists as long as countries do not oppose and abstention does not count as opposition. But a consensus document with only one abstention certainly carries more weight than a document with half a dozen or more abstentions. Worse still, it is highly probable that in the process of trying to reach agreement, to avoid abstentions (or outright opposition), the texts themselves may be significantly weakened. At the time of going to press, the preparations for the ICPD appeared to face precisely this danger. So far from Cairo advancing the international consensus on population, there seemed to be the real prospect that at least in some areas it might be rolled back.

The phrase 'couples and individuals', for example, had been negotiated with great difficulty at Bucharest in 1974.[21] Paragraph 14(f) of the *World Population Plan of Action* stated that 'All couples and individuals have the basic right to decide freely and responsibly the number and spacing of their children and to have the information, education and the means to do so...'[22] This language, including the term 'couples and individuals' was repeated in Recommendation 30 of the Mexico City consensus document.[23] The draft Programme of Action as submitted to PrepCom 3 referred to both 'couples and individuals' (para. 7.12) and 'individuals and couples' (7.15).

This was not just a semantic issue. It could affect the well-being of hundreds of millions. As Dr Halfdan Mahler, the Secretary-General of the International Planned Parenthood Federation, put it in his speech to PrepCom 3:

> In meeting the unmet demand we must recognize that the term 'unmet need' is a broad one that means different things to different people at different times. Women's perspectives and realities, when attempting to quantify and qualify unmet needs and demands in so-called family planning, have too often been ignored. For example, surveys have traditionally addressed only married women of reproductive age, leaving out the unmet needs of hundreds of millions who are active, or potentially so, but are not covered by these surveys. *For IPPF, unmet needs and demands refer not only to the hundreds of millions of couples, most of them poor and marginalized, living in urban slums and remote rural areas, who do not presently have access to acceptable and affordable quality family planning as an integral part of sexual and reproductive health care. It also refers to the hundreds of millions of young women and men who, at present, are excluded from such sexual and reproductive health care.* (emphasis added)

Globally, there are about 500 million adolescents aged 15 to 19, most of whom will become sexually active before age 20. The evidence appears to indicate that young people (who would be included in the term 'individuals') seldom use contraceptives and are at high risk of pregnancy, AIDS and other sexually-transmitted diseases (STDs). Yet in most countries, youth are not reached by existing reproductive health services. Recently, the World Health Organization (WHO) reviewed 35 studies in several countries, concluding that appropriate sexuality education does not encourage earlier initiation of intercourse, but often delays sexual activity and leads to safer sexual practices. WHO and other studies also show that access to contraceptive services is not associated with earlier sexual activity.[24]

Seen in this perspective, the Holy See's attempts to remove the word 'individuals' or Honduras' effort to replace the term 'couples and individuals' with the term 'men and women' appear bizarre, even grotesque. And though these delegations appear finally to have agreed to have let the phrase stand unbracketed for the time being, their reservations have been expressed for the record and there is no guarantee that the controversy will not be revived at Cairo.

ABORTION

As far as the question of abortion is concerned, no such spirit of compromise – if such it can be called – was on offer. When Section VII on Reproductive Rights, Sexual and Reproductive Health and Family Planning was considered by the Plenary on the final day of the PrepCom, Costa Rica, Argentina, Malta, Venezuela, Morocco and Ecuador argued passionately that they could not agree to any terms unless these were clearly defined so as to exclude abortion. That blanket reservation therefore extended to many of the expressions currently to be found in the population and family planning lexicon, including abortion, safe abortion, legal abortion, unsafe abortion, illegal abortion, fertility regulation, reproductive health, sexual health, safe motherhood, reproductive rights and even the phrase 'family planning' itself.

On April 22, 1994, the day PrepCom 3 ended, a revealing article by Susan Chira appeared in the *New York Times*. 'Pope John Paul II has campaigned vigorously against the United Nations plan,' Chira wrote. 'The Vatican is particularly troubled by the United States' shift on abortion since the last major population conference, in Mexico City in 1984, when Washington declared it would not give aid to family-planning programmes that offered abortion. President Clinton reversed that policy when he was elected.'

Susan Chira went on to write:

> '"It would be very sad if this were to become a conference about abortion" said Monsignor Diarmuid Martin, the Vatican delegate. 'The United States wants the question of abortion as a fundamental dimension of population policy throughout the world to be a major theme of the conference.'
>
> Timothy E. Worth, the United States representative to the conference, said: 'I think it is unfair that any group would say the US is out promoting abortion. That simply is not true. The US has been a wonderfully moderating influence. Clearly we will not get agreement on our position, which is that abortion should be safe legal and rare.'

* * * * *

At the time this last chapter was being written, the International Conference on Population and Development was still in the future. Four months or so from now, the final gavel will descend in Cairo and it will be clear at that moment just how much of the Draft Programme of Action has been retained as presented and how much has suffered significant modification as a result of the laborious intergovernmental process.

As noted above, though there are still some major disagreements to be resolved (particularly as far as the Vatican and its supporters are concerned), there has already been a great deal of progress towards an agreed text. Dr Nafis Sadik, the ICPD's Secretary-General, was herself optimistic about the outcome of PrepCom 3, referring to the 'warm reception the Draft Programme of Action received from the vast majority of delegates.' If that optimism turns out to be warranted, if the Cairo programme is finally adopted more or less in the form presented in January, then it will be fair to say that the international community has at last (and not before time) reached that definitive consensus on population which has so far eluded it. Most important of all, if the commitments as far as the allocation of resources – both external and domestic – are concerned, are actually firm and 'bankable', if in other words the Cairo Programme is given the political and material backing to put it into effect, there must be every prospect of attaining the goals which are proposed, both quantitative and qualitative (including, therefore, the goals relating to infant and maternal mortality, female education, reproductive health, family planning and, ultimately, population stabilization).

The challenge is great, but not insuperable. Agreeing a plan of action is one thing; actually carrying it out is something else. Success must depend in the end not just on the allocation of resources or on the creation or strengthening of appropriate institutions, but on the personal commitment of individual people.

Behind each demographic statistic – past, present and future – are real individuals, real couples, real families. The true heroes of this story are of necessity anonymous since they are the hundreds of millions of men and women, adolescents and children, who have participated over the last three decades in population and development programmes and who must continue to do so in ever-increasing measure in the future.

Oxford, England, May 1, 1994

NOTES

1. A/CONF.171/PC/5
2. E/Conf.60/19. See Chapter 6
3. E/CONF.76/19. See Chapter 8
4. See *The Earth Summit: The United Nations Conference on Environment and Development* (UNCED), Stanley P. Johnson, Graham and Trotman/Martinus Nijhoff, 1993, p. 126.
5. See, for example, Chapter 8 and Mr Rafael Salas' speech to the International Conference on Population, Mexico City, August 1994.
6. op. cit. para 6.3.
7. op. cit. para 3.21.
8. op. cit. para 3.23.
9. op. cit. para 3.16.
10. op. cit. para 8.5.
11. op. cit. para 1.10.
12. op. cit. para 8.15.
13. op. cit. para 7.10.
14. op. cit. para 7.13.
15. op. cit. para 11.5.
16. op. cit. para 12.10.
17. op. cit. para 13.14–13.20.
18. *Children by Choice not Chance*, UK Overseas Development Administration, August 1991.
19. op. cit. para 4.4
20. *Earth Negotiations Bulletin*, Vol. 6, No. 23 of 14 April 1994.
21. See World Population and the United Nations: Challenge and Response, Stanley P. Johnson, Cambridge University Press, 1987, p. 116.
22. E/CONF.60/19, p. 7
23. E/CONF.76/19, p. 24
24. See *Youth at Risk: Meeting the Sexual Health Needs of Adolescents,* by Stephanie L. Koontz and Shanti R. Conly, Population Action International, April 1994.

Annex A – Population and Social Indicators

Population Indicators

Country or territory	Population (millions) 1992	Population (millions) 2025	Average growth rate (%) 1990–95	Birth rate per 1000 1990–95	Death rate per 1000 1990–95	Life expectancy 1990–95	Infant Mortality per 1000 1990–95	Per cent urban 1992	Urban growth rate (%) 1990–95	Fertility rate per woman 1990–95
World total	55,4790.0	8,472.4	1.7	26	9	65	62	44	2.7	3.3
More developed regions (‡)	1,224.7	1,403.3	0.5	14	10	75	12	73	0.9	1.9
Less developed regions (+)	4,254.3	7,069.2	2.0	29	9	62	69	35	3.7	3.6
AFRICA	681.7	1,582.5	2.9	4.3	14	53	95	33	46	6.0
Eastern Africa (1)	207.4	516.0	3.1	48	16	49	108	20	5.8	6.8
Burundi	5.8	13.4	2.9	46	17	48	106	6	5.6	6.8
Ethiopia	53.0	130.7	3.1	49	18	47	122	13	4.9	7.0
Kenya	25.2	63.8	3.4	44	10	59	66	25	6.8	6.3
Madagascar	12.8	33.7	3.3	445	13	55	110	25	6.1	6.6
Malawi	10.4	24.9	3.3	54	21	44	142	12	6.2	7.6
Mauritius (2)	1.1	1.4	1.0	18	7	70	21	41	1.1	2.0
Mozambique	14.9	36.3	2.8	45	18	47	147	30	8.1	6.5
Rwanda	7.5	20.6	3.4	52	18	46	110	6	5.2	8.5
Somalia	9.2	23.4	3.2	50	19	47	122	25	4.5	7.0
Uganda	18.7	45.9	3.0	51	21	42	104	12	5.5	7.3
United Rep. of Tanzania	27.8	74.2	3.4	48	15	51	102	22	6.7	6.8
Zambia	8.6	21.0	2.8	46	18	44	84	42	3.4	6.3
Zimbabwe	10.6	22.9	3.0	41	11	56	59	30	5.5	5.3
Middle Africa (3)	75.1	190.0	3.1	46	15	51	96	33	4.7	6.5
Angola	9.9	26.6	3.7	51	19	46	124	30	6.5	7.2
Cameroon	12.2	29.3	2.8	41	12	56	63	42	5.1	5.7
Central African Republic	3.2	7.0	2.6	44	18	47	105	48	4.4	6.2
Chad	5.8	12.9	2.7	44	18	48	122	34	6.0	5.9
Congo	2.4	5.8	3.0	45	15	52	82	42	4.5	6.3
Gabon	1.2	2.9	3.3	43	16	54	94	47	5.3	5.3
Zaire	39.9	104.5	3.2	47	15	52	93	28	4.0	6.7

Population Indicators (*continued*)

Country or territory	Population (millions) 1992	Population (millions) 2025	Average growth rate (%) 1990–95	Birth rate per 1000 1990–95	Death rate per 1000 1990–95	Life expectancy 1990–95	Infant Mortality per 1000 1990–95	Per cent urban 1992	Urban growth rate (%) 1990–95	Fertility rate per woman 1990–95
Northern Africa (4)	147.7	280.4	2.5	34	9	61	69	45	3.5	4.7
Algeria	26.3	51.8	2.7	34	7	66	61	53	4.3	4.9
Egypt	54.8	93.5	2.2	31	9	62	57	44	2.6	4.1
Libyan Arab Jamahiriya	4.9	12.9	3.5	42	8	63	68	84	4.4	6.4
Morocco	26.3	47.5	2.4	32	8	63	68	47	2.4	4.4
Sudan	26.7	60.6	2.8	42	14	52	99	23	4.6	6.0
Tunisia	8.4	13.4	2.1	27	6	68	43	57	3.2	3.4
Southern Africa	45.3	85.3	2.4	32	9	63	55	47	3.3	4.2
Botswana	1.3	2.9	38	9	61	60	27	7.4	5.1	
Lesotho	1.8	3.8	2.5	34	10	61	79	21	6.1	4.7
Namibia	1.5	3.8	3.2	43	11	59	70	29	5.5	6.0
South Africa	39.8	73.2	2.4	31	9	63	53	50	3.1	4.1
Western Africa (5)	206.2	510.8	3.1	46	15	51	102	35	5.4	6.5
Benin	4.9	12.4	3.1	49	18	46	87	40	5.0	7.1
Burkina Faso	9.5	22.6	2.8	47	18	48	118	17	8.2	6.5
Côte d'Ivoire	12.9	37.9	3.7	50	15	52	91	42	5.3	7.4
Ghana	16.0	38.0	3.0	42	12	56	81	35	4.4	6.0
Guinea	6.1	15.1	3.0	51	20	45	134	27	5.9	7.0
Guinea-Bissau	1.0	2.0	2.1	43	21	44	140	21	4.5	5.8
Liberia	2.8	7.2	3.3	47	14	55	126	47	5.6	6.8
Mali	9.8	24.6	3.2	51	19	46	159	25	5.8	7.1
Mauritania	2.1	5.0	2.9	46	18	48	117	49	5.8	6.5
Niger	8.3	21.3	3.3	51.	19	47	124	21	6.9	7.1
Nigeria	115.7	285.8	3.1	45	14	53	96	37	5.5	6.4
Senegal	7.7	17.1	2.7	43	16	49	80	41	4.0	6.1
Sierra Leone	4.4	9.8	2.7	48	22	43	143	34	5.1	6.5
Togo	3.8	9.4	3.2	45	13	55	85	29	4.9	6.6

Population Indicators (continued)

Country or territory	Population (millions) 1992	Population (millions) 2025	Average growth rate (%) 1990–95	Birth rate per 1000 1990–95	Death rate per 1000 1990–95	Life expectancy 1990–95	Infant Mortality per 1000 1990–95	Per cent urban 1992	Urban growth rate (%) 1990–95	Fertility rate per woman 1990–95
ASIA	3,233.0	4,900.3	1.8	26	8	65	62	32	3.5	3.2
Eastern Asia (6)	1,387.9	1,762.2	1.3	20	7	72	26	35	3.4	2.1
China	1,188.0	1,539.8	1.4	21	7	71	27	28	4.4	2.2
Dem. Peo. Rep. of Korea	22.6	33.3	1.9	24	5	71	24	60	2.4	2.4
Hong Kong	5.8	6.4	0.8	13	6	78	6	94	1.0	1.4
Japan	124.5	127.0	0.4	11	7	79	5	77	0.6	1.7
Mongolia	2.3	4.6	34	8	64	60	59	3.7	4.6	
Republic of Korea	44.2	50.3	0.8	16	6	71	21	74	2.3	1.8
Southeastern Asia	461.5	715.6	1.9	28	8	63	55	30	3.8	3.4
Cambodia	8.8	16.7	2.5	39	14	51	116	12	4.6	4.5
Indonesia	191.2	283.3	1.8	27	8	63	65	30	4.3	3.1
Lao People's Dem. Rep.	4.5	9.4	3.0	45	15	51	97	20	6.3	6.7
Malaysia	18.8	31.3	2.4	29	5	71	14	45	4.3	3.6
Myanmar	43.7	75.6	2.1	33	11	58	81	25	3.3	4.2
Philippines	65.2	105.1	2.1	30	7	65	40	44	3.5	3.9
Singapore	2.8	3.3	1.0	16	6	74	8	100	1.0	1.7
Thailand	56.1	72.3	1.3	21	6	69	26	23	4.0	2.2
Viet Nam	69.5	117.0	2.0	29	9	64	36	20	2.9	3.9
Southern Asia	1,244.3	2,135.8	2.2	32	10	59	90	27	3.5	4.3
Afghanistan	19.1	45.8	6.7	53	22	43	162	19	8.9	6.9
Bangladesh	119.3	223.3	2.4	38	14	53	108	18	6.0	4.7
Bhutan	1.6	3.4	2.3	40	17	48	129	6	6.2	5.9
India	879.5	1,393.9	1.9	29	10	60	88	26	2.9	3.9
Iran (Islamic Republic of)	61.6	144.6	2.7	40	7	67	40	58	4.0	6.0
Nepal	20.6	40.1	2.5	37	13	54	99	12	7.2	5.5
Pakistan	124.8	259.6	2.7	41	10	59	98	33	4.4	6.2
Sri Lanka	17.7	24.7	1.3	21	6	72	24	22	2.2	2.5

Population Indicators (continued)

Country or territory	Population (millions) 1992	Population (millions) 2025	Average growth rate (%) 1990–95	Birth rate per 1000 1990–95	Death rate per 1000 1990–95	Life expectancy 1990–95	Infant Mortality per 1000 1990–95	Per cent urban 1992	Urban growth rate (%) 1990–95	Fertility rate per woman 1990–95
Western Asia (7)	139.3	286.6	2.7	34	7	66	54	65	4.2	4.7
Iraq	19.3	46.3	3.2	39	7	66	58	73	4.0	5.7
Israel	5.1	8.1	4.7	21	7	77	9	92	5.0	2.9
Jordan	4.3	10.8	3.4	40	5	68	36	69	4.5	5.7
Kuwait	2.0	2.8	-5.8	28	2	75	14	93	-5.4	3.7
Lebanon	2.8	4.5	2.0	27	7	69	34	86	2.8	3.1
Oman	1.6	4.7	3.6	40	5	70	30	12	7.4	6.7
Saudi Arabia	15.9	40.4	3.4	36	5	69	31	78	4.2	6.4
Syrian Arab Republic	13.3	35.3	3.6	42	6	67	39	51	4.5	6.1
Turkey	58.4	92.9	2.0	28	7	67	56	64	4.6	3.5
United Arab Emirates	1.7	2.8	2.3	21	4	71	22	82	3.1	4.5
Yemen	12.5	34.2	3.5	48	14	53	106	31	6.7	7.2
EUROPE	512.0	541.8	0.3	13	11	75	10	74	0.7	1.7
Eastern Europe	96.9	107.2	0.2	14	11	71	16	64	1.0	2.0
Bulgaria	9.0	8.8	-0.2	13	12	72	14	69	0.6	1.8
Czechoslovakia	15.7	17.9	0.3	14	11	73	10	79	1.2	2.0
Hungary	10.5	10.4	-0.2	12	14	70	14	66	0.9	1.8
Poland	38.4	43.8	0.3	14	10	72	15	63	1.0	2.1
Romania	23.3	26.3	0.3	16	11	70	23	55	1.2	2.1
Northern Europe (8)	92.8	97.8	0.2	14	11	76	7	83	0.4	1.9
Denmark	5.2	5.1	0.2	12	12	76	7	85	0.4	1.7
Estonia	1.6	1.7	-0.2	14	12	71	14	72	0.2	2.0
Finland	5.0	5.2	0.3	13	10	76	6	60	0.4	1.8
Ireland	3.5	3.6	-0.2	14	9	75	7	58	0.3	2.1
Latvia	2.7	2.8	-0.3	14	12	71	10	72	0.2	2.0

Population Indicators (continued)

Country or territory	Population (millions) 1992	Population (millions) 2025	Average growth rate (%) 1990–95	Birth rate per 1000 1990–95	Death rate per 1000 1990–95	Life expectancy 1990–95	Infant Mortality per 1000 1990–95	Per cent urban 1992	Urban growth rate (%) 1990–95	Fertility rate per woman 1990–95
Northern Europe (8) contd										
Lithuania	3.8	4.1	0.2	15	10	73	10	70	1.2	2.0
Norway	4.3	4.9	0.5	15	11	77	8	76	1.1	2.0
Sweden	8.7	9.5	0.5	14	11	78	6	84	0.7	2.1
United kingdom	57.7	60.3	0.2	14	11	76	7	89	0.3	1.9
Southern Europe (9)	144.6	143.2	0.2	11	10	76	12	67	0.9	1.5
Albania	3.3	4.5	0.8	23	5	73	23	36	1.7	2.7
Greece	10.2	10.1	0.3	10	10	78	8	63	1.1	1.5
Italy	57.8	56.2	0.1	10	10	77	8	70	0.5	1.3
Portugal	9.9	10.1	0.0	12	10	75	12	35	1.6	1.5
Spain	39.1	40.6	0.2	11	9	78	7	79	0.7	1.4
Yugoslavia (former)	23.9	26.1	0.3	14	10	72	23	58	1.9	1.9
Western Europe (10)	177.6	188.7	0.4	12	11	76	7	80	0.6	1.6
Austria	7.8	8.3	0.4	12	11	76	8	59	1.2	1.5
Belgium	10.0	9.9	0.1	12	11	76	8	96	0.2	1.7
France	57.2	60.8	0.4	13	10	77	7	73	0.4	1.8
Germany	80.3	83.9	0.4	11	11	76	7	86	0.7	1.5
Netherlands	15.2	17.7	0.7	14	9	77	7	89	0.8	1.7
Switzerland	6.8	7.7	0.7	13	10	78	7	62	1.5	1.7
LATIN AMERICA	457.7	701.6	1.8	26	7	68	47	73	2.6	3.1
Caribbean (11)	34.6	50.4	1.4	24	8	69	47	60	2.3	2.8
Cuba	10.8	13.0	0.9	17	7	76	14	74	1.5	1.9
Dominican Republic	7.5	11.4	2.0	28	6	68	57	62	3.4	3.3
Haiti	6.8	13.1	2.0	35	12	57	86	30	4.1	4.8
Puerto Rico	3.6	4.7	0.9	18	7	75	13	75	1.6	2.2
Trinidad and Tobago	1.3	1.8	1.1	23	6	71	18	65	1.6	2.7

Population Indicators (continued)

Country or territory	Population (millions) 1992	Population (millions) 2025	Average growth rate (%) 1990–95	Birth rate per 1000 1990–95	Death rate per 1000 1990–95	Life expectancy 1990–95	Infant Mortality per 1000 1990–95	Per cent urban 1992	Urban growth rate (%) 1990–95	Fertility rate per woman 1990–95
Central America (12)	118.6	199.2	2.2	30	6	69	39	67	3.0	3.5
Costa Rica	3.2	5.6	2.4	26	4	76	14	48	3.6	3.1
El Salvador	5.4	9.7	2.2	33	7	66	46	45	3.2	4.0
Guatemala	9.7	21.7	2.9	39	8	65	49	40	4.0	5.4
Honduras	5.5	11.5	3.0	37	7	66	60	45	4.9	4.9
Mexico	88.2	137.5	2.1	28	5	70	35	74	2.8	3.2
Nicaragua	4.0	9.1	3.7	40	7	67	52	61	4.9	5.0
Panama	2.5	3.9	1.9	25	5	73	21	54	2.7	2.9
South America (13)	304.5	451.9	1.7	24	7	67	51	76	2.4	2.9
Argentina	33.1	45.5	1.2	20	9	71	29	87	1.5	2.8
Bolivia	7.5	14.1	2.4	34	9	61	85	52	3.8	4.6
Brazil	154.1	219.7	1.6	23	7	66	57	76	2.5	2.7
Chile	13.6	19.8	1.6	23	6	72	17	85	1.9	2.7
Colombia	33.4	49.4	1.7	24	6	69	37	71	2.5	2.7
Ecuador	11.1	18.6	2.3	30	7	67	57	58	3.8	3.6
Paraguay	4.5	9.2	2.7	33	6	67	47	49	4.1	4.3
Peru	22.5	37.4	2.0	29	8	65	76	71	2.8	3.6
Uruguay	3.1	3.7	0.6	17	10	72	20	89	0.9	2.3
Venezuela	20.2	32.7	2.1	26	5	70	33	91	2.7	3.1
NORTHERN AMERICA (14)	282.7	360.5	1.1	16	9	76	8	76	1.3	2.0
Canada	27.4	38.4	1.4	14	8	77	7	78	1.6	1.8
United States of America	255.2	322.0	1.0	16	9	76	8	76	1.3	2.1

Population Indicators (continued)

Country or territory	Population (millions) 1992	Population (millions) 2025	Average growth rate (%) 1990–95	Birth rate per 1000 1990–95	Death rate per 1000 1990–95	Life expectancy 1990–95	Infant Mortallity per 1000 1990–95	Per cent urban 1992	Urban growth rate (%) 1990–95	Fertility rate per woman 1990–95
OCEANIA	27.5	41.3	11.5	19	8	73	22	71	1.6	2.5
Australia-New Zealand	21.1	29.5	1.3	15	8	77	7	85	1.4	1.9
Australia (15)	17.6	25.2	1.4	15	8	77	7	85	1.4	1.9
New Zealand	3.5	4.3	0.9	17	8	76	8	84	1.0	2.1
Melanesia (16)	5.5	10.2	2.2	32	9	59	49	21	3.8	4.6
Papau New Guinea	4.1	7.8	2.3	33	11	56	54	17	4.7	4.9
USSR (former) (17)	284.5	344.5	0.5	16	10	70	21	67	1.1	2.3

Demographic estimates for the newly independent states of the former USSR	Population (thousands) 1992	Growth rate (%) 1990–92	Crude birth rate per 1000	Crude death rate per 1000	Life expectancy at brith (years)	Infant Mortallity per 1000	Fertility rate per woman 1990–95
Armenia	3.489	2.3	23	6	71	23	2.6
Azerbaijan	7.283	0.8	27	7	70	28	2.8
Bearus	10.295	0.1	16	10	72	13	2.0
Georgia	5.471	0.1	18	9	72	22	2.3
Kazakhstan	17.048	0.8	24	8	69	28	3.0
Kyrgyzstan	4.518	1.3	31	7	68	36	4.0
Republic of Moldova	4.362	-0.0	21	10	68	24	2.6
Russian Federation	149.003	0.2	16	11	70	19	2.1
Tadjikistan	5.587	2.5	40	7	70	46	5.4
Turkmenistan	3.861	2.5	36	8	65	54	4.6
Ukraine	52.158	0.2	14	12	71	14	2.0

SOCIAL INDICATORS

Country of territory	Adult literacy M/F 1990	Secondary school enrolment M/F 1986–90	Births attended by health worker (%) 1983–91	Family planning users (%) 1975–91	Access to health services (%) 1985–88	Access to safe water (%) 1988–90	Food production per capita (1979–81=100) 1988–90	Agricultural population per hectare arable land 1988	GNP per capita (US$) 1990	% of central govt. expenditure 1980–90 Education	% of central govt. expenditure 1980–90 Health
AFRICA											
Eastern Africa (1)											
Burundi	61/40	5/3	19	9	61	38	95	3.5	210	..	..
Ethiopia	./..	17/12	14	4	46	19	85	2.5	120	..	..
Kenya	80/59	27/19	50	27	..	30	107	7.2	370	19.8	5.4
Madagascar	88/73	20/18	62	..	56	22	91	2.8	230	..	..
Malawi	./..	6/3	45	7	80	56	83	2.6	200	8.8	7.4
Mauritius (2)	./..	53/53	85	75	100	95	103	2.4	2,250	14.4	8.6
Mozambique	45/21	7/4	25	..	39	24	86	3.9	80	..	..
Rwanda	64/37	9/6	22	10	27	50	76	5.4	310	..	..
Somalia	36/14	13/7	2	..	27	37	99	4.9	120	..	..
Uganda	62/35	16/8	38	5	61	21	92	2.1	220	2.1	220....
United Rep. of Tanzania	93/88	5/4	60	10	76	56	88	3.9	110	..	..
Zambia	81/65	25/14	38	15	75	60	98	1.0	420	8.6	7.4
Zimbabwe	74/60	49/42	60	43	71	66	96	2.2	640	23.4	7.6
Middle Africa (3)											
Angola	56/29	17/9	15	..	30	35	80	1.9	..	..	..
Cameroon	66/43	31/20	45	16	41	42	90	1.0	960	12.0	3.4
Central African Republic	52/25	16/6	66	..	45	26	95	0.9	390	..	..
Chad	42/18	12/3	15	..	30	57	97	1.3	190	..	..
Congo	70/44	37/14	..	..	83	38	92	7.6	1,010	..	..
Gabon	74/49	./..	80	..	90	68	81	1.7	3,330	..	..
Zaire	84/61	32/16	..	..	26	33	97	2.8	220	1.4	0.7

Social Indicators *(continued)*

Country of territory	Adult literacy M/F 1990	Secondary school enrolment M/F 1986–90	Births attended by health worker (%) 1983–91	Family planning users (%) 1975–91	Access to health services (%) 1985–88	Access to safe water (%) 1988–90	Food production per capita (1979–81=100) 1988–90	Agricultural population per hectare arable land 1988	GNP per capita (US$) 1990	% of central govt. expenditure 1980–90 Education	% of central govt. expenditure 1980–90 Health
Northern Africa (4)											
Algeria	70/46	61/53	15	36	88	68	94	0.8	2,060	..	..
Egypt	63/34	91/71	35	48	..	73	123	8.0	600	13.4	2.8
Libyan Arab Jamahiriya	75/50	./..	76	..	..	94	103	0.3	..	..	..
Morocco	61/38	42/30	26	36	70	61	135	1.0	950	..	..
Sudan	43/12	23/17	69	9	51	46	75	1.2	..	..	..
Tunisia	74/56	50/39	68	50	90	92	94	0.4	1,440	16.3	6.1
Southern Africa											
Botswana	84/65	31/36	78	33	89	54	79	0.6	2,040	20.2	4.8
Lesotho	./..	21/31	40	5	80	48	81	4.2	530	15.2	7.4
Namibia	./..	./..	..	26	..	..	95	0.9	..	20.8	11.1
South Africa	./..	./..	..	50	..	..	88	0.4	..	..	..
Western Africa (5)											
Benin	32/16	23/9	45	9	18	54	118	1.5	360	..	..
Burkina Faso	28/9	9/5	30	..	49	69	114	2.0	330	..	..
Côte d'Ivoire	67/40	27/12	20	3	30	76	98	1.8	750	..	..
Ghana	70/51	49/30	55	13	60	57	109	2.5	390	25.7	9.0
Guinea	35/13	14/5	25	..	47	51	87	5.6	440	..	..
Guinea-Bissau	50/24	9/4	27	..	..	27	102	2.2	180	..	..
Liberia	50/29	./..	58	6	39	55	86	4.6	..	11.6	5.4
Mali	41/24	9/4	32	5	15	41	98	3.4	270	9.0	2.1
Mauritania	47/21	22/10	20	4	40	66	89	6.3	500	..	..
Niger	40/17	8/3	47	..	41	61	80	1.8	210	..	..
Nigeria	62/40	22/16	37	6	66	53	113	2.1	290	..	..
Senegal	52/25	21/11	41	11	40	47	104	1.0	710	..	..
Sierra Leone	31/11	23/11	25	..	..	36	88	1.4	240	10.4	3.6
Togo	56/31	33/10	15	16	61	59	98	1.6	410	..	..

Social Indicators *(continued)*

Country or territory	Adult literacy M/F 1990	Secondary school enrolment M/F 1986–90	Births attended by health worker (%) 1983–91	Family planning users (%) 1975–91	Access to health services (%) 1985–88	Access to safe water (%) 1988–90	Food production per capita (1979–81=100) 1988–90	Agricultural population per hectare arable land 1988	GNP per capita (US$) 1990	% of central govt. expenditure 1980–90 Education	% of central govt. expenditure 1980–90 Health
ASIA											
Eastern Asia (6)											
China	84/62	50/38	94	72	90	74	132	7.8	370	..	..
Dem. Peo. Rep. of Korea	./.	100/100	100	..	..	..	107	3.1	..	..	..
Hong Kong	./.	71/75	100	81	99	100	62	10.9	11,490	..	..
Japan	./.	94/97	100	58	..	..	95	1.8	25,430	..	..
Mongolia	./.	88/96	99	..	..	65	89	0.5	..	..	..
Republic of Korea	99/94	88/85	89	77	93	100	97	4.8	5,400	19.6	2.2
Southeastern Asia											
Cambodia	48/22	45/20	47	..	53	18	163	1.8	..	..	..
Indonesia	84/62	52/43	32	50	80	58	128	3.9	570	8.4	2.0
Lao People's Dem. Rep.	./.	31/22	..	..	67	35	121	3.1	200	..	..
Malaysia	87/70	58/59	82	51	..	79	155	1.1	2,320	16.8	4.6
Myanmar	89/72	25/23	57	..	33	31	101	1.9	..	16.9	4.1
Philippines	90/90	72/75	55	36	..	81	86	3.5	730	18.1	4.7
Singapore	./.	68/71	100	74	100	100	87	14.4	11,160	20.1	6.8
Thailand	96/90	32/28	71	66	90	93	105	1.7	1,420	..	..
Viet Nam	92/84	43/40	95	53	80	42	119	6.0	..	..	..
Southern Asia											
Afghanistan	44/14	11/5	9	..	29	21	85	1.1	..	..	4.8
Bangladesh	47/22	23/11	5	40	45	81	97	8.3	210	11.2	5.3
Bhutan	51/25	7/2	7	..	65	32	84	10.2	190	11.6	1.6
India	62/34	54/31	33	43	..	86	119	3.1	350	2.5	8.5
Iran (Islamic Republic of)	65/43	62/44	70	..	80	89	99	1.0	2,490	22.0	4.8
Nepal	38/13	42/17	6	14	//	37	113	7.1	170	10.9	0.7
Pakistan	47/21	28/12	40	12	55	56	104	3.0	380	2.0	5.4
Sri Lanka	93/84	71/76	94	62	93	60	88	4.6	470	9.9	

Social Indicators (continued)

Country of territory	Adult literacy M/F 1990	Secondary school enrolment M/F 1986–90	Births attended by health worker (%) 1983–91	Family planning users (%) 1975–91	Access to health services 1985–88	Access to safe water (%) 1988–90	Food production per capita (1979–81=100) 1988–90	Agricultural population per hectare arable land 1988	GNP per capita (US$) 1990	% of central govt. expenditure 1980–90 Education	% of central govt. expenditure 1980–90 Health
Western Asia (7)											
Iraq	70/49	58/37	50	14	93	92	90	0.7	..	..	4.1
Israel	./.	79/86	99	..	..	..	100	0.5	10,920	10.2	5.8
Jordan	89/70	80/78	87	35	97	99	113	0.5	1,240	14.2	7.4
Kuwait	77/67	93/87	99	35	100	..	..	7.1	..	14.0	..
Lebanon	88/73	57/56	45	..	..	92	145	0.9	..	..	..
Oman	./.	55/40	60	9	91	55	..	12.2	..	10.7	4.6
Saudi Arabia	73/48	53/39	90	..	97	94	277	4.5	7,050	..	..
Syrian Arab republic	78/51	63/45	61	20	75	70	83	0.5	1,000	8.6	1.3
Turkey	90/71	63/39	77	63	..	78	97	0.9	1,630	19.2	3.6
United Arab Emirates	58/38	60/69	99	..	99	95	..	1.1	19,860	15.0	6.9
Yemen	53/26	42/7	12	1	38	38	80	..	..	..	..
EUROPE											
Eastern Europe											
Bulgaria	./.	74/76	100	76	..	..	99	0.3	2,250	6.0	4.1
Czechoslovakia	./.	84/90	100	..	..	..	123	0.3	3,140	1.8	0.4
Hungary	./.	70/72	99	73	..	..	112	0.3	2,780	3.3	7.9
Poland	./.	80/83	100	75	..	..	109	0.5	1,690	..	..
Romania	./.	84/92	100	58	..	..	96	0.4	1,640	2.7	8.7
Northern Europe (8)											
Denmark	./.	106/107	100	63	..	..	129	0.1	22,080	9.3	1.1
Estonia	./.	./.									
Finland	./.	103/121	100	80	..	..	108	0.2	26,040	14.4	10.8
Ireland	./.	93/102	..	..	..	..	108	0.5	9,550	11.3	12.1
Latvia	./.	./.	..	..	..	..	..		..		..

Social Indicators *(continued)*

Country of territory	Adult literacy M/F 1990	Secondary school enrolment M/F 1986–90	Births attended by health worker (%) 1983–91	Family planning users (%) 1975–91	Access to health services (%) 1985–88	Access to safe water (%) 1988–90	Food production per capita (1979–81=100) 1988–90	Agricultural population per hectare arable land 1988	GNP per capita (US$) 1990	% of central govt. expenditure 1980–90 Education	% of central govt. expenditure 1980–90 Health
Northern Europe (8)											
Lithuania	./.	./.	..	..	..	..	..	0.3	..	..	..
Norway	./.	96/101	..	84	..	..	101	0.1	23,120	9.4	10.4
Sweden	./.	89/93	100	78	..	..	97	0.2	23,660	8.7	0.9
United Kingdom	./.	82/85	100	81	..	..	107		16,100	3.2	14.6
Southern Europe (9)											
Albania	./.	86/73	99	..	..	..	..	0.6	..	..	..
Greece	98/89	99/94	97	..	..	..	100	0.3	5,900	8.3	11.3
Italy	98/96	78/78	..	78	..	..	97	0.5	16,830		
Portugal	89/82	47/56	90	66	..	..	107	0.2	4,900		
Spain	97/93	100/111	96	59	..	..	112	0.6	11,020	5.6	12.8
Yugoslavia (former)	97/88	82/79	86	55	..	..	94		3,060		
Western Europe (10)											
Austria	./.	81/83	..	71	..	..	108	0.3	19,060	9.2	12.9
Belgium	./.	103/104	100	81	..	..	117	0.2	15,540		
France	./.	93/100	94	80	..	..	100	0.2	19,490	6.8	15.2
Germany	./.	92/88	99	78	..	..	112	0.3	..	0.6	19.3
Netherlands	./.	105/102	100	76	..	..	115	0.6	17,320	10.8	11.7
Switzerland	./.	./.	99	71	..	..	104	0.6	32,680		
LATIN AMERICA											
Caribbean (11)											
Cuba	95/93	84/94	90	70	..	..	101	0.6	..	..	..
Dominican Republic	85/82	./.	92	56	80	63	94	1.8	830	9.5	11.3
Haiti	59/47	20/19	20	10	50	36	93	4.2	370		
Jamaica	98/99	62/68	82	55	90	100	91	2.7	1,500		
Puerto Rico	./.	./.	..	70	..	..	..		..		
Trinidad and Tobago	./.	81/84	98	53	99	96	74	0.8	3,610		

Social Indicators (continued)

Country of territory	Adult literacy M/F 1990	Secondary school enrolment M/F 1986–90	Births attended by health worker (%) 1983–91	Family planning users (%) 1975–91	Access to health services (%) 1985–88	Access to safe water (%) 1988–90	Food production per capita (1979–81=100) 1988–90	Agricultural population per hectare arable land 1988	GNP per capita (US$) 1990	% of central govt. expenditure 1980–90 Education	% of central govt. expenditure 1980–90 Health
Central America (12)											
Costa Rica	93/93	41/42	93	70	80	92	91	1.4	1,900	19.0	26.3
El Salvador	76/70	26/26	50	47	56	48	94	2.6	1,110	16.2	7.8
Guatemala	63/47	21/19	34	23	34	62	95	2.4	900	19.5	9.9
Honduras	76/71	28/36	90	41	66	65	91	1.6	590	..	..
Mexico	90/85	53/53	77	53	78	71	96	1.1	2,490	13.9	1.9
Nicaragua	../..	28/46	73	27	83	54	61	1.1	..	..	..
Panama	88/88	56/63	96	64	80	84	88	1.0	1,830	18.5	17.9
South America (13)											
Argentina	96/95	69/78	87	..	71	65	95	0.1	2,370	9.3	2.0
Bolivia	85/71	36/31	54	30	63	53	107	0.8	630	18.0	2.3
Brazil	83/80	32/42	95	66	..	97	111	0.5	2,680	5.3	7.2
Chile	94/93	72/78	98	..	97	89	112	0.4	1,940	10.1	5.9
Colombia	88/86	52/53	94	66	60	88	109	1.7	1,260	..	..
Ecuador	88/84	55/57	56	53	75	58	108	1.2	980	18.2	11.0
Paraguay	92/88	28/30	66	48	61	34	119	0.9	1,110	12.7	4.3
Peru	92/79	68/61	52	59	75	61	100	2.1	1,160	16.2	5.1
Uruguay	97/96	68/76	96	..	82	73	113	0.3	2,560	7.4	4.5
Venezuela	87/90	50/62	69	49	..	90	94	0.5	2,560	..	..
NORTHERN AMERICA (14)											
Canada	../..	104/105	99	73	..	..	106	..	20,470	2.9	5.5
United States of America	../..	98/99	99	74	..	..	92	..	21,790	1.7	13.5

Social Indicators *(continued)*

Country of territory	Adult literacy M/F 1990	Secondary school enrolment M/F 1986–90	Births attended by health worker (%) 1983–91	Family planning users (%) 1975–91	Access to health services (%) 1985–88	Access to safe water (%) 1988–90	Food production per capita (1979–81=100) 1988–90	Agricultural population per hectare arable land 1988	GNP per capita (US$) 1990	% of central govt. expenditure 1980–90 Education	Health
OCEANIA											
Australia-New Zealand											
Australia (15)	./..	80/83	99	76	..	..	95	..	17,000	6.8	12.8
New Zealand	./..	87/89	99	70	..	97	104	0.6	12,680	12.5	12.7
Melanesia (16)	./..	./..	..	..	..	..					
Papua New Guinea	65/38	16/10	20	..	96	34	105	6.6	860	15.3	9.4
USSR (former) (17)	./..	./..	..	..	..	..	112	0.2	..	1.7	13.5

Selected Indicators for Less Populous Countries or Territories

Country or territory	Population (millions) 1992	Population (millions) 2025	Average growth rate (%) 1990–95	Birth rate per 1,000 1990–95	Death rate per 1,000 1990–95	Life expectancy 1990–95	Infant Mortality per 1,000 1990–95	Per cent urban 1992	Urban growth rate (%) 1990–95	Fertility rate per woman 1990–95	GNP per capita (US$) 1990
Bahamas	0.3	0.4	1.6	19	5	72	24	65	2.3	2.0	11,420
Bahrain	0.5	1.0	2.8	26	4	71	12	83	3.2	3.8	–
Barbados	0.3	0.3	0.3	16	9	76	10	46	1.7	1.8	6,540
Brunei Darussalam	0.3	0.4	2.2	24	4	74	8	58	2.2	3.1	–
Cape Verde	0.4	0.8	2.9	36	7	68	40	30	5.2	4.3	890
Comoros	0.6	1.6	3.7	48	12	56	89	29	5.9	7.1	480
Cyprus	0.7	0.9	0.9	17	8	77	9	54	2.2	2.3	8,020
Djibouti	0.5	1.2	3.0	46	16	49	112	82	3.6	6.6	–
East Timor	0.8	1.2	2.0	39	19	45	150	14	4.9	4.9	–
Equatorial Guinea	0.4	0.8	2.6	43	18	48	117	30	3.9	5.9	330
Fiji	0.7	1.0	1.0	24	5	71	23	40	1.7	3.0	1,780
French Polynesia	0.2	0.4	2.3	28	5	70	16	66	2.9	3.3	–
Gambia	0.9	1.9	2.6	44	19	45	132	24	5.1	6.1	260
Guadaloupe	0.4	0.5	1.2	19	7	75	12	49	2.3	2.2	–
Guyana	0.8	1.1	0.9	25	7	65	48	34	2.5	2.5	330
Iceland	0.3	0.3	1.0	17	7	78	5	91	1.3	2.2	21,400
Luxembourg	0.4	0.4	0.7	12	11	75	8	85	1.1	1.6	28,730
Maldives	0.2	0.5	3.0	38	8	63	55	31	5.7	6.2	450
Malta	0.4	0.4	0.7	15	8	76	9	88	1.0	2.1	6,610
Martinique	0.4	0.4	0.9	17	7	76	10	76	1.8	2.0	–
Micronesia (18)	0.4	0.9	2.5	32	6	67	36	49	4.4	4.4	–
Polynesia (19)	0.6	0.8	1.3	28	5	71	25	44	3.0	4.0	–
Qatar	0.5	0.7	2.8	23	4	70	26	90	3.1	4.4	15,860
Reunion	0.6	0.9	1.6	21	5	74	7	65	2.7	2.3	–
Solomon Islands	0.3	0.8	3.3	37	4	70	27	16	6.7	5.4	590
Suriname	0.4	0.7	1.9	26	6	70	28	49	3.1	2.7	3,050
Swaziland	0.8	1.7	2.7	37	10	58	73	28	6.2	4.9	810

Notes

All indicators are based on data compiled before 1 January 1992.

Data for small countries or area, generally those with populations of 200,000 or less in 1990, are not given separately. They have been included in regional population figures.

‡ More developed regions comprise Northern America, Japan, Europe, Australia-New Zealand and the former Union of Soviet Socialist Republics.

† Less developed regions comprise all regions of Africa, Latin America, Asia (excluding Japan), and Melanesia, Micronesia and Polynesia.

1 Including British Indian Ocean Territory and Seychelles.

2 Including Agalesa, Rodrigues and St. Brandon.

3 Including São Tomé and Principe.

4 Including Western Sahara.

5 Including St. Helena.

6 Including Macau.

7 Including Gaza Strip (Palestine).

8 Including Channel Islands, Faeroe Islands, and Isle of Man.

9 Including Andorra, Gibraltar, Holy See and San Marino.

10 Including Liechtenstein and Monaco.

11 Including Anguilla, Antigua and Barbuda, Aruba, British Virgin Islands, Cayman Islands, Dominica, Grenada, Montserrat, Netherlands Antilles, Saint Kitts and Nevis, Saint Lucia, Saint Vincent and the Grenadines, Turks and Caicos Islands, and United States Virgin Islands.

12 Including Belize.

13 Including Falkland Islands (Malvinas) and French Guiana.

14 Including Bermuda, Greenland, and St. Pierre and Miquelon.

15 Including Christmas Island, Cocos (Keeling) Islands, and Norfolk Island.

16 Including New Caledonia and Vanuatu.

17 Including Armenia, Azerbaijan, Belarus, Geogia, Kazakhstan, Kyrgyzstan, Republic of Moldova, Russian Federation, Tajikistan, Turkmenistan, Ukraine, and Uzbekistan, Estonia, Latvia and Lithuania are included in Northern Europe.

18 Comprising Federated States of Micronesia, Guam, Kiribati, Marshall Islands, Nauru, Northern Marians Islands, Pacific Islands (Palau), and Wake Island.

19 Comprising American Samoa, Cook Islands, Johnston Island, Pitcairn, Samoa, Tokelau, Tonga, Midway Islands, Tuvalu, and Wallis and Futuna Islands.

Sources:

Population indicators – United Nations Population Division, *World Pupulation Prospects: The 1992 Revisions*; Social indicators – Food and Agriculture Organization of the United Nations (FAO), *The State of Food and Agriculture 1991*; United Nations Children's Fund (UNICEF), *The State of the World's Children 1993*; United Nations Population Division, *World Monitoring Report 1993*, (draft); World Bank, *World Development Report 1992*.

Index